CORE TWELFTH EDITION

2012 ELECTION UPDATE

AMERICAN GOVERNMENT
POWER & PURPOSE

Theodore J. Lowi
Cornell University

Benjamin Ginsberg
The Johns Hopkins University

Kenneth A. Shepsle
Harvard University

Stephen Ansolabehere
Harvard University

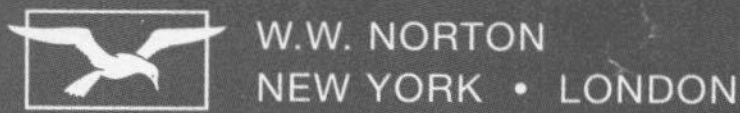

W.W. NORTON
NEW YORK • LONDON

W. W. Norton & Company has been independent since its founding in 1923, when William Warder Norton and Mary D. Herter Norton first published lectures delivered at the People's Institute, the adult education division of New York City's Cooper Union. The firm soon expanded its program beyond the Institute, publishing books by celebrated academics from America and abroad. By mid-century, the two major pillars of Norton's publishing program—trade books and college texts—were firmly established. In the 1950s, the Norton family transferred control of the company to its employees, and today—with a staff of four hundred and a comparable number of trade, college, and professional titles published each year—W. W. Norton & Company stands as the largest and oldest publishing house owned wholly by its employees.

Printed in the United States of America.

Editor: Ann Shin
Associate Editor: Jake Schindel
Editorial Assistant: Caitlin Cummings
Project Editor: Christine D'Antonio
Media Editor: Peter Lesser
Media Editorial Assistant: Jennifer Barnhardt
Marketing Manager: Sasha Levitt
Production Manager: Eric Pier-Hocking
Ancillaries Editor: Lorraine Klimowich
Book Designer: Kiss Me I'm Polish LLC, New York
Design Director: Rubina Yeh
Composition: Jouve North America—Brattleboro, VT
Manufacturing: Quad Graphics, Taunton

Library of Congress Cataloging-in-Publication Data

American government : power and purpose / Theodore J. Lowi . . . [et al.]. — Core 12th ed.
p. cm.
Includes bibliographical references and index.
ISBN 978-0-393-92188-5 (pbk.)
1. United States—Politics and government. I. Lowi, Theodore J.
JK276.L69 2012
320.473—dc23

2011050941

W. W. Norton & Company, Inc., 500 Fifth Avenue, New York, N.Y. 10110-0017
www.wwnorton.com

W. W. Norton & Company Ltd., Castle House, 75/76 Wells Street, London W1T 3QT

1 2 3 4 5 6 7 8 9 10

For Our Families

Angele, Anna, and Jason Lowi
Sandy, Cindy, and Alex Ginsberg
Rise, Nilsa, and Seth Shepsle
Laurie Gould and Rebecca and
Julia Ansolabehere

Contents

4 Civil Liberties 104

5 Civil Rights 146

Preface

This book was written for faculty and students who are looking for a little more than just "nuts and bolts," and who are drawn to an analytical perspective. No fact about American government is intrinsically difficult to grasp, and in an open society such as ours, facts abound. The philosophy of a free and open media in the United States makes information about the government that would be suppressed elsewhere readily available. The advent of the Internet and other new communication technologies has further expanded the opportunity to learn about our government. The ubiquity of information in our society is a great virtue. Common knowledge about the government gives our society a vocabulary that is widely shared among its citizens and enables us to communicate effectively with each other about politics. But it is also important to reach beyond that common vocabulary and develop a more sophisticated understanding of politics and government. The sheer quantity of facts in our society overwhelms us at times. In a 24/7 news cycle it can be hard to pick out what stories are important and to stay focused on them. The single most important task of the teacher of political science is to confront popular ideas and information and to choose from among them the small number of really significant concepts that help us make better sense of the world. This book aims to help instructors and students accomplish this task.

The analytical framework of this book is oriented around five principles that we use to help make sense of politics:

1. All political behavior has a purpose.
2. Institutions structure politics.
3. All politics is collective action.
4. Political outcomes are the products of individual preferences and institutional procedures.
5. How we got here matters.

This Twelfth Edition builds on the major revision we undertook in the Eleventh Edition. We have not changed the approach of the book. Rather, in this new edition, we have both sharpened the analytical approach developed in earlier editions and made it more teachable. Those who have used this book in the past are familiar with the narrative it presents about American government and politics—the storyline of how the United States government has evolved, how it operates, and the characters involved in the unfolding development of our polity. This book also presents an analytical approach based on the five principles outlined above. We are guided by the belief that students of government need an analytical framework for understanding political phenomena—a framework rooted in some of the most important insights the discipline of political science has to offer and that encourages students to draw out the general lessons about collective action and collective decision making.

The major changes in this Twelfth Edition are intended to provide a more contemporary and unified approach to the key topics in American government—and to make it easier to teach that approach. The most significant changes include:

- Part 3 on "Democratic Politics" provides a more current and integrated treatment of mass political behavior. Building on deep revisions of the chapters on public opinion, elections, and the media in the Eleventh Edition, this Twelfth Edition includes extensively revised chapters on parties and interest groups. Chapter 11 on elections has also been revised to provide analysis of the 2010 elections.
- Civil liberties and civil rights have been broken out into two separate chapters. Reviewers and instructors told us strong coverage of these important topics should be spread over two chapters. (However, the overall length of this section has only increased slightly as a result, so instructors who liked assigning both topics together should still be able to do so.)
- Seven new Analyzing the Evidence sections written by researchers in each specific area highlight the political science behind the information in the book. New Analyzing the Evidence units include:

  "Health Care Policy and the States" (Chapter 3)
  Contributed by Jenna Bednar, University of Michigan

  "Evaluating the Death Penalty" (Chapter 4)
  Contributed by Joseph Ura, Texas A&M University

  "Presidential Appointees in the Executive Branch" (Chapter 7)
  Contributed by David Lewis, Vanderbilt University

  "When Does Congress Rein in the Bureaucracy?" (Chapter 8)
  Contributed by Jamie Carson, University of Georgia

  "Ideological Voting on the Supreme Court" (Chapter 9)
  Contributed by Andrew D. Martin, Washington University in St. Louis, and Kevin M. Quinn, UC Berkeley School of Law

"The Electoral Impact of Congressional Redistricting" (Chapter 11)

"Interest Group Influence" (Chapter 13)
Contributed by Beth L. Leech, Rutgers University

For the Twelfth Edition we have profited greatly from the guidance of many teachers who have used earlier editions, and from the suggestions of numerous thoughtful reviewers. We thank them by name in the Acknowledgments. We recognize that there is no single best way to craft in an introductory text, and we are grateful for the advice we have received.

Theodore J. Lowi
Benjamin Ginsberg
Kenneth A. Shepsle
Stephen Ansolabehere

Acknowledgments

Our students at Cornell, Johns Hopkins, and Harvard have already been identified as an essential factor in the writing of this book. They have been our most immediate intellectual community, a hospitable one indeed. Another part of our community, perhaps a large suburb, is the discipline of political science itself. Our debt to the scholarship of our colleagues is scientifically measurable, probably to several decimal points, in the footnotes of each chapter. Despite many complaints that the field is too scientific or not scientific enough, political science is alive and well in the United States. Political science has never been at a loss for relevant literature, and without that literature, our job would have been impossible.

We are pleased to acknowledge our debt to the many colleagues who had a direct and active role in criticism and preparation of the manuscript. The First Edition was read and reviewed by Gary Bryner, Brigham Young University; James F. Herndon, Virginia Polytechnic Institute and State University; James W. Riddlesperger, Jr., Texas Christian University; John Schwarz, University of Arizona; Toni-Michelle Travis, George Mason University; and Lois Vietri, University of Maryland. We also want to reiterate our thanks to the four colleagues who allowed us the privilege of testing a trial edition of our book by using it as the major text in their introductory American Government courses: Gary Bryner, Brigham Young University; Allan J. Cigler, University of Kansas; Burnet V. Davis, Albion College; and Erwin A. Jaffe, California State University–Stanislaus.

For subsequent editions, we relied heavily on the thoughtful manuscript reviews we received from David Canon, University of Wisconsin; Russell Hanson, Indiana University; William Keech, Carnegie Mellon University; Donald Kettl, University of Wisconsin; Anne Khademian, University of Wisconsin; William McLauchlan, Purdue University; J. Roger Baker, Wittenburg University; James Lennertz, Lafayette College; Allan McBride, Grambling State University; Joseph Peek, Jr., Georgia State University; Grant Neeley, Texas Tech University; Mark Graber, University of Maryland; John Gilmour, College of

William and Mary; Victoria Farrar-Myers, University of Texas at Arlington; Timothy Boylan, Winthrop University; Robert Huckfeldt, University of California–Davis; Mark Joslyn, University of Kansas; Beth Leech, Rutgers University; Charles Noble, California State University, Long Beach.

For the Eighth Edition, we benefited from the comments of Scott Ainsworth, University of Georgia; Thomas Brunell, Northern Arizona University; Daniel Carpenter, Harvard University; Brad Gomez, University of South Carolina; Paul Gronke, Reed College; Marc Hetherington, Bowdoin College; Gregory Huber, Yale University; Robert Lowry, Iowa State University; and Anthony Nownes, University of Tennessee; Scott Adler, University of Colorado–Boulder; John Coleman, University of Wisconsin–Madison; Richard Conley, University of Florida; Keith Dougherty, University of Georgia; John Ferejohn, Stanford University; Douglas Harris, Loyola College; Brian Humes, University of Nebraska–Lincoln; Jeffrey Jenkins, Northwestern University; Paul Johnson, University of Kansas; Andrew Polsky, Hunter College–CUNY; Mark Richards, Grand Valley State University; Charles Shipan, University of Iowa; Craig Volden, Ohio State University; and Garry Young, George Washington University.

For the Ninth Edition, we were guided by the comments of John Baughman; Lawrence Baum, Ohio State University; Chris Cooper, Western Carolina State University; Charles Finochiaro, State University of New York–Buffalo; Lisa Garcia-Bellorda, University of California–Irvine; Sandy Gordon, New York University; Steven Greene, North Carolina State University; Richard Herrera, Arizona State University; Ben Highton, University of California–Davis; Trey Hood, University of Georgia; Andy Karch, University of Texas–Austin; Glen Krutz, University of Oklahoma; Paul Labedz, Valencia Community College; Brad Lockerbie, University of Georgia; Wendy Martinek, State University of New York–Binghamton; Nicholas Miller, University of Maryland Baltimore County; Russell Renka, Southeast Missouri State University; Debbie Schildkraut, Tufts University; Charles Shipan, University of Iowa; Chris Shortell, California State University, Northridge; John Sides, University of Texas–Austin; Sean Theriault, University of Texas–Austin; and Lynn Vavreck, University of California, Los Angeles.

For the Tenth Edition, we were grateful for the detailed comments of Christian Grose, Vanderbilt University; Kevin Esterling, University of California–Riverside; Martin Johnson, University of California–Riverside; Scott Meinke, Bucknell University; Jason MacDonald, Kent State University; Alan Wiseman, Ohio State University; Michelle Swers, Georgetown University; William Hixon, Lawrence University; Gregory Koger, University of Miami; and Renan Levine, University of Toronto.

For their advice on the Eleventh Edition, we thank Scott Ainsworth, University of Georgia; Bethany Albertson, University of Washington; Brian Arbour, John Jay College; James Battista, University at Buffalo, State University of New York; Lawrence Becker, California State University, Northridge; Damon Cann, Utah State University; Jamie Carson, University of Georgia; Suzanne Chod, Pennsylvania State University; Michael Crespin, University of Georgia; Ryan Emenaker, College of the Redwoods; Kevin Esterling, University of California–Riverside; Brad Gomez, Florida State University; Sanford Gordon, New York

University; Christian Grose, Vanderbilt University; James Hanley, Adrian College; Ryan Hurl, University of Toronto; Josh Kaplan, University of Notre Dame; Wendy Martinek, Binghamton University; Will Miller, Southeast Missouri State University; Evan Parker-Stephen, Texas A&M University; Melody Rose, Portland State University; Eric Schickler, University of California–Berkeley; John Sides, George Washington University; and Lynn Vavreck, University of California–Los Angeles.

We also thank the reviewers who advised us on this Twelfth Edition: John M. Aughenbaugh, Virginia Commonwealth University; Christopher Banks, Kent State University; Michael Berkman, Pennsylvania State University; Cynthia Bowling, Auburn University; Matthew Cahn, California State University, Northridge; Damon Cann, Utah State University; Tom Cioppa, Brookdale Community College; David Damore, University of Nevada, Las Vegas; Kevin Esterling, University of California, Riverside; Jessica Feezell, University of California, Santa Barbara; Charle J. Finocchiaro, University of South Carolina; Rodd Freitag, University of Wisconsin, Eau Claire; Kevin Jefferies, Alvin Community College; Nancy Jimeno, California State University, Fullerton; Gregory Koger, University of Miami; David E. Lewis, Vanderbilt University; Allison M. Martens, University of Louisville; Thomas M. Martin, Eastern Kentucky University; Michael Andrew McLatchy, Clarendon College; Ken Mulligan, Southern Illinois University, Carbondale; Geoffrey D. Peterson, University of Wisconsin, Eau Claire; Jesse Richman, Old Dominion University; Mark C. Rom, Georgetown University; Laura Schneider, Grand Valley State University; Scot Schraufnagel, Northern Illinois University; Ronald P. Seyb, Skidmore College; Martin S. Sheffer, Tidewater Community College; Charles R. Shipan, University of Michigan; Howard A. Smith, Florida Gulf Coast University; Michele Swers, Georgetown University; Charles Tien, Hunter College; Elizabeth Trentanelli, Gulf Coast State College; and Kenneth C. Williams, Michigan State University.

An important contribution to recent editions was made by the authors of the Analyzing the Evidence units. We are grateful to the authors of the new Analyzing the Evidence sections in the Twelfth Edition, who are named in the preface. In addition, Jamie Carson, Andrea Campbell, and Kevin Esterling contributed to this feature in earlier editions, and much of their work is still reflected in this edition. We thank the three of them for their excellent contributions to the book. We also thank Joe Williams, who provided valuable assistance in updating the data figures and tables throughout the book.

Perhaps above all, we wish to thank those who kept the production and all the loose ends of this Twelfth Edition coherent and in focus. Ann Shin has been a talented editor, offering numerous suggestions for this edition. Christine D'Antonio has been a superb project editor, following in the great tradition of her predecessors. Eric Pier-Hocking has been an excellent production manager, and Caitlin Cummings has been a helpful editorial assistant. Peter Lesser brought a vision to accompanying electronic resources, and Lorraine Klimowich oversaw the test bank and instructor's manual—both spent countless hours making these resources a reality.

We are more than happy, however, to absolve all these contributors from any flaws, errors, and misjudgments that this book contains. We wish it could be free of all production errors, grammatical errors, misspellings, misquotes, missed citations, etc. From that standpoint, a book ought to try to be perfect. But substantively we have not tried to write a flawless book; we have not tried to write a book to please everyone. We have again tried to write an effective book, a book that cannot be taken lightly. Our goal was not to make every reader a political scientist. Our goal was to restore politics as a subject of vigorous and enjoyable discourse, releasing it from the bondage of the 30-second sound bite and the 30-page technical briefing. Every person can be knowledgeable because everything about politics is accessible. One does not have to be a television anchorperson to profit from political events. One does not have to be a philosopher to argue about the requisites of democracy, a lawyer to dispute constitutional interpretations, an economist to debate public policy. We will be very proud if our book contributes in a small way to the restoration of the ancient art of political controversy.

Theodore J. Lowi
Benjamin Ginsberg
Kenneth A. Shepsle
Stephen Ansolabehere

AMERICAN GOVERNMENT
POWER & PURPOSE
2012 ELECTION UPDATE

1

FOUNDATIONS

Five Principles of Politics

Chapter Outline

- Making Sense of Government and Politics
- Five Principles of Politics
- Conclusion

American government and politics are extraordinarily complex. The United States has many levels of government: federal, state, county, city, and town—to say nothing of a host of special and regional authorities. Each of these governments operates under its own rules and statutory authority and is related to the others in complex ways. In many nations, regional and local governments are appendages of the national government. This is not true in the United States. America's state and local governments possess a considerable measure of independence and authority. Each level of government, moreover, consists of an array of departments, agencies, offices, and bureaus, each with its own policies, jurisdiction, and responsibilities, and undertaking a variety of sometimes overlapping tasks. At times this complexity gets in the way of effective governance, as in the case of governmental response to emergencies. America's federal, state, and local public safety agencies seldom share information and frequently use incompatible communications equipment, so they are often not even able to speak to each other. For example, on September 11, 2001, New York City's police and fire departments could not effectively coordinate their responses to the terrorist attack on the World Trade Center because their communications systems were not linked. While communication has improved in the last decade, it is still the case that many security and policy agencies, ranging from the Central Intelligence Agency (CIA) to the National Security Administration (NSA) to the Department of Homeland Security (DHS) to the Federal Bureau of Investigation (FBI), possess separate computer operating systems and databases that inhibit cooperation through sharing.

The complexity of America's government is no accident. Complexity was one element of the Founders' grand constitutional design. The framers of the Constitution hoped that an elaborate division of power among institutions and between the states and the federal government would allow a variety of competing groups, forces, interests, and ideas to have access to arenas of decision making and a voice in public affairs—while preventing any single group or coalition from monopolizing power. One set of interests might be active and powerful in some states, other forces would be influential in the national legislature, and still other groups might prevail in the executive branch. The overall pattern would disperse power and opportunity, allowing many groups to achieve at least some of their political goals. In this way, America's political tradition associates complexity with liberty and political opportunity.

But although America's institutional complexity creates many avenues and possibilities for political action, its complexity also places a considerable burden on citizens who might wish to achieve something through political participation, for they may not easily discern where particular policies are actually made, who the influential decision makers are, and what forms of political participation are most likely to be effective. This is one of the paradoxes of political life: In a dictatorship, lines of political authority may be simple, but opportunities to influence the use of power are few; in America, political opportunities are plentiful, but how they should be used is far from obvious. Indeed, precisely because America's institutional and political arrangements are so complex, many Americans are mystified by government. As we see in Chapter 10, many Americans have difficulty making sense of even the basic features of the Constitution.

If America's government seems complex, its politics can be utterly bewildering. Like the nation's governmental structure, its political processes have numerous components. For most Americans, the focal point of politics is the electoral process. As we see in Chapter 11, tens of millions of Americans participate in a host of national, state, and local elections, during which they listen to thousands of candidates debate a perplexing array of issues. Candidates inundate the media with promises, charges, and countercharges while an army

CORE OF THE ANALYSIS

- Five principles of politics can help us think analytically about American government and make sense of the apparent chaos and complexity of the political world. These five principles are:
- All political behavior has a purpose (rationality principle).
- Institutions structure politics (institution principle).
- All politics is collective action (collective-action principle).
- Political outcomes are the products of individual preferences and institutional procedures (policy principle).
- How we got here matters (history principle).

of pundits and journalists, whom we also discuss in Chapters 10 and 14, adds its own clamor to the din.

Politics, however, does not end on Election Day. Indeed, given the growing tendency of losers to challenge election results in the courts, even elections do not end on Election Day. The most famous of these, of course, was the resolution of the 2000 presidential election by the Supreme Court in *Bush v. Gore.* Long after the voters have spoken, political struggles continue in Congress, the executive branch, and the courts and embroil political parties, interest groups, and the mass media. In some instances, the participants in political struggles and their goals seem fairly obvious. For example, it is no secret that businesses and upper-income wage earners strongly support programs of tax reduction, farmers support maintenance of agricultural subsidies, and labor unions oppose increasing the eligibility age for Social Security. Each of these forces has created or joined organized groups to advance its cause. We examine some of these groups in Chapter 13.

In other instances, though, the participants in political struggles and their goals are not so clear. Sometimes corporate groups hide behind environmental causes to surreptitiously promote their economic interests. Strong environmental requirements make it difficult for prospective competitors to enter their markets. Other times groups claiming to want to help the poor and downtrodden seek only to help themselves. And to make matters worse, many of the government's policies are made behind closed doors, away from the light of publicity. Ordinary citizens can hardly be blamed for failing to understand bureaucratic rule making and other obscure techniques of government.

MAKING SENSE OF GOVERNMENT AND POLITICS

Can we find order in the apparent chaos of politics? The answer is that we can, and doing so is the purpose of this text. Finding order in the apparent chaos of politics is precisely what political scientists do. The discipline of political science, and especially the study of American politics, is devoted to identifying patterns and regularities in all the noise and maneuvering of everyday political life. This is motivated by two fundamental questions: What do we observe? And why?

The first question makes clear that political science is an *empirical* enterprise. By this we mean that it aims to identify facts and patterns that are true in the world around us. What do voters decide when they enter the polling booth? What strategies and tactics do candidates employ to capture votes? What decisions do legislators make about how to vote on bills? What groups organize and put pressure on the institutions of government? How do the media report politics? What tools are available to the president so he can get what he wants in dealing with Congress? How have courts intervened in regulating political life?

How do they come to the decisions they have made? These and many other questions have been explored by political science in an effort to observe and ascertain what is true about the political world, and will be taken up in great detail in later chapters.

The second question—why?—is the fundamental concern of science. We not only would like to know that something is true about the world. We also want to know why it is true. Knowing why something is true requires us to create a theory of how the world works. And a theory is constructed from basic principles. The remainder of this chapter will present a set of such basic principles. They will help us navigate the apparent chaos of politics and make sense of what we observe. In this way we not only describe politics, we analyze it.

One of the most important goals of this book is to help readers learn to analyze what they observe in American politics.[1] Analysis requires abstracting. For example, in political science, we are not much interested in an analysis that *only* explains why the Republicans gained congressional seats in the 2010 elections. Explanations that provide an account of a unique circumstance are the sorts of things in which pundits, journalists, and other commentators engage as soon as the polls close. You find them on television news programs as well as on the op-ed pages of newspapers. Rather, as political scientists, we seek a more general theory of voting choice that we can apply to particular instances—such as the 2010 elections.

In this chapter, we first discuss what we mean by *government* and *politics*. Then we introduce our five principles of politics. These principles are intentionally somewhat abstract, because we want them to apply to a wide range of circumstances. However, we provide concrete illustrations along the way, and in later chapters we apply the principles presented here more extensively to help us understand the specific features of politics and government in the United States. We conclude this chapter with a brief guide to analyzing evidence, something you will find useful as we examine empirical information throughout the rest of the book.

What Is Government?

Government is the term generally used to describe the formal political arrangements by which a land and its people are ruled. Government is composed of institutions and processes that rulers establish to strengthen and perpetuate their power or control over a land and its inhabitants. A government may be as simple as a tribal council that meets occasionally to advise the chief or as complex as our own vast establishment, with its elaborate procedures, laws, governmental bodies, and bureaucracies. This more complex government is sometimes called the state, an abstract concept referring to the source of all public authority.

government

The institutions and procedures through which a land and its people are ruled

1 For an entire book devoted to the issue of analysis, see Kenneth A. Shepsle, *Analyzing Politics: Rationality, Behavior, and Institutions*, 2nd ed. (New York: Norton, 2010).

Forms of Government

autocracy

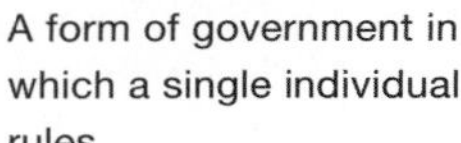

A form of government in which a single individual rules

oligarchy

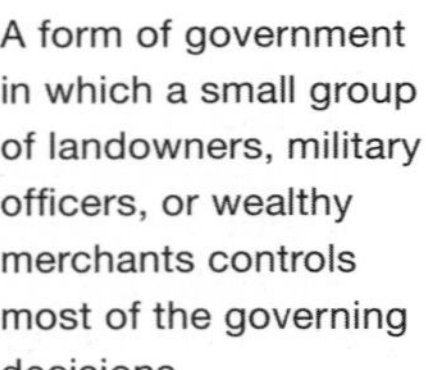

A form of government in which a small group of landowners, military officers, or wealthy merchants controls most of the governing decisions

democracy

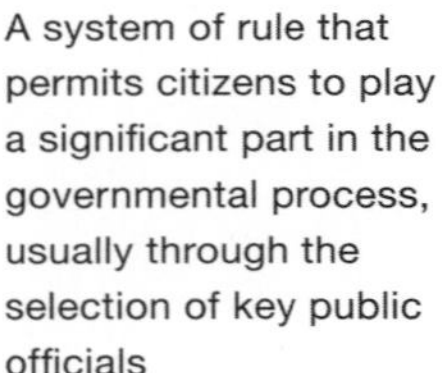

A system of rule that permits citizens to play a significant part in the governmental process, usually through the selection of key public officials

constitutional government

A system of rule in which formal and effective limits are placed on the powers of the government

authoritarian government

A system of rule in which the government recognizes no formal limits but may nevertheless be restrained by the power of other social institutions

Governments vary in their institutional structure, in their size, and in their modes of operation. Two questions are of special importance in determining how governments differ from each other: Who governs? And, how much government control is permitted?

In some nations political authority is vested in a single individual—a king or dictator, for example. This state of affairs is called an autocracy. When a small group of landowners, military officers, or wealthy merchants controls most of the governing decisions, the government is said to be an oligarchy. If more people participate and the populace is deemed to have some influence over decision making, the government is tending toward democracy.

Governments also vary considerably in terms of how they govern. In the United States and some other nations, governments are severely limited in terms of *what* they are permitted to control (they are restricted by substantive limits) as well as *how* they go about exercising that control (they are restricted by procedural limits). Governments that are so limited are called constitutional governments. In other nations, although the law imposes few real limits, a government is nevertheless kept in check by other political and social institutions that it is unable to control but must come to terms with, such as autonomous territories, an organized church, organized business groups, or organized labor unions. Such governments are generally called authoritarian. In a third, very small, group of nations, including the Soviet Union under Joseph Stalin, Nazi Germany, and present-day North Korea, governments not only are free of legal limits but also seek to eliminate those organized social groupings that might challenge or limit their authority. These governments typically attempt to dominate or control every sphere of political, economic, and social life and, as a result, are called totalitarian.

Politics

In its broadest sense, the term *politics* refers to conflicts over the character, membership, and policies of any organization to which people belong. As Harold Lasswell, a famous political scientist, once put it, politics is the struggle over "who gets what, when, how."[2] Although politics is a phenomenon that can be found in any organization, in this book politics refers only to conflicts and struggles over the leadership, structure, and policies of governments. The goal of politics, as we define it, is to have a share or a say in the composition of the government's leadership, how the government is organized, or what its policies are going to be.

Politics takes many forms. As they attempt to influence the policies and leadership of the government, individuals may run for office, vote, join political parties and movements, contribute money to candidates, lobby public officials, participate in demonstrations, write letters, talk to their friends and neighbors,

2 Harold D. Lasswell, *Politics: Who Gets What, When, How* (1936; repr., New York: Meridian, 1958).

go to court, and engage in numerous other activities. Some forms of politics are aimed at gaining power, some at influencing those in power, and others at bringing new people to power and throwing the old leaders out. Those in power use myriad means and strategies to try to achieve their goals. But even though it takes many forms, politics possesses an underlying logic that can be understood in terms of five simple principles:

1. All political behavior has a purpose.
2. Institutions structure politics.
3. All politics is collective action.
4. Political outcomes are the products of individual preferences, institutional procedures, and collective action.
5. How we got here matters.

Some of these principles may seem obvious or abstract. They prove useful, however, because they possess a distinct kernel of truth on the one hand, yet on the other hand are sufficiently general to help us understand politics in a wide variety of settings. Armed with these principles, we can perceive the order underlying the apparent chaos of political events whenever and wherever they take place.

totalitarian government

A system of rule in which the government recognizes no formal limits on its power and seeks to absorb or eliminate other social institutions that might challenge it

politics

The conflicts and struggles over the leadership, structure, and policies of government

FIVE PRINCIPLES OF POLITICS

The Rationality Principle: All Political Behavior Has a Purpose

One compelling reason that governments do what they do is that they respond to what people want. All people have goals and their political behavior is guided by these goals. For many citizens, political behavior is as simple as reading a headline or an editorial in the newspaper while drinking their morning coffee or discussing the latest local political controversy with a neighbor over the back fence. Though political, these actions are normal routines of everyday life. Beyond these very basic acts, citizens' political behavior broadens to include still relatively modest activities, such as watching a political debate on television, arguing about politics with a coworker, signing a petition, or attending a city-council meeting. These are understood to be explicitly political activities that require some forethought. Political behavior requiring even more premeditation and effort includes going to the polls and casting a vote in the November election (having first registered in a timely manner), contacting one's legislative representatives about a political issue, contributing time or money to a political campaign, or even running for local office.

Some of these acts require time, effort, financial resources, and resolve, whereas others place small, even insignificant demands on a person. Nevertheless, all of them are done for specific reasons. They are not random; they are not entirely automatic or mechanical, even the smallest of them; they are purposeful. Sometimes they are engaged in for the sake of entertainment (reading the front page in the morning) or just to be sociable (chatting about politics with a neighbor, coworker, or family member). At other times, they take on considerable personal importance explicitly because of their political content—because an individual cares about, and wants to influence, an issue, a candidate, a party, or a cause. We will treat all of this political activity as purposeful, as having a goal. Indeed, our attempts to identify the goals of various political activities will help us understand them better.

We've just noted that many of the political activities of ordinary citizens are hard to distinguish from conventional everyday behavior—reading newspapers, watching television news, discussing politics, and so on. For the professional politician, on the other hand—the legislator, executive, judge, party leader, bureau chief, or agency head—nearly every act is political. The legislator's decision to introduce a particular piece of legislation, give a speech in the legislative chamber, move an amendment to a pending bill, vote for or against that bill, or accept a contribution from a particular group requires his or her careful attention. There are pitfalls and dangers, and the slightest miscalculation can have huge consequences. Introduce a bill that appears to be too pro-labor in the eyes of your constituents, for example, and before you know it you're charged with being in bed with the unions during the next election campaign. Give a speech against job quotas for minorities, and you risk your standing with the minority communities in your state or district. Accept campaign contributions from industries known to pollute, and environmentalists think you are no friend of the earth. Nearly every move a legislator makes is fraught with risks. And because of these risks, legislators think about their moves before they make them—sometimes carefully, sometimes not; sometimes correctly, sometimes not. But whatever actions they take or decide against taking, they make their choices with forethought, with deliberation, with calculation. Their actions are not knee-jerk but are, in a word, instrumental. Individuals think through the benefits and the costs of a decision, speculate about future effects, and weigh the risks of their decision. Making decisions is all about weighing probabilities of various events and determining the personal value of various outcomes.

instrumental

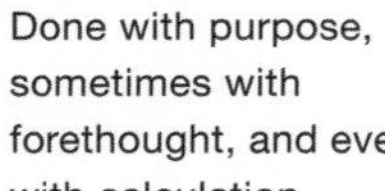

Done with purpose, sometimes with forethought, and even with calculation

To find examples of instrumental behavior, consider elected officials. Most politicians want to keep their positions or move up the political ladder to even more important positions. They like their jobs for a variety of reasons—salary, privileges, prestige, stepping-stones, and opportunities for accomplishment, to name just a few. So we can understand why politicians do what they do by thinking of their behavior as instrumental, with a goal of keeping their jobs. This is quite straightforward in regard to elected politicians. They often see no further than the next election and think mainly about how to prevail in that contest. To understand their routines and behaviors, it is essential to figure out who can help them win. "Retail" politics involves dealing directly with constituents, as when a politician helps an individual navigate a federal agency, find a misplaced Social Security check, or apply to a service academy. "Wholesale" politics involves appealing to collections of constituents, as when a legislator introduces a bill that would benefit a group that is active in her state or district (say, veterans), secures money for a bridge or public building in his hometown, or intervenes in an official proceeding on behalf of an interest group that will, in turn, contribute to the next campaign. Politicians may do any and all of these things because it is "right" or for ideological reasons. But we institute elections and provide incentives for politicians to help constituents as a means of winning those elections, just in case their generosity of spirit and personal ideology are insufficient. Elections and electoral politics are thus premised on instrumental behavior by politicians.

Political scientists have found it useful to explain the behavior of elected politicians by treating the "electoral connection" as the principal motivation.[3] Elected politicians, in this view, base their behavior on the goal of maximizing votes at the next election, or maximizing their probability of winning. Of course, politicians seek other things as well—public policy objectives, power in their institution (for legislators, this includes acquiring committee chairs and party leadership posts), and ambition for higher office (members of the House may want to become senators, and senators may want the presidency).[4] Primary emphasis on the electoral motivation is premised on the fact that re-election is a necessary condition for pursuing any of the other objectives.[5]

But what about political actors who are not elected? What do they want? Consider a few examples:

- Agency heads and bureau chiefs, motivated by policy preferences and power, seek to maximize their budgets.
- Legislative committee chairs (who are elected to Congress but appointed to committees) are "turf minded," intent on maximizing their committee's policy jurisdiction and thus its power.
- Voters cast ballots to influence the policies of government, with an eye to their own personal welfare as well as their conception of "what's best for the country."
- Justices, serving lifetime terms, maximize the prospects for their view of constitutional interpretation to prevail.[6]

---

3 The classic statement of this premise is David R. Mayhew, *Congress: The Electoral Connection* (New Haven, CT: Yale University Press, 1974). Although nearly four decades old, this book remains a source of insight and wisdom.

4 The classic statement of this additional premise is Richard F. Fenno, *Congressmen in Committees* (Boston: Little, Brown, 1973), another book that remains relevant decades after its publication.

5 As Vince Lombardi, the famous coach of the Green Bay Packers football team, once said, "Winning isn't everything; it's the only thing."

6 For most political actors, self-interest motivates their behavior. The motivations or purposes of judges and justices have proved more difficult to ascertain in light of the fact that they typically enjoy lifetime appointments (and thus are not looking ahead to the next election or occasion for "contract renewal"). For an interesting discussion of judicial motivations by an eminent law professor and incumbent judge, see Richard Posner, "What Do Judges Maximize? (The Same Thing Everybody Else Does)," *Supreme Court Economic Review* 3 (1993): 1–41.

In each of these instances, we can postulate motivations for political actors that seem to fit the political context in which they are found. These goals often have a strong element of self-interest, but they may be broadened out to incorporate "enlightened self-interest," including the welfare of others (such as their families), the entire society, or even all of humanity.

The Institution Principle: Institutions Structure Politics

In pursuing political goals, people—especially elected leaders and other government officials—confront certain recurring problems, and they develop routines and standard ways of addressing those problems. Routinized, structured relations are what we call institutions. Institutions are the rules and procedures that provide incentives for political behavior, thereby shaping politics. Institutions may discourage conflict, encourage coordination, enable bargaining, and thus facilitate decision making, cooperation, and collective action.

institutions

The rules and procedures that provide incentives for political behavior, thereby shaping politics

Institutions are part script and part scorecard. As scripts, they choreograph political activity. As scorecards, they list the players, their positions, what they want, what they know when they take actions, what they can do, and when they can do it. Although the Constitution sets the broad framework for American political institutions, much adaptation and innovation takes place as the institutions themselves are bent to the various purposes of strategic political actors who want to win for their side and defeat the other side. Our focus here will be on the authority that institutions provide politicians for the pursuit of public policies. The discussion is divided into four broad subjects: jurisdiction, agenda and veto power, decisiveness, and delegation.

Jurisdiction. A critical feature of an institution is the domain over which institutional members have the authority to make decisions. Political institutions are full of specialized jurisdictions over which individuals or subsets of members have authority. One feature of the U.S. Congress, for example, is the existence of "standing committees," whose jurisdictions are carefully defined by law. Most members of Congress become specialists in all aspects of the jurisdiction of their committees—and they often seek committee assignments based on the subjects in which they want to specialize. Committee members are granted specific authority within their jurisdiction to set the agenda of the larger parent chamber. For example, proposed legislation related to the military must pass through the Armed Services Committee before it can be voted on by the entire House or Senate. Thus, the politics of the legislative institution in the United States is affected by the way its jurisdiction-specific committees are structured. Similarly, a bureau or agency is established by law, and its jurisdiction—its scope of authority—is firmly fixed. For example, the Food and Drug Administration possesses well-defined authority to regulate the marketing of pharmaceuticals but is not permitted to regulate products falling outside its jurisdiction.

jurisdiction

The domain over which an institution or member of an institution has authority

Agenda Power and Veto Power. Agenda power describes who determines what will be taken up for consideration in an institution. Those who exercise some form of agenda power are said to engage in gatekeeping. They determine which alternatives may pass through the gate onto the institution's agenda and which alternatives will have the gate slammed in their face. Gatekeeping, in other words, consists of the power to make proposals and the power to block proposals from being made. The ability to keep something off an institution's agenda should not be confused with veto power. Veto power is the ability to defeat something even if it does become part of the agenda. In the legislative process, for example, the president has no general gatekeeping authority—he or she has no agenda power and thus cannot force the legislature to take up a proposal—but does have (limited) veto power provided by the Constitution. Congress, on the other hand, controls its own agenda—its members can place matters on the legislative agenda. Congress cannot be prevented from passing a measure, but a presidential veto can prevent a measure from becoming the law of the land. Thus, when it comes to legislation, agenda power is vested in the legislature. Veto power is possessed both by the legislature and the president (the assent of each is required for a bill to become a law). We'll examine these processes in more detail in Chapters 7 and 8.

agenda power

The control over what a group will consider for discussion

veto power

The ability to defeat something even if it has made it on to the agenda of an institution

Decisiveness. Another crucial feature of an institution is its rules for making decisions. It might sound like a straightforward task to lay out the rules for decision making, but in practice such rules often require a raft of conditions and qualifications. Every organization has rules of some sort, and the more an organization values participation by the broadest range of its members, the more it needs those rules: the requirement of participation must be balanced with the need to bring discussion and activity to a close at some point so that a decision can be made. This is why one of the motions that can be made on the floor of a legislature is to "move" the previous question, a motion to close the debate and move immediately to a vote.[7] In some legislatures, though, inaction seems to take precedence over action. In the U.S. House of Representatives, for example, a motion to adjourn (and thus not vote on a measure) takes precedence over a motion to move the previous question. In the U.S. Senate, to take another example, a supermajority (60 votes) is required to close debate and move to a vote. Decisiveness rules thus specify when votes may be taken and the sequence in which votes may occur, and—most important of all—how many individuals supporting a motion are sufficient for it to pass.

Delegation. A final aspect of institutional authority concerns delegation. Representative democracy is the quintessential instance of delegation. Citizens, through voting, delegate the authority to make decisions on their behalf

delegation

The transmission of authority to some other official or body for the latter's use (though often with the right of review and revision)

7 For a general discussion of motions to close debate and get on with the decision, see Henry M. Robert, *Robert's Rules of Order* (1876), items III. 21 and VI. 38. *Robert's* has achieved the status of an icon and now exists in an enormous variety of forms and shapes.

to representatives—chiefly legislators and executives—rather than exercising political authority directly. We can think of our political representatives as our *agents*, just as we may think of professionals and craftspeople whose services we retain—doctors, lawyers, accountants, plumbers, mechanics, and so on—as agents whom we hire to act on our behalf. Why would those with authority, whom we will call *principals*, delegate some of their authority to agents? This has to do with the virtues of decentralization and of division and specialization of labor. The answer is that both principals and agents benefit from it. Principals benefit because they are able to off-load to experts and specialists tasks that they themselves are less capable of performing. Ordinary citizens, for example, are not so well versed in the tasks of governance as are professional politicians. Thus by delegating, citizens do not have to be specialists and can focus their energies on other things. This is the rationale for representative democracy. Agents benefit as well, since delegation means there is a demand for their services, which enables them to exercise authority and receive compensation for their efforts.

Examples of principals and agents abound in politics. Elected officials are agents for citizen-principals. Leaders are agents for their followers. Government bureaus—called *agencies* after all—serve as agents for elected principals in the executive and legislative branches.[8] Law clerks are agents for the judges who employ them. Lobbyists are agents of special interests. In short, the political world is replete with links between principals and agents.

The relationship between a principal and agent allows the former to delegate to the latter with gains for both, which may seem almost too good to be true. But there is a dark side to this principal-agent relationship. As the eighteenth-century economist Adam Smith noted in his classic work, *The Wealth of Nations* (1776), economic agents are not motivated by the welfare of their customers to grow vegetables, make shoes, or weave cloth; rather, they do those things out of their own self-interest. Thus a principal must take care when delegating to agents that those agents are properly motivated to serve the principal's interests, either by sharing his or her interests or by deriving something of value (reputation, compensation, and so on) for acting to advance those interests. The principal will need to have some instruments by which to monitor and validate what his or her agent is doing and then reward or punish the agent accordingly. Nevertheless, a principal will not bother to eliminate entirely the agent's prospective deviations from the principal's interests. The reason is transaction costs. The effort necessary to negotiate and then police every aspect of a principal-agent relationship becomes, at some point, more costly than it is worth. In sum, the upside of delegation consists of the assignment of activities to precisely those agents who possess a comparative advantage in performing them. The downside is the prospective misalignment of the goals of agents with the goals of principals and thus the possibility of agents marching to the beat of their own drummers. Delegation is a double-edged sword.

principal-agent relationship

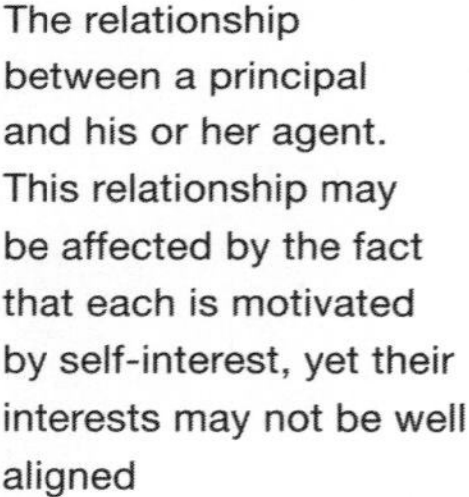
The relationship between a principal and his or her agent. This relationship may be affected by the fact that each is motivated by self-interest, yet their interests may not be well aligned

transaction costs 

The cost of clarifying each aspect of a principal-agent relationship and monitoring it to make sure arrangements are complied with

8 Thus, elected officials are simultaneously agents of their constituents and principals for bureaucrats to whom they delegate authority to implement policy.

Characterizing institutions in terms of jurisdiction, agenda and veto power, decisiveness, and delegation covers an immense amount of ground. Our purpose here has been to introduce the many ways collectivities arrange their business and routinize it, thereby enabling cooperation and facilitating political bargaining and decision making. A second purpose has been to highlight the potential diversity in institutional arrangements—there are so many ways to do things collectively. This diversity underscores the sophistication and intelligence of the framers of the U.S. Constitution in the institutional choices they made more than two centuries ago, as we discuss in the following chapter. Finally, we want to make clear that institutions not only make rules for governing but also present strategic opportunities for various political interests, depending on how the institutions are designed. As George Washington Plunkitt, the savvy and candid political boss of Tammany Hall, said of the institutional situations in which he found himself, "I seen my opportunities, and I took 'em."[9]

The Collective-Action Principle: All Politics Is Collective Action

The third factor that helps explain why governments do what they do is that political action is collective. It involves building, combining, mixing, and amalgamating people's individual goals. This sometimes occurs in highly institutionalized settings—a committee, legislature, or bureaucracy, for example. However, it also occurs in less institutionalized settings—a campaign rally, a get-out-the-vote drive, or a civil rights march. Moreover, collective action can be difficult to orchestrate because the individuals involved in the decision-making process often have different goals and preferences. The result is mixed motives for cooperation. Conflict is inevitable; the question is how it can be resolved. The most typical and widespread means of resolving collective dilemmas is bargaining among individuals. But when the number of parties involved is too large to engage in face-to-face bargaining, incentives must be provided to get everyone to act collectively.

Informal Bargaining. Political bargaining may be highly formal or entirely informal. Relations among neighbors, for example, are usually based on informal give-and-take. To present a personal example, one of this book's authors has a neighbor with whom he shares a hedge on their property line. First one takes responsibility for trimming the hedge and then the other, alternating from year to year. This arrangement (or bargain) is merely an understanding, not a legally binding agreement, and it was reached amicably and without much fuss or fanfare after a brief conversation. No organized effort—such as hiring

9 In the nineteenth century and well into the twentieth, Tammany Hall was the club that ran New York City's Democratic Party like a machine.

lawyers, drafting an agreement, and having it signed, witnessed, notarized, filed at the county courthouse, and so on—was required to reach this bargain.

Bargaining in politics can be similarly informal and unstructured. Whether called horse trading, back-scratching, logrolling, or wheeling and dealing, it has much the same flavor as the casual, over-the-fence negotiation between neighbors that was just described. Deals will be struck depending on the preferences and beliefs of the participants. If preferences are too incompatible or beliefs too inconsistent with one another, then a deal simply may not be possible. If preferences and beliefs are not too far out of line, then there will be a range of possible bargaining outcomes, some of which slightly advantage one party, others of which advantage other parties. In short, there will be room for a compromise.

In fact, much of politics *is* informal, unstructured bargaining. First, many disputes subjected to bargaining are of sufficiently low impact that establishing elaborate formal machinery for dealing with them is just not worth the effort. Rules of thumb often develop as a benchmark—such as "split the difference" or "take turns" (the outcome of the hedge-trimming example just given). Second, repetition can contribute to successful cooperation. If a small group engages in bargaining today over one matter and tomorrow over another—as neighbors bargain over draining a swampy meadow one day, fixing a fence another, and trimming a hedge on still another occasion—then patterns develop. If one party constantly tries to extract maximal advantage, then the other parties will cease doing business with him. If, on the other hand, each party "gives a little to get a little," then a pattern of cooperation develops over time. It is the repetition of similar, mixed-motive occasions that allows this pattern to emerge without formal trappings. Many political circumstances are either amenable to informal rules of thumb like those mentioned or are repeated with sufficient frequency as to allow cooperative patterns to emerge.[10]

Formal Bargaining. Other bargaining situations are governed by rules. The rules describe such things as who gets to make the first offer, how long the other parties have to consider it, whether other parties must take it or leave it or can make counteroffers, the method by which they convey their assent or rejection, what happens when all (or some decisive subset) of the others accept or reject it, what happens next if the proposal is rejected, and so on. It may be hard to imagine two neighbors deciding how to trim their common hedge under procedures as explicit and formal as these. It makes more sense, however, to imagine a bargaining session over wages and working conditions between labor and management at a large manufacturing plant proceeding in just this manner. The distinction suggests that some parties are more suited to formal proceedings, whereas others get on well enough without them. The same may be said about situations. A husband and wife are likely to divide household chores by informal

10 A wonderful description of how ranchers in Shasta County, California, organized their social lives and collective interactions in just this fashion is found in Robert C. Ellickson, *Order without Law: How Neighbors Settle Disputes* (Cambridge, MA: Harvard University Press, 1991).

bargaining, but this same couple would employ a formal procedure if they were dividing household assets in a divorce settlement.

Formal bargaining is often associated with events that take place in official institutions—legislatures, courts, party conventions, administrative and regulatory agencies. These are settings in which situations involving mixed motives arise over and over again. Year in and year out, legislatures pass statutes, approve executive budgets, and oversee the administrative branch of government. Courts administer justice, determine guilt or innocence, impose sentences, resolve differences between disputants, and render interpretive opinions about the meaning of the law. Party conventions nominate candidates and approve the platforms on which they base their campaigns. Administrative and regulatory agencies implement policy and make rulings about its applicability. All of these are instances of mixed-motive circumstances in which gains from cooperation are possible but bargaining failures are also a definite possibility. Consequently, the formal bargaining that takes place through institutions is governed by rules that regularize proceedings both to maximize the prospects of reaching agreement and to guarantee that procedural wheels don't have to be reinvented each time a similar bargaining problem arises. This is our first application of the institution principle: institutions facilitate collective action.

Collective Dilemmas and Bargaining Failures. Even when gains are possible from collective action—when people share some common objective, for example—it still may not be feasible to arrive at a satisfactory conclusion. Let us take the simple example of two farmers interested in mending a piece of fence that separates their properties. For simplicity, suppose that Farmer Jones and Farmer Smith each value the mended fence at some positive level, V. Suppose further that the total cost (in terms of time or effort) to do this chore is c, a big enough cost to make the job not worth the effort if a farmer had to do it all by himself. For example, if each farmer values the mended fence at \$700, but the cost to repair it on his own is \$1,000, the net benefit to one farmer repairing it alone (\$700 minus \$1,000) is less than zero—and thus not an attractive option. If they shared the cost equally, their net benefit would each be $V–c/2$, in our example, \$700 minus \$500—a positive net benefit of \$200 to both. If one of the farmers, however, could off-load the entire project on his neighbor, then he would not have to bear any of the cost and would enjoy the mended fence valued by him at V (\$700). The situation is displayed in the accompanying Figure 1.1. Each row gives the options available to Jones and each column the options available to Smith. The lower left entry in each cell of the figure is the payoff to Jones if he selects the row option and Smith selects the column option; the upper right entry in each cell is Smith's payoff. Thus if both choose to mend the fence (the upper left cell), then they each enjoy a (positive) net benefit of $V–c/2$. If, on the other hand, Jones takes on the job, but Smith does not—this is the upper right cell of the figure—then Jones pays the full price and receives $V–c$ (which is negative) and Smith gets the full value, V. The other two cells are filled in according to this logic.

Consider now how Jones might think about this problem. On the one hand, if Smith chooses to mend the fence (left column in the figure), then Jones gets $V–c/2$ if he does too, but he does even better, V, if he lets Smith do the whole

Figure 1.1
A COLLECTIVE DILEMMA

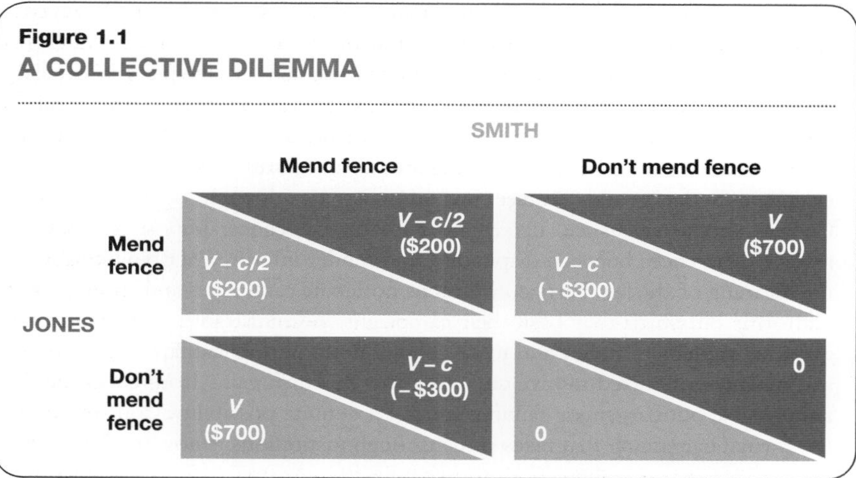

job. On the other hand, if Smith chooses not to mend the fence (right column in the figure), then Jones gets *V–c* if he goes ahead and does the job himself (this is negative) but gets zero if he too does not take up the task. Putting these together, Jones realizes that *no matter what Smith does, Jones is better off not mending the fence*. Following the same logic, Smith will arrive at the same conclusion. So, each chooses "don't mend fence," and each gets a payoff of zero, even though both would have been better off if both had chosen "mend the fence."

This is a famous dilemma in social science.[11] It is a dilemma because the two individuals actually share a common goal—mending the fence—but each person's individual rationality causes both of them to do worse than they needed to. Had they only "suspended" their rationality and contributed to the common objective, then each would have been better served than when both are behaving in a fully rational manner. Even if the two farmers sat down and tried to overcome this dilemma, the dilemma still persists, as each has a rational temptation to defect from a bargain in which both agree to mend the fence. Moreover, each is nervous that the other will defect, given the incentives of the situation, and so feels compelled to defect himself.

The broad point of this example is that bargaining, even with common values and objectives, is no guarantee that a positive outcome will occur. We encounter dilemmas and bargaining failures like the one facing the two farmers frequently in politics. We will also discover that people have invented some methods that partially mitigate bargaining failures.

Collective Action, Free Riders, Public Goods, and the Commons. The idea of political bargaining suggests an intimate kind of politics, involving face-to-face relations, negotiation, compromise, give-and-take, and so on. Such bargaining results from the combination of mixed motives and small

11 In another context, it is known as the prisoner's dilemma. We encounter it again in Chapter 13 when we discuss interest groups.

numbers. When the numbers of individuals or other actors become large, bargaining may no longer be practical. If 100 people own property bordering a swampy meadow, how does this community solve the swamp's mosquito problem? How does the community secure the benefits that arise from cooperation? In short, what happens if a simple face-to-face interaction, possibly amenable to bargaining, now requires coordination among a large number of people?

In the swamp meadow example, everyone shares some common value—eliminating the mosquito habitat—but they may disagree on other matters. Some may want to use pesticides in the meadow, while others are concerned about the environmental impact. And there are bound to be disagreements over how to pay for the project. A collective-action problem arises, as in this example, when there is something to be gained if the group can cooperate and assure one another that no one will get away with bearing less than their fair share of the effort. Face-to-face bargaining, however, is made impractical by sheer numbers. The issue, then, is how to accomplish some common objective among a large number of interested parties.

Groups of individuals intent on collective action will ordinarily establish some decision-making procedures—relatively formal arrangements by which to resolve differences, coordinate the group to pursue a course of action, and sanction slackers, if necessary. Workers in a manufacturing plant, for example, may attempt to form a union. Or, to take another example, like-minded citizens may organize a political party. Most groups will also require a leadership structure, which is necessary even if all the members of the group are in agreement about how to proceed. This structure is necessary to deal with a phenomenon known as free riding. Imagine that each owner of land bordering a swamp wants the area cleared of mosquitoes. If one or a few owners were to clear the swamp alone, their actions would benefit all the other owners as well, without any efforts on the part of these others. They would be free riders, enjoying the benefit of others' efforts without contributing themselves. (The same issue faced farmers Smith and Jones in the fence-mending problem described earlier.) It is this prospect of free riding that risks undermining collective action. A leadership structure will have to be in place to threaten and, if necessary, inflict punishments to discourage individuals from reneging on the individual contributions required to enable the group to pursue its common goals.

 **collective action**

The pooling of resources and the coordination of effort and activity by a group of people (often a large one) to achieve common goals

 **free riding**

Enjoying the benefits of some good or action while letting others bear the costs

Another way to think about this is to describe a commonly shared goal—in the present example a mosquito-free meadow—as a public good. A public good is a benefit that others cannot be denied from enjoying, once it has been provided. Once the meadow is mosquito free, it will constitute a benefit to *all* the members of the group, even those who have not contributed to its provision. More generally, a public good is one that can be "consumed" by individuals without using it up, and for which there are no means at hand to exclude individuals easily. A classic example is a lighthouse. Once it is erected, it aids all ships, and there is no simple way to charge a ship for its use. Another classic example is national defense. It protects tax payers and tax avoiders alike. A third example is clean air. Once enough people restrict their polluting, the air is cleansed and may be enjoyed even by those who have not restricted their polluting. (Imagine owners of hybrid vehicles whose reduced pollution makes for cleaner air enjoyed even by those

 **public good**

A good that (1) may be enjoyed by anyone if it is provided and (2) may not be denied to anyone once it has been provided

whose automobiles produce lots of noxious exhaust.) Because public goods have these properties, it is easy for some members of a group to free-ride on the efforts shouldered by others. And as a result, it may be difficult to get anyone to provide it in the first place. Collective action is required, and this in turn often requires leaders (or governments) with the capacity to induce all to contribute to its provision.

by-product theory

The idea that groups provide members with private benefits to attract membership. The possibility of group collective action emerges as a consequence

Various solutions to the collective-action problem have been proposed. The most famous is Mancur Olson's by-product theory.[12] Briefly, Olson's idea is this: The nub of free riding derives from the fact that most individuals in a large group don't make much difference to the final result, and they know it. This is why they may comfortably abstain from participation: they know that in following their inclination to avoid the costs of participation, they do not damage their prospects (or anyone else's) for receiving benefits. The problem is that although no one person's free riding does much harm, if enough people free ride, then the collective action will be compromised. What if, however, something of value were at stake that would be lost if the person abstained from participation? What if participants were given something special that nonparticipants were denied? That is, what if some benefits were contingent on contributing to the group effort? Many organizations use this tactic, giving dues-paying or effort-contributing members special insurance or education benefits, reduced-fare travel, free or subsidized subscriptions to magazines and newsletters, bowling and golf tournaments, soccer leagues, access to members-only social events, and so on. Olson argued that if members were prepared to "pay their dues" to join an organization partially (or even mainly) for these special benefits, of which they would otherwise be deprived—what Olson called selective benefits—then the collective cooperation would end up being provided as well, as a by-product, with whatever surplus the dues structure generated. A member's inclination to free ride would be diminished, not because of feelings of obligation to his or her fellow members, not because of a moral imperative to participate, and not even because of a desire for the collective benefit supplied by the group, but rather because of self-interest—the desire for selective benefits. Clearly this is an extreme version of the argument; the main point is that the selective benefits available only to participants and contributors—and denied to nonparticipants and noncontributors—are the key to successful collective action. A group that appeals to its members *only* on the basis of its common collective purposes is a group that will have trouble achieving those purposes.[13]

selective benefits

Benefits that do not go to everyone but, rather, are distributed selectively—only to those who contribute to the group enterprise

12 Mancur Olson, *The Logic of Collective Action: Public Goods and the Theory of Groups* (1965; repr., Cambridge, MA: Harvard University Press, 1971). On the general subject of collective action, the interested reader should also consult Shepsle, *Analyzing Politics*, chap. 9, where Olson's work, among that of others, is taken up.

13 Getting such an organizational effort up and running, however, is no small feat. Olson's argument appreciates what is necessary to keep a group going but underestimates what it takes to organize collective action in the first place. Put differently, a prior collective-action problem needs to be solved—and that is an organizational problem. The solution is leadership, and the individuals imaginative enough to see this need are referred to as political entrepreneurs. That is, there must be a selective benefit available to those who bear organizational burdens, thereby facilitating the collective action; the selective benefits of leadership include perquisites of office, financial reward, and honor and status.

One of the most notorious collective-action problems involves too much of a good thing. Known as the *tragedy of the commons*, this type of problem reveals how unbridled self-interest can have damaging collective consequences. A political party's reputation, for example, can be seen as something that benefits all politicians affiliated with the party. This collective reputation is not irreparably harmed if one legislator in the party pushes her advantage by getting approval for a minor amendment helpful to a special interest in her district. But if lots of party members do it, the party comes to be known as the champion of special interests, and its reputation is tarnished. A pool of resources is not much depleted if someone takes a little of it. But it does become depleted if lots of people take from it—a forest is lost a pine tree at a time; an oil reserve declines a barrel at a time; the atmosphere is polluted a particle at a time. The party's reputation, the forest, the oil reserve, and the atmosphere are all *commons*.[14] The problem to which they are vulnerable is *overgrazing*—a common resource that is irreparably depleted by individual actions.[15]

To summarize, individuals try to accomplish things not only as individuals but also as members of larger collectivities (families, friendship groups, clubs and associations, and political parties) and even larger categories (economic classes, ethnic groups, and nationalities). The rationality principle covers individual initiative. The collective action principle describes the paradoxes encountered, the obstacles that must be overcome, and the incentives necessary for individuals to work with others to coordinate their energies, accomplish collective purposes, and secure the dividends of cooperation. Much of politics is about doing this or failing to do this. The institution principle discussed previously takes this argument to its logical conclusion, focusing on collective activities that are regularized because they are both important and frequently occurring. Institutions do the public's business while relieving communities of having to reinvent collective action each time it is required. Thus we have a rationale for government.

The Policy Principle: Political Outcomes Are the Products of Individual Preferences and Institutional Procedures

At the end of the day, we are interested in the results of politics—the collective decisions that emerge from the political process. A Nebraska farmer, for example, cares about how public laws and rulings affect his welfare and that of

14 The original meaning is of a pasture on which cows graze. A most insightful discussion of "commons problems," of which these are examples, is Elinor Ostrom, *Governing the Commons: The Evolution of Institutions for Collective Action* (New York: Cambridge University Press, 1990).

15 The classic statement is Garrett Hardin, "The Tragedy of the Commons," *Science* 162 (1968): 1243–8.

his family, friends, and neighbors. He cares about how export policies affect the prices his crops and livestock products earn in international markets and how monetary policy influences inflation and, as a result, the cost of purchasing fuel, feed, seed, and fertilizer; about the funding of public and private research and development efforts in agriculture and their effect on the quality and reliability of the scientific information he obtains; and about the affordability of the state university, where he hopes to educate his children. He also cares, eventually, about inheritance laws and their effect on his ability to pass his farm on to his kids without Uncle Sam taking a huge chunk of it in estate taxes. As students of American politics, we need to consider the link between individual goals, institutional arrangements, collective action, and policy outcomes. How do all of these leave their marks on policy? What biases, predilections, and tendencies manifest themselves in public decisions?

The linchpin is the motivations of political actors. As we saw in our discussion of the rationality principle, their ambitions—ideological, personal, electoral, and institutional—provide politicians with the incentives to craft policies in particular ways. In fact, most policies make sense only as reflections of individual politicians' interests, goals, and beliefs. Examples include:

Personal interests: Congressman X is an enthusiastic supporter of subsidizing home heating oil (but opposes regulation to keep its price down) because some of his friends own heating-oil distributorships.[16]

Electoral ambitions: Senator Y, a well-known political moderate, has lately been introducing very conservative amendments to bills dealing with the economy to appeal to more conservative financial donors, who might then contribute to her budding presidential campaign.

Institutional ambitions: Representative Z has promised his vote and given a rousing speech on the House floor supporting a particular amendment because he knows it is near and dear to his party leader. He hopes his support will earn him her endorsement next year for an assignment to the prestigious Appropriations Committee.

These examples illustrate how policies are politically crafted according to both institutional procedures and individual aspirations. The procedures, as we saw in a previous discussion, are a series of chutes and ladders that shape, channel, filter, and prune the alternatives from which ultimate policy choices are made. The politicians who populate these institutions, as we have just noted, are driven both by private objectives and by public purposes, pursuing their

16 These friends would benefit from people's having the financial means to buy home heating oil but would not want the price they charge for the oil restricted.

own private interests while working on behalf of their conception of the public interest.

Because the institutional features of the American political system are complex and policy change requires success at every step, change is often impossibly difficult, meaning the status quo usually prevails. A long list of players must be satisfied with the change, or it won't happen. Most of these politicians will need some form of "compensation" to provide their endorsement and support.

Majorities are usually built by legislators drafting bills so as to spread the benefits to enough members of the legislature to get the requisite number of votes for that particular bill. Derisively, this is called pork-barrel legislation. It can be better understood by remembering that the overwhelming proportion of pork-barrel projects that are distributed to build policy majorities are justified to voters as valuable additions to the public good of the various districts. What may be pork to the critic is actual bridges, roads, and post offices.

Elaborate institutional arrangements, complicated policy processes, and intricate political motivations make for a highly combustible mixture. The policies that emerge are inevitably lacking in the neatness that citizens desire. But policies in the United States today are sloppy and slapdash for a clear reason: The tendency to spread the benefits broadly results when political ambition comes up against a decentralized political system.

The History Principle: How We Got Here Matters

There is one more aspect of our analysis that is important: we must ask how we have gotten where we are. How did we get the institutions and policies that are in place? By what series of steps? When by choice and when by accident? Every question and problem we confront has a history. History will not tell the same story for every institution. Nevertheless, without history, we have neither a sense of causation nor a full sense of how institutions are related to one another. In explaining the answer to why governments do what they do, we must turn to history to see what choices were available to political actors at a given time, what consequences resulted from those choices and what consequences might have flowed from the paths not chosen.

Imagine a tree growing from the bottom of the page. Its trunk grows upward from some root ball at the bottom, dividing into branches that continue to grow upward, further dividing into smaller branches. Imagine a path through this tree, from its very roots at the bottom of the page to the end of one of the highest branches at the top of the page. There are many such paths, from the one point at the bottom to many possible points at the top. If instead of a tree this were a time diagram, then the root ball at the bottom would represent some specific beginning point and all of the top-branch endings would represent some terminal time. Each path is now a possible history, the delineation of movement from some specific beginning to some concluding time. Alternative histories, like paths through trees, entail irreversibilities. Once one starts down a historical path (or up a tree), one cannot always retrace one's steps.[17] Once things happen, they cannot always un-happen. Some futures are foreclosed by the choices people have already made or, if not literally foreclosed, then made extremely unlikely.

path dependency 

The idea that certain possibilities are made more or less likely because of the historical path taken

It is in this sense that we explain a current situation at least in part by describing the historical path by which we arrived at it. Some scholars use the term path dependency to suggest that some possibilities are more or less likely because of events that occurred, and choices that were made, earlier in history. Both the status quo and the path from it significantly delimit future possibilities.

Three factors that help to explain why history commonly matters in political life are rules and procedures, loyalties and alliances, and historically conditioned points of view. As for the first of these factors, rules and procedures, choices made during one point in time continue to have important consequences for years, decades, or even centuries. For example, America's single-member-district plurality voting rules, established in the eighteenth century, continue to shape the nation's party system today.[18] Those voting rules, as we shall see in Chapter 12, help explain why the United States has a two-party system rather than the multiparty systems found in many other Western democracies. Thus a set of choices made 200 years ago affects party politics today.

A second way in which history often matters in politics is through the persistence of loyalties and alliances. Many of the political alliances that are important in American politics today are products of events that took place decades ago. For example, Jewish voters are among the Democratic Party's most loyal supporters, consistently giving 80 or 90 percent of their votes to Democratic presidential candidates. Yet on the basis of economic interest, Jews, one of the wealthier social groups in America, might be expected to vote for the Republicans. In recent years, moreover, the GOP has been a stronger supporter of Israel than the Democrats. Why, then, do Jews overwhelmingly support the Democrats? Part of the answer has to do with history. In the late nineteenth and early twentieth centuries, Jews suffered considerable discrimination in the United States. In the 1930s, though, under the leadership of Franklin Delano Roosevelt, the Democratic Party was one vehicle through which Jews in America began their climb to the success they enjoy today. This historical experience continues to shape Jewish political identity. Similar historical experiences help to explain the political loyalties of African Americans, Cuban Americans, and others.

17 Clearly with tree climbing this is not literally true, or once we started climbing a tree, we would never get down! So the tree analogy is not perfect here.

18 Single-member districts are arrangements in which one legislator is selected from each district. (Some electoral systems select multiple members from each district.) A plurality voting rule declares that the one legislator selected in a district is the one with the most votes (not necessarily a majority).

A third factor explaining why history matters is the fact that past events and experiences shape current viewpoints and perspectives. For example, many Americans now in their sixties and seventies view events in Iraq through the lens of the Vietnam War. Those influenced by the memory of Vietnam often see U.S. military involvement in a Third World country as likely to lead to a quagmire of costs and casualties. Interestingly, in the 1960s, many older Americans viewed events in Vietnam through the lens of the 1930s, when the Western democracies were slow to resist Adolf Hitler's Germany. Thus to those influenced by events of the 1930s and World War II, failure to respond strongly to aggression was seen as a form of appeasement that would only encourage hostile powers to use force against American interests. Both groups saw the world through perspectives that they had learned from their own histories.

CONCLUSION

This introductory chapter has asked much of the reader. We have set the stage for an analytical treatment of the phenomena that constitute American politics. This analytical approach requires attention to *argument* and *evidence*. To construct an argument about some facet of American politics—why were young voters attracted to Barack Obama in 2008 or Ronald Reagan in 1980? Why do incumbent legislators in the House and Senate have so much success in securing reelection? Why does the president dominate media attention?—we can draw on a set of five principles. The linchpin is the rationality principle, emphasizing individual goal seeking as a key explanation for behavioral patterns. But politics is a collective undertaking, and it is often structured by political arrangements, so we also focus on collective action and the institutions in which such action takes place (collective action principle, institution principle). The combination of goal-seeking individuals engaging in collective activity in institutional contexts provides leverage for understanding why governments govern as they do—making laws, passing budgets, implementing policies, rendering judicial judgments (policy principle). But we could not make entire sense of these activities without an appreciation of the broader historical path (history principle). These five principles, then, are tools of analysis. They are also tools of discovery, permitting the interested observer to uncover new ideas about why politics works as it does.

Arguments may be tight or loose, compelling or questionable, persuasive or dubious. To know if an argument truly contributes to our understanding of the real world around us, we need to look at evidence. In the study of American politics, much of this evidence takes the form of quantitative data, and much of it is easily accessible on Web sites. How to make sense of such evidence is what political scientists do in their workaday world. In the Analyzing the Evidence section beginning on page 26, we provide a brief glimpse of how to go about this task. We hope it proves helpful in allowing you to think analytically about political information as we move through the remaining chapters of the book.

Drawing on the lesson of the history principle, we begin in the remaining chapters of Part One by setting the historical stage. With analytical principles and strategies for analyzing evidence in hand, we are in a position to understand what influenced and inspired the founding generation more than two centuries ago to create a national government and a federal political system, while preserving individual rights and liberties.

For Further Reading

Bianco, William T. *American Politics: Strategy and Choice*. New York: Norton, 2001.

Dahl, Robert A. *Who Governs? Democracy and Power in an American City*. New Haven, CT: Yale University Press, 1961.

Downs, Anthony. *An Economic Theory of Democracy*. New York: Harper & Row, 1957.

Ellickson, Robert C. *Order without Law: How Neighbors Settle Disputes*. Cambridge, MA: Harvard University Press, 1991.

reader selection Hardin, Garrett, "The Tragedy of the Commons," *Science* 162 (1968): 1243–8.

Hindmoor, Andrew. *Rational Choice*. New York: Palgrave-Macmillan, 2006.

reader selection Kiewiet, D. Roderick, and Mathew McCubbins. *The Logic of Delegation*. Chicago: University of Chicago Press, 1991.

Mayhew, David R. *Congress: The Electoral Connection*. New Haven, CT: Yale University Press, 1974.

Mueller, Dennis. *Public Choice III*. New York: Cambridge, 2003.

reader selection Olson, Mancur, Jr. *The Logic of Collective Action: Public Goods and the Theory of Groups*. 1965. Reprinted with new preface and appendix. Cambridge, MA: Harvard University Press, 1971.

Putnam, Robert D. *Making Democracy Work: Civic Traditions in Modern Italy*. Princeton, NJ: Princeton University Press, 1993.

Riker, William H. *Liberalism against Populism: A Confrontation between the Theory of Democracy and the Theory of Social Choice*. San Francisco: Freeman, 1982.

Shepsle, Kenneth A. "Rational Choice Institutionalism," in R.A.W. Rhodes, Sarah A. Binder, and Bert A. Rockman, eds. *The Oxford Handbook of Political Institutions.* New York: Oxford University Press, 2006, pp. 23–39.

———. *Analyzing Politics: Rationality, Behavior, and Institutions.* 2nd ed. New York: Norton, 2010.

Visit **wwnorton.com/studyspace/** to access free review materials such as:

- Vocabulary Flashcards of All Key Terms
- Chapter Review Quizzes
- Complete Study Outlines

reader selection

Highlighted selections are included in *Readings in American Politics: Analysis and Perspectives*, Second Edition.

ANALYZING THE EVIDENCE

CHAPTER | 01

How Do Political Scientists Know What They Know?

The five principles introduced in this chapter provide a foundation for understanding and explaining the facts of political life; they capture the basic framework that underlies our analysis of politics. However, to make and test arguments about politics, we need more than just an analytical framework; we also need empirical evidence. We need to understand how political scientists uncover facts about politics and what tools they use to analyze and interpret these facts. What data are relevant to an argument about politics? How do we learn things from these data? How do we test arguments about the data?

Consider one of the most basic questions about voting: Why do people vote the way they do? In elections, Americans face two main alternatives in the form of the Democratic Party and the Republican Party. These parties have distinctive policy priorities, notably in the important area of economic policy. Since at least the 1930s, the Democratic Party has favored economic policies that redistribute income to poorer segments of society; Republicans, on the other hand, favor lower taxes and little or no redistribution. If those are the choices, we might argue that it makes sense to vote according to one's economic self-interest: choose the candidate from the party that maximizes your income. On reflection, however, we can see that other factors may also affect election outcomes and voting, including the candidates' personal qualities, important noneconomic issues, and even habits. Which best explains vote choice?

Table A Vote Cast for President, 2008

VOTE CAST	VOTE (%)
BARACK OBAMA (Democrat)	33%
JOHN MCCAIN (Republican)	28%
Other candidates	1%
Did not vote	38%

What Are Data? There is, in our example, a behavior that we generally want to explain, *vote choice*. We represent this general construct as a variable. A variable defines all possible outcomes that might have occurred and assigns them a unique label or value. Vote choice, for instance, may take four possible values or outcomes: vote for the Democratic Party candidate, vote for the Republican Party candidate, vote for another party or candidate, or don't vote.

The second step is to measure the behavior of interest. This stage requires the collection of data. Observation of a small set of events can be quite enlightening. We might, for instance, conduct in-depth interviews with a dozen or so people about how they decided to vote. However, we often require more evidence to support a given claim: a small number of people

Censuses and random sample surveys are staples of social science data collection. With a census we observe all individuals in a population at a given moment. Every 10 years, the United States conducts a comprehensive enumeration of all people living in the country, including information on families, educatio levels, income, race and ethnicity, commuting, housing, and employment. An election is a census of sorts as it is a comprehensive count of all votes cast in a given election. So we can measure vote choice by takin count of all electoral votes (Table A).

A survey, on the other hand, consists of a study of a relatively small subset of individuals. We call thi subset a sample. One of the most important social science research projects of the second half of th twentieth century is the American National Election Study, or ANES. The ANES is a national survey that ha been conducted during every presidential election and most midterm congressional elections since 194 to gauge how people voted and to understand why. In recent years, the ANES has used a sample c between 1,000 and 2,000 Americans to make inferences about the entire voting population of over 10 million. So voter behavior can also be measured through surveys. Today, most of the information used b public policy makers, businesses, and academic researchers, including estimates of unemployment an inflation, television and radio ratings, and most demographic characteristics of the population, are measured using surveys.

Summarizing Data. Communicating the information in a census or survey requires tools for summarizing data. First, we compute the frequency with which each value of a variable occurs. Frequency may b either the actual number of times that a specific behavior or value of a variable occurs or the percent of th observations in which it occurs.

Second, we construct a graph or statistic that summarizes the frequencies of all values of the variabl The distribution of a variable expresses how often each of the values of the variable occurs. A bar cha displays all possible values of a variable on one axis, usually the horizontal axis; the heights of the bars equa the frequency or percent of cases observed for each value (Figure A). In a pie chart, the frequency for eac value is depicted as a share of the whole (Figure B). A line graph is often used to show frequency over tim

Vote Cast for President, 2008

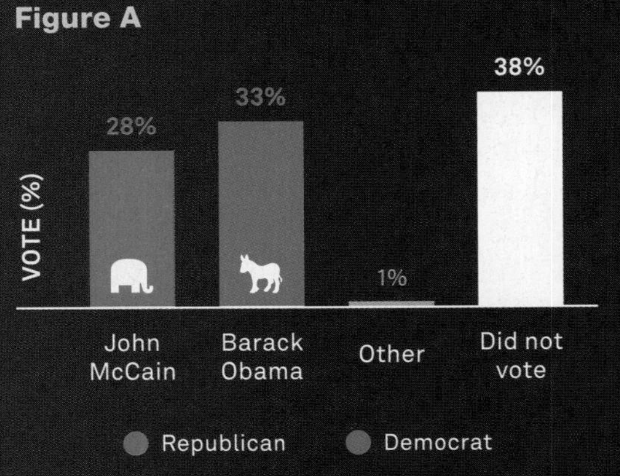

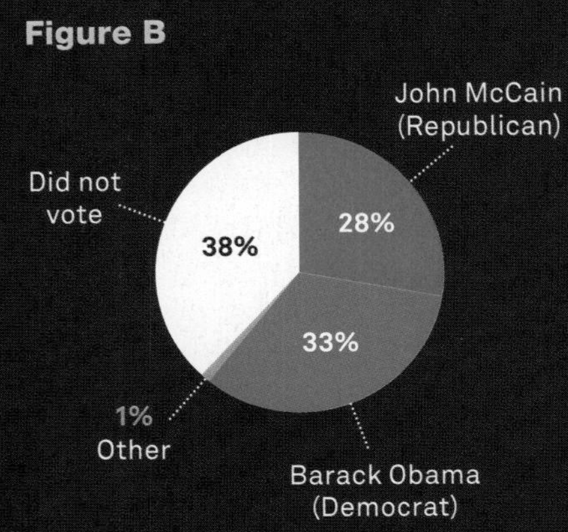

igure C Party Identification, 1952–2008

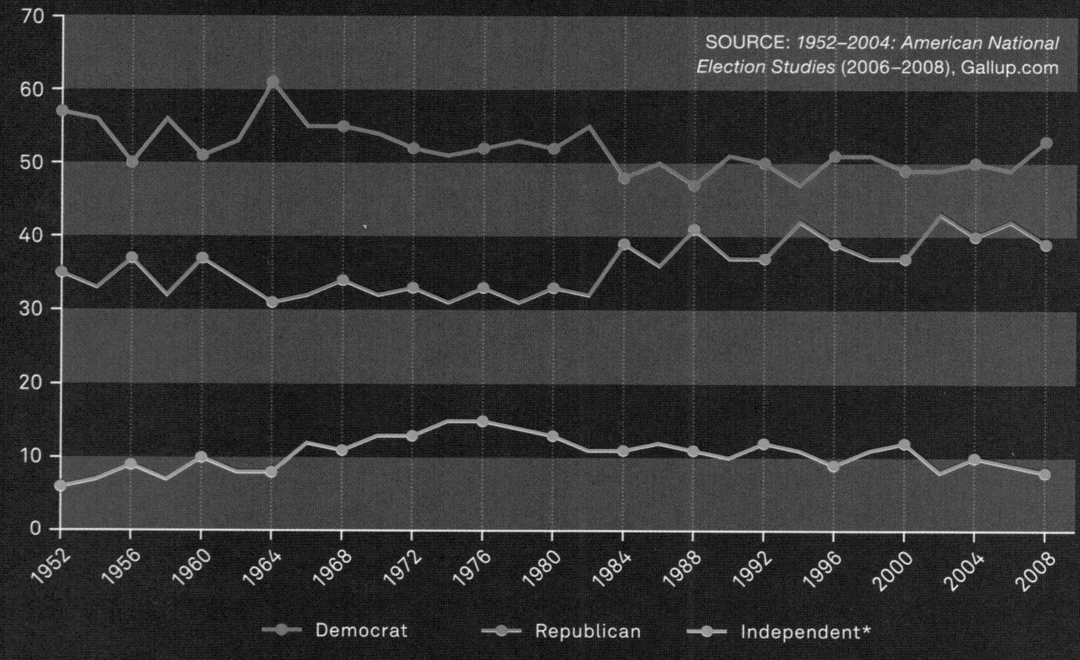

*Independents who said they leaned toward one party are counted with that party.

gure C). A statistical table typically displays the values of the variable along the left-hand side of the table d the frequencies, which may be the number or the percentage of occurrences, to the right (Table A).

The distribution of income in the United States offers a somewhat different example. This variable kes a range of values from the smallest household income to the largest household income, which we n organize in categories. In Figure D, the first category is "less than $10,000," the second category is 10,000 to $14,999," and so forth up to the top category, "$200,000 or more." All possible income levels e covered in this classification.

Variables such as income can also be characterized with statistics, such as the median or mean. In this ample, the **median** is the value of household income such that half of all households have income below e value and half have income above it. Fifty percent of all cases have income above the median value, d fifty percent have income below it; thus the median is also called the fiftieth percentile. The median usehold income in the United States in 2007 was $50,233, meaning that half of all households have come below that value and half have income above that amount. The **mean** is the average value for the iable. In the case of household income, the mean equals the sum of all households' incomes divided by e number of households. Personal income totaled approximately $11.6 trillion in 2007, and there were 117 lion households. So the average household income was $99,800.

Why do the median and mean differ? In calculating the median, every household is equal. We merely

Figure D Distribution of Household Income in the United States, 2007

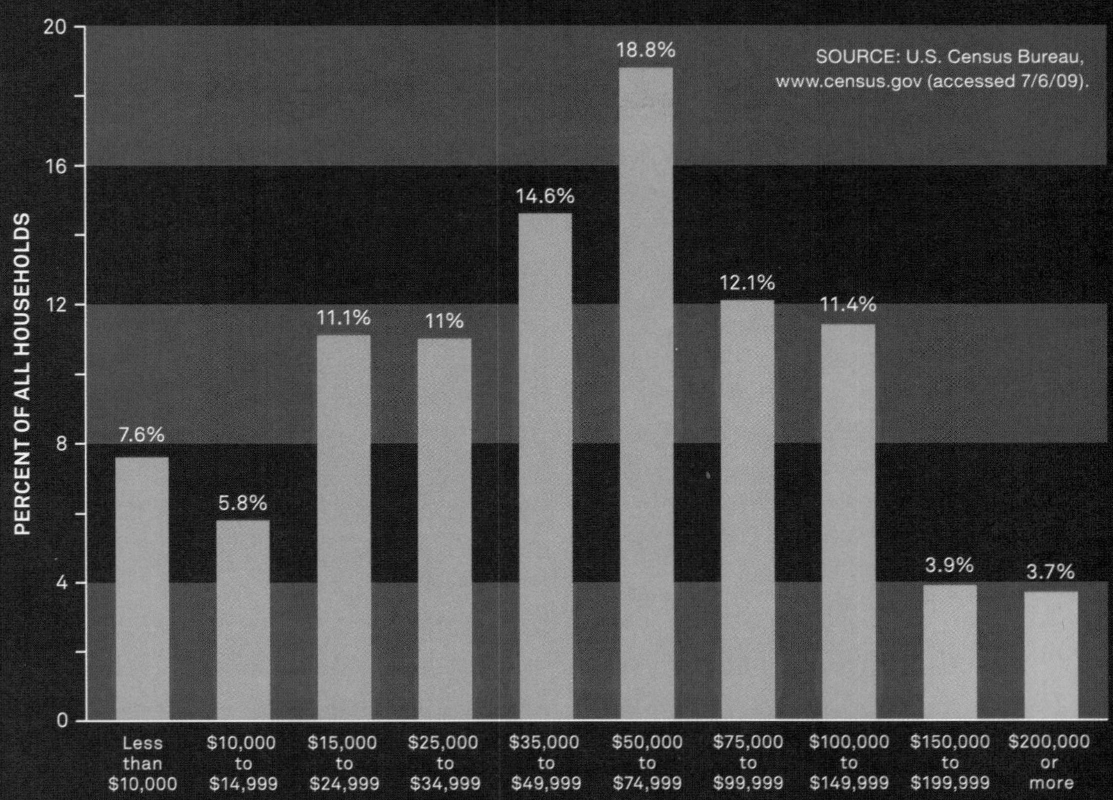

count the percent above and below a certain income level. The mean value weights households according to their incomes; consequently, a household with $200,000 income contributes 10 times as much to the calculation of the mean as a household with $20,000. If there were only small differences in income among households, the mean would be very close to the median. The difference between the median income and the mean income thus provides a way to measure inequality.

The concept of the median is particularly important in thinking about voting. In an election involving two parties or candidates, it takes at least 50 percent of the votes to win. In a legislature, any bill must receive at least half of the votes of those present in order to pass. Suppose a piece of legislation directly affects people's incomes by taxing those with income above a certain level, say $75,000, and redistributing that income to people who make less than that amount. Suppose also that people only care about their personal income when thinking about this bill. Based on the data in Figure D, if people voted only on the basis of their income—their economic self-interest—then the 31.1 percent with incomes over $75,000 would oppose the tax and 68.9 percent would support it. In such a setting, one could easily see that democracy would inevitably tax the rich and redistribute wealth.

Testing Arguments Using Data. The argument that democracy will tend to redistribute wealth depends on an important assumption—that people vote their economic self-interest. Is that assumption correct?

Usually, such conjectures take the form of a hypothesis that there is a strong relationship between two variables, such as income and the vote. To test the argument that people vote their economic self-interest, we want to know how much voting decisions depend on individuals' income levels. As stated earlier, in the United States today, the Republican Party generally favors lower income taxes and less income redistribution, and the Democratic Party favors higher income taxes and more income redistribution. We therefore want to know if those in high-income households vote Republican at a much higher rate than those in low-income households. The difference in voting behavior between these two groups is the effect of income on the vote.

Table B Vote by Level of Income in 2008 National Exit Polls

INCOME	OBAMA	McCAIN	OTHER
Under $15,000	73%	25%	2%
$15-30,000	60%	37%	3%
$30-50,000	55%	43%	2%
$50-75,000	48%	49%	3%
$75-100,000	51%	48%	1%
$100-150,000	48%	51%	1%
$150-200,000	48%	50%	2%
$200,000 or more (6%)	52%	46%	2%

To see whether the effect of income on the vote is indeed large, we can use the data in Table B to examine the actual voting behavior of different sorts of individuals. The national exit polls in 2008 reveal that 73 percent of voters with income less than $15,000 chose the Democrat, Barack Obama. By comparison, 52 percent of those with income over $200,000 chose Barack Obama. This large difference (21 percentage points) reveals that income is associated with vote choice, but it is not absolutely determinative: no income group voted overwhelmingly Republican in this election.

As we explore alternative arguments about vote choice, we can make many different comparisons—Democrats versus Republicans, men versus women, college graduates versus high school graduates, and so forth. Our goal is to find which, if any, of these potential explanations best accounts for the variation in vote choice. Throughout this book, we will consider other outcomes besides voter behavior, such as the support by members of Congress for different types of legislation and the percent of times that the executive succeeds in passing legislation—in each case, what we know about these phenomena in American

Many times we will look for a relationship or association between two variables to see if the predictions from an argument hold true, and if they do, we take that as evidence supporting the argument. A relationship or association between two variables, sometimes called a **correlation**, should not be taken to mean that one of the variables caused the other to occur. **Causation** is more difficult to establish. A correlation between two variables X (say, education) and Y (say, income) is consistent with a theory that says that education increases one's earning power. From a simple correlation, however, one cannot tell whether variable X caused variable Y or Y caused X or some other variable W (say, intelligence) caused both. Social scientists design experiments and carefully controlled comparisons (such as comparisons of twins) in order to measure causal relationships. Observing simple associations and correlations, though, is a first step in verifying our arguments, ideas, and theories about how politics works.

Be a Savvy Consumer of Quantitative Data. Beyond the figures and tables in this book, which reflect data from sources that we consider reliable and accurate, you will undoubtedly encounter other data about politics in the news and elsewhere. Before you take such data—and whatever argument they seem to support—at face value, it is worth asking a few questions about how the data were gathered and presented.

- What is the source of the data? Is it a respected source like a government office or a major mainstream news organization, which may be relied upon to gather and report data accurately? Or is it from a source that is likely to have a goal other than accurate presentation of the data, like an interest group or a campaign or an entertainment Web site?
- What is the date (or date range) for the data?
- What is being measured? For example, in a poll showing support for a candidate, is it the percent of all Americans? The percent of likely voters? The percent of Democrats or Republicans?
- Why are the data presented a certain way? Is this the best way to present these data? Does it distort the data in any way? What relationships and patterns do we observe in the data?

Thinking through the questions above can also help you better understand the information in the data figures and tables found throughout this book. In each of the chapters to follow, you will also find an Analyzing the Evidence section, highlighting arguments and evidence on some of the subjects of that chapter. Many of these sections discuss how political scientists use the basic methodology discussed above to test arguments about American politics. You will then have an opportunity to analyze related data yourself in accompanying exercises on the StudySpace student Web site (**wwnorton.com/studyspace**).

EXPLORE
POLITICAL DATA
FURTHER AT:
wwnorton.com/studyspace

2

PART ✕ 2 3 4

FOUNDATIONS

Constructing a Government: The Founding and the Constitution

Chapter Outline

- The First Founding: Interests and Conflicts
- The Second Founding: From Compromise to Constitution
- The Constitution
- The Fight for Ratification: Federalists versus Antifederalists
- Changing the Institutional Framework: Constitutional Amendment
- Reflections on the Founding: Ideals or Interests?

To really understand the character of the American Founding and the meaning of the American Constitution, it is essential to look beyond myths and rhetoric. Our first principle of politics is that all political behavior has a purpose. The men and women who became revolutionaries were guided by a number of purposes. Most of the nation's Founders, though highly educated, were not political theorists. They were, rather, hardheaded and pragmatic in their commitments and activities. Although their interests were not identical, they did agree that a relationship of political and economic dependence on a colonial power, one that did not treat them as full-fledged citizens of the empire, was intolerable. In the end, the decision to break away from Britain in 1776 and, over the succeeding decade, fashion institutions of self-governance was the consequence.

Many of those most active in the initial days of the Revolution felt backed into a corner, their decisions forced. For years, the imperial center in London, preoccupied by wars with France that had spread across several continents, had left the colonists to their own devices. These were years in which the colonists enjoyed an immense amount of local control and home rule. These institutional arrangements suited merchants, farmers, and planters in the separate colonies. Local control under the mild direction of colonial governors left colonists to tend to their own business for the most part. But suddenly, as the war with France drew to a close in the 1760s, the British presence became more onerous and more intrusive. This historical experience incited collective action. In reaction to English attempts to extract tax revenues to pay for the troops that were being sent to defend the colonial frontier, protests erupted throughout the colonies against the infamous Stamp Act of 1765. This act required that all printed and legal documents, including newspapers, pamphlets, advertisements, notes and bonds, leases, deeds, and licenses, be printed on official paper stamped and sold by English officials. To show their displeasure with the act, the colonists held mass meetings, participated in parades, lit bonfires, and conducted other demonstrations throughout the spring and summer of 1765. In Boston, for example, a stamp agent was hanged and burned in effigy, leading to his resignation. Later the home of the lieutenant governor was sacked because of a rumor that he supported the Stamp Act. By November 1765, business was proceeding and newspapers were being published without stamps; in March 1766, Parliament repealed the detested law. Through their protest, the nonimportation agreements that the colonists subsequently adopted, and the Stamp Act Congress that met in October 1765, the colonists took the first steps down a path that ultimately would lead to war and the establishment of a new nation.

This is where we begin our story in the present chapter. We first assess the political backdrop of the American Revolution. From the history principle we know that nearly a century of relatively light-handed colonial administration by London had produced a set of expectations among the colonists that later British actions unmistakably violated. Then we examine the Constitution that ultimately emerged—after a rather bumpy experience in self-government just after the Revolution—as the basis for America's government. This document is the quintessential institutional setup that structures political relationships, facilitates collective action, and encourages peaceful conflict resolution. We conclude with a reflection on the Founding period by emphasizing a lesson to be learned from the Founding that continues to be important throughout American history. The lesson is that politics, as James Madison said in *The Federalist Papers*, generally involves struggles among conflicting interests. In 1776, the main conflict was between pro-Revolutionary and anti-Revolutionary forces. In 1787, the major struggle was between the Federalists and the Antifederalists. Today the struggle is between the Democratic and Republican parties, each representing competing economic, social, and sectional interests. Often political ideas are

CORE OF THE ANALYSIS

The framers of the Constitution, although guided by underlying values, also had conflicting goals and interests.

These conflicting interests were accommodated through the rules and procedures—the institutions—set forth in the Constitution.

The Constitution not only provides a framework for government but also often guides the policy process—even to this day.

the weapons developed by competing interests to further their own causes. The New England merchants who cried "no taxation without representation" cared more about lower taxes than expanded representation. Yet today representation is one of the foundations of American democracy.

As we try to understand American politics, we see that institutions matter a good deal. In fact, institutions matter in two ways. First, the institution principle tells us that institutions shape politics and affect the results of political conflicts—who wins and who loses. Second, the policy principle tells us that institutional procedures (coupled with individual preferences) help to determine policy outcomes—what the government can and cannot do. In the United States, no set of institutions is more important than the Constitution. What are the basic rules embodied in the Constitution? What significance have constitutional precepts had for American life? These are key questions addressed in this chapter. Of course, the history principle suggests that the Constitution itself was affected by the events of the colonial and founding periods. So, let us first turn to the events that preceded and shaped America's basic law.

THE FIRST FOUNDING: INTERESTS AND CONFLICTS

Competing ideals often reflect competing interests, and so it was in Revolutionary America. The American Revolution and the Constitution were outgrowths and expressions of a struggle among economic and political forces within the colonies. Five sectors of society had interests that were important in colonial politics: (1) the New England merchants; (2) the southern planters; (3) the "royalists"—holders of royal lands, offices, and patents (licenses to engage in a profession or business activity); (4) shopkeepers, artisans, and laborers; and (5) small farmers. Throughout the eighteenth century, these groups were in conflict over issues of taxation, trade, and commerce. For the most part, however, the southern planters, the New England merchants, and the royal officeholders and patent holders—groups that together made up the colonial elite—were able to maintain a political alliance that held in check the more radical forces representing shopkeepers, laborers, and small farmers. After 1750, however, by seriously threatening the interests of New England merchants and southern planters, British tax and trade policies split the colonial elite. This split permitted radical forces to expand their political influence and set into motion a chain of events that culminated in the American Revolution.[1]

1 The social makeup of colonial America and some of the social conflicts that divided colonial society are discussed in Jackson Turner Main, *The Social Structure of Revolutionary America* (Princeton, NJ: Princeton University Press, 1965).

British Taxes and Colonial Interests

Beginning in the 1750s, the debts and other financial problems faced by the British government forced it to search for new revenue sources. This search rather quickly led to the Crown's North American colonies, which on the whole paid remarkably little in taxes to the mother country. The British government reasoned that a sizable fraction of its debt was, in fact, attributable to the expenses it had incurred in defense of the colonies during the recent French and Indian War, as well as to the continuing protection from Indian attacks that British forces were giving the colonists and to the protection that the British navy was providing for colonial shipping. Thus during the 1760s, Britain sought to impose new, though relatively modest, taxes on the colonists.

Like most governments of the period, the British regime had at its disposal only limited ways to collect revenues. The income tax, which in the twentieth century became the single most important source of government revenue, had not yet been developed. For the most part in the mid-eighteenth century, governments relied on tariffs, duties, and other taxes on commerce, and it was to such taxes, including the Stamp Act, that the British turned during the 1760s. British interests (revenue) and institutions (Parliament and colonial administration) combined to produce a plausible solution to an existing problem, as suggested by the policy principle.[2]

The colonists were accustomed to managing their own affairs and were resentful of British meddling. Moreover, the Stamp Act and other taxes on commerce, such as the Sugar Act of 1764, which taxed sugar, molasses, and other commodities, most heavily affected the two groups in colonial society whose commercial interests and activities were most extensive: the New England merchants and southern planters. Under the famous slogan "no taxation without representation," the merchants and planters together purposefully organized opposition to the new taxes. In the course of the struggle against British tax measures, the planters and merchants broke with their royalist allies and turned to their former adversaries—the shopkeepers, small farmers, laborers, and artisans—for help. With the assistance of these groups, the merchants and planters organized demonstrations and boycotts of British goods that ultimately forced the Crown to rescind most of its new taxes. It was in the context of this unrest that a confrontation between colonists and British soldiers in front of the Boston customs house on the night of March 5, 1770, resulted in what came to be known as the Boston Massacre. Nervous British soldiers opened fire on the

2 Parliament also enacted the Proclamation of 1763 as part of the British settlement with the Native Americans. This withdrew the right of colonists to settle lands west of the Allegheny Mountains, preserving them for native populations. Among others, the families of George Washington and Benjamin Franklin had speculated on these lands and thus faced serious financial loss. See Norman Schofield, *Architects of Political Change: Constitutional Quandaries and Social Choice Theory* (New York: Cambridge University Press, 2006), chap. 3. A compact version is found in Norman Schofield, "Evolution of the Constitution," *British Journal of Political Science* 32 (2002): 1–23.

mob surrounding them, killing five colonists and wounding eight others. News of this event quickly spread throughout the colonies and was used by radicals to fan anti-British sentiment.

From the perspective of the merchants and planters, however, the British government's decision to eliminate most of the hated taxes meant a victorious end to their struggle with the mother country. They were eager to end the unrest they had helped arouse, and they supported the British government's efforts to restore order. Indeed, most respectable Bostonians supported the actions of the British soldiers involved in the Boston Massacre. In their subsequent trial, the soldiers were defended by John Adams, a pillar of Boston society and a future president of the United States. Adams asserted that the soldiers' actions were entirely justified, provoked by a "motley rabble of saucy boys, negroes and mulattoes, Irish teagues and outlandish Jack tars." All but two of the soldiers were acquitted.[3]

Despite the efforts of the British government and the better-to-do strata of colonial society, it proved difficult to bring an end to the political strife. The more radical forces representing shopkeepers, artisans, laborers, and small farmers, who had been mobilized and energized by the struggle over taxes, continued to agitate for political and social change within the colonies. Dramatic events helped them to overcome early collective action problems. These radicals, led by individuals such as Samuel Adams, a cousin of John Adams, asserted that British power supported an unjust political and social structure within the colonies, and they began to advocate an end to British rule.[4] That the British revenue-raising policies backfired so dramatically was a result of their greatly underestimating colonial resistance. Although they seemed rational and sensible before the fact, the policies appeared mistaken after the fact and were rescinded. The rationality principle only requires people to do the best they can at the time they act. There are bound to be uncertainties that can only imperfectly be taken into account and thus necessitate subsequent adaptation. So the British attempts to raise revenue and then to adapt this strategy in the face of the resulting unrest were rational, but it proved difficult to undo the damage caused by their initial misreading of the situation.

Organizing resistance to the British authorities required widespread support. Collective action, as noted, may emerge spontaneously in certain circumstances, but the colonists' campaign against the British imperial power in late-eighteenth-century America was a series of encounters, maneuvers, and ultimately, confrontations that required planning, coalition building, bargaining, compromising, and coordinating—all elements of the give-and-take of politics.

3 Quoted in George B. Tindall and David E. Shi, *America: A Narrative History,* 8th ed. (New York: Norton, 2010), p. 202.

4 For a discussion of events leading up to the Revolution, see Charles M. Andrews, *The Colonial Background of the American Revolution: Four Essays in American Colonial History* (New Haven, CT: Yale University Press, 1924).

Conflicts among the colonists had to be resolved by bargaining, persuasion, and even force. Cooperation needed cultivation and encouragement. Leadership was clearly a necessary ingredient.

Political Strife and the Radicalizing of the Colonists

The political strife within the colonies was the background for the events of 1773–74. In 1773, the British government granted the politically powerful East India Company a monopoly on the export of tea from Britain, eliminating a lucrative form of trade for colonial merchants. To add to the injury, the East India Company sought to sell the tea directly in the colonies instead of working through the colonial merchants. Tea was an extremely important commodity in the 1770s, and these British actions posed a mortal threat to the New England merchants. The merchants once again called on their radical adversaries for support. The most dramatic result was the Boston Tea Party of 1773, led by Samuel Adams.

This event was of decisive importance in American history. The merchants had hoped to force the British government to rescind the Tea Act, but they did not support any demands beyond this one. They certainly did not seek independence from Britain. Samuel Adams and the other radicals, however, hoped to provoke the British government to take actions that would alienate its colonial supporters and pave the way for a rebellion. This was precisely the purpose of the Boston Tea Party, and it succeeded. By dumping the East India Company's tea into Boston Harbor, Adams and his followers goaded the British into enacting a number of harsh reprisals. Within five months of the incident in Boston, the British Parliament had passed a series of acts that closed the port of Boston to commerce, changed the provincial government of Massachusetts, provided for the removal of accused persons to Britain for trial, and most important, restricted movement to the West from the southern colonies—further alienating the southern planters who depended on access to new western lands. These acts of retaliation confirmed the worst criticisms of England and helped radicalize Americans and move them toward collective resistance to British rule.[5]

The choice of this course of action by British politicians looks puzzling in retrospect, but at the time it appeared reasonable to those who prevailed in Parliament that a show of force was required. The toleration of lawlessness and the making of concessions, they felt, would only egg on the more radical elements in the colonies to take additional liberties and demand further concessions. The British, in effect, drew a line in the sand. Their repressive reactions became a clear point around which dissatisfied colonists could rally. Radicals such as

5 For an intriguing take on the role of dense population networks in cities that promoted collective action against the British, see Edward L. Glaeser, "Revolution of Urban Rebels," *Boston Globe*, July 4, 2008, Section A.

Samuel Adams had been agitating for more violent measures to deal with Britain. But ultimately they needed Britain's political repression to create widespread support for independence.[6]

Thus the Boston Tea Party set into motion a cycle of provocations and retaliations that in 1774 resulted in the convening of the First Continental Congress, an assembly consisting of delegates from all parts of the colonies, which called for a total boycott of British goods and, under the prodding of the radicals, began to consider the possibility of independence from British rule. The eventual result was the Declaration of Independence.

The Declaration of Independence

In 1776, the Second Continental Congress appointed a committee consisting of Thomas Jefferson of Virginia, Benjamin Franklin of Pennsylvania, Roger Sherman of Connecticut, John Adams of Massachusetts, and Robert Livingston of New York to draft a statement of American independence from British rule. The Declaration of Independence, was written by Jefferson who drew many of his ideas from the thought of the British philosopher John Locke whose work was widely read in the colonies. Adopted by the Second Continental Congress, the Declaration was an extraordinary document in both philosophical and political terms. Philosophically, the Declaration was remarkable for its assertion—derived from Locke—that certain rights, called "unalienable rights"—including life, liberty, and the pursuit of happiness—could not be abridged by governments. In the world of 1776, a world in which some kings still claimed to rule by divine right, this was a dramatic statement. Politically, the Declaration was remarkable because, despite the differences of interest that divided the colonists along economic, regional, and philosophical lines, it identified and focused on problems, grievances, aspirations, and principles that might unify the various colonial groups. The Declaration was an attempt to identify and articulate a history and a set of principles that might help to forge national unity.[7]

Articles of Confederation and Perpetual Union

America's first written constitution. Adopted by the Continental Congress in 1777, the Articles of Confederation and Perpetual Union were the formal basis for America's national government until 1789, when they were superseded by the Constitution

The Articles of Confederation

Having declared their independence, the colonies needed to establish a governmental structure—a set of institutions through which to govern. In November 1777, the Continental Congress adopted the Articles of Confederation and Perpetual Union—the United States' first written constitution. Although it was not

6 For an extensive discussion of how misunderstandings and incorrect beliefs caused the situation to spin out of control, see Jack N. Rakove, Andrew R. Rutten, and Barry R. Weingast, "Ideas, Interest, and Credible Commitments in the American Revolution" 2008, http://ssrn.com/abstract=1153515 (accessed 2/3/09).

7 A "biography" of the Declaration is found in Pauline Maier, *American Scripture: Making the Declaration of Independence* (New York: Knopf, 1997).

ratified by all the states until 1781, it was the country's operative constitution for almost 12 years, until March 1789.

The Articles of Confederation formed a constitution concerned primarily with limiting the powers of the central government. The central government, first of all, was based entirely in Congress. Because it was not intended to be a powerful government, it was given no executive branch. Execution of its laws was to be left to the individual states. Second, Congress had little power. Its members were not much more than delegates or messengers from the state legislatures. They were chosen by the state legislatures, their salaries were paid out of the state treasuries, and they were subject to immediate recall by state authorities. In addition, each state, regardless of its size, had only a single vote.

Congress was given the power to declare war and make peace, to make treaties and alliances, to coin or borrow money, and to regulate trade with Native Americans. It could also appoint the senior officers of the U.S. Army. But it could not levy taxes or regulate commerce among the states. Moreover, the army officers it appointed had no army to serve in because the nation's armed forces were composed of the state militias. An especially dysfunctional aspect of the Articles of Confederation was that the central government could not prevent one state from discriminating against other states in the quest for foreign commerce.

In brief, the relationship between Congress and the states under the Articles of Confederation was much like the contemporary relationship between the United Nations and its member states, a relationship in which virtually all governmental powers are retained by the states. It was properly called a confederation because, as provided under Article II, "each state retains its sovereignty, freedom, and independence, and every power, jurisdiction, and right, which is not by this Confederation expressly delegated to the United States, in Congress assembled." Not only was there no executive but there was also no judicial authority and no other means of enforcing Congress's will. If there were to be any enforcement at all, it would be done for Congress by the states.[8] All told, the Articles of Confederation were an inadequate institutional basis for collective action. The states collectively could act only if each state individually were prepared to participate in and enforce that action.

THE SECOND FOUNDING: FROM COMPROMISE TO CONSTITUTION

Institutional arrangements, devised to accomplish various collective purposes by creating routines and processes, aren't always well suited to these tasks. The Declaration of Independence and the Articles of Confederation were not

8 See Merrill Jensen, *The Articles of Confederation* (Madison: University of Wisconsin Press, 1963).

sufficient to hold the nation together as an independent and effective nation-state. Almost from the moment of armistice with the British in 1783, moves were afoot to reform and strengthen the Articles of Confederation.

International Standing and Balance of Power

There was a special concern for the country's international position. Competition among the states for foreign commerce allowed the European powers to play the states against one another, creating confusion on both sides of the Atlantic. At one point during the winter of 1786–87, John Adams, a leader in the struggle for independence, was sent to negotiate a new treaty with the British, one that would cover disputes left over from the war. The British government responded that because the United States under the Articles of Confederation was unable to enforce existing treaties, it would negotiate with each of the 13 states separately.

At the same time, well-to-do Americans—in particular the New England merchants and southern planters—were troubled by the influence that "radical" forces exercised in the Continental Congress and in the governments of several of the states. The colonists' victory in the Revolutionary War not only had meant the end of British rule but also had significantly changed the balance of political power within the new states. As a result of the Revolution, one key segment of the colonial elite—the royal land, office, and patent holders—was stripped of its economic and political privileges. In fact, many of these individuals, along with tens of thousands of other colonists who considered themselves loyal British subjects, had left for Canada after the British surrender. And although the pre-Revolutionary elite was weakened, the pre-Revolutionary radicals were now better organized than ever before and were the controlling forces in such states as Pennsylvania and Rhode Island, where they pursued economic and political policies that struck terror in the hearts of the pre-Revolutionary political establishment. In Rhode Island, for example, between 1783 and 1785 a legislature dominated by representatives of small farmers, artisans, and shopkeepers had instituted economic policies, including drastic currency inflation, that frightened businessmen and property owners throughout the country. Of course, the central government under the Articles of Confederation was powerless to intervene.

The Annapolis Convention

The continuation of international weakness and domestic economic turmoil led many Americans to consider whether their newly adopted form of government might not already require revision. Experiments in governance don't always work out. After nearly a decade under the Articles, in the fall of 1786, many state leaders accepted an invitation from the Virginia legislature to attend a conference of representatives of all the states. Delegates from five states actually attended. This conference, held in Annapolis, Maryland, was the first step toward the second founding. One positive thing that came out of the Annapolis Convention was a carefully worded resolution calling on Congress to send commissioners to Philadelphia at a later time "to devise such further provisions as shall appear to them necessary to render the Constitution of the Federal Government adequate to the exigencies of the Union."[9] This resolution was drafted by Alexander Hamilton, a 34-year-old New York lawyer who had played a significant role in the Revolution as George Washington's secretary and would play a still more significant role in framing the Constitution and forming the new government in the 1790s. But the resolution did not necessarily imply any desire to do more than improve and reform the Articles of Confederation.

Shays's Rebellion

It is possible that the Constitutional Convention of 1787 in Philadelphia would never have taken place at all except for a single event that occurred soon after the Annapolis Convention: Shays's Rebellion. Like the Boston Tea Party, this was a focal event. It concentrated attention, coordinated beliefs, produced widespread fear and apprehension, and thus convinced waverers that something was broken and needed fixing. In short, it prompted collective action by providing politicians who had long been convinced that the Articles were flawed and insufficient with just the ammunition they needed to convince a much broader public of these facts.[10]

Daniel Shays, a former army captain, led a mob of farmers in a rebellion against the government of Massachusetts. The purpose of the rebellion was to prevent foreclosures on their debt-ridden land by keeping the county courts of western Massachusetts from sitting until after the next election. The state militia dispersed the mob, but for several days Shays and his followers terrified the state government by attempting to capture the federal arsenal at Springfield, provoking an appeal to Congress to help restore order. Within a few days, the state government regained control and captured fourteen of the rebels (all were eventually pardoned). In 1787, a newly elected Massachusetts legislature granted some of the farmers' demands. Although the incident ended peacefully, its effects lingered and spread.

Congress under the Confederation had been unable to act decisively in a time of crisis. This inadequacy provided critics of the Articles of Confederation with precisely the evidence they needed to push Hamilton's Annapolis resolution through the Congress. Thus the states were asked to send representatives to Philadelphia to discuss constitutional revision. Delegates were eventually sent by every state except Rhode Island.

9 Quoted in Samuel Eliot Morison, Henry Steele Commager, and William E. Leuchtenburg, *The Growth of the American Republic*, 6th ed. (New York: Oxford University Press, 1969), I: 244.

10 For an easy-to-read argument that supports this view, see Keith L. Dougherty, *Collective Action under the Articles of Confederation* (New York: Cambridge University Press, 2001).

The drama of Shays's Rebellion underscores the robustness and resistance to change of an institutional status quo—the Articles of Confederation regime. As the history principle suggests, the status quo prevails until and unless it is replaced. And to accomplish the latter, a spark or focal event is often necessary to coalesce the forces of change and enable them to overcome the biases in favor of doing nothing and keeping the status quo in place. In effect, Shays's Rebellion strengthened the resolve of supporters of change, convinced waverers, and generally coordinated the beliefs of many that something comprehensive needed to be done about the existing regime. Thus, the event facilitated collective action.

The Constitutional Convention

In May 1787, 29 of a total of 73 delegates selected by the state governments convened in Philadelphia, with political strife, international embarrassment, national weakness, and local rebellion fixed in their minds. Recognizing that these issues were symptoms of fundamental flaws in the Articles of Confederation, the delegates soon abandoned the plan to revise the Articles and committed themselves to a second founding—a second and ultimately successful attempt to create a legitimate and effective national system. This effort occupied the convention for the next five months. Americans had learned a good deal from what many saw as the shortcomings of the Articles of Confederation. They learned, for example, that executive power was a necessary component of effective government. They also learned that without an army or navy the government could not protect its citizens' interests. Demonstrating once again that history matters, Americans' experiences under the Articles helped shape the new Constitution.

A Marriage of Interest and Ideals. For years, scholars have disagreed about the motives of the Founders in Philadelphia. Among the most controversial views of the framers' motives is the "economic" interpretation put forward by the historian Charles Beard and his disciples.[11] According to Beard's account, America's Founders were a collection of securities speculators and property owners whose only aim was personal enrichment. From this perspective, the Constitution's lofty principles were little more than sophisticated masks behind which the most venal interests sought to enrich themselves. Although Beard's arguments are extreme in their exclusive emphasis on economics, there is some foundation for them. Northern economic interests feared debtor revolts, while southern planters feared slave revolts. Capital investment and its protection were weak under the Articles not only because of potential rebellions but also because of inflated currencies, limited credit markets, and outstanding public

---

11 Charles A. Beard, *An Economic Interpretation of the Constitution of the United States* (New York: Macmillan, 1913).

debt. Also, manufacturers needed protection from foreign competition, and exporters (primarily of southern cotton) needed the security of safe passage for their cargoes on the high seas.

Contrary to Beard's approach is the view that the framers of the Constitution were concerned with philosophical and ethical ideas. Indeed, the framers sought to devise a system of government consistent with the dominant philosophical and moral values of the day.[12]

Lurking in the background was a generalized suspicion of distant central government. As the historian Joseph Ellis observed, this was the "core argument used to discredit the authority of Parliament and the British monarch . . . an obsessive suspicion of any centralized political power that operated in far-away places."[13] But in fact, these interests and ideals belong together: the Founders' interests were reinforced by their principles. The convention that drafted the U.S. Constitution was chiefly organized by the New England merchants and southern planters. Although the delegates representing these groups did not all hope to profit personally from an increase in the value of their securities, as Beard would have it, they did hope to benefit in the broadest political and economic sense by breaking the power of their radical foes and establishing a system of government more compatible with their long-term economic and political interests. Thus the framers—in line with the rationality principle—sought to create a new government capable of promoting commerce and protecting property from radical state legislatures. They also sought to liberate the national government from the power of individual states and their sometimes venal and corrupt local politicians. At the same time, they hoped to fashion a government less susceptible than the existing state and national regimes to populist forces hostile to the interests of the commercial and propertied classes. These highly educated but practically experienced politicians were instrumentally motivated by both interests and ideals. The Constitutional Convention was a grand exercise in rationality and collective action.

The Great Compromise. The proponents of a new government fired their opening shot on May 29, 1787, when Edmund Randolph of Virginia offered a resolution that proposed corrections and enlargements in the Articles of Confederation. The proposal, which showed the strong influence of James Madison, was not a simple motion. It provided for virtually every aspect of a new government. Randolph later admitted it was intended to be an alternative draft constitution, and it did in fact serve as the framework for what ultimately became the Constitution.[14]

12 For an analytical treatment see Schofield, *Architects of Political Change*, chap. 4.

13 Joseph Ellis, *Founding Brothers: The Revolutionary Generation* (New York: Knopf, 2000), p. 7.

14 There is no verbatim record of the debates, but Madison was present during virtually all of the deliberations and kept full notes on them. Madison's notes, along with the somewhat less complete records kept by several other participants in the convention, are available in a four-volume set. See Max Farrand, ed., *The Records of the Federal Convention of 1787*, rev. ed., 4 vols. (New Haven, CT: Yale University Press, 1966).

This proposal, known as the Virginia Plan, provided for a system of representation in the national legislature based on the population of each state, the proportion of each state's revenue contribution, or both. (Randolph also proposed a second branch of the legislature, but it was to be elected by the members of the first branch.) Because the states varied enormously in size and wealth, the Virginia Plan was thought to be heavily biased in favor of the large states that would have greater representation in the proposed system.

While the convention was debating the Virginia Plan, additional delegates arriving in Philadelphia were beginning to mount opposition to it. Their resolution, introduced by William Paterson of New Jersey and known as the New Jersey Plan, did not oppose the Virginia Plan point for point. Instead, it concentrated on specific weaknesses in the Articles of Confederation, in the spirit of revision rather than radical replacement of that document. Supporters of the New Jersey Plan did not seriously question the convention's commitment to replacing the Articles. But their opposition to the Virginia Plan's scheme of representation was sufficient to send its proposals back to committee to be worked into a common document. In particular, delegates from the less populous states, which included Delaware, New Jersey, Connecticut, and New York, asserted that the more populous states, such as Virginia, Pennsylvania, North Carolina, Massachusetts, and Georgia, would dominate the new government if representation were to be determined by population. The smaller states argued that each state should be equally represented in the new regime regardless of its population.

The issue of representation was one that threatened to wreck the entire constitutional enterprise. Delegates conferred, factions maneuvered, and tempers flared. James Wilson of Pennsylvania told the small-state delegates that if they wanted to disrupt the Union they should go ahead. The separation could, he said, "never happen on better grounds." Small-state delegates were equally blunt. Gunning Bedford of Delaware declared that the small states might look elsewhere for friends if they were forced. "The large states," he said, "dare not dissolve the confederation. If they do the small ones will find some foreign ally of more honor and good faith, who will take them by the hand and do them justice." These sentiments were widely shared. The Union, as Oliver Ellsworth of Connecticut put it, was "on the verge of dissolution, scarcely held together by the strength of a hair." Convention delegates, acting as agents for the interests of their respective states, bargained, cajoled, and made attempts at persuasion in the rational pursuit of a result they would prefer.

Great Compromise

An agreement reached at the Constitutional Convention of 1787 that gave each state an equal number of senators regardless of its population but linked representation in the House of Representatives to population

The outcome of this debate was the Great Compromise, also known as the Connecticut Compromise. Under the terms of this compromise, in the first chamber of Congress—the House of Representatives—the members would be apportioned according to the number of inhabitants in each state. This, of course, was what delegates from the large states had sought. But in the second chamber—the Senate—each state would have an equal vote regardless of its size; this was to deal with the concerns of the small states. This compromise was not immediately satisfactory to all the delegates. Indeed, two of the most vocal supporters of the small-state faction, John Lansing and Robert Yates of New York, were so incensed by the concession that their colleagues had made to the large-state forces that they stormed out of the convention.

In the end, however, both sets of forces preferred compromise to the breakup of the Union, and the plan was accepted. The Analyzing the Evidence unit for this chapter explores, in more detail, the states' conflicting interests and how these shaped the eventual compromise.

The Question of Slavery: The Three-fifths Compromise. Many of the conflicts that emerged during the Constitutional Convention were reflections of the fundamental differences between the slave and nonslave states, differences that pitted the southern planters and New England merchants against each other. This was the first premonition of a conflict that would almost destroy the Republic in later years.

Over 90 percent of all slaves resided in five states—Georgia, Maryland, North Carolina, South Carolina, and Virginia—where they accounted for 30 percent of the total population. In some places, slaves outnumbered nonslaves by as much as 10 to 1. If the Constitution were to embody any principle of national supremacy, some basic decisions would have to be made about the place of slavery in the general scheme.

Northerners and southerners eventually reached agreement through the Three-fifths Compromise. The seats in the House of Representatives would be apportioned according to a "population" in which five slaves would count as three people. The slaves would not be allowed to vote, of course, but the number of representatives would be apportioned accordingly. This arrangement was supported by the slave states, which included some of the biggest and some of the smallest states at that time. It was also accepted by many delegates from nonslave states who strongly supported the principle of property representation, whether that property was expressed in slaves or in land, money, or stocks. The concern exhibited by most delegates was over how much slaves would count toward a state's representation rather than whether the institution of slavery would continue.

Three-fifths Compromise

An agreement reached at the Constitutional Convention of 1787 stipulating that for purposes of the apportionment of congressional seats, every slave would be counted as three-fifths of a person

The issue of slavery was the most difficult one faced by the framers, and it nearly destroyed the Union. Although some delegates believed slavery to be morally wrong, an evil and oppressive institution that made a mockery of the ideals and values espoused in the Constitution, morality was not the issue that caused the framers to support or oppose the Three-fifths Compromise. Whatever they thought of the institution of slavery, most delegates from the northern states opposed counting slaves in the distribution of congressional seats. Wilson of Pennsylvania, for example, argued that if slaves were citizens, they should be treated and counted like other citizens. If, on the other hand, they were property, then why should not other forms of property be counted toward the apportionment of Congress? But southern delegates made it clear that if the northerners refused to give in, they would never agree to the new government. Even southerners such as Edmund Randolph of Virginia, who conceded that slavery was immoral, insisted on including slaves in the allocation of congressional seats. This conflict between the southern and northern delegates was so divisive that many came to question the possibility of creating and maintaining a union of the two. Pierce Butler of South Carolina declared that the North and the South were as different as Russia and Turkey. Eventually the North and the

Voting at the Constitutional Convention

Under the Articles of Confederation, there was a unicameral Congress in which each state delegation received a single vote regardless of state population. So Virginia, with roughly 700,000 people, had the same share of votes as Rhode Island, with a population closer to 70,000. Among the issues considered by the framers at the Constitutional Convention, one of the most contentious involved how representation in the Congress would work under the new Constitution.

The larger states supported the Virginia Plan—because under this plan at least one of the chambers of Congress would be elected with representation proportional to population, giving the more populous states more of a voice in the national government. Given that the smaller, less populous states were poised to lose representation if votes in Congress were based on population, delegates from those states proposed the New Jersey Plan, which called for the creation of a unicameral legislature with one vote per state. Moreover, many of the delegates from the smaller states threatened to leave the convention if the Virginia Plan were ratified. In an attempt to prevent the smaller states from departing, Roger Sherman proposed the Connecticut Compromise. This plan called for a bicameral legislature, with representation based on population in the lower house and equal representation of states in the upper house. The plan ultimately passed by a 5–4 vote.

Votes on Two Plans

States*/Population**	VOTE ON VIRGINIA PLAN	VOTE ON CONNECTICUT COMPROMISE
VIRGINIA 747,550	YES	NO
PENNSYLVANIA 433,611	YES	NO
MASSACHUSETTS 378,556	YES	—
NEW YORK 340,241	NO	—
MARYLAND 319,728	—	YES
NORTH CAROLINA 395,005	YES	YES
SOUTH CAROLINA 249,073	YES	NO
CONNECTICUT 237,655	YES	YES
NEW JERSEY 184,139	NO	YES
GEORGIA 82,548	YES	NO
NEW HAMPSHIRE 141,899	—	—
DELAWARE 59,096	NO	YES
RHODE ISLAND 69,112	—	—

= 30,000 people

Free population

Slave population

* Maryland's delegates were split equally and thus did not vote. Delegates from New Hampshire never attended at the same time as those from New York, hence their lack of participation. Rhode Island did not send any delegates to attend the Convention.

** Population data are based on the 1790 census and therefore are only approximate with respect to populations in 1787.

Representation in the First Congress

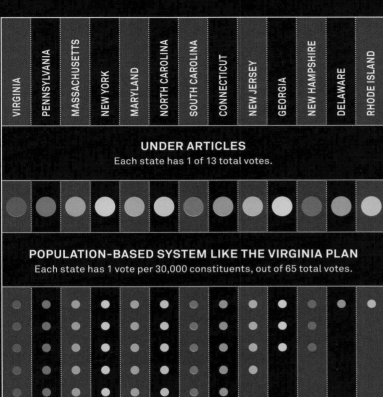

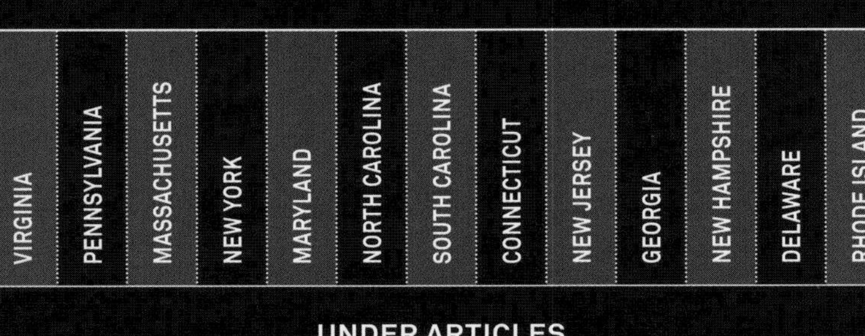

UNDER ARTICLES

Each state has 1 of 13 total votes.

POPULATION-BASED SYSTEM LIKE THE VIRGINIA PLAN

Each state has 1 vote per 30,000 constituents, out of 65 total votes.

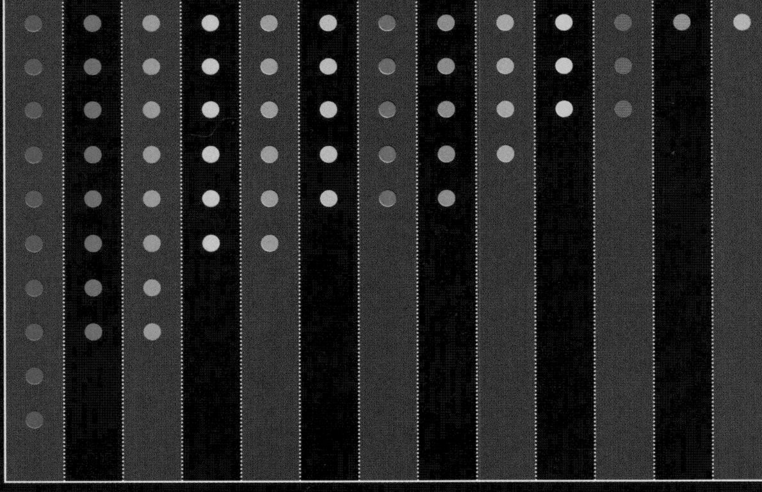

Note that the framers calculated the number of representatives per state using population estimates. The first census was not taken until 1790.

If we consider the number of representatives in Congress that each state would receive under the various plans, it becomes clear why individual states voted the way they did. Under the Articles and the proposed New Jersey Plan, even the smallest states had 1 out of 13 votes in the Congress.

Under a population-based system like the Virginia Plan, the smaller states would lose voting power in the Congress. For example, in a population-based system with one representative per 30,000 people, Delaware would only have 1 out of 65 votes—significantly less voting power than the 1 out of 13 these states enjoyed under the Articles and other arrangements that would give each state equal representation in Congress.

EXPLORE
THE DESIGN OF THE CONSTITUTION
FURTHER AT:
wwnorton.com/studyspace

SOURCES:

Keith L. Dougherty and Jac C. Heckelman, "A Pivotal Voter from a Pivotal State: Roger Sherman at the Constitutional Convention," *American Political Science Review 100* (May 2006): 297–302.

Clinton L. Rossiter, *1787: The Grand Convention* (New York: Macmillan Publishing

South compromised on the issue of slavery and representation. Indeed, northerners even agreed to permit a continuation of the odious slave trade to keep the South in the Union. But in due course, Butler proved to be correct, and a bloody war was fought when the disparate interests of the North and the South could no longer be reconciled.

THE CONSTITUTION

The political significance of the Great Compromise and the Three-fifths Compromise was to reinforce the unity of the mercantile and planter forces that sought to create a new government. The Great Compromise reassured those who feared that the importance of their own local or regional influence would be reduced by the new governmental framework. The Three-fifths Compromise temporarily defused the rivalry between the merchants and the planters. Their unity secured, members of the alliance supporting the establishment of a new government moved to fashion a constitutional framework consistent with their economic and political interests.

The framers of the Constitution understood that well-designed institutions make it easier to achieve collective goals. They understood also that the institutions they built could affect political outcomes for decades, if not centuries, to come. Accordingly, the framers took great care to construct institutions that over time would help the nation accomplish what they viewed as important political purposes.

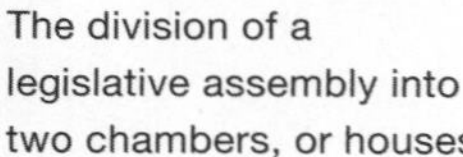

The division of a legislative assembly into two chambers, or houses

In particular, the framers sought first a new government that would be strong enough to promote commerce and protect property from radical state legislatures such as Rhode Island's. This goal became the basis for national control over commerce and finance, as well as for both the establishment of national judicial supremacy and the effort to construct a strong presidency. Second, the framers sought to prevent what they saw as the threat posed by the "excessive democracy" of the state and national governments under the Articles of Confederation. Here again the framers' historical experience mattered. This goal led to such constitutional principles as bicameralism (division of the Congress into two chambers), checks and balances, staggered terms of office, and indirect election (selection of the president by an electoral college rather than directly by the voters). Third, the framers, lacking the power to force the states or the public at large to accept the new form of government, sought to identify principles that would help secure support. This goal became the basis for the constitutional provision for direct popular election of representatives and, subsequently, the basis for the addition of the Bill of Rights to the Constitution. Finally, the framers wanted to be certain that the government they created did not use its power to pose even more of a threat to its citizens' liberties and property rights than did the radical state legislatures they feared and despised. To prevent the new government from abusing its power, the framers incorporated into the Constitution such principles as the separation of powers and federalism.

The framers provided us with a grand lesson in purposive behavior. They came to Philadelphia united by a common distaste for government under the Articles and animated by the agitation following Shays's Rebellion. They didn't always agree on what it was they disliked about the Articles. They certainly didn't agree on how to proceed—hence the necessity for the historic compromises we have just described. But they did believe that the acts of fostering commerce and protecting property could be served better by a set of institutional arrangements other than that provided by the Articles. They agreed that the institutional arrangements of government mattered for their lives and for those of their fellow citizens. They believed that both too much democracy and too much governmental power were threats to the common good, and they felt compelled to find instruments and principles that weighed against them. Let us assess the major provisions of the Constitution's seven articles to see how each relates to these objectives.

The Legislative Branch

The first seven sections of Article I of the Constitution provide for a Congress consisting of two chambers—a House of Representatives and a Senate. Members of the House of Representatives are given two-year terms of office and are to be elected directly by the people. Members of the Senate are to be appointed by the state legislatures (this provision was changed in 1913 by the Seventeenth Amendment, which instituted direct election of senators) for six-year terms. These terms, moreover, are staggered so that the appointments of one-third of the senators expire every two years. The Constitution assigns somewhat different tasks to the House and the Senate. Though the approval of each body is required for the enactment of a law, the Senate alone is given the power to ratify treaties and approve presidential appointments. The House, on the other hand, is given the sole power to originate revenue bills.

The character of the legislative branch is directly related to the framers' major goals. The House of Representatives was designed to be directly responsible to the people, to encourage popular consent for the new Constitution, and to help enhance the power of the new government. At the same time, to guard against "excessive democracy," the power of the House of Representatives was checked by the Senate, whose members are to be appointed rather than elected directly by the people and are to serve long (six-year) terms. The purpose of this provision, according to Alexander Hamilton, was to avoid "an unqualified complaisance to every sudden breeze of passion, or to every transient impulse which the people may receive."[15] Staggered terms of service in the Senate, moreover, were intended to make that body even more resistant to popular pressure. Because only one-third of the senators would be selected at any given time, the composition of the institution would be protected from changes in popular

15 Alexander Hamilton, James Madison, and John Jay, *The Federalist Papers*, Clinton Rossiter, ed. (New York: New American Library, 1961), no. 71.

preferences transmitted by the state legislatures. This would prevent what James Madison called "mutability in the public councils arising from a rapid succession of new members."[16] Thus the structure of the legislative branch was designed to contribute to governmental power, promote popular consent for the new government, and at the same time place limits on the popular political currents that many of the framers saw as a radical threat to the economic and social order.

The issues of power and consent are important throughout the Constitution. Section 8 of Article I lists the specific powers of Congress, which include the authority to collect taxes, borrow money, regulate commerce, declare war, and maintain an army and navy. By granting it these powers, the framers indicated clearly that they intended the new government to be far more influential than its predecessor. At the same time, by defining the new government's most important powers as belonging to Congress, the framers sought to promote popular acceptance of this critical change by reassuring citizens that their views would be fully represented whenever the government exercised its new powers.

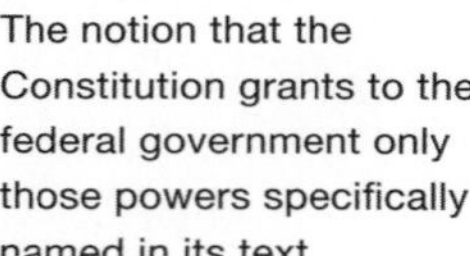

expressed power

The notion that the Constitution grants to the federal government only those powers specifically named in its text

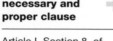

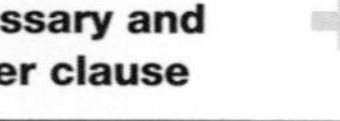

necessary and proper clause

Article I, Section 8, of the Constitution, which enumerates the powers of Congress and provides Congress with the authority to make all laws "necessary and proper" to carry them out; also referred to as the elastic clause

As a further guarantee to the people that the new government would pose no threat to them, the Constitution implies that any powers not listed are not granted at all. This is the doctrine of expressed power. The Constitution grants only those powers specifically expressed in its text. But the framers intended to create an active and powerful government, so they included the necessary and proper clause, sometimes known as the elastic clause, which signifies that the enumerated powers are meant to be a source of strength to the national government, not a limitation on it—that the government may employ means "necessary and proper" to implement the expressed powers. No new powers can be seized on by the national government without a constitutional amendment. In the absence of such an amendment, any power not enumerated is conceived to be "reserved" to the states (or the people).

The Executive Branch

The Constitution provides for the establishment of the presidency in Article II. As Alexander Hamilton commented, the presidential article was aimed toward creating "energy in the Executive." It did so in an effort to overcome the natural stalemate that was built into both the bicameral legislature and the separation of powers among the legislative, executive, and judicial branches. The Constitution afforded the president a measure of independence from the people and from the other branches of government, particularly Congress.

Some of the framers had argued for a plural executive or executive council in order to avoid the evils that many associated with a monarch. In *Federalist 70*, however, Hamilton argued that "energy" required a single rather than a plural executive. While abuse of power should be guarded against by checks and balances and other devices, energy also required that the executive should

16 *The Federalist,* no. 62.

be provided with "competent powers" to direct the nation's business.[17] These would include the unconditional power to accept ambassadors from other countries; this provision amounts to the power to "recognize" other countries. The president is also given the power to negotiate treaties, although their acceptance requires the approval of the Senate. The president is given the unconditional right to grant reprieves and pardons, except in cases of impeachment. And the president is provided with the power to appoint major departmental personnel, convene Congress in a special session, and veto congressional enactments. (The veto power is formidable, but it is not absolute because Congress can override it by a two-thirds vote.)[18]

The framers hoped to create a presidency that would make the federal government, rather than the states, the agency capable of timely and decisive action to deal with public issues and problems. This goal is the meaning of the "energy" that Hamilton hoped to impart to the executive branch.[19] At the same time, however, the framers sought to help the president withstand (excessively) democratic pressures by making the office subject to indirect rather than direct election (through selection by a separate electoral college). The extent to which the framers' hopes were realized is the topic of Chapter 7.

Of course, the most energetic and independent form of executive known to the framers was a monarch. Some of the anti-Federalist opponents of the Constitution averred that the framers had, in effect, created a new king in the office of the President.[20] But, even if some framers viewed the president as a sort of constitutional monarch, there was no chance that the convention might act to actually establish a monarchy in the United States. History matters, and Americans' experience with monarchs made that choice of institutions impossible.

The Judicial Branch

In establishing the judicial branch in Article III, the Constitution reflects the framers' preoccupations with enhancing the power of the national government and checking radical democratic impulses while guarding against potential interference with liberty and property from the new national government itself.

17 *The Federalist*, no. 70.

18 A modern description of executive-legislature relations is, "The president proposes; the Congress disposes." The president may propose to the legislature when the subject is a treaty or a major departmental appointment or a federal judge or justice, which must be approved by the Senate; then the president is a legislative "agenda setter." When, however, it is a proposed law or budget, it is a "suggestion" that the legislature may choose to ignore altogether. Such proposals are then said to be "dead on arrival" because Congress marches to the beat of its own drummer.

19 *The Federalist*, no. 70.

20 Herbert Storing, ed., *The Complete Anti-Federalist*, 7 vols. (Chicago: University of Chicago Press, 1981), p. 308.

Under the provisions of Article III, the framers created a court that was to be literally a supreme court of the United States and not merely the highest court of the national government. The most important expression of this intention was granting the Supreme Court the power to resolve any conflicts that might emerge between federal and state laws. In particular, the Supreme Court was given the right to determine whether a power was exclusive to the federal government, concurrent with the states, or exclusive to the states. The significance of this was noted by Justice Oliver Wendell Holmes, Jr., who observed, "I do not think the United States would come to an end if we lost our power to declare an act of Congress void. I do think the union would be imperilled if we could not make that declaration as to the laws of the several states."[21]

In addition, the Supreme Court was assigned jurisdiction over controversies between citizens of different states. The long-term significance of this provision was that as the country developed a national economy, it came to rely increasingly on the federal judiciary, rather than the state courts, for the resolution of disputes.

Judges were given lifetime appointments to protect them from popular politics and interference by the other branches. To further safeguard judicial independence, the Constitution also prohibited Congress from reducing the salary of any sitting judge. This did not mean, however, that the judiciary would remain totally impartial to political considerations or to the other branches, for the president appoints the judges and the Senate approves the appointments. Congress also has the power to create inferior (lower) courts, change the jurisdiction of the federal courts, add or subtract federal judges, and even change the size of the Supreme Court.

judicial review

The power of the courts to declare actions of the legislative and executive branches invalid or unconstitutional. The Supreme Court asserted this power in *Marbury v. Madison* (1803)

No direct mention is made of judicial review—the power of the courts to render the final decision when a conflict of interpretation of the Constitution or of laws arises between the courts and Congress, the courts and the executive branch, or the courts and the states. Scholars generally feel that judicial review is implicit in the very existence of a written constitution and in the power given directly to the federal courts over "all Cases . . . arising under this Constitution, the Laws of the United States, and Treaties made, or which shall be made, under their Authority" (Article III, Section 2). The Supreme Court eventually assumed the power of judicial review. Its assumption of this power, as we see in Chapter 9, was based not on the Constitution itself but on the politics of later decades and the membership of the Court.

National Unity and Power

Various provisions in the Constitution address the framers' concern with national unity and power, including Article IV's provisions for comity (reciprocity) among states and among the citizens of all states.

21 Oliver Wendell Holmes, Jr., *Collected Legal Papers* (New York: Harcourt, Brace, 1920), pp. 295–6.

Each state is prohibited from discriminating against the citizens of other states in favor of its own citizens, with the Supreme Court charged with deciding in each case whether a state has discriminated against goods or people from another state. The Constitution restricts the power of the states in favor of ensuring that the national government holds enough power to give the country a free-flowing national economy.

The framers' concern with national supremacy was also expressed in Article VI in the supremacy clause, which provides that national laws and treaties "shall be the supreme Law of the Land." This means that all laws made under the "Authority of the United States" are superior to all laws adopted by any state or any other subdivision and the states are expected to respect all treaties made under that authority. This provision was a direct effort to keep the states from dealing separately with foreign nations or businesses. The supremacy clause also binds the officials of all state and local, as well as federal, governments to take an oath of office to support the national Constitution. This means that every action taken by the U.S. Congress must be applied within each state as though the action were in fact state law.

supremacy clause

A clause of Article VI of the Constitution that states that all laws passed by the national government and all treaties are the supreme laws of the land and superior to all laws adopted by any state or any subdivision

Amending the Constitution

The Constitution establishes procedures for its own revision in Article V. Its provisions are so difficult that Americans have availed themselves of the amending process only 17 times since 1791, when the first 10 amendments were adopted. Many other amendments have been proposed in Congress, but fewer than 40 of them have come even close to fulfilling the Constitution's requirement of a two-thirds vote in Congress, and only a fraction have gotten anywhere near adoption by three-fourths of the states. The Constitution can also be amended by a constitutional convention. Occasionally proponents of particular measures, such as a balanced-budget amendment, have called for a constitutional convention to consider their proposals. Whatever the purpose for which it was called, however, such a convention would presumably have the authority to revise America's entire system of government.

It should be noted that any body of rules, including a national constitution, must balance the need to respond flexibly to changes on the one hand with the caution not to be too flexible on the other. An inflexible body of rules is one that cannot accommodate major change. It risks being rebelled against, a circumstance in which the slate is wiped clean and new rules are designed—or ignored altogether. Too much flexibility, however, is disastrous. It invites those who lose in normal everyday politics to replay battles at the constitutional level. If institutional change is too easy to accomplish, the stability of the political system becomes threatened. This means, as stated in the institution principle, that the institutional arrangements characterized in a constitution should structure politics by providing a framework, not rigidly specify political outcomes explicitly.

Ratifying the Constitution

The rules for ratification of the Constitution of 1787 are set forth in Article VII of the Constitution. This provision actually violated the amendment provisions of the Articles of Confederation. For one thing, it adopts a nine-state rule in place of the unanimity required by the Articles. For another, it provides for ratification to occur in special state conventions called for that purpose rather than in the state legislatures. All the states except Rhode Island eventually did set up state conventions to ratify the Constitution.

separation of powers

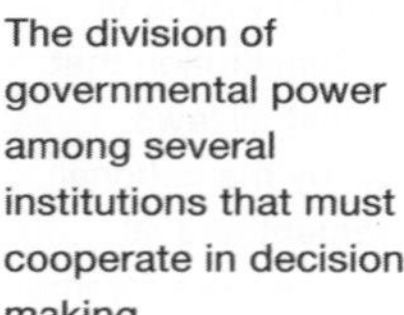

The division of governmental power among several institutions that must cooperate in decision making

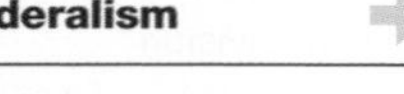

federalism

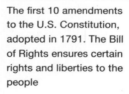

The system of government in which a constitution divides power between a central government and regional governments

Bill of Rights 

The first 10 amendments to the U.S. Constitution, adopted in 1791. The Bill of Rights ensures certain rights and liberties to the people

checks and balances 

The mechanisms through which each branch of government is able to participate in and influence the activities of the other branches

Constitutional Limits on the National Government's Power

As we have indicated, although the framers sought to create a powerful national government, they also wanted to guard against possible misuse of that power. To that end, the framers incorporated two key principles into the Constitution: the separation of powers and federalism (see Chapter 3). A third set of limitations, in the form of the Bill of Rights, was added to the Constitution to help secure its ratification when opponents of the document charged that it paid insufficient attention to citizens' rights.

The Separation of Powers. No principle of politics was more widely shared at the time of the 1787 Founding than the principle that power must be used to balance power. The French political theorist Baron de la Brède et de Montesquieu (1689–1755) believed that this balance was an indispensable defense against tyranny. His writings, especially his major work, *The Spirit of the Laws,* "were taken as political gospel" at the Philadelphia convention. Although the principle of the separation of powers was not explicitly stated in the Constitution, the entire structure of the national government was built precisely on Article I, the legislature; Article II, the executive; and Article III, the judiciary (see Figure 2.1).

However, separation of powers is nothing but mere words on parchment without a method to maintain the separation. The method became known by the popular label checks and balances. Each branch is given not only its own powers but also some power over the other two branches. Among the most familiar checks and balances are the president's veto as a power over Congress and Congress's power over the president through its control of appointments to high executive posts and to the judiciary. Congress also has power over the president with its control of appropriations and (by the Senate) the right of approval of treaties. The judiciary was assumed to have the power of judicial review over the other two branches.

Another important feature of the separation of powers is the principle of giving each of the branches a distinctly different constituency. Theorists such as Montesquieu called this a "mixed regime," with the president chosen indirectly by electors, the House by popular vote, the Senate (originally) by state legislature, and the judiciary by presidential appointment. By these means, the

Figure 2.1
THE SEPARATION OF POWERS

Passes federal laws

Controls federal appropriations

Approves treaties and presedential appointments

Regulates interstate commerce

Establishes lower-court system

Enforces laws

Serves as commander in chief of armed forces

Makes foreign treaties

Proposes laws

Nominates Supreme Court justices and federal court judges

Pardons those convicted in federal court

Reviews lower-court decisions

Decides constitutionality of laws

Decides cases involving disputes between states

occupants of each branch would tend to develop very different outlooks on how to govern, different definitions of the public interest, and different alliances with private interests.

Federalism. Compared with the confederation principle of the Articles of Confederation, federalism was a step toward greater centralization of power. The delegates agreed that they needed to place more power at the national level, without completely undermining the power of the state governments. Thus they devised a system of two sovereigns—the states and the nation—with the hope that competition between the two would be an effective limitation on the power of both.

The Bill of Rights. Late in the Philadelphia convention, a motion was made to include a bill of rights in the Constitution. After a brief debate, in which hardly a word was said in its favor and only one speech was made against it, the motion to include it was almost unanimously turned down. Most delegates sincerely believed that because the federal government was already limited to its expressed powers, any further protection of citizens was not needed. The delegates argued that the states should adopt bills of rights because their greater powers needed greater limitations. But almost immediately after the Constitution was ratified, there was a movement to adopt a national bill of rights. This is why the Bill of Rights, adopted in 1791, makes up the first 10 amendments to the Constitution and is not incorporated into the body of it. We have a good deal more to say about the Bill of Rights in Chapter 4.

THE FIGHT FOR RATIFICATION: FEDERALISTS VERSUS ANTIFEDERALISTS

The first hurdle faced by the new Constitution was ratification by state conventions of delegates elected by the people of each state. This struggle for ratification was carried out in 13 separate campaigns. Each involved different men, moved at a different pace, and was influenced by local as well as national considerations. Two sides faced off throughout the states, however, calling themselves Federalists and Antifederalists (Table 2.1).[22] The Federalists (who ought to have called themselves Nationalists but took their name to appear to follow in the Revolutionary tradition) supported the Constitution and preferred a strong national government. The Antifederalists opposed the Constitution and preferred a decentralized federal government; they took their name by default, in reaction to their better-organized opponents. The Federalists were united in their support of the Constitution, whereas the Antifederalists were divided in what they believed the alternative to the Constitution should be.

During the struggle over ratification of the proposed Constitution, Americans argued about great political issues and ideals. How much power should the national government be given? What safeguards were most likely to prevent the abuse of power? What institutional arrangements could best ensure adequate representation for all Americans? Was tyranny to be feared more from the many or from the few?

In political life, of course, ideals—and values—are seldom completely divorced from some set of interests. In 1787, Americans were divided along economic, regional, and political lines. These divisions inevitably influenced their attitudes toward the profound political questions of the day. Many well-to-do merchants and planters, as we saw earlier, favored the creation of a stronger central government that would have the capacity to protect property, promote commerce, and keep some of the more radical state legislatures in check. At the same time, many powerful state leaders, such as Governor George Clinton

22 An excellent analysis of the ratification campaigns—based on a quantitative assessment of the campaigners' own words as found in campaign documents, pamphlets, tracts, public letters, and the eighteenth-century equivalent of op-ed pieces (such as the individual essays that make up the *Federalist Papers*)—is William H. Riker, *The Strategy of Rhetoric: Campaigning for the American Constitution* (New Haven, CT: Yale University Press, 1996).

Table 2.1
FEDERALISTS VERSUS ANTIFEDERALISTS

	FEDERALISTS	ANTIFEDERALISTS
Who were they?	Property owners, creditors, merchants	Small farmers, frontiersmen, debtors, shopkeepers
What did they believe?	Elites are best fit to govern and "excessive democracy" is dangerous	Government should be close to the people and the concentration of power in the hands of the elites is dangerous
What system of government did they favor?	Strong national government; believed in "filtration" so that only elites would obtain governmental power	Retention of power by state governments and protection of individual rights
Who were their leaders?	Alexander Hamilton, James Madison, George Washington	Patrick Henry, George Mason, Elbridge Gerry, George Clinton

of New York, feared that strengthening the national government would reduce their own influence and status. Each of these interests, of course, justified its position with an appeal to basic values.

Ideas are often important weapons in political warfare, and seeing how and by whom they are wielded can illuminate their otherwise obscure implications. Even if an idea is invented and initially brandished to serve an interest, however, once it has been articulated, it can take on a life of its own and prove to have implications that transcend the narrow interests it was created to serve. For example, some opponents of the Constitution who criticized the absence of a bill of rights in the initial document did so simply with the hope of blocking the document's ratification. Yet the bill of rights that was added to the Constitution has proved for over two centuries to be a bulwark of civil liberty in the United States.

As this example shows, truly great political ideas transcend the interests that initially set them forth. The first step in understanding a political value is understanding why and by whom it is espoused. The second step is understanding the full implications of the idea itself—implications that may go far beyond the interests that launched it. Whatever the underlying clash of interests that may have guided them, the Federalists and the Antifederalists presented important alternative visions of America.

During the ratification struggle, thousands of essays, speeches, pamphlets, and letters were presented in support of and in opposition to the proposed Constitution. The best-known pieces supporting ratification of the Constitution were the 85 essays written under the name Publius by Alexander Hamilton, James Madison, and John Jay between the fall of 1787 and the spring of 1788. The *Federalist Papers*, as they are collectively known today, defended the principles of the Constitution and sought to dispel fears of a national authority. The Antifederalists published essays of their own, arguing that the new Constitution betrayed the Revolution and was a step toward monarchy. Among the best of the Antifederalist works were the essays, usually attributed to New York Supreme Court Justice Robert Yates, that were written under the name Brutus and published in the *New York Journal* at the same time the *Federalist Papers* appeared. The Antifederalist view was also ably presented in pamphlets and letters written by a former delegate to the Continental Congress and future U.S. senator, Richard Henry Lee of Virginia, using the pen name the Federal Farmer. These essays highlight the major differences of opinion between Federalists and Antifederalists. Federalists appealed to basic principles of government in support of their nationalist vision. Antifederalists cited equally fundamental precepts to support their vision of a looser confederacy of small republics.

The two sides engaged in what was almost certainly the very first nationwide political campaign in the history of the world. Though each side was itself only loosely organized, they did address their collective action problem—a rudimentary form of coordination and cooperation was manifest. This was especially evident in the division of labor among Hamilton, Madison, and Jay as they alternately wrote under the Publius pseudonym on different aspects of the newly drafted Constitution in an effort to effect its ratification in the state of New York.

Representation

One major area of contention between the two sides was the question of representation. The Antifederalists asserted that representatives must be "a true picture of the people, . . . [possessing] the knowledge of their circumstances and their wants."[23] This could be achieved, argued the Antifederalists, only in small, relatively homogeneous republics such as the existing states. In their view, the size and extent of the entire nation precluded the construction of a truly representative form of government.

The absence of true representation, moreover, would mean that the people would lack confidence in and attachment to the national government and would refuse to obey its laws voluntarily. As a result, according to the Antifederalists, the national government described by the Constitution would be compelled to resort to force to secure popular compliance. The Federal Farmer averred that laws of the remote federal government could be "in many cases disregarded, unless a multitude of officers and military force be continually kept in view, and

23 Melancton Smith, quoted in Herbert J. Storing, *What the Anti-Federalists Were For: The Political Thought of the Opponents of the Constitution* (Chicago: University of Chicago Press, 1981), p. 17.

employed to enforce the execution of the laws, and to make the government feared and respected."[24]

Federalists, for their part, did not long for pure democracy and saw no reason that representatives should be precisely like those they represented. In their view, government must be representative *of* the people but must also have a measure of autonomy *from* the people. Their ideal government was to be constructed such that it would be capable of serving the long-term public interest even if doing so conflicted with the public's current preference. In more contemporary terms, Federalists sought representatives who were *trustees* whereas Antifederalists sought *delegates*.

Federalists also dismissed the Antifederalist claim that the distance between representatives and constituents in the proposed national government would lead to popular disaffection and compel the government to use force to secure obedience. Federalists replied that the system of representation they proposed was more likely to produce effective government. In Hamilton's words, there would be "a probability that the general government will be better administered than the particular governments."[25] Competent government, in turn, should inspire popular trust and confidence more effectively than simple social proximity between rulers and ruled.

The Threats Posed by the Majority

A second important issue dividing Federalists and Antifederalists was the threat of tyranny—unjust rule by the group in power. Both opponents and defenders of the Constitution frequently affirmed their fear of tyrannical rule. Each side, however, had a different view of the most likely source of tyranny and, hence, of the way in which the threat was to be forestalled.

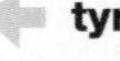 **tyranny**

Oppressive government that employs the cruel and unjust use of power and authority

From the Antifederalist perspective, the great danger was the tendency of all governments—including republican governments—to become gradually more and more "aristocratic" in character, with the small number of individuals in positions of authority using their stations to gain more and more power over the general citizenry. In essence, the few would use their power to tyrannize the many. For this reason, Antifederalists were sharply critical of those features of the Constitution that divorced governmental institutions from direct responsibility to the people—institutions such as the Senate, the executive, and the federal judiciary. The latter, appointed for life, presented a particular threat: "I wonder if the world ever saw . . . a court of justice invested with such immense powers, and yet placed in a situation so little responsible," protested Brutus.[26]

The Federalists, too, recognized the threat of tyranny. They were not naive about the motives and purposes of individuals and took them to be no less opportunistic and self-interested than the Antifederalists did. But the Federalists

24 "Letters from the Federal Farmer," no. 2, in Storing *The Complete Anti-Federalist.*

25 *The Federalist,* no. 27.

26 "Essays of Brutus," no. 15, in Storing, *The Complete Anti-Federalist.*

believed that the danger particularly associated with republican governments was not aristocracy but, instead, majority tyranny. The Federalists were concerned that a popular majority, "united and actuated by some common impulse of passion, or of interest, adverse to the rights of other citizens," would endeavor to "trample on the rules of justice."[27] From the Federalist perspective, it was precisely those features of the Constitution attacked as potential sources of tyranny by the Antifederalists that offered the best hope of averting the threat of oppression. The size and extent of the nation, for instance, were for the Federalists a bulwark against tyranny. In Madison's famous formulation, reflecting the logic of the collective action principle,

> The smaller the society, the fewer probably will be the distinct parties and interests . . . the more frequently will a majority be found of the same party; and the smaller the number of individuals composing a majority, and the smaller the compass within which they are placed, the more easily will they concert and execute their plans of oppression. Extend the sphere, and you take in a greater variety of parties and interests; you make it less probable that a majority of the whole will have a common motive to invade the rights of other citizens; or if such a common motive exists, it will be more difficult for all who feel it to discover their own strength, and to act in unison with each other.[28]

The Federalists understood that in a democracy, temporary majorities could abuse their power. The Federalists' misgivings about majority rule were reflected in the constitutional structure. The indirect election of senators, the indirect election of the president, the judicial branch's insulation from the people, the separation of powers, the president's veto power, the bicameral design of Congress, and the federal system were all means to curb majority tyranny. These features of the Constitution suggest, following the institution principle, the framers' awareness of the problems of majority rule and the need for institutional safeguards. Except for the indirect election of senators (which was changed in 1913), these aspects of the constitutional structure remain in place today.[29]

To some extent, the Federalists were influenced by an understanding of history that differed from that of the Antifederalists. Federalists believed that colonial history, to say nothing of the history of the Greeks, showed that republican governments were often endangered by mob rule. The Antifederalists, by contrast, thought that history revealed the dangers of aristocratic conspiracies against popular liberties. History matters, but it is always subject to interpretation.

27 *The Federalist,* no. 10.

28 *The Federalist,* no. 10.

29 A classic development of this theme is found in James M. Buchanan and Gordon Tullock, *The Calculus of Consent: Logical Foundations of Constitutional Democracy* (Ann Arbor: University of Michigan Press, 1962). For a review of the voting paradox and a case study of how it applies today, see Kenneth A. Shepsle, *Analyzing Politics, Rationality, Behavior and Institutions,* 2nd ed. (New York: Norton, 1997), pp. 53–89.

Governmental Power

A third major difference between Federalists and Antifederalists was the issue of governmental power. Both the opponents and the proponents of the Constitution agreed on the principle of limited government. They differed, however, on the fundamentally important question of how to place limits on governmental action. Antifederalists favored limiting and enumerating the powers granted to the national government in relation to both the states and the people at large. To them, the powers given the national government ought to be "confined to certain defined national objects."[30] Otherwise, the national government would "swallow up all the power of the state governments."[31] Antifederalists bitterly attacked the supremacy clause and the necessary and proper clause of the Constitution as unlimited and dangerous grants of power to the national government.[32]

Antifederalists also demanded that a bill of rights be added to the Constitution to place limits on the government's exercise of power over the citizenry. "There are certain things," wrote Brutus, "which rulers should be absolutely prohibited from doing, because if they should do them, they would work an injury, not a benefit to the people."[33] Similarly, the Federal Farmer maintained that "there are certain unalienable and fundamental rights, which in forming the social compact . . . ought to be explicitly ascertained and fixed."[34]

Federalists favored the construction of a government with broad powers. They wanted a government that had the capacity to defend the nation against foreign foes, guard against domestic strife and insurrection, promote commerce, and expand the nation's economy. Antifederalists shared some of these goals but still feared governmental power. Hamilton pointed out, however, that these goals could not be achieved without allowing the government to exercise the necessary power. Federalists acknowledged, of course, that every power could be abused but argued that the way to prevent misuse of power was not by depriving the government of the powers needed to achieve national goals. Instead, they argued that the threat of abuse of power would be mitigated by the Constitution's internal checks and controls. As Madison put it,

> The power surrendered by the people is first divided between two distinct governments, and then the portion allotted to each subdivided among distinct and separate departments. Hence a double security arises to the rights of the people. The different governments will control each other, at the same time that each will be controlled by itself.[35]

---

30 "Essays of Brutus," no. 7.

31 "Essays of Brutus," no. 6.

32 Storing, *What the Anti-Federalists Were For*, p. 28.

33 "Essays of Brutus," no. 9.

34 "Letters from the Federal Farmer," no. 2.

35 *The Federalist*, no. 51.

The Federalists' concern with avoiding unwarranted limits on governmental power led them to oppose a bill of rights, which they saw as nothing more than a set of unnecessary restrictions on the government.

The Federalists acknowledged that abuse of power remained a possibility but felt that the risk had to be taken because of the goals to be achieved. "The very idea of power included a possibility of doing harm," said the Federalist John Rutledge during South Carolina's ratification debates. "If the gentleman would show the power that could do no harm," Rutledge continued, "he would at once discover it to be a power that could do no good."[36]

CHANGING THE INSTITUTIONAL FRAMEWORK: CONSTITUTIONAL AMENDMENT

The Constitution has endured for more than two centuries as the framework of government. But it has not endured without change. Without change, the Constitution might have become merely a sacred relic, stored under glass.

Amendments: Many Are Called, Few Are Chosen

The need for change was recognized by the framers of the Constitution, and the provisions for amendment were incorporated into Article V. Since 1791, when the first 10 amendments, the Bill of Rights, were added, only 17 amendments have been adopted. And two of them—Prohibition and its repeal—cancel each other out, so that for all practical purposes only 15 amendments have been added to the Constitution since 1791. Despite vast changes in American society and its economy, only 12 amendments have been adopted since the Civil War amendments in 1868.

Four methods of amendment are provided for in Article V:

1. Passage in House and Senate by two-thirds vote; then ratification by majority vote of the legislatures of three-fourths (now 38) of the states.
2. Passage in House and Senate by two-thirds vote; then ratification by conventions called for that purpose in three-fourths of the states.
3. Passage in a national convention called by Congress in response to petitions by two-thirds (now 34) of the states; ratification by majority vote of the legislatures of three-fourths of the states.
4. Passage in a national convention, as in method 3; then ratification by conventions called for that purpose in three-fourths of the states.

36 Quoted in Storing, *What the Anti-Federalists Were For,* p. 30.

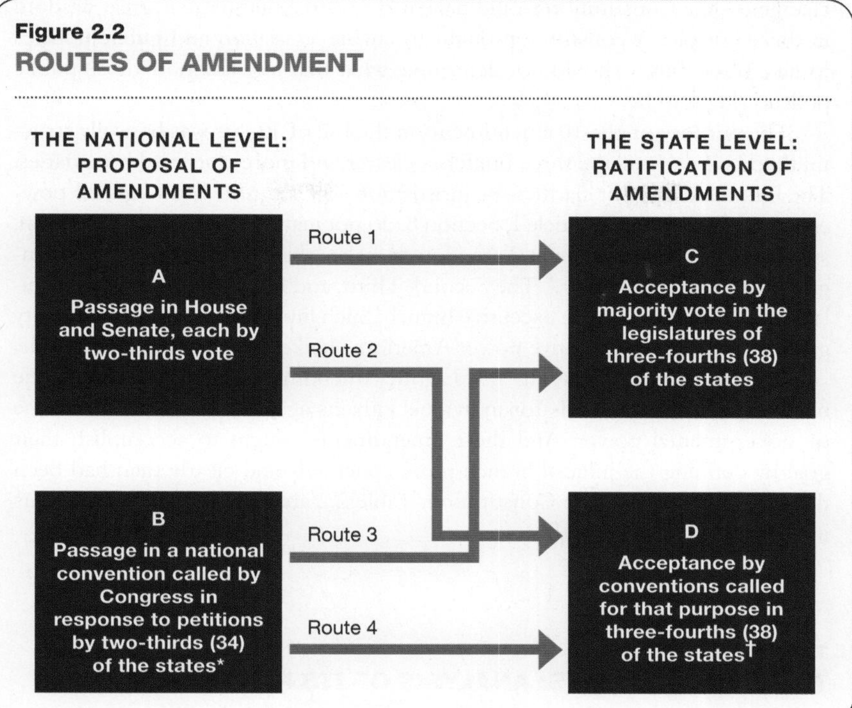
Figure 2.2
ROUTES OF AMENDMENT
THE NATIONAL LEVEL: PROPOSAL OF AMENDMENTS
THE STATE LEVEL: RATIFICATION OF AMENDMENTS
A
Passage in House and Senate, each by two-thirds vote
B
Passage in a national convention called by Congress in response to petitions by two-thirds (34) of the states*
Route 1
Route 2
Route 3
Route 4
C
Acceptance by majority vote in the legislatures of three-fourths (38) of the states
D
Acceptance by conventions called for that purpose in three-fourths (38) of the states†

* This method of proposal has never been employed. Thus amendment routes 3 and 4 have never been attempted.

† In each amendment proposal, Congress has the power to choose the method of ratification, the time limit for consideration by the states, and other conditions of ratification.

(Figure 2.2 illustrates each of these methods.) Because no amendment has ever been proposed by national convention, however, routes 3 and 4 have never been employed. And route 2 has been employed only once (for the Twenty-first Amendment, which repealed the Eighteenth, or Prohibition, Amendment). Thus route 1 has been used for all the others.

The Twenty-seven Amendments

The Constitution and its amendments are reproduced at the end of this book. Most of the Constitution's 27 amendments share a common characteristic: All but two are concerned with the structure or composition of government. This is consistent with the dictionary, which defines *constitution* as the "makeup or composition of a thing"—anything. And it is consistent with the concept of a constitution as higher law because the whole point and purpose of a higher law is to establish a framework within which government and the process of making ordinary law can take place. Even those who would have preferred more changes in the Constitution would have had to agree that there is great wisdom in this principle. A constitution ought to enable legislation and public policies to take place, but it should not determine what that legislation or those public policies ought to be.

The purpose of the 10 amendments in the Bill of Rights was basically structural: to give each of the three branches clearer and more restricted boundaries. The First Amendment clarifies the jurisdiction of Congress. Although the powers of Congress under Article I, Section 8, do not justify laws regulating religion, speech, and the like, the First Amendment makes this limitation explicit: "Congress shall make no law . . ." The Second, Third, and Fourth Amendments similarly spell out limits on the executive branch. Such limits were seen as a necessity given the abuses of executive power Americans had endured under British rule.

The Fifth, Sixth, Seventh, and Eighth Amendments contain some of the most important safeguards for individual citizens against the arbitrary exercise of governmental power. And these amendments sought to accomplish their goal by defining the judicial branch more concretely and clearly than had been done in Article III of the Constitution. Table 2.2 analyzes the 10 amendments included in the Bill of Rights.

Table 2.2

THE BILL OF RIGHTS: ANALYSIS OF ITS PROVISIONS

AMENDMENT	PURPOSE
I	Limits on Congress: Congress is not to make any law establishing a religion or abridging the freedom of speech, press, or assembly or the right to petition the government.
II, III, IV	Limits on the executive: The executive branch is not to infringe on the right of people to keep arms (II), is not to arbitrarily take houses for use by a militia (III), and is not to engage in the search or seizure of evidence without a court warrant swearing to a belief in the probable existence of a crime (IV).
V, VI, VII, VIII	Limits on the courts: The courts are not to hold trials for serious offenses without provision for a grand jury (V), a petit (trial) jury (VII), a speedy trial (VI), presentation of charges, and confrontation of hostile witnesses (VI). Individuals may not be compelled to testify against themselves (V) and are immune from trial more than once for the same offense (V). Neither bail nor punishment can be excessive (VIII), and no property can be taken without just compensation (V).
IX, X	Limits on the national government: All rights not enumerated are reserved to the states or the people.

Table 2.3

AMENDING THE CONSTITUTION TO EXPAND THE ELECTORATE

AMENDMENT	PURPOSE	YEAR PROPOSED	YEAR ADOPTED
XIV	Provided, in Section 1, a national definition of citizenship*	1866	1868
XV	Extended voting rights to all races	1869	1870
XIX	Extended voting rights to women	1919	1920
XXII	Extended voting rights to residents of the District of Columbia	1960	1961
XXIV	Extended voting rights to all classes by abolition of poll taxes	1962	1964
XXVI	Extended voting rights to citizens aged 18 and over	1971	1971

Five of the 17 amendments adopted since 1791 are directly concerned with expansion of the electorate (Table 2.3). These occasional efforts to expand the electorate were made necessary by the fact that the Founders were unable to establish a national electorate with uniform voting qualifications. Stalemated on that issue, the delegates decided to evade it by providing in the final draft of Article I, Section 2, that eligibility to vote in a national election would be the same as "the Qualifications requisite for Electors of the most numerous Branch of the State Legislature." Article I, Section 4, added that Congress could alter state regulations as to the "Times, Places and Manner of holding Elections for Senators and Representatives." Nevertheless, this meant that any important expansion of the American electorate would almost certainly require a constitutional amendment.

Six more amendments are also electoral in nature, although not concerned directly with voting rights and the expansion of the electorate (Table 2.4). These six amendments are concerned with the elective offices themselves (the Twentieth, Twenty-second, and Twenty-fifth) or with the relationship between elective offices and the electorate (the Twelfth, Fourteenth, and Seventeenth).

Table 2.4

AMENDING THE CONSTITUTION TO CHANGE THE RELATIONSHIP BETWEEN THE ELECTED OFFICES AND THE ELECTORATE

AMENDMENT	PURPOSE	YEAR PROPOSED	YEAR ADOPTED
XII	Provided a separate ballot for the vice president in the electoral college	1803	1804
XIV	Eliminated, in Section 2, the counting of slaves in the apportionment of House seats	1866	1868
XVII	Provided for the direct election of senators	1912	1913
XX	Eliminated "lame duck" sessions of Congress	1932	1933
XXII	Limited the presidential term	1947	1951
XXV	Provided for presidential succession in case of disability	1965	1967

Another five amendments have sought to expand or limit the powers of the national and state governments (Table 2.5).[37] The Eleventh Amendment protects the states from suits by private individuals and takes away from the federal courts any power to hear suits by private individuals of one state (or a foreign country) against another state. Three other amendments in Table 2.5 are obviously designed to reduce state power (the Thirteenth), reduce state power and expand national power (the Fourteenth), and expand national power (the Sixteenth). The Twenty-seventh puts a limit on Congress's ability to raise its own salary.

The two missing amendments underscore the meaning of the rest: the Eighteenth, or Prohibition, Amendment and the Twenty-first, its repeal. They

37 The Fourteenth Amendment is included in this table as well as in Table 2.3 because it not only seeks to define citizenship but also *seems* to intend that this definition of citizenship include, along with the right to vote, all the rights of the Bill of Rights, regardless of the state in which the citizen resides. A great deal more will be said about this in Chapter 4.

Table 2.5

AMENDING THE CONSTITUTION TO EXPAND OR LIMIT THE POWER OF GOVERNMENT

AMENDMENT	PURPOSE	YEAR PROPOSED	YEAR ADOPTED
XI	Limited the jurisdiction of federal courts over suits involving the states	**1794**	**1798**
XIII	Eliminated slavery and the rights of states to allow property in the form of persons	**1865***	**1865**
XIV	In Section 2, applied due process of the Bill of Rights to the states	**1866**	**1868**
XVI	Established the national power to tax income	**1909**	**1913**
XXVII	Limited Congress's power to raise its own salary	**1789**	**1992**

* The Thirteenth Amendment was proposed on January 31, 1865, and adopted less than a year later, on December 6, 1865.

represent the only instance in which the country tried to *legislate* by constitutional amendment. In other words, the Eighteenth is the only amendment that was designed to deal directly with some substantive social problem. And it was the only amendment ever to have been repealed. Two other amendments—the Thirteenth, which abolished slavery, and the Sixteenth, which established the power to levy an income tax—can be said to have had the effect of legislation. But the purpose of the Thirteenth Amendment was to restrict the power of the states by forever forbidding them to treat any human being as property. As for the Sixteenth Amendment, it is certainly true that income-tax legislation followed immediately; nevertheless, the amendment concerns itself strictly with establishing the power of Congress to enact such legislation. The legislation came later; and if down the line a majority in Congress had wanted to abolish the income tax, they could also have done so by legislation rather than through the arduous path of a constitutional amendment repealing the income tax.

For those whose hopes for change center on the Constitution, it must be emphasized that the amendment route to social change is, and always will be, extremely limited. This is "path dependency," as captured in the history principle, with a vengeance. The status quo—the original Constitution—and the arduousness of its amendment process provide durability on the one hand and constrain the prospects for change on the other. Through a constitution it is possible to establish a working structure of government, and through a constitution it is possible to establish basic rights of citizens by placing limitations and obligations on the powers of that government. Once these things have been accomplished, the real problem is how to extend rights to those people who do not already enjoy them.

REFLECTIONS ON THE FOUNDING: IDEALS OR INTERESTS?

At the start of this chapter, we stressed the need to look beyond the myths and rhetoric of the Founding era to analyze the goals of the Founders, their struggle to resolve their conflicts and reach their collective goals, and the institutions that resulted from their endeavor. The story of the Founding—the initial decision of Britain's New World colonies to chart a separate course (the Declaration of Independence), a successful revolution and the creation of a confederation of states with a weak central government (the Articles of Confederation), and the re-creation of an entirely elaborated new body of institutional arrangements (the Constitution), what Seymour Martin Lipset called the "first new nation"[38]—is a chronicle of purposeful collective action leading to the creation of a unique political scaffolding for governance.

The revolutionary generation, the politicians of the Articles years, and those who met in Philadelphia to create a new nation were rational actors with specific goals and purposes in mind. As we've seen, some scholars, such as Charles Beard, put a premium on economic self-interest. Northern merchants and manufacturers wanted property protection and security, unfettered opportunities to trade in domestic and international markets, and the financial security of sound currency, low taxes, and limited public debt. Southern planters also wanted property protection (with some of that property human in form), low tariffs to enable them to obtain manufactured goods cheaply, and access to international markets for their products and for slaves. Small farmers, tradesmen, and artisans wanted easy credit, relief from onerous taxes, and permissive policies toward debt. Other scholars have emphasized the idea of liberty and the "rights of Englishmen" that were compromised by clumsy interventions on the part of the mother country. Independence, loose federation, and finally a new

38 Seymour Martin Lipset, *The First New Nation* (New York: Norton, 1979).

nation with a central government capable of effective action were the goals, at different times, toward which the economic and political purposes of many of these groups pointed.

To orchestrate a revolution, organize a confederation, or draft a constitution requires a large variety of collective actions. Behaviors of many must be coordinated, participation must be induced, efforts must be focused on common objectives, and free riding must be discouraged. To accomplish all this, bargaining, cooperation, and compromise must prevail, and during the Founding period, political leaders facilitated this process. Jefferson and Adams brought the colonies to the point of separating from the motherland; Washington was pivotal in the revolutionary phase; a variety of politicians came together to bargain over the directions to be taken by the Confederation, often without success; Madison, Hamilton, Washington, and ultimately Franklin presided over the drafting of the Constitution. In sum, collective action, coordinated by motivated leadership, paved the historical path from colony to new nation.

We've also seen that new institutions were needed to organize the new government successfully. Colonial institutions were satisfactory for 150 years, especially in a context in which the mother country was preoccupied with events elsewhere. Independence and self-governance became institutional objectives when the burdens of colonialism began to weigh heavily on the economic circumstances and political freedoms of the colonists. Over a 15-year period (roughly 1775–90), the Founders experimented with and ultimately crafted a political order that, in most of its aspects, has survived more than two centuries. The final product of the Constitutional Convention has to be considered an extraordinary victory for the groups that had most forcefully called for the creation of a new system of government to replace the Articles of Confederation. Antifederalist criticisms forced the Constitution's proponents to accept the addition of a bill of rights designed to limit the powers of the national government. In general, however, it was the Federalist vision of America that triumphed. The Constitution adopted in 1789 created the framework for a powerful national government that has defended the nation's interests, promoted its commerce, and maintained national unity in the years since.

Though the Constitution was the product of a particular set of political forces, the form of government it established has a significance that goes far beyond the interests of its authors. As we have observed, political ideals often take on lives of their own. The great political values incorporated into the Constitution continue, more than two centuries later, to shape our political lives in ways that the framers may not have anticipated. For example, when they empowered Congress to regulate commerce among the states in Article I, Section 8, of the Constitution, they could hardly have anticipated that this provision would become the basis for many of the federal government's regulatory activities in areas as diverse as the environment and civil rights.

Two great constitutional notions, federalism and civil liberties, will be discussed in Chapters 3 and 4. As we close our discussion of the Founding and move on to an examination of federalism, it is worth reflecting on the Antifederalists. Although they were defeated in 1789, the Antifederalists present us with an important picture of a road not taken, an America that might have been. Would we have been worse off as a people if we had been governed by a confederacy of small republics linked by a national administration with severely limited powers? Were the Antifederalists correct in predicting that a government given great power in the hope that it might do good would, through "insensible progress," inevitably come to serve the interests of the few at the expense of the many? More than two centuries of government under the federal Constitution are not necessarily enough to definitively answer these questions. Only time will tell.

For Further Reading

Amar, Akhil Reed. *America's Constitution: A Biography*. New York: Random House, 2005.

Bailyn, Bernard. *The Ideological Origins of the American Revolution*. Cambridge, MA: Harvard University Press, 1967.

Beard, Charles A. *An Economic Interpretation of the Constitution of the United States*. New York: Macmillan, 1913.

Beeman, Richard. *Plain, Honest Men: The Making of the American Constitution*. New York: Random House, 2010.

Breyer, Stephen. *Active Liberty: Interpreting Our Democratic Constitution*. New York: Knopf, 2005.

Chernow, Ron. *Alexander Hamilton*. New York: Penguin, 2004.

Ellis, Joseph. *Founding Brothers: The Revolutionary Generation*. New York: Knopf, 2000.

———. *His Excellency, George Washington*. New York: Knopf, 2004.

Farrand, Max, ed. *The Records of the Federal Convention of 1787*. Rev. ed. 4 vols. New Haven, CT: Yale University Press, 1966.

Glaeser, Edward C. "Revolution of Urban Rebels." *Boston Globe*, July 4, 2008, Section A.

reader selection

Hamilton, Alexander, James Madison, and John Jay. *The Federalist Papers*. Clinton Rossiter, ed. New York: New American Library, 1961.

Keller, Morton. *America's Three Regimes: A New Political History*. New York: Oxford University Press, 2007.

Lutz, Donald. *Colonial Origins of the American Constitution.* New York: Liberty Fund, 2010.

Maier, Pauline. *American Scripture: Making the Declaration of Independence.* New York: Knopf, 1997.

Riker, William H. *The Strategy of Rhetoric: Campaigning for the American Constitution.* New Haven, CT: Yale University Press, 1996.

Storing, Herbert J., ed. *The Complete Anti-Federalist.* 7 vols. Chicago: University of Chicago Press, 1981.

reader selection

Visit **wwnorton.com/studyspace/** to access free review materials such as:

- Vocabulary Flashcards of All Key Terms
- Chapter Review Quizzes
- Complete Study Outlines

reader selection

Highlighted selections are included in *Readings in American Politics: Analysis and Perspectives*, Second Edition.

PART X 2 3 4

FOUNDATIONS

3

Federalism and the Separation of Powers

Chapter Outline

- Who Does What? Federalism and Institutional Jurisdictions
- The Separation of Powers
- Federalism and the Separation of Powers: Collective Action or Stalemate?

The great achievement of American politics was the fashioning of an effective constitutional structure of political institutions. Although it is an imperfect and continuously evolving work in progress, this structure of law and political practice has served its people well for more than two centuries by managing conflict, providing inducements for bargaining and cooperation, and facilitating collective action. It has had at least one major failure: the cruel practice of slavery, which ended only after a destructive civil war. But the basic configuration of institutions first formulated in Philadelphia in 1787 survived that tragedy and has otherwise stood the test of time.

Two of America's most important institutional features are federalism and the separation of powers. Federalism seeks to limit government by dividing it into two levels, national and state, each with sufficient independence to compete with the other, thereby restraining the power of both.[1] The separation of powers seeks to limit the power of the national government by dividing government against itself—by giving the legislative, executive, and judicial branches separate functions, thus forcing them to share power.

In Chapter 1 we observed that institutions organize political life. Institutions, however, take many forms and can choreograph collective action in a variety of ways. One important difference among political institutions is the manner in which they distribute decision, agenda, and veto powers. The institutions

1 The notion that federalism requires separate spheres or jurisdictions in which lower and higher levels of government are uniquely decisive is developed fully in William H. Riker, *Federalism: Origin, Operation, Significance* (Boston: Little, Brown, 1964). This American version of federalism is applied to the emerging federal arrangements in the People's Republic of China during the 1990s in a paper by Barry R. Weingast, "The Economic Role of Political Institutions: Market-Preserving Federalism and Economic Development," *Journal of Law, Economic, and Organization* 11 (1995): 1–32.

established by authoritarian regimes are usually designed to concentrate power in the hands of a small group of leaders who determine what will be considered, make the final decisions, and seek to block the actions of others. In democratic states, in contrast, political institutions are usually designed to allow a variety of groups to participate in decision making and provide at least a measure of agenda and veto power to a number of actors.

In the United States, the framers of the Constitution created institutions that would widely disperse involvement in decision making, along with agenda and veto power. Federalism assigns agenda-setting power, decision-making power, and veto powers to the federal government and to each of the 50 states. The separation of powers gives several federal institutions a degree of control over the agenda, the power to affect decisions, and the ability to block the actions of the others. The framers feared that concentrating power in a small number of hands would threaten citizens' liberties, and they were surely correct. Yet, although the constitutional dispersion of power among federal institutions and between the federal government and the states may well protect our liberties, it often seems to make it impossible to get anything done collectively. This lack of decisiveness sometimes appears to negate the most important reason for building institutions in the first place.

Since the adoption of the Constitution, ambitious politicians have developed a variety of strategies for overcoming the many impediments to policy change that inevitably arise in our federal system of separated powers. Most commonly, those seeking to promote a new program may try to find ways of dispersing the program's benefits so that other politicians controlling institutional veto powers will be persuaded that it is in their interest to go along. Thus, federalism and the separation of powers have given rise to the federal pork

CORE OF THE ANALYSIS

Two of the most important institutional features of America's government are federalism and the separation of powers.

Federalism assigns agenda-setting, decision-making, and veto powers to the federal government and the 50 states.

The apportionment of powers between the federal government and the states has shifted over time.

The separation of powers delineates the authority of the executive, Congress, and the courts, giving each a degree of control over the agenda, the power to affect decisions, and the ability to block the actions of the others.

barrel, to the defense subcontracting system, and to grants-in-aid and other forms of policy that reflect the dispersion of decision, agenda, and veto powers. For example, if the executive branch hopes to win congressional support for a new weapons system, it generally sees to it that portions of the new system are subcontracted to firms in as many congressional districts as possible. In this way, dispersion of benefits helps to overcome the separation of powers between the executive and legislative branches. Similarly, as we see below, federal officials often secure state cooperation with national programs by offering the states funding, called grants-in-aid, in exchange for their compliance. These programs help to overcome the limitations of federalism. Thus, consistent with our discussion of the five principles of politics in Chapter 1, America's public policies are shaped by the institutional arrangements through which individual efforts must flow.

However, institutions are not carved in stone. Once created, they are subject to revision and modification as competing forces seek new decision rules that will give them an advantage, and as the leaders of institutions seek to strengthen their own power and expand their own jurisdictions at the expense of other institutions. In recent decades, the presidency has increased in power relative to Congress, and the federal government has grown in jurisdiction relative to the states. Nevertheless, these two core institutional features, federalism and the separation of powers, remain at the heart of the American system of government. Let us examine these features and assess their consequences for American government.

WHO DOES WHAT? FEDERALISM AND INSTITUTIONAL JURISDICTIONS

federalism

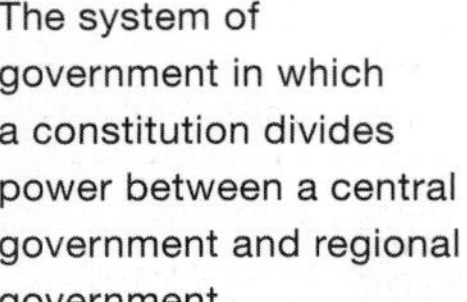
The system of government in which a constitution divides power between a central government and regional government

sovereignty

Supreme and independent political authority

Federalism can be defined as the division of powers and functions between the national government and the state governments. Federalism limits national and state power by creating two levels of government—the national government and the state governments, each with a large measure of sovereignty and thus the ability to restrain the power of the other. As we saw in Chapter 2, the states existed as individual colonies before independence, and for nearly 13 years they were virtually autonomous units under the Articles of Confederation. In effect, the states had retained too much power relative to the national government, a problem that led directly to the Annapolis Convention in 1786 and to the Constitutional Convention in 1787. Under the Articles, disorder within states was beyond the reach of the national government (see Shays's Rebellion, discussed in Chapter 2), and conflicts of interest between states were not manageable. For example, states were making their own trade agreements with foreign countries and companies, which might then play off one state against another for special advantages. Some states adopted trade tariffs and further barriers to foreign commerce that were contrary to the interests of other states.[2] Tax and other barriers were also being erected between the states.[3] But even after the ratification of the Constitution, the states continued to be more important than the national government. For nearly a century and a half, virtually all of the fundamental policies governing the lives of Americans were made by the state legislatures, not by Congress.

Why Keep the States: The Importance of History. Many of the Constitution's framers, particularly Alexander Hamilton, had hoped to create something close to a unitary national government and to circumscribe severely the power of the individual states. The fact that the framers established a federal system in which the states retained significant powers is an illustration of the importance of history. Each of the states had a well-established set of governmental institutions staffed by legislators, judges, and executive officials who had no desire to see their power and autonomy submerged in a new national government. New York's governor George Clinton, for example, opposed the idea of a stronger national government mainly because he enjoyed his position as the chief executive of what amounted to an important independent nation. At the same time, citizens identified with their own states. The people of North America were not Americans. Instead, they had already had several generations to become Virginians, New Yorkers, Pennsylvanians, and so on. Well-established popular identification with the 13 states was another reason that even the most nationalistic of the framers was forced to accept the idea that the states would continue as important entities. In a sense, the framers were faced by the same historically given realities faced today by advocates of a stronger European Union (EU). The nations of Europe have historically distinct identities, well-entrenched governments, and loyal citizens. Given the force of history, uniting these nations is no easy matter. Like America's Founders, the architects of the EU, bowing to history, have generally sought to erect the new regime on federal foundations.

Federalism in the Constitution: Who Decides What

American federalism recognized two sovereigns in the original Constitution and reinforced the principle in the Bill of Rights by granting a few expressed powers to the national government and reserving the rest to the states. Thus, the Constitution defined the jurisdiction of each level of government.

expressed powers

Powers specifically granted to the federal government in the text of the Constitution

The Powers of the National Government. As we saw in Chapter 2, the expressed powers granted to the national government are found in Article I,

2 For a good treatment of these conflicts of interest between states, see Forrest McDonald, *E Pluribus Unum: The Formation of the American Republic, 1776–1790* (Boston: Houghton Mifflin, 1965), chap. 7, esp. pp. 319–38.

3 See David M. O'Brien, *Constitutional Law and Politics*, 3rd ed. (New York: Norton, 1997), I:602–3.

Section 8, of the Constitution. These 17 powers include the powers to collect taxes, coin money, declare war, and regulate commerce (which became a very important power for the national government). Article I, Section 8, also contains an important source of power for the national government: the implied powers that enable Congress "to make all Laws which shall be necessary and proper for carrying into Execution the foregoing Powers." Not until several decades after the Founding did the Supreme Court allow Congress to exercise the power granted in this necessary and proper clause, but as we see later in this chapter, this doctrine allowed the national government to expand considerably the scope of its authority, although the process was a slow one. In addition to these expressed and implied powers, the Constitution affirms the power of the national government in the supremacy clause (Article VI), which makes all national laws and treaties "the supreme Law of the Land."

implied powers

Powers derived from the necessary and proper clause (Article I, Section 8) of the Constitution. Such powers are not specifically expressed but are implied through the expansive interpretation of delegated powers

necessary and proper clause 

Article I, Section 8, of the Constitution, which enumerates the powers of Congress and provides Congress with the authority to make all laws "necessary and proper" to carry them out; also referred to as the elastic clause

The Powers of State Government. One way in which the framers sought to preserve a strong role for the states was through the Tenth Amendment to the Constitution. The Tenth Amendment presents a decision rule, or general principle governing decisions, stating that the powers the Constitution does not delegate to the national government or deny to the states are "reserved to the States respectively, or to the people." The Antifederalists, who feared that a strong central government would encroach on individual liberty, repeatedly pressed for such an amendment as a way of limiting national power. Federalists agreed to the amendment because they did not think it would do much harm, given the powers the Constitution already granted to the national government. The Tenth Amendment is also called the reserved powers amendment because it aims to reserve powers to the states.

reserved powers 

Powers, derived from the Tenth Amendment to the Constitution, that are not specifically delegated to the national government or denied to the states; these powers are reserved to the states

The most fundamental power retained by the states is that of coercion—the power to develop and enforce criminal codes, administer health and safety rules, and regulate the family via marriage and divorce laws. The states have the power to regulate individuals' livelihoods: if you're a doctor or a lawyer or a plumber or a barber, you must be licensed by the state. Even more fundamental, the states had the power to define private property: private property exists because state laws against trespass define who is and who is not entitled to use a piece of property. If you own a car, your ownership isn't worth much unless the state is willing to enforce your right to possession by making it a crime for anyone else to drive your car without your permission. These are fundamental matters, and the powers of the states regarding such domestic issues are much greater than the powers of the national government, even today. For example, in its 2008 decision in the case of *District of Columbia v. Heller*, the Supreme Court ruled that a District of Columbia handgun control ordinance that made it virtually impossible for a district resident to legally possess a handgun was unconstitutional.[4] The Court based its ruling on the Second Amendment, which guarantees the right to bear arms. The Court's majority, however, indicated that the Second Amendment applied only to the federal government and that the District's

4 *District of Columbia v. Heller*, 554 U.S. 570 (2008).

ordinance was invalidated only because the District of Columbia was legally an agency of the federal government.[5] Two years later, in the case of *McDonald v. Chicago*, the Court struck down a Chicago gun ordinance, this time declaring that the Second Amendment applied to the states as well as the federal government.[6]

A state's authority to regulate these fundamental matters is commonly referred to as the police power of the state and encompasses the state's power to regulate the health, safety, welfare, and morals of its citizens. Policing is what states do—they coerce you in the name of the community in order to maintain public order. And this was exactly the type of power the Founders intended the states to exercise.

police power

The power reserved to the government to regulate the health, safety, and morals of its citizens

In some areas, the states share concurrent powers with the national government: they retain and share some power to regulate commerce and affect the currency—for example, by chartering banks, granting or denying corporate charters, granting or denying licenses to engage in a business or practice a trade, and regulating the quality of products or the conditions of labor. This issue of concurrent versus exclusive power has come up from time to time in our history, but wherever there has been a direct conflict of laws between the federal and the state levels, the issue has most often been resolved in favor of national supremacy.

concurrent powers

The authority possessed by *both* state and national governments, such as the power to levy taxes

States' Obligations to Each Other. The Constitution also creates obligations among the states. These obligations, spelled out in Article IV, were intended to promote national unity. By requiring the states to recognize actions and decisions taken in other states as legal and proper, the framers aimed to make the states less like independent countries and more like parts of a single nation.

Article IV, Section 1, calls for "Full Faith and Credit" among states, meaning that each state is normally expected to honor the "public Acts, Records, and Proceedings" that take place in any other state. So, for example, if two people are married in Texas—marriage being regulated by state law—Missouri must recognize that marriage even though the couple was not married under Missouri state law.

full faith and credit clause

The provision in Article IV. Section 1, of the Constitution requiring that each state normally honors the public acts and judicial decisions that take place in another state

This full faith and credit clause has recently become entangled in the controversy over gay marriage. In several states, individuals of the same sex may marry. A number of other states, though, have passed "defense of marriage acts" that define marriage only as a union between a man and a woman. Eager to show its disapproval of gay marriage, Congress passed the federal Defense of Marriage Act in 1996, declaring that states will *not* have to recognize a same-sex marriage legally contracted in another state. The Supreme Court may eventually be asked to clarify this issue.

Article IV, Section 2, known as the comity clause, also seeks to promote national unity. It provides that citizens enjoying the privileges and immunities

privileges and immunities

The provision in Article IV, Section 2, of the Constitution stating that a state cannot discriminate against someone from another state or give its own residents special privileges

5 Jess Bravin and Susan Davis, "In a First, High Court Affirms Gun Rights," *Wall Street Journal*, June 22, 2008, p. A1.

6 *McDonald v. Chicago*, 130 S. Ct. 3020 (2010).

of one state should be entitled to similar treatment in other states. What this clause has come to mean is that a state cannot discriminate against someone from another state or give special privileges to its own residents. For example, in the 1970s, when Alaska passed a law that gave residents preference over nonresidents in obtaining work on the state's oil and gas pipelines, the Supreme Court ruled the law illegal because it discriminated against citizens of other states.[7] This clause also regulates criminal justice among the states by requiring states to return fugitives to the states from which they have fled. Thus in 1952, when an inmate escaped from an Alabama prison and sought to avoid being returned to Alabama on the grounds that he was being subjected to "cruel and unusual punishment" there, the Supreme Court ruled that he must be returned, according to Article IV, Section 2.[8] This example highlights the difference between the obligations among states and those among different countries. Recently France refused to return an American fugitive because he might be subject to the death penalty, which does not exist in France.[9] The Constitution clearly forbids states from doing something similar.

Limitations on the States. Although most of the truly coercive powers of government are reserved to the states, the Constitution does impose some significant limitations. One example was given in the discussion of the privileges and immunities clause: that one state cannot discriminate against a person residing in another state. But the most prominent application of this clause is extradition; any person in any state "who shall flee from Justice . . . [to] another State, shall on Demand . . . be delivered up . . . to the State having Jurisdiction" (Article IV, Section 2). In the last section, we gave the example of the case of an Alabama inmate.

Another potential limit on states is in a clause in Article I, Section 10, that provides that "no State shall, without the Consent of Congress, . . . enter into any Agreement or Compact with another State." Compacts are a way for two or more states to reach a legally binding agreement about how to solve a problem that crosses state lines. In the early years of the Republic, states turned to compacts primarily to settle border disputes. Today with the support of the federal government they are used for a wide range of issues but are especially important in regulating the distribution of river water, addressing environmental concerns, and operating transportation systems that cross state lines.[10] A well-known contemporary example is the Port of New York Authority, a compact formed between New York and New Jersey in 1921. Without it, such public works as the bridge connecting Brooklyn and Staten Island, the bridges connecting New

7 *Hicklin v. Orbeck*, 437 U.S. 518 (1978).

8 *Sweeney v. Woodall*, 344 U.S. 86 (1953).

9 Marlise Simons, "France Won't Extradite American Convicted of Murder," *New York Times*, December 5, 1997, p. A9.

10 Patricia S. Florestano, "Past and Present Utilization of Interstate Compacts in the United States," *Publius* (Fall 1994): 13–26.

Jersey and Staten Island, the Lincoln Tunnel, the George Washington Bridge, the expansion and integration of the New York port area, and the expansion and integration of the three major airports and countless approaches and transfer facilities could not have been financed or completed.[11] In 1972, the name of the agency was appropriately changed to the Port Authority of New York and New Jersey.

Local Government and the Constitution. Local government, including counties, cities, and towns occupies a peculiar but very important place in the American system. In fact, the status of American local government is probably unique in world experience. First, it must be pointed out that local government has no status in the American Constitution. *State* legislatures created local governments, and *state* constitutions and laws permit local governments to take on some of the responsibilities of the state governments. Most states amended their own constitutions to give their larger cities home rule—a guarantee of noninterference in various areas of local affairs. But local governments enjoy no such recognition in the Constitution. Local governments have always been mere conveniences of the states.[12]

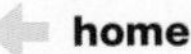

home rule

The power delegated by the state to a local unit of government to manage its own affairs

Local governments became administratively important in the early years of the Republic because the states possessed little administrative capability. They relied on local governments—cities and counties—to implement the laws of the state. Local government was an alternative to a statewide bureaucracy.

The Slow Growth of the National Government's Power

Before the 1930s, America's federal system could have been characterized as one of dual federalism, a two-layered system—national and state—in which the states and their local principalities did most of the governing. That is, the jurisdiction of the states was greater than that of the federal government. The structure of dual federalism is demonstrated in Table 3.1. The items in each column (disregarding the local-level functions discussed in the previous section) are the important types of public policies that governed America for the first century and a half under the Constitution. We refer to it here as the traditional system precisely because almost nothing about our pattern of government changed

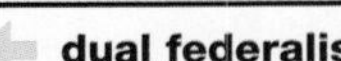

dual federalism

The system of government that prevailed in the United States from 1789 to 1937, in which fundamental governmental powers were shared between the federal and state governments, with the states exercising the most important powers

11 A good discussion of the status of the New York Port Authority in politics is found in Wallace Sayre and Herbert Kaufman, *Governing New York City—Politics in the Metropolis* (New York: Russell Sage Foundation, 1960), chap. 9.

12 A good discussion of the constitutional position of local governments is in York Y. Willbern, *The Withering Away of the City* (Bloomington: Indiana University Press, 1971). For more on the structure and theory of federalism, see Thomas R. Dye, *American Federalism: Competition among Governments* (Lexington, MA: Lexington Books, 1990), chap. 1; and Martha Derthick, "Up-to-Date in Kansas City: Reflections on American Federalism," *PS: Political Science and Politics* 25 (December 1992): 671–5.

Table 3.1

THE FEDERAL SYSTEM: SPECIALIZATION OF GOVERNMENTAL FUNCTIONS IN THE TRADITIONAL SYSTEM, 1789–1937

NATIONAL GOVERNMENT JURISDICTION (DOMESTIC)	STATE GOVERNMENT JURISDICTION	LOCAL GOVERNMENT JURISDICTION
Internal improvements	Property laws (including slavery)	Adaptation of state laws to local conditions (variances)
Subsidies	Estate and inheritance laws	Public works
Tariffs	Commerce laws	Contracts for public works
Public lands disposal	Banking and credit laws	Licensing of public accommodations
Patents	Corporate laws	Assessable improvements
Currency	Insurance laws Family laws Morality laws Public health laws Education laws General penal laws Eminent domain laws Construction codes Land-use laws Water and mineral laws Criminal procedure laws Electoral and political party laws Local government laws Civil service laws Occupations and professions laws	Basic public services

during two-thirds of our history. That is, of course, with the exception of the four years of the Civil War, after which we returned to the traditional system.

But there was more to dual federalism than merely the existence of two tiers. The two tiers were functionally quite different from one another. There have been debates every generation over how to divide responsibilities between the two tiers. As we have seen in this chapter, the Constitution delegated a list of specific powers to the national government and reserved all the rest to the states. That left a lot of room for interpretation, however, because of the final, "elastic" clause of Article I, Section 8. The three formal words *necessary and proper* amounted to an invitation to struggle over the distribution of powers between national and state governments. We confront this struggle throughout the book. However, the most remarkable thing about the history of American federalism is that federalism remained dual for nearly two-thirds of that history, with the national government remaining steadfastly within a "strict construction" of Article I, Section 8. The results are clear in Table 3.1.

The best example of the potential elasticity inherent in Article I, Section 8, is in the commerce clause, which delegates to Congress the power "to regulate Commerce with foreign Nations, and *among the several States* and with the Indian Tribes" [emphasis added]. This clause can be interpreted broadly or narrowly, and in fact the Supreme Court embraced the broad interpretation throughout most of the nineteenth century. Yet Congress chose not to take the Court's invitation to be expansive. The first and most important case favoring national power was *McCulloch v. Maryland*.[13] The issue was whether Congress had the power to charter a bank, in particular the Bank of the United States (created by Congress in 1791 over Thomas Jefferson's constitutional opposition), because no express power to create banks was found anywhere in Article I, Section 8. Chief Justice John Marshall, speaking for the Supreme Court, answered that such a power could be "implied" from the other specific powers in Article I, Section 8, plus the final clause enabling Congress "to make all Laws which shall be necessary and proper for carrying into Execution the foregoing Powers." Thus the Court created the potential for significant increases in national governmental power by creating a decision rule that favored the national government over the states. Essentially, Marshall's ruling said that if a goal was allowed in the Constitution and Congress's chosen means to achieve the goal was not prohibited by the Constitution, Congress could act. This ruling gave the national government wide latitude.

commerce clause

Article I, Section 8, of the Constitution, which delegates to Congress the power "to regulate Commerce with foreign Nations, and among the several States, and with the Indian Tribes." This clause was interpreted by the Supreme Court to favor national power over the economy

A second question of national power arose in *McCulloch v. Maryland*: the question of whether Maryland's attempt to tax the bank was constitutional. Once again Marshall and the Supreme Court took the side of the national government, arguing that a legislature representing all the people (Congress) could not be taxed out of business by a state legislature (Maryland) representing only a small portion of the American people. This opinion was accompanied by Marshall's immortal dictum that "the power to tax is the power to destroy."

13 *McCulloch v. Maryland*, 4 Wheaton 316 (1819).

It was also in this case that the Supreme Court recognized and reinforced the supremacy clause: whenever a state law conflicts with a federal law, the state law should be deemed invalid because "the Laws of the United States . . . shall be the supreme Law of the Land." (The concept of federal supremacy was introduced in Chapter 2 and will come up again in Chapter 9.)

This nationalistic interpretation of the Constitution was reinforced by another major case, that of *Gibbons v. Ogden* in 1824. The important but relatively narrow issue was whether the state of New York could grant a monopoly to Robert Fulton's steamboat company to operate an exclusive service between New York and New Jersey. Aaron Ogden had secured his license from Fulton's company, whereas Thomas Gibbons, a former partner of Ogden's, had secured a competing license from the U.S. government. Chief Justice Marshall argued that Gibbons could not be kept from competing because the state of New York did not have the power to grant this particular monopoly affecting other states' interests. To reach his decision, it was necessary for Marshall to define what Article I, Section 8, meant by "Commerce . . . among the several States." Marshall insisted that the definition was "comprehensive" but added that the comprehensiveness was limited "to that commerce which concerns more states than one." This opinion gave rise to what later came to be called interstate commerce.[14]

Although *Gibbons* was an important case, the precise meaning of interstate commerce would remain uncertain for several decades of constitutional discourse. However, one thing was certain: "interstate commerce" was a source of power for the national government as long as Congress sought to improve commerce through subsidies, services, and land grants (Table 3.1, col. 1). Later in the nineteenth century, when the national government sought to use its power to *regulate* the economy rather than merely promote economic development, the concept of interstate commerce began to operate as a restraint rather than as a source of national power. Any effort by the federal government to regulate commerce in such areas as fraud, the production of impure goods, the use of child labor, or the existence of dangerous working conditions or long hours was declared unconstitutional by the Supreme Court as a violation of the concept of interstate commerce. Regulation in these areas would mean the federal government was entering the factory and the workplace, areas inherently local because the goods produced there had not yet passed into commerce and crossed state lines. Any effort to enter these local workplaces was an exercise of police power, a power reserved to the states. No one questioned the power of the national government to regulate certain kinds of businesses, such as railroads, gas pipelines, and waterway transportation, because they intrinsically involved interstate commerce.[15] But well into the twentieth century, most other efforts by Congress

---

14 *Gibbons v. Ogden*, 9 Wheaton 1 (1824).

15 In *Wabash, St. Louis, and Pacific Railway Company v. Illinois*, 118 U.S. 557 (1886), the Supreme Court struck down a state law prohibiting rate discrimination by a railroad; in response, Congress passed the Interstate Commerce Act of 1887, creating the Interstate Commerce Commission (ICC), the first federal regulatory agency.

to regulate commerce were blocked by the Supreme Court's interpretation of federalism, with the concept of interstate commerce as the primary barrier.

For example, in the 1918 case of *Hammer v. Dagenhart*, the Supreme Court struck down a statute prohibiting the interstate shipment of goods manufactured with the use of child labor. Congress had been careful to avoid outlawing the production of such goods which took place within states and only prohibited their interstate shipment. The Court, however, declared that the intent of Congress had been to outlaw the manufacture of the products in question and declared that the statutory language was merely a ruse.[16]

After his election in 1932, President Franklin Delano Roosevelt was eager to expand the power of the national government. His "New Deal" depended on governmental power to regulate the economy and to intervene in every facet of American society. Roosevelt's efforts provoked sharp conflicts between the president and the federal judiciary. After threatening to expand the size of the Supreme Court and a host of new judicial appointments, Roosevelt was able to bend the judiciary to his will. Beginning in the late 1930s, the Supreme Court issued a series of decisions converting the commerce clause from a barrier to a source of national power.

Among the most important of these cases was *National Labor Relations Board v. Jones & Loughlin Steel Company*.[17] At issue was the National Labor Relations Act, known as the Wagner Act, which prohibited corporations from interfering with the efforts of employees to organize into unions, to bargain collectively over wages and working conditions, and to go on strike and engage in picketing. The newly formed National Labor Relations Board (NLRB) had ordered Jones & Loughlin to reinstate workers fired because of their union activities. The appeal reached the Supreme Court because the steel company had made a constitutional issue over the fact that its manufacturing activities were local and therefore beyond the government's reach. The Supreme Court rejected this argument declaring that a large corporation with subsidiaries and suppliers in many states was inherently involved in interstate commerce and hence subject to congressional regulation. In other decisions, the Court upheld minimum wage laws, the Social Security Act and, in the case of *Wickard v. Filburn*, federal rules controlling how much of any given commodity local farmers might grow.[18]

After 1937, the Supreme Court threw out the old distinction between interstate and intrastate commerce. The Court began to refuse even to review appeals challenging acts of Congress that protected the rights of employees to organize and engage in collective bargaining, regulated the amount of farmland in cultivation, extended low-interest credit to small businesses and farmers, and restricted the activities of corporations dealing in the stock market, as well as many other laws that contributed to the construction of the "regulatory state" and the "welfare state."

---

16 *Hammer v. Dagenhart*, 247 U.S. 251 (1918).

17 *National Labor Relations Board v. Jones & Loughlin Steel Company*, 301 U.S. 1 (1937).

18 *Wickard v. Filburn*, 317 U.S. 111 (1942).

Cooperative Federalism and Grants-in-Aid: Institutions Shape Policies

Roosevelt was able to overcome judicial resistance to expansive New Deal programs. Congress, however, forced him to recognize the continuing importance of the states by crafting a number of programs in such a way as to encourage the states to pursue nationally set goals while leaving them some leeway to administer programs according to local values and needs.

If the traditional system of two sovereigns performing highly different functions can be called dual federalism, the system since the 1930s can be called cooperative federalism, which generally refers to supportive relations, sometimes partnerships, between the national government and the state and local governments. It comes in the form of federal subsidization of special state and local activities; these subsidies are called grants-in-aid. But make no mistake about it: although many of these state and local programs would not exist without the federal grant-in-aid, the grant-in-aid is also an important form of federal influence. (Another form of federal influence, the mandate, is covered in the next section.)

cooperative federalism

A type of federalism existing since the New Deal era, in which grants-in-aid have been used strategically to encourage states and localities (without commanding them) to pursue nationally defined goals. Also known as intergovernmental cooperation

A grant-in-aid is really a kind of bribe, or a "carrot," whereby Congress appropriates money for state and local governments with the condition that the money be spent for a particular purpose as defined by Congress. Congress uses grants-in-aid because it does not have the political or constitutional power to command local governments to do its bidding. Federalism gives the states the power to veto many national government efforts. For example, some states have threatened to opt out of the federal No Child Left Behind education law and thus veto it in their own jurisdictions. When you can't command, a monetary inducement becomes a viable alternative. The grant-in-aid is one more example of the fact that institutions shape policies. America's constitutional system gives the states de facto vetoes over many potential national government programs. As a result, the central government has learned to craft policies likely to elicit the states' cooperation.

grants-in-aid

A general term for funds given by Congress to state and local governments

This approach came to be applied to cities as well. Congress set national goals, such as public housing and assistance to the unemployed, and provided grants-in-aid to meet them. World War II temporarily stopped the distribution of these grants. But after the war, Congress resumed the provision of grants for urban development and school lunches. The value of such categorical grants-in-aid increased from $2.3 billion in 1950 to over $450 billion in 2008 (Figure 3.1). Sometimes Congress requires the state or local government to match the national contribution dollar for dollar, but for some programs, such as the interstate highway system, the congressional grant-in-aid provides a significant percentage of the cost. The nationwide speed limit of 55 miles per hour was not imposed on individual drivers by an act of Congress. Instead, Congress bribed the state legislatures by threatening to withdraw the federal highway grants-in-aid if the states did not set that speed limit. In the early 1990s, Congress began to ease up on the states, permitting them, under certain conditions, to go back to the 65-mile-per-hour (or higher) limit without losing their highway grants.

categorical grants-in-aid

Funds given by Congress to states and localities and that are ear-marked by law for specific categories, such as education or crime prevention

Figure 3.1
THE HISTORICAL TREND OF FEDERAL GRANTS-IN-AID

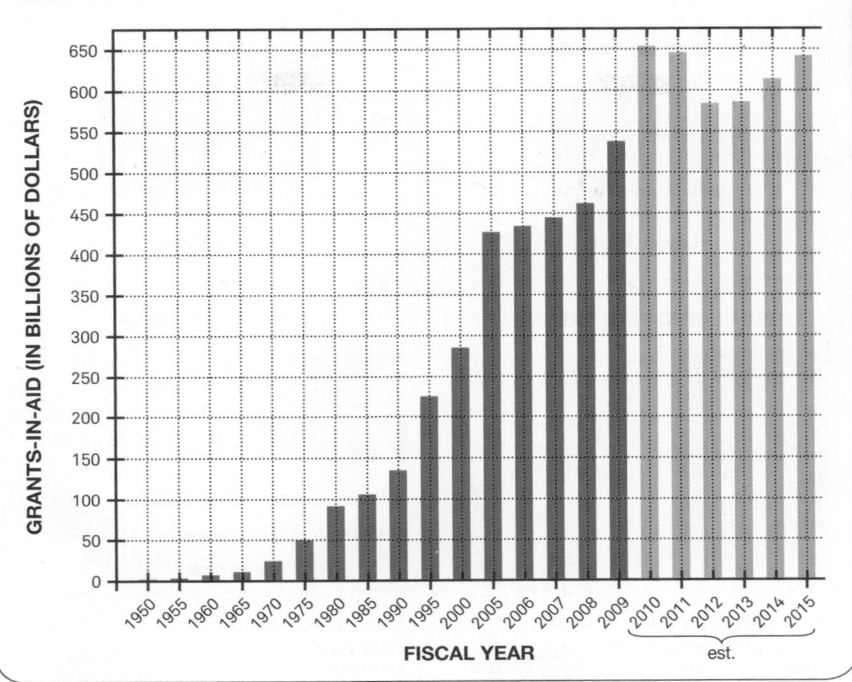

NOTE: Excludes outlays for national defense, international affairs, and net interest.
SOURCE: Office of Management and Budget, *Budget of the U.S. Government, Fiscal Year 2011*, www.whitehouse.gov/omb/budget/fy2011/pdf/hist.pdf (accessed 11/17/11).

ANALYZING THE EVIDENCE

Federal grants-in-aid began to expand dramatically during the 1960s. What political trends might explain this expansion?

For the most part, the categorical grants created before the 1960s simply helped the states perform their traditional functions, such as educating and policing.[19] In the 1960s, however, the national role expanded, and the number of categorical grants increased dramatically. For example, during the 89th Congress (1965–66) alone, the number of categorical grant-in-aid programs grew from 221 to 379.[20] The grants authorized during the 1960s announced national purposes much more strongly than did earlier grants. Central to that national purpose was the need to provide opportunities to the poor.

Many of the categorical grants enacted during the 1960s were project grants, which require state and local governments to submit proposals to federal agencies. In contrast to the older formula grants, which used a formula (composed of such elements as need and state and local capacities) to distribute funds, the

project grants Grant programs in which state and local governments submit proposals to federal agencies and for which funding is provided on a competitive basis

formula grants Grants-in-aid in which a formula is used to determine the amount of federal funds a state or local government will receive

19 Kenneth T. Palmer, "The Evolution of Grant Policies," in *The Changing Politics of Federal Grants,* Lawrence D. Brown, James W. Fossett, and Kenneth T. Palmer, eds. (Washington, DC: Brookings Institution, 1984), p. 15.

20 Palmer, "Grant Policies," p. 6.

Figure 3.2
FOUR VIEWS OF FEDERALISM

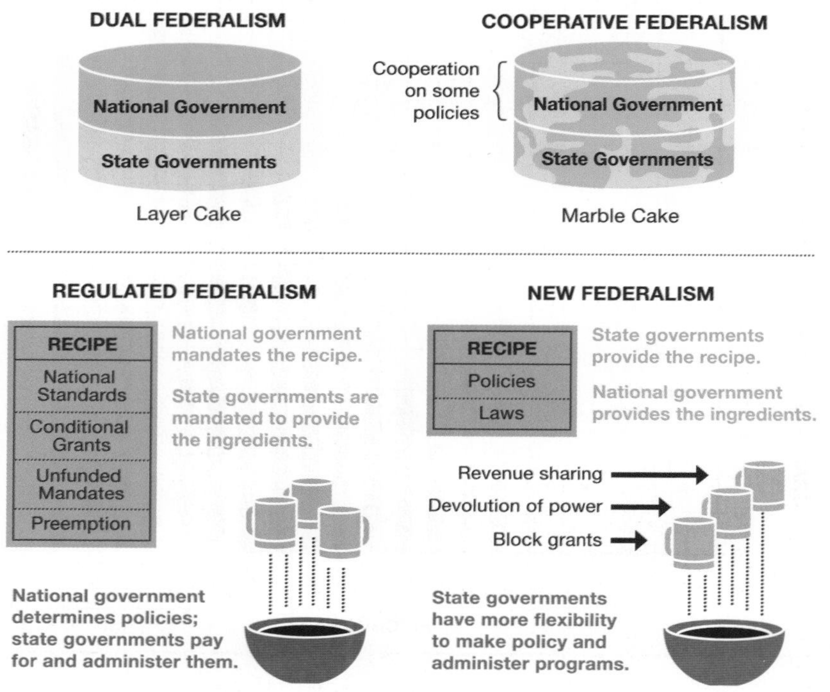

DUAL FEDERALISM

National Government
State Governments
Layer Cake

COOPERATIVE FEDERALISM

Cooperation on some policies
National Government
State Governments
Marble Cake

REGULATED FEDERALISM

RECIPE
National Standards
Conditional Grants
Unfunded Mandates
Preemption

National government mandates the recipe.
State governments are mandated to provide the ingredients.

National government determines policies; state governments pay for and administer them.

NEW FEDERALISM

RECIPE
Policies
Laws

State governments provide the recipe.
National government provides the ingredients.

Revenue sharing
Devolution of power
Block grants

State governments have more flexibility to make policy and administer programs.

new project grants made funding available on a competitive basis. Federal agencies would give grants to the proposals they judged to be the best. In this way, the national government acquired substantial control over which state and local governments got money, how much they got, and how they spent it.

The political scientist Morton Grodzins characterized the shift to post–New Deal cooperative federalism as a move from "layer cake federalism" to "marble cake federalism,"[21] in which the line distinguishing intergovernmental cooperation and sharing has blurred, making it difficult to say where the national government ends and the state and local governments begin. Figure 3.2 demonstrates the basis of the marble cake idea. In the late 1970s, federal aid contributed 25 to 30 percent of the operating budgets of all the state and local governments in

21 Morton Grodzins, "The Federal System," in *Goals for Americans*, ed. President's Commission on National Goals (Englewood Cliffs, NJ: Prentice-Hall, 1960), p. 265. In a marble cake, the white cake is distinguishable from the chocolate cake, but the two are streaked rather than arranged in distinct layers.

Figure 3.3
THE RISE, DECLINE, AND RECOVERY OF FEDERAL AID

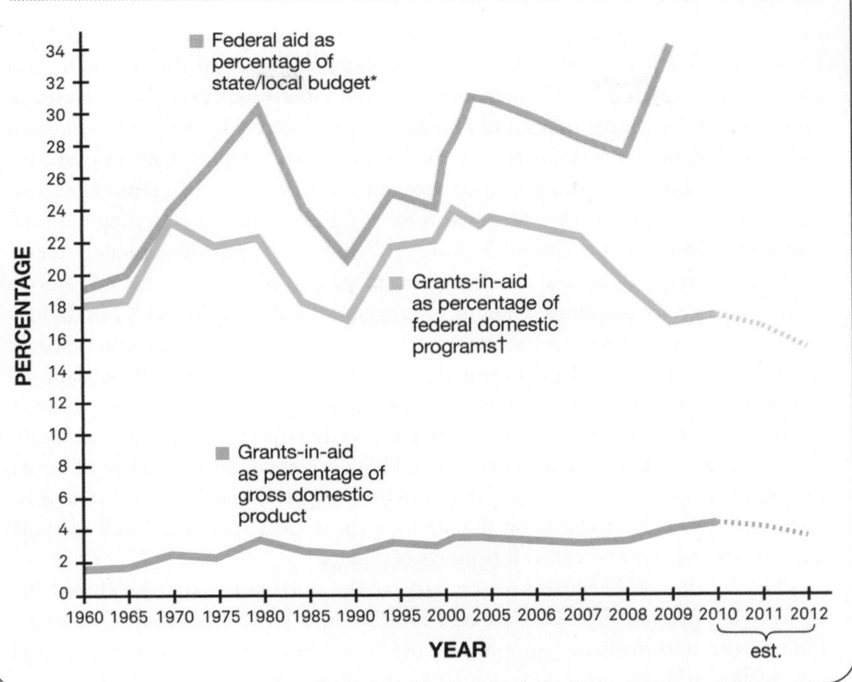

ANALYZING THE EVIDENCE

The extent to which state and local governments rely upon federal funding has varied a great deal over time. What difference does it make if the states are fiscally dependent upon the federal government?

*Federal aid as a percentage of state and local expenditures after transfers.
†Federal aid as a percentage of federal expenditures from the federal government's own funds.
SOURCES: U.S. Census, www.census.gov/compendia/statab/2011/tables/11s0429.pdf (accessed 8/16/11), and Office of Management and Budget, www.whitehouse.gov/omb/budget/historicals (accessed 11/17/11).

the country (Figure 3.3). In 2009, federal aid accounted for more than 33 percent of state and local budgets. This increase was temporary, resulting from the Obama administration's $787 billion stimulus package designed to help state and local governments weather the 2008–10 recession. Briefly, however, federal aid became the single largest source of state revenue, exceeding sales and property tax revenues for the first time in U.S. history.

Regulated Federalism and National Standards

Developments from the 1960s to the present have moved well beyond cooperative federalism to what might be called regulated federalism.[22] Regulated federalism is

22 The concept and the best discussion of this modern phenomenon are found in Donald F. Kettl, *The Regulation of American Federalism* (1983; repr., Baltimore: Johns Hopkins University Press, 1987), esp. pp. 33–41.

an important new decision rule, enhancing the national government's power. In some areas, the national government actually regulates the states by threatening to withhold grant money unless state and local governments conform to national standards. The most notable instances of this kind of regulated federalism are in the areas of civil rights, poverty programs, and environmental protection. This focus reflects a general shift in federal regulation away from the oversight and control of strictly economic activities toward "social regulation"—intervention on behalf of individual rights and liberties, environmental protection, workplace safety, and so on. In these instances, the national government provides grant-in-aid financing but sets conditions the states must meet to keep the grants (see again Figure 3.2). The national government refers to these policies as "setting national standards." Important examples include the Asbestos Hazard Emergency Act of 1986, which requires school districts to inspect for asbestos hazards and remove them from school buildings when necessary, and the Americans with Disabilities Act of 1990, which requires all state and local governments to promote access for the handicapped to all government buildings. The net effect of these national standards is that state and local policies are more uniform from coast to coast. National regulations and standards provide coordination across states and localities and solve collective action problems. However, there are a number of other programs in which the national government engages in regulated federalism by imposing national standards on the states without providing any funding at all. These have come to be called unfunded mandates.[23]

unfunded mandates

National standards or programs imposed on state and local governments by the federal government without accompanying funding or reimbursement

These burdens became a major part of the rallying cry that produced the famous Republican Congress elected in 1994 and its Contract with America. One of the first measures adopted by the Republican 104th Congress in 1995 was an act to limit unfunded mandates: the Unfunded Mandates Reform Act (UMRA). UMRA was considered a triumph of lobbying efforts by state and local governments, and it was "hailed as both symbol and substance of a renewed congressional commitment to federalism."[24] Under this law, any mandate with an uncompensated state and local cost estimated at greater than $50 million a year, as determined by the Congressional Budget Office, can be stopped by a point of order raised on the House or Senate floor. This so-called stop, look, and listen requirement forced Congress to take positive action to own up to a mandate and its potential costs.

The effect of UMRA has not been revolutionary. UMRA does not prevent members of Congress from passing unfunded mandates; it only makes

23 John J. DiIulio and Donald F. Kettl report that in 1980 there were 36 laws that could be categorized as unfunded mandates. And despite the concerted opposition of the administrations of Ronald Reagan and George H. W. Bush, another 27 laws qualifying as unfunded mandates were adopted between 1982 and 1991. See John DiIulio, Jr., and Donald F. Kettl, *Fine Print: The Contract with America, Devolution, and the Administrative Realities of American Federalism* (Washington, DC: Brookings Institution, 1995), p. 41.

24 Paul Posner, "Unfunded Mandate Reform: How Is It Working?" *Rockefeller Institute Bulletin* (1998): 35.

them think twice before they do. Moreover, the act exempts several areas from coverage. And states must still enforce antidiscrimination laws and meet other requirements in order to receive federal assistance. On the other hand, UMRA is a serious effort to move the national-state relationship a bit further toward the state side.

New Federalism and the National-State Tug-of-War

Federalism in the United States can be understood in part as a tug-of-war between those seeking more uniform national standards and those seeking more room for variability from state to state. Presidents Richard Nixon and Ronald Reagan called their efforts to reverse the trend toward national standards and reestablish traditional policy making and implementation the new federalism. They helped craft national policies whose purpose was to return more discretion to the states. Examples of these policies include Nixon's revenue sharing and Reagan's block grants, which consolidated a number of categorical grants into one larger category, leaving the state (or local) government more discretion to decide how to use the money.

block grants

Federal funds given to state governments to pay for goods, services, or programs, with relatively few restrictions on how the funds may be spent

President Barack Obama, on the other hand, seemed to believe firmly in regulated federalism. In 2009, Obama proposed a record-shattering $3 trillion national budget that included hundreds of millions of dollars in grants to the states for public works and infrastructural improvements as part of his plan to stimulate the nation's faltering economy. Obama, however, told the state governors that he would be watching to see that they spent the money wisely and in a manner consistent with the federal government's purposes. Once again, the national government seemed to view the states as administrative arms more than independent laboratories.

This same idea seemed manifest in the Obama administration's new health care reform law. Under the law, every state was required to establish an insurance exchange where individuals in need of health insurance could shop for the best rate. States were also required to expand their Medicaid programs, adding as many as 15 million Americans to the Medicaid rolls. A number of states were concerned that the costs of the new program would fall on their already strained budgets and 12 state attorneys general brought suit in federal courts charging that the program's mandates violated the Tenth Amendment. Following conflicting rulings in the lower federal courts, the Supreme Court considered the issue in 2012 and upheld major provisions of the legislation, although the Court ruled that the federal government cannot require that Medicaid rolls be expanded.

states' rights

The principle that states should oppose increases in the authority of the national government. This view was most popular before the Civil War

The Supreme Court as Referee. The courts establish the decision rules that determine the relationship between federal and state power. For much of the nineteenth century, federal power remained limited. The Tenth Amendment was used to bolster arguments about states' rights, which in their

ANALYZING THE EVIDENCE

Health Care Policy and the States

CHAPTER 03

Contributed by
Jenna Bednar
University of Michigan

Responsibility for health care policy and poverty relief is entangled in the 2010 Patient Protection and Affordable Care Act (ACA), an attempt by Congress to standardize access to health care nationally and contain costs. The primary federalism question in the ACA is what level of government, state or federal, should set Medicaid eligibility criteria. Medicaid is a program to provide health care coverage to the poor and is jointly financed by the federal and state governments. Prior to passage of the ACA, the states set the eligibility requirements, prescribing an income threshold, denoted as a percentage of the federal poverty level (FPL), above which a resident is ineligible to receive Medicaid-funded benefits. States set widely varying thresholds for Medicaid eligibility.

The first map below shows the Medicaid eligibility thresholds for parents of Medicaid-eligible children. The thresholds are expressed as a percentage of the FPL, which in 2009 was $22,050 for a family of four. In 2009, a family of four living in Minnesota could earn up to $47,408 (215 percent of FPL) and the parents would still qualify for Medicad benefits (children are insured separately), while the same family living in Texas would be ineligible if they earned more than $5,733 (26 percent of FPL). The second map shows the percentage of people without health insurance in each state.

Medicaid Eligibility Thresholds and Percentage Uninsured[1]

MEDICAID ELIGIBILITY
Percentage of FPL

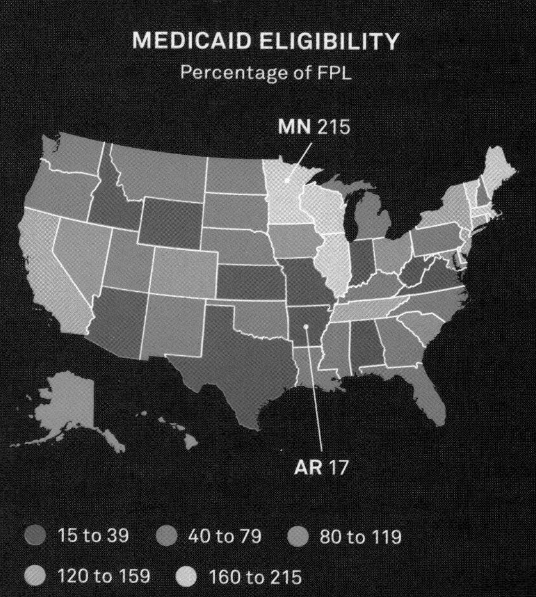

UNINSURED
Non-elderly with incomes up to 139% of FPL

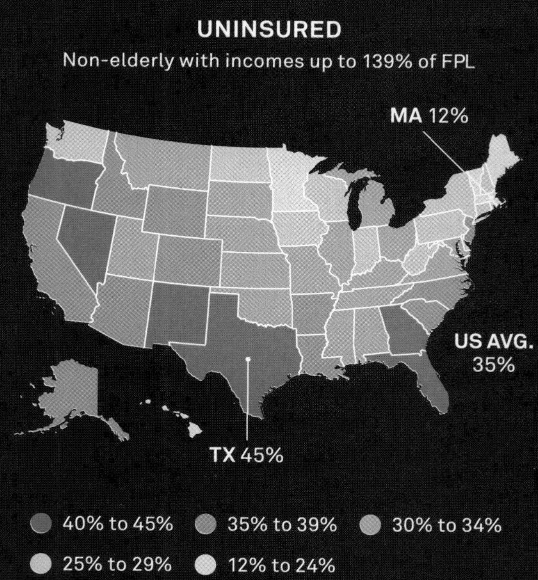

When public policy is decentralized in a federal system, not only can states set policy according to their own preferences and capacity, as demonstrated by the variation in Medicaid eligibility, but states may also innovate to improve policy. For example, in 2006 Massachusetts enacted a law that required residents to obtain insurance but subsidized or offered free coverage for the poor. In the graph below, we see the proportion of the non-elderly Massachusetts population without health insurance compared with the proportion of non-elderly without health insurance nationwide. Although Massachusetts already had a far lower rate of uninsured than the national average, the introduction of health policy reform further reduced the percentage of uninsured at a time when the national average was increasing. The program has expanded coverage, but Massachusetts's per capita health care spending continues to rise.

The ACA is modeled on the Massachusetts plan. Two aspects have been politically controversial: the requirement that all individuals obtain insurance and the standardization of Medicaid eligibility to 133 percent of FPL (in 2010, that meant any family of four making $29,327 or less would be eligible). The ACA expands health care access for the poor in states that had previously set very low income thresholds for eligibility but does so by centralizing authority, reducing the state's control over health care policy and poverty relief.

Through their representation in Congress, states negotiated significant fiscal relief: the federal government will pay over 95 percent of the cost of expanded coverage for the first six years of the act's life and 90 percent of the costs thereafter. Since the bill passed, the attorneys general of 26 states and one governor have filed a suit challenging the constitutionality of the ACA.[2] Ultimately, the fate of health care responsibility will rest with the American public, as they come to accept or reject the arguments made on both sides in this ongoing debate.

Percentage of Population without Health Insurance[3]

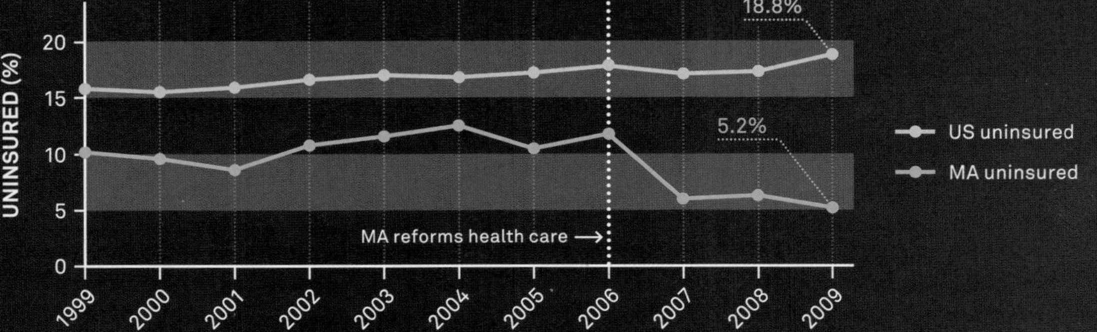

1 SOURCES: U.S. Census Bureau, The Annual Social and Economic Supplement to the Current Population Survey, "Income, Poverty and Health Insurance Coverage in the United States: 2009" (P60-238); Kaiser Family Foundation, 50 State Comparisons, Health Coverage & Uninsured, www.statehealthfacts.org (accessed 7/25/11).

2 *Florida v. U.S. Department of Health and Human Services* (3:10-CV-91-RV/EMT). A twenty-seventh state, Iowa, is both a plaintiff and a supporter of the ACA. The attorney general has filed a brief in support of the legislation while the governor, Terry Branstad, has filed a motion to join the suit against it.

3 SOURCE: U.S. Census Bureau, Current Population Survey, "Annual Social and Economic Supplements 2010," Table HIA-6.

EXPLORE
FEDERALISM AND HEALTH CARE POLICY
FURTHER AT:
wwnorton.com/studyspace

extreme version claimed that the states did not have to submit to national laws when they believed the national government had exceeded its authority. Arguments in favor of states' rights were voiced less often after the Civil War. But the Supreme Court continued to use the Tenth Amendment to strike down laws that it thought exceeded national power, including the Civil Rights Act passed in 1875.

In the early twentieth century, however, the Tenth Amendment appeared to lose its force. Reformers began to press for national regulations to limit the power of large corporations and to preserve the health and welfare of citizens. The Supreme Court approved some of these laws, but it struck down others, including a law combating child labor. The Court stated that the law violated the Tenth Amendment because only states should have the power to regulate conditions of employment. By the late 1930s, however, the Supreme Court had approved such an expansion of federal power that the Tenth Amendment appeared irrelevant. In fact, in 1941, Justice Harlan Fiske Stone declared that the Tenth Amendment was simply a "truism," that it had no real meaning.[25]

Recent years have seen a revival of interest in the Tenth Amendment and important Supreme Court decisions limiting federal power. Much of the renewed interest stems from conservatives who believe that a strong federal government encroaches on individual liberties. They believe freedom is better protected by returning more power to the states through the process of devolution. In 1996, the Republican presidential candidate, Bob Dole, carried a copy of the Tenth Amendment in his pocket as he campaigned, pulling it out to read at rallies.[26] Around the same time, the Eleventh Amendment concept of state sovereign immunity was revived by the Court. This legal doctrine holds that states are immune from lawsuits by private individuals or groups claiming that the state violated a statute enacted by Congress.

state sovereign immunity

A legal doctrine holding that states cannot be sued for violating an act of Congress

The Supreme Court's ruling in *United States v. Lopez* in 1995 fueled further interest in the Tenth Amendment. In that case, the Court, stating that Congress had exceeded its authority under the commerce clause, struck down a federal law that barred handguns near schools.[27] It was the first time since the New Deal that the Court had limited congressional powers in this way. The Court further limited the power of the federal government over the states in a 1996 ruling based on the Eleventh Amendment. That ruling prevented Seminole Indians from suing the state of Florida in federal court. A 1988 law had given Indian tribes the right to sue a state in federal court if the state did not negotiate in good faith issues related to gambling casinos on tribal land. The Supreme Court's ruling appeared to signal a much broader limitation on national power by raising new questions about whether individuals can sue a state if it fails to uphold federal law.[28]

25 *United States v. Darby,* 312 U.S. 100 (1941).

26 W. John Moore, "Pleading the 10th," *National Journal,* July 29, 1995, p. 1940.

27 *United States v. Lopez,* 514 U.S. 549 (1995).

28 *Seminole Tribe v. Florida,* 517 U.S. 44 (1996).

Another significant decision involving the relationship between the federal government and state governments was the 1997 case of *Printz v. United States*, in which the Court struck down a key provision of the Brady bill, enacted by Congress in 1993 to regulate gun sales. Under the terms of the act, state and local law enforcement officers were required to conduct background checks on prospective gun purchasers. The Court held that the federal government cannot require states to administer or enforce federal regulatory programs.[29] Because the states bear administrative responsibility for a variety of other federal programs, this decision could have far-reaching consequences. Finally, in another major ruling from the 1996–97 term, in *City of Boerne v. Flores*, the Court ruled that Congress had gone too far in restricting the power of the states to enact regulations they deemed necessary for the protection of public health, safety, or welfare (see Chapter 4).[30] These rulings signal a move toward a much more restricted federal government.

This trend continued with the 2006 *Gonzales v. Oregon* case. The *Gonzales* case involved Oregon's physician-assisted suicide law, which permitted doctors to prescribe lethal doses of medication for terminally ill patients who requested help ending their lives. In 2001, then U.S. attorney general John Ashcroft issued an order declaring that any physician involved in such a procedure would be prosecuted for violating the federal Controlled Substances Act. The state of Oregon joined several physicians and patients in a suit against Ashcroft's order. Eventually, the U.S. Supreme Court ruled that the federal government could not overrule state laws determining how drugs should be used so long as the drugs were not prohibited by federal law.[31]

These developments put federalism and the Court directly in the line of fire. But there is nothing new in this. The Court under John Marshall was, in essence, a nationalizing court. Marshall's successor, Chief Justice Roger Taney, gave us the most extreme denationalizing period, virtually inventing the concept of states' rights, as slavery and its extension were endangering the Union. The Court in place when Franklin Delano Roosevelt was first elected was extremely antinational; it declared virtually all the novel New Deal programs unconstitutional. And most notoriously, that same Court, after Roosevelt's landslide 1936 reelection, followed public opinion into the longest and most profound pro-nationalizing era. (It should be explained once again that the national government was permitted to expand, but not at the expense of the states.) The only remarkable thing about the current era has been the moderation and patience of the Burger and Rehnquist Courts in turning the tendency back toward the states. This tug-of-war between state and national levels of government will almost certainly continue.

29 *Printz v. United States*, 521 U.S. 898 (1997).

30 *City of Boerne v. Flores*, 521 U.S. 507 (1997).

31 *Gonzales v. Oregon*, 546 U.S. 243 (2006).

THE SEPARATION OF POWERS

As we noted at the beginning of this chapter, the separation of powers gives several different federal institutions the ability to influence the nation's agenda, to affect decisions, and to prevent the other institutions from taking action—dividing agenda, decision, and veto power. This arrangement may be cumbersome, but the Constitution's framers saw it as an essential means of protecting liberty.

In his discussion of the separation of powers, James Madison quoted the originator of the idea, the French political thinker Baron de Montesquieu: "There can be no liberty where the legislative and executive powers are united in the same person . . . [or] if the power of judging be not separated from the legislative and executive powers."[32] Using this same reasoning, many of Madison's contemporaries argued that there was not *enough* separation among the three branches, and Madison had to backtrack to insist that complete separation was not required:

> Unless these departments [branches] be so far connected and blended as to give to each a constitutional control over the others, the degree of separation which the maxim requires, as essential to a free government, can never in practice be duly maintained.[33]

This is the secret of how Americans have made the separation of powers effective: they have made it self-enforcing by giving each branch of government the means to participate in, and partially or temporarily obstruct, the workings of the other branches.

Checks and Balances: A System of Mutual Vetoes

checks and balances

The mechanisms through which each branch of government is able to participate in and influence the activities of the other branches

The means by which each branch of government interacts with the others is known informally as checks and balances. This arrangement gives each branch agenda and veto power, under a decision that requires all the branches to agree on national policies (see Figure 3.4). The best-known examples are the presidential power to veto legislation passed by Congress; the power of Congress to override the veto by a two-thirds majority vote, the power of Congress to impeach the president, and the power of the Senate to approve presidential appointments; the power of the president to appoint the members of the Supreme Court and the other federal judges with Senate approval; and the power of

32 Alexander Hamilton, James Madison, and John Jay, *The Federalist Papers*, Clinton L. Rossiter, ed. (New York: New American Library, 1961), no. 47, p. 302.

33 *The Federalist*, no. 48, p. 308.

Figure 3.4

CHECKS AND BALANCES

EXECUTIVE OVER LEGISLATIVE

President can veto acts of Congress

President can call a special session of Congress

President carries out, and thereby interprets, laws passed by Congress

Vice president casts tiebreaking vote in the Senate

JUDICIAL OVER LEGISLATIVE

Court can declare laws unconstitutional

Chief justice presides over Senate during hearing to impeach the president

LEGISLATIVE OVER EXECUTIVE

Congress can override presidential veto

Congress can impeach and remove president

Senate can reject president's appointments and refuse to ratify treaties

Congress can conduct investigations into president's actions

Congress can refuse to pass laws or provide funding that president requests

LEGISLATIVE OVER JUDICIAL

Congress can change size of federal court system and number of Supreme Court justices

Congress can propose constitutional amendments

Congress can reject Supreme Court nominees

Congress can impeach and remove federal judges

Congress can amend court jurisdictions

Congress controls appropriations

JUDICIAL OVER EXECUTIVE

Court can declare executive actions unconstitutional

Court has the power to issue warrants

Chief justice presides over impeachment of president

EXECUTIVE OVER JUDICIAL

President nominates Supreme Court justices

President nominates federal judges

President can pardon those convicted in federal court

President can refuse to enforce the courts' decisions

the Supreme Court to engage in judicial review (discussed below). The framers sought to guarantee that the three branches would in fact use the checks and balances as weapons against each other by giving each branch a different political constituency: direct, popular election of the members of the House and indirect election of senators (until the Seventeenth Amendment, adopted in 1913); indirect election of the president (still in effect, at least formally); and appointment of federal judges for life. All things considered, the best characterization of the separation-of-powers principle in action is, as we said in Chapter 2, "separated institutions sharing power."[34]

Legislative Supremacy

legislative supremacy 

The preeminent position assigned to Congress by the Constitution

Although each branch was to be given adequate means to compete with the other branches, it is also clear that within the system of separated powers the framers provided for legislative supremacy by making Congress the preeminent branch. Legislative supremacy made the provision of checks and balances in the other two branches all the more important.

The most important indication of the intention of legislative supremacy was made by the framers when they decided to place the provisions for national powers in Article I, the legislative article, and to treat the powers of the national government as powers of Congress. In a system based on the "rule of law," the power to make the laws is the supreme power. Section 8 provides in part that "*Congress* shall have Power To lay and collect Taxes . . . ; To borrow Money . . . ; To regulate Commerce" [emphasis added]. The Founders also provided for legislative supremacy in their decision to give Congress the sole power over appropriations and to give the House of Representatives the power to initiate all revenue bills. Madison recognized legislative supremacy as part and parcel of the separation of powers:

> It is not possible to give to each department an equal power of self-defense. In republican government, the legislative authority necessarily predominates. The remedy for this inconveniency is to divide the legislature into different branches; and to render them, by different modes of election and different principles of action, as little connected with each other as the nature of their common functions and their common dependence on the society will admit.[35]

In other words, Congress was so likely to dominate the other branches that it would have to be divided against itself, into House and Senate. One almost could say that the Constitution provided for four branches, not three.

Although "presidential government" gradually supplanted legislative supremacy after 1937, the relative power position of the executive and legislative branches since that time has varied. The degree of conflict between the president and

34 Richard E. Neustadt, *Presidential Power and the Modern Presidents: The Politics of Leadership from Roosevelt to Reagan* (1960; rev. ed., New York: Free Press, 1990), p. 33.

35 *The Federalist,* no. 51, p. 322.

Congress has changed with the rise and fall of political parties, and it has been especially tense during periods of divided government, when one party controls the White House and another controls Congress, as has been the case almost continuously since 1969.

divided government

The condition in American government in which the presidency is controlled by one party while the opposing party controls one or both houses of Congress

Checks and Balances: The Rationality Principle at Work

The framers' idea that the president and Congress would check and balance one another rests, in part, on an application of the rationality principle. The framers assumed that each branch would seek to maintain or even expand its power and would resist what the framers called "encroachments" on its prerogatives by the other branch. This idea certainly seems consistent with the behavior of presidents and congressional leaders. At least since the Nixon administration, presidents and members of Congress have battled almost constantly over institutional prerogatives. For example, what culminated in the Watergate struggle between Congress and President Richard Nixon began when Nixon sought to implement a reorganization of the executive branch that would have increased presidential control and reduced congressional oversight powers.[36] After Nixon's resignation, Congress enacted several pieces of legislation, including the War Powers Act, to delimit presidential power. When he took office, President Ronald Reagan worked to undo Congress's efforts and to bolster the power of the White House. Reagan had a good deal of success, though Congress ultimately put a stop to his efforts through investigations into presidential wrongdoing in the so-called Iran-Contra affair. During the Clinton era, Congress impeached the president but failed to convict him. During President George W. Bush's second term in office, Congress and the president battled constantly over the president's frequent refusals to disclose information to Congress on the basis of executive privilege and his assertions that only the White House was competent to manage the nation's security. "I am the decider," the president famously averred. During his first months in office, President Obama had little reason to clash with Congress. Both houses were controlled by Democrats, and the Democratic leadership was eager to cooperate with the new president. However, this "honeymoon" between Obama and Congress ended when the GOP took control of the House of Representatives in 2010 and vowed to fight the president's programs.

executive privilege

The claim that confidential communications between the president and the president's close advisers should not be revealed without the consent of the president

Though each institution has registered success and failures in this struggle, over time, the president has possessed a distinct advantage. The president is a unitary actor, whereas Congress, as a collective decision maker, suffers from collective action problems (see Chapter 13). That is, each member of Congress may have individual interests that are inconsistent with the collective interests of Congress as a whole. For example, when Congress initially registered its support for President Bush's plan to use force in Iraq in 2003, members were uneasy about the fact that the president was asserting that he actually did not need

36 Benjamin Ginsberg and Martin Shefter, *Politics by Other Means*, 3rd ed. (New York: Norton, 2002), chap. 1.

congressional approval—that he was the only decider. The president was using the war to underline claims of institutional power, but few members of Congress thought it would be politically safe to express that viewpoint when the public was clamoring for action. These considerations help explain why, over time, the powers of the presidency have grown and those of Congress diminished.[37] We will return to this topic in Chapter 7.

The Role of the Supreme Court: Establishing Decision Rules

The role of the judicial branch in the separation of powers has depended on the power of judicial review (see Chapter 9), a power not provided for in the Constitution but asserted by Chief Justice Marshall in 1803:

> If a law be in opposition to the Constitution; if both the law and the Constitution apply to a particular case, so that the Court must either decide that case conformable to the law, disregarding the Constitution, or conformable to the Constitution, disregarding the law; the Court must determine which of these conflicting rules governs the case: This is of the very essence of judicial duty.[38]

Marshall's decision was an extremely important assertion of judicial power and has been the basis of the judiciary's influence in American life ever since. In effect, Marshall declared that whenever there was doubt or disagreement about which rule should apply in a particular case, the Court would decide. In this way, Marshall made the Court the arbiter of all future debates between Congress and the president and between the federal and state governments.

In terms of numbers of cases, judicial review of the constitutionality of acts of the president or Congress is relatively rare. For example, there were no Supreme Court reviews of congressional acts in the 50 plus years between *Marbury v. Madison* (1803) and *Dred Scott v. Sandford* (1857). In the century or so between the Civil War and 1970, 84 acts of Congress were held unconstitutional (in whole or in part), but there were long periods of complete Supreme Court deference to Congress, punctuated by flurries of judicial review during times of social upheaval. The most significant of these was 1935–36, when 12 acts of Congress were invalidated, blocking virtually the entire New Deal program.[39] Then, after 1935, when the Court made its great reversals, no significant acts

---

37 Matthew Crenson and Benjamin Ginsberg, *Presidential Power: Unchecked and Unbalanced* (New York: Norton, 2007).

38 *Marbury v. Madison*, 1 Cranch 137 (1803).

39 The Supreme Court struck down eight out of ten New Deal statutes. For example, in *Panama Refining Company v. Ryan*, 293 U.S. 388 (1935), the Court ruled that a section of the National Industrial Recovery Act of 1933 was an invalid delegation of legislative power to the executive branch. And in *Schechter Poultry Corporation v. United States*, 295 U.S. 495 (1935), the Court found the National Industrial Recovery Act itself to be invalid for the same reason.

were voided until 1983, when the Court declared unconstitutional the legislative veto, a practice in which Congress authorized the president to take action but reserved the right to rescind presidential actions with which it disagreed.[40] Another decision, in 1986, struck down the Gramm-Rudman Act of 1985, which mandated a balanced budget. That act, the Court held, delegated too much power to the comptroller general, a congressional official, to direct the president to reduce the budget.[41] The Supreme Court became much more activist (that is, less deferential to Congress) after the elevation of Justice William H. Rehnquist to the position of chief justice in 1986.[42] All of the cases in Table 3.2 altered some aspect of federalism by declaring unconstitutional all or an important portion of an act of Congress, and the end of this episode of judicial activism against Congress is not over. Between 1995 and 2002, at least 26 acts or parts of acts of Congress were struck down on constitutional grounds.[43]

Since the New Deal period, the Court has been far more deferential toward the president, with only five significant confrontations. One was the so-called steel seizure case of 1952, in which the Court refused to permit President Harry Truman to use "emergency powers" to force workers back into the steel mills during the Korean War.[44] A second case was *United States v. Nixon*, in which the Court declared unconstitutional President Nixon's refusal to respond to a subpoena to make available the infamous White House tapes as evidence in a criminal prosecution. The Court argued that although executive privilege did protect confidentiality of communications to and from the president, this protection did not extend to data in presidential files or tapes linked to criminal prosecutions.[45] During the heat of the Clinton scandal, the Supreme Court rejected the claim that the pressures and obligations of the office of president were so demanding that all litigation "but the most exceptional cases" should be deferred until the end of the president's term.[46] But of far greater importance, the Supreme Court struck down the Line Item Veto Act of 1996 on the grounds that it violated Article I, Section 7, which prescribes procedures for congressional enactment, and presidential acceptance or veto, of statutes. The Court held that any such change in the procedures of adopting laws would have to be made by amendment to the Constitution, not by legislation.[47]

The fifth confrontation came after the September 11, 2001, terrorist attacks. But because of the terrorism scare, it was the least restrictive of the five. In *Rasul v. Bush*, the Court held that the estimated 650 "enemy combatants" detained

---

40 *Immigration and Naturalization Service v. Chadha*, 462 U.S. 919 (1983).

41 *Bowsher v. Synar*, 478 U.S. 714 (1986).

42 Cass R. Sunstein, "Taking Over the Courts," *New York Times*, November 9, 2002, p. A19.

43 Sunstein, "Taking Over the Courts."

44 *Youngstown Sheet and Tube Company v. Sawyer*, 343 U.S. 579 (1952).

45 *United States v. Nixon*, 418 U.S. 683 (1974).

46 *Clinton v. Jones*, 520 U.S. 681 (1997).

47 *Clinton v. City of New York*, 524 U.S. 417 (1998).

Table 3.2

A NEW FEDERAL SYSTEM? THE CASE RECORD, 1995–2006

CASE	DATE	COURT HOLDING
United States v. Lopez, 514 U.S. 549	**1995**	Voids federal law barring handguns near schools: it is beyond Congress's power to regulate commerce.
Seminole Tribe v. Florida, 517 U.S. 44	**1996**	Voids federal law giving tribes the right to sue a state in federal court: "sovereign immunity" requires a state's permission to be sued.
Printz v. United States, 521 U.S. 898	**1997**	Voids key provision of Brady law requiring states to make background checks on gun purchases: as an "unfunded mandate," it violated state sovereignty under the Tenth Amendment.
City of Boerne v. Flores, 521 U.S. 507	**1997**	Restricts Congress's power under the Fourteenth Amendment to regulate city zoning and health and welfare policies to "remedy" rights: Congress may not expand those rights.
Alden v. Maine, 527 U.S. 706	**1999**	Declares states "immune" from suits by their *own* employees for overtime pay under the Fair Labor Standards Act of 1938. (See also the *Seminole* case.)
United States v. Morrison, 529 U.S. 598	**2000**	Extends *Seminole* case by invalidating Violence against Women Act: states may not be sued by individuals for failing to enforce federal laws.
Gonzales v. Oregon, 546 U.S.	**2006**	Upholds state assisted-suicide law over attorney general's objection.

without formal charges at the U.S. Naval Station at Guantánamo Bay, Cuba, had the right to seek release through a writ of *habeas corpus*.[48] However, in Section 7 of the 2006 Military Commissions Act, Congress declared that enemy combatants held at Guantánamo Bay could not avail themselves of the right of *habeas corpus*. Then, in 2008, the Supreme Court responded by striking down Section 7 and affirming that the Guantánamo detainees had the right to challenge their detentions in federal court.[49] The Court noted that *habeas corpus* was among the most fundamental constitutional rights and was included in the Constitution even before the Bill of Rights was added.

writ of *habeas corpus*

A court order demanding that an individual in custody be brought into court and shown the cause for detention. *Habeas corpus* is guaranteed by the Constitution and can be suspended only in cases of rebellion or invasion

FEDERALISM AND THE SEPARATION OF POWERS: COLLECTIVE ACTION OR STALEMATE?

Institutions are designed to solve collective action problems, but the solutions can take many different forms. The framers of the American Constitution believed that agenda, decision, and veto powers should be dispersed among many different institutions. And because history matters and the 13 existing states already possessed considerable autonomy when the Constitution was drafted, the framers had little choice but to relinquish a considerable measure of agenda, decision, and veto powers to them as well. The result was our federal system of separated powers.

Critics of the American constitutional framework have often pointed to this dispersion of governmental power as a source of weakness and incoherence in America's policy-making processes. Because of federalism, America's national government is often unable to accomplish what might be a matter of course in most nations. For example, in the case of *United States v. Lopez*, cited earlier, the Supreme Court invalidated a federal statute prohibiting the possession of firearms near schools, saying that it was an unconstitutional encroachment on the sovereignty of the states. In a country with a unitary system of government, this statute would not face this type of hurdle.

Because of the separation of powers, Congress often finds itself stymied by the president—or the president by Congress—in efforts to bring about changes in policy. The president possesses a veto over congressional action. Congress can, by legislation, seek to limit the powers of the executive. In 2008, for example, Congress attempted to express its displeasure with the president's conduct of the war on terrorism by enacting legislation outlawing a number of harsh methods authorized by the president for the interrogation of terrorist suspects.

48 *Rasul v. Bush*, 542 U.S. 466 (2004).

49 *Boumediene v. Bush*, 06-1195 (2008).

The president responded with a veto. In 2011, the newly elected Republican House of Representatives promised to repeal the president's recently enacted health care program. The Senate, still controlled by the Democrats, seemed unlikely to agree, and the president was almost certain to veto any bill that threatened what he viewed as the major achievement of his first term in office. In the meantime, though, challenges to the new law in the federal courts meant that the Supreme Court would eventually weigh in on the matter, perhaps forcing major modifications in the program. Sometimes it may appear that the dispersion of power among different institutions of government ensures that there will be no collective action.

The framers, though, did not want to make collective action too easy. They thought it was important to provide checks and balances that would protect the nation from the tyrannical actions of a small number of leaders, as well as from precipitous and thoughtless actions on the part of larger groups—the framers called this latter possibility "majority tyranny." The framers believed that well-constructed institutions should diminish the likelihood of inappropriate and unwise collective action, even at the cost of occasional stalemate. In recent years, the U.S. government often has been criticized more for what it *has* done, especially with regard to the wars in Iraq and Afghanistan, than what it *has not* done. Many Americans believe that Congress should have done more to thwart presidential war policies and hope the judiciary will do more to delimit presidential war powers in the future. The framers likely would have understood this desire to check the executive branch. Stalemate is not always the worst collective outcome.

For Further Reading

Bednar, Jenna. *The Robust Federation.* New York: Cambridge University Press, 2008.

Campbell, Tom. *Separation of Powers in Practice.* Palo Alto, CA: Stanford University Press, 2004.

Crenson, Matthew, and Benjamin Ginsberg. *Presidential Power: Unchecked and Unbalanced.* New York: Norton, 2007.

Ferejohn, John A., and Barry R. Weingast, eds. *The New Federalism: Can the States Be Trusted?* Stanford, CA: Hoover Institution Press, 1997.

Fisher, Louis. *Constitutional Conflicts between Congress and the President.* 7th ed. Lawrence: University of Kansas Press, 2007.

reader selection Hamilton, Alexander, James Madison, and John Jay. *The Federalist Papers.* Clinton Rossiter, ed. New York: New American Library, 1961.

Karmis, Dimitrios, and Wayne Norman. *Theories of Federalism: A Reader.* New York: Palgrave, Macmillan, 2005.

LaCroix, Alison L. *The Ideological Origins of American Federalism.* Cambridge, MA: Harvard University Press, 2010.

Noonan, John T. *Narrowing the Nation's Power: The Supreme Court Sides with the States.* Berkeley: University of California Press, 2002.

Posner, Richard. *Not a Suicide Pact: The Constitution in a Time of National Emergency.* New York: Oxford University Press, 2006.

Riker, William H. *Federalism: Origin, Operation, Significance.* Boston: Little, Brown, 1964.

reader selection

Samuels, David, and Matthew Shugart, *Presidents, Parties and Prime Ministers: How the Separation of Powers Affects Party Organization and Behavior.* New York: Cambridge University Press, 2010.

Smith, Rogers M. *Civic Ideals: Conflicting Visions of Citizenship in U.S. History.* New Haven, CT: Yale University Press, 1997.

Van Horn, Carol E. *The State of the States.* 4th ed. Washington, DC: CQ Press, 2004.

Winston, Pamela. *Welfare Policymaking in the States: The Devil in Devolution.* Washington, DC: Georgetown University Press, 2002.

Visit **wwnorton.com/studyspace/** to access free review materials such as:

- ➜ Vocabulary Flashcards of All Key Terms
- ➜ Chapter Review Quizzes
- ➜ Complete Study Outlines

reader selection

Highlighted selections are included in *Readings in American Politics: Analysis and Perspectives*, Second Edition.

PART ✖ 2 3 4

FOUNDATIONS

4

Civil Liberties

Chapter Outline

- Origins of the Bill of Rights
- Nationalizing the Bill of Rights
- The Bill of Rights Today

Institutions are designed to solve collective action problems, and in the United States among the most important constitutional instruments created for this purpose are civil liberties and civil rights. To "solve," however, does not mean simply to facilitate collective action. Instead, the constitutional principles of civil liberties and civil rights presented in the Bill of Rights also *regulate* collective action. Civil liberties are limitations or restrictions on collective action. In effect, the concept of civil liberties defines certain spheres of activity, such as speech or worship, in which the government's authority to interfere with individual conduct is limited. Civil rights are the rules determining who may participate or be represented in collective decision-making processes, as well as regulating the ways in which the government can and cannot treat its citizens. Thus, generally speaking, civil liberties limit collective action by restricting the government's jurisdiction. Civil rights, on the other hand (as we will see in Chapter 5), regulate collective action by establishing important decision rules for the government's conduct.

Jurisdiction over civil liberties and civil rights issues is primarily exercised by the courts, which have developed myriad decision rules and procedures designed to resolve controversies in these realms. The U.S. Supreme Court, in particular, asserts a good deal of agenda and veto power when it comes to the interpretation of constitutional principles, and we will examine many Supreme Court decisions in this chapter and in Chapter 5. But consistent with the concept of checks and balances, other actors—particularly the U.S. Congress—also claim agenda and veto power in these realms. The Supreme Court's jurisdiction over constitutional issues is derived from Article III of the Constitution, from statutes, and from prior decisions of the Court itself. Congress's jurisdiction stems from Article II of the Constitution, which gives Congress the power to make the laws, and from its role in the process of amending the Constitution, as defined in Article V.

In their rulings, the courts are heavily influenced by history. Every court decision recites the history of prior court decisions relating to the principles at hand. This use of history is called *precedent.* When courts issue their decisions, they constantly refer to the opinions of prior courts to justify their interpretations, logic, and ultimate findings. Seldom will a court depart from established precedent. Even the Supreme Court is always careful to justify its decisions by pointing to numerous precedents and will seldom overturn established legal principles. Because the job of a court is to apply rather than to make the law, history in the form of precedent is an important factor limiting judicial discretion.

As we observed in our discussion of federalism and the separation of powers, institutional principles are not carved in stone. Over the past century, a number of civil liberties have been strengthened, placing greater limits on collective action. In the realm of civil rights, as Chapter 5 will show, African Americans and others who were once excluded from participation in many collective processes have won the right to be included. In both areas, change came as a result of political struggles and was punctuated by battles within and between Congress and the courts. With these considerations in mind, let us examine the character and evolution of civil liberties in America to be followed by a discussion of civil rights in the next chapter.

ORIGINS OF THE BILL OF RIGHTS

When the first Congress under the new Constitution met in late April 1789 (having been delayed since March 4 by the lack of a quorum because of bad winter roads), the most important item of business was consideration of a proposal to

CORE OF THE ANALYSIS

Civil liberties are rules that limit the government's authority to interfere in certain spheres of activity. They restrict the government's jurisdiction in areas such as free speech and religion.

Americans' most important civil liberties are to be found in the Constitution's Bill of Rights—which might have been called the Bill of Liberties.

Today's conception of civil liberties has been shaped by the historical development of these ideas and their interpretation by key political actors, especially the Supreme Court.

add a bill of rights to the Constitution. Such a proposal by the Virginia delegate George Mason had been turned down with little debate in the waning days of the Constitutional Convention in September 1787 because of arguments by Alexander Hamilton and other Federalists that a bill of rights was irrelevant in a constitution providing the national government with only delegated powers. How could the national government abuse powers not given to it in the first place? Hamilton was also concerned that a bill of rights would weaken the new government by limiting its jurisdiction even before it had an opportunity to organize itself. But when the Constitution was submitted to the states for ratification, Antifederalists, most of whom had *not* been delegates in Philadelphia, picked up on the argument of Thomas Jefferson (who also had not been a delegate) that the omission of a bill of rights was a major imperfection of the new Constitution. Whatever the merits of Hamilton's or Jefferson's positions, to gain ratification, the Federalists in Massachusetts, South Carolina, New Hampshire, Virginia, and New York made an "unwritten but unequivocal pledge" to add a bill of rights and a promise to confirm (in what became the Tenth Amendment) the understanding that all powers not delegated to the national government or explicitly prohibited to the states were reserved to the states.[1]

James Madison, who had been a delegate to the Philadelphia convention and later became a member of Congress, may still have believed privately that a bill of rights was not needed. But in 1789, recognizing the urgency of obtaining the Antifederalists' support for the Constitution and the new government, he fought for a bill of rights, arguing that the ideals it embodied would acquire "the character of fundamental maxims of free Government, and as they become incorporated with the national sentiment, counteract the impulses of interest and passion."[2]

"After much discussion and manipulation . . . at the delicate prompting of Washington and under the masterful prodding of Madison," the House adopted 17 amendments; the Senate adopted 12 of these. Ten of the amendments were ratified by the necessary three-fourths of the states, making them part of the Constitution on December 15, 1791—from the start, these 10 were called the Bill of Rights.[3]

civil liberties

The protections of citizens from improper governmental action

Civil liberties can be defined as protections of citizens from improper governmental action. When adopted in 1791, the Bill of Rights was seen as guaranteeing a private sphere of personal liberty free of governmental restrictions. As Jefferson had put it, a bill of rights "is what people are entitled to against every government on earth." In this sense, we could call the Bill of Rights a bill of

1 Clinton L. Rossiter, *1787: The Grand Convention* (New York: Norton, 1987), p. 302.

2 Quoted in Milton Konvitz, "The Bill of Rights: Amendments I–X," in *An American Primer*, 2 vols., Daniel J. Boorstin, ed. (Chicago: University of Chicago Press, 1966), I: 159.

3 Rossiter, *1787*, p. 303, where he also reports that "in 1941 the States of Connecticut, Massachusetts, and Georgia celebrated the sesquicentennial of the Bill of Rights by giving their hitherto withheld and unneeded assent."

liberties because the amendments focus on what government must *not* do. For example (with emphasis added),

1. "Congress shall make *no* law . . ." (I)
2. "The right . . . to . . . bear Arms, shall *not* be infringed." (II)
3. "*No* Soldier shall . . . be quartered . . ." (III)
4. "*No* Warrants shall issue, but upon probable cause . . ." (IV)
5. "*No* person shall be held to answer . . . unless on a presentment or indictment of a Grand Jury . . ." (V)
6. "Excessive bail shall not be required . . . *nor* cruel and unusual punishments inflicted." (VIII)

Thus the Bill of Rights is a series of "thou shalt nots"—restraints addressed to government, limiting its jurisdiction. Some of these restraints are *substantive*, putting limits on *what* the government shall and shall not have the power to do, such as establishing a state religion, quartering troops in private homes without consent, or seizing private property without just compensation. Other restraints are procedural, dealing with how the government is supposed to act. For example, even though the government has the substantive power to declare certain acts to be crimes and to arrest and imprison persons who violate its criminal laws, it may not do so except by fairly meticulous observance of procedures designed to protect the accused. The best-known procedural rule is that a person is presumed innocent until proven guilty. This rule does not question the government's power to punish someone for committing a crime; it questions only the way the government determines who committed the crime. Substantive and procedural restraints together identify the realm of civil liberties. Proponents of the Bill of Rights wished to make it clear that their enumeration of rights and liberties should not be deemed exhaustive. Americans might be entitled to other constitutional protections not formally included in the Bill of Rights. This concern was addressed by the Ninth Amendment, which declares that the enumeration in the Constitution of some rights "shall not be construed" to mean that the people do not retain others rights as well.

NATIONALIZING THE BILL OF RIGHTS

The First Amendment provides that "Congress shall make no law respecting an establishment of religion . . . or abridging the freedom of speech, or of the press; or the right of . . . [assembly and petition]." But this is the only amendment in the Bill of Rights that addresses itself exclusively to the national government. For example, the Second Amendment provides that "the right of the people to keep and bear Arms, shall not be infringed." The Fifth Amendment says, among other things, that *no person* "shall . . . be twice put in jeopardy of life or limb" for the same crime, that *no person* "shall be compelled in any criminal case to be a witness against himself," that *no person* shall "be deprived of life, liberty, or property, without due process of law," and that private property cannot be taken "without just compensation."[4] Because the First Amendment is the only part of the Bill of Rights that is explicit in its intention to put limits on the national government, a fundamental question inevitably arises: Do the remaining amendments of the Bill of Rights put limits on state governments, or do they put them only on the national government?

Dual Citizenship

The question of whether the Bill of Rights also limits state governments was settled in 1833 in a way that may seem odd to Americans today. The 1833 case was *Barron v. Baltimore*, and the facts were simple. In paving its streets, the city of Baltimore had disposed of so much sand and gravel in the water near John Barron's wharf that the value of the wharf for commercial purposes was virtually destroyed. Barron brought the city into court on the grounds that it had, under the Fifth Amendment, unconstitutionally deprived him of his property.

Here Chief Justice Marshall, in one of the most significant Supreme Court decisions ever handed down, said:

> The Constitution was ordained and established by the people of the United States for themselves, for their own government, and not for the government of individual States. Each State established a constitution for itself, and in that constitution provided such limitations and restrictions on the powers of its particular government as its judgment dictated. . . . If these propositions be correct, *the fifth amendment must be understood as restraining the power of the General Government, not as applicable to the States.*[5] [Emphasis added]

In other words, if an agency of the *national* government had deprived Barron of his property, there would have been little doubt about Barron's winning his case. But if the constitution of the state of Maryland contained no such provision protecting citizens of Maryland from such action, then Barron had no legal leg to stand on against Baltimore, an agency of the state of Maryland.

---

4 It would be useful at this point to review all the provisions of the Bill of Rights to confirm this distinction between the wording of the First Amendment and the wording of the rest (see the Appendix). The emphasis in the examples is not in the original. For a spirited and enlightening essay on the extent to which the entire Bill of Rights is about equality, see Martha Minow, "Equality and the Bill of Rights," in *The Constitution of Rights: Human Dignity and American Values*, Michael J. Meyer and William A. Parent, eds. (Ithaca, NY: Cornell University Press, 1992), pp. 118–28.

5 *Barron v. Mayor and City of Baltimore*, 32 U.S. 243 (1833).

Barron v. Baltimore confirmed "dual citizenship"—that is, that each American was a citizen of the national government and separately a citizen of one of the states. This meant that the Bill of Rights did not apply to decisions or procedures of state (or local) governments. Even slavery could continue because the Bill of Rights could not protect anyone from state laws treating people as property. In fact, the Bill of Rights did not become a vital instrument for the extension of civil liberties for anyone until after a bloody civil war and the revolutionary Fourteenth Amendment intervened. And even so, nearly another century would pass before the Bill of Rights would truly come into its own. This is a case where America's history has truly mattered. America's states predated the creation of the federal government. The states joined the Union voluntarily, retaining many of their sovereign powers. In many other nations, subnational governments were created by and for the administrative convenience of the central government. In the United States, the nationalization of governmental powers has proceeded slowly and in fits and starts.

The Fourteenth Amendment

From a constitutional standpoint, the defeat of the South in the Civil War settled one question and raised another. It probably settled forever the question of whether secession was an option for any state. After 1865, there was to be more "united" than "states" to the United States. But this left unanswered just how much the states were obliged to obey the Constitution and, in particular, the Bill of Rights. Just reading the words of the Fourteenth Amendment, anyone might think it was almost perfectly designed to impose the Bill of Rights on the states and thereby reverse *Barron v. Baltimore.* The very first words of the Fourteenth Amendment point in that direction:

> All persons born or naturalized in the United States, and subject to the jurisdiction thereof, are citizens of the United States and of the State wherein they reside.

This provides for a single national citizenship, and at a minimum that means civil liberties should not vary drastically from state to state. That would seem to be the spirit of the Fourteenth Amendment: to nationalize the Bill of Rights by nationalizing the definition of citizenship.

This interpretation of the Fourteenth Amendment is reinforced by the next clause of the Amendment:

> No State shall make or enforce any law which shall abridge the privileges or immunities of citizens of the United States; nor shall any State deprive any person of life, liberty, or property, without due process of law.

All of this sounds like an effort to extend the Bill of Rights in its entirety to citizens wherever they might reside. But this was not to be the Supreme Court's interpretation for nearly a century. Within five years of ratification of the

Fourteenth Amendment in 1868, the Court was making decisions as though the amendment had never been adopted. The shadow of *Barron* grew longer and longer. In an important 1873 decision known as *the Slaughter House Cases*, the Supreme Court determined that the federal government was under no obligation to protect the "privileges and immunities" of citizens of a particular state against arbitrary actions by that state's government. The Court argued that the framers of the Fourteenth Amendment could not have intended to incorporate the entire Bill of Rights.[6] Yet when the Civil Rights Act of 1875 attempted to protect blacks from discriminatory treatment by proprietors of hotels, theaters, and other public accommodations, the Supreme Court disregarded its own primary argument in the previous case and held the act unconstitutional, declaring that the Fourteenth Amendment applied only to discriminatory actions by state officials, "operating under cover of law," and not to discrimination against blacks by private individuals, even though these private individuals were companies offering services to the public.[7] Such narrow interpretations raised the inevitable question of whether the Fourteenth Amendment had incorporated any of the Bill of Rights. The Fourteenth Amendment remained shadowy until the mid-twentieth century. The shadow was *Barron v. Baltimore* and the Court's unwillingness to "nationalize" civil liberties—that is, to interpret the civil liberties expressed in the Bill of Rights as imposing limitations not only on the federal government but also on the states.

It was not until the very end of the nineteenth century that the Supreme Court began to nationalize the Bill of Rights by incorporating its civil liberties provisions into the Fourteenth Amendment. Table 4.1 outlines the major steps in this process. The only change in civil liberties during the first 60 years after the adoption of the Fourteenth Amendment came in 1897, when the Supreme Court held that the due process clause of the Fourteenth Amendment did in fact prohibit states from taking property for a public use without just compensation.[8] This effectively overruled *Barron* because it meant that the citizen of Maryland, or any state, was henceforth protected from a "public taking" of property even if the state constitution did not provide such protection. The power of public agencies to seize private property is called eminent domain. According to the Fifth Amendment, private owners must be paid "just compensation" by the government if it decides that it needs their property. In a broader sense, however, *Barron* still cast a shadow because the Supreme Court had "incorporated" into the Fourteenth Amendment only the property protection provision of the Fifth Amendment and no other clause, let alone the other amendments of the Bill of Rights. In other words, although due process applied to the taking of life and liberty as well as property, only property was incorporated into the Fourteenth Amendment as a limitation on state power.

6 *The Slaughter House Cases*, 83 U.S. 36 (1873).

7 *The Civil Rights Cases*, 109 U.S. 3 (1883).

8 *Chicago, Burlington, and Quincy Railroad Company v. Chicago*, 166 U.S. 226 (1897).

Table 4.1

INCORPORATION OF THE BILL OF RIGHTS INTO THE FOURTEENTH AMENDMENT

SELECTED PROVISIONS AND AMENDMENTS	DATE "INCORPORATED"	KEY CASES
Eminent domain (V)	1897	*Chicago, Burlington, and Quincy Railroad v. Chicago*
Freedom of speech (I)	1925	*Gitlow v. New York*
Freedom of the press (I)	1931	*Near v. Minnesota ex rel. Olson*
Free exercise of religion (I)	1934	*Hamilton v. Regents of the University of California*
Freedom of assembly (I)	1939	*Hague v. Committee for Industrial Organization*
Freedom from unnecessary search and seizure (IV)	1949	*Wolf v. Colorado*
Freedom from warrantless search and seizure ("exclusionary rule") (IV)	1961	*Mapp v. Ohio*
Freedom from cruel and unusual punishment (VIII)	1962	*Robinson v. California*
Right to counsel in any criminal trial (VI)	1963	*Gideon v. Wainwright*
Right against self-incrimination and forced confessions (V)	1964	*Mallory v. Hogan* *Escobedo v. Illinois*
Right to privacy (III, IV, and V)	1965	*Griswold v. Connecticut*
Right to remain silent (V)	1966	*Miranda v. Arizona*
Right against double jeopardy (V)	1969	*Benton v. Maryland*
Right to bear arms (II)	2010	*McDonald v. Chicago*

No further expansion of civil liberties through incorporation occurred until 1925, when the Supreme Court held that freedom of speech is "among the fundamental personal rights and 'liberties' protected by the due process clause of the Fourteenth Amendment from impairment by the states."[9] In 1931, the Court added freedom of the press to that short list of civil rights protected by the Bill of Rights from state action; in 1934, it added freedom of religion; and in 1939, it added freedom of assembly.[10] But that was as far as the Court was willing to go. This one-by-one application of the provisions of the Bill of Rights is known as *selective incorporation* as distinguished from the notion of "total incorporation" advocated by some scholars. Total incorporation is the idea that all of the provisions of the Bill of Rights were applied to the states by the Fourteenth Amendment. As late as 1937, the Supreme Court was still loath to nationalize civil liberties beyond the First Amendment. In fact, the Court in that year took one of its most extreme turns backward toward *Barron v. Baltimore*.

The state of Connecticut had indicted a man named Frank Palko for first-degree murder, but a lower court found him guilty of only second-degree murder and sentenced him to life in prison. Unhappy with the verdict, the state of Connecticut appealed the conviction to its highest court, won the appeal, got a new trial, and succeeded in getting Palko convicted of first-degree murder. Palko appealed to the Supreme Court on what seemed an open-and-shut case of double jeopardy—being tried twice for the same crime. Yet though a majority of the Court agreed that this could indeed be considered a case of double jeopardy, the justices decided that double jeopardy was *not* one of the provisions of the Bill of Rights incorporated into the Fourteenth Amendment as a restriction on the powers of the states. Justice Benjamin Cardozo, considered one of the ablest Supreme Court justices of the twentieth century, rejected the argument made by Palko's lawyer that "whatever is forbidden by the Fifth Amendment is forbidden by the Fourteenth also." Cardozo responded tersely, "There is no such general rule." Palko was eventually executed for the crime—because he lived in the state of Connecticut rather than in a state whose constitution included a guarantee against double jeopardy.

Cases like *Palko* extended the shadow of *Barron* into its second century, despite adoption of the Fourteenth Amendment. The Constitution, as interpreted by the Supreme Court, left standing the framework in which the states had the power to determine their own law on a number of fundamental issues. It left states with the power to pass laws segregating the races—and 13 states chose to exercise that power. The constitutional framework also left states with the power to engage in searches and seizures without a warrant, indict accused persons without benefit of a grand jury, deprive persons of trial by jury, force

---

9 *Gitlow v. New York*, 268 U.S. 652 (1925).

10 *Near v. Minnesota ex rel. Olson*, 283 U.S. 697 (1931); *Hague v. Committee for Industrial Organization*, 307 U.S. 496 (1939).

persons to testify against themselves, deprive accused persons of their right to confront adverse witnesses, and as we have seen, prosecute accused persons more than once for the same crime.[11] All of these were implicitly identified in the *Palko* case as "not incorporated" into the Fourteenth Amendment as limitations on the powers of the states.

The Constitutional Revolution in Civil Liberties

For more than 30 years after the *Palko* case, the nineteenth-century framework was sustained, but signs of change came after 1954, in *Brown v. Board of Education*, when the Supreme Court overturned the infamous *Plessy v. Ferguson*.[12] *Plessy* was a civil rights case involving the "equal protection" clause of the Fourteenth Amendment but was not an issue of applying the Bill of Rights to the states. (We will discuss *Plessy*'s significance for civil rights in the next chapter.) Nevertheless, *Brown* indicated clearly that the Supreme Court was going to be expansive about civil liberties because in that case the Court effectively promised that it was actively going to subject the states and all actions affecting civil rights and civil liberties to *strict scrutiny*. In retrospect, one could say that this constitutional revolution was given a jump start by the *Brown* decision,[13] even though the results were not apparent until after 1961, when the number of incorporated civil liberties increased (Table 4.1).

Nationalizing the Bill of Rights. As with the federalism revolution, the constitutional revolution in civil liberties was a movement toward nationalization. But the two revolutions required opposite motions on the part of the Supreme Court. In the area of commerce (the first revolution), the Court had to decide to assume a passive role by not interfering as Congress expanded the meaning of the commerce clause of Article I, Section 8. This expansion has been so extensive that the national government can now constitutionally reach a single farmer growing 20 acres of wheat or a small restaurant selling barbecue to local "whites only" without the farmer's or the restaurant's being anywhere near interstate commerce routes. In the second revolution, involving the Bill of Rights and the Fourteenth Amendment rather than the commerce clause, the Court had to assume an active role, which required close review not of Congress but of the laws of state legislatures and the decisions of state courts to apply a

---

11 *Palko v. Connecticut*, 302 U.S. 319 (1937), was explicitly reversed in *Benton v. Maryland*, 395 U.S. 784 (1969), in which the Court said that double jeopardy was in fact incorporated into the Fourteenth Amendment as a restriction on the states.

12 *Brown v. Board of Education*, 347 U.S. 483 (1954); *Plessy v. Ferguson*, 163 U.S. 537 (1896).

13 The first constitutional revolution began with *National Labor Relations Board v. Jones and Laughlin Steel Corporation*, 301 U.S. 1 (1937).

single national Fourteenth Amendment standard to the rights and liberties of all citizens.

Table 4.1 shows that until 1961, only the First Amendment had been fully and clearly incorporated into the Fourteenth Amendment.[14] After 1961, several other important provisions of the Bill of Rights were incorporated. Of the cases that expanded the Fourteenth Amendment's reach, among the most famous (partly because it became the subject of a best-selling book and a popular movie) is *Gideon v. Wainwright*, which established the right to counsel in a criminal trial.[15] In *Mapp v. Ohio*, the Court held that evidence obtained in violation of the Fourth Amendment ban on unreasonable searches and seizures would be excluded from trial.[16] This "exclusionary rule" was particularly irksome to police and prosecutors because it meant that patently guilty defendants sometimes got to go free because the evidence that clearly damned them could not be used. In *Miranda*, the Court's ruling required that arrested persons be informed of the rights to remain silent and have counsel present during interrogation.[17] This is the basis of the Miranda rule of reading persons their rights, which is familiar to most Americans from movies and TV police shows. By 1969, in *Benton v. Maryland*, the Supreme Court had come full circle regarding the rights of the criminally accused, explicitly reversing the *Palko* ruling and thereby incorporating double jeopardy.

Miranda rule

The convention derived from the Supreme Court's 1966 ruling in the case of *Miranda v. Arizona* whereby persons under arrest must be informed of their legal rights, including their right to counsel, before undergoing police interrogation

During the 1960s and early 1970s, the Court expanded another important area of civil liberties: rights to privacy. When the Court began to take a more activist role in the mid-1950s and the 1960s, the idea of a right to privacy was revived. In 1958, the Supreme Court recognized "privacy in one's association" in its decision to prevent the state of Alabama from using the membership list of the National Association for the Advancement of Colored People (NAACP) in its investigations.[18] As we see later in this chapter, legal questions about the right to privacy have come to the fore in more recent cases concerning birth control, abortion, homosexuality, and assisted suicide.

14 The one exception was the right to a public trial (the Sixth Amendment), but the 1948 case did not mention the right to a public trial as such; it was cited in a 1968 case as establishing the right to a public trial as part of the Fourteenth Amendment. The 1948 case was *In re Oliver*, 333 U.S. 257, where the issue was put more generally as "due process," and public trial itself was not mentioned. Later opinions, such as *Duncan v. Louisiana*, 391 U.S. 145 (1968), cited the *Oliver* case as the precedent for incorporating public trials as part of the Fourteenth Amendment.

15 Anthony Lewis, *Gideon's Trumpet* (New York: Random House, 1964); *Gideon v. Wainwright*, 372 U.S. 335 (1963).

16 *Mapp v. Ohio*, 367 U.S. 643 (1961).

17 *Miranda v. Arizona*, 384 U.S. 436 (1966).

18 *NAACP v. Alabama*, 357 U.S. 449 (1958).

THE BILL OF RIGHTS TODAY

Since liberty requires restraining the power of government, the general status of civil liberties can never be considered fixed and permanent.[19] Every provision in the Bill of Rights is subject to interpretation, and in any dispute involving a clause of the Bill of Rights, interpretations will always be shaped by the interpreter's interest in the outcome. As we have seen, the Court continuously reminds everyone that if it has the power to expand the Bill of Rights, it also has the power to contract it.[20]

One good way to examine the Bill of Rights today is the simplest way: to take the provisions one at a time. Some of these provisions are settled areas of law, and some are not. Any one of them can be reinterpreted by the Court at any time.

The First Amendment and Freedom of Religion

> Congress shall make no law respecting an establishment of religion, or prohibiting the free exercise thereof; or abridging the freedom of speech, or of the press; or the right of the people peaceably to assemble, and to petition the Government for a redress of grievances.

The Bill of Rights begins by guaranteeing freedom, and the First Amendment provides for that freedom in two distinct clauses: "Congress shall make no law [1] respecting an establishment of religion, or [2] prohibiting the free exercise thereof." The first clause is called the establishment clause, and the second is called the free exercise clause. Let us examine the meaning of each clause.

Separation between Church and State. The establishment clause and the idea of "no law" regarding the establishment of religion could be interpreted in several possible ways. One interpretation, which probably reflects the views of many of the First Amendment's authors, is that the government is prohibited from establishing an official church. Official state churches, such as the Church of England, were common in the eighteenth century and were viewed by many Americans as inconsistent with a republican form of government. Indeed, many American colonists had fled Europe to escape persecution for having rejected state-sponsored churches. A second possible interpretation is the "nonpreferentialist" or "accommodationist" view, which holds that the

establishment clause

The First Amendment clause that says, "Congress shall make no law respecting an establishment of religion." This law means that a wall of separation exists between church and state

19 This section is taken from Benjamin Ginsberg, Theodore J. Lowi, and Margaret Weir, *We the People: An Introduction to American Politics*, 8th ed. (New York: Norton, 2011).

20 For a lively and readable treatment of the possibilities of restricting provisions of the Bill of Rights without actually reversing prior decisions, see David G. Savage, *Turning Right: The Making of the Rehnquist Supreme Court* (New York: Wiley, 1992).

government may not take sides among competing religions but is not prohibited from providing assistance to religious institutions or ideas so long as it shows no favoritism. The United States accommodates religious beliefs in a variety of ways, from the reference to God on U.S. currency to the prayer that begins every session of Congress. These forms of establishment have never been struck down by the courts.

The third view regarding religious establishment, which for many years dominated Supreme Court decision making in this realm, is the idea of a "wall of separation" between church and state that cannot be breached by the government. The concept of a wall of separation was Jefferson's own formulation, and it has figured in many Supreme Court cases arising under the establishment clause. For two centuries, Jefferson's words have had a powerful impact on our understanding of the proper relationship between church and state in America.

Despite the absolute sound of the phrase *wall of separation*, there is ample room to disagree on how high the wall is or of what materials it is composed. For example, the Court has been consistently strict in cases of school prayer, striking down such practices as Bible reading,[21] nondenominational prayer,[22] a moment of silence for meditation, and pregame prayer at public sporting events.[23] In each of these cases, the Court reasoned that school-sponsored observations, even of an apparently nondenominational character, are highly suggestive of school sponsorship and therefore violate the prohibition against establishment of religion. On the other hand, the Court has been quite permissive (and some would say inconsistent) about the public display of religious symbols, such as city-sponsored Nativity scenes in commercial or municipal areas.[24] And although the Court has consistently disapproved of government-financed support for religious schools, even when the purpose has been purely educational and secular, it has permitted certain direct aid to students of such schools in the form of busing, for example. In 1971, after 30 years of cases involving religious schools, the Court attempted to specify some criteria to guide its decisions and those of lower courts, indicating, for example, in a decision invalidating state payments for the teaching of secular subjects in parochial schools, circumstances under which the Court might allow certain financial assistance. The case was *Lemon v. Kurtzman*; in its decision, the Supreme Court established three criteria to guide future cases, in what came to be called the *Lemon* test. The Court held that government aid to religious schools would be accepted as constitutional if (1) it had a secular purpose, (2) its effect was neither to advance nor to inhibit religion, and (3) it did not entangle government and religious institutions in one another's affairs.[25]

***Lemon* test**

Rule articulated in *Lemon v. Kurtzman* according to which governmental action in respect to religion is permissible if it is secular in purpose, does not lead to "excessive entanglement" with religion, and neither promotes nor inhibits the practice of religion

21 *Abington School District v. Schempp*, 374 U.S. 203 (1963).

22 *Engel v. Vitale*, 370 U.S. 421 (1962).

23 *Wallace v. Jaffree*, 472 U.S. 38 (1985).

24 *Lynch v. Donnelly*, 465 U.S. 668 (1984).

25 *Lemon v. Kurtzman*, 403 U.S. 602 (1971). The *Lemon* test is still good law, but as recently as the 1994 Court term, four justices urged that it be abandoned. Here is a settled area of law that may become unsettled.

Although these restrictions make the *Lemon* test a hard test to pass, imaginative authorities have found ways to do so, and the Supreme Court has demonstrated a willingness to let them, perhaps moving toward a more accommodationist view of the establishment clause. In 1995, for example, the Court narrowly ruled that a student religious group at the University of Virginia could not be denied student activities funds merely because it was a religious group espousing a particular viewpoint about a deity. The Court called the denial "viewpoint discrimination" and declared that it violated the free speech rights of the group.[26] This led two years later to a new, more conservative approach to the separation of church and state. In 1997, the Court accepted the practice of sending public-school teachers into parochial schools to provide remedial education to disadvantaged children.[27]

In 2004, the question of whether the phrase "under God" in the Pledge of Allegiance violates the establishment clause was brought before the Court. Written in 1892, the pledge had been used in schools without any religious references. But in 1954, in the midst of the Cold War, Congress voted to change the pledge, in response to the "godless Communism" of the Soviet Union. The conversion was made by adding two key words, so that the revised version read, "I pledge allegiance to the flag of the United States of America and to the Republic for which it stands, one nation *under God*, indivisible, with liberty and justice for all" [emphasis added].

Ever since the change was made, there has been a constant murmuring of discontent from those who object to an officially sanctioned profession of belief in a deity as a violation of the religious freedom clause of the First Amendment. In 2003, Michael Newdow, the father of a kindergarten student in a California elementary school, forced the issue to the surface when he brought suit against the local school district. Newdow, an atheist, argued that the reference to God turned the daily recitation of the pledge into a religious exercise. A federal court ruled that although students were not required to recite the pledge at all, having to stand and listen to others say "under God" still violated the First Amendment's establishment clause. The case was appealed to the Supreme Court, and on June 14, 2004—50 years to the day after the adoption of "under God" in the pledge—the Court ruled that Newdow lacked a sufficient personal stake in the case to bring the complaint.[28] This inconclusive decision by the Court left "under God" in the pledge while keeping the issue alive for possible resolution in a future case.

In two cases in 2005, the Supreme Court ruled, also inconclusively, on government-sponsored displays of religious symbols. Both cases involved displays of the Ten Commandments. In *Van Orden v. Perry*, the Court said in a 5–4 decision that a display of the Ten Commandments in the Texas state capital did

26 *Rosenberger v. University of Virginia,* 515 U.S. 819 (1995).

27 *Agostini v. Felton,* 521 U.S. 203 (1997). The case being overruled was *Aguilar v. Felton,* 473 U.S. 402 (1985).

28 *Elk Grove Unified School District v. Newdow,* 542 U.S. 1 (2004).

not violate the Constitution.[29] However, in *McCreary v. ACLU*, decided at the same time and also by a 5–4 margin, the Court determined that a display of the Ten Commandments inside two Kentucky court houses was unconstitutional.[30] Justice Breyer, the swing vote in the two cases intimated that the difference had been the purpose of the displays. Most legal observers, though, could see little difference between the two and assume that the Court will provide further clarification in future cases.

free exercise clause

The First Amendment clause that protects a citizen's right to believe and practice whatever religion he or she chooses

Free Exercise of Religion. The free exercise clause protects the right to believe and practice whatever religion one chooses; it also protects the right to be a nonbeliever. Generally speaking, problems arise under the free exercise clause not because the government specifically decides to interfere with religion. Rather, they arise, because generally applicable secular laws happen to intrude on the beliefs of one or another group. The precedent-setting case involving free exercise was *West Virginia State Board of Education v. Barnette* (1943), which involved the children of a family of Jehovah's Witnesses who refused to salute and pledge allegiance to the American flag on the grounds that their religious faith did not permit it. Three years earlier, the Court had upheld such a requirement and had permitted schools to expel students for refusing to salute the flag. But the entry of the United States into a war to defend democracy coupled with the ugly treatment to which the Jehovah's Witnesses' children had been subjected induced the Court to reverse itself and endorse the free exercise of religion even when it may be offensive to the beliefs of the majority.[31]

Although the Supreme Court has been fairly consistent and strict in protecting the free exercise of religious belief, it has taken pains to distinguish between religious beliefs and *actions* based on those beliefs. In one case, for example, two Native Americans had been fired from their jobs for smoking peyote, an illegal drug. They claimed they had been fired from their jobs illegally because smoking peyote was a religious sacrament protected by the free exercise clause. The Court disagreed with their claim in an important 1990 decision,[32] but Congress supported the claim and went on to engage in an unusual controversy with the Court, involving the separation of powers as well as the proper application of the separation of church and state. Congress literally reversed the Court's 1990 decision with the enactment of the Religious Freedom Restoration Act (RFRA) of 1993, which forbids any federal agency or state government to restrict a person's free exercise of religion unless the federal agency or state government demonstrates that its action "furthers a compelling government interest" and "is

29 *Van Orden v. Perry*, 545 U.S. 677 (2005).

30 *McCreary v. ACLU*, 545 U.S. 844 (2005).

31 *West Virginia State Board of Education v. Barnette*, 319 U.S. 624 (1943). The case it reversed was *Minersville School District v. Gobitus*, 310 U.S. 586 (1940).

32 *Employment Division v. Smith*, 494 U.S. 872 (1990).

the least restrictive means of furthering that compelling governmental interest." One of the first applications of the RFRA was to a case brought by St. Peter's Catholic Church against the city of Boerne, Texas, which had denied permission to the church to enlarge its building because the building had been declared a historic landmark. The case went to federal court on the argument that the city had violated the church's religious freedom as guaranteed by Congress in the RFRA. The Supreme Court declared the RFRA unconstitutional, but on grounds rarely utilized, if not unique to this case: Congress had violated the separation-of-powers principle, infringing on the powers of the judiciary by going so far beyond its lawmaking powers that it ended up actually expanding the scope of religious rights rather than just enforcing them. The Court thereby implied that questions requiring a balancing of religious claims against public policy claims were reserved strictly to the judiciary.[33]

The *City of Boerne* case did settle some matters of constitutional controversy over the religious exercise and the establishment clauses of the First Amendment, but it left a lot more unsettled. What about the refusal of some Amish parents to send their children to school beyond eighth grade because of their belief that exposing their children to "modern values" undermines their religious commitment? In this example, the Court decided in favor of the Amish and endorsed a very strong interpretation of the protection of free exercise.[34] Or, what if free exercise of religion clashes with other values such as nondiscrimination? A 2010 case involved a public law school in California that denied the use of school funds and facilities to a Christian student group that excluded gays and non-Christians. In a 5–4 ruling, the Court said the school was acting to prevent discrimination, not interfering with the student group's right to exercise its religion.[35]

The First Amendment and Freedom of Speech and the Press

> Congress shall make no law . . . abridging the freedom of speech, or of the press.

Because democracy depends on an open political process and politics is basically talk, freedom of speech and freedom of the press are considered critical. For this reason, they were given a prominence in the Bill of Rights equal to that of freedom of religion. In 1938, freedom of speech (which in all important respects includes freedom of the press) was given extraordinary constitutional status when the Supreme Court established that any legislation that attempts

---

33 *City of Boerne v. Flores,* 521 U.S. 507 (1997).

34 *Wisconsin v. Yoder,* 406 U.S. 205 (1972).

35 *Christian Legal Society v. Martinez,* No.08-1371 (2010).

to restrict these fundamental freedoms "is to be subjected to a more exacting judicial scrutiny . . . than are most other types of legislation."[36]

The Court was saying that the democratic political process must be protected at almost any cost. This higher standard of judicial review came to be called *preferred position.* Preferred position implies that speech—at least some kinds of speech—will be protected almost absolutely. In 2011, for example, the Supreme Court ruled 8–1 that the Westboro Baptist Church, a tiny Kansas institution, had a First Amendment right to picket the funerals of American soldiers killed in action while displaying signs reading "Thank God for Dead Soldiers." Members of the church believe that these deaths represent divine punishment for America's tolerance of homosexuality and other matters. In his opinion, Chief Justice Roberts wrote, "As a nation we have chosen to protect even hurtful speech on public issues to ensure that we do not stifle public debate."[37] But, even though we do protect many types of speech with which most Americans strongly disagree, it turns out that only some types of speech are fully protected against restrictions. Many forms of speech are less than absolutely protected—even though they are entitled to a preferred position.

Political Speech. Political speech was the activity of greatest concern to the framers of the Constitution, even though they found it the most difficult provision to observe. Within seven years of the ratification of the Bill of Rights, Congress adopted the infamous Alien and Sedition Acts, which, among other things, made it a crime to say or publish anything that might tend to defame or bring into disrepute the government of the United States. Quite clearly, the acts' intentions were to criminalize the very conduct given absolute protection by the First Amendment. Fifteen violators, including several newspaper editors, were indicted, and a few were convicted before the relevant portions of the acts were allowed to expire.

The first modern free speech case arose immediately after World War I. It involved persons who had been convicted under the federal Espionage Acts of 1917 for opposing American involvement in the war. The Supreme Court upheld the act and refused to protect the speech rights of the defendants on the grounds that their activities—appeals to draftees to resist the draft—constituted a "clear and present danger" to security.[38] This is the first and most famous test of when government intervention or censorship can be permitted, though it is no longer used by courts.

clear and present danger

The criterion used to determine whether speech is protected or unprotected, based on its capacity to present a "clear and present danger" to society

It was only after the 1920s that real progress toward a genuinely effective First Amendment was made. Since then, political speech has been consistently protected by the courts even when it has been deemed "insulting" or

36 *United States v. Carolene Products Company*, 304 U.S. 144 (1938), 384. This footnote is one of the Court's most important doctrines. See Alfred H. Kelly, Winfred A. Harbison, and Herman Belz, *The American Constitution: Its Origins and Development*, 7th ed., 2 vols. (New York: Norton, 1991), II: 519–23.

37 *Snyder v. Phelps*, 09-751 (2011).

38 *Schenck v. United States*, 249 U.S. 47 (1919).

"outrageous." Here is the way the Supreme Court put it in one of its most important statements on the subject:

> The constitutional guarantees of free speech and free press do not permit a State to forbid or proscribe advocacy of the use of force or of law violation *except where such advocacy is directed to inciting or producing imminent lawless action and is likely to incite or produce such action.*[39] [Emphasis added]

This statement was made in the case of a Ku Klux Klan leader, Charles Brandenburg, who had been arrested and convicted of advocating "revengent" action against the president, Congress, and the Supreme Court, among others, if they continued "to suppress the white, Caucasian race." Although Brandenburg was not carrying a weapon, some members of his audience were. Nevertheless, the Supreme Court reversed the state courts and freed Brandenburg while declaring Ohio's Criminal Syndicalism Act unconstitutional because it punished persons who "advocate, or teach the duty, necessity, or propriety [of violence] as a means of accomplishing industrial or political reform" or who publish materials or "voluntarily assemble . . . to teach or advocate the doctrines of criminal syndicalism." The Supreme Court argued that the statute did not distinguish "mere advocacy" from "incitement to imminent lawless action." It would be difficult to go much further in protecting freedom of speech. Typically, the federal courts will strike down restrictions on speech if they are deemed to be "overbroad," "vague," or lacking "neutrality" in terms of the content of the speech, for example, if a statute prohibited the views of the political left but not the political right, or vice versa.

Another area of recent expansion of political speech—the participation of wealthy persons and corporations in political campaigns—was opened up in 1976 with the Supreme Court's decision in *Buckley v. Valeo.*[40] Campaign finance reform laws of the early 1970s, arising out of the Watergate scandal, sought to put severe limits on campaign spending, and a number of important provisions were declared unconstitutional on the basis of a new principle that spending money by or on behalf of candidates is a form of speech protected by the First Amendment. The issue came up again in 2003, after passage of a new and still more severe campaign finance law, the Bipartisan Campaign Reform Act (BCRA) (2002). In *McConnell v. Federal Election Commission*, the majority seriously reduced the area of speech protected by the *Buckley v. Valeo* decision by holding that Congress was well within its power to put limits on the amounts individuals could spend, plus severe limits on the amounts of "soft money" that could be spent by corporations and their PACs and limits on issue advertising prior to election day. The Court argued that "the selling of access . . . has given rise to the appearance of undue influence [that justifies] regulations impinging on First

39 *Brandenburg v. Ohio*, 395 U.S. 444 (1969).

40 *Buckley v. Valeo*, 424 U.S. 1 (1976).

Amendment rights . . . in order to curb corruption or the appearance of corruption."[41] In 2007, however, in the case of *Federal Election Commission v. Wisconsin Right to Life*, the Supreme Court struck down a key portion of BCRA, finding that the act's limitations on political advertising violated the First Amendment's guarantee of free speech.[42] In 2008, in the case of *Davis v. Federal Election Commission*, the Supreme Court struck down another element of BCRA, the so-called millionaire's amendment, which had increased contribution limits for opponents of self-funded, wealthy candidates.[43] And, in *Citizens United v. Federal Election Commission*, in 2010, the Court ruled that corporate funding of independent election ads could not be limited under the First Amendment.[44]

Symbolic Speech, Speech Plus, and the Rights of Assembly and Petition. The First Amendment treats the freedoms of assembly and petition as equal to the freedoms of religion and political speech. Freedom of assembly and freedom of petition are closely associated with speech but go beyond it to speech associated with action. Since at least 1931, the Supreme Court has sought to protect actions that are designed to send a political message. (Usually the purpose of a symbolic act is not only to send a direct message but also to draw a crowd—to do something spectacular in order to draw spectators to the action and thus strengthen the message.) Thus the Court held unconstitutional a California statute making it a felony to display a red flag "as a sign, symbol or emblem of opposition to organized government."[45] Although today there are limits on how far one can go with actions that symbolically convey a message, the protection of such action is very broad. Thus although the Court upheld a federal statute making it a crime to burn draft cards to protest the Vietnam War on the grounds that the government had a compelling interest in preserving draft cards as part of the conduct of the war itself, it considered the wearing of black armbands to school a protected form of assembly. In these sorts of cases, a court will often use the standard it articulated in the draft card case, *United States v. O'Brien*, and now known as the "*O'Brien* test."[46] Under the terms of the *O'Brien* test, a statute restricting expressive or symbolic speech must be justified by a compelling government interest and be narrowly tailored toward achieving that interest.

Another example is the burning of the American flag as a symbol of protest. In 1984, at a political rally held during the Republican National Convention in Dallas, a political protester burned an American flag in violation of a Texas statute that prohibited desecration of a venerated object. In a 5–4 decision,

---

41 *McConnell v. Federal Election Commission*, 540 U.S. 93 (2003).

42 *Federal Election Commission v. Wisconsin Right to Life*, 551 U.S. 449 (2007).

43 *Davis v. Federal Election Commission*, 554 U.S. 724 (2008).

44 *Citizens United v. FEC*, 130 S. Ct. 876 (2010).

45 *Stromberg v. California*, 283 U.S. 359 (1931).

46 *United States v. O'Brien*, 391 U.S. 367 (1968).

the Supreme Court declared the Texas law unconstitutional on the grounds that flag burning is expressive conduct protected by the First Amendment.[47] Congress reacted immediately with a proposal for a constitutional amendment reversing the Court's decision, and when the amendment failed to receive the necessary two-thirds majority in the Senate, Congress passed the Flag Protection Act of 1989. Protesters promptly violated this act, and their prosecution moved quickly into the federal district court, which declared the new law unconstitutional. The Supreme Court, in another 5–4 decision, affirmed the lower court's decision.[48] In 2003, the Supreme Court struck down a Virginia cross-burning statute, ruling that states could make cross burning a crime as long as the statute required prosecutors to prove that the act of setting fire to the cross was intended to intimidate. Justice Sandra Day O'Connor wrote for the majority that the First Amendment permits the government to forbid cross burning as a "particularly virulent form of intimidation" but not when the act was "a form of symbolic expression."[49] This decision will almost inevitably become a more generalized First Amendment protection of any conduct, including flag burning, that can be shown to be a form of symbolic expression.

Closer to the original intent of the assembly and petition clause is the category of speech plus—following speech with physical activity such as picketing, distributing leaflets, and other forms of peaceful demonstration or assembly. Such assemblies are consistently protected by courts under the First Amendment; state and local laws regulating such activities are closely scrutinized and frequently overturned. But the same assembly on private property is quite another matter and can in many circumstances be regulated. For example, the directors of a shopping center can lawfully prohibit an assembly protesting a war or supporting a ban on abortion. Assemblies in public areas can also be restricted under some circumstances, especially when the assembly or demonstration jeopardizes the health, safety, or rights of others. This condition was the basis of the Supreme Court's decision to uphold a lower-court order restricting the access that abortion protesters had to the entrances of abortion clinics.[50]

speech plus

Speech accompanied by activities such as sit-ins, picketing, and demonstrations. Protection of this form of speech under the First Amendment is conditional, and restrictions imposed by state or local authorities are acceptable if properly balanced by considerations of public order

Freedom of the Press. For all practical purposes, freedom of speech implies and includes freedom of the press. With the exception of the broadcast media, which are subject to federal regulation, the press is protected under the doctrine prohibiting prior restraint. Beginning with the landmark 1931 case of *Near v. Minnesota*,[51] the Supreme Court has held that except under the most

prior restraint

An effort by a government agency to block the publication of material it deems libelous or harmful in some other way; censorship. In the United States, the courts forbid prior restraint except under the most extraordinary circumstances

47 *Texas v. Johnson*, 491 U.S. 397 (1989).

48 *United States v. Eichman*, 496 U.S. 310 (1990).

49 *Virginia v. Black*, 538 U.S. 343 (2003).

50 For a good general discussion of "speech plus," see Louis Fisher, *American Constitutional Law* (New York: McGraw-Hill, 1990), pp. 544–6. The case upholding the buffer zone against the abortion protesters is *Madsen v. Women's Health Center*, 512 U.S. 753 (1994).

51 *Near v. Minnesota ex rel. Olson*, 283 U.S. 697 (1931).

extraordinary circumstances, the First Amendment prohibits government agencies from seeking to prevent newspapers or magazines from publishing whatever they wish. Indeed, in the case of *New York Times v. United States*, the so-called Pentagon Papers case, the Supreme Court ruled that the government could not even block publication of secret Defense Department documents furnished to the *New York Times* by an opponent of the Vietnam War who had obtained the documents illegally.[52] In a 1990 case, however, the Supreme Court upheld a lower-court order restraining the Cable News Network (CNN) from broadcasting tapes of conversations between the former Panamanian dictator Manuel Noriega and his lawyer, supposedly recorded by the American government. By a vote of 7–2, the Court held that CNN could be restrained from broadcasting the tapes until the trial court in the Noriega case had listened to the tapes and decided whether their broadcast would violate Noriega's right to a fair trial.[53]

Libel and Slander. Some speech is not protected at all. If a written statement is made in "reckless disregard of the truth" and is considered damaging to the victim because it is "malicious, scandalous, and defamatory," it can be punished as libel. If an oral statement of such nature is made, it can be punished as slander.

libel

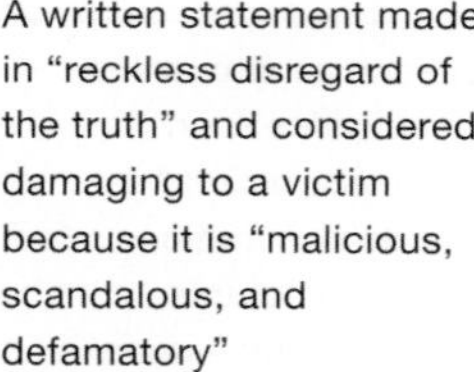

A written statement made in "reckless disregard of the truth" and considered damaging to a victim because it is "malicious, scandalous, and defamatory"

slander

An oral statement made in "reckless disregard of the truth" and considered damaging to a victim because it is "malicious, scandalous, and defamatory"

Today most libel suits involve freedom of the press, and the realm of free press is enormous. Historically, newspapers were subject to the law of libel, which provided that newspapers that printed false and malicious stories could be compelled to pay damages to those they defamed. In recent years, however, American courts have greatly narrowed the meaning of libel and made it extremely difficult, particularly for politicians or other public figures, to win a libel case against a newspaper. In the important case of *New York Times v. Sullivan*, the Court held that to be deemed libelous a story about a public official not only had to be untrue but also had to result from "actual malice" or "reckless disregard" for the truth.[54] In other words, the newspaper had to *deliberately* print false and malicious material. In practice, it is nearly impossible to prove that a paper deliberately printed maliciously false information, and it is especially difficult for a politician or other public figure to win a libel case. Essentially, the print media have been able to publish anything they want about a public figure.

In at least one recent case, however, the Court has opened up the possibility of public officials' filing libel suits against the press. In 1985, the Court held that the press was immune from libel only when the printed material was "a matter of public concern." In other words, in future cases a newspaper would have to show that the public official was engaged in activities that were indeed *public*.

52 *New York Times v. United States*, 403 U.S. 713 (1971).

53 *Cable News Network v. Noriega*, 111 S. Ct. 451 (1990).

54 *New York Times v. Sullivan*, 376 U.S. 254 (1964).

This new principle has made the press more vulnerable to libel suits, but it still leaves an enormous realm of freedom for the press. For example, the late Reverend Jerry Falwell, a cofounder of the Moral Majority, lost his libel suit against *Hustler* magazine even though the magazine had published a cartoon depicting Falwell having drunken intercourse with his mother in an outhouse. A unanimous Supreme Court rejected a jury verdict in favor of damages for "emotional distress" on the grounds that parodies, no matter how outrageous, are protected because "outrageousness" is too subjective a test and thus would interfere with the free flow of ideas protected by the First Amendment.[55]

Obscenity and Pornography. If libel and slander cases can be difficult because of the problem of determining the truth of statements and whether those statements are malicious and damaging, cases involving pornography and obscenity can be even stickier. It is easy to say that pornography and obscenity fall outside the realm of protected speech, but it is impossible to draw a clear line defining where protection ends and unprotected speech begins. Not until 1957 did the Supreme Court confront this problem, and it did so with a definition of obscenity that may have caused more confusion than it cleared up. Justice William Brennan, in writing the Court's opinion, defined obscenity as speech or writing that appeals to the "prurient interest"—that is, books, magazines, films, and other material whose purpose is to excite lust as this appears "to the average person, applying contemporary community standards." Even so, Brennan added, the work should be judged obscene only when it is "utterly without redeeming social importance."[56] Brennan's definition, instead of clarifying the Court's view, caused more confusion. In 1964, Justice Potter Stewart confessed that although he found pornography impossible to define, "I know it when I see it."[57]

All attempts by the courts to define pornography and obscenity have proved impractical because each instance required courts to screen thousands of pages of print material or feet of film alleged to be pornographic. The vague and impractical standards that had been developed meant ultimately that almost nothing could be banned on the grounds that it was pornographic and obscene. An effort was made to strengthen the restrictions in 1973, when the Supreme Court expressed its willingness to define pornography as a work that as a whole is deemed prurient by the "average person" according to "community standards," depicts sexual conduct "in a patently offensive way," and lacks "serious literary, artistic, political, or scientific value." This definition meant that pornography would be determined by local rather than national standards. Thus a local bookseller might be prosecuted for selling a volume that was a best-seller

---

55 *Hustler Magazine v. Falwell,* 485 U.S. 46 (1988).

56 *Roth v. United States,* 354 U.S. 476 (1957).

57 Concurring opinion in *Jacobellis v. Ohio,* 378 U.S. 184 (1964).

nationally but was deemed pornographic locally.[58] This new definition of standards did not help much either, and not long after 1973 the Court again began to review all such community antipornography laws, reversing most of them. Consequently, today there is a widespread fear that Americans are free to publish any and all variety of intellectual expression, whether there is any "redeeming social value" or not. Yet this area of free speech is far from settled.

In recent years, the battle against obscene speech has focused on pornography on the Internet. Opponents of this form of expression argue that it should be banned because of the easy access children have to the Internet. The first major effort to regulate the content of the Internet occurred on February 1, 1996, when the 104th Congress passed major telecommunications legislation. Attached to the Telecommunications Act was an amendment, called the Communications Decency Act (CDA), that was designed to regulate the online transmission of obscene material. The constitutionality of the CDA was immediately challenged in court by a coalition of interests led by the American Civil Liberties Union (ACLU). In the 1997 Supreme Court case of *Reno v. ACLU*, the Court struck down the CDA, ruling that it suppressed speech that "adults have a constitutional right to receive."[59] Congress again tried to limit children's access to Internet pornography with the 2001 Children's Internet Protection Act, which required public libraries to install antipornography filters on all library computers with Internet access. The law was challenged, and in 2003 the Court upheld it, asserting that its provisions did not violate library patrons' First Amendment rights.[60] In 2003, Congress enacted the Prosecutorial Remedies and Other Tools to end the Exploitation of Children Today (PROTECT) Act, which outlawed efforts to sell child pornography via the Internet. The Supreme Court upheld this act in the 2008 case of *United States v. Williams*, in which the majority said that criminalizing efforts to pander child pornography did not violate free-speech guarantees.[61]

In 2000, the Supreme Court also extended the highest degree of First Amendment protection to cable (not broadcast) television. In *United States v. Playboy Entertainment Group*, the Court struck down a portion of the Telecommunications Act of 1996 that required cable TV companies to limit the broadcast of sexually explicit programming to late-night hours. In its decision, the Court noted that the law already provided parents with the means to restrict access to sexually explicit cable channels through various blocking devices. Moreover, such programming could come into the home only if parents decided to purchase such channels in the first place.[62]

58 *Miller v. California*, 413 U.S. 15 (1973).

59 *Reno v. ACLU*, 521 U.S. 844 (1997).

60 *United States v. American Library Association*, 539 U.S. 194 (2003).

61 *United States v. Williams*, 553 U.S. 385 (2008).

62 *United States v. Playboy Entertainment Group, Inc.*, 529 U.S. 803 (2000).

Fighting Words. Speech can also lose its protected position when it moves toward the sphere of action. "Expressive speech," for example, is protected until it moves from the symbolic realm to the realm of actual conduct—to direct incitement of damaging conduct with the use of so-called fighting words. In 1942, the Supreme Court upheld the arrest and conviction of a man who had violated a state law forbidding the use of offensive language in public. He had called the arresting officer a "goddamned racketeer" and "a damn Fascist." When his case reached the Supreme Court, the arrest was upheld on the grounds that the First Amendment provides no protection for such offensive language because such words "are no essential part of any exposition of ideas."[63] This case was reaffirmed in a much more famous and more important case decided at the height of the Cold War, when the Supreme Court held that

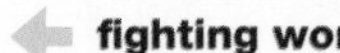
fighting words

Speech that directly incites damaging conduct

> there is no substantial public interest in permitting certain kinds of utterances: the lewd and obscene, the profane, the libelous, and the insulting or "fighting" words—those which by their very utterance inflict injury or tend to incite an immediate breach of the peace.[64]

Since that time, however, the Supreme Court has reversed almost every conviction based on arguments that the speaker had used "fighting words." But again, it does not mean this is an absolutely settled area. In recent years, the increased activism of minority and women's groups has prompted a movement against words that might be construed as offensive to members of a particular group. This movement has come to be called, derisively, political correctness, or PC. In response to this movement, many organizations have attempted to impose codes of etiquette that acknowledge these enhanced sensitivities. These efforts to formalize the restraints on the use of certain words in public are causing great concern over their possible infringement on freedom of speech. But how should we determine what words are "fighting words" and therefore fall outside the protections of the freedom of speech?

One category of conditionally protected speech is the free speech of high school students in public schools. In 1986, the Supreme Court backed away from a broad protection of student free speech rights by upholding the punishment of a high school student for making a sexually suggestive speech. The Court opinion held that such speech interfered with the school's goal of teaching students the limits of socially acceptable behavior.[65] Two years later the Supreme Court took another conservative step by restricting students' speech and press

63 *Chaplinsky v. State of New Hampshire,* 315 U.S. 568 (1942).

64 *Dennis v. United States,* 341 U.S. 494 (1951), which upheld the infamous Smith Act of 1940, which provided criminal penalties for those who "willfully and knowingly conspire to teach and advocate the forceful and violent overthrow and destruction of the government."

65 *Bethel School District No. 403 v. Fraser,* 478 U.S. 675 (1986).

rights even further, defining them as part of the educational process and not to be treated with the same standard as adult speech in a regular public forum.[66] An even more recent case involving high school students is the 2007 case of *Morse v. Frederick*.[67] This case dealt with the policies of Juneau-Douglas High School in Juneau, Alaska. In 2002, the Olympic torch relay passed Juneau on its way to Salt Lake City for the opening of the Winter Olympics. As the torch passed Juneau-Douglas High, a senior, Joseph Frederick, unfurled a banner that read, "Bong Hits 4 Jesus." The school's principal promptly suspended Frederick, who then brought suit for reinstatement, alleging that his free-speech rights had been violated. Like most of America's public schools, Juneau High prohibits assemblies or expressions on school grounds that advocate illegal drug use. Schools say that some federal aid is contingent on this policy. Civil libertarians, of course, see such policies as restricting students' right to free speech—a right that has been recognized by the Supreme Court since a 1969 case in which it said an Iowa public school could not prohibit students from wearing antiwar armbands. Unfortunately for Frederick, today's Supreme Court has a much more conservative cast than its 1969 counterpart. Speaking for the Court's majority, Chief Justice Roberts said that the First Amendment did not require schools to permit students to advocate illegal drug use.

In addition, scores of universities have attempted to develop speech codes to suppress utterances deemed to be racial or ethnic slurs. What these universities often find, however, is that the codes may produce more problems than they solve. Speech codes at public universities have been struck down by federal judges as unconstitutional infringements of speech. Such concerns are not limited to universities, although universities have probably moved furthest toward efforts to formalize "politically correct" speech guidelines. Similar developments have taken place in large corporations, both public and private, in which many successful complaints and lawsuits have been brought, alleging that the words of employers or their supervisors create a "hostile or abusive working environment." The Supreme Court has held that "sexual harassment" that creates a "hostile working environment" includes "unwelcome sexual advances, requests for sexual favors, and other *verbal* or physical conduct of a sexual nature"[68] [emphasis added]. A fundamental free speech issue is involved in these regulations of hostile speech.

Hate Speech. Many jurisdictions have drafted ordinances banning forms of expression designed to assert hatred toward one or another group, be they African Americans, Jews, Muslims, or others. Such ordinances seldom pass constitutional muster. The leading Supreme Court case in this realm is the 1992 decision in *R.A.V. v. City of St. Paul*.[69] Here, a white teenager was arrested for burning a

66 *Hazelwood School District v. Kuhlmeier*, 484 U.S. 260 (1988).

67 *Morse v. Frederick*, 551 U.S. 393 (2007).

68 *Meritor Savings Bank v. Vinson*, 477 U.S. 57 (1986).

69 *R.A.V. v. City of St. Paul*, 506 U.S. 377 (1992).

cross on the lawn of a black family in violation of a municipal ordinance that banned cross burning. The Court ruled that such an ordinance must be *content neutral*, that is, not prohibiting actions directed at some groups but not others. The statute in question prohibited only cross burning—typically an expression of hatred of African Americans. Since a statute banning all forms of hateful expression would be deemed overly broad, the *R.A.V.* standard suggests that virtually all hate speech is constitutionally protected.

Commercial Speech. Commercial speech, such as newspaper or television advertising, does not have full First Amendment protection because it cannot be considered political speech. Initially considered to be entirely outside the protection of the First Amendment, commercial speech has made gains during the twentieth century. Some commercial speech is still unprotected and therefore regulated. For example, the regulation of false and misleading advertising by the Federal Trade Commission is an old and well-established power of the federal government. The Supreme Court long ago approved the constitutionality of laws prohibiting the electronic media from carrying cigarette advertising.[70] The Court has upheld a state-university ban on Tupperware parties in college dormitories.[71] It has upheld city ordinances prohibiting the posting of all signs on public property (as long as the ban is total, so that there is no hint of censorship).[72] And the Supreme Court, in a heated 5–4 decision written by Chief Justice William Rehnquist, upheld Puerto Rico's statute restricting gambling advertising aimed at residents of Puerto Rico.[73]

However, the gains far outweigh the losses in the effort to expand the protection commercial speech enjoys under the First Amendment. As the scholar Louis Fisher explains, "In part, this reflects the growing appreciation that commercial speech is part of the free flow of information necessary for informed choice and democratic participation."[74] For example, the Court in 1975 struck down a state statute making it a misdemeanor to sell or circulate newspapers encouraging abortions; the Court ruled that the statute infringed on constitutionally protected speech and the right of the reader to make informed choices.[75] On a similar basis, the Court reversed its own earlier decisions upholding laws that prohibited dentists and other professionals from advertising their services. For the Court, medical-service advertising was a matter of health that could be advanced by the free flow of information.[76] In a 1983 case, the Supreme Court

70 *Capital Broadcasting Company v. Acting Attorney General*, 405 U.S. 1000 (1972).

71 *Board of Trustees, State University of New York v. Fox*, 492 U.S. 469 (1989).

72 *City Council v. Taxpayers for Vincent*, 466 U.S. 789 (1984).

73 *Posadas de Puerto Rico Associates v. Tourism Company of Puerto Rico*, 478 U.S. 328 (1986).

74 Fisher, *American Constitutional Law*, p. 546.

75 *Bigelow v. Virginia*, 421 U.S. 809 (1975).

76 *Virginia State Board of Pharmacy v. Virginia Citizens Consumer Council*, 425 U.S. 748 (1976). Later cases restored the rights of lawyers to advertise their services.

struck down a congressional statute that prohibited the unsolicited mailing of advertisements for contraceptives. In 1996, the Court struck down Rhode Island laws and regulations banning the advertisement of liquor prices as a violation of the First Amendment.[77] And in a 2001 case, the Court ruled that a Massachusetts ban on all cigarette advertising violated the First Amendment right of the tobacco industry to advertise its products to adult consumers.[78] These instances of commercial speech are significant in themselves, but they are all the more significant because they indicate the breadth and depth of the freedom existing today to direct appeals broadly to a large public, not only to sell goods and services but also to mobilize people for political purposes.

The Second Amendment and the Right to Bear Arms

> A well regulated Militia, being necessary to the security of a free State, the right of the people to keep and bear Arms, shall not be infringed.

The point and purpose of the Second Amendment is the provision for militias; they were to be the backing of the government for the maintenance of local public order. *Militia* was understood at the time of the Founding to be a military or police resource for state governments, and militias were specifically distinguished from armies and troops, which came within the sole constitutional jurisdiction of Congress. Some individuals, though, have always argued that the Second Amendment also establishes an individual right to bear arms. In its 2008 decision in the case of *District of Columbia v. Heller*, the Supreme Court ruled that the federal government could not prohibit individuals from owning guns for self-defense in their homes.[79] The case involved a District of Columbia ordinance that made it virtually impossible for residents to possess firearms legally. The District of Columbia is an entity of the federal government, and the Court did not indicate that its ruling applied to state firearms laws. However, in the 2010 case of *McDonald v. Chicago*, the Court struck down a Chicago firearms ordinance and applied the Second Amendment to the states as well.[80]

Rights of the Criminally Accused

Except for the First Amendment, most of the battle to apply the Bill of Rights to the states was fought over the various protections granted to individuals who are accused of a crime, who are suspects in the commission of a crime, or

77 *44 Liquormart, Inc., and Peoples Super Liquor Stores, Inc., Petitioners v. Rhode Island and Rhode Island Liquor Stores Association*, 517 U.S. 484 (1996).

78 *Lorillard Tobacco v. Reilly*, 533 U.S. 525 (2001).

79 *District of Columbia v. Heller*, 554 U.S. 570 (2008).

80 *McDonald v. Chicago*, 130 S. Ct. 3020 (2010).

who are brought before the court as a witness to a crime. The Bill of Rights entitles every American to due process of law. The concept of due process of law means that the government must respect all the legal rights to which every individual is entitled. The Fourth, Fifth, Sixth, and Eighth Amendments, taken together, are the essence of the due process of law, even though this fundamental concept does not appear until the very last words of the Fifth Amendment. In the next sections, we look at specific cases that illuminate the dynamics of this important constitutional issue. The procedural safeguards that we shall discuss may seem remote to most law-abiding citizens, but they help define the limits of governmental action against the personal liberty of every citizen. Many Americans believe that "legal technicalities" are responsible for setting many criminals free. In many cases, that is absolutely true. In fact, setting defendants free is the very purpose of the requirements that constitute due process. One of America's traditional and most strongly held juridical values is that "it is far worse to convict an innocent man than to let a guilty man go free."[81] In civil suits, verdicts rest on "the preponderance of the evidence"; in criminal cases, guilt has to be proved "beyond a reasonable doubt"—a far higher standard. The provisions for due process in the Bill of Rights were added in order to improve the probability that the standard of reasonable doubt will be respected.

due process

Proceeding according to law and with adequate protection for individual rights

The Fourth Amendment and Searches and Seizures

> The right of the people to be secure in their persons, houses, papers, and effects, against unreasonable searches and seizures, shall not be violated, and no Warrants shall issue, but upon probable cause, supported by Oath or affirmation, and particularly describing the place to be searched, and the persons or things to be seized.

The purpose of the Fourth Amendment is to guarantee the security of citizens against unreasonable (that is, improper) searches and seizures. In 1990, the Supreme Court summarized its understanding of the Fourth Amendment brilliantly and succinctly: "A search compromises the individual interest in privacy; a seizure deprives the individual of dominion over his or her person or property."[82] But how are we to define what is reasonable and what is unreasonable?

The 1961 case of *Mapp v. Ohio* illustrates the beauty and the agony of one of the most important of the procedures that have grown out of the Fourth Amendment—the exclusionary rule, which prohibits evidence obtained during an illegal search from being introduced in a trial. Dollree (Dolly) Mapp was "a Cleveland woman of questionable reputation" (by some accounts), the ex-wife

exclusionary rule

The ability of courts to exclude evidence obtained in violation of the Fourth Amendment

81 *In re Winship*, 397 U.S. 358 (1970). An outstanding treatment of due process in issues involving the Fourth through Seventh Amendments is found in Fisher, *American Constitutional Law*, chap. 13.

82 *Horton v. California*, 496 U.S. 128 (1990).

of one prominent boxer, and the fiancée of an even more famous one. Acting on a tip that Dolly Mapp was harboring a suspect in a bombing incident, several policemen forcibly entered her house, claiming they had a warrant to look for the suspect. The police did not find the suspect but did find some materials connected to the local numbers racket (an illegal gambling operation) and a quantity of "obscene materials," which were in violation of an Ohio law banning possession of such materials. Although the warrant was never produced, the evidence that had been seized was admitted by a court, and Mapp was charged and convicted of illegal possession of obscene materials.

By the time Mapp's appeal reached the Supreme Court, the issue of obscene materials had faded into obscurity, and the question before the Court was whether any evidence produced under the circumstances of the search of her home was admissible. The Court's opinion affirmed the exclusionary rule: under the Fourth Amendment (applied to the states through the Fourteenth Amendment), "all evidence obtained by searches and seizures in violation of the Constitution . . . is inadmissible." This means that even people who are clearly guilty of the crime of which they are accused must not be convicted if the only evidence for their conviction was obtained illegally. This idea was expressed by Supreme Court Justice Benjamin Cardozo nearly a century ago when he wrote that "the criminal is to go free because the constable has blundered."

The exclusionary rule is the most severe restraint ever imposed by the Constitution and the courts on the behavior of the police. The exclusionary rule is a dramatic restriction because it rules out precisely the evidence that produces a conviction; it frees those people who are *known* to have committed the crime of which they have been accused. Because it works so dramatically in favor of persons known to have committed a crime, the Court has since softened the application of the rule. In recent years, the federal courts have relied on a discretionary use of the exclusionary rule, whereby they make a judgment as to the "nature and quality of the intrusion." It is thus difficult to know ahead of time whether a defendant will or will not be protected from an illegal search under the Fourth Amendment.[83]

Another recent issue involving the Fourth Amendment is the controversy over mandatory drug testing. Such testing is most widely used on public employees, and in an important case the Supreme Court upheld the U.S. Customs Service's drug-testing program for its employees.[84] That same year the Court approved drug and alcohol tests for railroad workers if the workers were involved in a serious accident.[85] After Court approvals of those two cases in 1989, more than 40 federal agencies initiated mandatory employee drug tests. The practice of drug testing was reinforced by a presidential executive order widely touted as the "campaign for a drug-free federal workplace." These growing practices

83 For a good discussion of the issue, see Fisher, *American Constitutional Law*, pp. 884–9.

84 *National Treasury Employees Union v. Von Raab*, 489 U.S. 656 (1989).

85 *Skinner v. Railroad Labor Executives Association*, 489 U.S. 602 (1989).

gave rise to public appeals against the general practice of "suspicionless testing" of employees. Regardless of any need to limit the spread of drug abuse, doing so by testing public employees seemed patently unconstitutional, in violation of the Fourth Amendment. A 1995 case, in which the Court upheld a public school district's policy requiring that all students participating in interscholastic sports submit to random drug tests, surely contributed to the efforts of federal, state, and local agencies to initiate random and suspicionless drug and alcohol testing.[86] The most recent cases suggest, however, that the Court is beginning to consider limits on the "war" against drugs. In a decisive 8–1 decision, the Court applied the Fourth Amendment as a shield against "state action that diminishes personal privacy" when the officials in question are not performing high-risk or safety-sensitive tasks.[87] Using random and suspicionless drug testing as a symbol to fight drug use was, in the Court's opinion, carrying the exceptions to the Fourth Amendment too far.

More recently, the Court found it unconstitutional for police to use trained dogs in roadblocks set up to look for drugs in cars. Unlike drunk-driving roadblocks, where public safety is directly involved, narcotics roadblocks "cannot escape the Fourth Amendment's requirement that searches be based on suspicion of individual wrongdoing."[88] The Court also ruled that the police may not use thermal-imaging devices to detect suspicious patterns of heat emerging from private homes without obtaining the usual search warrant.[89] In 2009 the court ruled against an Arizona school district that conducted a strip search of a 13-year-old student suspected of hiding drugs in her underwear.[90]

The Fifth Amendment

> No person shall be held to answer for a capital, or otherwise infamous crime, unless on a presentment or indictment of a Grand Jury, except in cases arising in the land or naval forces, or in the Militia, when in actual service in time of War or public danger; nor shall any person be subject for the same offense to be twice put in jeopardy of life or limb; nor shall be compelled in any criminal case to be a witness against himself, nor be deprived of life, liberty, or property, without due process of law; nor shall private property be taken for public use, without just compensation.

Grand Juries. The first clause of the Fifth Amendment, the right to have a grand jury determine whether a trial is warranted, is considered "the oldest

grand jury

A jury that determines whether sufficient evidence is available to justify a trial. Grand juries do not rule on the accused's guilt or innocence

86 *Vernonia School District v. Acton*, 515 U.S. 646 (1995).

87 *Chandler et al. v. Miller, Governor of Georgia et al.*, 520 U.S. 305 (1997).

88 *Indianapolis v. Edmund*, 531 U.S. 32 (2000).

89 *Kyllo v. United States*, 533 U.S. 27 (2001).

90 *Safford Unified School District No.1 v. Redding*, 08-479 (2009).

institution known to the Constitution."[91] Grand juries play an important role in federal criminal cases. However, the provision for a grand jury is the one important civil liberties provision of the Bill of Rights that was not incorporated by the Fourteenth Amendment to apply to state criminal prosecutions. Thus some states operate without grand juries. In such states, the prosecuting attorney simply files a "bill of information" affirming that there is sufficient evidence available to justify a trial. If the accused person is to be held in custody, the prosecutor must take the available information before a judge to determine whether the evidence shows probable cause.

double jeopardy 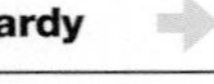

The Fifth Amendment right providing that a person cannot be tried twice for the same crime

Double Jeopardy. "Nor shall any person be subject for the same offense to be twice put in jeopardy of life or limb" is the constitutional protection from double jeopardy, or being tried more than once for the same crime. The protection from double jeopardy was at the heart of the *Palko* case in 1937, which, as we saw earlier in this chapter, also helped establish the principle of selective incorporation of the Bill of Rights. It took more than 30 years for the Court to nationalize the constitutional protection against double jeopardy.

Self-Incrimination. Perhaps the most significant liberty found in the Fifth Amendment, and the one most familiar to many Americans who watch television crime shows, is the guarantee that no citizen "shall be compelled in any criminal case to be a witness against himself." The most famous case concerning self-incrimination is one of such importance that Chief Justice Earl Warren assessed its results as going "to the very root of our concepts of American criminal jurisprudence." Twenty-three-year-old Ernesto Miranda was sentenced to between 20 and 30 years in prison for the kidnapping and rape of an eighteen-year-old woman. The woman had identified him in a police lineup, and, after two hours of questioning Miranda confessed, subsequently signing a statement that his confession had been made voluntarily, without threats or promises of immunity. These confessions were admitted into evidence, served as the basis for Miranda's conviction, and also served as the basis of the appeal of his conviction all the way to the Supreme Court. In one of the most intensely and widely criticized decisions ever handed down by the Supreme Court, Ernesto Miranda's case produced the rules the police must follow before questioning an arrested criminal suspect.

The reading of a person's "Miranda rights" has become a standard scene in every police station and on virtually every dramatization of police action on television and in the movies. *Miranda* advanced the civil liberties of accused persons not only by expanding the scope of the Fifth Amendment clause covering coerced confessions and self-incrimination but also by confirming the right to counsel. The Supreme Court under Warren Burger and William Rehnquist considerably softened the Miranda restrictions, making the job of the police a little easier, but the Miranda rule still stands as a protection against egregious

91 E. S. Corwin and Jack Peltason, *Understanding the Constitution* (New York: Wadsworth, 2007), p. 286.

police abuses of arrested persons. The Supreme Court reaffirmed Miranda in *Dickerson v. United States*.[92] However, in the 2010 case of *Berghuis v. Thomkins*, the Supreme Court did introduce an important qualification to the *Miranda* rule, saying in a 5–4 decision that statements made by suspects who did not expressly waive their rights (usually by signing a form) could still be used against them.[93] The dissenting justices expressed the fear that this decision would open the way for police abuses.

Eminent Domain. Another fundamental clause of the Fifth Amendment is the "takings clause," which extends to each citizen a protection against the taking of private property "without just compensation." Although this part of the amendment is not specifically concerned with protecting persons accused of crimes, it is nevertheless a fundamentally important instance where the government and the citizen are adversaries. As discussed earlier in this chapter, the power of any government to take private property for a public use is called eminent domain. This power is essential to the very concept of sovereignty. The Fifth Amendment neither invented eminent domain nor took it away; its purpose was to put limits on that inherent power through procedures that require a demonstration of a public purpose and the provision of fair payment for the seizure of someone's property. This provision is now universally observed in all American principalities, but it has not always been meticulously observed.

eminent domain

The right of the government to take private property for public use, with reasonable compensation awarded for the property

The first modern case confronting the issue of public use involved a mom-and-pop grocery store in a rundown neighborhood on the southwest side of the District of Columbia. In carrying out a vast urban-redevelopment program in the 1950s, the city government of Washington, D.C., took the property as one of a large number of privately owned lots to be cleared for new housing and business construction. The owner of the grocery store and his successors, after his death, took the government to court on the grounds that taking property from one private owner and eventually turning that property back, in altered form, to another private owner was an unconstitutional use of eminent domain. The store owners lost their case. The Supreme Court's argument was a curious but very important one: The "public interest" can mean virtually anything a legislature says it means. In other words, since the overall slum clearance and redevelopment project was in the public interest, according to the legislature, the eventual transfers of property that were going to take place were justified.[94] In 1984 and again in 2005 the Supreme Court reaffirmed that decision.[95]

92 *Dickerson v. United States*, 530 U.S. 428 (2000).

93 *Berghuis v. Thomkins*, 560 U.S. ___ (2010).

94 *Berman v. Parker*, 348 U.S. 26 (1954). For a thorough analysis of the case, see Benjamin Ginsberg, "*Berman v. Parker*: Congress, the Court, and the Public Purpose," *Polity* 4 (1971): 48–75.

95 *Hawaii Housing Authority v. Midkiff*, 469 U.S. 2321 (1984) and *Kelo v. City of New London*, 545 U.S. (2005).

The Sixth Amendment and the Right to Counsel

> In all criminal prosecutions, the accused shall enjoy the right to a speedy and public trial, by an impartial jury of the State and district wherein the crime shall have been committed, which district shall have been previously ascertained by law, and to be informed of the nature and cause of the accusation; to be confronted with the witnesses against him; to have compulsory process for obtaining witnesses in his favor, and to have the Assistance of Counsel for his defense.

Like the exclusionary rule of the Fourth Amendment and the self-incrimination clause of the Fifth Amendment, the "right to counsel" provision of the Sixth Amendment is notable for freeing defendants who seem to the public to be patently guilty as charged. Other provisions of the Sixth Amendment, such as the right to a speedy trial and the right to confront witnesses before an impartial jury, are less controversial in nature.

Gideon v. Wainwright is the perfect case study because it involved a disreputable person who seemed patently guilty of the crime for which he was convicted. In and out of jails for most of his 51 years, Clarence Earl Gideon received a five-year sentence for breaking into and entering a poolroom in Panama City, Florida. While serving time in jail, Gideon became a fairly well qualified "jailhouse lawyer," made his own appeal on a handwritten petition, and eventually won the landmark ruling on the right to counsel in all felony cases.[96] *Gideon* was decided in 1963, and the following year, in *Escobedo v. Illinois*, the Supreme Court ruled that suspects had a right to counsel during police interrogations, not just when their cases reached trial.[97]

The right to counsel has been expanded during the past few decades. For example, although at first the right to counsel was met by judges' assigning lawyers from the community as a formal public obligation, most states and cities have now created an office of public defender whose state-employed professional defense lawyers typically provide poor defendants with much better legal representation. And although these defendants cannot choose their private defense attorneys, they do have the right to appeal a conviction on the grounds that the counsel provided by the state was deficient. For example, in 2003 the Supreme Court overturned the death sentence of a Maryland death-row inmate, holding that the defense lawyer had failed to fully inform the jury of the defendant's history of "horrendous childhood abuse."[98] Moreover, the right to counsel extends beyond serious crimes to any trial, with or without a jury, that holds the possibility of imprisonment.[99]

---

96 For a full account of the story of the trial and release of Clarence Earl Gideon, see Lewis, *Gideon's Trumpet*.

97 *Escobedo v. Illinois*, 378 U.S. 478 (1964).

98 *Wiggins v. Smith*, 539 U.S. 510 (2003).

99 For further discussion of these issues, see Corwin and Peltason, *Understanding the Constitution*, pp. 319–23.

The Eighth Amendment and Cruel and Unusual Punishment

The Eighth Amendment prohibits "excessive bail," "excessive fines," and "cruel and unusual punishment." Virtually all the debate over Eighth Amendment issues focuses on the last clause of the amendment: the protection from "cruel and unusual punishment." One of the greatest challenges in interpreting this provision consistently is that what is considered "cruel and unusual" varies from culture to culture and from generation to generation. And unfortunately, it also varies by class and race.

By far the biggest issue in the inconsistency of class and race as constituting cruel and unusual punishment arises over the death penalty. In 1972, the Supreme Court overturned several state death-penalty laws not because they were cruel and unusual but because they were being applied in a capricious manner.[100] Very soon after that decision, a majority of states revised their capital-punishment provisions to provide clear standards.[101] Since 1976, the Court has consistently upheld state laws providing for capital punishment, although it also continues to review numerous death penalty appeals each year.

Between 1976 and 2009, states executed 1,161 people. Most of those executions occurred in southern states, with Texas leading the way at 430. As of 2002, 38 states had adopted some form of capital punishment, a move approved of by about three-quarters of all Americans. (See the Analyzing the Evidence section on the following page.)

Although virtually all criminal conduct is regulated by the states, Congress has also jumped on the bandwagon, imposing capital punishment for more than 50 federal crimes. Despite the seeming popularity of the death penalty, the debate has become, if anything, more intense. In 1997, for example, the American Bar Association passed a resolution calling for a halt to the death penalty until concerns about its fairness—that is, whether its application violates the principle of equality—and concerns about ensuring due process are addressed. In 2000, the governor of Illinois imposed a moratorium on the death penalty and created a commission to review the capital punishment system. After a two-year study by the commission, Illinois adopted a number of reforms, including a ban on executions of the mentally retarded. In June 2002, the Supreme Court banned all executions of mentally retarded defendants, a decision that could move 200 or more people off death row. In 2008, the Court issued a number of death penalty opinions, declaring that death was too harsh a penalty for a child rapist[102] and invalidating a death sentence for a black defendant where the prosecutor had improperly excluded African Americans from the jury.[103] In

100 *Furman v. Georgia,* 408 U.S. 238 (1972).

101 *Gregg v. Georgia,* 428 U.S. 153 (1976).

102 *Kennedy v. Louisiana,* 554 U.S. 407 (2008).

103 *Snyder v. Louisiana,* 552 U.S. 472 (2008).

ANALYZING THE EVIDENCE

Evaluating the Death Penalty

CHAPTER | 04

Contributed by
Joseph Ura
Texas A&M University

Statistical analysis of the relationship between the availability of the death penalty as a punishment and murder rates produces mixed evidence of the deterrent effect of the death penalty. In general, analysis of national crime data indicates that there is a negative relationship between the use of the death penalty and the murder rate over the last half-century. That is, as the number of executions goes up or down, the rate of murders nationwide moves in the opposite direction. In contrast, analysis that compares murder rates in states with the death penalty to states without it often finds that states that continue to utilize the death penalty have crime rates that are comparable to states that do not utilize the death penalty.

Evaluating the effectiveness of the death-penalty deterrent presents substantial challenges for social science. The association between the use of the death penalty and crime rates over time is complicated by the close association between the number of executions and other law enforcement and penal policy changes. For example, increasing numbers of executions during the 1980s and 1990s were part of a larger trend of sending greater numbers of convicted criminals to prison for longer periods of time. Likewise, it is difficult to simply compare crime rates in death-penalty states and non-death-penalty states, since the comparisons are complicated by economic, social, and demographic differences among states,which are associated with variance in state crime rates.

Executions and the Murder Rate

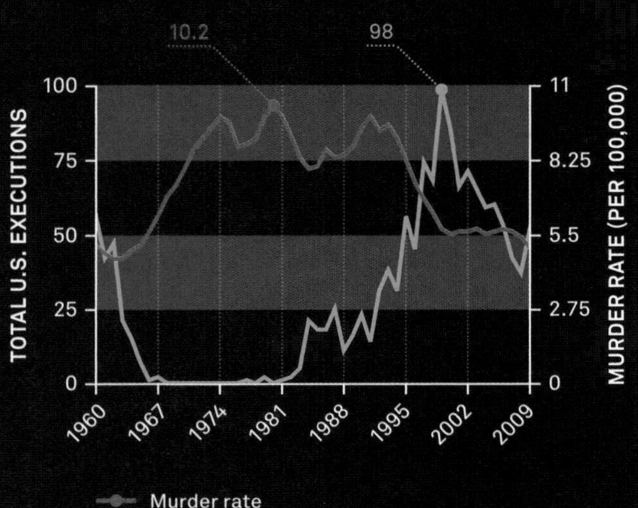

Over time, there is a reasonably strong negative relationship between the annual number of executions and the murder rate (-0.59 for the years 1960–2009). Murder rates in the United States began to rise dramatically around 1967 and remained substantially above rates observed in the early 1960s until the mid-1990s. The sharp rise in violent crime and its later decline correspond to periods of declining and then increasing use of the death penalty. This aggregate correlation supports claims that the use of the death penalty deters potential murders.

SOURCE: Bureau of Justice Statistics, *FBI Uniform Crime Report.*

ncarceration and the Murder Rate

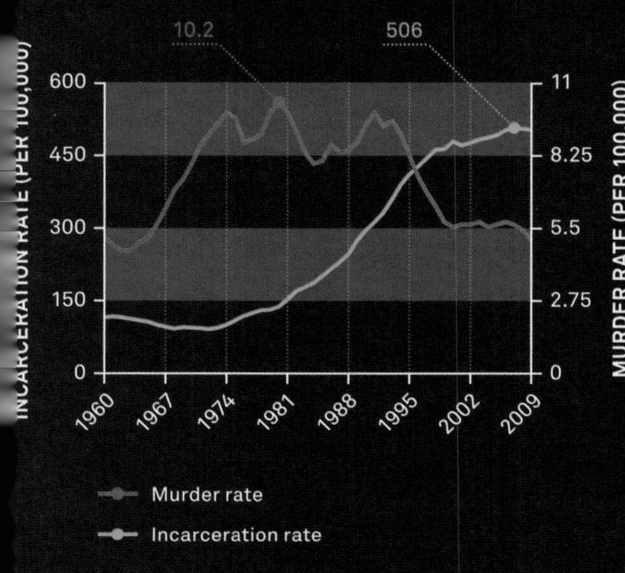

The increased use of the death penalty in the United States during the 1990s was part of a larger trend of increased utilization of the criminal justice system. The rate of incarceration in the United States grew steadily through the 1980s before jumping dramatically over the 1990s. The growth of the penal population in the United States was also coincident with other policy changes designed to reduce crime, including a dramatic increase in the number of police officers, and changes in the American criminal landscape, such as stabilization of the market for illegal drugs. It is therefore difficult to pinpoint the effects of a single causal force out of several reinforcing developments that occur at more or less the same time.

SOURCE: Sourcebook of Criminal Justice Statistics, www.albany.edu/sourcebook (accessed 10/31/11).

Executions and the Murder Rate per State, 2009

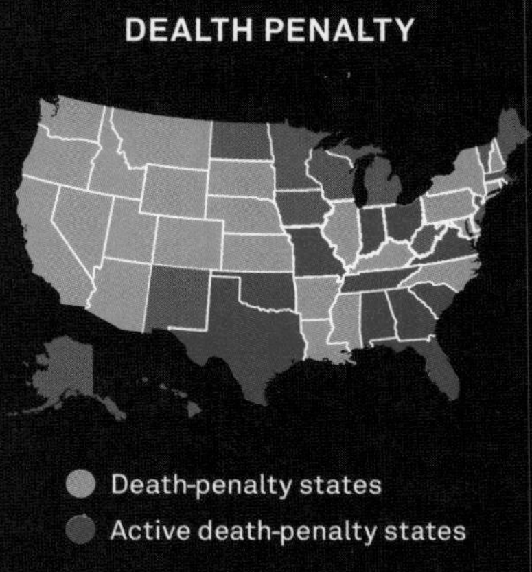

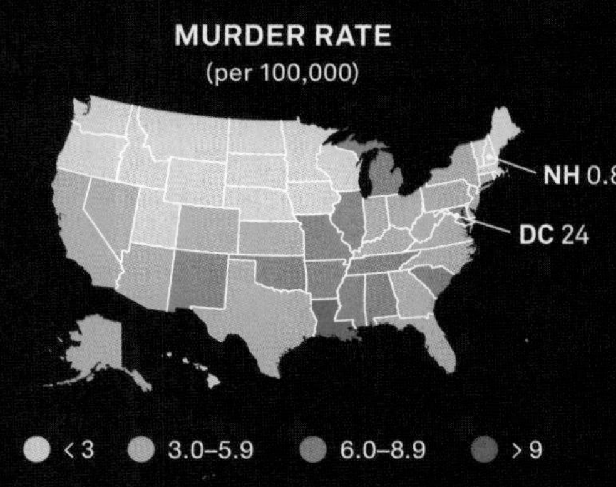

Across states, the relationship between the use of the death penalty and murder rates provides little evidence of a deterrent effect. In 2009, the murder rate in the 14 states that had abolished the death penalty completely was 4.5. Among the death-penalty states, the murder rate averaged 4.7. And, in the 11 states that conducted at least one execution, the murder rate averaged 5.8. The 2009 data pattern is typical, which challenges the idea that criminals are deterred from committing murder by the availability of the death penalty.

EXPLORE **THE DEATH PENALTY** FURTHER AT: **wwnorton.com/studyspace**

SOURCE: Bureau of Justice Statistics, *FBI Uniform Crime Report*

a decision which received worldwide attention, the Court ruled that the International Court of Justice had no authority to order a Texas court to reopen a death penalty case involving a foreign national.[104]

Many death penalty supporters praise its deterrent effects on other would-be criminals. Although studies of capital crimes usually fail to demonstrate any direct deterrent effect, the punishment's failure to act as a deterrent may be due to the lengthy delays—typically years and even decades—between convictions and executions. A system that eliminates undue delays would surely enhance deterrence. And deterring even one murder or other heinous crime, proponents argue, is more than ample justification for such laws. Beyond that argument, the death penalty is seen as a proper expression of retribution, echoed in the biblical phrase "an eye for an eye." People who commit vicious crimes deserve to forfeit their lives in exchange for the suffering they have inflicted. If the world applauded the execution of Nazis after World War II, for example, how could it deny the right of society to execute a serial killer?

Constitutional objections to the death penalty often invoke the Eighth Amendment's protection against punishments that are "cruel and unusual." Yet the death penalty can hardly be considered a violation of this protection, say supporters, since it was commonly used in the eighteenth century and was supported by most early American leaders. And although the poor, men, blacks, and Latinos are more likely than others to find themselves sitting on death row, this fact reflects the painful reality that these categories of individuals are more likely to commit crimes.

Death penalty opponents are quick to point out that the death penalty has not been proved to deter crime, either in the United States or abroad. In fact, America is the only Western nation that still executes criminals. The fact that American states execute criminals debases rather than elevates society by extolling vengeance. If the government is to serve as an example of proper behavior, say foes, it has no business sanctioning killing when incarceration will similarly protect society. As for the Constitution, most of the Founders surely supported the death penalty. But, foes note, they also countenanced slavery and lived at a time when society was both less informed about, and more indifferent to, the human condition. Modern Americans' greater civility should be reflected in how the society defines individual rights.

Furthermore, according to death penalty foes, execution is expensive—more expensive than life imprisonment—precisely because the government must make every effort to ensure that it is not executing an innocent person. Curtailing legal appeals would make the possibility of a mistake too great. And although most Americans do support the death penalty, people also support life without the possibility of parole as an alternative. Race also intrudes in death penalty cases: people of color (who are more likely to face economic deprivation) are

104 *Medellin v. Texas,* 552 U.S. 491 (2005).

disproportionately more likely to be sentenced to death, whereas whites charged with identical crimes are less likely to be given the ultimate punishment. Finally, according to opponents, a life sentence may be a worse punishment than the death penalty.

The Right to Privacy

Some of the people all of the time and all of the people some of the time would just like to be left alone, to have their own private domain into which no one—friends, family, government, church, or employer—has the right to enter without permission.

Many Jehovah's Witnesses felt that way in the 1930s. They risked serious punishment in 1940 by telling their children not to salute the flag or say the Pledge of Allegiance in school because of their understanding of the first commandment's prohibition of the worship of "graven images." As noted in our discussion of the free exercise of religion, they lost their appeal, the children were expelled, and the parents were punished. However, the Supreme Court later concluded that the 1940 decision had been "wrongly decided." These two cases arose under the freedom of religion provisions of the First Amendment, but they were also the first cases to confront the possibility of another right that is not mentioned anywhere in the Constitution or the Bill of Rights: the right to be left alone. When the Court began to take a more activist role in the mid-1950s and 1960s, the idea of a right to privacy was revived. In 1958, the Supreme Court recognized "privacy in one's association" in its decision to prevent the state of Alabama from using the membership list of the NAACP in the state's investigations. The Constitution does not specifically mention a right to privacy, but recall that the Ninth Amendment declares that the rights enumerated by the Constitution are not an exhaustive list.

right to privacy

The right to be let alone, which has been interpreted by the Supreme Court to entail free access to birth control and abortions

Birth Control. The sphere of privacy was drawn in earnest in 1965, when the Court ruled that a Connecticut statute forbidding the use of contraceptives violated the right of marital privacy. Estelle Griswold, the executive director of the Planned Parenthood League of Connecticut, was arrested by the state of Connecticut for providing information, instruction, and medical advice about contraception to married couples. She and her associates were found guilty as accessories to the crime and fined $100 each. The Supreme Court reversed the lower court's decisions and declared the Connecticut law unconstitutional because it violated "a right of privacy older than the Bill of Rights—older than our political parties, older than our school system." Justice William O. Douglas, author of the majority decision in the *Griswold* case, argued that this right of privacy is also grounded in the Constitution because it fits into a "zone of privacy" created by a combination of the Third, Fourth, and Fifth Amendments. A concurring opinion, written by Justice Arthur Goldberg, attempted to strengthen Douglas's argument by adding that "the concept of liberty . . . embraces the right of marital privacy though that right is not mentioned explicitly in the Constitution [and] is supported by numerous decisions of this Court . . . and *by the language and history of the Ninth Amendment*"[105] [emphasis added].

Abortion. The right to privacy was confirmed and extended in 1973 in the most important of all privacy decisions and one of the most important Supreme Court decisions in American history: *Roe v. Wade*. This decision established a woman's right to seek an abortion and prohibited states from making abortion a criminal act.[106] The Burger Court's decision in *Roe* took a revolutionary step toward establishing the right to privacy. It is important to emphasize that the preference for privacy rights and for their extension to include the rights of women to control their own bodies was not something invented by the Supreme Court in a vacuum. Most states did not regulate abortions in any fashion until the 1840s, at which time only 6 of the 26 states had any regulations governing abortion at all. In addition, many states had begun to ease their abortion restrictions well before the 1973 *Roe* decision, although in recent years a number of states have reinstated some restrictions on the procedure.

By extending the umbrella of privacy, this sweeping ruling dramatically changed abortion practices in America. In addition, it galvanized and nationalized the abortion debate. Groups opposed to abortion, such as the National Right to Life Committee, organized to fight the new liberal standard, while abortion rights groups sought to maintain that protection. In recent years, the legal standard shifted against abortion rights supporters in three key Supreme Court cases.

In *Webster v. Reproductive Health Services*, the Court narrowly upheld (by a 5–4 majority) the constitutionality of restrictions on the use of public medical facilities for abortion.[107] And in the 1992 case of *Planned Parenthood v. Casey*, another 5–4 majority of the Court upheld *Roe* but narrowed its scope, refusing to invalidate a Pennsylvania law that significantly limits freedom of choice. The Court's decision defined the right to an abortion as a "limited or qualified" right subject to regulation by the states as long as the regulation does not constitute an "undue burden."[108] More recently, the Court had another opportunity to rule on what constitutes an undue burden. In the 2000 case of *Stenberg v. Carhart*, the Court, by a vote of 5–4, struck down Nebraska's ban on partial-birth abortions

105 *Griswold v. Connecticut*, 381 U.S. 479 (1965) and *Griswold v. Connecticut*, concurring opinion. In 1972, in *Eisenstadt v. Baird*, 405 U.S. 438 (1972), the Court extended the privacy right to unmarried women.

106 *Roe v. Wade*, 410 U.S. 113 (1973).

107 *Webster v. Reproductive Health Services*, 492 U.S. 490 (1989), which upheld a Missouri law that restricted the use of public medical facilities for abortion. The decision opened the way for other states to limit the availability of abortion.

108 *Planned Parenthood v. Casey*, 505 U.S. 833 (1992).

because the law had the "effect of placing a substantial obstacle in the path of a woman seeking an abortion."[109]

Homosexuality. In the last two decades, the right to be left alone began to include the privacy rights of gays. One morning in Atlanta in the mid-1980s, Michael Hardwick was arrested by a police officer who discovered him in bed with another man. The officer had come to serve a warrant for Hardwick's arrest for failure to appear in court to answer charges of drinking in public. One of Hardwick's unknowing housemates invited the officer to look in Hardwick's room, where he found Hardwick and another man engaging in "consensual sexual behavior." Hardwick was then arrested under Georgia's laws against heterosexual and homosexual sodomy. Hardwick filed a lawsuit against the state, challenging the constitutionality of the Georgia law, and won his case in the federal court of appeals. The state of Georgia, in an unusual move, appealed the court's decision to the Supreme Court. The majority of the Court reversed the lower-court decision, holding against Hardwick on the grounds that "the federal Constitution confers [no] fundamental right upon homosexuals to engage in sodomy" and that there was therefore no basis to invalidate "the laws of the many states that still make such conduct illegal and have done so for a very long time."[110]

Seventeen years later, and to most everyone's surprise, the Court overturned *Bowers v. Hardwick* with a dramatic pronouncement that gays are "entitled to respect for their private lives" as a matter of constitutional due process. With *Lawrence v. Texas*, state legislatures no longer had the authority to make private sexual behavior a crime.[111] Drawing from the tradition of negative liberty, the Court maintained, "In our tradition the State is not omnipresent in the home. And there are other spheres of our lives and existence outside the home, where the State should not be a dominant presence." Explicitly encompassing lesbians and gay men within the umbrella of privacy, the Court concluded that the "petitioners are entitled to respect for their private lives. The State cannot demean their existence or control their destiny by making their private sexual conduct a crime." This decision added substance to the Ninth Amendment "right of privacy."

The Right to Die. Another area ripe for further litigation and public discourse is the so-called right to die. A number of highly publicized physician-assisted suicides in the 1990s focused attention on whether people have a right to choose their own death and receive assistance in carrying it out. Can this become part of the privacy right, or is it a new substantive right? In the 2006 case of

---

109 *Stenberg v. Carhart,* 530 U.S. 914 (2000).

110 *Bowers v. Hardwick,* 478 U.S. 186 (1986).

111 *Lawrence and Garner v. Texas,* 539 U.S. 558 (2003).

Gonzales v. Oregon, the Supreme Court upheld an Oregon law that allowed doctors to use drugs to facilitate the deaths of terminally ill patients who requested such assistance.[112] This decision is not a definitive ruling on the right-to-die question, but it does suggest that the Court is not hostile to the idea.

Civil Liberties and the History Principle

Constitutional guarantees of civil rights and civil liberties often seem clear in the abstract, but they inevitably produce thousands of complex questions and controversies every year when they are applied to concrete cases. Every government agency, for example, is constitutionally required to respect Americans' civil liberties. The government, though, is also obligated to protect the public's health and safety. This duty is sometimes called the "police power" and is exercised by the federal government and the governments of the states. Suppose that Congress enacts a law allowing national security agencies to sift through millions of phone calls searching for evidence of terrorist plots. Is such a law an unjustified intrusion on civil liberties or a necessary and legitimate effort to prevent bloodshed? In 2008, the Supreme Court declined to hear a case brought by a civil liberties group that wanted to halt a large-scale federal wiretapping program aimed at identifying possible terrorist communications. This action let stand a lower-court ruling that had allowed the program to continue. As this example suggests, the precise character of constitutional limitations on collective action is always open to debate however much we may agree on the basic principles.

For Further Reading

Ackerman, Bruce. *Before the Next Attack: Preserving Civil Liberties in an Age of Terrorism.* New Haven, CT: Yale University Press, 2006.

reader selection

District of Columbia v. Heller, 554 U.S. 570, 2008.

Dworkin, Ronald. *Justice in Robes.* Cambridge, MA: Belknap Press, 2006.

Gerstmann, Evan. *Same-Sex Marriage and the Constitution.* New York: Cambridge University Press, 2004.

Levy, Leonard W. *Freedom of Speech and Press in Early America: Legacy of Suppression.* New York: Harper & Row, 1963.

Lewis, Anthony. *Freedom for the Thought That We Hate: A Biography of the First Amendment.* New York: Basic Books, 2010.

112 *Gonzales v. Oregon*, 546 U.S. 243 (2006).

———. *Gideon's Trumpet.* New York: Random House, 1964.

O'Brien, David. *Constitutional Law and Politics: Civil Rights and Civil Liberties.* 8th ed. New York: Norton, 2011.

Posner, Richard. *Not a Suicide Pact: The Constitution in a Time of National Emergency.* New York: Oxford University Press, 2006.

Rosenberg, Gerald N. *The Hollow Hope: Can Courts Bring About Social Change?* Chicago: University of Chicago Press, 1991.

Visit **wwnorton.com/studyspace/** to access free review materials such as:

- ➔ Vocabulary Flashcards of All Key Terms
- ➔ Chapter Review Quizzes
- ➔ Complete Study Outlines

reader selection

Highlighted selections are included in *Readings in American Politics: Analysis and Perspectives*, Second Edition.

PART ☒ 2 3 4

FOUNDATIONS

Civil Rights

Chapter Outline

- The Struggle for Civil Rights

As we observed in Chapter 4, civil liberties limit collective action by restricting the government's jurisdiction. Civil rights, the topic of this chapter, regulate citizens' participation in and treatment by collective decision-making processes. In essence, civil rights are rules the government must follow with regard to the treatment of citizens when collective decisions are made and implemented.

In some nations, citizens have few if any civil rights. They have no right to vote or to be represented in decision making or to be judged by their peers if accused of a crime. They are often subject to arbitrary imprisonment and capricious punishment. Americans, on the other hand, began life as a nation with a number of civil rights guaranteed by their federal and state constitutions. State constitutions provided voting rights and the federal Constitution provided such rights as representation in Congress (Article I, Section 2) and the privilege of habeas corpus (Article I, Section 9).

Yet, America's early conception of civil rights was much narrower than it is today. The Founders' initial decision rules permitted widely disparate treatment of different categories of individuals, including women, members of minority racial and ethnic groups, and others. Women were denied the right to vote and hampered in other ways from taking part in collective political action. Members of minority ethnic groups faced many forms of legally sanctioned discrimination. Black people were, of course, held in slavery in a number of states and possessed virtually no political rights.

Prior to the Civil War, roughly 4 million African Americans were slaves in the southern states where they were the backbone of the agricultural economy of the region. Slavery was prohibited in most of the Northern states and the issue of whether or not slavery should be allowed in America's western territories bitterly divided the nation. In the 1857 case of *Dred Scott v. Sandford*, involving the fate of an escaped slave, the Supreme Court ruled that slaves were not citizens, could not bring suit in court, and were merely their masters' personal property. Moreover, said the Court, slavery could not be excluded from the territories.[1] This decision inflamed sectional divisions, infuriated antislavery groups in the North, and helped to provoke the Civil War. In the aftermath of the Civil War came the adoption of the Thirteenth, Fourteenth, and Fifteenth Amendments, which ended slavery and began the nation's long struggle to define and redefine civil rights.

With the adoption of the Fourteenth Amendment in 1868, civil rights became part of the Constitution, guaranteed to each citizen through "equal protection of the laws." These words launched a century of political movements and legal efforts to press for racial equality. African Americans' quest for civil rights in turn inspired many other groups—including members of other racial and ethnic groups, women, people with disabilities, and gay men and lesbians—to seek new laws and constitutional guarantees of their civil rights.

civil rights

The legal or moral claims that citizens are entitled to make on the government

Congress passed the Fourteenth Amendment, and the states ratified it in the aftermath of the Civil War. Together with the Thirteenth Amendment, which abolished slavery, and the Fifteenth Amendment, which guaranteed voting rights to black men, it seemed to provide a guarantee of civil rights for the newly freed enslaved blacks. But the general language of the Fourteenth Amendment meant that its support for civil rights could be far reaching. The very simplicity of the equal protection clause of the Fourteenth Amendment left it open to interpretation:

equal protection clause

The provision of the Fourteenth Amendment guaranteeing citizens "the equal protection of the laws." This clause has been the basis for the civil rights of African Americans, women, and other groups

> No State shall make or enforce any law which shall . . . deny to any person within its jurisdiction the equal protection of the laws. Under the Constitution today, no American may be excluded from participation or representation in collective decision-making processes or treated adversely by decision makers on account of such factors as race, gender, or ethnic background. However, as we see in this chapter, the enforcement of this guarantee was hard-won, and debates over the extent of the government's responsibility in ensuring equal protection persist.

CORE OF THE ANALYSIS

Civil rights are rules that govern collective decision-making processes and outcomes. They curb the power of majorities to exclude or harm individuals on the basis of factors such as race, gender, or ethnic background.

Today's conception of civil rights has been shaped by the historical development of these ideas and their interpretation by key political actors, especially the Supreme Court.

1 *Dred Scott v. Sandford*, 60 U.S. 393 (1857).

THE STRUGGLE FOR CIVIL RIGHTS

The Supreme Court was initially no more ready to enforce the civil rights aspects of the Fourteenth Amendment than it was to enforce the civil liberties provisions. The Court declared the Civil Rights Act of 1875 unconstitutional on the grounds that it sought to protect blacks from discrimination by *private* businesses, whereas the Fourteenth Amendment, according to the Court's interpretation, was intended to protect individuals from discrimination only in the case of actions by *public* officials of state and local governments.

Plessy v. Ferguson: "Separate but Equal"

In 1896, the Court went still further, in the infamous case of *Plessy v. Ferguson.* It upheld a Louisiana statute that *required* segregation of the races on trolleys and other public carriers (and, by implication, in all public facilities, including schools). Homer Plessy, a man defined as "one-eighth black," had violated a Louisiana law that provided for "equal but separate accommodations" on trains and a $25 fine for any white passenger who sat in a car reserved for blacks or any black passenger who sat in a car reserved for whites. The Supreme Court held that the Fourteenth Amendment's "equal protection of the laws" was not violated by racial distinction as long as the law applied to both races equally. People generally pretended they were treated equally as long as some accommodation existed. The Court said that although

> the object of the [Fourteenth] Amendment was undoubtedly to enforce the absolute equality of the two races before the law, . . . it could not have intended to abolish distinctions based on color, or to enforce social, as distinguished from political, equality, or a commingling of the two races upon terms unsatisfactory to either.[2]

What the Court was saying in effect was that the use of race as a criterion of exclusion in public matters was not unreasonable. This was the origin of the "separate but equal" rule, which was not reversed until 1954.

"separate but equal" rule

The doctrine that public accommodations could be segregated by race but still be equal

Racial Discrimination after World War II

The Supreme Court had begun to change its position on racial discrimination before World War II by defining more strictly the criterion of equal facilities in the "separate but equal" rule. In 1938, the Court rejected Missouri's policy of paying qualified blacks' tuition to out-of-state law schools rather than admitting them to the University of Missouri Law School.[3]

2 *Plessy v. Ferguson*, 163 U.S. 537 (1896).

3 *Missouri ex rel. Gaines v. Canada*, 305 U.S. 337 (1938).

After the war, modest progress resumed. In 1950, the Court rejected Texas's claim that its new "law school for Negroes" afforded education equal to that of the all-white University of Texas Law School; without confronting the "separate but equal" principle itself, the Court's decision anticipated *Brown v. Board of Education* by opening the question of whether any segregated facility could be truly equal.[4] The same was true in 1944, when the Supreme Court struck down the southern practice of "white primaries," which legally excluded blacks from participation in the process of nominating candidates. Here the Court simply recognized that primaries could no longer be regarded as the private affairs of the parties but were an integral aspect of the electoral process. This decision made parties "an agency of the State," and any practice of discrimination against blacks was therefore "state action within the meaning of the Fifteenth Amendment."[5] The most important pre-1954 decision was probably *Shelley v. Kraemer*,[6] in which the Court ruled against the widespread practice of "restrictive covenants," whereby the seller of a home added a clause to the sales contract requiring the buyers to agree not to sell their home to any nonwhite, non-Christian, and so on. The Court ruled that although private persons could sign such restrictive covenants, they could not be judicially enforced because the Fourteenth Amendment prohibits any organ of the state, including the courts, from denying equal protection of its laws.

However, none of these pre-1954 cases confronted head on the principle of "separate but equal" as such and its legal and constitutional support for racial discrimination. Each victory by the Legal Defense Fund of the NAACP was celebrated for itself and was seen, it was hoped, as a trend, but each was still a small victory, not a leading case. The massive effort by the southern states to resist direct desegregation and to prevent further legal actions against it by making a show of equalizing the quality of white and black schools convinced the NAACP that the Supreme Court was unready for a full confrontation with the constitutional principle sustaining segregation. But the continued unwillingness of Congress after 1948 to consider fair employment legislation seemed to convince the NAACP that the courts were its only hope. Thus by 1951, the NAACP had decided to attack the principle of segregation itself as unconstitutional and, in 1952, instituted cases in South Carolina, Virginia, Kansas, Delaware, and the District of Columbia. The strategy was to file suits simultaneously in different federal districts so that inconsistent results between any two states would more quickly lead to Supreme Court acceptance of at least one appeal.[7] Of these suits, the Kansas case became the

4 *Sweatt v. Painter, 339 U.S. 629 (1950).*

5 *Smith v. Allwright*, 321 U.S. 649 (1944).

6 *Shelley v. Kraemer*, 334 U.S. 1 (1948).

7 The best reviews of strategies, tactics, and goals is found in John Hope Franklin, *From Slavery to Freedom: A History of Negro Americans*, 4th ed. (New York: Knopf, 1974), chap. 22; and Richard Kluger, *Simple Justice: The History of* Brown v. Board of Education *and Black America's Struggle for Equality* (New York: Vintage, 1977), chaps. 21 and 22.

chosen one. It seemed to be ahead of the pack in its district court, and it had the special advantage of being located in a state outside the Deep South.[8]

Oliver Brown, the father of three girls, lived "across the tracks" in a low-income, racially mixed Topeka neighborhood. Every school-day morning, Linda Brown took a school bus to the Monroe School for black children, about a mile away. In September 1950, Oliver Brown took Linda to the all-white Sumner School, which was closer to home, to enter her in the third grade, in defiance of state law and local segregation rules. When they were refused, Brown took his case to the NAACP, and soon thereafter *Brown v. Board of Education* was born. In mid-1953, the Court announced that the several cases on their way up would be reargued within the context of a set of questions having to do with the intent of the Fourteenth Amendment. Almost exactly a year later, the Court responded to those questions in one of the most important decisions in its history.

In deciding the case, the Court, to the surprise of many, basically rejected as inconclusive all the learned arguments about the intent and the history of the Fourteenth Amendment and committed itself to considering only the consequences of segregation:

> Does segregation of children in public schools solely on the basis of race, even though the physical facilities and other "tangible" factors may be equal, deprive the children of the minority group of equal educational opportunities? We believe that it does. . . . We conclude that, in the field of public education, the doctrine of "separate but equal" has no place. Separate educational facilities are inherently unequal.[9]

The *Brown* decision altered the constitutional framework in two fundamental respects. First, after *Brown*, the states would no longer have the power to use race as a criterion of discrimination in law. Second, the national government would from then on have the constitutional basis for extending its power (hitherto in doubt, as we saw earlier) to intervene with strict regulatory policies against the discriminatory actions of state or local governments, school boards, employers, and many others in the private sector.

Civil Rights after *Brown v. Board of Education*

Although *Brown v. Board of Education* withdrew all constitutional authority to use race as a criterion of exclusion, this historic decision was merely a small opening move. First, most states refused to cooperate until sued, and many ingenious

---

8 The District of Columbia case came up too, but because the District of Columbia is not a state, the case did not directly involve the Fourteenth Amendment and its equal protection clause. It confronted the Court on the same grounds, however: that segregation is inherently unequal. Its victory in effect was incorporation in reverse, with equal protection moving from the Fourteenth Amendment to become part of the Bill of Rights. See *Bolling v. Sharpe*, 347 U.S. 497 (1954).

9 *Brown v. Board of Education*, 347 U.S. 483 (1954).

schemes were employed to delay obedience (such as paying the tuition of white students to attend newly created "private" academies). Second, even as southern school boards began to cooperate by eliminating their legally enforced (de jure) segregation, extensive actual (de facto) school segregation remained in the North and the South as a consequence of racially segregated housing, which could not be affected by the 1954 *Brown* principles. Third, discrimination in employment, public accommodations, juries, voting, and other areas of social and economic activity was not directly touched by *Brown*.

de jure segregation

Racial segregation that is a direct result of law or official policy

de facto segregation

Racial segregation that is not a direct result of law or government policy but is, instead, a reflection of residential patterns, income distributions, or other social factors

A decade of frustration following *Brown* made it fairly obvious that adjudication alone would not succeed. The goal of equal protection required positive, or affirmative, action by Congress and administrative agencies. And given massive southern resistance and generally negative national public opinion toward racial integration, progress would not be made through courts, Congress, or agencies without intense, well-organized support. The number of peaceful civil rights demonstrations for voting rights and public accommodations increased greatly during the first 14 years following *Brown*.[10]

Organized civil rights demonstrations began to mount slowly but surely after *Brown v. Board of Education*. By the 1960s, the many organizations that made up the civil rights movement had accumulated experience and built networks capable of launching massive direct-action campaigns against southern segregationists. The Southern Christian Leadership Conference, the Student Nonviolent Coordinating Committee, and many other organizations had built a movement that stretched across the South. That movement used the media to attract nationwide attention and support. In the massive March on Washington in 1963, the Reverend Martin Luther King, Jr., staked out the movement's moral claims in his "I Have a Dream" speech. Also in the 1960s, images of protesters being beaten, attacked by police dogs, and set on with fire hoses did much to win broad sympathy for the cause of black civil rights and discredit state and local governments in the South. In this way, the movement created intense pressure for a reluctant federal government to take more assertive steps to defend black civil rights.

Why Fight for Civil Rights? Collective Action and Selective Benefits. One of the tenets of our five principles of politics from Chapter 1 is that individuals have little incentive to participate in mass-action politics. After all, what possible difference could one person make by taking part in a civil rights protest? Participation is costly in terms of time, and in the case of civil rights marchers even one's health or life was endangered. The risks outweighed the potential benefits, yet hundreds of thousands of people *did* participate. Why?

Even though little scholarly attention has been paid by those who apply this perspective to the civil rights movements,[11] a general answer is available. Most

10 Jonathan D. Casper, *The Politics of Civil Liberties* (New York: Harper & Row, 1972), p. 90.

11 One notable exception is Dennis Chong, *Collective Action and the Civil Rights Movement* (Chicago: University of Chicago Press, 1991).

TIME LINE

CAUSE AND EFFECT IN THE CIVIL RIGHTS MOVEMENT

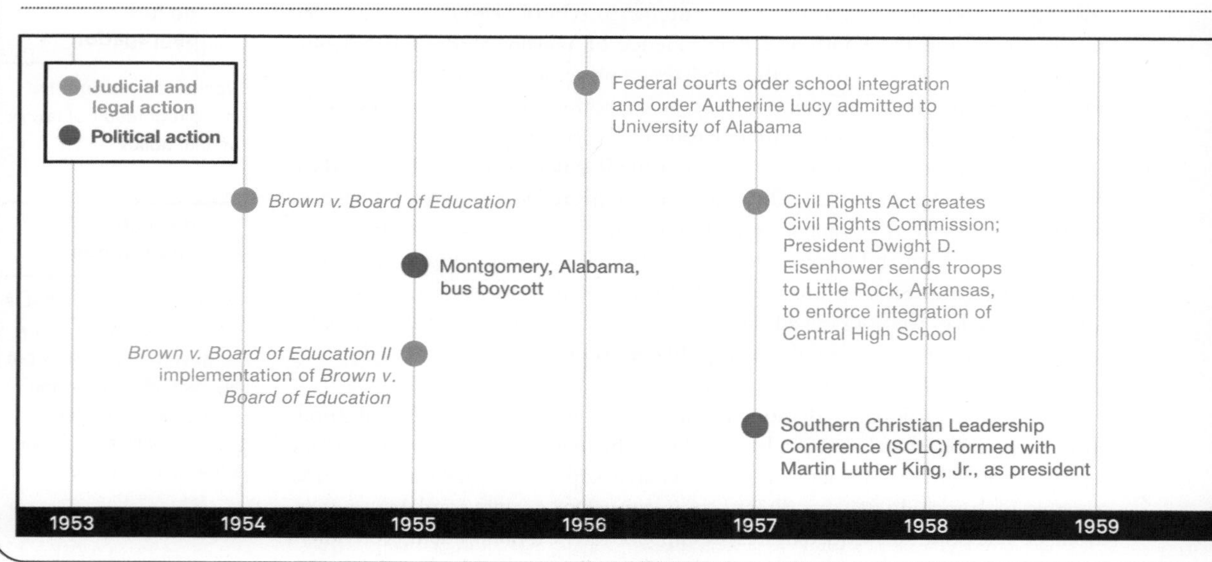

Judicial and legal action
Political action
Federal courts order school integration and order Autherine Lucy admitted to University of Alabama
Brown v. Board of Education
Civil Rights Act creates Civil Rights Commission; President Dwight D. Eisenhower sends troops to Little Rock, Arkansas, to enforce integration of Central High School
Montgomery, Alabama, bus boycott
Brown v. Board of Education II implementation of Brown v. Board of Education
Southern Christian Leadership Conference (SCLC) formed with Martin Luther King, Jr., as president
1953
1954
1955
1956
1957
1958
1959

rational analysis takes behavior to be *instrumental*—motivated by and directed toward some purpose or objective. But behavior may also be *experiential.* People do things, on this account, because they like doing them—they feel good inside, they feel free of guilt, they take pleasure in the activity for its own sake. We maintain that this second view of behavior is entirely compatible with rational accounts. Instrumental behavior may be thought of as *investment activity*, whereas experiential behavior may be thought of as *consumption activity*. With the latter, it is the behavior itself that generates utility, rather than the consequences produced by the behavior. To take a specific illustration of collective action, many people certainly attended the 1963 March on Washington because they cared about civil rights. But it is unlikely that many deluded themselves into thinking their individual participation made a large difference to the fate of the civil rights legislation they supported through the march. Rather, they attended because they wanted to be part of a social movement, hear Martin Luther King, Jr., speak, and identify with the hundreds of thousands of others who felt the same way. Also—and this should not be minimized—many participated because they anticipated that the march would be fun, an adventure of sorts.

So experiential behavior is consumption-oriented activity predicated on the belief that the activity in question is fulfilling, apart from its consequences. Individuals are bound to be animated both by the consumption value of a particular behavior and by its instrumental value, the rational (investment) explanation that we have used throughout this book. To insist on only one of these complementary forms of rationality while excluding the other is to provide but a partial explanation.

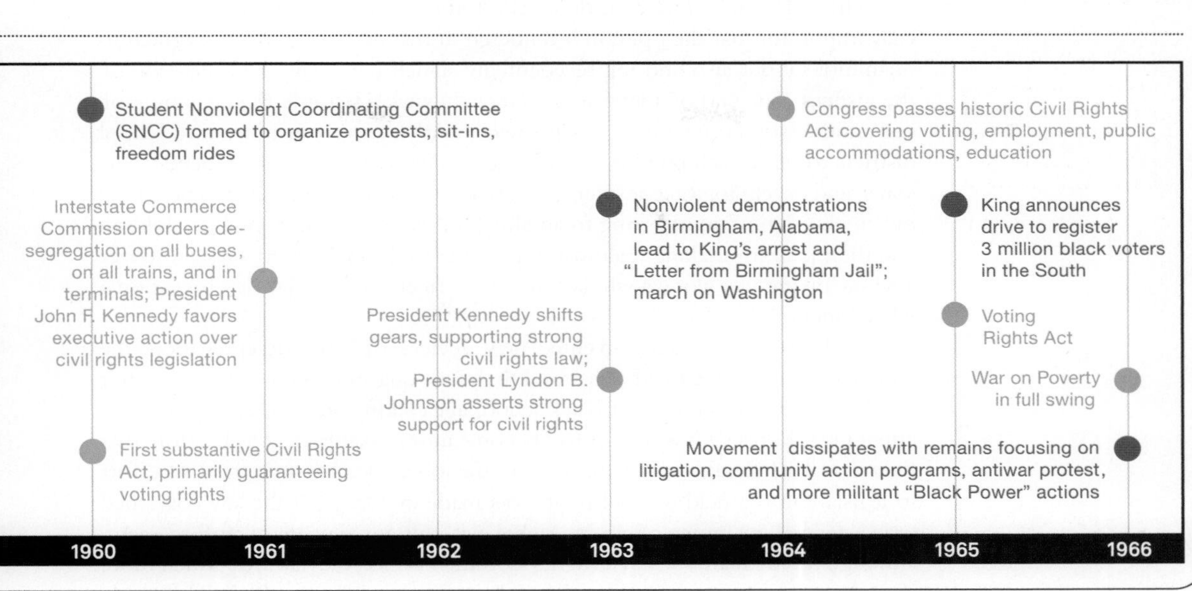
Student Nonviolent Coordinating Committee (SNCC) formed to organize protests, sit-ins, freedom rides
Interstate Commerce Commission orders desegregation on all buses, on all trains, and in terminals; President John F. Kennedy favors executive action over civil rights legislation
First substantive Civil Rights Act, primarily guaranteeing voting rights
President Kennedy shifts gears, supporting strong civil rights law; President Lyndon B. Johnson asserts strong support for civil rights
Nonviolent demonstrations in Birmingham, Alabama, lead to King's arrest and "Letter from Birmingham Jail"; march on Washington
Congress passes historic Civil Rights Act covering voting, employment, public accommodations, education
King announces drive to register 3 million black voters in the South
Voting Rights Act
War on Poverty in full swing
Movement dissipates with remains focusing on litigation, community action programs, antiwar protest, and more militant "Black Power" actions
1960
1961
1962
1963
1964
1965
1966

School Desegregation, Phase One. Although the District of Columbia and some of the school districts in the border states began to respond almost immediately to court-ordered desegregation, the states of the Deep South responded with a carefully planned delaying tactic known as *massive resistance.* Southern politicians stood shoulder to shoulder to declare that the Supreme Court's decisions and orders were without effect. The legislatures in these states enacted statutes ordering school districts to maintain segregated schools and state superintendents to terminate state funding wherever there was racial mixing in the classroom. Some southern states violated their own long traditions of local school autonomy by centralizing public school authority under the governor or the state board of education and giving states the power to close schools and provide alternative private schooling wherever local school boards might be tending to obey the Supreme Court.

Most of these plans of massive resistance were tested in the federal courts and struck down as unconstitutional.[12] But southern resistance was not confined to legislation. In 1957, for example, Governor Orval Faubus mobilized the Arkansas National Guard to intercede against enforcement of a federal court

12 The two most important cases were *Cooper v. Aaron,* 358 U.S. 1 (1958), which required Little Rock, Arkansas, to desegregate, and *Griffin v. Prince Edward County School Board,* 377 U.S. 218 (1964), which forced all the schools of that Virginia county to reopen after they had been closed for five years to avoid desegregation.

order to integrate Little Rock's Central High School, and President Dwight D. Eisenhower was forced to deploy U.S. troops and place the city under martial law. The Supreme Court considered the Little Rock confrontation so historically important that the opinion it rendered in that case not only was agreed to unanimously but also and unprecedentedly signed personally by every one of the justices. The end of massive resistance, however, became the beginning of still another southern strategy, "pupil placement" laws, which authorized school districts to place each pupil in a school according to a variety of academic, personal, and psychological considerations, never mentioning race at all. These laws put the burden of transferring to an all-white school on the nonwhite children and their parents, making it almost impossible for a single court order to cover a whole district, let alone a whole state. The effect was to delay desegregation a while longer.[13]

As the southern states invented new devices to avoid desegregation, the federal courts followed with cases and decisions quashing them. Ten years after *Brown,* fewer than 1 percent of black school-age children in the Deep South were attending schools with whites. It had become unmistakably clear well before that time that the federal courts could not do the job alone. The first modern effort to legislate in the field of civil rights was made in 1957, but the law contained only a federal guarantee of voting rights, without any powers of enforcement, although it did create the Civil Rights Commission to study abuses. Much more important legislation for civil rights followed, especially the Civil Rights Act of 1964. It is important to observe here the mutual dependence of the courts and the legislatures—not only do the legislatures need constitutional authority to act, but the courts also need legislative and political assistance, through the power of the purse, the power to organize administrative agencies to implement court orders, and the ability to focus political support. Consequently, even as Congress finally moved into the field of school desegregation (and other areas of equal protection), the courts continued to exercise their powers, not only by issuing court orders against recalcitrant school districts but also by extending and reinterpreting aspects of the equal protection clause to support legislative and administrative actions.

School Desegregation: Busing and Beyond. The most important judicial extension of civil rights in education after 1954 was probably the *Swann* decision of 1971, which held that state-imposed desegregation could be brought about by busing children across school districts even where relatively long distances were involved. But the decision went beyond that, adding that under certain limited circumstances even racial quotas could be used as the "starting point in shaping a remedy to correct past constitutional violations" and that the

13 *Shuttlesworth v. Birmingham Board of Education,* 358 U.S. 101 (1958), upheld a pupil placement plan purporting to assign pupils on various bases, with no mention of race. This case interpreted *Brown* to mean that school districts must stop explicit racial discrimination but were under no obligation to take positive steps to desegregate. For a while, black parents were doomed to case-by-case approaches.

Figure 5.1

THE PERCENTAGE OF SOUTHERN BLACK SCHOOLCHILDREN ATTENDING SCHOOL WITH WHITES, 1955–73

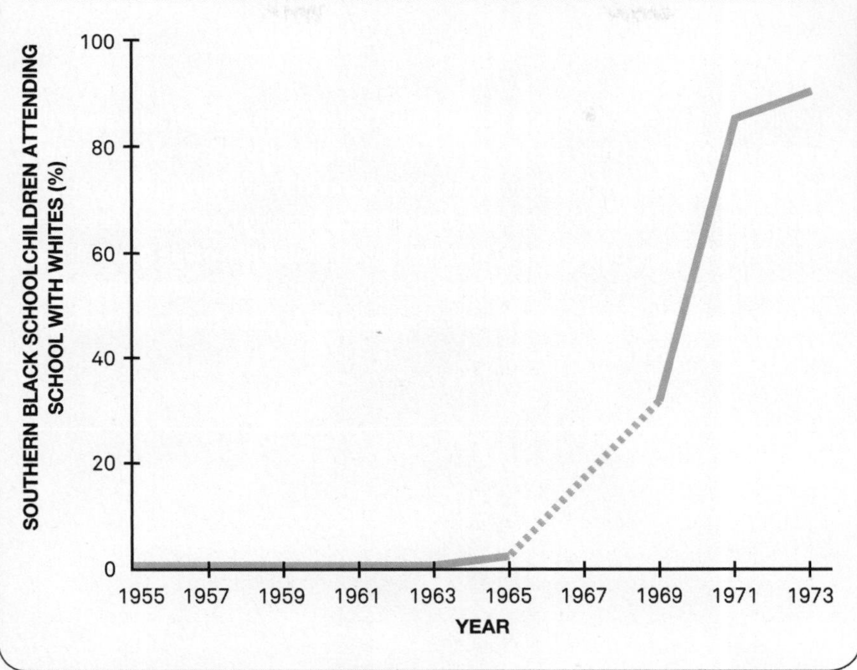

ANALYZING THE EVIDENCE

What happened in 1964 that accounts for the upward trend beginning in 1965?

NOTE: Dashed line indicates missing data.
SOURCE: Gerald N. Rosenberg, *The Hollow Hope: Can Courts Bring About Social Change?* (Chicago: University of Chicago Press, 1991), pp. 50–51.

pairing or grouping of schools and the reorganizing of school attendance zones would also be acceptable (Figure 5.1).[14]

Three years later, however, the *Swann* case was severely restricted when the Supreme Court determined that only cities found guilty of deliberate and de jure racial segregation (segregation in law) would have to desegregate their schools. This decision was handed down in the 1974 case of *Milliken v. Bradley*, involving the city of Detroit and its suburbs.[15] The *Milliken* ruling had the effect of exempting most northern states and cities from busing because school segregation in northern cities is generally de facto (segregation in fact), resulting from segregated housing and thousands of acts of private discrimination against blacks and other minorities.

14 *Swann v. Charlotte-Mecklenburg Board of Education*, 402 U.S. 1 (1971).

15 *Milliken v. Bradley*, 418 U.S. 717 (1974).

ANALYZING THE EVIDENCE

Racial Equality

As we discuss in this chapter, civil rights is a major political issue in the United States. Especially since the 1960s, most forms of racial discrimination have been prohibited by law, and a large number of government programs have been designed to promote greater political, social, and economic equality between black and white Americans. Despite these efforts, progress in the direction of racial equality has been uneven. As we see in the following figures and tables, some data suggest that the United States has made great strides toward the color-blind society envisioned by the early leaders of the civil rights movement. Other data, though, indicate that we have a long way to go. The fact that America's president is black does not mean that complete racial equality has been achieved in the United States.

High School Graduation Rates

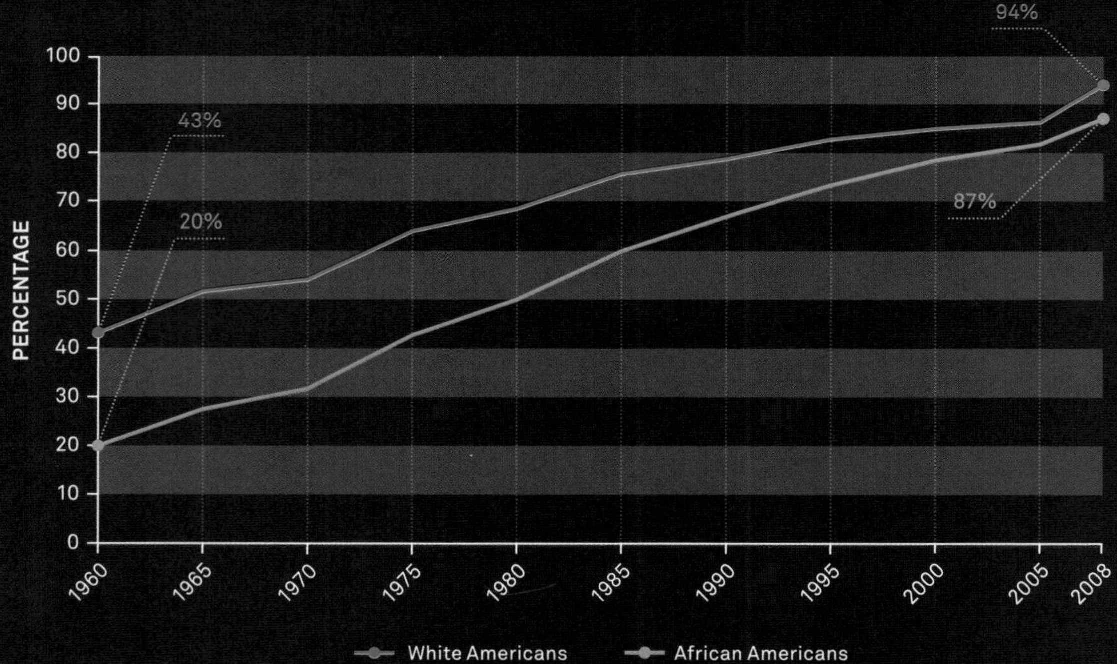

One encouraging statistic is the change over the past 45 years in black versus white levels of educational attainment. In 1960, black Americans were less than half as likely to finish high school or graduate from college as whites. Today, the percentage of blacks graduating from high school is nearly identical to the percentage of whites who earn diplomas.

African Americans Elected to Office

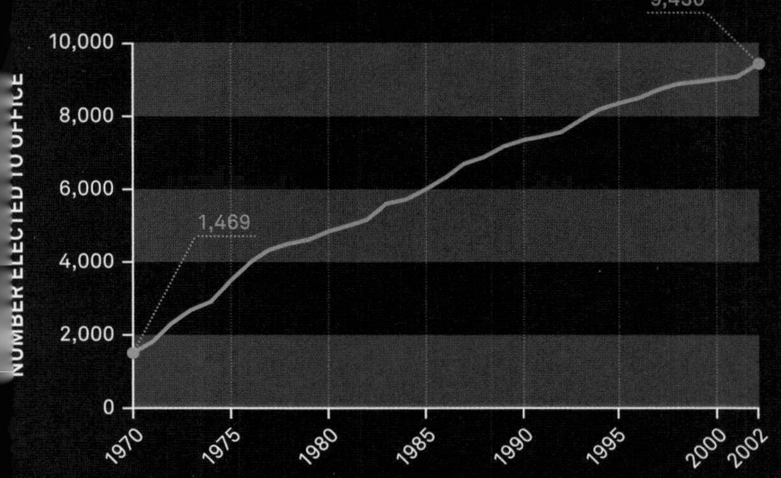

Progress has also been made in the political arena. As recently as 1970, only 1,469 African Americans held elected office in the United States—this out of approximately half a million federal, state, and local offices. By 2002, the last year the government collected data, there were more than 9,400 black elected officials. This represented an increase of more than 600 percent.

Median Income

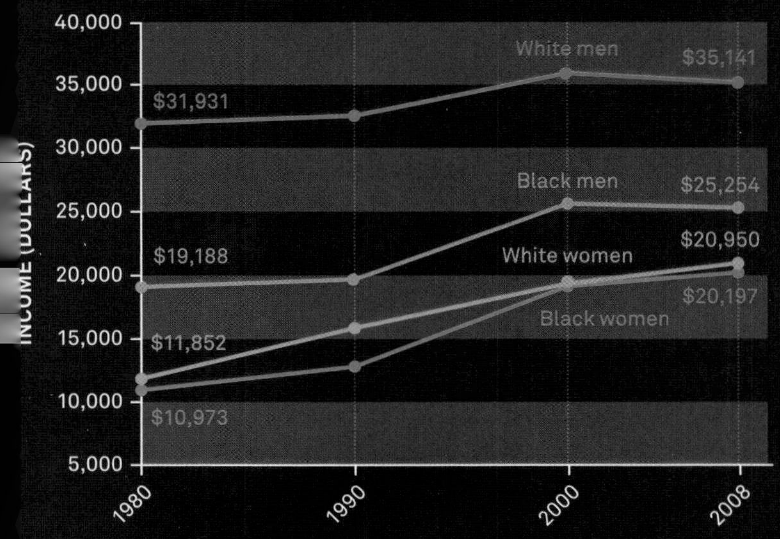

In the economic realm, the gap between blacks and whites has decreased more slowly. In 2008, the median income of black men was only 71 percent of the mean income for white men. This represented only slight progress for black men since 1980. Black women's mean income was close to that of white women in 2008, but women of both races trailed men by a wide margin. The graph at the left shows *median* income, which also reflects this gap.

SOURCES:

High School Graduation Rates: National Center for Educational Statistics, "Digest of Education Statistics," Table 115.

African Americans Elected to Office: Joint Center for Political and Economical Studies, "Black Elected Officials," www.jointcenter.org/BD/detail/BEO.htm (accessed 6/22/09), and U.S. Census Bureau, *2011 Statistical Abstract*, Table 700.

Median Income: U.S. Census Bureau, www.census.gov (accessed 6/22/09), and *2011 Statistical Abstract*, Table 413.

EXPLORE
RACIAL EQUALITY
FURTHER AT:
wwnorton.com/studyspace

Additional progress in the desegregation of schools is likely to be extremely slow unless the Supreme Court decides to permit federal action against de facto segregation and the various kinds of private schools and academies that have sprung up for the purpose of avoiding integration. The prospects for further school integration diminished with a series of Supreme Court decisions handed down in the 1990s. In 1995, for example, in *Missouri v. Jenkins*, the Court signaled to the lower courts that they should "disengage from desegregation efforts."[16] This is a direct and explicit threat to the main basis of the holding in the original 1954 *Brown v. Board of Education* decision.

The Rise of the Politics of Rights

Despite the agonizingly slow progress of school desegregation, there was some progress in other areas of civil rights during the 1960s and 1970s. Voting rights were established and fairly quickly began to revolutionize southern politics, and service on juries was no longer denied to minorities. But progress in securing the right to participate in politics and government dramatized the relative lack of progress in the economic domain, and it was in this area that battles over civil rights were increasingly fought.

Outlawing Discrimination in Employment. The federal courts and the Justice Department entered this area through Title VII of the Civil Rights Act of 1964, which outlaws job discrimination by all private and public employers, including government agencies (such as fire and police departments), that employ more than 15 workers. We have already seen that the Supreme Court gave "interstate commerce" such a broad definition that Congress had the constitutional authority to ban discrimination by virtually any local employers.[17] Title VII makes it unlawful to discriminate in employment on the basis of color, religion, sex, or national origin, as well as race.

A possible problem with Title VII is that the complaining party has to show that deliberate discrimination was the cause of the failure to get a job or a training opportunity. Rarely does an employer explicitly admit discrimination on the basis of race, sex, or any other illegal reason. Recognizing the rarity of such an admission, the courts have allowed aggrieved parties (the plaintiffs) to make their case if they can show that an employer's hiring practices had the *effect* of exclusion. A leading case in 1971 involved a class action by several black employees in North Carolina attempting to show with statistical evidence that blacks had been relegated to one department of the Duke Power Company, which involved the least desirable of manual-labor jobs, and that they had been

16 *Missouri v. Jenkins*, 515 U.S. 70 (1995). The quotation is from David M. O'Brien, *Supreme Court Watch 1996* (New York: Norton, 1996), p. 220.

17 See especially *Katzenbach v. McClung*, 379 U.S. 294 (1964).

kept out of contention for the better jobs because the employer had added high-school education and passing grades on specially prepared aptitude tests as qualifications for those jobs. The Supreme Court held that although the statistical evidence did not prove intentional discrimination and the requirements were race neutral in appearance, their effects were sufficient to shift the burden of justification to the employer to show that the requirements were a "business necessity" that bore "a demonstrable relationship to successful performance."[18] The ruling in this case was subsequently applied to other hiring, promotion, and training programs.[19] In recent years, though, the Supreme Court has placed a number of limits on employment discrimination suits. In 2007, for example, in the case of *Ledbetter v. Goodyear Tire and Rubber Co.* the Court said that a complaint of gender discrimination must be brought within 180 days of the time the discrimination was alleged to have occurred.[20] This blocks suits based on events that might have taken place in the past. In 2009, Congress enacted the Ledbetter Fair Pay Act to overturn the Court's decision and give workers more time to file pay discrimination claims. In a pair of important 2008 decisions, also, the Court helped individuals who sought to bring employment discrimination complaints by declaring that employers were barred from retaliating against them.[21] Fear of retaliation is a powerful force discouraging employees from seeking to assert their legal rights.

Women and Gender Discrimination. In the decades prior to the Civil War, American women began to organize and engage in collective action to advance their political and social rights, including the right to vote. In 1848, women (and men) attending the Seneca Falls Convention issued the "Declaration of Sentiments and Resolutions" asserting that women were entitled to rights in every way equal to those of men. By the 1880s, the issue of voting rights for women was the subject of mass meetings, parades, and protests. A new organization, the National American Woman Suffrage Association (NAWSA), formed in 1890 and claimed 2 million members by 1917. In 1920, the Nineteenth Amendment was ratified, granting women the right to vote in federal elections.

Despite their possession of voting rights, women continued to suffer discrimination in a variety forms, particularly in the realm of employment. Here, women benefitted from the Civil Rights movement and, especially, from Title VII.

Title VII not only provided a valuable tool for the growing women's movement in the 1960s and 1970s, but in many ways the law actually fostered the

18 *Griggs v. Duke Power Company*, 401 U.S. 424 (1971). See also Allan P. Sindler, *Bakke, DeFunis, and Minority Admissions: The Quest for Equal Opportunity* (New York: Longman, 1978), pp. 180–9.

19 For a good treatment of these issues, see Charles O. Gregory and Harold A. Katz, *Labor and the Law*, 3rd ed. (New York: Norton, 1979), chap. 17.

20 *Ledbetter v. Goodyear Tire and Rubber Co.*, 550 U.S. 618 (2007).

21 *CBOC West v. Humphries*, 553 U.S. 442 (2008), *Gomez-Perez v. Potter*, 553 U.S. 474 (2006).

growth of the women's movement.[22] The first major campaign of the National Organization for Women (NOW) involved picketing the Equal Employment Opportunity Commission (EEOC) for its refusal to ban sex-segregated employment advertisements. NOW also sued the *New York Times* for continuing to publish such ads after the passage of Title VII. Another organization, the Women's Equity Action League (WEAL), pursued legal action on a wide range of sex discrimination issues, filing lawsuits against law schools and medical schools for their discriminatory admission policies, for example.

Building on these victories and the growth of the women's movement, feminist activists sought an equal rights amendment (ERA) to the Constitution. The proposed amendment was short: its substantive passage stated that "equality of rights under the law shall not be denied or abridged by the United States or by any State on account of sex." The amendment's supporters believed that such a sweeping guarantee of equal rights was a necessary tool for ending all discrimination against women and for making gender roles more equal. Opponents charged that it would be socially disruptive and would introduce changes—such as coed restrooms—that most Americans did not want. The amendment easily passed Congress in 1972 and won quick approval in many state legislatures but fell 3 states short of the 38 needed to ratify the amendment by the 1982 deadline for its ratification.[23]

Despite the failure of the ERA, gender discrimination expanded dramatically as an area of civil rights law. In the 1970s, the conservative Burger Court helped to establish gender discrimination as a major and highly visible civil rights issue. Although the Burger Court refused to treat gender discrimination as the equivalent of racial discrimination,[24] it did make it easier for plaintiffs to file and win suits on the basis of gender discrimination by applying an "intermediate" level of review to these cases.[25] This intermediate scrutiny is midway between traditional rules of evidence, which put the burden of proof on the plaintiff, and the doctrine of strict scrutiny, which requires the defendant to show not only that a particular classification is reasonable but also that there is a need or compelling interest for it. Intermediate scrutiny shifts the burden of proof partially onto the defendant, rather than leaving it entirely on the plaintiff.

intermediate scrutiny

The test used by the Supreme Court in gender discrimination cases. Intermediate scrutiny places the burden of proof partially on the government and partially on the challengers to show that the law in question is constitutional

One major step was taken in 1992, when the Court decided in *Franklin v. Gwinnett County Public Schools* that violations of Title IX of the 1972 Education Act could be remedied with monetary damages.[26] Title IX forbids gender

22 This and the next five sections are from Benjamin Ginsberg, Theodore J. Lowi, and Margaret Weir, *We the People: An Introduction to American Politics*, 8th ed. (New York: Norton, 2011).

23 See Jane J. Mansbridge, *Why We Lost the ERA* (Chicago: University of Chicago Press, 1986), and Gilbert Steiner, *Constitutional Inequality* (Washington, DC: Brookings Institution, 1985).

24 See *Frontiero v. Richardson*, 411 U.S. 677 (1973).

25 See *Craig v. Boren*, 423 U.S. 1047 (1976).

26 *Franklin v. Gwinnett County Public Schools*, 503 U.S. 60 (1992).

discrimination in education, but it initially sparked little litigation because of its weak enforcement provisions. The Court's 1992 ruling opened the door for more legal action in the area of education. The greatest impact has been in the areas of sexual harassment—the subject of the *Franklin* case—and in equal treatment of women's athletic programs. The potential for monetary damages has made universities and public schools take the problem of sexual harassment more seriously. Colleges and universities have also started to pay more attention to women's athletic programs. In the two years after the *Franklin* case, complaints to the Education Department's Office for Civil Rights about unequal treatment of women's athletic programs nearly tripled. In several high-profile legal cases, some prominent universities have been ordered to create more women's sports programs; many other colleges and universities have begun to add more women's programs in order to avoid potential litigation.[27] In 1997, the Supreme Court refused to hear a petition by Brown University challenging a lower-court ruling that the university establish strict sex equity in its athletic programs. The Court's decision meant that in colleges and universities across the country, varsity athletic positions for men and women must reflect their overall enrollment numbers.[28]

In 1996, the Supreme Court made another important decision about gender and education by putting an end to all-male schools supported by public funds. It ruled that the Virginia Military Institute's policy of not admitting women was unconstitutional.[29] Along with the Citadel, an all-male military college in South Carolina, Virginia Military Institute (VMI) had never admitted women. It argued that the unique educational experience it offered, including intense physical training and the harsh treatment of freshmen, would be destroyed if women were admitted. The Court, however, ruled that the male-only policy denied "substantial equality" to women. Two days after the Court's ruling, the Citadel announced that it would accept women. VMI considered becoming a private institution in order to remain all male, but in September 1996 the school board finally voted to admit women. The legal decisions may have removed formal barriers to entry, but the experience of the female cadets at these schools has not been easy. The first female cadet at the Citadel, Shannon Faulkner, won admission in 1995 under a federal court order but quit after four days. Although four women were admitted to the Citadel after the Supreme Court decision, two of them quit several months later. They charged harassment by male students, including attempts to set the female cadets on fire.[30]

Courts began to find sexual harassment a form of sex discrimination during the late 1970s. Although sexual harassment law applies to education, most of the

27 Jennifer Halperin, "Women Step Up to Bat," *Illinois Issues* 21 (September 1995): 11–4.

28 Joan Biskupic and David Nakamura, "Court Won't Review Sports Equity Ruling," *Washington Post*, April 22, 1997, p. A1.

29 *United States v. Virginia*, 518 U.S. 515 (1996).

30 Judith Havemann, "Two Women Quit Citadel over Alleged Harassment," *Washington Post*, January 13, 1997, p. A1.

law of sexual harassment has been developed by courts through interpretation of Title VII of the Civil Rights Act of 1964. In 1986, the Supreme Court recognized two forms of sexual harassment—the quid pro quo type, which involves sexual extortion, and the hostile-environment type, which involves sexual intimidation.[31] Employers and many employees have worried that hostile-environment sexual harassment is too ambiguous. When can an employee bring charges? When is the employer liable? In 1986, the Court said that sexual harassment may be legally actionable even if the employee did not suffer tangible economic or job-related losses in relation to it. And in 1993, the Court said that sexual harassment may be legally actionable even if the employee did not suffer tangible psychological costs as a result of it.[32] In two 1998 cases, the Court further strengthened the law when it said that whether or not sexual harassment results in economic harm to the employee, an employer is liable for the harassment if it was committed by someone with authority over the employee—by a supervisor, for example. But the Court also said that an employer may defend itself by showing that it had a sexual harassment prevention and grievance policy in effect.[33]

The development of gender discrimination as an important part of the civil rights struggle has coincided with the rise of women's politics as a discrete movement in American politics. As with the struggle for racial equality, the relationship between changes in government policies and political action suggests that changes in government policies to a great degree produce political action. Today the existence of a powerful women's movement derives in large measure from the enactment of Title VII of the Civil Rights Act of 1964 and from the Burger Court's vital steps in applying that law to the protection of women. The recognition of women's civil rights has become an issue that in many ways transcends the usual distinctions of American political debate. In the heavily partisan debate over the federal crime bill enacted in 1994, for instance, the section of the bill that enjoyed the widest support was the Violence against Women Act, whose most important feature was that it defined gender-biased violent crimes as a matter of civil rights and created a civil rights remedy for women who have been the victims of such crimes. But since the act was ruled unconstitutional by the Supreme Court in 2000, the struggle for women's rights will likely remain part of the political debate.

Latinos. The labels "Latino" and "Hispanic" encompass a wide range of groups with diverse national origins, distinctive cultural identities, and particular experiences. For example, the early political experiences of Mexican Americans were shaped by race and region. In 1898, Mexican Americans were given formal political rights, including the right to vote. In many places, however, and especially in Texas, Mexican Americans were segregated and prevented from

---

31 *Meritor Savings Bank v. Vinson,* 477 U.S. 57 (1986).

32 *Harris v. Forklift Systems,* 510 U.S. 17 (1993).

33 *Burlington Industries v. Ellerth,* 524 U.S. 742 (1998); *Faragher v. City of Boca Raton,* 524 U.S. 775 (1998).

voting by such means as the white primary and the poll tax.[34] Region made a difference too. In contrast to the northeastern and midwestern cities in which most European immigrants settled, the Southwest did not have a tradition of ethnic mobilization associated with machine politics. Particularly after the political reforms enacted in the first decade of the twentieth century, city politics in the Southwest was dominated by a small group of white elites. In the countryside, when Mexican Americans participated in politics, it was often as part of a political organization dominated by a large white landowner, or *patron*.

The earliest independent Mexican American political organizations, the League of United Latin American Citizens (LULAC) and the American GI Forum, worked to stem discrimination against Mexican Americans in the years after World War II. By the late 1950s, the first Mexican American had been elected to Congress, and four others followed in the 1960s. In the late 1960s, a new kind of Mexican American political movement was born. Inspired by the black civil rights movement, Mexican American students launched boycotts of high school classes in Los Angeles, Denver, and San Antonio. Students in colleges and universities across California joined in as well. Among their demands were bilingual education, an end to discrimination, and greater cultural recognition. In Crystal City, Texas, which had been dominated by Anglo politicians despite a population that was overwhelmingly Mexican American, the newly formed La Raza Unida Party took over the city government.[35]

Discrimination against Mexican Americans and other Latinos in the Southwest was pervasive prior to World War II, with segregated schools common in Texas and California along with housing and employment restrictions. In 1947, LULAC won an important court victory in the case of *Mendez v. Westminster* which overturned an Orange County, California policy of school segregation aimed at Mexican Americans.[36] The *Mendez* case was an important precedent for *Brown v. Board of Education* and is now recognized as a major landmark in the civil rights struggle.

In recent years, Latino political strategy has developed along two tracks. One is a traditional ethnic-group path of voter registration and voting along ethnic lines. This strategy is helped by the enormous growth of the Latino population resulting in part from immigration. The second is a legal strategy using the various civil rights laws designed to ensure fair access to the political system. The Mexican American Legal Defense and Education Fund (MALDEF) has played a key role in designing and pursuing the latter strategy.

---

34 New Mexico had a different history because not many Anglos settled there initially. (*Anglo* is the term for a non-Hispanic white of European background.) Mexican Americans had considerable power in territorial legislatures between 1865 and 1912. See Lawrence H. Fuchs, *The American Kaleidoscope* (Hanover, NH: University Press of New England, 1990), pp. 239–40.

35 On the La Raza Unida Party, see Carlos Muñoz, Jr., and Mario Barrera, "La Raza Unida Party and the Chicano Student Movement in California," in *Latinos and the Political System*, F. Chris Garcia, ed. (Notre Dame, IN: University of Notre Dame Press, 1988), pp. 213–35.

36 *Mendez v. Westminster*, 161 F. 2d. 744 (Ninth Cir., 1947).

Asian Americans. The early Asian experience in the United States was shaped by a series of naturalization laws dating back to 1790, the first of which declared that only white aliens were eligible for citizenship. Chinese immigrants had begun arriving in California in the 1850s, drawn by the boom of the gold rush. They were immediately met with hostility. The virulent antagonism toward Chinese immigrants in California led Congress in 1870 to declare Chinese immigrants ineligible for citizenship. In 1882, the first Chinese Exclusion Act suspended the entry of Chinese laborers.

At the time of the Exclusion Act, the Chinese community was composed predominantly of single male laborers, with few women and children. The few Chinese children in San Francisco were initially denied entry to the public schools; only after parents of American-born Chinese children pressed legal action were the children allowed to attend public school. Even then, however, they were made to attend a separate Chinese school. American-born Chinese children could not be denied citizenship, however; this right was confirmed by the Supreme Court in 1898, when it ruled in *United States v. Wong Kim Ark* that anyone born in the United States was entitled to full citizenship.[37] Still, new Chinese immigrants were barred from the United States until 1943; China by then had become a key wartime ally, and Congress repealed the Chinese Exclusion Act and permitted Chinese residents to become citizens.

Immigration climbed rapidly after the 1965 Immigration and Nationality Services Act, which lifted discriminatory quotas. In spite of this and other developments, limited English proficiency barred many Asian Americans and Latinos from full participation in American life. Two developments in the 1970s, however, established rights for language minorities. In 1974, the Supreme Court ruled in *Lau v. Nichols*, a suit filed on behalf of Chinese students in San Francisco, that school districts have to provide education for students whose English is limited.[38] It did not mandate bilingual education, but it established a duty to provide instruction that students could understand. The 1970 amendments to the Voting Rights Act of 1965 permanently outlawed literacy tests in all 50 states and mandated bilingual ballots or oral assistance for those who speak Spanish, Chinese, Japanese, Korean, Native American languages, or Eskimo languages.

Immigration and Rights. Asian Americans, Latinos, and other groups have also been concerned about the impact of immigration laws on their civil rights. Many Asian American and Latino organizations opposed the Immigration Reform and Control Act of 1986 because it imposes sanctions on employers who hire undocumented workers. Such sanctions, they feared, would lead employers to discriminate against Latinos and Asian Americans. These suspicions were confirmed in a 1990 report by the General Accounting Office that

37 *United States v. Wong Kim Ark,* 169 U.S. 649 (1898).

38 *Lau v. Nichols,* 414 U.S. 563 (1974).

found employer sanctions had created a "widespread pattern of discrimination" against Latinos and others who appear foreign.[39] Organizations such as MALDEF and the Asian Law Caucus monitor and challenge such discrimination. These groups have turned their attention to the rights of legal and illegal immigrants as anti-immigrant sentiment has grown in recent years.

The Supreme Court has ruled that illegal immigrants are eligible for education and medical care but can be denied other social benefits; legal immigrants are to be treated much the same as citizens. But growing immigration—including an estimated 300,000 illegal immigrants per year—and mounting economic insecurity have undermined these practices. Groups of voters across the country now strongly support drawing a sharper line between immigrants and citizens. Not surprisingly, the movement to deny benefits to noncitizens began in California, which experienced sharp economic distress in the early 1990s and has the highest levels of immigration of any state. In 1994, Californians voted in favor of Proposition 187, which denied illegal immigrants all services except emergency medical care. Supporters of the measure hoped to discourage illegal immigration and pressure illegal immigrants already in the country to leave. Opponents contended that denying basic services to illegal immigrants risked creating a subclass of residents in the United States whose lack of education and poor health would threaten all Americans. In 1994 and 1997, a federal court declared most of Proposition 187 unconstitutional, affirming previous rulings that illegal immigrants should be granted public education.

The question of the rights of illegal immigrants points to an even tougher problem. Congress has the power to deny public benefits to this group, but doing so would go against long-standing traditions in American political culture. Legal immigrants have traditionally enjoyed most of the rights and obligations of citizens (such as paying taxes). As the constitutional scholar Alexander Bickel points out, the Constitution begins with "We the People of the United States"; likewise the Bill of Rights refers to the rights of *people*, not the rights of citizens. But even as Congress continues to debate immigration policy, several states, led by Arizona, have enacted their own laws aimed at identifying and deporting illegal immigrants within their borders. Immigration continues to be a divisive issue in American politics.

Native Americans. The political status of Native Americans was left unclear in the Constitution. But by the early 1800s, the courts had defined each of the Indian tribes as a nation. As members of Indian nations, Native Americans were declared noncitizens of the United States. The political status of Native Americans changed in 1924, when congressional legislation granted citizenship to all those who were born in the United States. A variety of changes in federal policy toward Native Americans during the 1930s paved the way for a later resurgence of their political power. Most important was the

39 Dick Kirschten, "Not Black and White," *National Journal*, March 2, 1991, p. 497.

federal decision to encourage Native Americans on reservations to establish local self-government.[40]

The Native American political movement gathered force in the 1960s as Indians began to use protest, litigation, and assertion of tribal rights to improve their situation. In 1968, Dennis Banks cofounded the American Indian Movement (AIM), the most prominent Native American protest organization. AIM won national attention in 1969 when 200 of its members, representing 20 tribes, took over the famous prison island of Alcatraz in San Francisco Bay, claiming it for Native Americans. In 1973, AIM members took over the town of Wounded Knee, South Dakota, the site of the massacre of over 200 Sioux men, women, and children by the U.S. Army in December 1890. The federal government responded to the rise in Indian activism with the Indian Self-determination and Education Assistance Act (1975), which began to give Indians more control over their own land.[41]

As a language minority, Native Americans were also affected by the 1975 amendments to the Voting Rights Act and the *Lau* decision, which established the right of Native Americans to be taught in their own languages. This ruling marked quite a change from the boarding schools once run by the Bureau of Indian Affairs, at which members of Indian tribes were forbidden to speak their own languages. Native Americans have also sought to expand their rights on the basis of their sovereign status. Since the 1920s and 1930s, Native American tribes have sued the federal government for illegally seizing land, seeking monetary reparations and land as damages. Both types of damages have been awarded in such suits, but only in small amounts. Native American tribes have been more successful in winning federal recognition of their sovereignty. Sovereign status has, in turn, allowed them to exercise greater self-determination. Most significant economically was a 1987 Supreme Court decision that freed Native American tribes from most state regulations prohibiting gambling.[42] The establishment of casino gambling on Native American lands has brought a substantial flow of new income into desperately poor reservations.

Americans with Disabilities. The concept of rights for people with disabilities began to emerge in the 1970s as the civil rights model spread to other groups. The seed was planted in a little-noticed provision of the 1973 Rehabilitation Act that outlawed discrimination against individuals on the basis of disabilities. As in many other cases, the law itself helped give rise

40 Not all Indian tribes agreed with this, including the Navajos. See Ronald Takaki, *A Different Mirror: A History of Multicultural America* (Boston: Little, Brown, 1993), pp. 238–48.

41 On the resurgence of Indian political activity, see Stephen Cornell, *The Return of the Native: American Indian Political Resurgence* (New York: Oxford University Press, 1990), and Dee Brown, *Bury My Heart at Wounded Knee* (New York: Holt, 1971).

42 *California v. Cabazon Band of Mission Indians*, 480 U.S. 202 (1987).

to the movement demanding rights.[43] Modeling itself on the NAACP's Legal Defense Fund, the disability movement founded a Disability Rights Education and Defense Fund to press its legal claims. The movement achieved its greatest success with the passage of the Americans with Disabilities Act (ADA) of 1990, which guarantees the disabled equal employment rights and access to public businesses. Claims of discrimination in violation of this act are considered by the EEOC. The impact of the law has been far reaching as businesses and public facilities have installed ramps, elevators, and other devices to meet its requirements.[44]

In 1998, the Supreme Court interpreted the ADA to apply to people with HIV. Until then, ADA was interpreted as applying to people with AIDS but not people with HIV. The case arose when a dentist was asked to fill a cavity for a woman with HIV; he would do it only if the procedure was done in a hospital setting. The woman sued, and her complaint was that HIV had already disabled her because it was discouraging her from having children. (The act prohibits discrimination in employment, housing, and health care.) Although there have been widespread concerns that the ADA was being expanded too broadly and the costs were becoming too burdensome, corporate America did not seem to be disturbed by the Court's ruling. Stephen Bokat, general counsel of the U.S. Chamber of Commerce, said businesses in general had already been accommodating people with HIV as well as those with AIDS and the case presented no serious problem.[45]

The Aged. The 1967 federal Age Discrimination in Employment Act (ADEA) made age discrimination illegal when practiced by employers with at least 20 employees. Many states have added to the federal provisions with their own age-discrimination laws, and some of the state laws are stronger than the federal provisions. The major lobbyist for seniors, AARP (formerly the American Association of Retired Persons), with its claim to more than 30 million members, has been active in keeping these laws on the books and making sure they are vigorously implemented.

Gay Men and Lesbians. In less than 30 years, the gay movement has become one of the largest civil rights movements in contemporary America. Beginning with street protests in the 1960s, it has grown into a well-financed and sophisticated lobby. The Human Rights Campaign is the primary national PAC

43 See the discussion in Robert A. Katzmann, *Institutional Disability: The Saga of Transportation Policy for the Disabled* (Washington, DC: Brookings Institution, 1986).

44 For example, after pressure from the Justice Department, one of the nation's largest rental-car companies agreed to make special hand controls available to any customer requesting them. See "Avis Agrees to Equip Cars for Disabled," *Los Angeles Times*, September 2, 1994, p. D1.

45 The case and the interview with Stephen Bokat were reported in Margaret Warner, "Expanding Coverage: Defining Disability," *Online NewsHour*, June 30, 1998, www.pbs.org/newshour/bb/law/jan-june98/hiv_6-30.html (accessed 2/16/09).

focused on gay rights; it provides campaign financing and volunteers to work for candidates endorsed by the group. The movement has also formed legal rights organizations, including the Lambda Legal Defense and Education Fund.

Gay rights drew national attention in 1993, when President Bill Clinton confronted the question of whether gays should be allowed to serve in the military. As a candidate, Clinton had said he favored lifting the ban on gays in the military. The issue set off a huge controversy in the first months of his presidency. After nearly a year of deliberation, the administration enunciated a compromise: its "don't ask, don't tell" policy, which allows gay men and lesbians to serve in the military as long as they do not openly proclaim their sexual orientation or engage in homosexual activity. The administration maintained that the ruling would protect gay men and lesbians from witch-hunting investigations, but many gay advocates expressed disappointment, charging the president with reneging on his campaign promise.

But until 1996, there was no Supreme Court ruling or national legislation explicitly protecting gay men and lesbians from discrimination. The first gay rights case that the Court decided, *Bowers v. Hardwick* (1986), ruled against a right to privacy that would protect consensual homosexual activity. After the *Bowers* decision, the gay rights movement sought suitable legal cases to test the constitutionality of discrimination against gay men and lesbians, much as the civil rights movement had done in the late 1940s and 1950s. As one advocate put it, "lesbians and gay men are looking for their *Brown v. Board of Education*."[46] Among the cases tested were those stemming from local ordinances restricting gay rights (including the right to marry), job discrimination, and family-law issues such as adoption and parental rights. In 1996, in *Romer v. Evans*, the Supreme Court explicitly extended fundamental civil rights protections to gay men and lesbians by declaring unconstitutional a 1992 amendment to the Colorado state constitution that prohibited local governments from passing ordinances to protect gay rights.[47] The decision's forceful language highlighted the connection between gay rights and civil rights as it declared discrimination against gay people unconstitutional.

In *Lawrence v. Texas* (2003), the Court overturned *Bowers* and struck down a Texas statute criminalizing certain intimate sexual conduct between consenting partners of the same sex.[48] A victory for lesbians and gay men every bit as significant as *Roe v. Wade* was for women, *Lawrence v. Texas* extends at least one aspect of civil liberties to sexual minorities: the right to privacy. However, this decision by itself does not undo the various exclusions that deprive lesbians and gay men of full civil rights, including the right to marry, which became a hot-button issue.

Early in 2004, the Supreme Judicial Court of Massachusetts ruled that under that state's constitution same-sex couples were entitled to marry. The state senate then requested the court to rule on whether a civil-union statute

---

46 Quoted in Joan Biskupic, "Gay Rights Activists Seek a Supreme Court Test Case," *Washington Post*, December 19, 1993, p. A1.

47 *Romer v. Evans*, 517 U.S. 620 (1996).

48 *Lawrence and Garner v. Texas*, 539 U.S. 558 (2003).

(avoiding the word *marriage*) would, as it did in Vermont, satisfy the court's ruling, in response to which the court ruled negatively, asserting that civil unions are too much like the "separate but equal" doctrine that maintained legalized racial segregation from 1896 to 1954. In San Francisco, meanwhile, hundreds of gay men and women responded to the opportunity provided by the mayor, who had directed the city clerk to issue marriage licenses to same-sex couples, in defiance of California law. Since that time, same-sex marriage has been put to voters in numerous states. In November 2004, voters in 11 states approved bans on same-sex marriage. In 2008, California voters changed the state constitution to prohibit same-sex marriage, although this action was subsequently overturned by a federal judge. In 2012, voters in Maine, Maryland, and Washington approved constitutional amendments legalizing same-sex marriage, while voters in Minnesota voted down a proposed constitutional amendment that would have defined marriage as being solely a union between a man and a woman.

Affirmative Action

The politics of rights not only spread to increasing numbers of groups in society but also expanded its goal. The relatively narrow goal of equalizing opportunity by eliminating discriminatory barriers had been developing toward the far broader goal of affirmative action—compensatory action to overcome the consequences of past discrimination and encourage greater diversity. An affirmative action policy tends to involve two novel approaches: (1) positive or benign discrimination in which race or some other status is taken into account, but for compensatory action rather than mistreatment, and (2) compensatory action to favor members of the disadvantaged group who themselves may never have been the victims of discrimination. Quotas may be—but are not necessarily—involved in affirmative action policies.

 **affirmative action**

A policy or program designed to redress historic injustices committed against specific groups by making special efforts to provide members of these groups with access to educational and employment opportunities

In 1965, President Lyndon Johnson attempted to inaugurate affirmative action by executive orders directing agency heads and personnel officers to pursue vigorously a policy of minority employment in the federal civil service and in companies doing business with the national government. But affirmative action did not become a prominent goal until the 1970s.

The Supreme Court and the Burden of Proof. As this movement spread, it began to divide civil rights activists and their supporters. The whole issue of qualification versus minority preference was addressed in the case of Allan Bakke. Bakke, a white man with no minority affiliation, brought suit against the University of California Medical School at Davis on the grounds that in denying him admission the school had discriminated against him on the basis of his race (that year the school had reserved 16 of 100 available slots for minority applicants). He argued that his grades and test scores had ranked him well above many students who had been accepted at the school and that the only possible explanation for his rejection was that the others were black or Hispanic and he was white. In 1978, Bakke won his case before the Supreme Court and was admitted to the medical school, but he did not succeed in getting affirmative action declared unconstitutional. The Court rejected the procedures at the University of California because its medical school had used both a quota and a separate admissions system for minorities. The Court agreed with Bakke's argument that racial categorizations are suspect categories that place a severe burden of proof on those using them to show a "compelling public purpose." The Court went on to say that achieving "a diverse student body" was such a public purpose, but the method of a rigid quota of student slots assigned on the basis of race was incompatible with the equal protection clause. Thus the Court permitted universities (and other schools, training programs, and hiring authorities) to continue to take minority status into consideration but limited severely the use of quotas to situations in which previous discrimination had been shown and the quotas were used more as a guideline for social diversity than as a mathematically defined ratio.[49]

For nearly a decade after *Bakke*, the Supreme Court was tentative and permissive about efforts by corporations and governments to experiment with affirmative action programs in employment.[50] But in 1989, the Court returned to the *Bakke* position, ruling that any "rigid numerical quota" is suspect. In *Wards Cove v. Atonio*, the Court further weakened affirmative action by easing the way for employers to prefer white men, holding that the burden of proof of unlawful discrimination should be shifted from the defendant (the employer) to the plaintiff (the person claiming to be the victim of discrimination).[51] This decision virtually overruled the Court's prior holding.[52] That same year, the Court ruled that any affirmative action program already approved by federal courts could be challenged by white men who alleged that the program discriminated against them.[53]

In 1995, the Supreme Court's ruling in *Adarand Constructors v. Pena* further weakened affirmative action. This decision stated that race-based policies, such as preferences given by the government to minority contractors must survive strict scrutiny, placing the burden on the government to show that such affirmative action programs serve a compelling government interest and are narrowly tailored to address identifiable past discrimination.[54]

Other developments in the courts and the states also worked to restrict affirmative action in important ways. One of the most significant was the *Hopwood* case, in which white students challenged admissions practices at the University of Texas Law School, charging that the school's affirmative action program discriminated against whites. In 1996, a federal court ruling on the case (the U.S.

---

49 *Regents of the University of California v. Bakke*, 438 U.S. 265 (1978).

50 *United Steelworkers of America v. Weber*, 443 U.S. 193 (1979), and *Fullilove v. Klutznick*, 448 U.S. 448 (1980).

51 *Wards Cove Packing Company v. Atonio*, 490 U.S. 642 (1989).

52 *Griggs v. Duke Power Company*, 401 U.S. 424 (1971).

53 *Martin v. Wilks*, 490 U.S. 755 (1989).

54 *Adarand Constructors v. Pena*, 515 U.S. 200 (1995).

Court of Appeals for the Fifth Circuit) stated that race could never be considered in granting admissions and scholarships at state colleges and universities.[55] This decision effectively rolled back the use of affirmative action permitted by the 1978 *Bakke* case. In *Bakke*, as noted earlier, the Supreme Court had outlawed quotas but said that race could be used as one factor among many in admissions decisions. Many universities and colleges have since justified affirmative action as a way of promoting racial diversity among their student bodies. What was new in the *Hopwood* decision was the ruling that race could *never* be used as a factor in admissions decisions, even to promote diversity. In 1996, the Supreme Court refused to hear a challenge to the *Hopwood* case. This meant that its ruling remains in effect in the states covered by the Fifth Circuit—Texas, Louisiana, and Mississippi—but does not apply to the rest of the country.

The weakening of affirmative action in the courts was underscored in a case the Supreme Court agreed to hear in 1998. A white schoolteacher in New Jersey who had lost her job had sued her school district, charging that her layoff was racially motivated: a black colleague hired on the same day was not laid off. Under former president George H. W. Bush, the Justice Department had filed a brief on her behalf in 1989, but in 1994 the Clinton administration formally reversed course in a new brief supporting the school district's right to make distinctions based on race as long as they did not involve the use of quotas. Three years later, the administration, worried that the case was weak and could result in a broad decision against affirmative action, reversed course again and filed a brief with the Court urging a narrow ruling in favor of the dismissed worker. Because the school board had justified its actions on the grounds of preserving diversity, the administration feared that a broad ruling by the Supreme Court could totally prohibit the use of race in employment decisions, even as one factor among many designed to achieve diversity. But before the Court could issue a ruling, a coalition of civil rights groups brokered and arranged to pay for a settlement. This unusual move reflected the widespread fear of a sweeping negative decision. Cases involving dismissals, as the New Jersey case did, are generally viewed as much more difficult to defend than cases that concern hiring. In addition, the particular facts of the New Jersey case—two equally qualified teachers hired on the same day—were seen as unusual and unfavorable to affirmative action.[56]

This betwixt-and-between status of affirmative action was where things stood in 2003, when the Supreme Court took two cases against the University of Michigan that were virtually certain to clarify, if not put closure on, affirmative action. The first suit, *Gratz v. Bollinger*, alleged that by using a point-based ranking system that automatically awarded 20 points (out of 150) to African American, Latino, and Native American applicants, the university's undergraduate admissions policy discriminated unconstitutionally against white students with otherwise

55 *Hopwood v. State of Texas*, 78 F. 3d 932 (Fifth Cir., 1996).

56 Linda Greenhouse, "Settlement Ends High Court Case on Preferences," *New York Times*, November 22, 1997, p. A1; Barry Bearak, "Rights Groups Ducked a Fight, Opponents Say," *New York Times*, November 22, 1997, p. A1.

equal or superior academic qualifications. The Supreme Court agreed, 6–3, arguing that something tantamount to a quota was involved because undergraduate admissions lacked the necessary "individualized consideration," employing instead a "mechanical one," based too much on the favorable minority points.[57] The Court's ruling in *Gratz v. Bollinger* was not surprising, given *Bakke*'s holding against quotas and recent decisions calling for strict scrutiny of all racial classifications, even those that are intended to remedy past discrimination or promote future equality.

The second case, *Grutter v. Bollinger*, broke new ground. Barbara Grutter sued the University of Michigan Law School on the grounds that it had discriminated in a race-conscious way against white applicants with grades and law boards equal or superior to those of minority applicants. A precarious vote of 5–4 aligned the majority of the Supreme Court with Justice Lewis Powell's opinion in *Bakke* for the first time. In *Bakke*, Powell had argued that diversity in education is a compelling state interest and that constitutionally race could be considered a positive factor in admissions decisions. In *Grutter*, the Court reiterated Powell's holding and, applying strict scrutiny to the law school's policy, found that its admissions process was narrowly tailored to the school's compelling state interest in diversity because it gave a "highly individualized, holistic review of each applicant's file," in which race counted but was not used in a "mechanical way."[58]

Throughout the 1990s, federal courts, including the Supreme Court, had subjected public affirmative action programs to strict scrutiny to invalidate them. *Adarand Constructors v. Pena* (1995) definitively established the Supreme Court's view that constitutionally permissible use of race must serve a compelling state interest. Between *Korematsu v. United States* (1944)[59] and *Grutter*, no consideration of race had survived strict scrutiny. Such affirmative action plans that had survived constitutional review did so before 1995, under a lower standard of review, one reserved for policies intended to remedy racial injustice. For affirmative action to survive under the post-1995 judicial paradigm, the Court needed to find that sometimes racial categories can be deployed to serve a compelling state interest. That the Court found exactly this in *Grutter* puts affirmative action on stronger ground—at least if its specific procedures pass the Supreme Court's muster and until the Court's majority changes. A recent affirmative action case that attracted wide attention was *Ricci v. DeStefano*, in which the Court ruled that New Haven, Connecticut, officials had discriminated against white firefighters when they threw out a promotions exam because no nonwhite candidate received a high enough score for promotion.[60] The Court said that employers must show "a strong basis in evidence" under Title VII of the Civil Rights Act and may not rely simply on a test's outcome to show racial discrimination.

57 *Gratz v. Bollinger*, 539 U.S. 244 (2003).

58 *Grutter v. Bollinger*, 539 U.S. 306 (2003).

59 *Korematsu v. United States*, 323 U.S. 214 (1944).

60 *Ricci v. DeStefano*, 129 S. Ct. 2658 (2009).

Referenda on Affirmative Action. The courts have not been the only center of action: challenges to affirmative action have also emerged in state and local politics, in the form of ballot initiatives or referendums that ask voters to decide the issue. One of the most significant state actions was the passage of the California Civil Rights Initiative, also known as Proposition 209, in 1996. Proposition 209 outlawed affirmative action programs in the state and local governments of California, thus prohibiting state and local governments from using race or gender preferences in their decisions about hiring, contracting, and university admissions. The political battle over Proposition 209 was heated, and supporters and defenders took to the streets and airwaves to make their case. When the referendum was held, the measure passed with 54 percent of the vote, including 27 percent of the black vote, 30 percent of the Latino vote, and 45 percent of the Asian American vote.[61] In 1997, the Supreme Court refused to hear a challenge to the new law.

Many observers predicted that the success of California's ban on affirmative action would provoke similar movements in states and localities across the country. But the political factors that contributed to the success of Proposition 209 in California may not exist in many other states. Winning a controversial state referendum takes leadership and lots of money. The popular California Republican governor Pete Wilson led with a strong anti-affirmative action stand (favoring Proposition 209), and his campaign had a lot of money for advertising. But similar conditions did not exist elsewhere. Few prominent Republican leaders in other states were willing to come forward to lead the anti-affirmative action campaign. Moreover, the outcome of any referendum, especially a complicated and controversial one, depends greatly on how the issue is drafted and placed on the ballot. California's Proposition 209 was framed as a civil rights initiative: "The state shall not discriminate against, or grant preferential treatment to, any individual or group on the basis of race, sex, color, ethnicity, or national origin." Different wording can produce quite different outcomes, as a 1997 vote on affirmative action in Houston revealed. There the ballot initiative asked voters whether they wanted to ban affirmative action in city contracting and hiring, not whether they wanted to end preferential treatment. In that city, 55 percent of voters decided in favor of affirmative action.[62]

Civil Liberties and Civil Rights: Limiting and Regulating Collective Action

Over the past century, America has strengthened its citizens' liberties and expanded their rights. Both civil liberties and civil rights are solutions to collective action problems. Strengthening the former means imposing more restrictions

61 Michael A. Fletcher, "Opponents of Affirmative Action Heartened by Court Decision," *Washington Post*, April 13, 1997, p. A21.

62 See Sam Howe Verhovek, "Houston Vote Underlined Complexity of Rights Issue," *New York Times*, November 6, 1997, p. A1.

on some forms of collective action. Expanding the later means allowing more individuals to take part in collective decision making and imposing restrictions on the sorts of decisions that can be reached.

Institutions help to solve collective action problems, but no particular solution is carved in stone. Contending political forces continually seek to change the institutional rules to serve their particular purposes. In the United States today, for example, some groups argue the need for additional rights for gay men and lesbians, immigrants, and others who have often faced political, social, and economic discrimination. Opponents of this idea assert that the expansion of civil rights to include such matters as same-sex marriage or social and educational benefits for illegal immigrants is inappropriate. The outcomes of this and other struggles over liberties and rights are never certain. Institutions matter, but exactly how they will matter in the years to come is always subject to change.

For Further Reading

Baer, Judith, and Leslie Goldstein. *The Constitutional and Legal Rights of Women.* Los Angeles: Roxbury, 2006.

reader selection *Brown v. Board of Education of Topeka*, 347 U.S. 483, 1954.

reader selection Dawson, Michael. *Behind the Mule: Race and Class in African-American Politics.* Princeton, NJ: Princeton University Press, 1995.

Dworkin, Ronald. *Justice in Robes.* Cambridge, MA: Belknap Press, 2006.

Garrow, David J. *Bearing the Cross: Martin Luther King, Jr., and the Southern Christian Leadership Conference: A Personal Portrait.* New York: Morrow, 1986.

Gerstmann, Evan. *Same-Sex Marriage and the Constitution.* New York: Cambridge University Press, 2004.

Glendon, Mary Ann. *Rights Talk: The Impoverishment of Political Discourse.* New York: Free Press, 1991.

Jackson, Thomas. *From Civil Rights to Human Rights.* Philadelphia: University of Pennsylvania Press, 2006.

Klarman, Michael. *From Jim Crow to Civil Rights: The Supreme Court and the Struggle for Racial Equality.* New York: Oxford University Press, 2004.

Lewis, Anthony. *Gideon's Trumpet.* New York: Random House, 1964.

Meltsner, Michael. *The Making of a Civil Rights Lawyer.* Charlottesville: University of Virginia Press, 2006.

O'Brien, David. *Constitutional Law and Politics: Civil Rights and Civil Liberties.* 8th ed. New York: Norton, 2011.

Rosenberg, Gerald N. *The Hollow Hope: Can Courts Bring About Social Change?* 2nd ed. Chicago: University of Chicago Press, 2008.

reader selection

Sugrue, Thomas. *Sweet Land of Liberty: The Forgotten Struggle for Civil Rights in the North.* New York: Random House, 2009.

Tushnet, Mark, and Michael Olivas. *Colored Men and Hombres Aqui:* Hernandez v. Texas *and the Emergence of Mexican American Lawyering.* Houston: Arte Publico Press, 2006.

Yoshino, Kenji. *Covering: The Hidden Assault on Our Civil Rights.* New York: Random House, 2007.

Visit **wwnorton.com/studyspace/** to access free review materials such as:

- Vocabulary Flashcards of All Key Terms
- Chapter Review Quizzes
- Complete Study Outlines

reader selection

Highlighted selections are included in *Readings in American Politics: Analysis and Perspectives*, Second Edition.

6

PART 1 X 3 4

INSTITUTIONS

Congress: The First Branch

Chapter Outline

- Representation
- Problems of Legislative Organization
- The Organization of Congress
- Rules of Lawmaking: How a Bill Becomes a Law
- How Congress Decides
- Beyond Legislation: Additional Congressional Powers
- Power and Representation
- Conclusion

The U.S. Congress is the "first branch" of government under Article I of our Constitution and is also among the world's most important representative bodies. Most of the world's representative bodies only represent—that is, their governmental functions consist mainly of affirming and legitimating the national leadership's decisions. The U.S. Congress is one of the few national representative bodies that actually possesses powers of governance. For example, the U.S. Congress never accedes to the president's budget proposals without making major changes, but both the British House of Commons and the Japanese Diet always accept the budget exactly as proposed by the government.

This unique status of the American Congress provides an illustration of the institution principle. In the separation-of-powers regime institutionalized by the U.S. Constitution, the American executive cannot govern alone. The legislature, in particular, actively participates. In Richard Neustadt's memorable phrase, the executive and the legislature in the United States are "separated institutions sharing power."[1] In parliamentary regimes, such as Britain or Japan, in contrast, the executive controls its majority in parliament. These different institutional arrangements give different powers to different players. In the American case, the institutional arrangements were intended to give Congress a great deal of power relative to the president.

Congress controls a formidable battery of powers that it uses to shape policies and, when necessary, defend its prerogatives against the executive branch. Congress has vast authority over the two most important powers given to any government: the power of force (control over the nation's military forces) and the power over money. Specifically, according to Article I, Section 8, Congress can "lay and collect Taxes," deal with indebtedness and bankruptcy, impose

1 Richard E. Neustadt, *Presidential Power: The Politics of Leadership* (New York: Wiley, 1960), p. 42.

duties, borrow and coin money, and generally control the nation's purse strings. It also may "provide for the common Defence and general Welfare," regulate interstate commerce, undertake public works, acquire and control federal lands, promote science and "useful Arts" (pertaining mostly to patents and copyrights), and regulate the militia.

In the realm of foreign policy, Congress has the power to declare war, deal with piracy, regulate foreign commerce, and raise and regulate the armed forces and military installations. These powers over war and the military are supreme—even the president, as commander in chief of the military, must obey the laws and orders of Congress *if* Congress chooses to assert its constitutional authority. (In the past century, Congress has usually surrendered this authority to the president.) Further, the Senate has the power to approve treaties (by a two-thirds vote) and the appointment of ambassadors. Capping these powers, Congress is charged to make laws "which shall be necessary and proper for carrying into Execution the foregoing Powers, and all other Powers vested by this Constitution in the Government of the United States, or in any Department or Officer thereof."

If it seems to you that many of these powers, especially those having to do with war and spending, actually belong to the president, that is because modern presidents do exercise great authority in these areas. The modern presidency is a more powerful institution than it was two centuries ago, and much of that power has come from Congress, either because Congress has delegated the

CORE OF THE ANALYSIS

Members of Congress, like all politicians, are ambitious and thus eager to serve the interests of their constituents in order to improve their chances of re-election.

Congress is the most important representative institution of American government. In many ways, Congress works because its system of representation harnesses individual legislators' ambitions and puts them to use.

The internal organization of Congress solves the collective action problems that arise due to the many and varied goals of individual legislators.

Rules matter in the legislative process, and the process through which a bill becomes a law affects which proposed bills succeed and in what form.

power to the president by law or because Congress has simply allowed, or even urged, presidents to be more active in these areas.[2] As we noted in Chapter 1, institutions evolve over time, as the various players seek to adapt them to their purposes. This helps explain why today the executive branch seems like a more important branch of government than Congress. Still, the constitutional powers of Congress remain intact in the document. As we shall see, congressional power cannot be separated from congressional representation. Indeed, there is a reciprocal relationship between the two. Without its array of powers, Congress could do little to represent effectively the views and interests of its constituents. At the same time, the power of Congress is ultimately a function of its capacity to represent important groups and forces in American society effectively. All five principles of politics from Chapter 1 are important to our understanding of the institutional structure of the contemporary Congress.

We begin our discussion with a brief consideration of representation. Then we examine the institutional structure of the contemporary Congress and the manner in which congressional powers are organized and employed. Throughout, we point out the connections between these two aspects—the ways in which representation affects congressional operations (especially through "the electoral connection") and the ways in which congressional institutions enhance or diminish representation (especially Congress's division-of-labor and specialization-of-labor committee system).

REPRESENTATION

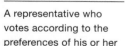

constituency

The district making up the area from which an official is elected

Congress is the most important representative institution in American government. Each member's primary responsibility is to the district, to his or her constituency, not to the congressional leadership, a party, or even Congress itself. Yet the task of representation is not a simple one. Views about what constitutes fair and effective representation differ, and constituents can make very different kinds of demands on their representatives. Members of Congress must consider these diverse views and demands as they represent their districts (Figure 6.1).

delegate

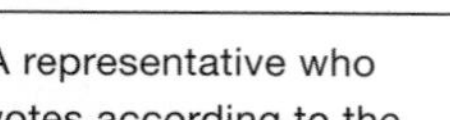

A representative who votes according to the preferences of his or her constituency

Legislators generally vary in the weight they give to personal priorities and the things their campaign contributors and past supporters desire. Some see themselves as perfect agents of others: they have been elected to do the bidding of those who sent them to the legislature, and they act as delegates. Others see

2 On the issue of congressional delegation to the executive, two valuable sources are D. Roderick Kiewiet and Mathew D. McCubbins, *The Logic of Delegation: Congressional Parties and the Appropriations Process* (Chicago: University of Chicago Press, 1991), and David Epstein and Sharyn O'Halloran, *Delegating Powers: A Transaction Cost Politics Approach to Policy Making under Separate Powers* (New York: Cambridge University Press, 1999).

Figure 6.1
HOW MEMBERS OF CONGRESS REPRESENT THEIR DISTRICTS

MEMBERS OF CONGRESS

Individual constituents	Organized interests	District as a whole
Solve problems with agencies Provide jobs Sponsor private bills Sponsor appointments to service academies Answer complaints Provide information	Introduce legislation Intervene with regulatory agencies Obtain federal grants and contracts Help with importing or exporting Help in securing favorable tax status Make promotional speeches and symbolic gestures	Obtain federal projects Obtain grants and contracts that promote employment Support policies that enhance economic prosperity, safety, cultural resources, and so on Participate in state and regional caucuses

themselves as having been selected by their fellow citizens to do what they think is "right," and they act as trustees. Most legislators are a mix of these two types. And all, one way or another, need to survive the next election in order to pursue whatever role they formulate for themselves. Rational agents necessarily must focus on survival.

trustee

A representative who votes based on what he or she thinks is best for his or her constituency

Legislators not only represent others; they may be representative *of* others as well. The latter is especially salient today when it comes to gender and race, where descriptive representation is symbolically significant at the very least. Descriptive characteristics permit women members and representatives drawn from minority groups to serve and draw support from those with whom they share an identity, both inside their formal constituency and in the nation at large.

As we discussed in Chapter 1, one person might be trusted to speak for another if the two are formally bound together so that the representative is in some way accountable to those he or she purports to represent. If representatives can somehow be punished or held to account for failing to speak properly for their constituents, then we know they have an incentive to provide good representation even if their own backgrounds, views, and interests differ from those of the people they represent. This idea is called agency representation—the sort of representation that takes place when constituents have the power to hire and fire their representatives (who act as their agents). Frequent competitive elections are an important means by which constituents hold their representatives to account and keep them responsive to their own views and preferences. The idea of a representative as agent is similar to the relationship between lawyer and client. True, the relationship between the member of Congress and as many as 630,000 "clients" in the district or that between the senator and possibly millions of clients in the state is very different from that of the lawyer and client. But the criteria of performance are comparable.

agency representation

The type of representation according to which representatives are held accountable to their constituents if they fail to represent them properly. That is, constituents have the power to hire and fire their representatives

We would expect at the very least that each representative will constantly be seeking to discover the interests of the constituency and will be speaking for those interests in Congress and other centers of government.[3] We expect this because we believe that members of Congress, like politicians everywhere, are ambitious. For many, this ambition is satisfied simply by maintaining a hold on their present office and advancing up the rungs of power in that body. Some, however, may be looking ahead to the next level—to higher legislative office, as when a representative seeks a Senate seat, or to an executive office, as when a legislator returns home to run for the state's governorship, or at the highest level, when a legislator seeks the presidency.[4] This means that members of Congress may not only be concerned with their present *geographic* constituency. They may want to appeal to a different geographic constituency, for instance, or seek support from a broader gender, ethnic, or racial community. We shall return to this topic shortly in a discussion of elections. But we can say here that in each of these cases the legislator is eager to serve the interests of constituents, either to enhance his or her prospects of contract renewal at the next election or to improve the chances of moving to another level. In short, the agency conception of representation works in proportion to the ambition of politicians (as "agents") and the capacity of constituents (as "principals") to reward or punish on the basis of the legislator's performance and reputation.[5]

3 The classic description of interactions between politicians and "the folks back home" is given by Richard F. Fenno, Jr., *Home Style: House Members in Their Districts* (Boston: Little, Brown, 1978). Essays elaborating on Fenno's classic are found in Morris P. Fiorina and David W. Rohde, eds., *Home Style and Washington Work* (Ann Arbor: University of Michigan Press, 1989).

4 For more on political careers generally, see John R. Hibbing, "Legislative Careers: Why and How We Should Study Them," *Legislative Studies Quarterly* 24 (1999): 149–71. See also Cherie D. Maestas, Sarah Lutton, L. Sandy Maisel, and Walter J. Stone, "When to Risk It? Institutions, Ambitions, and the Decision to Run for the U.S. House," *American Political Science Review* 100, no. 2 (May 2006): 195–208.

5 Constituents aren't a legislative agent's only principals. He or she may also be beholden to party leaders and special interests, as well as to members and committees in the chamber. See Forrest Maltzman, *Competing Principals* (Ann Arbor: University of Michigan Press, 1997).

House and Senate: Differences in Representation

The framers of the Constitution provided for a bicameral legislature—a legislative body consisting of two chambers. As we saw in Chapter 2, the framers intended each of these chambers, the House and the Senate, to represent a different constituency. Members of the House were to be "close to the people," elected by popular vote every two years. Members of the Senate, on the other hand, were appointed by state legislatures for six-year terms, were to represent the elite members of society, and were to be attuned more to the interests of property than to those of the population. Today members of both the House and the Senate are elected directly by the people. The 435 members of the House are elected from districts apportioned according to population; the 100 members of the Senate are elected by state, with two senators from each. Senators continue to have longer terms in office and usually represent much larger and more diverse constituencies than do their counterparts in the House of Representatives (Table 6.1).

bicameral legislature

A legislative assembly composed of two chambers, or houses

The House and the Senate play different roles in the legislative process. In essence, the Senate is the more deliberative of the two bodies: it is the forum in which any and all ideas can receive a thorough public airing. The House is the more centralized and the more organized of the two bodies: it is better equipped to play a routine role in the governmental process. In part, this difference stems from the different rules governing the two bodies. These rules give House leaders more control over the legislative process and provide for House members to specialize in certain legislative areas. The rules of the much

Table 6.1

DIFFERENCES BETWEEN THE HOUSE AND THE SENATE

	HOUSE	SENATE
Minimum age of member	25 years	30 years
Length of U.S. citizenship	At least 7 years	At least 9 years
Length of term	2 years	6 years (staggered)
Number per state	Depends on population: 1 per 30,000 in 1789; 1 per 630,000 today	2 per state
Constituency	Tends to be local	Is both local and national

smaller, more free-wheeling Senate give its leadership relatively little power and discourage specialization. This is the institution principle at work. The two legislative chambers are organized in very different ways, reflecting not only their differences in size but also their differences in electoral rhythm, constituencies, and roles. House members specialize, their specialized activities take place mainly in committees, and deliberations by the full House take place mainly in response to committee proposals. The institution is organized to facilitate expeditious consideration of committee bills. The Senate does many of the same things. But senators are less specialized, partly because of their more heterogeneous constituencies, and therefore involve themselves in many more areas of policy. Senate proceedings permit wider participation and more open-ended deliberation.

Both formal and informal factors also contribute to the differences between the two chambers of Congress. Differences in the length of terms and the requirements for holding office specified by the Constitution generate differences in how the members of each body develop their constituencies and exercise their powers of office. The result is that members of the House more effectively and more frequently serve as the agents of well-organized local interests with specific legislative agendas—for instance, used-car dealers seeking relief from regulation, labor unions seeking more favorable legislation, or farmers looking for higher subsidies. The small size and relative homogeneity of their constituencies and the frequency with which they must seek re-election make House members more attuned than senators to the legislative needs of local interest groups. This is what the framers intended when they drafted the Constitution—namely, that the House of Representatives would be "the people's house" and that its members would reflect and represent public opinion in a timely manner.

Senators, on the other hand, serve larger and more heterogeneous constituencies. As a result, they are somewhat better able than members of the House to serve as the agents of groups and interests organized on a statewide or national basis. Moreover, with longer terms in office, senators have the luxury of considering "new ideas" or seeking to bring together new coalitions of interests, rather than simply serving existing ones. This, too, was the intent of the Constitution's drafters—that the Senate should provide a balance to the more responsive House, with its narrower and more homogenous constituencies. The Senate was said to be the saucer that cools the tea, bringing deliberation, debate, inclusiveness, calm, and caution to policy formulation.

For much of the late twentieth century, the House exhibited more intense partisanship and ideological division than the Senate. Because of their diverse constituencies, senators tended to be more inclined to seek compromise positions that offended as few voters and interest groups as possible. Members of the House, in contrast, with their party's domination in more homogeneous districts, were less inclined to seek compromises and more willing to stick to their partisan and ideological guns. For instance, the House divided almost exactly along partisan lines on the 1998 vote to impeach President Bill Clinton. In the Senate, by contrast, 10 Republicans joined Democrats to acquit Clinton of obstruction of justice charges, and in a separate vote five Republicans joined

Democrats to acquit Clinton of perjury.[6] However, beginning with the presidency of George W. Bush, even the Senate grew more partisan and polarized—especially on social issues and the war in Iraq.[7] In the first two years of Barack Obama's presidency, many of the president's initiatives dealing with the economic crisis, health care, gay rights, financial rescues, and most other areas have received virtually no Republican support.

The Electoral System

In light of their role as agents of various constituencies in their states and districts and the importance of elections as a mechanism by which principals (constituents) reward and punish their agents, representatives are very much influenced by electoral considerations. Three factors related to the American electoral system affect who gets elected and what he or she does once in office. The first set of issues concerns who decides to run for office and which candidates have an edge over others. The second issue is that of the incumbency advantage. Finally, the way congressional district lines are drawn can greatly affect the outcome of an election. Let us examine more closely the impact of these considerations on who serves in Congress.

Running for Office. Voters' choices are restricted from the start by who decides to run for office. In the past, decisions about who would run for a particular elected office were made by local party officials. A person who had a record of service to the party, or who was owed a favor, or whose "turn" had come up might be nominated by party leaders for an office.[8] Today few

---

6 Eric Pianin and Guy Gugliotta, "The Bipartisan Challenge: Senate's Search for Accord Marks Contrast to House," *Washington Post*, January 8, 1999, p. 1.

7 On the confirmation of Supreme Court nominations, however, even in an atmosphere of elevated partisanship moderates from both parties in the Senate have prevented partisan extremism from dominating. Chief Justice John Roberts was easily confirmed in 2005, and Justice Samuel Alito, though given a rougher ride during confirmation hearings, was approved with support from both parties in 2006. Likewise, in 2009 and 2010, respectively, Democrat Obama's nominees to the Supreme Court, Sonia Sotomayor and Elena Kagan, were confirmed with some Republican support. Senate Democrats did block a number of lower court appointments proposed by the Bush administration. And the same practice has been followed by Senate Republicans in response to Obama's judicial nominations.

8 In the nineteenth century, it was often considered an *obligation*, not an honor, to serve in Congress. The real political action was back home in the state capital or a big city, not in Washington. So the practice of "rotation" was devised, according to which a promising local politician would do a tour of duty in Washington before being slated for an important local office. This is not to say that electoral incentives—the so-called electoral connection, in which a legislator's behavior was motivated by the desire to retain the seat for himself or his party—was absent in nineteenth-century America. See, for example, Jamie L. Carson and Erik J. Engstrom, "Assessing the Electoral Connection Evidence from the Early United States," *American Journal of Political Science* 49 (2005): 746–57. See also William T. Bianco, David B. Spence, and John D. Wilkerson, "The Electoral Connection in the Early Congress: The Case of the Compensation Act of 1816," *American Journal of Political Science* 40 (1996): 145–71.

party organizations have the power to slate candidates in that way. Instead, the decision to run for Congress is a more personal choice. One of the most important factors determining who runs for office is a candidate's ambition.[9] A potential candidate may also assess whether he or she can attract enough money to mount a credible campaign. The ability to raise money depends on connections to other politicians, interest groups, and the national party organization. Wealthy individuals may finance their own races. In 2000, for example, the New Jersey Democrat and former investment banker Jon Corzine spent more than $60 million of his own money to win a U.S. Senate seat. (In 2005, he spent a similar amount of money to win the governorship of New Jersey. But money isn't everything. Despite his wealth, Corzine lost this post four years later.)

Features distinctive to each congressional district also affect the field of candidates. Among them is the range of other political opportunities that may lure potential candidates away. In addition, the way the congressional district overlaps state legislative boundaries may affect a candidate's decision to run. A state-level representative or senator who is considering a run for the U.S. Congress is more likely to assess his or her prospects favorably if the state district coincides with the congressional district (because the voters will already know him or her). For similar reasons, U.S. representatives from small states, whose congressional districts cover a large portion of the state, are far more likely to run for statewide office than members of Congress from large states. For example, John Thune was elected as the lone representative from South Dakota in 1996. His constituency thus completely overlapped those of Senators Tim Johnson and Tom Daschle. In 2002, Thune challenged Johnson, losing by barely 500 votes. In 2004, he defeated Daschle, then the Democratic leader in the Senate. For any candidate, decisions about running must be made early because once money has been committed to declared candidates, it is harder for new candidates to break into a race. Thus the outcome of a November election is partially determined many months earlier, when decisions to run are finalized.[10]

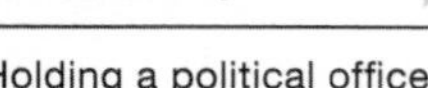

incumbency

Holding a political office for which one is running

Incumbency. Incumbency plays a very important role in the American electoral system and in the kind of representation citizens get in Washington. Once in office, members of Congress are typically eager to remain in office and make politics a career. Over the course of the twentieth century, Congress developed into a professional legislature, a legislature whose members serve full time for

9 See Linda L. Fowler and Robert D. McClure, *Political Ambition: Who Decides to Run for Congress* (New Haven, CT: Yale University Press, 1989), and Alan Ehrenhalt, *The United States of Ambition: Politicians, Power, and the Pursuit of Office* (New York: Times Books, 1991).

10 Thus the timing of Hurricane Katrina was especially propitious for the Democrats and unfortunate for the Republicans. Occurring in September 2005, the poor response by the Bush administration in the aftermath of the hurricane gave the Democrats a long lead time in which to recruit high-quality candidates to contest the November 2006 congressional elections while discouraging high-quality Republican candidates. On the thesis of "strategic candidacy," see Gary C. Jacobson, *The Politics of Congressional Elections*, 7th ed. (New York: Pearson Longman, 2008).

Figure 6.2

TURNOVER IN THE HOUSE OF REPRESENTATIVES

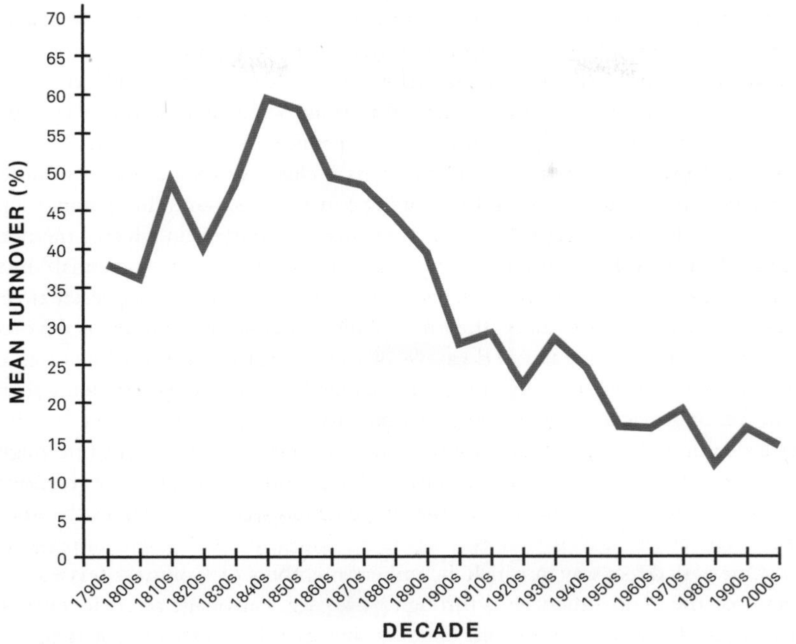

NOTE: Overall for this period, the mean turnover was 30.7 percent.
SOURCE: Based on John Swain, Stephen A. Borelli, Brian C. Reed, and Sean F. Evans, "A New Look at Turnover in the U.S. House of Representatives, 1789–1998," *American Politics Quarterly* 28 (2000): 435–57.

multiple terms (Figure 6.2).[11] The career ambitions of members of Congress are helped by an array of tools that they can use to stack the deck in favor of their re-election. These tools have been created by incumbent legislators themselves to aid their own cause—the rationality principle at work once again. Through effective use of this arsenal of weapons, an incumbent establishes a reputation for competence, imagination, and responsiveness—the attributes most principals look for in an agent.

Perhaps the most important advantage of incumbency is the opportunity legislators have to serve on legislative committees. Especially in the House, but often in the Senate as well, incumbent legislators are able to burnish their policy credentials, to develop expertise and, critically, to be in a position to help constituents, either through affecting the legislative agenda or interceding with

11 Nelson W. Polsby, "The Institutionalization of the U.S. House of Representatives," *American Political Science Review* 62, no. 1 (March 1968): 144–68.

the bureaucracy. It is here—on committees—that incumbents establish a track record of accomplishments that compares favorably with the mere promises of electoral challengers. This advantage is especially powerful when a legislator's committees deal with issues central to the lives of his or her constituents. (And, party leaders in Congress are adept at matching their members to the "right" committees—yet another example of the rationality principle at work.) Finally, the advantage of committee membership is cumulative: continuous service on a committee not only enhances a legislator's policy credentials and expertise but also positions him or her for committee leadership posts.

casework 

An effort by members of Congress to gain the trust and support of constituents by providing personal service. One important type of casework consists of helping constituents obtain favorable treatment from the federal bureaucracy

The opportunity to help constituents is a clear advantage that committee membership gives incumbents. But helping constituents—and thus gaining support in the district—goes beyond the particular committees in which a member serves. In establishing an attractive political reputation and a "personal" relationship with his or her constituents, well over a quarter of a representative's time and nearly two-thirds of the time of his or her staff members is devoted to constituency service (termed casework). This service is not merely a matter of writing and mailing letters. It includes talking to constituents, providing them with minor services, presenting special bills for them, and attempting to influence decisions by regulatory commissions on their behalf. Indeed, one might think of the member's legislative staff and office operation as a congressional enterprise, much like a firm, with the member himself or herself as the chief executive officer.[12]

patronage 

The resources available to higher officials, usually opportunities to make partisan appointments to offices and confer grants, licenses, or special favors to supporters

One very direct way in which incumbent members of Congress serve as the agents of their constituencies is through patronage. Patronage refers to a variety of forms of direct services and benefits that members provide for their districts. One of the most important forms of patronage is pork-barrel legislation. Through pork-barrel legislation, representatives seek to capture federal projects and federal funds for their districts (or states in the case of senators) and thus "bring home the bacon."

pork-barrel legislation 

The appropriations made by legislative bodies for local projects that often are not needed but are created so that local representatives can carry their home district in the next election

A common form of pork barreling is the earmark, the practice through which members of Congress insert into otherwise pork-free bills language that provides special benefits for their own constituents.[13] For example, among the more outrageous earmarks in a 2005 transportation bill was a bridge in Alaska that cost more than $10 million and connected the mainland to an island on which no one lives (the so-called "bridge to nowhere"). This earmark proved so embarrassing to the Republicans once they began receiving adverse publicity that they rescinded the appropriation.

12 For more on the congressional office as an enterprise that processes the casework demands of constituents, see Robert H. Salisbury and Kenneth A. Shepsle, "Congressman as Enterprise," *Legislative Studies Quarterly* 6 (1981): 559–76.

13 For a study of academic earmarking, see James D. Savage, *Funding Science in America: Congress, Universities, and the Politics of the Academic Pork Barrel* (New York: Cambridge University Press, 1999). For a general study of pork-barrel activity, see the excellent book by Diana Evans, *Greasing the Wheels: Using Pork Barrel Projects to Build Majority Coalitions in Congress* (New York: Cambridge University Press, 2004).

By 2010 House Republicans had sworn off earmarks altogether and their partisan colleagues in the Senate, though less enthusiastically, seemed willing to go along. In one of the last actions taken by the 111th Congress—the lame-duck session following the November 2010 elections—a spending bill funding government operations through March 2011 was stripped of nearly all earmarks.

Pork-barrel activities by incumbent legislators bring a number of our principles from Chapter 1 into play. Incumbent legislators engage in the practice because it furthers their electoral objectives (the rationality principle). They succeed to the degree that they are able to join with fellow legislators in exchanging support for each other's projects (the collective action principle). These efforts are facilitated by institutional procedures: amendments to appropriations bills, omnibus legislation, opportunities to insert special provisions into bills (the institution principle). And they decidedly influence the mix and location of spending by the federal government (the policy principle). From time to time, as with the "bridge to nowhere," the practice becomes so egregious that Congress establishes procedures to restrict the activity, thereby constraining the actions of members of Congress in the future (the history principle).

Finally we should note that all of these incumbent benefits are publicized though another incumbency advantage—the franking privilege. Under a law enacted by the 1st Congress in 1789, members of Congress may send mail to their constituents free of charge to keep them informed of governmental business and public affairs. Under current law, members receive an average of about $100,000 in free postage for mailings to their constituents. There is a great variety of franked mail. Some target special groups on issues of direct interest to them—for example, news about minimum wage legislation sent to union households in the district. Most common of all are "your congressman at work" newsletters, which are sent to households in an entire district on a regular basis.

Members may not use these funds to send mail outside their districts, however, or to send mass mailings within 90 days of a primary or general election. Despite the restrictions, the franking privilege provides incumbents with a valuable resource for publicizing their activities and making themselves visible to voters.

The incumbency advantage is evident in the high rates of re-election among congressional incumbents: over 90 percent for House members and nearly 90 percent for members of the Senate in recent years (Figure 6.3).[14] In 2008, 95 percent of House incumbents running in the general election were successful, and 85 percent of incumbent senators were re-elected. In the 2010 elections, dozens of incumbent Democrats lost their seats to Republican challengers in the House, but still a majority of all incumbents (from both parties) who ran

14 Norman J. Ornstein, Thomas E. Mann, and Michael J. Malbin, *Vital Statistics on Congress, 1995–1996* (Washington, DC: CQ Press, 1996), pp. 60–61 (see also subsequent editions); Robert S. Erickson and Gerald C. Wright, "Voters, Candidates, and Issues in Congressional Elections," in *Congress Reconsidered*, 8th ed., Lawrence C. Dodd and Bruce I. Oppenheimer, eds. (Washington, DC: CQ Press, 2005), pp. 77–106; and John R. Alford and David W. Brady, "Personal and Partisan Advantage in U.S. Congressional Elections, 1846–1990," in *Congress Reconsidered*, 5th ed., Lawrence C. Dodd and Bruce I. Oppeheimer, eds. (Washington, DC: CQ Press, 1993), pp. 141–57.

Figure 6.3
THE POWER OF INCUMBENCY

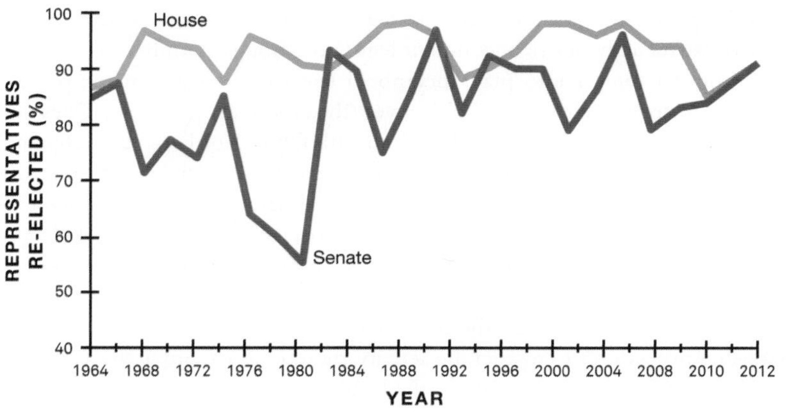

SOURCES: Center for Responsive Politics, www.opensecrets.org/bigpicture/reelect.php?cycle=2010 and authors' update.

held onto their seats—nearly 80 percent of Democrats and more than 98 percent of Republicans. In 2012, 91 percent of those incumbents running for re-election in each chamber won. In the Senate 10 of the 33 incumbents left the body, but 21 of the 23 running for re-election were successful; in the House 42 members retired, 13 lost primaries, and 27 lost in the general election, leaving 356 of 393 successful.

An additional incumbency advantage to include on your list is in fund-raising. Incumbents with their "brand name" are in a position to raise campaign funds throughout their term, often in such quantities as to scare off prospective challengers. Thus, the incumbency advantage is evident in what is called sophomore surge—the tendency for candidates to win a higher percentage of the vote when seeking their second term in office than they won in their initial election victory. Members of Congress almost always are able to outspend their challengers (Figure 6.4).[15] Over the past quarter century, and despite many campaign finance regulations that were meant to level the playing field, the gap between incumbent and challenger spending has grown. Members of the majority party in the House and Senate are particularly attractive to donors who want access to those in power.[16]

15 Stephen Ansolabehere and James Snyder, "Campaign War Chests and Congressional Elections," *Business and Politics* 2 (2000): 9–34.

16 Gary W. Cox and Eric Magar, "How Much Is Majority Status in the U.S. Congress Worth?" *American Political Science Review* 93, no. 2 (June 1999): 299–309.

Figure 6.4
HOUSE AND SENATE CAMPAIGN EXPENDITURES

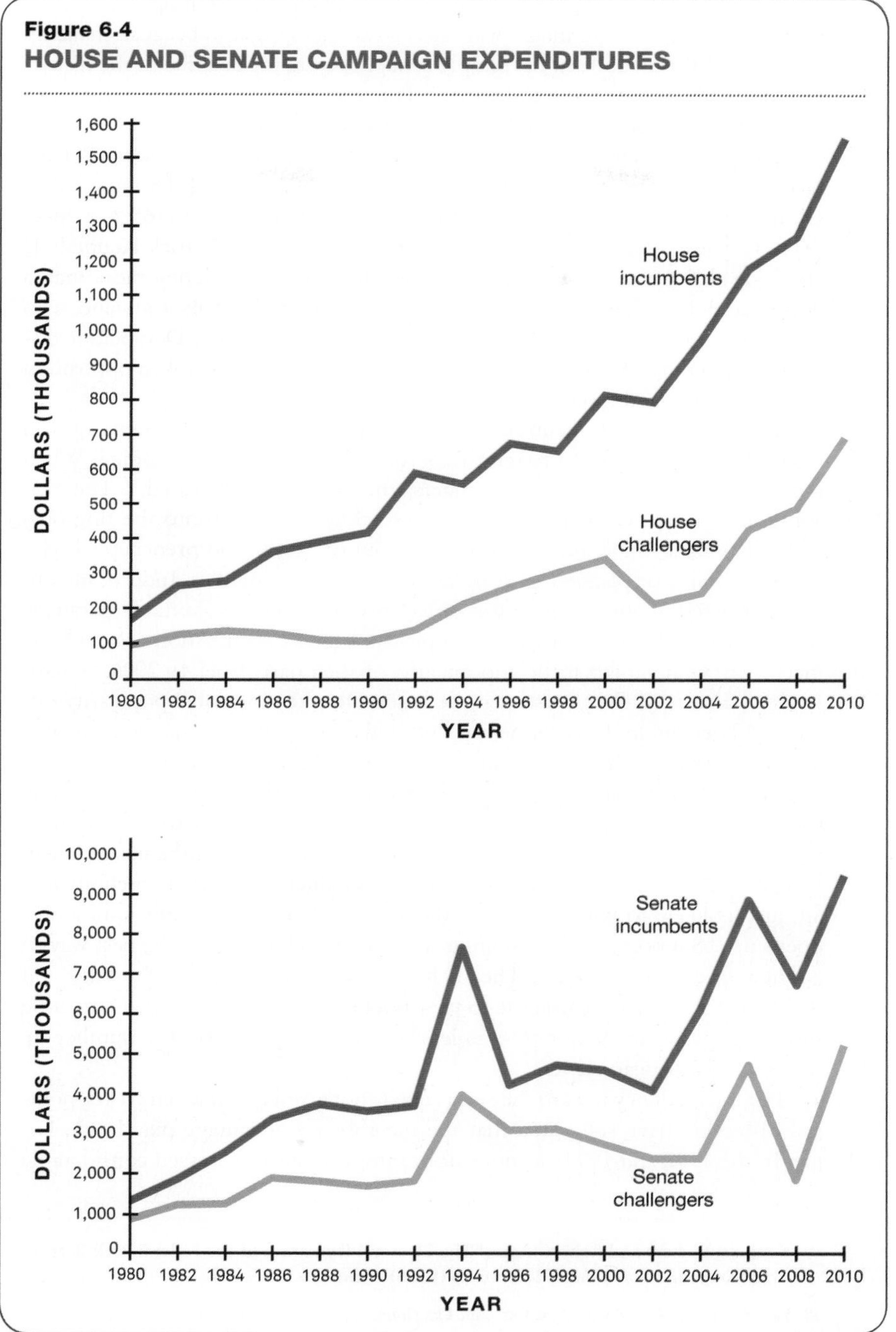

SOURCES: Norman J. Ornstein, Thomas E. Mann, and Michael J. Malbin, *Vital Statistics on Congress, 2001–2002* (Washington, DC: American Enterprise Institute, 2002), pp. 87, 93, and Campaign Finance Institute, www.cfinst.org (accessed 8/8/11).

Incumbency can help a candidate by discouraging potential opponents, not only because of an incumbent's war-chest advantages but also because challengers fear that the incumbent has simply brought too many benefits to the district or is too well liked or too well known.[17] Potentially strong challengers may also decide that a district's partisan leanings are too unfavorable.

The eighth district of Massachusetts provides a notable example. Represented by, among others, John F. Kennedy (1947–52) and Thomas "Tip" O'Neill (1953–86), who became president and Speaker of the House, respectively, this seat became vacant when the incumbent Joseph Patrick Kennedy II (1987–98) left office. A wide-open Democratic primary, attracting more than a dozen candidates, barely selected the mayor of Somerville, Mike Capuano, who went on to win the general election easily in this urban, heavily Democratic district. Capuano has remained in this seat ever since, facing only token opposition in each election and rolling up huge majorities.

The advantage of incumbency thus tends to preserve the status quo in Congress by discouraging potentially strong challengers from running. When incumbents do face strong challengers, they are often defeated.[18] The reason is that strong challengers are willing to throw their hat into the ring only when they believe the incumbent is weak, out of touch, too preoccupied with national affairs, or plagued by scandal or declining capabilities. Indeed, incumbents afflicted in any of these ways may choose to retire voluntarily (strategic retirement) instead of facing the high probability of defeat. Another source of incumbent vulnerability is the unpopularity of their party label. In 2006, Senator Lincoln Chafee (R-R.I.) illustrated the latter. Despite a personal popularity rating of 62 percent in the polls, he was defeated as many Rhode Islanders signaled their displeasure with the Bush administration and the Republican Congress.

The role of incumbency also has implications for the social composition of Congress. For example, the incumbency advantage makes it harder for women to increase their numbers in Congress because most incumbents are men. Female candidates who run for open seats (for which there are no incumbents) are just as likely to win as male candidates but they have to wait until a seat opens up.[19] Supporters of term limits argue that such limits are the best way to get new faces into Congress. They believe that the incumbency advantage and the tendency of many legislators to view politics as a career mean that very little turnover will occur in Congress unless limits are imposed on the number of terms a legislator can serve.

But the tendency toward the status quo is not absolute. In recent years, political observers have suggested that the incumbency advantage may be declining. In the 1992 and 1994 elections, for example, voters expressed considerable

17 Kenneth Bickers and Robert Stein, "The Electoral Dynamics of the Federal Pork Barrel," *American Journal of Political Science* 40 (1996): 1300–26.

18 Jacobson, *The Politics of Congressional Elections.*

19 See Barbara C. Burrell, *A Woman's Place Is in the House, Campaigning for Congress in the Feminist Era* (Ann Arbor: University of Michigan Press, 1994), and David Broder, "Key to Women's Political Parity: Running," *Washington Post*, September 8, 1994, p. A17.

anger and dissatisfaction with incumbents, producing a 25 percent turnover in the House in 1992 and a 20 percent turnover in 1994. Yet the defeat of incumbents was not the main factor at work in either of these elections; 88.3 percent of House incumbents who sought re-election were re-elected in 1992, and 90.2 percent won re-election in 1994. In 1992, it was an exceptionally high retirement rate (20 percent, as opposed to the norm of 10 percent) among members of Congress that created more open seats and brought new faces into Congress.[20] In 1994, a large number of open seats combined with an unprecedented mobilization of Republican voters to shift control of Congress to the Republican Party. In 2006, the reverse happened. The Democrats needed to gain 15 seats to capture the House, and they won double that number; in the Senate, they captured the six Republican seats they needed to win control of that chamber. The election in 2010 saw another reversal as Republicans easily exceeded the gains required to capture the House and barely fell short of capturing the Senate.

Congressional Districts. The final factor that affects who wins a seat in Congress is the way congressional districts are drawn. Every 10 years, state legislatures must redraw congressional districts to reflect population changes. In 1929, Congress enacted a law fixing the total number of congressional seats at 435. As a result, when states with fast-growing populations gain districts, they do so at the expense of states with slower population growth. In recent decades, this has meant that the nation's growth areas in the South and West have gained congressional seats at the expense of the Northeast and the Midwest (Figure 6.5). After the 2010 census, for example, Texas gained four seats and Florida two, whereas New York and Ohio lost two each. Redrawing congressional districts is a highly political process: districts are shaped to create an advantage for the majority party in the state legislature, which controls the redistricting process. In this complex process, those charged with drawing districts use sophisticated computer technologies to come up with the most favorable district boundaries. Redistricting can create open seats and may pit incumbents of the same party against each other, ensuring that one of them will lose. Redistricting can also give an advantage to one party by clustering voters with some ideological or sociological characteristics in a single district or by separating those voters into two or more districts. Gerrymandering can have a major effect on the outcome of congressional elections. Before 1980, for example, California's House seats had been almost evenly divided between the two parties. After the 1980 census, a redistricting effort controlled by the Democrats, who held both houses of the state legislature as well as the governorship, resulted in Democrats' taking control of two-thirds of the state's seats in the U.S. House of Representatives.[21]

gerrymandering

The apportionment of voters in districts in such a way as to give unfair advantage to one political party

20 The reason for the high voluntary retirement rate that year is interesting. Congress had passed a reform making it impossible for members to pocket money left in their office accounts when they retired. The last year in which pocketing this money was permitted was 1992, and a number of members took that opportunity to retire, some enriching themselves by hundreds of thousands of dollars.

21 David Butler and Bruce Cain, *Congressional Redistricting: Comparative and Theoretical Perspectives* (New York: Macmillan, 1992).

Figure 6.5
APPORTIONMENT OF HOUSE SEATS BY REGION, 1910 AND 2010

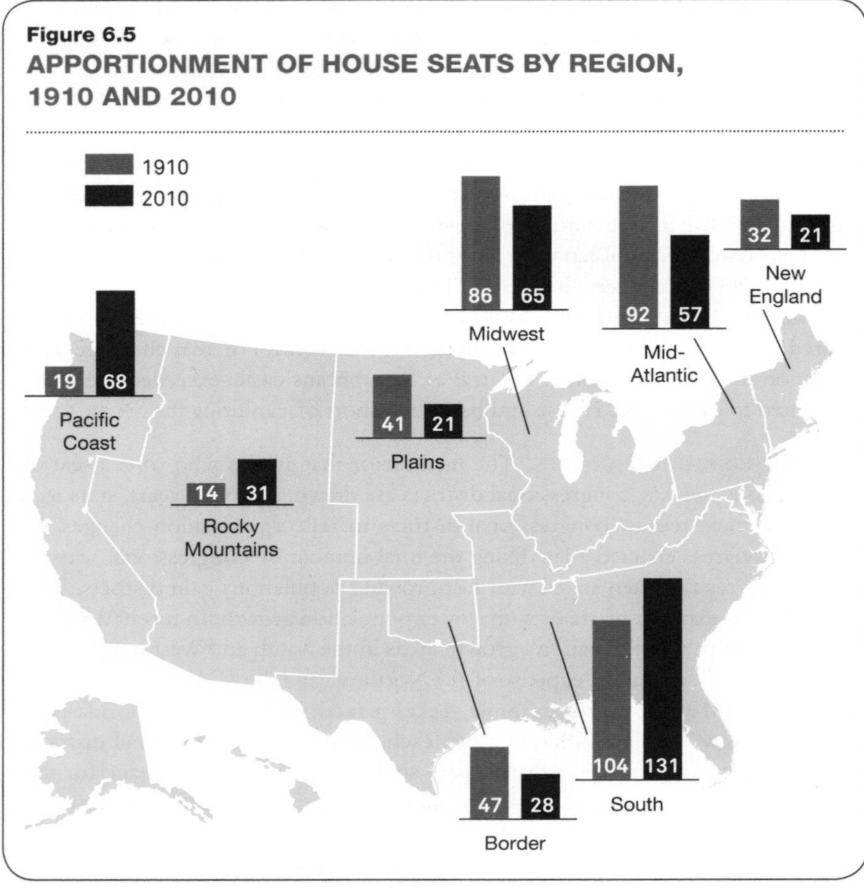

SOURCES: Norman J. Ornstein, Thomas E. Mann, and Michael J. Malbin, eds., *Vital Statistics on Congress, 2001–2002* (Washington, DC: American Enterprise Institute, 2002), p. 59; U.S. Census Bureau, "Change in Number of Seats in the U.S. House of Representatives, by State, Ordered by Seats Gained and Lost: 1940 to 2010," www.census.gov/population/apportionment/data/files/1940-2010%20seat%20change%20by%20state.pdf (accessed 11/1/11).

Another more recent case benefited the Republicans. The 2002 congressional election was the first one under the redistricting required by the 2000 census. In 2003, the Texas legislature, controlled by the Republicans, set to work drawing up a *new* set of congressional districts. Ordinarily this exercise is performed once per decade, after the constitutionally required census. But, argued the Texas Republicans, nothing prohibits a state from doing it more frequently. Democrats in the Texas state legislature were furious and twice staged walkouts, even fleeing across the border to Oklahoma to avoid a posse of Texas Rangers sent to retrieve them. These walkouts delayed proceedings by making it difficult to assemble enough legislators to meet the minimum requirements to do legislative business. Finally, however, the Republicans prevailed, redrawing the federal districts in a way that was very favorable to them. In the next election in 2004, the Republicans gained five seats in Texas, defeating four Democratic incumbents, in part as a result of their redistricting maneuver.[22] Examples such as these explain why the two parties invest substantial resources in state legislative and gubernatorial contests during the electoral cycle that precedes the year in which congressional district boundaries will be redrawn. The "Analyzing the Evidence" unit in Chapter 11 takes a closer look at redistricting, looking ahead to how district lines were redrawn after the 2010 census.

As we see in Chapter 11, since the passage of the 1982 amendments to the 1965 Voting Rights Act, race has become a major—and controversial—consideration in drawing voting districts. These amendments, which encouraged the creation of districts in which members of racial minorities have decisive majorities, have greatly increased the number of minority representatives in Congress. After the 1991–92 redistricting, the number of predominantly minority districts doubled, from 26 to 52. Among the most fervent supporters of the new minority districts were white Republicans, who used the opportunity to create more districts dominated by white Republican voters.[23] These developments raise thorny questions about representation. Some analysts argue that although the system may grant minorities greater sociological representation, it has made it more difficult for them to win substantive policy goals.[24]

PROBLEMS OF LEGISLATIVE ORGANIZATION

The U.S. Congress is not only a representative assembly. It is also a legislative body. For Americans, representation and legislation go hand in hand. Many parliamentary bodies, however, are representative yet lack the power to legislate. It is no small achievement that the U.S. Congress both represents *and* governs.

Governing is a challenge. It is extraordinarily difficult for a large, representative assembly to formulate, enact, and implement laws. Just the internal complexities of conducting business within Congress—the legislative process—are daunting. In addition, many individuals and institutions have the capacity to influence the legislative process. Because successful legislation requires the confluence of so many distinct factors, it is little wonder that most of the thousands

22 In late 2004, the U.S. Supreme Court ordered a lower federal court to reconsider the "extra" Texas redistricting plan. This case worked its way back to the Supreme Court. In June 2006, the Court ruled that the Texas legislature was within its rights to redistrict more than once per decade; however, it also ruled that some of the particular decisions about district boundaries violated the rights of Latino voters.

23 David Lublin, *The Paradox of Representation: Racial Gerrymandering and Minority Interests in Congress* (Princeton, NJ: Princeton University Press, 1997).

24 Lani Guinier, *The Tyranny of the Majority: Fundamental Fairness in Representative Democracy* (New York: Free Press, 1995). See also David Epstein and Sharyn O'Halloran, "Measuring the Electoral and Policy Impact of Majority-Minority Voting Districts," *American Journal of Political Science* 42 (1999): 367–95.

of bills considered by Congress each year are defeated long before they reach the president.

The supporters of legislative proposals often feel that the formal rules of the congressional process are deliberately designed to prevent their own deserving proposals from ever seeing the light of day. But these rules allow Congress to play an important role in lawmaking. If it wants to be more than a rubber stamp for the executive branch, like so many other representative assemblies around the world, a national legislature such as Congress must develop a division of labor, set an agenda, maintain order through rules and procedures, and place limits on discussion. If it wants to accomplish these things in a representative setting in which a veritable diversity of political preferences exists, then it must find the ways and means to allow cooperation despite the variety of interests and coalitions and to make compromises despite conflicts. We will first take up the general issues that face any legislature or decision-making group possessing diverse preferences: the problems of cooperation, coalitions, and compromises.

Cooperation in Congress

A number of factors make cooperation difficult in Congress. A popularly elected legislative assembly—the Boston City Council, the Kansas state legislature, the U.S. Congress, the French National Assembly, or the European Parliament—consists of politicians who harbor a variety of political objectives. Because they got where they are by winning an election and many hope to stay where they are or possibly advance their political careers, these politicians are intimately aware of whom they must please to do so:

- Because campaigns are expensive propositions, most politicians are eager to please those who can supply resources for the next campaign—campaign donors, PACs, important endorsers, party officials, volunteer activists.
- The most recent campaign—one that the politicians won—provides them with information about just why their victory was secured. It is sometimes quite difficult to sort out the myriad factors, but at the very least the politicians have a good sense of what categories of voters supported them and may be prepared to support them again if performance is adequate.
- Many politicians not only aim to please campaign contributors and voters but also have an agenda of their own. Whether for private gain or public good, politicians come to the legislature with policy goals of personal importance.

Congress consists of a heterogeneous group of legislators, and the specific public policies that they want to pursue are thus many and varied. They may be considered from two perspectives. First, owing to their different constituencies, legislators will give priority to different realms of public policy. A Cape Cod congressman will be interested in shipping, fishing, coastal preservation, harbor development, tourism, and shipbuilding. An inner-city Philadelphia congresswoman may not care much at all about those issues, focusing instead on welfare reform, civil rights policy, aid to inner-city school systems, and job-retraining programs. Montana's sole member of Congress is probably not interested in coastal preservation or inner-city schools but rather in ranching, agriculture, mining, and public land use. Evidently, Congress encompasses a mélange of legislative priorities.

Second, the opinions its members hold on any given issue are diverse. Although interest in environmental protection, for example, ranges from high among those who count many Sierra Club members among their constituents to low among those who have other fish to fry, once environmental protection is on the agenda there is a broad range of preferences for specific initiatives. Some want pollution discharges carefully monitored and regulated by a relatively powerful watchdog agency. Others believe that more decentralized and less intrusive means, such as marketable pollution permits, are the way to go—so-called "cap and trade" policies. Still others think the entire issue is overblown, that any proposed cure is worse than the disease, and that the country would be best served by leaving well enough alone.

Diversity in both priorities and preferences among legislators is sufficiently abundant that the view of no group of legislators predominates. Legislative consensus must be built—this is what legislative politics is all about. Each legislator clamors to get his or her priority issue the attention he or she believes it deserves or to make sure his or her position on a given issue prevails. But neither effort is likely to succeed on its own merits. Support must be assembled, deals consummated, and promises and threats used. In short, legislators intent on achieving their objectives must cooperate, coalesce, and compromise. And these activities are facilitated by rules and procedures. This system leads to the division and specialization of legislative work, the regularization of procedures, and the creation of agenda power. All of these organizational features of Congress arise as part of a governance structure to allow for cooperation and coalition building—activities that yield compromise policies.

Underlying Problems and Challenges

Before we can understand why Congress selects particular ways to institutionalize its practices, we need a finer appreciation of other underlying problems with which legislators must grapple. Then we can consider how the U.S. Congress deals with these problems.

Matching Influence and Interest. Legislatures are highly egalitarian institutions. Each legislator has one vote on any issue coming before the body. Whereas a consumer has a cash budget that she may allocate in any way she wishes to categories of consumer goods, a legislator is not given a vote budget in quite the same sense. Instead, his budget of votes is "dedicated"—one vote for each motion before the assembly. He cannot aggregate the votes in his possession and cast all or some large fraction of them for a motion on a subject near and dear to his heart (or the hearts of his constituents). This is a source of frustration because, as we have noted, the premise of instrumental behavior dictates that legislators would, if they could, concentrate whatever resources they commanded on those subjects of highest priority to them. The egalitarian arrangement thus forces legislators to make deals with one another—"I'll support you on this motion if you support me on a future motion."

Information. Legislators do not vote for outcomes directly but, rather, for instruments (or policies) whose effects produce outcomes. Thus legislators, to vote intelligently, must know the connection between the instruments they vote for and the effects they desire. In short, they must have information and knowledge about how the world works.

Few legislators—indeed, few people in general—know how the world works in very many policy domains except in the most superficial of ways. Nearly everyone in the legislature would benefit from the production of valuable information, at the very least information that would allow all of them to eliminate policy instruments that make very little difference in solving social problems or even make matters worse. Producing such information, however, is not a trivial matter. Simply to digest the knowledge that is being produced outside the legislature by knowledge-industry specialists (academics, scientists, journalists, interest groups) is a taxing task. Clearly institutional arrangements that provide incentives to some legislators to produce, evaluate, and disseminate this knowledge for others will permit public resources to be used more effectively. Because legislatures are in competition with other branches of government—particularly the executive—legislators need to meet certain informational requirements just to keep up with the competition.

Compliance. The legislature is not the only game in town. The promulgation of public policies is a joint undertaking in which judges, executives, bureaucrats, and others participate alongside legislators. If the legislature develops no means with which to monitor what happens after a bill becomes law, then it risks seeing public policies implemented in ways other than those it intended when the law was passed. Cooperation does not end with the successful passage of a law. If legislators wish to have an impact on the world around them, especially on those matters to which their constituents give priority, then it is necessary to attend to policy implementation, not just policy formulation. But it is just not practical for all 435 representatives and all 100 senators to march down to this or that agency on Pennsylvania Avenue to ensure appropriate implementation by the executive bureaucracy. Compliance will not just happen, and like the production and dissemination of reliable information at the policy-formulation stage, the need for oversight of the executive bureaucracy is but an extension of the cooperation that produced legislation in the first place. It, too, must be institutionalized.

What we have suggested in this abstract discussion about legislative institutions and practices is that Congress is a place in which different kinds of representatives congregate and try to accomplish things so that they may reap the support of their respective constituents back home. This very diversity is problematic—it requires cooperation, coalitions, and compromise. In addition, there is a mismatch of influence and interest (owing to one person, one vote), information about the effectiveness of alternative policies is in short supply, and the legislature must worry about how its product—public laws—gets treated by the other branches of government. These are the problems that legislatures, including the U.S. Congress, devise institutional arrangements to solve or at least mitigate. This is where the rationality principle and institution principle join forces.

THE ORGANIZATION OF CONGRESS

We now examine the organization of Congress and the legislative process, particularly the basic building blocks of congressional organization: political parties, the committee system, congressional staff, the caucuses, and the parliamentary rules of the House and Senate. Each of these factors plays a key role in the organization of Congress and in the process through which Congress formulates and enacts laws. We also look at powers Congress has in addition to lawmaking and explore the future role of Congress in relation to the powers of the executive.

Party Leadership and Organization in the House and the Senate

One significant aspect of legislative life is not even part of the *official* organization: political parties. The legislative parties—primarily Democratic and Republican in modern times but numerous others over the course of American history—are organizations that foster cooperation, coalitions, and compromise. They are the vehicles of collective action, both for legislators sharing common policy objectives inside the legislature and for those very same legislators as candidates in periodic election contests back home.[25] In short, political parties in Congress are the fundamental building blocks from which policy coalitions are fashioned to pass legislation and monitor its implementation, thereby providing a track record on which members build electoral support.

25 For a historically grounded analysis of the development of political parties as well as a treatment of their general contemporary significance, see John H. Aldrich, *Why Parties? The Origin and Transformation of Political Parties in America* (Chicago: University of Chicago Press, 1995). For an analysis of the parties in the legislative process, see Gary W. Cox and Mathew D. McCubbins, *Legislative Leviathan: Party Government in the House*, 2nd ed. (Berkeley: University of California Press, 2006). See also their *Setting the Agenda: Responsible Party Government in the U.S. House of Representatives* (New York: Cambridge University Press, 2005). A provocative essay questioning the role of parties is Keith Krehbiel, "Where's the Party?" *British Journal of Political Science* 23 (1993): 235–66.

party caucus, or party conference

A normally closed meeting of a political or legislative group to select candidates or leaders, plan strategy, or make decisions regarding legislative matters

Speaker of the House

The chief presiding officer of the House of Representatives. The Speaker is elected at the beginning of every Congress on a straight party vote. He or she is the most important party and House leader

majority leader

The elected leader of the party holding a majority of the seats in the House of Representatives or the Senate. In the House, the majority leader is subordinate in the party hierarchy to the Speaker

minority leader

The elected leader of the party holding less than a majority of the seats in the House or Senate

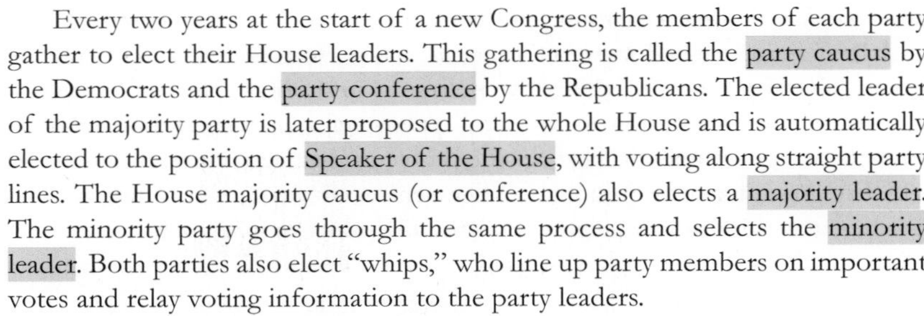

Every two years at the start of a new Congress, the members of each party gather to elect their House leaders. This gathering is called the party caucus by the Democrats and the party conference by the Republicans. The elected leader of the majority party is later proposed to the whole House and is automatically elected to the position of Speaker of the House, with voting along straight party lines. The House majority caucus (or conference) also elects a majority leader. The minority party goes through the same process and selects the minority leader. Both parties also elect "whips," who line up party members on important votes and relay voting information to the party leaders.

In December 2006, in the wake of the November elections, the Democrats become the majority party in both chambers. In the House, they selected Nancy Pelosi of California as Speaker, Steny Hoyer of Maryland as majority leader, and James Clyburn of South Carolina as whip. The Republicans, who had in the previous Congress made John Boehner of Ohio their majority leader, kept him on as minority leader, as well as Roy Blunt of Missouri as minority whip. In 2008, Republicans chose Eric Cantor of Virgina to replace Blunt as whip, but otherwise the leadership from both parties remained the same. In 2010 there was another reversal of fortune as the Republicans stormed back into the majority. Both parties kept their top leaders: Boehner and Cantor as Speaker and majority leader, respectively, and Pelosi and Hoyer as their minority counterparts. As the 2012 election continued Republican control of the House, the leadership remained the same.

At one time, party leaders strictly controlled committee assignments, using them to enforce party discipline. Today representatives often expect to receive the assignments they want and resent leadership efforts to control assignments. The leadership's best opportunities to use committee assignments as rewards and punishments come when more than one member seeks a seat on a committee.

Generally representatives seek assignments that will allow them to influence decisions of special importance to their districts. Representatives from farm districts, for example, may request seats on the Agriculture Committee.[26] This is one method by which the egalitarian allocation of power in the legislature is overcome. Even though each legislator has just one vote on each issue in the full chamber, he or she, by serving on the right committees, is able to acquire extra influence in areas important to his or her constituents. Seats on powerful committees such as Ways and Means, which is responsible for tax legislation, and Energy and Commerce, responsible for health, energy, and regulatory policy, are especially popular.

We now turn to the Senate, where the president pro tempore, a position designated in the Constitution, exercises mainly ceremonial leadership. Usually the majority party designates the member with the greatest seniority to serve in this

26 For an extensive discussion of the committee-assignment process in the U.S. House, see Kenneth A. Shepsle, *The Giant Jigsaw Puzzle: Democratic Committee Assignments in the Modern House* (Chicago: University of Chicago Press, 1978), and Scott A. Frisch and Sean Q. Kelly, *Committee Assignment Politics in the U.S. House of Representatives* (Norman: University of Oklahoma Press, 2006). See also E. Scott Adler, *Why Congressional Reforms Fail: Reelection and the House Committee System* (Chicago: University of Chicago Press, 2002).

capacity. Real power is in the hands of the majority and minority leaders, each elected by party caucus. Together they control the Senate's calendar, or agenda, for legislation. In addition, the senators from each party elect a whip.

The 2002 elections gave the Republican Party a one-seat majority in the Senate. In the 2004 election, they gained an additional four seats, for a 55-to-45 majority. Republicans re-elected Bill Frist of Tennessee as majority leader, while Democrats replaced the recently defeated Tom Daschle of South Dakota with Harry Reid of Nevada as the minority leader. After their six-seat gain in the 2006 election, the Democrats named Reid majority leader. The Republicans elected Mitch McConnell of Kentucky to the post of minority leader. Both were re-elected to these positions after the 2008, 2010, and 2012 elections.

Party leaders reach outside their respective chambers in an effort to augment their power and enhance prospects for their party programs. One important external strategy involves fund-raising. In recent years, congressional leaders have established their own political action committees. Interest groups are usually eager to contribute to these "leadership PACs" in order to curry favor with powerful members of Congress. The leaders, in turn, use the funds to support the various campaigns of their party's candidates and thereby create a sense of obligation and loyalty among those they help.[27]

In addition to the tasks of organizing Congress, congressional party leaders set the legislative agenda. Not only do the party leaders have considerable sway over Congress's agenda in the large, but they also regulate the fine-grained deliberation over specific items on the agenda. This aspect of agenda setting is multifaceted. At the outset, for example, a bill is initially filed with the clerk of the House as a legislative proposal. The Speaker of the House then determines which committee has jurisdiction over it. Indeed, since the mid-1970s, the Speaker has been given additional bill-assignment powers, known as multiple referral, permitting him or her to assign different parts of a bill to different committees or the same parts sequentially or simultaneously to several committees.[28] The steering and agenda setting by party leaders work, however, within an institutional framework consisting of structures and procedures. The Analyzing the Evidence unit on page 200 takes a closer look at parties and agenda control.

27 Rank-and-file members, especially those from safe districts who face limited electoral challenges, have also created their own PACs, which enable them to contribute to their party and its candidates. See Eric S. Heberlig, "Congressional Parties, Fundraising, and Committee Ambition," *Political Research Quarterly* 56 (2003): 151–61.

28 For a historical look, see David W. Rohde and Kenneth A. Shepsle, "Leaders and Followers in the House of Representatives: Reflections on Woodrow Wilson's *Congressional Government*," *Congress and the Presidency* 14 (1987): 111–33. An analysis of the House leadership is Eric Schickler and Kathryn Pearson, "The House Leadership in an Era of Partisan Warfare," in *Congress Reconsidered*, 8th ed., pp. 207–26. A companion piece on the Senate is C. Lawrence Evans and Daniel Lipinski, "Obstruction and Leadership in the U.S. Senate," in *Congress Reconsidered*, 8th ed., pp. 227–48. An update is Kathryn Pearson and Eric Schickler, "The Transition to Democratic Leadership in a Polarized House," in *Congress Reconsidered*, 9th ed., Lawrence C. Dodd and Bruce I. Oppenheimer, eds. (Washington, DC: CQ Press, 2008), pp. 165–89.

rties and Agenda ntrol in Congress

CHAPTER

Contributed by
Jamie Carson
University of Georgia

ssing the influence of political parties on legislative politics, political scientists often ask how utcomes in Congress. One approach might be to look for evidence of arm-twisting and pr y party leaders, both of which can be used to influence members' roll-call vote choices. Yet, ir cholars have responded to this question by looking for evidence of agenda manipulation y party. If the majority party can control what gets voted on—through their control of the ttee and other committees, combined with the party leaders' scheduling power—then it car es even where the party leaders cannot effectively twist arms and promise favors. Thus, a qu s taken center stage in congressional research is, who controls the agenda in Congress?

lican and Democratic Agendas, 2011

REPUBLICAN AGENDA 2011
REPEAL HEALTH CARE REFORM
REDUCE DISCRETIONARY SPENDING
EXTEND BUSH-ERA TAX CUTS
NATIONAL SECURITY
BUDGET/DEFICIT MANAGEMENT
TERRORISM/HOMELAND SECURITY
SOCIAL SECURITY REFORM
JOB CREATION

DEMOCRATIC AGENDA 2011
ECONOMIC RECOVERY
ENERGY INDEPENDENCE
AFGHANISTAN TROOP WITHDRAWAL
ONGOING HEALTH CARE REFORM
REGULATORY REFORM
DEFICIT REDUCTION
BANKING INDUSTRY REFORM
REDUCE GLOBAL WARMING

genda control so important in Congress? Whichever party controls a greater number of seats in either r the Senate decides which issues will come to the floor for consideration. In addition to all the perks th ority control, the party with a majority is able to push items on its specific agenda. As we see from the t f the most prominent agenda items, there are clear differences between Republicans and Democrats in

House Rolls on Final-Passage Votes, 99th–111th Congresses

Congress	Majority party	Final passage votes	Majority party rolls	Majority party roll rate	Minority party rolls	Minority party roll rate
99th	DEMOCRATS	89	1	1.1%	35	39%
100th	DEMOCRATS	116	2	1.7%	40	34%
101st	DEMOCRATS	118	1	0.9%	39	36%
102nd	DEMOCRATS	142	0	0.0%	39	27%
103rd	DEMOCRATS	160	1	0.6%	56	35%
104th	REPUBLICAN	136	1	0.7%	63	46%
105th	REPUBLICAN	133	3	2.3%	51	38%
106th	REPUBLICAN	136	4	2.9%	51	39%
107th	REPUBLICAN	93	1	1.1%	31	37%
108th	REPUBLICAN	119	1	0.8%	46	33%
109th	REPUBLICAN	146	2	1.4%	64	39%
110th	DEMOCRATS	161	4	2.5%	102	63%
111th	DEMOCRATS	116	1	0.9%	92	79%

One specific way of thinking about agenda control in Congress is in terms of the winners and losers on particular pieces of legislation, because this may tell us how much influence the majority party actually has. The most prominent example of this approach has been to look at partisan roll rates. A party (or group of members) is "rolled" when a majority of its members winds up on the losing side of a vote that passes. In focusing specifically on final-passage votes in the U.S. House, the political scientists Gary Cox and Mathew McCubbins have found that, at the aggregate level, the majority party is almost never rolled. In contrast, and as we see from the table above, the minority party is significantly more likely to be on the losing side on final-passage votes. This suggests that the majority party controls the agenda and prevents legislation that it opposes (and is likely to lose on) from coming to a vote. The dramatic increase in the minority party roll rate during recent congresses also most likely reflects high levels of partisan polarization within the House.

SOURCES:

Republican and Democratic Agendas, 2011: Major Garrett and Susan Davis, *National Journal*, "The GOP Blueprint," November 6, 2010.

House Rolls on Final-Passage Votes, 99th–111th Congresses: Gary W. Cox and Mathew D. McCubbins, *Setting the Agenda: Responsible Party Government in the U.S. House of Representatives* (New York: Cambridge University Press, 2005); calculated by author.

EXPLORE **PARTIES AND AGENDA CONTROL** FURTHER AT:

wwnorton.com/studyspace

Having described some of the powers of party leaders, we might pause and ask an even more basic question: Why do members allow themselves to be governed by powerful party leaders? Leaders, after all, are elected by their rank-and-file members, and in their respective party caucuses the rank and file determine how powerful they will permit their leaders to be. Indeed, the power of party leaders has ebbed and flowed over time. From the end of World War II until as late as the 1970s, for example, when the Democrats were the majority party most of the time, party leaders were relatively weak. Speaker of the House Sam Rayburn (D-Tex.), to give one example, was beloved by his followers and was quite successful at persuading members to toe the party line during the 1940s and 1950s. But persuasion was just about the only tool at his disposal. Later party leaders possessed more potent tools. Jim Wright (D-Tex.), for example, who served as Speaker in the 1980s, was provided with considerable power over committee assignments and chaired most of the party committees that formulated policy objectives for the Democrats. Why did party leaders become more powerful?

The political scientists John Aldrich and David Rohde have sought to understand these ebbs and flows in the power of a party over its members, or what they call "conditional party government." They suggest that the institutional strength of party leaders is conditional; it depends on particular circumstances. The circumstance they emphasize is the degree to which party members share policy goals. If the rank and file are relatively homogeneous in this respect, they will endow their leaders with considerable power to prosecute the shared agenda. If, on the other hand, party members are heterogeneous in their goals, they will be less disposed to empower a leader (indeed, they will be suspicious of any exercise of power by a leader). Thus the Democratic Party of the 1940s and 1950s, with its northern liberal wing and its southern conservative wing, was heterogeneous in the extreme and provided its leaders with few power resources. The effects of the Voting Rights Act of 1965, one of which was that formerly Democratic constituencies in the South started electing Republicans, began to be felt in the 1970s, reducing the diversity in the Democratic ranks and thus rendering the party more homogeneous. Under this changed circumstance, Democratic Party legislators, who were more focused than before on moderate and liberal goals, were prepared to empower their leaders.[29]

---

29 A now-classic treatment of the ebbs and flows of parties and their leaders in the modern era is David W. Rohde, *Parties and Leaders in the Post-reform House* (Chicago: University of Chicago Press, 1991). For a more historical perspective, see David W. Rohde, John H. Aldrich, and Mark M. Berger, "The Historical Variability in Conditional Party Government, 1877–1986," in *Party, Process, and Political Change in Congress: New Perspectives on the History of Congress*, David W. Brady and Mathew D. McCubbins, eds. (Palo Alto, CA: Stanford University Press, 2002), pp. 17–35. For a development of the analytical argument, see David W. Rohde and John H. Aldrich, "The Logic of Conditional Party Government: Revisiting the Electoral Connection," in *Congress Reconsidered*, 7th ed., Lawrence C. Dodd and Bruce I. Oppenheimer, eds. (Washington, DC: CQ Press, 2001), pp. 265–92. A complementary theoretical perspective is offered by the political scientists Gary Cox and Mathew McCubbins in both *Legislative Leviathan* and *Setting the Agenda*.

The Committee System: The Core of Congress

If the system of leadership in each party and chamber constitutes the first set of organizational arrangements in the U.S. Congress, then the committee system provides it with a second set of organizational structures. But these are more a division-of-labor and specialization-of-labor system than the hierarchy-of-power system that determines leadership arrangements.

Congress began as a relatively unspecialized assembly, with each legislator participating equally in every step of the legislative process in all realms of policy. By the time of the War of 1812, if not earlier, Congress had begun employing a system of specialists—the committee system—because members with different interests and talents wished to play disproportionate roles in some areas of policy making while ceding influence in areas in which they were less interested.[30] If, Rip van Winkle–like, a congressman had fallen asleep in 1805 and woke up in 1825, he would have found himself in an entirely transformed legislative world. The legislative chambers in the beginning of that period consisted of bodies of generalists. By the end of the period, in policy area after policy area, the legislative agenda was dominated by groups of specialists serving on standing committees. If, on the other hand, our legislator had fallen asleep in 1825 and awoke a *century* later, the legislature would not seem so very different. In short, organizational decisions in the first quarter of the nineteenth century affected legislative activity over a long horizon. This is the history principle at work.

The congressional committee system consists of a set of standing committees, each with its own jurisdiction, membership, and authority to act. Each standing committee is given a permanent status by the official rules, with a fixed membership, officers, rules, a staff, offices, and above all, a jurisdiction that is recognized by all other committees and, usually, the leadership as well (Table 6.2). The jurisdiction of each standing committee is defined by the subject matter of legislation. Except for the Rules Committee in the House and the Rules and Administration Committee in the Senate, all the important committees receive proposals for legislation and process them into official bills. The House Rules Committee decides the order in which bills come up for a vote and determines the rules that govern the length of debate and opportunity for amendments. The jurisdictions of the standing committees usually parallel those of the major departments or agencies in the executive branch. There are important exceptions—Appropriations and Rules in both chambers, for example—but by and large the division of labor is self-consciously designed to parallel executive-branch organization.

standing committee

A permanent legislative committee that considers legislation within its designated subject area; the basic unit of deliberation in the House and Senate.

Jurisdiction. The world of policy is partitioned into policy jurisdictions, which become the responsibility of committees. The members of the Armed Services Committee, for example, become specialists in all aspects of military

30 The story of the evolution of the standing committee system in the House and the Senate in the early part of the nineteenth century is told in Gerald Gamm and Kenneth A. Shepsle, "Emergence of Legislative Institutions: Standing Committees in the House and Senate, 1810–1825," *Legislative Studies Quarterly* 14 (1989): 39–66.

Table 6.2

STANDING COMMITTEES OF CONGRESS, 2011*

HOUSE COMMITTEES	
Agriculture	Judiciary
Appropriations	Natural Resources
Armed Services	Oversight and Government Reform
Budget	Rules
Education and Workforce	Science, Space, and Technology
Energy and Commerce	Small Business
Financial Services	Standards of Official Conduct (Ethics)
Foreign Affairs	Transportation and Infrastructure
Homeland Security	Veterans' Affairs
House Administration	Ways and Means
SENATE COMMITTEES	
Agriculture, Nutrition, and Forestry	Finance
Appropriations	Foreign Relations
Armed Services	Health, Education, Labor, and Pensions
Banking, Housing, and Urban Affairs	Homeland Security and Governmental Affairs
Budget	Judiciary
Commerce, Science, and Transportation	Rules and Administration
Energy and Natural Resources	Small Business and Entrepreneurship
Environment and Public Works	Veterans' Affairs

*These were the committees in the 112th Congress (2011–12). Committee names and jurisdictions change over time, as does the number of committees.

affairs, the subject matter defining their committee's jurisdiction. Legislators tend to have disproportionate influence in their respective committee jurisdictions, not only because they have become the most knowledgeable members of the legislature in that area of policy but also because they are given the opportunity to exercise various forms of agenda power, a subject we develop further in the next section.

Dividing up institutional activities among jurisdictions, thereby encouraging participants to specialize, has its advantages. But it has its costs, too. If the Armed Services Committee of the House of Representatives had no restraints, its members would undoubtedly shower their districts with military facilities and contracts. In short, the delegation of authority and resources to specialist subunits exploits the advantages of the division and specialization of labor but risks jeopardizing the collective objectives of the group as a whole. The monitoring of committee activities thus goes hand in hand with delegation.

Sometimes new issues arise that fit neatly into no jurisdiction. Some, such as the issue of energy supplies that emerged during the 1970s, are so multifaceted that bits and pieces of them are spread across many committee jurisdictions. Other issues, such as the regulation of tobacco products, fall into the gray area claimed by several committees. In this case in the House, the Energy and Commerce Committee, with its traditional claim on health-related issues, fought with the Agriculture Committee, whose traditional domain includes crops such as tobacco, for jurisdiction over this issue. Still others, like Homeland Security, arise at the time of crisis, overlap with the jurisdictions of other committees, and take time to sort out turf responsibilities. Turf battles between committees of Congress are notorious.[31] These battles involve committee chairs, the Office of the Parliamentarian, the political leadership of the chamber, and from time to time, select committees appointed to realign committee jurisdictions.

Authority. Committees may be thought of as agents of the parent body to which jurisdiction-specific authority is provisionally delegated. In this section, we describe committee authority in terms of gatekeeping and after-the-fact authority.

Normally any member of the legislature can submit a bill calling for changes in some policy area. Almost automatically this bill is assigned to the committee of jurisdiction, and very nearly always, there it languishes. In a typical session in the House of Representatives, about 8,000 bills are submitted, fewer than 1,000 of which are acted on by the appropriate committee of jurisdiction. In effect, then, although any member is entitled to make proposals, committees get to decide whether to open the gates and allow the bill to be voted on by the full chamber. Related to gatekeeping authority is a committee's proposal power. After a bill is referred to a committee, the committee may take no further action

gatekeeping authority

The right and power to decide if a change in policy will be considered

proposal power

The capacity to bring a proposal before the full legislature

31 An outstanding description and analysis of these battles is found in David C. King, "The Nature of Congressional Committee Jurisdictions," *American Political Science Review* 88, no. 1 (March 1994): 48–63. See also King's *Turf Wars: How Congressional Committees Claim Jurisdiction* (Chicago: University of Chicago Press, 1997).

on it, amend the legislation in any way, or even write its own legislation before bringing the bill to the floor for a vote. Committees, then, are lords of their jurisdictional domains, setting the table, so to speak, for their parent chamber.[32]

after-the-fact authority

The authority to follow up on the fate of a proposal once it has been approved by the full chamber

conference committee

A joint committee created to work out a compromise for House and Senate versions of a piece of legislation

oversight

The effort by Congress, through hearings, investigations, and other techniques, to exercise control over the activities of executive agencies

A committee also has responsibilities for bargaining with the other chamber and for conducting oversight, or after-the-fact authority. Because the U.S. Congress is bicameral, once one chamber passes a bill, the bill must be considered by the other chamber. If the other chamber passes a bill different from the one passed in the first chamber and the first chamber refuses to accept the changes made, then the two chambers ordinarily meet in a conference committee, in which representatives from each chamber hammer out a compromise. In the great majority of cases, conferees are drawn from the committees that had original jurisdiction over the bill. For example, in a sample of Congresses in the 1980s, of the 1,388 House members who served as conferees for various bills during a three-year period, only 7 were not on the committee of original jurisdiction; similarly, in the Senate on only 7 of 1,180 occasions were conferees not drawn from the "right" committee.[33] The committee's effective authority to represent its chamber in conference-committee proceedings constitutes the first manifestation of after-the-fact power that complements its before-the-fact gatekeeping and proposal powers.

A second manifestation of after-the-fact committee authority consists of the committee's primacy in legislative oversight of policy implementation by the executive bureaucracy. Even after a bill becomes a law, it is not always (indeed, it is rarely) self-implementing. Executive agents—bureaucrats in the career civil service, commissioners in regulatory agencies, political appointees in the executive branch—march to their own drummers. Unless legislative actors hold their feet to the fire, they may not do precisely what the law requires (especially in light of the fact that statutes are often vague and ambiguous). Congressional committees are continuously watchful of the manner in which legislation is implemented and administered. They play this after-the-fact role by allocating staff and resources to track what the executive branch is doing and, from time to time, holding oversight hearings in which particular policies and programs are given intense scrutiny. This, in turn, gives congressional committees an additional source of leverage over policy in their jurisdictions. Oversight is discussed further in Chapter 8 on the bureaucracy.

32 This setup clearly gives committee members extraordinary power in their respective jurisdictions, allowing them to push policy into line with their own preferences—but only up to a point. If the abuse of their agenda power becomes excessive, the parent body has structural and procedural remedies available to counteract the committee's actions—such as stacking the committee with more compliant members, deposing a particularly obstreperous committee chair, or removing policies from a committee's jurisdiction. These are the clubs behind the door that only rarely have to be employed; their mere presence suffices to keep committees from the more outrageous forms of advantage taking.

33 See Kenneth A. Shepsle and Barry R. Weingast, "The Institutional Foundations of Committee Power," *American Political Science Review* 81, no. 1 (March 1987): 85–104.

Subcommittees. The standing committees of the U.S. House are divided into about 100 even more specialized subcommittees. These subcommittees serve their full committees in precisely the same manner as the full committees serve the parent chamber. Thus, in their narrow jurisdictions they have gatekeeping, proposal, interchamber-bargaining, and oversight powers. For a bill on wheat to be taken up by the full Agriculture Committee, for example, it first has to clear the subcommittee on General Farm Commodities. All of the issues involving assignments, jurisdictions, and authority that we discussed earlier regarding full committees apply at the subcommittee level as well.

Hierarchy. At the committee level, the mantle of leadership falls on the committee chair. He or she, together with the party leaders, determines the committee's agenda and then coordinates the committee's staff, investigatory resources, and subcommittee structure.[34] This coordination includes scheduling hearings, "marking up" bills—that is, transforming legislative drafts into final versions—and scripting the process by which a bill goes from committee to floor proceedings to final passage. For many years, Congress followed a rigid seniority rule for the selection of committee chairs. The benefits of this rule are twofold. First, the chair will be occupied by someone knowledgeable in the committee's jurisdiction, familiar with interest-group and executive-branch players, and politically experienced. Second, the larger institution will be spared divisive leadership contests that reduce the legislative process to efforts in vote grubbing. There are costs, however: senior individuals may be unenergetic, out of touch, even senile.

 **seniority**

The priority or status ranking given to an individual on the basis of length of continuous service on a congressional committee

The U.S. House operated according to a strict seniority principle from about 1910 (and, informally, even earlier) until the mid-1970s, when most members felt that the burdens of this arrangement were beginning to outweigh its advantages. Committee chairs are now elected by the majority-party members of the full legislature, though there remains a presumption (which may be rebutted) that the most senior committee member will normally assume the chair.[35]

Decisiveness on Committees. When a committee goes about its business, its chair exercises agenda power, as noted. But he or she is not a dictator. Any proposal made to the committee by the chair must ultimately secure the support of a committee majority. In this setting, who is *decisive*? That is, whose vote is necessary and sufficient for a motion to pass? The answer is provided by the *median-voter theorem*. This theorem can be stated as follows: if the alternatives under consideration can be represented as points on a line, if individuals have a most-preferred point, and their preferences decrease steadily for points farther away, then the most-preferred point of the median (middle) voter can defeat any other point in a majority contest.

34 Because subcommittee chairs do essentially the same things in their narrower jurisdictions, we won't provide a separate discussion of them.

35 Beginning with the Republican takeover of the House in 1995, committee chairs have been term limited. After three terms, a chair must step down. It appears that party leaders exert more authority today in the appointment of new chairs.

Figure 6.6
THE MEDIAN VOTER IN CONGRESSIONAL COMMITTEES

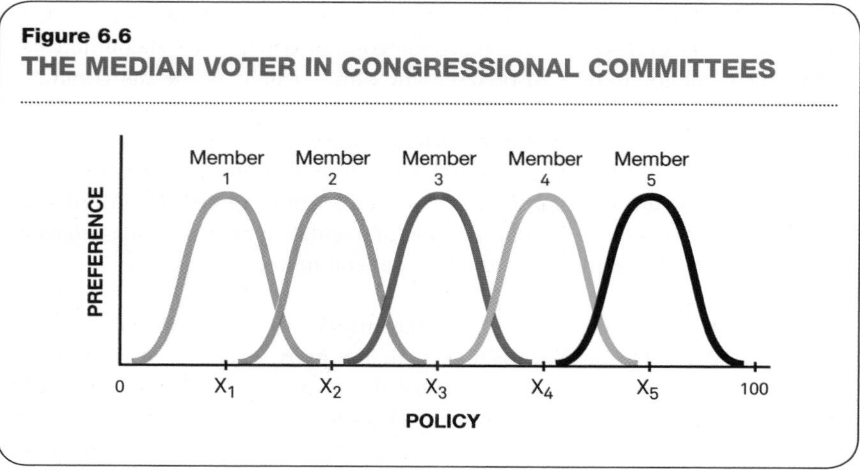

In Figure 6.6 we have a five-person committee that must choose a point on the line ranging from 0 to 100. Each member has a favorite point, represented by the peak of her curve, and her preferences decline steadily as points farther and farther away are considered. The median-voter theorem asserts that the favorite point of member 3 can beat any other point in a majority contest. A majority comprising members 3, 4, and 5 prefers 3's favorite to any point to its left; a majority comprising members 1, 2, and 3 prefers 3's favorite to any point to its right; therefore 3's favorite can prevail against *any* point. We will discuss the median-voter theorem again in Chapter 11 in the context of elections.

Monitoring Committees. If unchecked, committees might easily take advantage of their authority. Indeed, what prevents committees from exploiting their before-the-fact proposal power and their after-the-fact bargaining and oversight authority? As we saw in Chapter 1, in our discussion of the principal-agent problem, principals must be certain that agents are properly motivated to serve the principal's interests, either by actually sharing the principal's interests themselves or by deriving something of value (reputation, compensation, and so on) for acting to advance those interests. Alternatively, the principal will need to have some instruments by which to monitor and validate what his or her agent is doing, rewarding or punishing the agent accordingly.

Consider again the example of congressional committees. The House or Senate delegates responsibility to its Committee on Agriculture to recommend legislative policy in the field of agriculture. Not surprisingly, legislators from farm districts are most eager to get onto this committee, and for the most part their wishes are accommodated. The Committee on Agriculture, consequently, is composed mainly of farm legislators. And nonfarm legislators are relieved at not having to spend their time on issues of little material interest to them or their constituents. In effecting this delegation, however, the parent legislature is putting itself in the hands of its farm colleagues, benefiting from their expertise on farm-related matters, to be sure, but laying itself open to the danger of planting the fox squarely in the henhouse. The Committee on Agriculture becomes not only a collection of specialists but also a collection of advocates for farm interests. How can the parent body know for certain, therefore, that a recommendation from that committee is not more a reflection of its advocacy than a reflection of its expertise? This is the risk inherent in delegation in principal-agent relationships.

And it is for this reason that the parent legislature maintains a variety of tools and instruments to protect itself from being exploited by its agents. First, it does not allow committees to make final decisions on policy; it allows only recommendations, which the parent legislature retains the authority to accept, amend, or reject. A committee has agenda power, but it is not by itself decisive. Second, the parent body relies on the committee's concern for its own reputation. Making a recommendation on a piece of legislation is not a one-shot action; the committee knows it will return to the parent body time and time again with legislative recommendations, and it will not want to tarnish its reputation for expertise by too much advocacy. Third, the parent body relies on competing agents—interest groups, expert members not on the committee, legislative specialists in the other chamber of the legislature, executive-branch specialists, and even academics—to keep its own agents honest. Fourth, party leaders, through their control of plenary time on the floor, monitor committee products to make sure they are compatible with party goals. Finally, in the House there is an institutional club behind the door—the discharge petition. A committee that is sitting on a bill, not permitting it to be taken up by the full chamber, can be discharged of responsibility for the bill if a petition to that effect is signed by a majority of the chamber.

Nevertheless, a principal will not bother to eliminate *entirely* these prospective deviations from his or her interests by agents who have interests of their own. A principal will suffer some agency loss from having delegated authority to a "hired hand"; therefore, nearly all principal-agent relationships will be imperfect in some respects from the principal's perspective. Agents will be in a position to extract some advantage from the privileged relationship they have with their principal—not too much, or it will undermine the relationship altogether, but enough to diminish the benefits of the relationship a bit from the principal's point of view. The Committee on Agriculture, for example, cannot get away with spending huge proportions of the federal budget on agricultural subsidies to farmers. But it can insert small items into agriculture bills from time to time—an experimental grain-to-fuel conversion project in an important legislator's state or district, for example, or special funds to the U.S. trade representative to give priority to agriculture-related trade issues. The parent body, as we suggested, will find it worth its while to keep an eye on the Agriculture Committee, but it won't be worth its while to take action on every instance of indulgence by the committee. The cost of doing that—the transaction cost of monitoring and overseeing committee performance—gets excessive if perfection is the objective.

 **agency loss**

The difference between what a principal would like an agent to do and the agent's performance

Thus we see the institution principle providing some guidance on how a group of legislators organizes itself for business. The legislators take advantage of the division and specialization of labor, dividing themselves into specialized subgroups (committees and subcommittees) and thus enjoying the benefits of expertise from these subunits. But they also guard against the subunits' going off half cocked in pursuit of their own narrower interests. The parent legislature in effect uses institutional arrangements to regulate and oversee its subunits' activities.

Committee Reform. Over the years, Congress has reformed its organizational structure and operating procedures. Most changes have been made to improve efficiency, but some reforms have also represented a response to political considerations. In the 1970s, a series of reforms substantially altered the organization of power in Congress. Among the most important changes put into place at that time were the election of committee chairs, an increase in the number of subcommittees, greater autonomy for subcommittee chairs, the opening of most committee deliberations to the public, and a system of multiple referral of bills that allowed several committees to consider one bill at the same time. One of the driving impulses behind these reforms was an effort to reduce the power of committee chairs.

As a consequence of those reforms, power became more fragmented, making it harder to reach agreement on legislation. In 1995, the Republican leadership of the 104th Congress sought to concentrate more authority in the party leadership. One of the ways the House achieved this was by abandoning the principle of seniority in the selection of a number of committee chairs, appointing them instead according to their loyalty to the party. This move tied committee chairs more closely to the leadership. In addition, the Republican leadership eliminated 25 of the House's 115 subcommittees and gave committee chairs more power over their subcommittees. The result was an unusually cohesive congressional majority, which pushed forward a common agenda. House Republicans also agreed to impose a three-term limit on committee and subcommittee heads. As a result, all the chairs were replaced in 2001, when the 107th Congress convened. In many instances, chairs were replaced by the most senior Republican committee member, but the net result was a redistribution of power in the House of Representatives. Since 2001 some of the earlier practices have slowly begun to reassert themselves. Speaker Nancy Pelosi and the Democratic majority in 2007 observed seniority in the appointment of nearly all committee chairs. But it is not automatic, and committee chairs are on notice that significant deviations from a party policy consensus will not be tolerated. For example, in 2009 a newly enlarged Democratic majority replaced John Dingell (D-Mich.), a fixture in the House for half a century, as chair of the Commerce and Energy Committee with Henry Waxman (D-Calif.), a less senior member of the committee.

In the midst of the financial crisis during Obama's first term, especially 2009–11, fiscal matters figured very prominently. Taxing and spending committees in both chambers played major roles in shepherding a stimulus package and a rescue of the auto industry through both chambers, as well as follow-up monitoring of the earlier rescue of banks and other financial players. During this period, the banking committees produced major regulatory reforms for their industry. At the same time, the health committees produced what ultimately became Obama's health care policy. In all these activities, Speaker Pelosi and Majority Leader Reid conducted and choreographed. The legislative record of the 111th Congress was testimony both to an efficient division- and specialization-of-labor committee system *and* to authoritative and strong party leadership.

The Staff System: Staffers and Agencies

A congressional institution ranking just below committees and parties in importance is the staff system. Every member of Congress employs a large number of staff members, whose tasks include handling constituency requests and, to a large and growing extent, dealing with legislative details and the activities of administrative agencies. Increasingly, staffers bear the primary responsibility for formulating and drafting proposals, organizing hearings, dealing with administrative agencies, and negotiating with lobbyists. Indeed, legislators typically deal with each other through staff members rather than through direct, personal contact. Representatives and senators together employ nearly 11,000 staffers in their Washington and home offices. In addition to the personal staffs of individual senators and representatives, Congress also employs roughly 2,000 committee staffers. These individuals make up the permanent staff, who often stay regardless of turnover in Congress and are attached to every House and Senate committee. They are responsible for organizing and administering the committee's work, doing research, scheduling, organizing hearings, and drafting legislation.

Not only does Congress employ personal and committee staffs, but it has also established three staff agencies designed to provide the legislative branch with resources and expertise independent of the executive branch. These agencies enhance Congress's capacity to oversee administrative agencies and evaluate presidential programs and proposals. They are the Congressional Research Service, which performs research for legislators who wish to know the facts and competing arguments relevant to policy proposals or other legislative business; the Government Accountability Office, through which Congress can investigate the financial and administrative affairs of any government agency or program; and the Congressional Budget Office, which assesses the economic implications and likely costs of proposed federal programs, such as the Bush administration rescue packages for the failing financial system in 2008 and Barack Obama's stimulus package in 2009.

staff agencies

The agencies responsible for providing Congress with independent expertise, administration, and oversight capability

congressional caucus

An association of members of Congress based on party, interest, or social characteristics such as gender or race

Informal Organization: The Caucuses

In addition to the official organization of Congress, an unofficial organizational structure also exists: the caucuses, formally known as legislative service organizations (LSOs). A congressional caucus is a group of senators or representatives who share certain opinions, interests, or social characteristics. There are ideological caucuses such as the liberal Democratic Study Group and the conservative Democratic Forum. There are also a large number of caucuses composed of legislators representing particular economic or policy interests, such as the Travel and Tourism Caucus, the Steel Caucus, the Mushroom Caucus, and the Concerned Senators for the Arts. Legislators who share common backgrounds or social characteristics have organized such caucuses as the Congressional Black Caucus, the Congressional Caucus for Women's Issues, and the Hispanic Caucus. All these caucuses seek to advance the interests of the groups they represent by promoting legislation, encouraging Congress to hold hearings, and pressing administrative agencies for favorable treatment.

RULES OF LAWMAKING: HOW A BILL BECOMES A LAW

The institutional structure of Congress is one key factor that helps shape the legislative process. A second and equally important set of factors is made up of the rules of congressional procedure. These rules govern all the procedures from introducing a bill through submitting it to the president for signing. Not only do these regulations influence the fate of every bill, but they also help determine the distribution of power in Congress.[36]

Committee Deliberation

Even if a member of Congress, the White House, or a federal agency has spent months developing and drafting a piece of legislation, it does not become a bill until a senator or a representative officially submits it to the clerk of the House or Senate and it is referred to the appropriate committee for deliberation. No floor action on any bill can take place until the committee with jurisdiction over it has taken all the time it needs to deliberate.[37] During the course of its deliberations, the committee typically refers the bill to one of its subcommittees, which may hold hearings, listen to expert testimony, and amend the proposed

36 We should emphasize, although we don't mean to confuse the reader, that a legislature "suspends" its rules as often as it follows them. There are unorthodox ways to proceed in order to avoid procedural logjams, and the House and, especially, the Senate frequently resort to these unorthodox ways. See Barbara Sinclair, *Unorthodox Lawmaking: New Legislative Processes in the U.S. Congress*, 3rd ed. (Washington, DC: CQ Press, 2007).

37 A bill can be pulled from a committee by a discharge petition, but this is an extreme measure and is resorted to only rarely. Other parliamentary tricks may also be attempted, but it is fair to say that most of the time at least it is the committee of jurisdiction that influences the course of a bill.

legislation before referring it to the full committee for its consideration. The full committee may accept the recommendation of the subcommittee or hold its own hearings and prepare its own amendments. Even more frequently, the committee and subcommittee may do little or nothing with a bill and simply allow it to die in committee. In a typical congressional session, roughly 8,000 bills are introduced, and 85 to 90 percent of them die in committee—an indication of the power of the congressional committee system.

Once a bill's assigned committee or committees in the House of Representatives have acted affirmatively, the whole bill or various parts of it are transmitted to the Rules Committee, which determines the specific rules under which the legislation will be considered by the full House. Together with the Speaker, it influences when debate will be scheduled, for how long, what amendments will be in order, and the order in which they will be considered. The Speaker also rules on all procedural points of order and points of information raised during the debate. A bill's supporters generally prefer what is called a closed rule, which puts severe limits on floor debate and amendments. Opponents of a bill usually prefer an open rule, which permits potentially damaging floor debate and makes it easier to add amendments that may cripple the bill or weaken its chances of passing.

 **closed rule**

The provision by the House Rules Committee that prohibits the introduction of amendments during debate

 **open rule**

The provision by the House Rules Committee that permits floor debate and the addition of amendments to a bill

Debate

Party control of the agenda is reinforced by the rule giving the Speaker of the House and the majority leader of the Senate the power of recognition during debate on a bill. Usually the chair knows the purpose for which a member intends to speak well in advance of the occasion. Spontaneous efforts to gain recognition are often foiled. For example, the Speaker may ask, "For what purpose does the member rise?" before deciding whether to grant recognition. In general, the party leadership in the House has total control over debate. In the Senate, each member has substantial power to block the close of debate. A House majority can override opposition, whereas it takes an extraordinary majority (60 votes) to close debate in the Senate. In recent years, with partisanship in both chambers on the rise, prolonging debate, using procedural delays, and generally dragging one's feet have been potent tools for the minority to frustrate the majority.

In the House, virtually all of the time allotted by the Rules Committee for debate on a given bill is controlled by the bill's sponsor and its leading opponent. These two participants are, by rule and tradition, granted the power to allocate most of the debate time in small amounts to members who are seeking to speak for or against the measure.

In the Senate, other than the power of recognition, the leadership has much less control over floor debate. Indeed, the Senate is unique among the world's legislative bodies for its commitment to unlimited debate. Once given the floor, a senator may speak for as long as he or she wishes unless an extraordinary majority votes to end debate. On a number of memorable occasions, senators have used this right to prevent action on legislation they opposed. Through this tactic, called the filibuster, small minorities or even one individual in the Senate

 **filibuster**

A tactic used by members of the Senate to prevent action on legislation they oppose by continuously holding the floor and speaking until the majority backs down. Once given the floor, senators have unlimited time to speak, and it requires a cloture vote of three-fifths of the Senate to end a filibuster

can force the majority to give in to his or her demands. During the 1950s and 1960s, for example, opponents of civil rights legislation often sought to block its passage by adopting the filibuster. Sixty votes are needed to end a filibuster. This procedure is called cloture.[38]

cloture

A rule allowing a supermajority of the members of a legislative body to set a time limit on debate over a given bill

Although it is the best known, the filibuster is not the only technique used to block Senate action. Under Senate rules, members have a virtually unlimited ability to propose amendments to a pending bill. Each amendment must be voted on before the bill can come to a final vote. The introduction of new amendments can be stopped only by unanimous consent. This, in effect, can permit a determined minority to filibuster by amendment, indefinitely delaying the passage of a bill.

Senators can also place "holds," or stalling devices, on bills to delay debate. Senators place holds on bills when they fear that openly opposing them will be unpopular. Because holds are kept secret, the senators placing the holds do not have to take public responsibility for their actions.[39]

Once a bill is debated on the floor of the House and the Senate, the leaders schedule it for a vote on the floor of each chamber. By then, congressional leaders know what the vote will be; leaders do not bring legislation to the floor unless they are fairly certain it is going to pass. As a consequence, it is unusual for the leadership to lose a bill on the floor. On rare occasions, however, the last moments of the floor vote can be dramatic, as each party's leadership puts its whip organization into action to make sure wavering members vote with the party. In October 2008, a massive Treasury-sponsored plan to rescue failing financial institutions was defeated in the House *despite* the support of the leadership of both parties. Because the vote came just before the 2008 elections, members were afraid to buck strong constituency opposition to the rescue plan. (A modified version passed a week later, though still with substantial and vocal opposition.) In 2010 the stimulus package proposed by the Obama administration to pump money into an economy deep in recession passed in both chambers. In the House, it passed easily—246 to 183—the only uncertainty being whether there would be any Republicans supporting it; there weren't. In the Senate, there was genuine excitement; the critical vote there was 60 to 40, just enough to close down a prospective filibuster and allow for final passage.

Conference Committee: Reconciling House and Senate Versions of a Bill

Getting a bill out of committee and through one of the houses of Congress is no guarantee that it will be enacted. Frequently bills that began with similar provisions in both chambers emerge with little resemblance to one another.

38 It should be noted that the modern filibuster is used mostly as a "threat." An indication by a senator that he or she intends to filibuster is often sufficient to induce the majority leader to move on to another topic rather than waste the Senate's valuable plenary time.

39 This and other features of the Senate rules have come under intense scrutiny in the 112th Congress.

Alternatively, a bill may be passed by one chamber but undergo substantial revision in the other chamber. If the differences cannot be worked out by passing the revised version back to the other chamber, a conference committee composed of the senior members of the committees or subcommittees that initiated the bills may be required to iron out differences. Sometimes members or leaders will let objectionable provisions pass on the floor with the idea that they will be eliminated in conference. Conference agreement requires majority support from each of the two delegations. Legislation that emerges successfully from a conference committee is more often a compromise than a clear victory of one set of forces over another.

When a bill comes out of conference, it faces one more hurdle. Before it can be sent to the president for signing, the House-Senate conference report must be approved on the floor of each chamber. It must be voted up or down; no amendments are in order. Usually such approval is given quickly. Occasionally, however, a bill's opponents use the report as one last opportunity to defeat a piece of legislation.

Presidential Action

Once adopted by the House and the Senate, a bill goes to the president, who may choose to sign the bill into law or veto it (Figure 6.7). The veto is the president's constitutional power to reject a piece of legislation. To veto a bill, the president returns it within 10 days to the house of Congress in which it originated, along with objections to it. If Congress adjourns during the 10-day period and the president has taken no action, the bill is also considered to have been vetoed—by means of the pocket veto. The possibility of a presidential veto affects the willingness of members of Congress to push for different pieces of legislation at different times. If they think a proposal is likely to be vetoed, they might shelve it for a later time. Alternatively, the sponsors of a popular bill opposed by the president might push for passage to force the president to pay the political costs of vetoing it.[40] During the entire first term of President George W. Bush (2001–05), not one bill was vetoed. In the next two years, the president vetoed a single bill. In the 110th Congress (2007–08) the Republican president faced a Congress controlled by the Democrats. The president vetoed 11 bills, and four of his vetoes were overridden. In President Obama's first term, he exercised his veto power only twice, ranking him near the bottom of the list of presidential veto frequency. He vetoed only two bills, one on a Defense Department funding resolution and another minor bill on notaries.

veto

The president's constitutional power to turn down acts of Congress within 10 days of their passage while Congress is in session. A presidential veto may be overridden by a two-thirds vote of each house of Congress

pocket veto

A veto that is effected when Congress adjourns during the time a president has to approve a bill and the president takes no action on it

A presidential veto may be overridden by a two-thirds vote in both the House and the Senate. A veto override says much about the support that a president can expect from Congress, and it can deliver a stinging blow to the executive

40 John B. Gilmour, *Strategic Disagreement: Stalemate in American Politics* (Pittsburgh: University of Pittsburgh Press, 1995).

ANALYZING THE EVIDENCE

A bill must pass through many stages and succeed at all of them in order to become a law. To prevent a bill from becoming a law, opponents need prevail at only one stage. What effects do the complications in the process have on policy outcomes?

Figure 6.7

HOW A BILL BECOMES A LAW

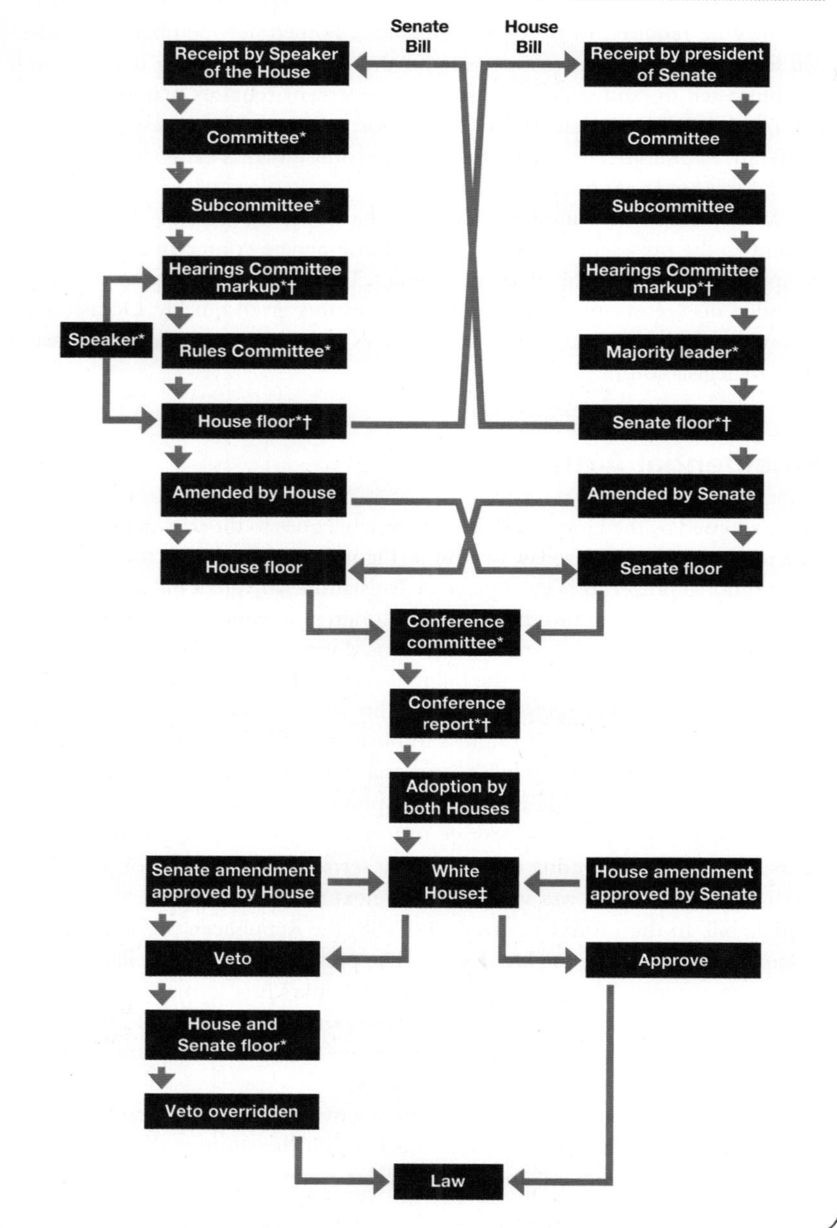

* Points at which the bill can be amended.

† Points at which the bill can die.

‡ If the president neither signs nor vetoes the bill within 10 days, it automatically becomes law.

branch. In 2007, a popular pork-barrel bill, the Water Resources Development Act, was vetoed by President Bush. His message to Congress, in part, stated:

> I am returning herewith without my approval H.R. 1495, the "Water Resources Development Act of 2007."
>
> This bill lacks fiscal discipline. I fully support funding for water resources projects that will yield high economic and environmental returns to the Nation and each year my budget has proposed reasonable and responsible funding. . . . However, this authorization bill makes promises to local communities that the Congress does not have a track record of keeping. The House of Representatives took a $15 billion bill into negotiations with a $14 billion bill from the Senate and instead of splitting the difference, emerged with a Washington compromise that costs over $23 billion. This is not fiscally responsible. . . . The bill's excessive authorization for over 900 projects and programs exacerbates the massive backlog of ongoing Corps construction projects, which will require an additional $38 billion in future appropriations to complete.[41]

Despite his opposition, both houses overwhelmingly overrode his veto. Presidents will often back down from their threat to veto a bill if they believe Congress will override the veto. These strategic interactions between the legislature and the executive branch are taken up in the next chapter.

Procedures in Congress: Regular and Unorthodox

We have noted that although there is a regular procedure in each chamber, it is often abandoned, and an abnormal, or unorthodox, procedure is devised. The treatment of appropriations bills in the period leading up to the November 2004 election provides an excellent example.

According to its regular procedure, the House passes 13 separate appropriations bills after each one has passed through an appropriations process, beginning with a subcommittee hearing, followed by full Appropriations Committee deliberations, and concluding with passage by the full House. These 13 measures are then transmitted to the Senate, which subjects each of them to its own regular appropriations process. Each of the bills (13 in all) now has a House version and a Senate version. Thirteen separate conference committees are set up to compromise on the differences between each pair. The 13 compromised versions are then sent back to each chamber for final approval. And in principle, though rarely in practice, this entire process is completed before October 1, the day on which the new fiscal year begins.

But 2004 was an election year, and members up for re-election really did not want to remind the voters that the appropriations bills they were passing were

41 *Congressional Record,* at 2007 H12458.

going to produce the largest deficit in history. So an unorthodox procedure was invented. Different versions of the appropriations bill to fund the legislative branch passed the House and the Senate through the normal process and was sent to conference. During the conference, the other 12 bills were tacked on, making a single appropriations bill. This omnibus bill was sent to each chamber for a single up-or-down vote. In voting for the omnibus measure, a member was "innoculated" against local objections from constituents. He or she could respond, "I know, I know. The omnibus bill is not ideal. But what was I to do? Defeating it would have shut the government down."

Even more unorthodox was the final passage of President Obama's health care bill in 2010. The House initially passed a health care bill in November 2009 with no Republican support and much grumbling from some Democrats who were unhappy with various aspects. But the Senate was the real battleground. A Senate version of the health care bill passed on Christmas Eve 2009. Upon their return after the holiday recess, Democratic leaders in the House and Senate plotted how to combine the two versions. But there was a shock that disrupted their plans—on January 19, 2010, Scott Brown, a Republican, won the Massachusetts Senate seat, vacant because of the death of Ted Kennedy (a Democrat and strong supporter of health care reform). The Senate was now no longer filibuster-proof, since the number of Democratic senators dropped below the magic cloture threshold. So any further vote in the Senate, which would be necessary to approve changes to the bill, could now be blocked by the Republican minority. What was to be done?

The Democrats took an unusual route. Speaker Pelosi and the Democratic leadership convinced Democrats in the House to support the Senate version of the bill, passing it 219 to 212. The identical bill was thus passed by both chambers, and no further vote was needed in the Senate. House Democrats were not happy with the Senate version, but they were placated by the promise of a second bill in which their concerns would be addressed. The second bill employed the so-called reconciliation procedure, a relatively arcane method that only requires a simple majority in each chamber. This way it was able to avoid a filibuster in the Senate. On March 26, the Senate passed this second bill, 56 to 43, the House passed it, 220 to 207, and the way was clear for Obama to sign health care reform into law.

Before leaving this topic, it is worth noting that normal and abnormal procedures involve either the conventional or the creative application of existing rules. Each chamber, however, is granted by the Constitution the privilege of formulating its own rules of procedure. So from time to time, the House or the Senate will change its rules of procedure. At other times, a dominant coalition in a chamber will threaten to do this unless it is allowed its way under the existing rules. Here we see the confluence of the rationality principle and the institution principle as rational legislators seek to (re)arrange their chamber's institutional procedures in order to accomplish particular purposes or realize particular goals.

This phenomenon was dramatically illustrated in May 2005. Even though Republicans were in the majority in the Senate, President Bush's judicial nominations were threatened by a filibuster by Democratic senators. (The Senate must formally approve a president's nominations to the federal judiciary.) In the face of nominations whose approval looked vulnerable to a blocking action by the minority party, Bill Frist, the Senate majority leader, unveiled what came to be known as the *nuclear option*. It entailed a clever parliamentary maneuver in which debate could be brought to a close not by securing the 60 votes normally required (which the Republicans did not control) but by a simple majority. This would be executed by formally requesting the president of the Senate (Vice President Dick Cheney) to end debate without a cloture vote because the issue before the Senate was the constitutional one of "advising and consenting" on a presidential judicial nomination. It was expected that any such move on the part of the Republicans would be followed by the Democrats' appealing any ruling by the Senate president to end debate. But that ruling required only a majority vote to be sustained. In this manner, the Republicans could end-run the practice of unlimited debate that normally prevails in the Senate, on constitutional issues at least. The nuclear option was never implemented, however. The very threat of it induced a number of moderate senators to agree to support a motion to end debate (thereby producing the 60 needed votes) and bring a presidential nominee forward for a final vote. These senators were willing to accommodate a vote so long as the president and the Republican majority did not abuse this concession by bringing forward "extremist" nominees.[42] With fortunes reversed in 2011—a Democratic president and a filibuster-inclined Senate Republican minority—it was Democrats who clamored for a nuclear option.

The Distributive Tendency in Congress

To pass a policy, it is necessary to authorize the policy—that is, to provide statutory authority to a government agency to implement the legislation—and then provide appropriations to fund the implementation. The list of politicians whose consent is required in these processes is extraordinarily long. At a minimum, it includes majorities of the relevant committee and subcommittee of each chamber (almost certainly including their chairs), the Appropriations Committee and the appropriate subcommittee in each chamber (including their chairs), the House Rules Committee, chamber majorities (including leaders of the majority party), and the president. Some of the legislators may go along without requiring much for their states or districts on the assumption that their turn will come on another bill. But most of these politicians will need some form of "compensation" in order to provide their endorsement and support.

42 For a model of the judicial confirmation process, see David W. Rohde and Kenneth A. Shepsle, "Advising and Consenting in the 60-Vote Senate: Strategic Appointments to the Supreme Court," *Journal of Politics* 69 (2007): 664–77.

With so many hurdles to clear before a legislative initiative can become a law, the benefits must be spread broadly. It is as though a bill had to travel on a toll road past a number of tollbooths, each one housing a collector with his or her hand out for payment. On rare occasions, the required toll takes the form of a personal bribe—a contract to a firm run by a congressman's brother, a job for a senator's daughter, a boondoggle "military inspection" trip to a Pacific isle for a legislator and his or her companion. Occasionally there is a wink-and-a-nod understanding, usually given by the majority leader or committee chair, that support from a legislator today will result in reciprocal support for legislation of interest to him or her down the road. Most frequently features of the bill are drafted initially or revised so as to be more inclusive, spreading the benefits widely among beneficiaries. This is the distributive tendency.

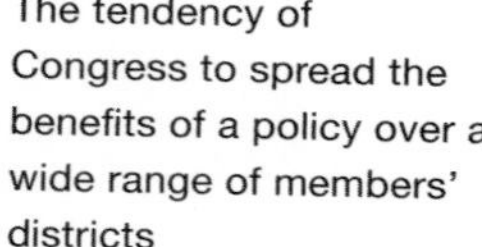

distributive tendency

The tendency of Congress to spread the benefits of a policy over a wide range of members' districts

The distributive tendency is part of the American system of representative democracy. Legislators, in advocating the interests of their constituents, are eager to advertise their ability to deliver for their state or district. They maneuver to put themselves in a position to claim credit for good things that happen there and duck blame for bad things. This is the way they earn trust back home, deter strong challengers in upcoming elections, and defeat those who do run against them. It means that legislators must take advantage of every opportunity that presents itself. In some instances, the results may seem bizarre. In April 2003, for example, Senator Thad Cochran (R-Miss.) was able to insert into the bill funding the war in Iraq language that provided $250 million for "disaster relief" for southern catfish farmers.[43] Most Americans would never have guessed that driving Saddam Hussein from power would have an effect on catfish farming in Mississippi.

This system, which is practiced in Washington and most state capitals, means that political pork gets spread around; it is not controlled by a small clique of politicians or concentrated in a small number of states or districts. But it also means that public authority and appropriations do not go where they are most needed. The most impoverished cities do not get so much money as is appropriate because some of the available money must be diverted to buy political support. The neediest individuals often do not get tax relief, health care, or occupational subsidies for reasons unrelated to philosophy or policy grounds. It is the distributive tendency at work. And it is one of the unintended consequences of the separation of powers and multiple veto points.[44] As the policy principle suggests, rationality combines with institutional practices to leave their marks on the shape of policy.[45]

43 Dan Morgan, "War Funding Bill's Extra Riders," *Washington Post*, April 8, 2003, p. A4.

44 See George Tsebelis, *Veto Players: How Political Institutions Work* (Princeton, NJ: Princeton University Press, 2002).

45 Since the 2010 elections, involving major Republican gains across the boards, there has been an anti-spending sentiment in the air in Washington. Earmarks, another name for pork-barrel projects, have been targeted. Legislators are of mixed minds about eliminating earmarks—they love being on record against spending but hate losing *their* earmarks.

HOW CONGRESS DECIDES

What determines the kinds of legislation that Congress ultimately produces? The process of creating a legislative agenda, drawing up a list of possible measures, and deciding among them is very complex. In this process, a variety of influences from inside and outside government play important roles. External influences include a legislator's constituency and various interest groups. Influences from inside government include party leadership, congressional colleagues, and the president. Let us examine each of these influences individually and then consider how they interact to produce congressional policy decisions.

Constituency

Because members of Congress want to be re-elected, the views of their constituents have a key influence on the decisions legislators make. Yet constituency influence is not so straightforward as we might think. In fact, most constituents do not even know what policies their representatives support. The number of citizens who *do* pay attention to such matters—the attentive public—is usually very small. Nonetheless, members of Congress spend a lot of time worrying about what their constituents think because these representatives realize that their choices may be scrutinized in a future election and used as ammunition by an opposing candidate. Because of this possibility, members of Congress try to anticipate their constituents' policy views.[46] Legislators are more likely to be influenced by those views if they think voters will take them into account during elections. In this way, constituents may affect congressional policy choices even when there is little direct evidence of their awareness of those choices.[47]

Interest Groups

Interest groups are another important external influence on the policies that Congress produces. When members of Congress are making voting decisions, interest groups that have some connection to constituents in the districts of

46 See John W. Kingdon, *Congressmen's Voting Decisions* (New York: Harper & Row, 1973), chap. 3, and R. Douglas Arnold, *The Logic of Congressional Action* (New Haven, CT: Yale University Press, 1990). See also Joshua Clinton, "Representation in Congress: Constituents and Roll Calls in the 106th House," *Journal of Politics* 68 (2006): 397–409.

47 Interest groups from the state or district (which we discuss later) can be useful to legislators in this respect when they provide information concerning the significance of particular issues for various constituency groups. In effect, they provide legislators with heads-up signals and wake-up calls. See Kenneth W. Kollman, *Outside Lobbying: Public Opinion and Interest Group Strategies* (Princeton, NJ: Princeton University Press, 1998).

particular members are most likely to be influential. For this reason, interest groups with the ability to mobilize followers in many congressional districts may be especially influential in Congress. The small-business lobby, for example, played an important role in defeating President Clinton's proposal for comprehensive health-care reform in 1993–94. The mobilization of networks of small businesses across the country meant that virtually every member of Congress had to take their views into account. In 2009, the Obama administration brought small business groups and the insurance industry to the table on health care very early in the process precisely because of this.

In addition to mobilizing voters, interest groups contribute money. In the 2012 electoral cycle, interest groups and PACs gave many millions of dollars in campaign contributions to incumbent legislators and challengers. What does this money buy? A popular conception is that campaign contributions buy legislative votes. In this view, legislators vote for whichever proposal favors the bulk of their contributors. Although the vote-buying hypothesis makes for good campaign rhetoric, it has little factual support. Empirical studies by political scientists show little evidence that contributions from large PACs influence legislative voting patterns.[48]

If contributions don't buy votes, what do they buy? Our claim is that campaign contributions influence legislative behavior in ways that are difficult for the public to observe and political scientists to measure. The institutional structure of Congress provides opportunities for interest groups to influence legislation outside the public eye, which legislators and contributors prefer.

Committee proposal power enables legislators, if they are on the relevant committee, to introduce legislation that favors contributing groups. Gatekeeping power enables committee members to block legislation that harms contributing groups. The fact that certain provisions are *excluded* from a bill is as much an indicator of PAC influence as the fact that certain provisions are *included*. The difference is that it is hard to measure what you don't see. Committee oversight powers enable members to intervene in bureaucratic decision making on behalf of contributing groups.

The point here is that voting on the floor, the alleged object of campaign contributions according to the vote-buying hypothesis, is a highly visible, highly public act, one that could get a legislator in trouble with his or her broader electoral constituency. The committee system, on the other hand, provides loads of opportunities for legislators to deliver "services" to PAC contributors and other donors that are more subtle and better hidden from public view. Thus we suggest that the most appropriate places to look for

---

48 See Janet M. Grenke, "PACs and the Congressional Supermarket: The Currency Is Complex," *American Journal of Political Science* 33, no. 1 (February 1989): 1–24. More generally, see Jacobson, *The Politics of Congressional Elections*. For a view that interest groups spend too little, not too much, money, see Stephen Ansolabehere, John de Figueiredo, and James Snyder, "Why Is There So Little Money in U.S. Politics?" *Journal of Economic Perspectives* 17 (2003): 105–30.

traces of campaign-contribution influence on the legislative process are in the manner in which committees deliberate, mark up proposals, and block legislation from the floor; outside public view, these are the primary arenas for interest-group influence.[49]

Interest groups mobilize voters and contribute campaign finance, but that's not all they do. They also convey information. While it is true that legislators become specialists, acquire expertise, and hire expert staff to assist them, much specialized knowledge, especially about how various aspects of policy will affect local constituencies, is possessed by lobbyists. Informational lobbying is a very important inside-the-beltway activity. Interest group expenditures on lobbying dwarf money given in campaign contributions.[50]

Party Discipline

In both the House and the Senate, party leaders have a good deal of influence over the behavior of their party members. This influence, sometimes called party discipline, was once so powerful that it dominated the lawmaking process. Let us define as a party vote a vote on which 50 percent or more of the members of one party take one position while at least 50 percent of the members of the other party take the opposing position. At the beginning of the twentieth century, most roll-call votes in the House of Representatives were party votes. The frequency of party votes declined through most of the twentieth century as legislative parties grew more ideologically diverse. Democrats included liberals from the big cities and conservatives from the South. Republicans included conservatives from the Midwest and West and moderates from the Northeast. The tail end of this decline in party voting can be observed in Figure 6.8 between 1955 and 1970. Beginning in the 1970s, however, legislative parties grew more homogeneous and more polarized. Conservative southern districts began electing Republicans, and liberal northeastern districts began sending Democrats to Congress. The data shown in the figure reflect this, with party votes ticking upward from the 1970s onward. Some of this change is the result of the intense partisan struggles that began during the administrations of Ronald Reagan and George H. W. Bush. Straight party-line voting was also seen briefly in the 103rd Congress (1993–94) after Bill Clinton's election in 1992. The situation soon gave way, however, to the many long-term factors working against party discipline

party vote

A roll-call vote in the House or Senate in which at least 50 percent of the members of one party take a particular position and are opposed by at least 50 percent of the members of the other party. Party votes are less common today than they were in the nineteenth century

roll-call votes

Votes in which each legislator's yes or no vote is recorded

49 A complementary effect of campaign contributions is not to buy votes that would otherwise be unavailable to a contributor. It is, rather, to increase the likelihood that legislators *already sympathetic* will be re-elected. Interest groups thus primarily support their friends with contributions rather than attempting to convert opponents to their cause.

50 See Sven E. Feldmann and Morten Bennedsen, "Informational Lobbying and Political Contributions," *Journal of Public Economics* 90 (2006): 631–56.

Party voting has ticked up since the 1970s but began to tail off after reaching a peak in the mid-1990s. What contributes to party voting?

Figure 6.8

PARTY UNITY SCORES BY CHAMBER

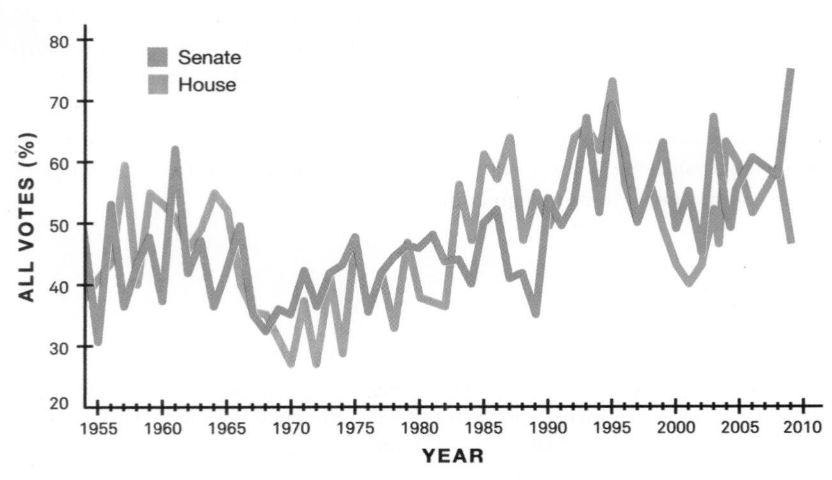

NOTE: The scores represent the percentage of recorded votes on which the majority of one party voted against the majority of the other party.

SOURCE: Voteview, http://pooleandrosenthal.com/party_unity.htm (accessed 6/27/11).

in Congress, as seen in the decline in party voting over the rest of the 1990s.[51] Since the election of George W. Bush, accompanied by Republican congressional control, party voting again ticked upward. And in the first two years of the Obama administration, party voting in both chambers was strong—Republican votes supporting Obama initiatives are quite rare.

To some extent, party divisions are based on ideology and background. Republican members of Congress are more likely than Democrats to be drawn from rural or suburban areas. Democrats are likely to be more liberal on economic and social questions than their Republican colleagues. This ideological gap has been especially pronounced since 1980 (Figure 6.9).[52] Ideological differences certainly help explain roll-call divisions between the two parties.[53]

---

51 There were fluctuations during George W. Bush's presidency—declines in party voting following September 11 and then surges and declines in subsequent years (see Figure 6.8).

52 This figure is slightly misleading in showing Southern Democrats becoming more liberal. It is true, but for a nonobvious reason: there are fewer and fewer Southern Democrats, with the ones remaining most likely to be urban and/or minority legislators.

53 Keith T. Poole and Howard Rosenthal, *Congress: A Political-Economic History of Roll Call Voting* (New York: Oxford University Press, 1997). As a result, it is hard to sort out the effects of party and ideology. On this latter issue, see Krehbiel, "Where's the Party?"

Figure 6.9

THE WIDENING IDEOLOGICAL GAP BETWEEN THE PARTIES

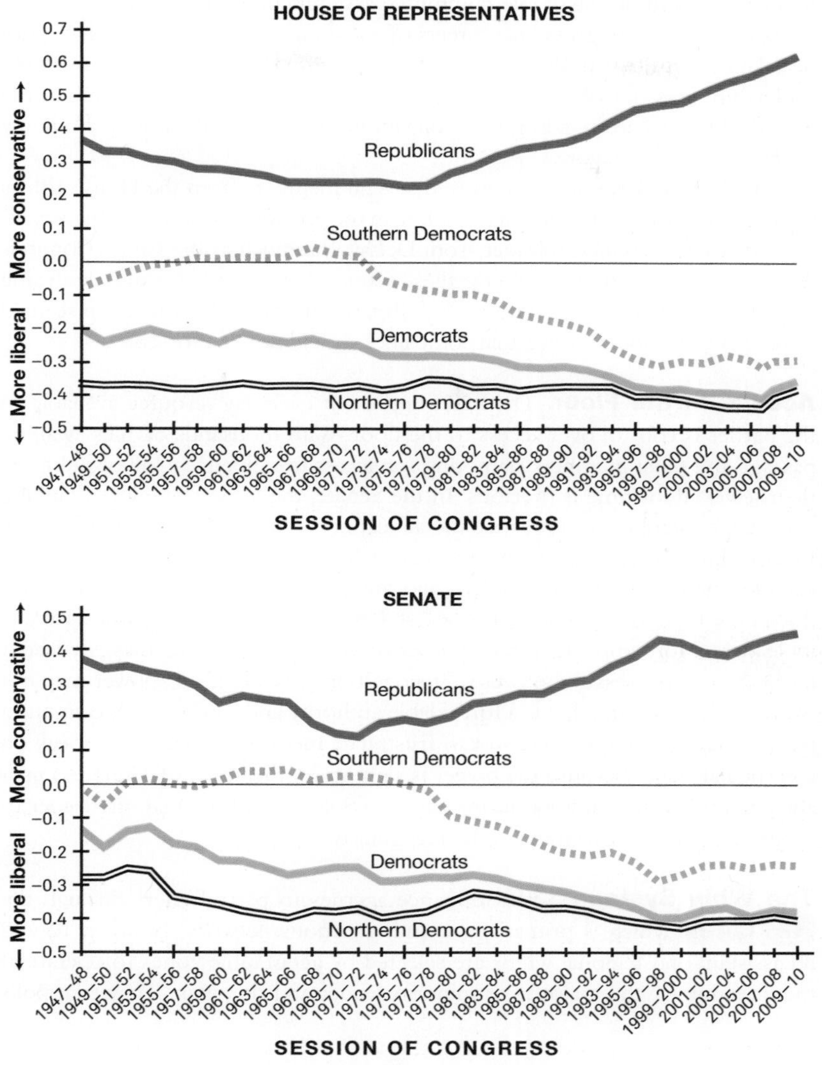

HOUSE OF REPRESENTATIVES

More conservative → / ← More liberal

0.7, 0.6, 0.5, 0.4, 0.3, 0.2, 0.1, 0.0, −0.1, −0.2, −0.3, −0.4, −0.5

Republicans

Southern Democrats

Democrats

Northern Democrats

1947–48, 1949–50, 1951–52, 1953–54, 1955–56, 1957–58, 1959–60, 1961–62, 1963–64, 1965–66, 1967–68, 1969–70, 1971–72, 1973–74, 1975–76, 1977–78, 1979–80, 1981–82, 1983–84, 1985–86, 1987–88, 1989–90, 1991–92, 1993–94, 1995–96, 1997–98, 1999–2000, 2001–02, 2003–04, 2005–06, 2007–08, 2009–10

SESSION OF CONGRESS

SENATE

More conservative → / ← More liberal

0.5, 0.4, 0.3, 0.2, 0.1, 0.0, −0.1, −0.2, −0.3, −0.4, −0.5

Republicans

Southern Democrats

Democrats

Northern Democrats

1947–48, 1949–50, 1951–52, 1953–54, 1955–56, 1957–58, 1959–60, 1961–62, 1963–64, 1965–66, 1967–68, 1969–70, 1971–72, 1973–74, 1975–76, 1977–78, 1979–80, 1981–82, 1983–84, 1985–86, 1987–88, 1989–90, 1991–92, 1993–94, 1995–96, 1997–98, 1999–2000, 2001–02, 2003–04, 2005–06, 2007–08, 2009–10

SESSION OF CONGRESS

SOURCE: Voteview, Party Polarization: 1879–2010, http://voteview.com/polarizedamerica.asp#POLITICALPOLARIZATION (accessed 6/27/11).

Ideology and background, however, are only part of the explanation of party unity. The other part has to do with party organization and leadership. Although party organization has weakened since the beginning of the twentieth century, today's party leaders still have some resources at their disposal: (1) committee assignments, (2) access to the floor, (3) the whip system, (4) logrolling, and

(5) the presidency. These resources are regularly used and are often effective in securing the support of party members.[54]

Committee Assignments. Leaders can create debts among members by helping them get favorable committee assignments. These assignments are made early in the congressional careers of most members and ordinarily cannot be taken from them if they later balk at party discipline. Nevertheless, if the leadership goes out of its way to get the right assignment for a member, the effort is likely to create a bond of obligation that can be called on without any other payments or favors.

In 2005, the Republicans removed several members from the House Ethics Committee because of their participation, in the previous Congress, in investigating the House Republican leader, Tom DeLay. Inasmuch as the Ethics Committee is seen as a bipartisan watchdog, these actions were regarded as muscle-flexing responses by the Republican leadership. Bipartisan or not, the leadership seemed to be saying, as noted earlier, that some lines should not be crossed.

Access to the Floor. The most important everyday resource available to the parties is control over access to the floor. With thousands of bills awaiting passage and most members clamoring for access to influence a bill or publicize themselves, floor time is precious. In the Senate, the leadership allows ranking committee members to influence the allocation of floor time—who will speak for how long. In the House, the Speaker, as head of the majority party (in consultation with the minority leader), allocates large blocks of floor time. Thus floor time is allocated in both houses of Congress by the majority and minority leaders. More important, the Speaker of the House and the majority leader in the Senate possess the power of recognition. Although this power may not appear to be substantial, it is a formidable authority and can be used to stymie a piece of legislation completely or to frustrate a member's attempts to speak on a particular issue. Because the power is significant, members of Congress usually attempt to stay on good terms with the Speaker and the majority leader to ensure that they will continue to be recognized.[55]

whip system 

A communications network in each house of Congress. Whips poll the membership to learn their intentions on specific legislative issues and assist the majority and minority leaders in various tasks

The Whip System. Some influence accrues to party leaders through the whip system, which is primarily a communications network. Between 12 and 20 assistant and regional whips are selected by geographic zones to operate at the direction of the majority or minority leader and the whip. They take polls

54 Legislative leaders may behave in ways that enhance their reputation for being willing to punish party members who stray from the party line. The problem of developing such a credible reputation is analyzed in Randall Calvert, "Reputation and Legislative Leadership," *Public Choice* 55 (1987): 81–120, and is summarized in Kenneth A. Shepsle, *Analyzing Politics: Rationality, Behavior, Institutions* (New York: Norton, 2010), 2nd ed., pp. 460–8.

55 A recent analysis of how floor time is allocated is found in Cox and McCubbins, *Setting the Agenda.*

of all the members to learn their intentions on specific bills. This information enables the leaders to know if they have enough support to allow a vote and whether the vote is so close that they need to put pressure on a few swing votes. Leaders also use the whip system to convey their wishes and plans to the members, but only in very close votes do they exert pressure on a member. In those instances, the Speaker or a lieutenant will go to a few party members who have indicated they will switch if their votes are essential. The whip system helps the leaders limit the practice of pressuring members to a few times per session. It helps maintain party unity in both houses of Congress, but it is particularly critical in the House of Representatives because of the large number of legislators whose positions and votes must always be accounted for.

Logrolling. An agreement between two or more members of Congress who have nothing in common except the need for mutual support is called logrolling. The agreement states, in effect, "You support me on bill X, and I'll support you on a bill of your choice." Because party leaders are the center of the communications networks in the two chambers, they can help members create large logrolling coalitions. Hundreds of logrolling deals are made each year, and although there are no official records, it would be a poor party leader whose whips did not know who owed what to whom.[56] In some instances, logrolling produces strange alliances. A seemingly unlikely alliance emerged in Congress in June 1994, when 119 mainly conservative senators and representatives from oil-producing states met with President Clinton to suggest that they might be willing to support the president's health care proposals in exchange for his support for a number of tax breaks for the oil industry. Senator J. Bennett Johnston of Louisiana, a leader of the oil-state representatives, contended that the issues of health care and oil production were closely related because both "affected the long-term economic security of the nation." Ironically, the oil-producing groups that promoted this alliance are generally among the most conservative forces in the nation. When asked what he thought of the president's health care proposal, George Alcorn, a leading industry lobbyist involved in the logrolling effort, dismissed Clinton's plan as "socialized medicine." Another alliance of strange bedfellows was the 1994 "corn for porn" logroll in which liberal urbanites supported farm programs in exchange for rural support for National Endowment for the Arts funding (at a time when many conservatives thought that the art

 **logrolling**

A legislative practice wherein reciprocal agreements are made between legislators, usually in voting for or against a bill. In contrast to bargaining, logrolling unites parties that have nothing in common but their desire to exchange support

56 For an analysis of the formal problems that logrolling (or vote trading) both solves and creates, see Shepsle, *Analyzing Politics*, pp. 374–6. It is argued there that logrolling cannot be the entire solution to the problem of assembling majority coalitions out of the diverse preferences found in any political party. The reason is that although party leaders can try to keep track of who owes what to whom, the bookkeeping is imperfect and highly complex at best. Nevertheless, if anyone is positioned to orchestrate a system of logrolling, it is the party leaders. And of all those who have tried to facilitate such "cooperation," Robert Byrd (D-W.Va.), who served as both majority whip and majority leader in the Senate, was the acknowledged master. For an insightful analysis of the ways party leaders build majority coalitions through the strategic use of pork-barrel projects, see Evans, *Greasing the Wheels*.

produced by some NEA grantees bordered on the pornographic). Good log-rolling, it would seem, is not hampered by minor ideological concerns.[57] In this case, the rationality principle (exemplified by a willingness to support a policy to which one is opposed in exchange for reciprocal support for a policy one cares passionately about) and the institution principle (in which the separation of powers allows the president and legislators to cut deals) work in unusual ways to produce policy outcomes.

The Presidency. Of all the influences that maintain the clarity of party lines in Congress, the influence of the presidency is probably the most important. Indeed, it is a touchstone of party discipline in Congress. Since the late 1940s, under President Harry Truman, presidents each year have identified a number of bills to be considered part of their administration's program. By the mid-1950s, both parties in Congress began to look to the president for these proposals, which became the most significant part of Congress's agenda. The president's support is a criterion for party loyalty, and party leaders are able to use it to rally some members.

Weighing Diverse Influences

Clearly many factors affect congressional decisions. But at various points in the decision-making process, some are likely to be more influential than others. For example, interest groups may be more effective at the committee stage, when their expertise is especially valued and their visibility is less obvious. Because committees play a key role in deciding what legislation reaches the floor of the House or the Senate, interest groups can often put a halt to bills they dislike, or they can ensure that the options that do reach the floor are those that the group's members support.

Once legislation reaches the floor and members of Congress are deciding among alternatives, constituent opinion will become more important. Legislators are also influenced very much by other legislators: many of their assessments about the substance and politics of legislation come from fellow members of Congress.

The influence of the external and internal forces described in the preceding section also varies according to the kind of issue being considered. On policies of great importance to powerful interest groups—farm subsidies, for example—those groups are likely to have considerable influence. On other issues, members of Congress may be less attentive to narrow interest groups and more willing to consider what they see as the general interest.

Finally, the mix of influences varies according to the historical moment. The Republicans' 1994 electoral victory allowed their party to control both houses of Congress for the first time in 40 years. That fact, combined with

57 Allen R. Meyerson, "Oil-Patch Congressmen Seek Deal with Clinton," *New York Times*, June 14, 1994, p. D2.

an unusually assertive Republican leadership, meant that party leaders became especially important in decision making. The willingness of moderate Republicans to support measures they had once opposed indicated the unusual importance of party leadership in this period. As the House Democratic minority leader, Richard Gephardt, put it, "When you've been in the desert forty years, your instinct is to help Moses."[58] In a reversal of fortune, the Democrats bounced back in 2006, with party leaders both working with the president *and* investigating the executive branch with equal levels of commitment. The Bush administration's financial "rescue package" of 2008 was itself rescued by *Democratic* leadership activism and *Democratic* votes. The election in 2010 represented yet another reversal of fortune with Republicans recapturing the House, increasing their numbers in the Senate, and positioning themselves to attempt to block new administrative victories. On this, the Republicans were successful, but to little avail: in the 2012 elections, the Democrats gained seats in both chambers.

BEYOND LEGISLATION: ADDITIONAL CONGRESSIONAL POWERS

In addition to the power to make the law, Congress has at its disposal an array of other instruments through which it can influence the process of government.

Advice and Consent: Special Senate Powers

The Constitution has given the Senate a special power, one that is not based on lawmaking: the president has the power to make treaties and appoint top executive officers, ambassadors, and federal judges—but only "with the Advice and Consent of the Senate" (Article II, Section 2). For treaties, two-thirds of those senators present must concur; for appointments, a majority is required.

The power to approve or reject presidential requests also involves the power to set conditions. The Senate only occasionally exercises its power to reject treaties and appointments. Only nine Supreme Court nominees have been rejected by the Senate during the past century, while most have been approved.[59]

More common than the Senate rejection of presidential appointees is a senatorial "hold" on an appointment. By Senate tradition, any member may place an indefinite hold on the confirmation of a mid- or lower-level presidential appointment. The hold may be a signal of a senator's willingness to filibuster

58 Quoted in David Broder, "At 6 Months, House GOP Juggernaut Still Cohesive," *Washington Post*, July 17, 1995, p. A1.

59 Of President George W. Bush's three nominees, however, although two were confirmed, one nominee withdrew because of a concern that she could not succeed.

a nomination, but it is typically used by senators trying to wring concessions from the White House on matters having nothing to do with the appointment in question. After Bush came to power in January 2001, the Democrats in the Senate actively scrutinized judicial nominations. Senate Democrats prevented final confirmation votes on a dozen especially conservative nominees, a matter about which President Bush frequently complained during the 2004 re-election campaign. Of course, Republicans had done exactly the same thing to many judicial nominations in the preceding Clinton administration and continued the practice in the Obama administration.

Judicial nomination politics loomed large during Bush's second term. Bush, who had not had a single opportunity to name a Supreme Court justice in his first term, was confronted with a flurry of opportunities during a few short months in his second term. During the summer of 2005, Justice Sandra Day O'Connor (the first woman to serve on the Court) announced her retirement. Bush nominated John Roberts, a sitting federal judge, as her replacement. But before he could be confirmed, Chief Justice William Rehnquist died. O'Connor agreed to remain on the Court until her replacement was confirmed, so President Bush withdrew Roberts's nomination and then renominated him to replace Rehnquist as chief justice. Roberts was confirmed in time for the opening of the Court's term in October. Bush now turned to O'Connor's replacement. His initial nominee, presidential confidante and White House Counsel Harriet Miers, was forced to withdraw amid charges of cronyism and lack of experience. Bush then nominated Samuel Alito, a federal appeals court judge with a substantial track record and solidly conservative credentials.

During his first term in office, President Obama had the opportunity to name two new justices when David Souter and John Paul Stevens announced their retirements. To replace Souter, Obama chose federal appeals court judge Sonia Sotomayor, the first Hispanic to serve on the Supreme Court. To take Stevens's place, Obama named Solicitor General Elena Kagan. Republicans grumbled that both nominees were too liberal but made only token objections since Sotomayor and Kagan would be replacing liberal justices and so would not change the balance of power on the Court.

executive agreement

An agreement between the president and another country that has the force of a treaty but does not require the Senate's "advice and consent"

Senatorial advice and consent is also required on treaties. Thus, at the end of the first Congress of the Obama presidency—one featuring frequent obstruction from Republicans—it was surprising that they joined Democrats in consenting to the New Start treaty with Russia to reduce nuclear arsenals. Most presidents make every effort to take potential Senate opposition into account in treaty negotiations and will frequently resort to executive agreements with foreign powers instead of treaties. The Supreme Court has held that such agreements are equivalent to treaties, but they do not need Senate approval.[60] In the

60 *United States v. Pink,* 315 U.S. 203 (1942). For a good discussion of the problem, see James W. Davis, *The American Presidency: A New Perspective* (New York: Harper & Row, 1987), chap. 8. A recent analysis is found in William G. Howell, *Power without Persuasion: The Politics of Direct Presidential Action* (Princeton, NJ: Princeton University Press, 2003).

past, presidents sometimes concluded secret agreements without informing Congress of the agreements' contents or even their existence. For example, American involvement in the Vietnam War grew in part out of a series of secret arrangements made between American presidents and the South Vietnamese during the 1950s and 1960s. Congress did not even learn of the existence of these agreements until 1969. In 1972, Congress passed the Case Act, which requires that the president inform Congress of any executive agreement within 60 days of its having been reached. This provides Congress with the opportunity to cancel agreements that it opposes. In addition, Congress can limit the president's ability to conduct foreign policy through executive agreement by refusing to appropriate the funds needed to implement an agreement. In this way, for example, Congress can modify or even cancel executive agreements to provide economic or military assistance to foreign governments.

Impeachment

The Constitution, in Article II, Section 4, also grants Congress the power of impeachment over the president, vice president, and other executive officials. Impeachment means charging a government official (president or otherwise) with "Treason, Bribery, or other high Crimes and Misdemeanors" and bringing him or her before Congress to determine guilt. Impeachment is thus like a criminal indictment, in which the House of Representatives acts like a grand jury, voting (by simple majority) on whether the accused ought to be impeached. If a majority of the House votes to impeach, the impeachment trial is held in the Senate, which acts like a trial jury by voting whether to convict and forcibly remove the person from office (this vote requires a two-thirds majority).

 **impeachment**

The charging of a government official (president or otherwise) with "Treason, Bribery, or other high Crimes and Misdemeanors" and bringing him or her before Congress to determine guilt

Controversy over Congress's impeachment power has arisen over the grounds for impeachment, especially the meaning of "high Crimes and Misdemeanors." A strict reading of the Constitution suggests that the only impeachable offense is an actual crime. But a more commonly agreed on definition is that "an impeachable offense is whatever the majority of the House of Representatives considers it to be at a given moment in history."[61] In other words, impeachment, especially impeachment of a president, is a political decision.

The United States came closest to impeaching and convicting a president in 1867. Andrew Johnson, a southern Democrat who had battled a congressional Republican majority over Reconstruction, was impeached by the House but saved from conviction by one vote in the Senate. At the height of the Watergate scandal in 1974, the House started impeachment proceedings against President Richard Nixon, but Nixon resigned before the House could proceed. The possibility of impeachment arose again in 1998, when President Clinton was accused

61 Carroll J. Doherty, "Impeachment: How It Would Work," *Congressional Quarterly Weekly Report*, January 31, 1998, p. 222.

of lying under oath and obstructing justice in the investigation into his sexual affair with White House intern Monica Lewinsky. In October 1998, the House voted to impeach the president. At the conclusion of the Senate trial in 1999, Democrats, joined by a handful of Republicans, acquitted the president of both charges.

The impeachment power is a considerable one; its very existence in the hands of Congress is a highly effective safeguard against the executive tyranny so greatly feared by the framers of the Constitution.

POWER AND REPRESENTATION

Because they feared both executive and legislative tyranny, the framers of the Constitution pitted Congress and the president against each other. And as the history principle suggests, this has provided us with a legacy of interbranch competition. During the first century of American government, Congress was the dominant institution. American foreign and domestic policy was formulated and implemented by Congress, and generally the most powerful figures in American government were the Speaker of the House and the leaders of the Senate—not the president. During the nineteenth century, Congress—not the president—dominated press coverage on "the affairs of government."[62] The War of 1812 was planned and fought by Congress; President Madison's resolve against the war dissolved under relentless pressure from congressional warhawks led by Speaker of the House Henry Clay. The great sectional compromises before the Civil War were formulated in Congress without much intervention from the executive branch. Even during the Civil War, a period of extraordinary presidential leadership, a joint congressional committee on the conduct of the war played a role in formulating war plans and campaign tactics—and even had a hand in the promotion of officers. After the Civil War, when President Andrew Johnson sought to interfere with congressional plans for Reconstruction, he was summarily impeached, saved from conviction by only one vote. Subsequent presidents understood the moral and did not attempt to thwart Congress.

This congressional preeminence began to diminish at the beginning of the twentieth century, so that by the 1960s the executive had become, at least temporarily, the dominant branch of American government. The major domestic policy initiatives of the twentieth century—Franklin D. Roosevelt's New Deal, Harry Truman's Fair Deal, John F. Kennedy's New Frontier, and Lyndon

62 Samuel Kernell and Gary C. Jacobson, "Congress and the Presidency as News in the Nineteenth Century," *Journal of Politics* 49 (1987): 1016–35.

Johnson's Great Society—all included some congressional involvement but were essentially developed, introduced, and implemented by the executive. In the area of foreign policy, although Congress continued to be influential during the twentieth century, the focus of decision-making power clearly moved into the executive branch. The War of 1812 may have been a congressional war, but in the twentieth century American entry into World War I, World War II, Korea, Vietnam, Iraq, Afghanistan, and a host of lesser conflicts was essentially a presidential—not a congressional—decision. In the last 40 years, there has been a good deal of resurgence of congressional power vis-à-vis the executive. This has occurred mainly because Congress has sought to represent many important political forces, such as the civil rights, women's, environmental, consumer, and peace movements, which in turn became constituencies for congressional power. It also has been helped along by the creation of congressional agencies, especially the Congressional Budget Office, the Congressional Research Service, and the Government Accountability Office, to provide the legislature with informational support independent of the executive branch. During the mid-1990s, Congress became more receptive to a variety of new conservative political forces, including groups on the social and religious right as well as more traditional economic conservatives. After Republicans won control of both houses in the 1994 elections, Congress took the lead in developing programs and policies supported by these groups. These efforts won Congress the support of conservative forces in its battles for power against a Democratic White House.

To herald the new accessibility of Congress, Republican leaders instituted a number of reforms designed to eliminate many of the practices that they had long criticized as examples of Democratic arrogance. Republican leaders reduced the number of committees and subcommittees, eliminated funding of the various unofficial caucuses, imposed term limits on committee chairs, eliminated the practice of proxy voting, reduced committee staffs by one-third, ended Congress's exemption from the labor, health, and civil rights laws that it imposed on the rest of the nation, and prohibited members from receiving most gifts. With these reforms, Republicans hoped to make Congress both more effective and more representative. Term limits and bans on gifts were seen as increasing the responsiveness of Congress to new political forces and to the American people in general. Simplification of the committee structure was seen as making Congress more efficient and thus potentially more effective and more powerful. To some extent, unfortunately, the various reforms worked at cross-purposes. Simplification of the committee structure and elimination of funding for the caucuses increased the power of the leadership, thereby muting the effectiveness of more representative elements. In another instance, when term limits for committee and subcommittee chairs were finally imposed in 2001, the result was confusion because experienced leaders were forced to step down, spreading power around in a more representative manner but diminishing committee effectiveness. This is the dilemma of congressional reform. Efficiency and representation are often competing principles in our system of government, and we must be wary of gaining one at the expense of the other. In the next chapter, we turn to the second branch of American government, the presidency, to view this dilemma from a somewhat different angle.

CONCLUSION

Our discussion in this chapter has been both descriptive and analytical. The Constitution sets the stage by describing Congress's role in politics. The U.S. Congress is a two-chamber legislature with the authority to develop and pass legislation (with the concurrence of the president) on the one hand, and the power to oversee policy implementation by the president and executive bureaucracy on the other hand. It is present at the creation, so to speak, and has a continuing responsibility after a law is crafted. Each chamber keeps an eye on the other chamber and ultimately must come to terms with that other chamber on joint legislative products that are sent on to the president for his or her signature. But each chamber has a life of its own as well. Each is organized by its majority party, itself possessing an organizational structure of leaders and followers. For efficiency reasons, and to accommodate the career and policy ambitions of its members, committee systems in the House and Senate allow for the division and specialization of labor; each of these committees is a "little legislature"[63] with committee leaders and a subcommittee structure. In addition to pursuing substantive policy objectives through legislation by authorizing new programs and reauthorizing existing ones, the two chambers have a special role to play in the financial realm—raising revenue from taxes and appropriating monies to fund authorized programs. In addition, the Constitution gives the Senate further responsibilities, including the approval of treaties and the confirmation of federal judges, Supreme Court justices, and high administrative officers.

In analytical terms, the U.S. Congress is an institutional arrangement. First, in light of the rationality principle, it arranges itself in accordance with the policy and career ambitions of its members. These goals encompass re-election, the achievement of personal policy objectives, and the attainment of influence and position inside the legislative chamber. Politicians are ambitious for themselves, their party, and their constituencies. To accomplish at least some of the personal objectives of 435 individuals in one chamber and 100 in the other, politicians must engage in bargaining, coordination, and cooperation. These activities are orchestrated by institutional rules, structures, and procedures, the effects of which are found in the policies ultimately produced. It should be

63 The classic statement is George Goodwin, *The Little Legislatures* (Amherst: University of Massachusetts Press, 1970).

noted that, given the size of majorities required in each chamber to produce results, policy benefits must be distributed widely in what we called the *distributive tendency*. The resulting product isn't always pretty; there are occasional "bridges to nowhere" and other undesirable pork-barrel projects. But this is what it takes to accomplish things in a diverse, multiperson, elected body. Over the course of more than two centuries, each chamber has created ways of doing business, reformed them, and sometimes engineered entirely new ways of conducting its affairs. The history of what has gone before channels this institutional engineering.

The two chambers of the American legislature do not operate in a vacuum. In front of them are the president, the executive bureaucracy, and the courts, which jointly participate in lawmaking and its implementation. Behind them is public opinion, which ultimately renders judgment on their efforts by rewarding or punishing individuals through elections. In the next three chapters we take up the presidency, the executive branch, and the court system. In Part III we explore public opinion and elections.

For Further Reading

Adler, E. Scott. *Why Congressional Reforms Fail: Reelection and the House Committee System.* Chicago: University of Chicago Press, 2002.

Aldrich, John H., and David W. Rohde. "The Republican Revolution and the House Appropriations Committee," *Journal of Politics* 62 (2000): 1–33.

Arnold, R. Douglas. *The Logic of Congressional Action.* New Haven, CT: Yale University Press, 1990.

Binder, Sarah. *Stalemate: Causes and Consequences of Legislative Gridlock.* Washington, DC: Brookings Institution, 2003.

——— and Paul Quirk, eds. *Institutions of Democracy: The Legislative Branch.* New York: Oxford University Press, 2004.

Brady, David W., and Mathew D. McCubbins, eds. *Party, Process, and Political Change in Congress: New Perspectives on the History of Congress.* Palo Alto, CA: Stanford University Press, 2002 (vol. 1); 2007 (vol. 2).

Brady, David W., and Craig Volden. *Revolving Gridlock: Politics and Policy from Carter to Bush.* 2nd ed. Boulder, CO: Westview Press, 2005.

Cox, Gary C., and Jonathon Katz, *Elbridge Gerry's Salamander: The Electoral Consequences of the Reapportionment Revolution.* Cambridge, UK: Cambridge University Press, 2002.

reader selection

———— and Mathew D. McCubbins. *Setting the Agenda: Responsible Party Government in the U.S. House of Representatives.* New York: Cambridge University Press, 2005.

————. *Legislative Leviathan: Party Government in the House.* 2nd ed. Berkeley: University of California Press, 2006.

reader selection

Fenno, Richard F., Jr. *Home Style: House Members in Their Districts.* Boston: Little, Brown, 1978.

————. *The United States: A Bicameral Perspective.* Washington, DC: American Enterprise Institute, 1982.

Fiorina, Morris P. *Congress: Keystone of the Washington Establishment.* 2nd ed. New Haven, CT: Yale University Press, 1989.

Frisch, Scott A., and Sean Q. Kelly. *Committee Assignment Politics in the U.S. House of Representatives.* Norman: University of Oklahoma Press, 2006.

Gamm, Gerald, and Kenneth A. Shepsle. "Emergence of Legislative Institutions: Standing Committees in the House and the Senate, 1810–1825," *Legislative Studies Quarterly* 14 (1989): 39–66.

Jacobson, Gary C. *The Politics of Congressional Elections.* 7th ed. New York: Longman, 2008.

Krehbiel, Keith. *Pivotal Politics: A Theory of U.S. Lawmaking.* Chicago: University of Chicago Press, 1998.

reader selection

Mayhew, David R. *Congress: The Electoral Connection.* New Haven, CT: Yale University Press, 1974.

Polsby, Nelson W. *How Congress Evolves.* New York: Oxford University Press, 2004.

Rohde, David W. *Parties and Leaders in the Post-reform House.* Chicago: University of Chicago Press, 1991.

Smith, Steven S., and Christopher J. Deering. *Committees in Congress.* 3rd ed. Washington, DC: Congressional Quarterly Press, 1997.

Stewart, Charles H. *Analyzing Congress.* New York: Norton, 2001.

Strom, Gerald. *The Logic of Lawmaking.* Baltimore, MD: Johns Hopkins University Press, 1990.

Wawro, Gregory, and Eric Schickler. *Filibuster: Obstruction and Lawmaking in the United States Senate.* Princeton, NJ: Princeton University Press, 2006.

Visit **wwnorton.com/studyspace/** to access free review materials such as:

- Vocabulary Flashcards of All Key Terms
- Chapter Review Quizzes
- Complete Study Outlines

reader selection

Highlighted selections are included in *Readings in American Politics: Analysis and Perspectives*, Second Edition.

7

INSTITUTIONS

The Presidency as an Institution

Chapter Outline

- The Constitutional Basis of the Presidency
- The Constitutional Powers of the Presidency
- The Rise of Presidential Government
- Presidential Government
- Presidential Power: Myths and Realities

America's last eight presidents have left office under political clouds and, in five cases, sooner than they wanted. Lyndon Johnson did not run for re-election in 1968 when the Vietnam War turned large segments of his own party against him. Richard Nixon was forced to resign in 1974, before completing his second term, as the Watergate scandal unfolded. Nixon's appointed successor, Gerald Ford, was defeated for election to a full term in 1976. Jimmy Carter, who ousted Ford, was, himself, denied re-election by Ronald Reagan. Reagan won re-election to a second term but left office with a reputation damaged by the Iran-Contra scandal. Reagan's successor, George H. W. Bush, was defeated for re-election by Bill Clinton. Clinton served two full terms but only after surviving an impeachment and numerous scandals. And, of course, Clinton's successor, George W. Bush, will be remembered as the least popular president in the history of opinion polling. Given this backdrop, it might be difficult to understand why Barack Obama ever aspired to the office.

Yet even as our presidents have limped out of the White House, the presidency as an institution has grown in power and prominence. Indeed, over the past century, the presidency has become America's most powerful institution in the realms of foreign and military policy and, arguably, in arenas of domestic policy as well. One reason that presidential power has grown despite the difficulties presidents have faced has to do with the character of the presidency as an institution. The presidency is America's only political institution characterized by unitary rather than collective decision-making processes. Members of Congress and the judiciary must deliberate, compromise, and vote before reaching decisions. The president may wish to seek advice from many sources but, in the end, exercises the powers of the office on his or her own authority. As former president George W. Bush once said, "I am the decider."

Unitary "deciders" are usually better able to accrue power than collective decision makers. To begin with, the unitary decider usually sees a direct relationship between the power of the institution and the ability to achieve whatever political goals he or she might have. Presidents Reagan and Clinton, for example, worked diligently and successfully to expand the president's power of regulatory review (discussed later in the chapter), so that they could use the bureaucratic rule-making process to achieve their policy goals without the need for congressional approval. For members of collective decision-making bodies such as Congress, on the other hand, the situation is not so simple. Members of Congress are often confronted with collective action problems and motivated to put their immediate political interests ahead of the long-term power of the institution. For example, in October 2008, Congress responded to enormous political pressure for quick action to deal with the nation's financial crisis by giving the executive branch unprecedented new economic powers. Few members considered how their vote would affect the long-term balance of power between the legislative and executive branches. Typically, as one observer put it in an earlier context, few members are prepared to "speak up for the institutional interests of Congress."[1]

At the same time, as the foregoing example suggests, collective decision makers often feel pressure to cede power to unitary deciders when expeditious

CORE OF THE ANALYSIS

The Constitution endows the president with only a small number of expressed powers, so the presidency is an office whose powers are primarily delegated to it by Congress or claimed by presidents without specific statutory authority.

Over time, the presidency has accumulated more and more power relative to the other institutions of government, partly because the president doesn't face the same collective action problems as Congress.

Presidents can broaden their powers through successful execution of the law.

Presidential power can also be enhanced through strategic interactions with other political actors, and through a president's ability to build popular support.

Historic events requiring bold action and leadership by the president, such as the Great Depression, can also contribute to the president's power.

1 Robert G. Kaiser, "Congress-s-s-s: That Great Hissing Sound You Hear Is Congress Giving Up Its Clout," *Washington Post*, March 14, 2004, p. B1.

action seems of paramount importance. During times of crisis, when a quick response is needed and the public is impatient with constitutional limitations on collective action, Congress and the judiciary typically accede to presidential demands for new executive powers to deal expeditiously with the emergency.

Hence, the character of the presidency as an institution—the fact that the president is a unitary decider—helps to explain why the presidency has gained in power over time at the expense of other institutions, particularly Congress. Of course, the fact that the president is a unitary decider, coupled with the growth of presidential power, also helps to explain why presidents usually become quite unpopular over the course of their terms. Unlike members of Congress and other participants in collective decision making, presidents cannot escape responsibility for their decisions and are invariably blamed when things go wrong. The problem with being the decider in more and more policy spheres is that presidents have opportunities to make more mistakes and generate more opposition. Thus, ironically, the growing power of the presidency as an institution is one reason that so many of our recent presidents have seen their own popularity fade after a few years in office.

Our focus in this chapter is on the development of the institutional character of the presidency, the power of the presidency, and the relationship between the two. The chapter concerns itself with three major topics. First, we review the constitutional origins and powers of the presidency. Second, we review the history of the American presidency to see how the office has evolved from its original status under the Constitution. Third, we assess the means by which presidents can enhance their own ability to govern.

THE CONSTITUTIONAL BASIS OF THE PRESIDENCY

The presidency as an institution was established by Article II of the Constitution. Article II begins by asserting, "The executive Power shall be vested in a President of the United States of America." It goes on to describe the qualifications for the office (one must be a natural-born citizen, at least thirty-five years of age, and a resident of the United States for at least 14 years), the manner in which the president is to be chosen, and the basic powers of the presidency. By vesting the executive power in a single president, the framers were emphatically rejecting proposals for various forms of collective leadership. Some delegates to the Constitutional Convention had argued in favor of a multiheaded executive or an "executive council" to avoid undue concentration of power in the hands of one individual. Most of the framers, however, hoped the president would be capable of taking quick and aggressive action. The framers thought a unitary executive would be more energetic than some form of collective leadership. They believed that a powerful executive would help protect the nation's interests vis-à-vis other nations and promote the federal government's interests relative to the states. In other words, the framers opted for a decider rather than a deliberative body.

Immediately following the first sentence of Article II, Section 1, of the Constitution, the manner in which the president is to be chosen is defined. This is an odd sequence, and it says something about the difficulty the delegates were having over how to provide great power of action to the executive and at the same time balance that power with limitations. This reflected the twin struggles deeply etched in the memories of the founding generation—against the powerful executive authority of King George III and the dismal low energy of the government under the Articles of Confederation. There was disagreement between those delegates who wanted the president to be selected by, and thus responsible to, Congress and those delegates who preferred that the president be elected directly by the people. Direct popular election would create a more independent and more powerful presidency. With the adoption of a scheme of indirect election through an electoral college, in which the electors would be selected by the state legislatures (and close elections would be resolved in the House of Representatives), the framers hoped to achieve a "republican" solution: a strong president responsible to state and national legislators rather than directly responsible to the electorate. This indirect method of electing the president dampened the power of most presidents in the nineteenth century by denying them a political base of support and legitimacy independent of Congress and the state legislatures.

The constitutional basis of the presidency is but a beginning, one subject to a variety of evolutionary pressures. Thus, the presidency was strengthened somewhat in the 1830s with the introduction of the national convention system of nominating presidential candidates. Until then, candidates had been nominated by their party's congressional delegates. That was the caucus system of nominating candidates, and it was derisively called King Caucus because any candidate for president had to be beholden to the party's leaders in Congress to get the party's nomination and the support of the party's congressional delegation in the presidential election. The convention system quickly became the most popular method of nominating candidates for all elective offices and remained so until well into the twentieth century. In the nineteenth century, it was seen as a victory for democracy over the congressional elite, giving the presidency a base of power independent of Congress. This additional independence did not immediately transform the presidency into the office we recognize today, but the national convention did begin to open the presidency to larger social forces and newly organized interests in society.

 **caucus system**

A normally closed meeting of a political or legislative group to select candidates, plan strategy, or make decisions regarding legislative matters

THE CONSTITUTIONAL POWERS OF THE PRESIDENCY

Whereas Article II, Section 1, explains how the president is to be chosen, Sections 2 and 3 outline the powers and duties of the president. These two sections identify two sources of presidential power. One source is the specific language of the Constitution. For example, the president is specifically authorized to

expressed powers 

Specific powers granted to the president under Article II, Sections 2 and 3, of the Constitution

delegated powers

Constitutional powers that are assigned to one government agency but exercised by another agency with the express permission of the first

inherent powers 

Powers claimed by a president that are not expressed in the Constitution but are inferred from it

make treaties, grant pardons, and nominate judges and other public officials. These clearly defined powers are called the expressed powers of the office and cannot be revoked by Congress or any other agency without an amendment to the Constitution. Other expressed powers include the power to receive ambassadors and to command the military forces of the United States.

The second source of presidential power lies in the declaration in Article II that the president "shall take Care that the Laws be faithfully executed." Because the laws are enacted by Congress, this language implies that Congress is to delegate to the president the power to implement or execute its will. Powers given to the president by Congress are called delegated powers. In principle, Congress delegates to the president only the power to identify or develop the means through which to carry out its decisions. So, for example, if Congress determines that air quality should be improved, it might delegate to a bureaucratic agency in the executive branch the power to identify the best means of bringing about such an improvement, as well as the power to implement the cleanup process. In practice, of course, decisions about how to clean the air are likely to have an enormous effect on businesses, organizations, and individuals throughout the nation. As it delegates power to the executive, Congress substantially enhances the importance of the presidency and the executive branch. In most cases, Congress delegates power to bureaucratic agencies in the executive branch rather than to the president. As we shall see, however, contemporary presidents have found ways to capture a good deal of this delegated power for themselves.

Presidents have claimed a third source of institutional power beyond expressed and delegated powers. These are powers that are not specified in the Constitution or the law but are said to stem from "the rights, duties and obligations of the presidency."[2] They are referred to as the inherent powers of the presidency and are most often asserted by presidents in times of war or national emergency. For example, after the fall of Fort Sumter and the outbreak of the Civil War, President Lincoln issued a series of executive orders although he had no clear legal basis for doing so. Without even calling Congress into session, Lincoln combined the state militias into a 90-day national volunteer force, called for 40,000 new volunteers, enlarged the regular army and navy, diverted $2 million in unspent appropriations to military needs, instituted censorship of the U.S. mails, ordered a blockade of southern ports, suspended the writ of *habeas corpus* in the border states, and ordered military police to arrest individuals whom he deemed to be guilty of engaging in or even contemplating treasonous

2 In the case of *In re Neagle*, 135 U.S. 1 (1890), David Neagle, a deputy U.S. marshal, had been authorized by the president to protect a Supreme Court justice whose life had been threatened by an angry litigant. When the litigant attempted to carry out his threat, Neagle shot and killed him. Neagle was then arrested by local authorities and tried for murder. His defense was that his act was "done in pursuance of a law of the United States." Although the law was not an act of Congress, the Supreme Court declared that it was an executive order of the president and that the protection of a federal judge was a reasonable extension of the president's power to "take Care that the Laws be faithfully executed."

actions.[3] Lincoln asserted that these extraordinary measures were justified by the president's inherent power to protect the nation.[4] Subsequent presidents, including Franklin Delano Roosevelt and George W. Bush, have had similar views.

Expressed Powers

The president's expressed powers, as defined by Article II, Sections 2 and 3, fall into several categories:

1. *Military.* Article II, Section 2, provides for the power as "Commander in Chief of the Army and Navy of the United States, and of the Militia of the several States, when called into the actual Service of the United States."
2. *Judicial.* Article II, Section 2, provides the "Power to grant Reprieves and Pardons for Offences against the United States, except in Cases of Impeachment."
3. *Diplomatic.* Article II, Section 2, provides the "Power, by and with the Advice and Consent of the Senate, to make Treaties." Article II, Section 3, provides the power to "receive Ambassadors and other public Ministers."
4. *Executive.* Article II, Section 3, authorizes the president to see to it that all the laws are faithfully executed. Section 2 gives the chief executive power to appoint, remove, and supervise all executive officers and appoint all federal judges.
5. *Legislative.* Article I, Section 7, and Article II, Section 3, give the president the power to participate authoritatively in the legislative process.

Military Power. The president's military powers are among the most important of the powers exercised by the chief executive. The position of commander in chief makes the president the highest military authority in the United States, with control of the entire defense establishment. The president is also head of the nation's intelligence network, which includes not only the Central Intelligence Agency (CIA) but also the National Security Council (NSC), the National Security Agency (NSA), the Federal Bureau of Investigation (FBI), and a host of less well known but very powerful international and domestic security agencies.

commander in chief

The power of the president as commander of the national military and the state national guard units (when called into service)

War and Inherent Presidential Power. The Constitution, of course, gives Congress the power to declare war. Presidents, however, have gone a long way toward capturing this power for themselves. Congress has not declared war since December 1941, and yet since then American military forces have engaged in numerous campaigns throughout the world under orders of the president.

3 James G. Randall, *Constitutional Problems under Lincoln* (New York: Appleton, 1926), chap. 1.

4 E. S. Corwin, *The President: Office and Powers*, 4th ed. (New York: New York University Press, 1957), p. 229.

When North Korean forces invaded South Korea in June 1950, Congress was prepared to declare war, but President Harry S. Truman decided not to ask for congressional action. Instead, Truman asserted the principle that the president, and not Congress, could decide when and where to deploy America's military might. Truman dispatched U.S. forces to Korea without a congressional declaration, and in the face of the emergency Congress felt it had to acquiesce. It passed a resolution approving the president's actions, and this sequence of events became the pattern for future congressional-executive relations in the military realm. The wars in Vietnam, Bosnia, Afghanistan, and Iraq, as well as a host of lesser conflicts, were all fought without declarations of war.

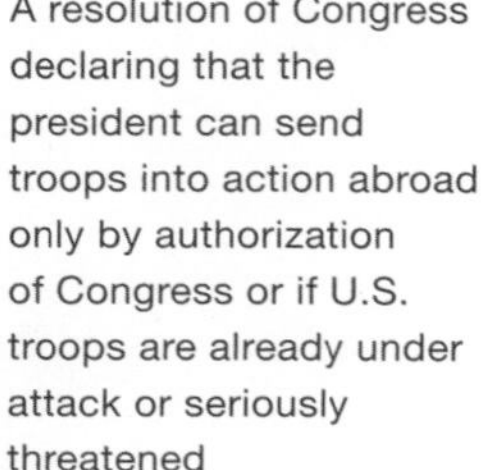

War Powers Resolution

A resolution of Congress declaring that the president can send troops into action abroad only by authorization of Congress or if U.S. troops are already under attack or seriously threatened

In 1973, Congress responded to presidential unilateralism by passing the War Powers Resolution—over President Richard Nixon's veto. This resolution reasserted the principle of Congress's power to declare war, required the president to inform Congress of any planned military campaign, and stipulated that forces must be withdrawn within 60 days in the absence of a specific congressional authorization for their continued deployment. Presidents have generally ignored the War Powers Resolution, however, claiming inherent executive power to defend the nation. Thus, for example, in 1989 President George H. W. Bush ordered an invasion of Panama without consulting Congress. In 1990, the same President Bush received congressional authorization to attack Iraq but had already made it clear that he was prepared to go to war with or without congressional assent. In 1995, President Bill Clinton ordered a massive bombing campaign against Serbian forces in the former nation of Yugoslavia without congressional authorization. And of course President George W. Bush responded to the 2001 attacks by Islamic terrorists by organizing a major military campaign to overthrow the Taliban regime in Afghanistan, which had sheltered the terrorists. In 2002, Bush ordered a major U.S. campaign against Iraq, which he accused of posing a threat to the United States. American forces overthrew the government of the Iraqi dictator Saddam Hussein and occupied the country. In both of these most recent instances, Congress passed resolutions approving the president's actions, but President Bush was careful to assert that he did not need congressional authorization. The War Powers Resolution was barely mentioned on Capitol Hill and was ignored by the White House.

Most American presidents have been attentive to the importance of history. George Washington, for example, always carried himself in a regal manner to establish, from the start, the dignity of the office. Beginning with Ronald Reagan, presidents were very conscious of the fact that the more times they ignored the War Powers Act and got away with so doing, the weaker the act became. Reagan, Clinton, and both Bushes deliberately refrained from using the law's procedures in order to undermine and, ultimately, negate the War Powers Act. Congress, for its part, seldom had the stomach to confront presidential claims that the nation's security demanded quick action and could not wait for the cumbersome war-powers process to run its course. Precisely because presidents know that history matters, they seize every opportunity to write a history favorable to their own goals and to the power of the presidency as an institution.

However, the fact that presidents since 1974 have ignored the War Powers Resolution, with virtually no objection from Congress, does not mean that tensions stemming from the separation of powers between the president and Congress have ceased. The relationship between the branches is encased in layers of institutional fabric, and as our institution principle suggests, tensions emerge within this complex institutional arrangement. The powers of the purse and of investigation give Congress levers with which to constrain even the most freewheeling executive. And for all these reasons, the president restrains himself, often self-censoring to minimize adverse political consequences.[5]

Military Sources of Domestic Power. The president's military powers extend into the domestic sphere. Article IV, Section 4, provides that "the United States shall . . . [protect] every State . . . against Invasion . . . and . . . domestic Violence." Congress has made this an explicit presidential power through statutes directing the president as commander in chief to discharge these obligations.[6] The Constitution restrains the president's use of domestic force by providing that a state legislature (or governor when the legislature is not in session) must request federal troops before the president can send them into the state to provide public order. Yet this proviso is not absolute. First, presidents are not obligated to deploy national troops merely because a state legislature or governor makes such a request. And more important, the president may deploy troops in a state or city without a specific request from a state legislature or governor if the president considers it necessary to maintain an essential national service during an emergency, enforce a federal judicial order, or protect federally guaranteed civil rights.

One historic example of the unilateral use of presidential emergency power to protect the states against domestic disorder, even when the states do not request it, was the decision by President Dwight Eisenhower in 1957 to send troops into Little Rock, Arkansas, against the wishes of the state of Arkansas in order to enforce court orders to integrate Little Rock's Central High School. As we saw in Chapter 5, the governor, Orval Faubus, had posted the Arkansas National Guard at the entrance of the school to prevent the court-ordered admission of nine black students. After an effort to negotiate with the governor failed, President Eisenhower reluctantly sent 1,000 paratroopers to Little Rock; they stood watch while the black students took their places in the all-white classrooms. This case makes quite clear that the president does not have to wait for a request by a state legislature or a governor before acting as a domestic commander in chief.[7] More recently, President George W. Bush sent various military

---

5 On this point, see William G. Howell and Jon C. Pevehouse, *While Dangers Gather: Congressional Checks on Presidential Power* (Princeton, NJ: Princeton University Press, 2007).

6 These statutes are contained mainly in Title 10 of the United States Code, Sections 331, 332, and 333.

7 A now classic study covering all aspects of the domestic use of the military is that of Adam Yarmolinsky, *The Military Establishment* (New York: Harper & Row, 1971). A famous instance of a president's unilateral use of the power to protect a state "against domestic violence" was President Grover Cleveland's response to the Pullman strike of 1894. The Supreme Court case that ensued was *In re Debs*, 158 U.S. 564 (1895).

units to the Gulf Coast in response to Hurricanes Katrina and Rita in 2005, and, in 2010, President Obama sent Coast Guard and teams from other agencies to participate in the rescue and cleanup following the BP *Deepwater Horizon* explosion and oil spill in the Gulf of Mexico. In most instances of domestic disorder—whether a result of human or natural events—presidents tend to exercise unilateral power by declaring a "state of emergency," thereby making available federal grants, insurance, and direct assistance.

Military emergencies have typically also led to expansion of the domestic powers of the executive branch. This was true during World Wars I and II and has been the case during the "war on terrorism" as well. Within a month of the September 11 attacks, the White House had drafted, and Congress had enacted, the USA PATRIOT Act, expanding the power of government agencies to engage in domestic surveillance, including electronic surveillance, and restricting judicial review of such efforts. The following year Congress created the Department of Homeland Security, combining offices of 22 federal agencies into one huge new cabinet department that would be responsible for protecting the nation from attack.

Judicial Power. The presidential power to grant reprieves, pardons, and amnesties involves the power of life and death over all individuals who may be a threat to the security of the United States. Presidents may use this power on behalf of a particular individual, as did Gerald Ford when he pardoned Richard Nixon in 1974 "for all offenses against the United States which he . . . has committed or may have committed." Or they may use it on a large scale, as Andrew Johnson did in 1868 when he gave full amnesty to all Southerners who had participated in the "Late Rebellion" and as Jimmy Carter did in 1977 when he declared an amnesty for all Vietnam War draft evaders. President Clinton issued a number of controversial pardons during his last weeks in office.

Diplomatic Power. The president is America's "head of state," its chief representative in dealings with other nations. As head of state, the president has the power to make treaties for the United States (with the advice and consent of the Senate). When President George Washington received Edmond Genet ("Citizen Genet") as the formal emissary of the revolutionary government of France in 1793 and had his cabinet officers and Congress back his decision, he established a greatly expanded interpretation of the power to "receive Ambassadors and other public Ministers," extending it to the power to "recognize" other countries. That power gives the president the almost unconditional authority to review the claims of any new ruling group to determine whether it indeed controls the territory and population of its country and therefore can, in the president's opinion, legitimately commit it to treaties and other agreements.

In recent years, presidents have expanded the practice of using executive agreements instead of treaties to establish relations with other countries.[8]

8 In *United States v. Pink*, 315 U.S. 203 (1942), the Supreme Court confirmed that an executive agreement is the legal equivalent of a treaty despite the absence of Senate approval.

An executive agreement is like a treaty because it is a contract between two countries, but an executive agreement does not require approval by the Senate. (A treaty does require a two-thirds vote of approval by the Senate.) Ordinarily executive agreements are used to carry out commitments already made in treaties or to arrange for matters well below the level of policy. But when presidents have found it expedient to use an executive agreement in place of a treaty, Congress has typically acquiesced.

executive agreement

An agreement between the president and another country that has the force of a treaty but does not require the Senate's "advice and consent"

Executive Power. The most important basis of the president's power as chief executive is found in Article II, Section 3, which stipulates that the president must see that all the laws are faithfully executed, and Section 2, which provides that the president will appoint, remove, and supervise all executive officers and appoint all federal judges (with Senate approval). The power to appoint the principal executive officers and to require each of them to report to the president on subjects relating to the duties of their departments makes the president the true chief executive officer (CEO) of the nation. In this manner, the Constitution focuses executive power and legal responsibility on the president. The famous sign on President Truman's desk, "The buck stops here," was not merely an assertion of Truman's personal sense of responsibility but was in fact evidence of his recognition of the legal and constitutional responsibility of the president. The president is subject to some limitations because the appointment of all such officers, including ambassadors, cabinet officers and other high-level administrators, and federal judges, is subject to majority approval by the Senate.

In this, the Congress (the Senate in particular) has *not* acquiesced, often refusing to confirm presidential nominees or holding them hostage by failing even to bring them up for an up-or-down vote. Table 7.1 shows, for Bush's last Congress and Obama's first, that the former had a confirmation success rate of about two-thirds, while the latter's was less than half. Congress, through its committees and the budgetary process, has oversight responsibilities for executive agencies. The George W. Bush administration, supported by conservative scholars, argued that Article II of the Constitution vests all executive power in the president, who, by implication, is in full control of the executive branch. This idea is called the theory of the unitary executive. The theory is often disputed in principle, but presidents often act as though they believe it.

Table 7.1
NOMINATIONS TO FEDERAL COURTS

PRESIDENT	CONGRESS	NOMINATIONS	CONFIRMED	WITHDRAWN	REJECTED	EXPIRED	PENDING
George W. Bush	110th	104	68	6	0	30	N/A
Barack Obama	111th	97	41	1	7	N/A	48

SOURCE: Library of Congress, http://thomas.loc.gov/ (accessed 10/21/10).

The theory of the unitary executive is controversial in part because it denies Congress a significant role in managing the bureaucracy, concentrating this authority instead in the hands of the executive. This undermines the view of the American separation of powers system that executive and legislature are two branches "sharing powers."[9]

executive privilege 

The claim that confidential communications between the president and the president's close advisers should not be revealed without the consent of the president

Another component of the president's power as chief executive is executive privilege. Executive privilege is the claim that confidential communications between a president and close advisers should not be revealed without the consent of the president. Presidents have made this claim ever since George Washington refused a request from the House of Representatives to deliver documents concerning negotiations of an important treaty. Washington refused (successfully) on the grounds that, first, the House was not constitutionally part of the treaty-making process and, second, that diplomatic negotiations required secrecy.

Executive privilege became a popular part of the checks-and-balances counterpoint between president and Congress, and presidents have usually had the upper hand when invoking it. Although many presidents have claimed executive privilege, the concept was not tested in the courts until the 1974 Watergate affair, during which President Nixon refused congressional demands that he turn over secret White House tapes that congressional investigators thought would establish Nixon's complicity in illegal activities. In *United States v. Nixon*, the Supreme Court ordered Nixon to turn over the tapes.[10] The president complied with the order and was forced to resign from office. *United States v. Nixon* is often seen as a blow to presidential power, but in actuality the Court's ruling recognized for the first time the validity of a claim of executive privilege, although holding that it did not apply in this instance. Subsequent presidents have cited *United States v. Nixon* in support of their claims of executive privilege. For example, the administration of George W. Bush invoked executive privilege when it refused to give Congress documents relating to the president's decision to make use of warrantless wiretaps and the so-called CIA leak case, in which the identity of a CIA operative was revealed after her husband criticized the administration. The Bush administration also invoked executive privilege when it refused to obey congressional subpoenas demanding materials pertaining to the firing of a number of assistant U.S. attorneys.[11]

The President's Legislative Power. The president plays a role not only in the administration of government but also in the legislative process. Two constitutional provisions are the primary sources of the president's power in

9 For a famous statement of this, see Richard E. Neustadt, *Presidential Power* (1960; rev. ed. New York: Free Press, 1980).

10 *United States v. Nixon,* 418 U.S. 683 (1974).

11 A recent extension of executive power by President George W. Bush is the "signing statement" which is discussed later in this chapter.

the legislative arena. The first of these is the provision in Article II, Section 3, providing that the president "shall from time to time give to the Congress Information of the State of the Union, and recommend to their Consideration such Measures as he shall judge necessary and expedient." The second of the president's legislative powers is of course the veto power assigned by Article I, Section 7.[12]

Delivering a State of the Union address might not appear to be of any great import. It is a mere obligation on the part of the president to make recommendations for Congress's consideration. But as political and social conditions favored an increasingly prominent role for presidents, each president, especially since Franklin Delano Roosevelt, has relied on this provision to become the primary initiator of proposals for legislative action in Congress and the principal source for public awareness of national issues, as well as the most important single individual participant in legislative decisions. Few today doubt that the president, together with the executive branch as a whole, is the primary source of many important congressional actions.

The veto is the president's constitutional power to turn down acts of Congress (Figure 7.1). It alone makes the president the most important single legislative leader.[13] No bill vetoed by the president can become law unless both the House and Senate override the veto by a two-thirds vote. In the case of a pocket veto, Congress does not have the option of overriding the veto but must reintroduce the bill in the next session. A pocket veto can occur when the president is presented with a bill during the last 10 days of a legislative session. Usually if a president does not sign a bill within 10 days, it automatically becomes law. But this is true only while Congress is in session. If a president chooses not to sign a bill presented within the last 10 days that Congress is in session, then the 10-day limit expires while Congress is out of session, and instead of becoming law, the bill is considered vetoed. In 1996, a new power was added to the president's lineup—the line-item veto—giving the president power to strike specific spending items from appropriations bills passed by Congress unless they are reenacted by a two-thirds vote of both the House and the Senate. In 1997, President Clinton used this power 11 times to strike 82 items from the federal budget. But in 1998 the Supreme Court ruled that the Constitution does not authorize the line-item veto.[14] Only a constitutional amendment would restore this power to the president.

 **veto**

The president's constitutional power to turn down acts of Congress within 10 days of their passage while Congress is in session. A presidential veto may be overridden by a two-thirds vote of each house of Congress

 **pocket veto**

A veto that is effected when Congress adjourns during the time a president has to approve a bill and the president takes no action on it

 **line-item veto**

The power of the executive to veto specific provisions (lines) of a bill passed by the legislature

12 There is a third source of presidential power implied in the provision for faithful execution of the laws. This is the president's power to impound funds—that is, to refuse to spend money Congress has appropriated for certain purposes. One author referred to this as a "retroactive veto power" (Robert E. Goosetree, "The Power of the President to Impound Appropriated Funds," *American University Law Review*, January 1962).

13 For more on the veto, see Chapter 6. Also see Robert J. Spitzer, *The Presidential Veto: Touchstone of the American Presidency* (Albany: State University of New York Press, 1988), and Charles M. Cameron, *Veto Bargaining: Presidents and the Politics of Negative Power* (New York: Cambridge University Press, 2000).

14 *Clinton v. City of New York*, 524 U.S. 417 (1998).

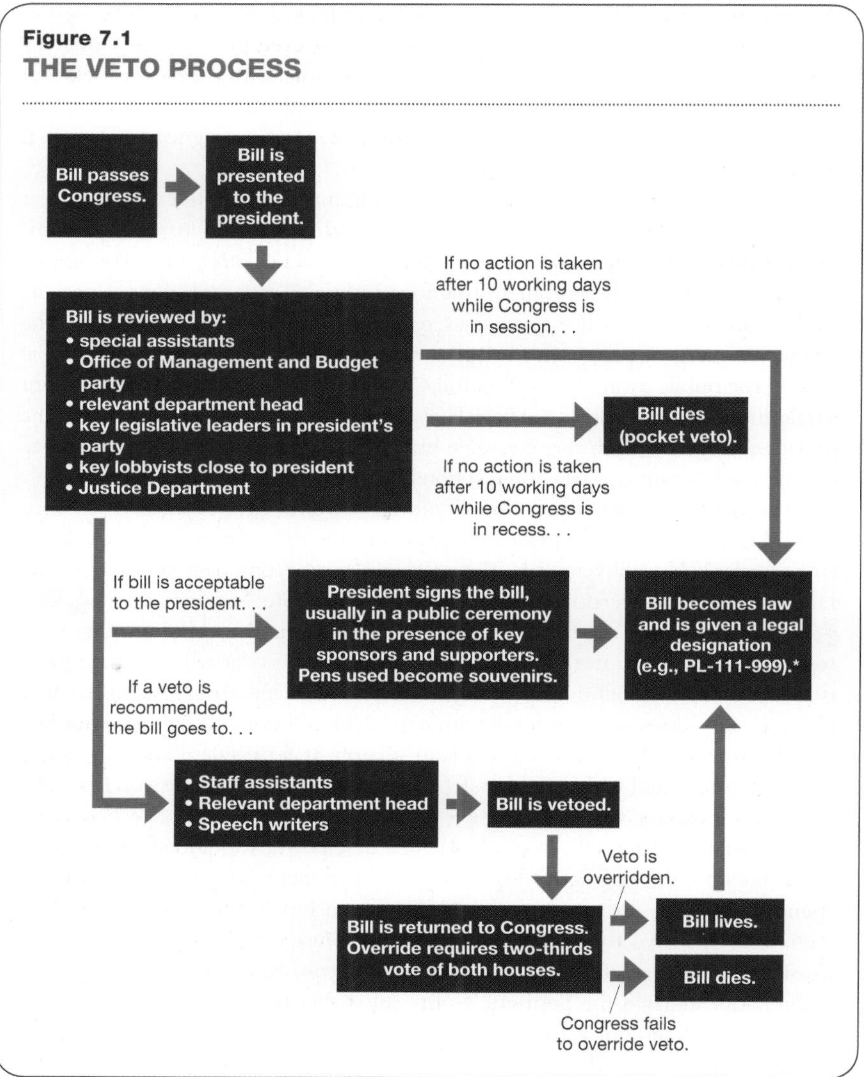
Figure 7.1
THE VETO PROCESS
Bill passes Congress.
Bill is presented to the president.
Bill is reviewed by:
• special assistants
• Office of Management and Budget party
• relevant department head
• key legislative leaders in president's party
• key lobbyists close to president
• Justice Department
If no action is taken after 10 working days while Congress is in session. . .
Bill dies (pocket veto).
If no action is taken after 10 working days while Congress is in recess. . .
If bill is acceptable to the president. . .
President signs the bill, usually in a public ceremony in the presence of key sponsors and supporters. Pens used become souvenirs.
Bill becomes law and is given a legal designation (e.g., PL-111-999).*
If a veto is recommended, the bill goes to. . .
• Staff assistants
• Relevant department head
• Speech writers
Bill is vetoed.
Veto is overridden.
Bill is returned to Congress. Override requires two-thirds vote of both houses.
Bill lives.
Bill dies.
Congress fails to override veto.

*PL stands for "public law"; 111 is the Congress (e.g., the 111th Congress was in session in 2009–11); 999 is the number of the law.

The Games Presidents Play: The Veto. Use of the veto varies according to the political situation that each president confronts. George W. Bush vetoed no bill during his first term, a period in which his party controlled both houses of Congress. He vetoed only one bill during the first two years of his second term, another period during which Congress was controlled by his party.[15] In the last two years of his second term, with Congress controlled by the Democrats, he vetoed 11 bills. In President Obama's first term, with

Democratic control of both the House and the Senate, he vetoed only two bills, both in the first two years. He vetoed no bills in the second two years, after the Democrats lost their House majority and had their Senate majority pared down, but this was mainly because the Republican strategy of obstruction, especially in the Senate, produced very little legislative product.[16] In general, presidents have used the veto to equalize or perhaps upset the balance of power with Congress. While the simple power to reject or accept legislation in its entirety might seem like a crude tool for making sure that legislation adheres to a president's preferences, the politics surrounding the veto is complicated, and it is rare that vetoes are used simply as bullets to kill legislation. Instead, vetoes are usually part of an intricate bargaining process between the president and Congress, involving threats of vetoes, the repassage of legislation, and second vetoes.[17]

The fact that presidents rarely veto legislation does not mean that vetoes and veto bargaining have an insignificant influence over the policy process. The fact that presidents vetoed only several hundred of the more than 20,000 public bills that Congress sent to them between 1945 and 2010 belies the centrality of the veto to presidential power. Many of these bills were insignificant and not worth the veto effort. Thus it is important to separate "significant" legislation, for which vetoes frequently occur, from insignificant legislation.[18] Vetoes can also be effective—even though they are rarely employed—because individuals will condition their actions on the basis of how they think others will respond.[19] With respect to vetoes, this means that members of Congress will alter the content of a bill to make it more to a president's liking in order to discourage a veto. Thus the veto power can be influential even when the veto pen rests in its inkwell.[20]

Rhetoric and reputation take on particular importance when vetoes become part of a bargaining process. Bargaining between Congress and the president is strategic and an example of the rationality principle in action. The president tries to influence legislators' beliefs about what they must do to keep the president from using the veto power. The key to veto bargaining is uncertainty. Members of Congress are often unsure about the president's policy preferences and therefore don't know which bills the president is willing to sign. When the policy preferences of the president and Congress diverge, as they typically do in a divided government, the president tries to convince Congress that his

---

15 A caveat: President George W. Bush, as observed in an earlier footnote, relied on signing statements as something of a substitute for the veto. Had the Supreme Court declared the maneuver unconstitutional, the president would have been forced to face squarely the decision to use the power of the veto.

16 For the complete list, see www.senate.gov/reference/Legislation/vetoes/vetoCounts.htm

17 Charles M. Cameron, *Veto Bargaining*. See also David W. Rohde and Dennis Simon, "Presidential Vetoes and Congressional Response: A Study of Institutional Conflict," *American Journal of Political Science* 29 (1985): 397–427.

18 David R. Mayhew, *Divided We Govern: Party Control, Lawmaking, and Investigations, 1946–1990* (New Haven, CT: Yale University Press, 1991).

19 Jack H. Nagel, *The Descriptive Analysis of Power* (New Haven, CT: Yale University Press, 1975).

20 See Rohde and Simon, "Presidential Vetoes and Congressional Response."

preferences are more extreme than they really are in order to get Congress to enact legislation that is closer to what he really wants. If members of Congress knew the president's preferences ahead of time, they would pass a bill that was close to what *they* wanted, subject to minimally satisfying the president. Through strategic use of the veto and veto threats, a president tries to shape Congress's beliefs about his policy preferences in order to gain greater concessions from Congress. Reputation is central to presidential effectiveness in this process.[21] By influencing congressional beliefs, the president is building a policy reputation that will affect future congressional behavior.

During the first year of his presidency, Barack Obama threatened to veto a defense spending bill that contained $369 billion in funding for the production of the F-22 fighter as well as a congressional resolution that would have blocked the release of about $350 billion in economic stimulus funds. After meeting with the president, members of Congress agreed to release the stimulus funds. On the issue of the F-22, however, Congress was reluctant to concede. Nevertheless, on July 21, 2009, with the backing of Defense Secretary Robert Gates and former Republican presidential nominee John McCain, Obama's position was sustained by a vote in the Senate, stripping funds for the F-22 from a defense appropriations measure. The House, which had previously voted to appropriate the funds, followed the Senate's lead on July 30, agreeing to eliminate the funds.

What about the relationship between mass public support for the president and the use of the veto? At least for the modern presidency, a crucial resource for the president in negotiating with Congress has been public approval as measured by opinion polls.[22] In some situations, members of Congress pass a bill not because they want to change policy but because they want to force the president to veto a popular bill that he disagrees with in order to hurt his approval ratings.[23] The key is that the public, uncertain of the president's policy preferences, uses information implied by vetoes to reassess what it knows about his preferences. As a result, vetoes may come at a price to the president. A president must, according to the rationality principle, weigh the advantages of using the veto or threatening to do so—to gain concessions from Congress—against the hit he may take in his popularity. The president may be reluctant to use the veto or the threat of a veto to gain concessions from Congress if it will hurt him in the polls. But in some cases, the president will take a hit in his approval ratings by vetoing a bill if it is drastically inconsistent with his policies.[24]

---

21 Neustadt, *Presidential Power*.

22 Theodore J. Lowi, *The Personal President: Power Invested, Promise Unfulfilled* (Ithaca, NY: Cornell University Press, 1985).

23 Timothy Groseclose and Nolan McCarty, "The Politics of Blame: Bargaining before an Audience," *American Journal of Political Science* 45 (2001): 100–19.

24 For a study of the ways presidents involve and mobilize mass public opinion on behalf of policies they pursue, see Brandice Canes-Wrone, *Who Leads Whom? Presidents, Policy, and the Public* (Chicago: University of Chicago Press, 2006). Also see Lawrence R. Jacobs and Robert Y. Shapiro, *Politicians Don't Pander: Political Manipulation and the Loss of Democratic Responsiveness* (Chicago: University of Chicago Press, 2000).

Legislative Initiative. Although not explicitly stated, the Constitution provides the president with the power of legislative initiative. To initiate means to originate, and in government that can mean power. The framers of the Constitution clearly saw legislative initiative as one of the keys to executive power. Initiative obviously implies the ability to formulate proposals for important policies, and the president, as an individual with a great deal of staff assistance, is able to initiate decisive action more frequently than Congress, with its large assemblies that have to deliberate and debate before taking action. With some important exceptions, Congress banks on the president to set the agenda of public policy. And quite clearly there is power in initiative: there is power in being able to set the terms of discourse in the making of public policy.

legislative initiative

The president's inherent power to bring a legislative agenda before Congress

For example, during the weeks immediately following September 11, 2001, George W. Bush took many presidential initiatives to Congress, and each was given almost unanimous support: from commitments to pursue Al Qaeda, remove the Taliban, and reconstitute the Afghanistan regime all the way to almost unlimited approval for mobilization of both military power and power over the regulation of American civil liberties. Bush's faced more difficulty in his second term, however. Growing problems (and casualties) in Iraq, administrative scandals, and a financial crisis plagued the president. As presidential popularity ebbed in the polls, so, too, did Bush's agenda power.

In 2009, soon after taking office, President Obama presented Congress with a record-breaking $3 trillion budget proposal that included a host of new programs in such areas as health and human services, transportation, housing, and education. Obama told Congress that he would soon be requesting several hundred billion more for the financial bailout designed to rescue America's banks and revive the nation's credit markets. Not only was Congress responsive to the president's initiatives but lawmakers also expected the president to take the lead in responding to America's financial emergency and other problems.

Together with the Democratic 111th Congress, President Obama achieved a number of legislative results in his first two years: the Lilly Ledbetter Fair Pay Act, the Children's Health Insurance Program Reauthorization Act of 2009, the American Recovery and Reinvestment Act of 2009, financial reform legislation, and, of course, health care reform legislation. Table 7.2 shows how Congress voted on each of these bills. In working to get these bills passed, Obama's team was strategic in how they pursued their goals and mindful of the institutional rules and practices that would affect the outcomes. Despite Obama's efforts to assemble bipartisan support, Republicans mainly opposed, as the votes in this table display. Comfortable Democratic majorities in each chamber gave him his victories.[25]

There were also legislative disappointments. Obama took on enormous political risks when he staked his presidency on legislative accomplishments. The first risk was that he would fail to accomplish what he had set out to do. For

25 During a "lame duck" session after the 2010 elections but before the new 112th Congress was seated, President Obama enjoyed some additional legislative successes, including Senate approval of a new nuclear treaty with Russia, extension of unemployment benefits, the prevention of tax hikes for middle- and upper-class families, and a free-trade agreement with South Korea.

Table 7.2A
FINAL PASSAGE VOTE TALLIES: HOUSE OF REPRESENTATIVES

	TOTAL		DEMOCRATS		REPUBLICANS	
LEGISLATION	**YEAS**	**NAYS**	**YEAS**	**NAYS**	**YEAS**	**NAYS**
The Lilly Ledbetter Fair Pay Act	250	177	247	5	3	172
The Children's Health Insurance Program Reauthorization Act of 2009	290	135	250	2	40	133
The American Recovery and Reinvestment Act of 2009	246	183	246	7	0	163
The Fraud Enforcement and Recovery Act of 2009	338	52	224	0	114	52
The Helping Families Save Their Homes Act of 2009	367	54	244	3	123	51
The Credit Card Accountability Responsibility and Disclosure Act of 2009	279	147	105	145	174	2
The Dodd-Frank Wall Street Reform and Consumer Protection Act	237	192	234	19	3	173
The Patient Protection and Affordable Care Act	219	212	219	34	0	178
Middle Class Tax Relief and Job Creation Act of 2012	293	132	147	41	146	91

SOURCE: Library of Congress, http://thomas.loc.gov/ (accessed 10/21/10).

example, President Jimmy Carter's inability to realize his big plans contributed greatly to his defeat in the 1980 election and to the impression that his presidency was "a failure."

The second risk is that the messy and often ugly process of legislation will frustrate a president's efforts to meet these goals. There is a reason that the German statesman Otto von Bismarck said, "Laws are like sausages. It's better not to see them being made." Compromise is at the heart of politics in a democracy. When the president gives special favors to those whose vote might help his legislation pass or when the majority leader tries to pass amendments

Table 7.2 B

FINAL PASSAGE VOTE TALLIES: SENATE

	TOTAL		DEMOCRATS		REPUBLICANS	
LEGISLATION	YEAS	NAYS	YEAS	NAYS	YEAS	NAYS
The Lilly Ledbetter Fair Pay Act	61	36	56	0	5	36
The Children's Health Insurance Program Reauthorization Act of 2009	66	32	57	0	9	32
The American Recovery and Reinvestment Act of 2009	60	38	57	0	3	38
The Fraud Enforcement and Recovery Act of 2009	92	5	56	0	36	4
The Helping Families Save Their Homes Act of 2009	91	5	56	0	35	5
The Credit Card Accountability Responsibility and Disclosure Act of 2009	90	5	55	1	35	4
The Dodd-Frank Wall Street Reform and Consumer Protection Act	60	39	57	1	3	38
The Patient Protection and Affordable Care Act	60	39	60	0	0	39
Middle Class Tax Relief and Job Creation Act of 2012	60	36	46	5	14	31

SOURCE: Library of Congress, http://thomas.loc.gov/ (accessed 10/21/10).

that favor a particular senator or representative, the seamy side of politics is rearing its head. During the attempt to pass health care reform, critics of bartering political favors for crucial votes had a field day. For example, Nebraska was given a Medicare exemption that no other state received solely to secure the vote for Obamacare of the pivotal Nebraska senator, something the media publicized and Obama opponents took great pains to point out. For a president who campaigned on "changing politics as we know it," it looked an awful lot like old-school politics. The Republicans were free to point out the inconsistencies between Democratic pledges for open, honest government and the closed-door negotiations, proposals, and counterproposals that were taking place. Even worse, elements of the coalitions that supported President Obama in the campaign had to watch as their objectives were sacrificed or ignored in the quest to get *something* done. Compromise is all well and good unless your pet policy is the one that's about to be compromised away, and public legislative bargaining alienated some supporters. In short, the messiness of the political process negatively affected the Democrats and left the Republicans largely unscathed.

Even when the president takes great pains to understand his political situation, he sometimes fails to meet his objectives. Most notably, Obama has not passed significant environmental legislation or comprehensive immigration reform. Both goals were announced at the outset of his presidency. Each was sacrificed as higher priorities dominated (and exhausted) the legislative agenda.

The 112th Congress, created by the 2010 elections, proved to be an altogether different experience for Obama. With majority control in the House ceded to the Republicans, the opposition exploited its new strength to obstruct or restrict administration initiatives. Legislative successes for Obama were few, far between, and only the result of constant struggle. Nevertheless, Obama prevailed in his 2012 re-election bid, at least in part because he did, in fact, deliver early in his term and could blame Republican obstructionism for his lack of success later on.

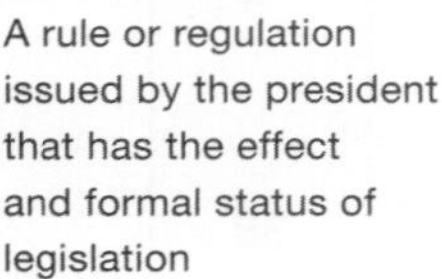

A rule or regulation issued by the president that has the effect and formal status of legislation

The president's initiative does not end with policy making involving Congress and the making of laws in the ordinary sense of the term. The president has still another legislative role (in all but name) within the executive branch. This is designated as the power to issue executive orders. The executive order is foremost a normal tool of management, a power virtually any CEO possesses to make company policy—rules setting procedures, etiquette, chains of command, functional responsibilities, and so on. But evolving from this normal management practice is a recognized presidential power to promulgate rules that have the effect and formal status of legislation. Most of the executive orders of the president provide for the reorganization of structures and procedures or otherwise direct the affairs of the executive branch—either to be applied across the board to all agencies or to be applied in some important respect to a single agency or department. The power to issue executive orders illustrates that although reputation and persuasion are typically required in presidential policy making, the practice of issuing executive orders, within limits, allows a president to govern without the necessity to persuade.[26] We take a closer look at how modern presidents have used executive orders later in the chapter.

Delegated Powers

Many of the powers exercised by the president and the executive branch are not set forth in the Constitution but are the products of congressional statutes and resolutions. Over the past three-quarters of a century, Congress has voluntarily

26 This point is developed in both Kenneth R. Mayer, *With the Stroke of a Pen: Executive Orders and Presidential Power* (Princeton, NJ: Princeton University Press, 2001), and William G. Howell, *Power without Persuasion: The Politics of Direct Presidential Action* (Princeton, NJ: Princeton University Press, 2003).

delegated a great deal of its own legislative authority to the executive branch. To some extent, this delegation of power has been an almost inescapable consequence of the expansion of governmental activity in the United States since the New Deal. Given the vast range of the federal government's responsibilities, Congress cannot execute and administer all the programs it creates and the laws it enacts. Inevitably Congress must turn to the hundreds of departments and agencies in the executive branch or, when necessary, create new agencies to implement its goals. Thus, for example, in 2002, when Congress sought to protect America from terrorist attacks, it established the Department of Homeland Security and gave it broad powers in the realms of law enforcement, public health, and immigration. Similarly, in 1970, when Congress enacted legislation designed to improve the nation's air and water quality, it assigned the task of implementing its goals to the new Environmental Protection Agency created by Nixon's executive order. Congress gave the EPA substantial power to set and enforce air- and water-quality standards.

As they implement congressional legislation, federal agencies collectively develop thousands of rules and regulations and issue thousands of orders and findings every year. Agencies interpret Congress's intent, promulgate rules aimed at implementing that intent, and issue orders to individuals, firms, and organizations throughout the nation designed to impel them to conform to the law. When it establishes an agency, Congress sometimes grants it only limited discretionary authority, providing very specific guidelines and standards that must be followed by the administrators charged with the program's implementation. Take the Internal Revenue Service (IRS), for example. Most Americans view the IRS as a powerful agency whose dictates can have an immediate and sometimes unpleasant effect on their lives. Yet congressional tax legislation is specific and detailed and leaves little to the discretion of IRS administrators.[27] The agency certainly develops numerous rules and procedures to enhance tax collection. It is Congress, however, that establishes the structure of the tax liabilities, tax exemptions, and tax deductions that determine each taxpayer's burdens and responsibilities.

In many instances, however, congressional legislation is not very detailed. Often Congress defines a broad goal or objective and delegates enormous discretionary power to administrators to determine how that goal is to be achieved. For example, the 1970 act creating the Occupational Safety and Health Administration (OSHA) states that Congress's purpose is "to assure so far as is possible every working man and woman in the nation safe and healthful working conditions." The act, however, neither defines such conditions nor suggests how they might be achieved.[28] The result is that agency administrators have enormous discretionary power to draft rules and regulations that have the effect of law. Indeed, the courts treat these administrative rules like congressional statutes.

27 Kenneth F. Warren, *Administrative Law*, 3rd ed. (Upper Saddle River, NJ: Prentice-Hall, 1996), p. 250.

28 Theodore J. Lowi, *The End of Liberalism: The Second Republic of the United States*, 2nd ed. (New York: Norton, 1979), pp. 117–8.

For all intents and purposes, when Congress creates an agency such as OSHA or the EPA, giving it a broad mandate to achieve some desirable outcome, it transfers its own legislative power to the executive branch.

In the nineteenth and early twentieth centuries, Congress typically wrote laws that provided fairly clear principles and standards to guide executive implementation. For example, the 1922 Tariff Act empowered the president to increase or decrease duties on certain manufactured goods in order to reduce the difference in cost between products produced domestically and those manufactured abroad. The act authorized the president to make the final determination, but his discretionary authority was quite constrained. The statute listed the criteria the president was to consider, fixed the permissible range of tariff changes, and outlined the procedures to be used to calculate the cost differences between foreign and domestic goods. When an importer challenged a particular executive decision as an abuse of delegated power, the Supreme Court had no difficulty finding that the president was merely acting in accordance with Congress's directives.[29]

At least since the New Deal, however, Congress has tended to give executive agencies broad mandates and draft legislation that offers few clear standards or guidelines for implementation by the executive. For example, the 1933 National Industrial Recovery Act, a major piece of New Deal legislation, gave the president the authority to set rules to bring about fair competition in key sectors of the economy without ever defining what the term meant or how it was to be achieved. Similarly, the 1938 Agricultural Adjustment Act, which led to a system of commodity price supports and agricultural production restrictions, authorized the secretary of agriculture to make agricultural marketing "orderly" without offering any guidance regarding the commodities to be affected, how markets were to be organized, or how prices should be determined. All these decisions were left to the discretion of the secretary and his or her agents.[30] This pattern of broad delegation became typical in the ensuing decades. The 1972 Consumer Product Safety Act, for example, authorizes the Consumer Product Safety Commission to reduce unreasonable risk of injury from household products but offers no suggestions to guide the commission's determination of what constitutes reasonable and unreasonable risks or how these are to be reduced.[31]

This shift from the nineteenth-century pattern of issuing relatively well defined congressional guidelines to administrators to the more contemporary pattern of broadly delegating congressional power to the executive branch is, to be sure, partially a consequence of the great scope and complexity of the tasks that America's contemporary government has undertaken. During much of the nineteenth century, the federal government had relatively few domestic responsibilities, and Congress could pay close attention to details. Today the operation of an enormous executive establishment and thousands of programs under

---

29 *J. W. Hampton & Company. v. United States*, 276 U.S. 394 (1928).

30 David Schoenbrod, *Power without Responsibility: How Congress Abuses the People through Delegation* (New Haven, CT: Yale University Press, 1993), pp. 49–50.

31 Lowi, *The End of Liberalism*, p. 117.

varied and changing circumstances requires that administrators be allowed some considerable measure of discretion to carry out their jobs. Nevertheless, the result is to shift power from Congress to the executive branch.[32]

THE RISE OF PRESIDENTIAL GOVERNMENT

Most of the real influence of the modern presidency derives from the powers granted by the Constitution and the laws made by Congress. Presidential power is institutional. Thus any person properly elected and sworn in as president will possess almost all the power held by the strongest presidents in American history. Even when they are lame ducks, presidents still possess all the power of the office. For example, in 2008, lame-duck president Bush secured the enactment of a major piece of legislation aimed at ameliorating the nation's economic crisis.

What variables account for a president's success in exercising these powers? Why are some presidents considered great successes, others colossal failures, and most somewhere in between? These questions relate broadly to the very concept of presidential power. Is it a reflection of the attributes of the person, or is it more characteristic of the political situations that a president encounters? The personal view of presidential power dominated political scientists' thinking for several decades,[33] but recently scholars have argued that presidential power should be analyzed in terms of the strategic interactions that a president has with other political actors.[34] With the occasional exception, however, it took more than a century, perhaps as much as a century and a half, before presidents came to be seen as consequential players in these strategic encounters. A bit of historical review will be helpful in understanding how the presidency has risen to its current level of influence.

The Legislative Epoch, 1800–1933

In 1885, a then-obscure political science professor named Woodrow Wilson titled his general textbook *Congressional Government* because American government was just that, congressional government. There is ample evidence that Wilson's

32 It must be noted that, to some extent, the shift in power is illusory. What authority Congress delegates, it can recover. The wise president or executive branch administrator is eminently aware of this and conditions his or her discretionary decisions with one eye cast over a shoulder at a watchful Congress.

33 Neustadt, *Presidential Power and the Modern Presidents.*

34 Charles M. Cameron, "Bargaining and Presidential Power," in *Presidential Power: Forging the Presidency for the Twenty-first Century,* Robert Y. Shapiro, Martha Joynt Kumar, and Lawrence R. Jacobs, eds. (New York: Columbia University Press, 2000). See also Samuel Kernell, *Going Public: New Strategies of Presidential Leadership,* 4th ed. (Washington, DC: Congressional Quarterly Press, 2006).

description of the national government was consistent not only with nineteenth-century reality but also with the intentions of the framers. Within the system of three separate and competing powers, the clear intent of the Constitution was legislative supremacy. In the early nineteenth century, some observers saw the president as little more than America's chief clerk. Indeed, most historians agree that after Thomas Jefferson and until the beginning of the twentieth century, Presidents Andrew Jackson and Abraham Lincoln were the only exceptions to a succession of weak presidents. Both Jackson and Lincoln are considered great presidents because they used their great power in momentous ways. But it is important in the history of the presidency that neither of them left his powers as an institutional legacy to his successors. That is to say, once Jackson and Lincoln left office, the presidency reverted to the subordinate role that it played during the nineteenth century.

One of the reasons so few great men became president in the nineteenth century is that there was only occasional room for greatness.[35] As Chapter 3 indicated, the national government of that period was not a particularly powerful entity. The presidency of the nineteenth century was also weak because during this period the presidency was not closely linked to major national political and social forces. Indeed, there were few important *national* political or social forces to which presidents could have linked themselves even if they had wanted to. Federalism had taken very good care of this by fragmenting political interests and diverting the energies of interest groups toward the state and local levels of government, where most key decisions were being made.

As discussed earlier in the chapter, the presidency was strengthened in the 1830s when the national convention system of nominating presidential candidates was introduced. However, this additional independence did not change the presidency into the office we see today because the parties disappeared, returning to their states and Congress once the national election was over. In addition, as the national government grew, Congress kept a tight rein on the president's power. For example, when Congress began to make its first efforts to exert power over the economy (beginning in 1887 with the adoption of the Interstate Commerce Act and in 1890 with the adoption of the Sherman Antitrust Act), it sought to keep this power away from the president and the executive branch by placing the new regulatory policies in "independent regulatory commissions" responsible to Congress rather than to the president (see also Chapter 8).

The New Deal and the Presidency

As discussed earlier, the key moment in the history of American national government came during Franklin Delano Roosevelt's administration. The Hundred Days at the outset of the Roosevelt administration in 1933 had no parallel

35 For related appraisals, see Jeffrey Tulis, *The Rhetorical Presidency* (Princeton, NJ: Princeton University Press, 1987); Stephen Skowronek, *The Politics Presidents Make: Leadership from John Adams to Bill Clinton* (Cambridge, MA: Harvard University Press, 1997); and Robert J. Spitzer, *President and Congress: Executive Hegemony at the Crossroads of American Government* (Philadelphia: Temple University Press, 1993).

in U.S. history. But it was only the beginning. The policies proposed by President Roosevelt and adopted by Congress during the first 1,000 days of his administration so changed the size and character of the national government that they constitute a moment in American history equivalent to the Founding or the Civil War. The president's constitutional obligation to see "that the laws be faithfully executed" became, during Roosevelt's presidency, virtually a responsibility to shape the laws before executing them.

Many of the New Deal programs were extensions of the traditional national government approach, which was described in Chapter 3 (see especially Table 3.1). But the New Deal went well beyond the traditional approach, adopting types of policies never before tried on a large scale by the national government; it began intervening in economic life in ways that had hitherto been reserved to the states. In other words, the national government discovered that it, too, had "police power" and could directly regulate individuals as well as provide roads and other services.

The new programs were such dramatic departures from the traditional policies of the national government that their constitutionality was in doubt. The Supreme Court in fact declared several of them unconstitutional, mainly on the grounds that in regulating the conduct of individuals or their employers, the national government was reaching beyond "*inter*state" and involving itself in "*intra*state"—essentially local—matters. Most of the New Deal remained in constitutional limbo until 1937, five years after Roosevelt was first elected and one year after his landslide 1936 re-election.

The turning point came with *National Labor Relations Board v. Jones and Laughlin Steel Corporation*, a Supreme Court case challenging the federal government's authority over the regulation of labor relations. The Court affirmed a federal role in the regulation of the national economy.[36] After the end of the New Deal, the Court has never again seriously questioned the legitimacy of interventions of the national government in the economy or society.[37]

The most important constitutional effect of Congress's actions and the Supreme Court's approval of those actions during the New Deal was the enhancement of presidential power. Most major acts of Congress in this period involved significant exercises of control over the economy. But few programs specified the actual controls to be used. Instead, Congress authorized the president or, in some cases, a new agency to determine what the controls would be. Some of the new agencies were independent commissions responsible to Congress. But most of the new agencies and new programs of the New Deal were placed in the executive branch directly under presidential authority. The institutional power of the presidency had been greatly increased.

36 *National Labor Relations Board v. Jones and Laughlin Steel Corporation,* 301 U.S. 1 (1937).

37 Some will argue that there are exceptions to this statement. One was *National League of Cities v. Usery,* 426 U.S. 833 (1976), which declared unconstitutional Congress's effort to supply national minimum wage standards to state and local government employees. But the Court reversed itself on this nine years later, in *Garcia v. San Antonio Metropolitan Transit Authority,* 469 U.S. 528 (1985). Another was *Bowsher v. Synar,* 478 U.S. 714 (1986). But cases such as these are few and far between, and they touch on only part of a law, not the constitutionality of an entire program.

Technically this form of congressional act, as we noted earlier, is the delegation of power. In theory, the delegation of power works as follows: (1) Congress recognizes a problem; (2) Congress acknowledges that it has neither the time nor the expertise to deal with the problem; and (3) Congress therefore sets the basic policies and then delegates to an agency the power to fill in the details. But in practice, Congress was delegating to the executive branch not merely the power to fill in the details but also real policy-making powers—that is, real legislative powers.

No modern government can avoid the delegation of significant legislative powers to the executive branch. But the fact remains that this delegation produced a fundamental shift in the American constitutional framework. During the 1930s, the growth of the national government through acts delegating legislative power tilted the national structure away from a Congress-centered government toward a president-centered government.[38] Make no mistake, Congress continues to be the constitutional source of policy. Legislative supremacy remains a constitutional fact of life, even in the twenty-first century, because delegations of power are contingent. And not all delegations are the same. A Democratic Congress, for example, is unwilling to empower a Republican president, and vice versa; unified governments are more likely than divided governments to engage in broad delegation.[39] In short, Congress can rescind these delegations of power, restrict them with subsequent amendments, and oversee the exercise of delegated power through congressional hearings, oversight agencies, budget controls, and other administrative tools. However, it is fair to say that presidential government has become an administrative fact of life as government by delegation has expanded greatly over the past century. The world of Woodrow Wilson's *Congressional Government* is forever changed. But Congress has many clubs behind its door with which to influence the manner in which the executive branch exercises its newly won power.

PRESIDENTIAL GOVERNMENT

The locus of policy decision making shifted to the executive branch because, as we just noted, Congress made delegations of authority to the president. Congress delegated authority to the executive for instrumental reasons, much as a principal

38 The Supreme Court did in fact *dis*approve broad delegations of legislative power by declaring the National Industrial Recovery Act of 1933 unconstitutional on the grounds that Congress did not accompany the broad delegations with sufficient standards or guidelines for presidential discretion (*Panama Refining Co. v. Ryan*, 293 U.S. 388 [1935], and *Schechter Poultry Corporation v. United States*, 295 U.S. 495 [1935]). The Supreme Court has never reversed those two decisions, but neither has it really followed them. Thus broad delegations of legislative power from Congress to the executive branch can be presumed to be constitutional. See Sotirios A. Barber, *The Constitution and the Delegation of Congressional Power* (Chicago: University of Chicago Press, 1975).

39 David Epstein and Sharyn O'Halloran, *Delegating Powers: A Transaction Cost Politics Approach to Policy Making under Separate Powers* (New York: Cambridge University Press, 1999).

delegates to an agent. An expanded agenda of political demands, necessitated first by economic crisis—the Great Depression—but also by an accumulation of the effects of nearly a century's worth of industrialization, urbanization, and greater integration into the world economy, confronted the national government, forcing Congress's hand. The legislature itself was limited in its ability to expand its own capacity to undertake these growing responsibilities, so delegation proved a natural administrative strategy. These acts of delegation gave a far greater role to the president, empowering this "agent" to initiate in his own right.

In the case of Franklin Roosevelt, his New Deal launched an era of presidential government. Congress certainly retained many tools with which to threaten, cajole, encourage, and persuade its executive agent to do its bidding. But presidents in general, and Roosevelt in particular, are not *only* agents of Congress and not *only* dependent on Congress for resources and authority. They are also agents of national constituencies for whom they are eager to demonstrate their capacity for leadership in executing constituency policy agendas.[40]

Likewise, congressional delegations of power are not the only resources available to a president. Presidents have at their disposal a variety of other formal and informal resources that have important implications for their ability to govern. Indeed, without these other resources, presidents would lack the ability—the tools of management and public mobilization—to make much use of the power and responsibility given to them by Congress. Let us first consider the president's formal or official resources and then turn to the more informal resources that affect a president's capacity to govern, in particular the president's base of popular support.

What Are the Formal Resources of Presidential Power?

The Cabinet. In the American system of government, the Cabinet is the traditional but informal designation for the heads of all the major departments of the federal government (Figure 7.2). The Cabinet has no constitutional status. In contrast to the United Kingdom and many other parliamentary countries, where the cabinet is the government, the American Cabinet is not a collective body. It meets but makes no decisions as a group. Each appointment must be approved by the Senate, but cabinet members are not responsible to the Senate or to Congress at large. Cabinet appointments help build party and popular support, but the Cabinet is not a party organ. The Cabinet is made up of directors but is not a true board of directors. Because cabinet appointees generally have not shared political careers with the president or with each other and because they may meet each other for the first time after their selection, the formation of an effective governing group out of this motley collection of appointments is unlikely.

 **Cabinet**

The secretaries, or chief administrators, of the major departments of the federal government. Cabinet secretaries are appointed by the president with the consent of the Senate

40 See Terry M. Moe, "Presidents, Institutions, and Theory," in *Researching the Presidency: Vital Questions, New Approaches,* George C. Edwards III, John H. Kessel, and Bert A. Rockman, eds. (Pittsburgh: University of Pittsburgh Press, 1993), p. 367.

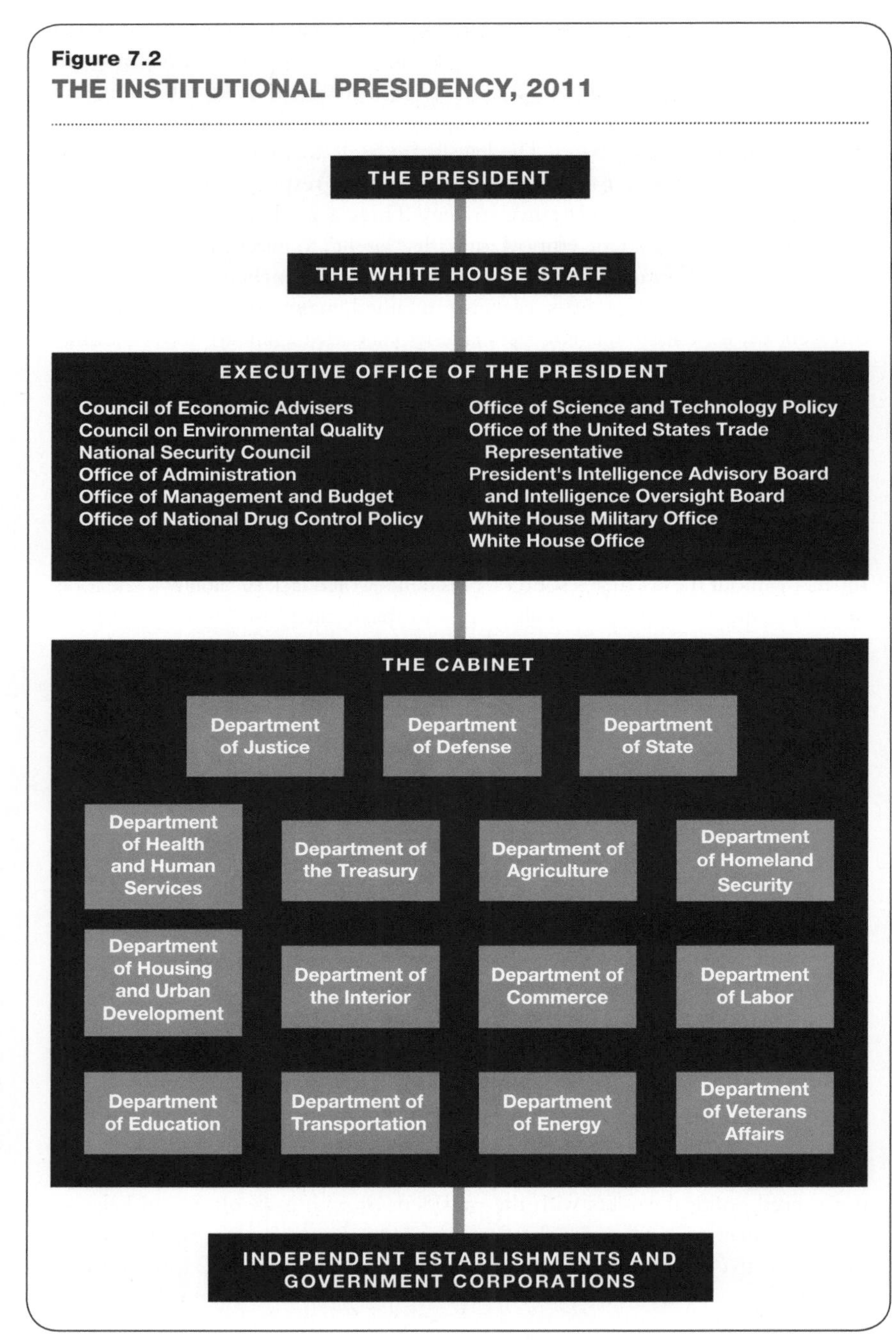
Figure 7.2
THE INSTITUTIONAL PRESIDENCY, 2011
THE PRESIDENT
THE WHITE HOUSE STAFF
EXECUTIVE OFFICE OF THE PRESIDENT
Council of Economic Advisers
Council on Environmental Quality
National Security Council
Office of Administration
Office of Management and Budget
Office of National Drug Control Policy
Office of Science and Technology Policy
Office of the United States Trade Representative
President's Intelligence Advisory Board and Intelligence Oversight Board
White House Military Office
White House Office
THE CABINET
Department of Justice
Department of Defense
Department of State
Department of Health and Human Services
Department of the Treasury
Department of Agriculture
Department of Homeland Security
Department of Housing and Urban Development
Department of the Interior
Department of Commerce
Department of Labor
Department of Education
Department of Transportation
Department of Energy
Department of Veterans Affairs
INDEPENDENT ESTABLISHMENTS AND GOVERNMENT CORPORATIONS

Some presidents have relied more heavily on an "inner cabinet," the National Security Council (NSC). The NSC, established by law in 1947, is composed of the president, the vice president, the secretary of state, the secretary of defense, and other officials invited by the president. It has its own staff of foreign policy specialists run by the assistant to the president for national security affairs. For these highest appointments, presidents usually turn to people from outside Washington, often longtime associates. President Obama (at least in his early months in office) relied heavily on his chief of staff, Rahm Emanuel, who resigned in 2010 to become mayor of Chicago (after several replacements, the position is now held by Jacob Lew); his former chief campaign strategist and now senior adviser, David Axelrod; the deputy chief of staff, Jim Messina (replaced by Nancy-Ann DePerle in 2012); and the press secretary, Robert Gibbs (replaced by Jay Carney in 2011). Collectively, this tight-knit group of Obama loyalists was known in Washington as "the boys."

National Security Council (NSC)

A presidential foreign policy advisory council composed of the president, the vice president, the secretary of state, the secretary of defense, and other officials invited by the president

Presidents have obviously been uneven in their reliance on the NSC and other subcabinet bodies because executive management is inherently a personal matter. Despite all the personal variations, however, one generalization can be made: presidents have increasingly preferred the White House staff to the Cabinet as their means of managing the gigantic executive branch.

The White House Staff. The White House staff is composed mainly of analysts and advisers.[41] Although many of the top White House staff members are given the title "special assistant" for a particular task or sector, the types of judgments they are expected to make and the kinds of advice they are supposed to give are a good deal broader and more generally political than those coming from the Executive Office of the President or the cabinet departments. The members of the White House staff also tend to be more closely associated with the president than other presidentially appointed officials.

White House staff

The analysts and advisers to the president, often given the title "special assistant"

From an informal group of fewer than a dozen people (popularly called the kitchen cabinet) and no more than four dozen at the height of Roosevelt's prewar administration, the White House staff has grown substantially with each successive president.[42] Richard Nixon employed 550 people in 1972. President Carter, who found so many of the requirements of presidential power distasteful and publicly vowed to keep his staff small and decentralized, built an even larger and more centralized staff. President Clinton reduced the White House staff by 20 percent, but a large White House staff is still essential and the staff remained large under Presidents George W. Bush and Barack Obama.

kitchen cabinet

An informal group of advisers to whom the president turns for counsel and guidance. Members of the official cabinet may or may not also be members of the kitchen cabinet

The White House staff is a crucial information source and management tool for the president. But it may also insulate the president from other sources

41 A substantial portion of this section is taken from Lowi, *The Personal President*, pp. 141–50.

42 All the figures since 1967, and probably since 1957, are understated because additional White House staff members have been on "detailed" service, borrowed from the military and various cabinet departments (some secretly assigned) and are not counted here because they were not on the White House payroll.

of information. Managing this trade-off between in-house expertise and access to independent outside opinion is a major challenge for the president. Sometimes it is botched, as when President George W. Bush depended too heavily on his staff for information about weapons of mass destruction (WMD) in Iraq, leading him to erroneous conclusions.[43]

Executive Office of the President (EOP)

The permanent agencies that perform defined management tasks for the president. Created in 1939, the EOP includes the Office of Management and Budget, the Council of Economic Advisers, the National Security Council, and other agencies

The Executive Office of the President. The development of the White House staff can be appreciated only in its relation to the still-larger Executive Office of the President (EOP). Created in 1939, the EOP is a major part of what is often called the institutional presidency—the permanent agencies that perform defined management tasks for the president. The most important and the largest EOP agency is the Office of Management and Budget (OMB). Its roles in preparing the national budget, designing the president's program, reporting on agency activities, and overseeing regulatory proposals make OMB personnel part of virtually every conceivable presidential responsibility. The status and power of the OMB have grown in importance with each successive president. The process of budgeting at one time was a bottom-up procedure, with expenditure and program requests passing from the lowest bureaus through the departments to "clearance" in OMB and hence to Congress, where each agency could be called in to reveal what its original request had been before it was revised by the OMB. Now the budgeting process is top-down: OMB sets the terms of discourse for agencies as well as for Congress. The director of OMB is now one of the most powerful officials in Washington.

The staff of the Council of Economic Advisers (CEA) constantly analyzes the economy and economic trends and attempts to give the president the ability to anticipate events rather than waiting and reacting to events. The Council on Environmental Quality was designed to do for environmental issues what the CEA does for economic issues. The members of the National Security Council meet regularly with the president to give advice on the large national security picture. The staff of the NSC assimilates and analyzes data from all intelligence-gathering agencies (the CIA, and so on). Other EOP agencies perform more specialized tasks.

Somewhere between 1,500 and 2,000 highly specialized staffers work for EOP agencies.[44] The importance of each agency in the EOP varies according to the personal orientation of the president. For example, the NSC staff was of immense importance under President Nixon, especially because it served essentially as the personal staff of the presidential assistant Henry Kissinger before his elevation to the office of secretary of state. But it was of less importance

43 See George Krause, "The Secular Decline in Presidential Domestic Policymaking: An Organizational Perspective," *Presidential Studies Quarterly* 34 (2004): 779–92. On the general issue, see James P. Pfiffner, ed., *The Managerial Presidency,* 2nd ed. (College Station: Texas A&M University Press, 1999).

44 The actual number is difficult to estimate because, as with the White House staff, some EOP personnel, especially those in national security work, are detailed to the office from outside agencies.

to President George H. W. Bush, who looked outside the EOP altogether for military policy matters, turning much more to the Joint Chiefs of Staff and its chair at the time, General Colin Powell.

The Vice Presidency. The vice presidency is a constitutional anomaly, even though the office was created by the Constitution along with the presidency. The vice president exists for two purposes only: to succeed the president in case of death, resignation, or incapacitation and to preside over the Senate, casting a tie-breaking vote when necessary.[45]

The main value of the vice presidency as a political resource for the president is electoral. Traditionally a presidential candidate's most important rule for the choice of a running mate is that he or she bring the support of at least one state (preferably a large one) not otherwise likely to support the ticket. Another rule holds that the vice-presidential nominee should provide some regional balance and, wherever possible, some balance among various ideological or ethnic subsections of the party. It is very doubtful that John Kennedy would have won in 1960 without his vice-presidential candidate, Lyndon Johnson, and the contribution Johnson made to winning in Texas. George W. Bush's choice of Dick Cheney in 2000 was almost completely devoid of direct electoral value, since Cheney comes from one of our least populous states (Wyoming, which casts only three electoral votes). But given Cheney's stalwart right-wing record both in Congress and as President George H. W. Bush's secretary of defense, coupled with his even more prominently right-wing wife, Lynne Cheney, his inclusion on the Republican ticket was clearly an effort to consolidate the support of the restive right wing of the Republican Party. In 2008, Barack Obama chose Senator Joseph Biden of Delaware as his vice-presidential running mate. Obama had often been criticized for lacking background in the realm of foreign policy. Biden, chair of the Senate Foreign Relations Committee, brought considerable foreign policy experience to the ticket.

As the institutional presidency has grown in size and complexity, most presidents of the past 25 years have sought to use their vice presidents as management resources after the election. George H. W. Bush, as President Reagan's vice president, was kept within the loop of decision making because Reagan delegated so much power. President Bush did not take such pains to keep Vice President Dan Quayle in the loop, but President Clinton relied greatly on his vice president, Al Gore, and Gore emerged as one of the most trusted and effective figures in the Clinton White House. The presidency of George W. Bush resulted in unprecedented power and responsibility for his vice president, Dick Cheney. Known as a hands-on vice president, Cheney played an active role in cabinet meetings and policy formation as well as in organizing the war on terror and launching the Iraq War. Cheney was widely viewed as one of the most—if not the most—influential vice presidents in American history. In the Obama administration, Vice President Joe Biden has wielded considerable influence.

45 Article I, Section 3, provides that "the Vice President . . . shall be President of the Senate, but shall have no Vote, unless they be equally divided." This is the only vote the vice president is allowed.

Drawing on his vast experience in the Senate, he has played an important role as liaison to the Congress. He has also been an important sounding board on matters involving foreign affairs, as Biden previously was a senior member of the Senate Foreign Relations Committee.

The President and Policy. The president's powers and institutional resources, taken together, give the chief executive a substantial voice in the nation's policy-making processes. Strictly speaking, presidents cannot introduce legislation. Only members of Congress can formally propose new programs and policies. However, presidents often do send proposals to Congress. Congress, in turn, takes up these proposals by referring them to the relevant committee of jurisdiction. Sometimes these proposals are said to be dead on arrival, an indication that presidential preferences are at loggerheads with those in the House or Senate. This is especially common during periods of divided government. In such circumstances, presidents and legislators engage in bargaining, although in the end the status quo may prevail—a situation sometimes termed "gridlock" by pundits and the media. Presidents are typically in a weak position in these circumstances, especially if they have grand plans to change the status quo.[46] During periods of unified government, the president has fellow partisans in charge of each chamber; in these cases, the president may indeed seize the initiative, seeking to coordinate policy initiatives from the White House. The political scientist Charles Cameron suggests that the distinction between unified and divided government is quite consequential for presidential "style": it makes the chief executive either bargainer in chief or coordinator in chief.[47]

Congress has come to expect the president to propose the government's budget, and the nation has come to expect presidential initiatives to deal with major problems. Some of these initiatives have come in the form of huge packages of programs—Franklin Delano Roosevelt's New Deal and Lyndon Johnson's Great Society. Sometimes presidents craft a single program they hope will have a significant effect on both the nation and their political fortunes. For example, George W. Bush made the war on terrorism the centerpiece of his administration. To fight this war, Bush brought about the creation of a new cabinet department, the Department of Homeland Security, and the enactment of such pieces of legislation as the USA PATRIOT Act to give the executive branch more power to deal with the terrorist threat. For President Obama there has been a series of successful legislative initiatives (some listed earlier in Table 7.2), the most important of which is health care.

At one time, historians and journalists liked to debate the question of strong versus weak presidents. Today every president is strong. This strength is not so much a function of personal charisma or political savvy as it is a reflection of the increasing power of the institution of the presidency.

46 D. Roderick Kiewiet and Mathew D. McCubbins, *The Logic of Delegation: Congressional Parties and the Appropriations Process* (Chicago: University of Chicago Press, 1991).

47 Cameron, "Bargaining and Presidential Power."

The Contemporary Bases of Presidential Power

In the nineteenth century, when Congress was America's dominant institution of government, its members sometimes treated the president with disdain. Today, however, no one would assert that the presidency is an unimportant institution. Presidents seek to dominate the policy-making process and claim the inherent power to lead the nation in time of war. The expansion of presidential power over the course of the past century has come about not by accident but as the result of an ongoing effort by successive presidents to enlarge the powers of the office. Some of these efforts have succeeded, and others have failed. As the framers of the Constitution predicted, presidential ambition has been a powerful and unrelenting force in American politics.

Generally presidents can expand their power by three means: party, popular mobilization, and administration. In the first instance, presidents may construct or strengthen national partisan institutions with which to exert influence in the legislative process and through which to implement their programs. Alternatively or in addition to the first tactic, presidents may use popular appeals to create a mass base of support that will allow them to subordinate their political foes. This tactic has sometimes been called the strategy of going public, or the "rhetorical" presidency.[48] In the third instance, presidents may seek to bolster their control of established executive agencies or create new administrative institutions and procedures that will reduce their dependence on Congress and give them a more independent governing and policy-making capability. Presidents' use of executive orders to achieve their policy goals in lieu of seeking to persuade Congress to enact legislation is, perhaps, the most obvious example.

Party as a Source of Power. All presidents have relied on the members and leaders of their own party to implement their legislative agendas. President George W. Bush, for example, worked closely with congressional GOP leaders on such matters as energy policy and Medicare reform. But the president does not control his own party; party members have considerable autonomy. On immigration policy, for example, the Bush proposals in 2006 were supported in most respects by the Republican-controlled Senate. The Republican-controlled House, however, passed much more punitive policies. The two chambers, despite being controlled by the president's party, were unable to agree on a compromise and ended up settling on elements of the House bill that the president least desired. Nevertheless, he signed the measure in October 2006, noting it was only the first step in comprehensive immigration reform. President Obama made immigration reform one of his priorities, but failed to induce the 111th Congress, controlled by his party, to take up the issue.

President Obama initially declared that he would seek bipartisan support for all of his programs. Congressional Republicans, however, calculated that they had little to gain from supporting Obama and much to lose if his administration was successful. Hence, the GOP opposed the president's domestic and

48 Kernell, *Going Public;* see also Tulis, *The Rhetorical Presidency.*

Figure 7.3
THE PRESIDENTIAL BATTING AVERAGE: PRESIDENTIAL SUCCESS ON CONGRESSIONAL VOTES, 1953–2010

ANALYZING THE EVIDENCE

Presidential success ebbs and flows, especially with the partisan character of Congress. Compare success rates when the president and the legislature were of the same party (for example, Clinton's first two years) and when they were not (for example, Clinton's last six years).

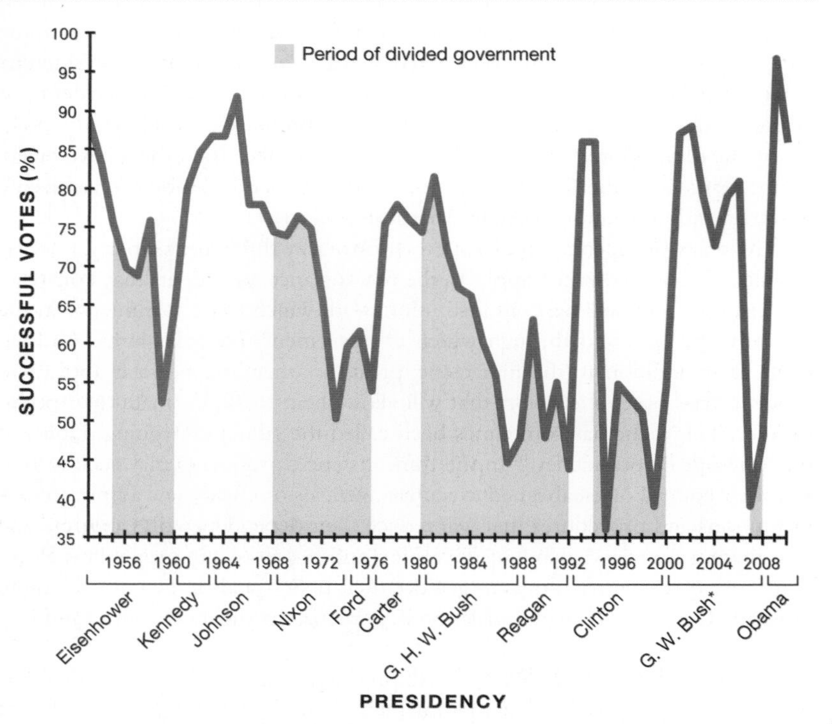

*In 2001, the government was divided for only part of the year.
NOTE: Percentages are based on votes on which presidents took a position.
SOURCES: *Congressional Quarterly Weekly Report*, January 3, 2011, pp. 18–24, and authors' update.

foreign policy initiatives. With overwhelming Democratic majorities in both houses of Congress, President Obama found that he had no difficulty turning to the Democratic leadership for support. Indeed, Republican opposition helped Democratic leaders unite their fractious followers behind the president's budget proposals in 2009. Indeed, most of Obama's successes (see Table 7.2) involved overwhelming Democratic support prevailing over nearly unanimous Republican opposition in his first two years.

In America's system of separated powers, the president's party may be in the minority in Congress and unable to do much for the chief executive's programs (Figure 7.3). Consequently, although their party is valuable to chief executives, it has not been a fully reliable presidential tool. The more unified the president's party is in supporting his legislative requests, the more unified the opposition party is likely to be. Unless the majority of the president's party is very large, he must also appeal to the opposition to make up for the inevitable defectors within the ranks of his own party. Thus the president often poses as being above partisanship to win "bipartisan" support in Congress. But to the extent that he pursues a bipartisan strategy, he cannot throw himself fully into building the party loyalty and the party discipline that would maximize the value of his own party's support in Congress. This is a dilemma for every president, particularly those faced with an opposition-controlled Congress.

The role of the filibuster in the Senate should not be underestimated in this context (see Chapter 6). Even a president with a large majority in the House and a good working majority in the Senate may not have the 60 votes needed to shut down debate in the Senate. This is especially apparent in the case of presidential appointments, where individual senators can place a hold on a nomination, putting everyone on notice that the president's pursuit of a particular candidate will trigger a filibuster.[49] Filibuster power was especially prominent in 2005 as President Bush sought Senate confirmation of federal judges and two Supreme Court justices. The Democrats, who were in the minority, were in a position to filibuster nominations they regarded as "extremist," forcing the president (and his majority partisans in the Senate) to negotiate. The Democrats lifted the filibuster threat in exchange for some moderation on the part of the president, and they allowed up-or-down votes on some nominees. Obama encountered similar resistance in the Senate where the powerful "Senator #60" was usually a Republican. Because they cannot always rely on their party in Congress, contemporary presidents are more likely to use two other methods—popular mobilization and executive administration—to achieve their political goals.

Going Public. Popular mobilization as a technique of presidential power has its historical roots in the presidencies of Theodore Roosevelt and Woodrow Wilson and subsequently became a weapon in the political arsenals of most presidents after the mid-twentieth century. During the nineteenth century, it was considered rather inappropriate for presidents to engage in personal campaigning on their own behalf or in support of programs and policies. When Andrew Johnson broke this unwritten rule and made a series of speeches vehemently seeking public support for his Reconstruction program, even some of his most ardent supporters were shocked at what was seen as a lack of decorum and dignity. The president's opponents cited his "inflammatory" speeches in one of the articles of impeachment drafted by Congress pursuant to the first effort in American history to oust an incumbent president.[50]

The president who used public appeals perhaps most effectively was Franklin Delano Roosevelt. The political scientist Sidney Milkis observes that Roosevelt was "firmly persuaded of the need to form a direct link between the executive office and the public."[51] Roosevelt developed a number of tactics aimed at forging

49 A powerful argument that invokes this logic is that of Keith Krehbiel in *Pivotal Politics: A Theory of U.S. Lawmaking* (Chicago: University of Chicago Press, 1998).

50 Tulis, *The Rhetorical Presidency,* p. 91.

51 Sidney M. Milkis, *The President and the Parties: The Transformation of the American Party System since the New Deal* (New York: Oxford University Press, 1993), p. 97.

such a link. Like his predecessors, he often embarked on speaking trips around the nation to promote his programs. On one such tour, he told a crowd, "I regain strength just by meeting the American people."[52] In addition, Roosevelt made limited but important use of the new electronic medium, radio, to reach millions of Americans. In his famous "fireside chats," the president, or at least his voice, came into living rooms across the country to discuss programs and policies and generally to assure Americans that Franklin Delano Roosevelt was aware of their difficulties and working diligently toward solutions.[53] Another executive, Mayor Fiorello La Guardia of New York City, also "went public," using radio to read comic strips to Depression-era city children during a long newspaper strike. A brilliant political ploy, it deeply impressed voting-age citizens while entertaining the young ones.

Roosevelt was also an innovator in the realm of what now might be called press relations. When he entered the White House, he faced a mainly hostile press typically controlled by conservative members of the business establishment. As the president wrote, "All the fat-cat newspapers—85 percent of the whole—have been utterly opposed to everything the Administration is seeking."[54] Roosevelt hoped to be able to use the press to mold public opinion, but to do so he needed to circumvent the editors and publishers who were generally unsympathetic to his goals. To this end, the president worked to cultivate the reporters who covered the White House. Roosevelt made himself available for twice-weekly press conferences, during which he offered candid answers to reporters' questions and made certain to make important policy announcements that would provide the reporters with significant stories to file with their papers.[55] Roosevelt was the first president to designate a press secretary (Stephen Early), who was charged with organizing the press conferences and making certain that reporters observed the informal rules distinguishing presidential comments that were off the record from those that could be attributed directly to the president.

Every president since Roosevelt has sought to craft a public relations strategy that emphasized his strengths and maximized his popular appeal. One Clinton innovation was to make the White House Communications Office an important institution within the EOP. In a practice continued by George W. Bush, the Communications Office became responsible not only for responding to reporters' queries but also for developing and implementing a coordinated communications strategy: promoting the president's policy goals, developing responses to unflattering news stories, and making certain that a favorable image

52 Quoted in James MacGregor Burns, *Roosevelt: The Lion and the Fox* (New York: Harcourt, Brace, 1956), p. 317.

53 The distribution of radio ownership in the 1930s was quite uneven, however. Roosevelt reinforced his "going public" radio addresses with a similarly uneven distribution of relief funds during the Depression. Counties with a high concentration of radio ownership received more relief funds, even after controlling for income and unemployment. Popular mobilization and public policy worked hand in hand. See David Strömberg, "Radio's Impact on Public Spending," *Quarterly Journal of Economics* 119 (2004): 189–221.

54 Burns, *Roosevelt*, p. 317.

55 Kernell, *Going Public*, p. 79.

of the president would, insofar as possible, dominate the news. Consistent with President Obama's successful use of social networking in his 2008 election campaign, the Obama administration's communications office has emphasized social networking techniques, including "tweeting," to reach newsmakers and the American people directly. For example, in May 2009, the White House posted a 140-character "tweet" on the swine flu. Of course, unlike ordinary tweets, presidential tweets must, under the terms of the Presidential Records Act, be recorded and stored for posterity.

In addition to using the media, recent presidents, have reached out directly to the American public to gain its approval (see Figure 7.4). During his first full month in office, for example, President Obama addressed Congress and the American people on the nation's financial crisis. Obama said nothing new but sought to reassure the public and to mobilize its support for his policies. During his first year in office, Obama made additional major speeches in the United States and abroad designed to generate both domestic and international support for his programs. In his speeches, the president frequently sought to explain how his approaches would differ from those of the Bush administration. In a nationally televised May 2009 speech on national security, for example, Obama declared that the security policies employed by the Bush administration, including harsh interrogations, indefinite detention of suspects, and other violations of America's customary rule of law were both inconsistent with American values and ineffective. He promised to craft an approach that would protect both liberty and the nation's security. In a June 2009 speech delivered in Cairo, Egypt, Obama sought to reassure the Arab world that the United States was not its enemy. Obama began his speech with the traditional Muslim greeting, "Assalamu Alaykum," and made reference in his text to the "holy Koran." The speech was well received, though many listeners wondered if the president's words would be followed by changes in policy.

The Limits of Going Public. Some presidents have been able to make effective use of popular appeals to overcome congressional opposition. Popular support, though, has not been a firm foundation for presidential power. To begin with, it is notoriously fickle. President George W. Bush maintained an approval rating of over 70 percent for more than a year after the September 11 terrorist attacks. By 2003, however, his approval rating had fallen nearly 20 points as American casualties in Iraq mounted; by the end of 2005, it had fallen almost another 20 points, to the high 30s, where it remained through much of 2006. Such declines in popular approval during a president's term in office are nearly inevitable and follow a predictable pattern (Figure 7.5). Presidents generate popular support by promising to undertake important programs that will contribute directly to the well-being of large numbers of Americans. Almost inevitably, presidential performance falls short of those promises and popular expectations, leading to a sharp decline in public support and an ensuing collapse of presidential influence. Reagan and Clinton are the exceptions among modern presidents—leaving office at least as popular as when they arrived.

Presidents certainly have not abandoned the tool of going public, but they no longer use it frequently as they once did—there has been, for example, a decline in presidential appearances on prime-time television over the past five

ANALYZING THE EVIDENCE

In the nineteenth century, presidents seldom made public speeches or other public appearances. By the end of the twentieth century, the number of times presidents went public had increased dramatically. What accounts for the growth in public appearances? What do presidents hope to accomplish through speeches and other public events? What risks do presidents take when they seek to develop and use popular support as a political tool?

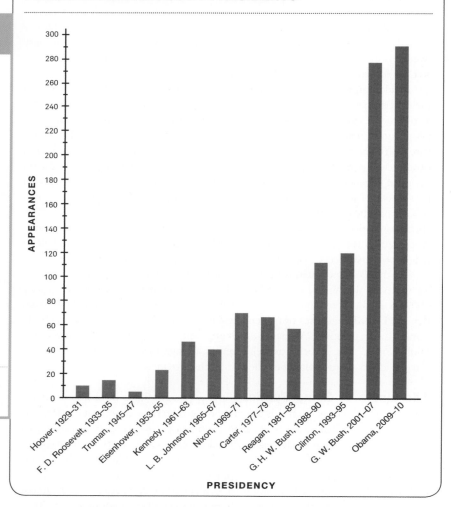

Figure 7.4
PUBLIC APPEARANCES BY PRESIDENTS

NOTE: Only the first two years of each term are included, because the last two years include many purely political appearances for the president's re-election campaign.

SOURCES: Kernell, *Going Public*, p.118, Lyn Ragsdale, *Vital Statistics on the Presidency*, 3rd ed. (Washington, DC: CQ Press, 2009), Table 4-9, pp. 202–3; POTUS Tracker, *Washington Post*, http://projects.washingtonpost.com/potus-tracker/ (accessed 8/8/11); and authors' updates.

administrations.[56] Instead, presidents have employed institutionalized public and media relations efforts more to create a generally favorable public image than to promote specific policies. Thus in 2002, President George W. Bush made several speeches to boost the proposed creation of the Homeland Security Department. At the same time, however, the White House Communications Office

56 Kernell, *Going Public*, p. 114.

Figure 7.5
PRESIDENTIAL PERFORMANCE RATINGS

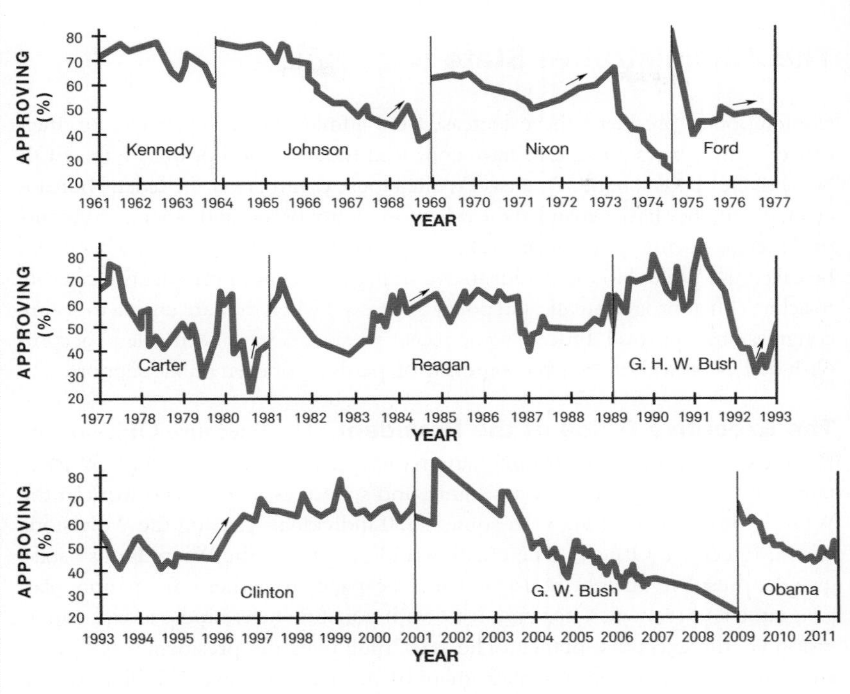

NOTE: Arrows indicate pre-election upswings.

SOURCES: Gallup and Louis Harris and Associates.

ANALYZING THE EVIDENCE

In the presidential performance-rating poll, respondents are asked, "Do you approve of the way the president is handling his job?" The graphs show the percentage of positive responses. What factors help explain changes in presidential approval ratings? Does popular approval really affect presidential power? How can popular feelings about the president affect the president's conduct and influence?

was engaged in a nonstop, seven-day-a-week effort to promote news and feature stories aimed at bolstering the president's more general public image. Stories emphasized the president's empathy for retirees hurt by the downturn of stock prices, the president's anger over corporate abuses, the president's concern for the environment, the president's determination to prevent terrorism, the president's support for Israel, and so forth. These are all examples of image polishing rather than going public on behalf of specific programs. Confronted with the limitations of a strategy of popular mobilization, presidents have shifted from an offensive strategy to a more defensive mode in this domain.

Technological change has also affected the tactics of going public. The growing heterogeneity of media outlets—cable stations, streamed radio, the blogosphere—and the declining viewership and readership of mainstream outlets has fragmented the public. This has necessitated newly crafted approaches—"narrowcasting" to reach targeted demographic categories rather than broadcasting to reach "the public." Instead of going "capital P" public, new approaches seek to appeal to myriad "small p" publics (plural). Shrinking and fragmented audiences have raised the costs and cast doubt on the effectiveness of presidential efforts to educate and mobilize public opinion. The limitations of going public as a route to presidential power have also led contemporary presidents to make use of a third technique: expanding their administrative capabilities.

The Administrative State

Contemporary presidents have increased the administrative capabilities of their office in three ways. First, they have enhanced the reach and power of the EOP. Second, they have sought to increase White House control over the federal bureaucracy. Third, they have expanded the role of executive orders and other instruments of direct presidential governance. Taken together, these components of what might be called the White House administrative strategy have given presidents a capacity to achieve their programmatic and policy goals even when they are unable to secure congressional approval. Indeed, some recent presidents have been able to accomplish quite a bit without much congressional, partisan, or even public support.

The Executive Office of the President. The Executive Office of the President has grown from 6 administrative assistants in 1939 to today's 39 assistants to the president, deputy assistants, and special assistants who work in the White House office, along with some 1,850 individuals staffing the 9 divisions of the Executive Office.[57] The creation and growth of the White House staff give the president an enormously enhanced capacity to gather information, plan programs and strategies, communicate with constituencies, and exercise supervision of the executive branch. The staff multiplies the president's eyes, ears, and arms, serving as a critical instrument of presidential power.[58] In light of the degree to which Congress delegates to the executive branch, as described earlier in this chapter, the president has greatly enhanced his capacity as an agent of policy formulation and implementation.

In particular, the OMB serves as a potential instrument of presidential control over federal spending and hence as a mechanism through which the White House has greatly expanded its power. The OMB has the capacity to analyze and approve not only budgetary requests but all legislative proposals emanating from all federal agencies before they are submitted to Congress. This procedure, now a matter of routine, greatly enhanced the president's control over the entire executive branch. All executive orders also go through the OMB.[59] Thus through one White House agency the president has the means to exert major influence over the flow of money as well as the shape and content of national legislation.

57 Harold W. Stanley and Richard G. Niemi, *Vital Statistics on American Politics, 2005–2006* (Washington, DC: Congressional Quarterly Press, 2005), pp. 250–1. For the FY 2012 estimates see "Executive Office of the President Fiscal Year 2012 Congressional Budget Submission," p. 15. It may be found at www.whitehouse.gov/sites/default/files/2012-eop-budget.pdf (accessed 3/9/2011).

58 Milkis, *The President and the Parties*, p. 128.

59 Milkis, *The President and the Parties*, p. 160.

Appointments and Regulatory Review. Presidents have also sought to increase their influence through bureaucratic appointments and regulatory review. By appointing loyal supporters to top jobs in the bureaucracy, presidents make it more likely that agencies will follow the president's wishes. As the Analyzing the Evidence section on the following page shows, recent presidents have increased the number of political appointees in the bureaucracy.

Through regulatory review, presidents have tried to control rule making by the agencies of the executive branch (see also Chapter 15). Whenever Congress enacts a statute, its actual implementation requires the promulgation of hundreds of rules by the agency charged with administering the law and giving effect to the will of Congress. Some congressional statutes are quite detailed and leave agencies with relatively little discretion. Typically, however, Congress enacts a relatively broad statement of legislative intent and delegates to the appropriate administrative agency the power to fill in many important details.[60] In other words, Congress typically says to an administrative agency, "Here is the problem. Deal with it."[61]

The discretion Congress delegates to administrative agencies has provided recent presidents with an important avenue for expanding their power. For example, President Clinton believed the president had full authority to order agencies of the executive branch to adopt such rules as the president thought appropriate, and he issued 107 directives to administrators ordering them to propose specific rules and regulations. In some instances, the language of the rule to be proposed was drafted by the White House staff; in other cases, the president asserted a priority but left it to the agency to draft the precise language of the proposal. Presidential rule-making directives covered a wide variety of topics. For example, Clinton ordered the Food and Drug Administration (FDA) to develop rules designed to restrict the marketing of tobacco products to children. White House and FDA staffers then spent several months preparing nearly 1,000 pages of new regulations affecting tobacco manufacturers and vendors.[62] Republicans denounced Clinton's actions as a usurpation of power.[63] After he took office, however, President George W. Bush made no move to surrender the powers Clinton had claimed. Bush continued the Clinton-era practice of issuing presidential directives to agencies to spur them to issue new rules and regulations. When he assumed office, President Obama appointed the Harvard law professor Cass Sunstein to head his regulatory review effort. Sunstein, an expert on the regulatory process who served for three years in the post, made regulatory review an even more important arrow in the president's quiver.

Governing by Decree: Executive Orders. A third mechanism through which contemporary presidents have sought to enhance their power to govern unilaterally is the use of executive orders and other forms of presidential

60 The classic critique of this process is Lowi, *The End of Liberalism.*

61 Kenneth Culp Davis, *Administrative Law Treatise* (St. Paul, MN: West, 1958), p. 9.

62 Elena Kagan, "Presidential Administration," *Harvard Law Review* 114 (2001): 2265.

63 For example, Douglas W. Kmiec, "Expanding Power," in *The Rule of Law in the Wake of Clinton,* Roger Pilon, ed. (Washington, DC: Cato Institute Press, 2000), pp. 47–68.

ANALYZING THE EVIDENCE

Presidential Appointees in the Executive Branch

CHAPTER 07

Contributed by
David Lewis
Vanderbilt University

Article II of the Constitution states that "The executive power shall be vested in a President of the United States of America" and details one of the president's most important constitutional roles, leading the executive branch. This means the president must manage 15 cabinet departments and 55–60 independent agencies—and the over 2 million civilian employees that work in the federal government. Given the system of separation of powers, the president often competes with Congress for control of the executive branch. Congress also has a legitimate interest in the actions of executive branch officials since Congress creates programs and agencies and determines their budgets. The stakes of this competition between the branches are increasing. As the scope and complexity of government work have grown, Congress has delegated important policy-making responsibility to government officials working in the executive branch. These officials determine important public policies such as allowable levels of pollutants in the environment, eligibility rules for government benefits like medical care and Social Security, and safety rules in workplaces. Modern presidents have sought to exert more control over these agencies by a number of means, including increasing the number of presidential appointments.

Civil Service Systems

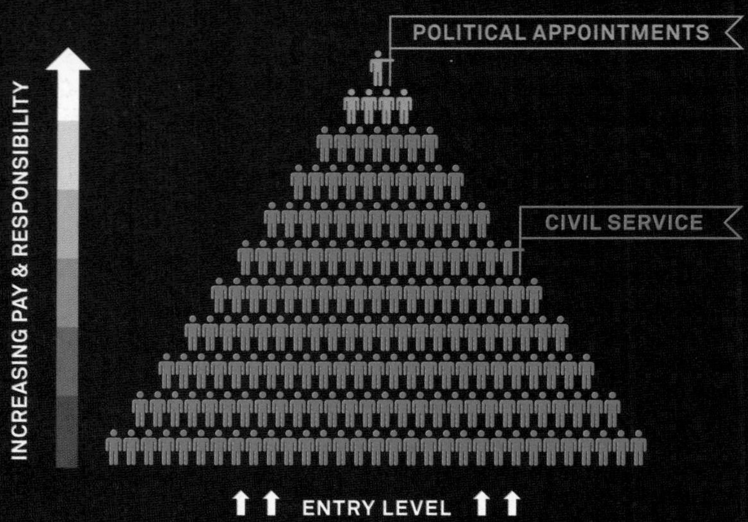

Government agencies are generally staffed by a mix of two types of employees: civil servants and political appointees. Civil servants staff the lower strata of government agencies and are to be hired, fired, promoted, and demoted on the basis of merit, and they cannot be removed without good cause. Political appointees, however, are generally selected from outside the civil service by the president, and most can be removed at the president's discretion.

SOURCE: David E. Lewis, *The Politics of Presidential Appointments* (Princeton, NJ: Princeton University Press, 2008).

Total Number of Federal Government Appointees and Percentage Appointed*

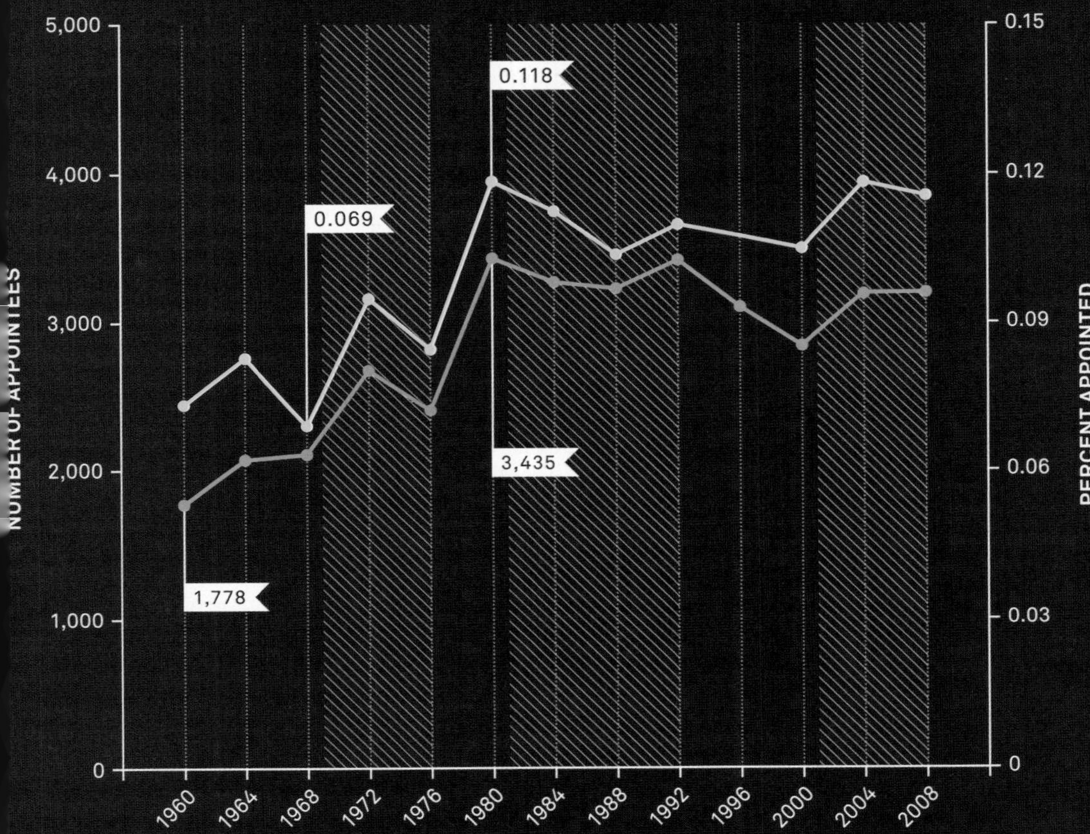

* Note: Includes salaried Senate-confirmed appointees and lower-level appointees that do not require Senate confirmation. Excludes ambassadors, U.S. marshals, U.S. attorneys, and advisory positions.

Number of appointees — Percent appointed — Republican president

Presidents since the middle of the twentieth century have sought to push down the dividing line between appointees and civil servants in government agencies. The figure above graphs the number and percentage of political appointees in the U.S. government over the last five decades. Interestingly, the proportion of federal employees that are appointees has grown during this time period, as presidents have tried to exert greater influence over the executive branch.

SOURCE: David E. Lewis, "Modern Presidents and the Transformation of the Federal Personnel System," *The Forum* 7(4): Article 6 (2010), www.bepress.com/forum/vol7/iss4/art6 (accessed 10/24/11).

EXPLORE **PRESIDENTIAL POWER** FURTHER AT: **wwnorton.com/studyspace**

decrees, including executive agreements, national security findings and directives, proclamations, reorganization plans, signing statements, and a host of others.[64] Executive orders have a long history in the United States and, as we saw earlier, have been the vehicles for a number of important government policies. These include the purchase of Louisiana, the annexation of Texas, the emancipation of the slaves, the internment of the Japanese, the desegregation of the military, the initiation of affirmative action, and the creation of important federal agencies, among them the Environmental Protection Agency (EPA), the Food and Drug Administration (FDA), and the Peace Corps.[65]

Although wars and national emergencies produce the highest volume of executive orders, such presidential actions also occur frequently in peacetime (Figure 7.6). In the realm of foreign policy, unilateral presidential actions in the form of executive agreements have virtually replaced treaties as the nation's chief foreign-policy instruments.[66] Presidential decrees, however, are often issued for purely domestic purposes.

Presidents may not use executive orders to issue whatever commands they please. The use of such decrees is bound by law. If a president issues an executive order, proclamation, directive, or the like, in principle he does so pursuant to the powers granted to him by the Constitution or delegated to him by Congress, usually through a statute. When presidents issue such orders, they generally state the constitutional or statutory basis for their actions. For example, when President Truman ordered the desegregation of the armed services, he did so pursuant to his constitutional powers as commander in chief. In a similar vein, when President Johnson issued Executive Order No. 11246, he asserted that the order was designed to implement the 1964 Civil Rights Act, which prohibited employment discrimination. Where an executive order has no statutory or constitutional basis, the courts have held it to be void. The most important case illustrating this point is *Youngstown Sheet and Tube Company v. Sawyer*, the so-called steel seizure case of 1952.[67] Here the Supreme Court ruled that President Truman's seizure of the nation's steel mills during the Korean War had no statutory or constitutional basis and was thus invalid.

A number of court decisions, though, have established broad boundaries that leave considerable room for presidential action. By illustration, the courts have held that Congress might approve a presidential action after the fact or, in effect, ratify a presidential action through "acquiescence"—for example, by not objecting for long periods of time or by continuing to provide funding for programs established by executive orders. In addition, the courts have indicated that some areas, most notably the realm of military policy, are presidential

---

64 A complete inventory is provided in Harold C. Relyea, *Presidential Directives: Background and Review,* Congressional Research Service Report for Congress, 98–611 GOV, 9 November 2001.

65 Terry M. Moe and William G. Howell, "The Presidential Power of Unilateral Action," *Journal of Law, Economics, and Organization* 15 (1999): 133–4. Also see William G. Howell, *Power without Persuasion.*

66 Moe and Howell, "Unilateral Action," p. 164.

67 *Youngstown Sheet and Tube Company v. Sawyer*, 343 U.S. 579 (1952).

Figure 7.6
SIGNIFICANT EXECUTIVE ORDERS, 1900–95

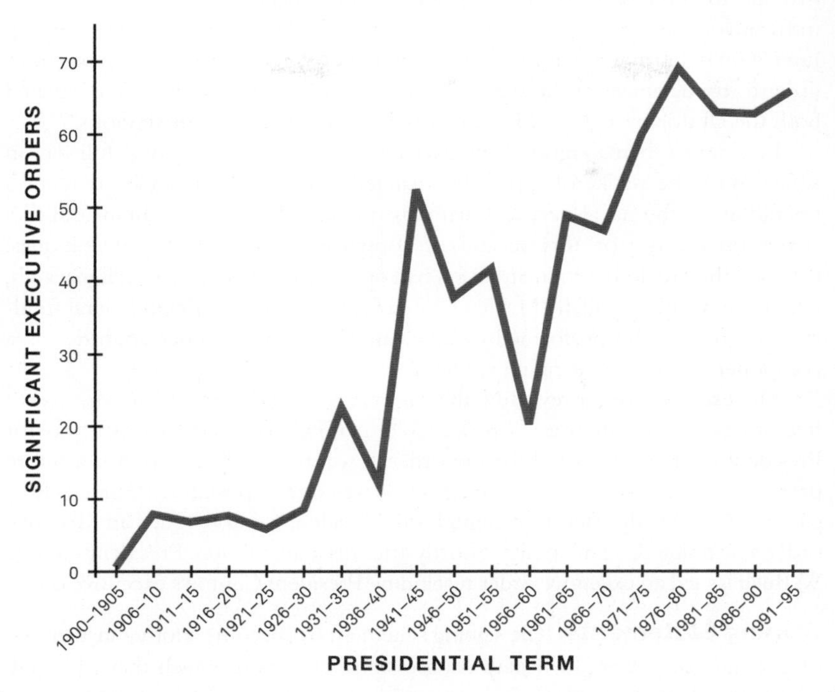

SOURCE: William G. Howell, "The President's Powers of Unilateral Action: The Strategic Advantages of Acting Alone" (Ph.D. diss., Stanford University, 1999).

ANALYZING THE EVIDENCE

During the twentieth century, presidents made increasingly frequent use of executive orders to accomplish their policy goals. What factors explain this development? How have Congress and the courts responded to increased presidential assertiveness?

in character, and they have allowed presidents wide latitude to make policy by executive decree. Thus within the very broad limits established by the courts, presidential orders can be and have been important policy tools.

President Clinton issued numerous orders designed to promote a coherent set of policy goals: protecting the environment, strengthening federal regulatory power, shifting the focus of America's foreign policy from unilateral to multilateral, expanding affirmative action programs, and helping organized labor in its struggles with employers.[68] Clinton certainly did not issue more executive orders than previous presidents. His innovation was to take an instrument that had been used sporadically and show that an activist president could develop and implement a significant policy agenda without legislation—a lesson that surely was not lost on his successors.

Indeed, just as he continued the practice of using regulatory review as a policy instrument, President George W. Bush did not hesitate to use executive orders. In November 2001, for example, Bush issued a directive authorizing the creation of military tribunals to try noncitizens accused of involvement in acts

68 Todd Gaziano, "The New 'Massive Resistance,'" *Policy Review* (May/June 1998): 283.

of terrorism against the United States. The presidential directive also prohibits defendants from appealing their treatment to any federal or state court. In 2005 and 2006, it came to light that Bush had ordered the National Security Administration to conduct a massive program of domestic surveillance of telephone traffic involving suspected terrorists. In *Hamdan v. Rumsfeld*, the Supreme Court in June 2006 determined that the military tribunals established by Bush's executive order to try detainees at the U.S. naval base at Guantánamo Bay, Cuba, violated both the Uniform Code of Military Justice and the Geneva Conventions.[69]

President Obama signed four executive orders on his second full day in office. With the stroke of a pen, he changed government policy on detention operations at the naval base at Guantanamo Bay; clarified his administration's stance on the use of torture and/or controversial interrogation techniques; reversed the previous administration's ban on certain types of stem cell research; and reversed the so-called "Mexico City gag rule," which restricted federal funding for groups who performed or advocated abortion in other countries as a component of family-planning services.

The executive order reversing the gag rule is a good example of why executive orders are in some ways less desirable than new laws. As easy as it was for President Obama to rescind the old order, it will be equally as easy for a future president to reinstate it. In fact, the gag rule was first imposed by President Reagan in 1984. Shortly after his inauguration, President Clinton issued an executive order rescinding Reagan's policy. Shortly after his inauguration, President George W. Bush issued an executive order rescinding President Clinton's executive order.

Signing Statements. The signing statement has become another instrument of presidential power. To negate congressional actions to which they objected, recent presidents have made frequent and calculated use of presidential signing statements when signing bills into law.[70] A signing statement is an announcement made by the president at the time of signing a congressional enactment into law, sometimes presenting the president's interpretation of the law as well as usually innocuous remarks predicting the many benefits the new law would bring to the nation. Occasionally, presidents have used signing statements to point to sections of the law they deemed improper or even unconstitutional, and to instruct executive branch agencies how they were to execute the law.[71] President Harry Truman, for example, accompanied his approval of the 1946 Hobbs Anti-Racketeering Act with a message offering his interpretation of ambiguous sections of the statute and indicating how the federal government would implement the new law.[72]

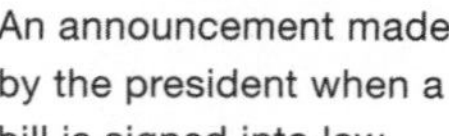

An announcement made by the president when a bill is signed into law

Presidents have made signing statements throughout American history, though many were not recorded and so did not become part of the official legislative

69 *Hamdan v. Rumsfeld*, 548 U.S. (2006).

70 Mark Killenbeck, "A Matter of Mere Approval? The Role of the President in the Creation of Legislative History," 48 *University of Arkansas Law Review* 239 (1995).

71 Philip J. Cooper, *By Order of the President: The Use and Abuse of Presidential Direct Action* (Lawrence: University Press of Kansas, 2002), p. 201.

72 Edward S. Corwin, *The President: Office and Powers*, 4th ed. (New York: New York University Press, 1957), p. 283.

record. Ronald Reagan's attorney general, Edwin Meese, is generally credited with transforming the signing statement into a routine tool of presidential direct action.[73] Meese believed that carefully crafted signing statements would provide a basis for action by executive agencies and, perhaps even more important, would become part of the history and context of a piece of legislation if and when judicial interpretation became necessary. Indeed, to make certain that signing statements became part of the legislative history, Meese reached an agreement with the West Publishing Company to include them in its authoritative texts.[74] With the way paved, Reagan proceeded to use detailed and artfully designed signing statements—prepared by the Department of Justice—to attempt to reinterpret congressional enactments. For example, when signing the Safe Drinking Water Amendments of 1986, President Reagan issued a statement that interpreted sections of the act to allow discretionary enforcement when Congress seemed to call for mandatory enforcement.

This strategy, to be sure, is not always successful. When he signed the Competition in Contracting Act in 1984, President Reagan declared that portions of the law were unconstitutional and directed executive branch officials not to comply with them. Subsequently, U.S. District Court Judge Harold Ackerman upheld the act and decried the notion that the president had the power to declare acts of Congress unconstitutional.[75] The same conclusion was later reached by the Ninth Circuit Court of Appeals, which declared that the president did not have the authority to "excise or sever provisions of a bill with which he disagrees."[76]

Despite these adverse rulings, however, the same tactic of reinterpreting and nullifying congressional enactments was continued by Reagan's successor, George H. W. Bush. When he signed the 1991 Civil Rights Act, Bush asserted his concern that one of its provisions might be unfairly applied to businesses. By so doing, the president established his own reading to shape the act's legislative history, provided guidance to administrators regarding the law's implementation, and attempted to influence future court interpretations.[77]

For the most part, Presidents Reagan and Bush used signing statements to limit the scope of affirmative action programs, to block expansion of business regulation, to reduce the impact of environmental programs, and to thwart new labor laws. Bill Clinton followed the examples set by Reagan and Bush and made extensive use of signing statements both to reinterpret and nullify congressional enactments. But, of course, Clinton's agenda was far different from that of his two immediate predecessors. Faced with Republican-controlled congresses for six of his eight years in office, Clinton used his signing statements to attempt to block constriction of affirmative action programs, to limit efforts to weaken environmental standards, and to protect the rights of individuals with disabilities.

Presidential use of signing statements to challenge legislative provisions and to declare that provisions not favored by the president would not be enforced

73 Cooper, *By Order of the President*, p. 201.

74 Cooper, *By Order of the President*, p. 203.

75 *AMERON, Inc. v. U.S. Army Corps of Engineers*, 610 F.Supp. 750 (D.N.J. 1985).

76 *Lear, Siegler v. Lehman*, 842 F.2nd 1102 (1988).

77 Cooper, *By Order of the President*, p. 207.

increased sharply during the George W. Bush years. President Reagan used signing statements to attack 71 legislative provisions, and President Clinton made 105 significant signing statements. Bush challenged more than 800 legislative provisions with his signing statements, including a number of important domestic and security matters, such as a congressional effort, led by Senator John McCain, to ban the use of torture by American interrogators. During the 2008 presidential campaign, Democrats denounced Bush's use of signing statements. In March 2009, however, President Obama made use of the same tactic employed by his predecessors. After he signed a $410 billion budget bill into law, Obama declared five provisions of the act to be unconstitutional and nonbinding, including a provision to prevent punishment of whistleblowers.

Ed Meese's contrivance has become a full-blown instrument of presidential power. Adding to the importance of this power in recent years, as presidents had hoped, courts have given weight to presidential signing statements when interpreting the meaning of statutes.[78]

The Advantages of the Administrative Strategy. Through the course of American history, party leadership and popular appeals have played important roles in presidential efforts to overcome political opposition. Both parties and appeals to the people continue to be instruments of presidential power. Reagan's tax cuts and Clinton's budget victories were achieved with strong partisan support. George W. Bush, lacking the oratorical skills of a Reagan or a Roosevelt, nevertheless made good use of sophisticated communications strategies to promote his agenda. Yet, as we saw, in the modern era, parties have waned in institutional strength, and the effects of popular appeals have often proved evanescent. The limitations of the alternatives have increasingly impelled presidents to try to expand the administrative capabilities of the office and their own capacity for unilateral action as means of achieving their policy goals. And in recent decades, the expansion of the Executive Office, the development of regulatory review, and the use of executive orders, signing statements, and the like have given presidents a substantial capacity to achieve significant policy results despite congressional opposition to their legislative agendas.

To be sure, the administrative strategy does not always succeed. In some instances over the years, as just noted, the federal courts have struck down unilateral actions by the president. And occasionally Congress acts to reverse presidential orders. For example, in 1999, Congress enacted legislation prohibiting the Department of Education from carrying out a presidential directive to administer national tests of reading and mathematics.[79] And before that, in 1996, in response to President Clinton's aggressive regulatory review program, the Republican-controlled Congress moved to strengthen its capacity to block the president's use of administrative directives by enacting the Congressional Review Act (CRA). This piece of legislation requires federal agencies to send

78 Kristy Carroll, "Whose Statute Is It Anyway? Why and How Courts Should Use Presidential Signing Statements When Interpreting Federal Statutes," 16 *Catholic University Law Review* 475 (1997).

79 Kagan, "Presidential Administration," p. 2351.

all proposed regulations to Congress for review 60 days before they take effect. It also creates a fast-track procedure to allow the House and Senate to enact a joint resolution of disapproval that would not only void the regulation but also prohibit the agency from subsequently issuing any substantially similar rule.

In principle, perhaps, Congress could respond more vigorously than it has to unilateral policy making by the president. Certainly a Congress willing to impeach a president should have the mettle to overturn his administrative directives. But the president has significant advantages in such struggles with Congress. In battles over presidential directives and orders, Congress is on the defensive, reacting to presidential initiatives. The framers of the Constitution saw "energy," or the ability to take the initiative, as a key feature of executive power.[80] When the president takes action by issuing an order or an administrative directive, Congress must initiate the cumbersome and time-consuming lawmaking process, overcome internal divisions, and enact legislation that the president may ultimately veto. Moreover, as the political scientist Terry Moe has argued, in such battles Congress faces a significant collective action problem insofar as members are likely to be more sensitive to the substance of a president's action and its effects on their constituents than to the more general implications of presidential power for the long-term vitality of their institution.[81]

PRESIDENTIAL POWER: MYTHS AND REALITIES

We began this chapter by observing that presidents had a distinct institutional advantage vis-à-vis other governmental actors. Presidents were unitary "deciders," whereas other political actors were members of institutions whose decision-making processes were collective, requiring deliberation, debate, compromise, and voting. This institutional difference has contributed to the steady growth of presidential power, which has occasioned an ongoing debate between the advocates of a strong presidency and those who favor America's traditional separation of powers system, with its built-in limitations and constraints on collective action, discussed in Chapter 1.

Emergency Power

Advocates of presidential power have typically advanced three arguments for deferring to the White House. The first, which echoes themes articulated by Alexander Hamilton and others among the nation's Founders, is that executive power is

80 Alexander Hamilton, James Madison, and John Jay, *The Federalist Papers,* Clinton L. Rossiter, ed. (New York: New American Library, 1961), no. 70, pp. 423–30.

81 Terry M. Moe, "The Presidency and the Bureaucracy: The Presidential Advantage," in *The Presidency and the Political System,* 7th ed., Michael Nelson, ed. (Washington, DC: Congressional Quarterly Press, 2003), pp. 425–57.

needed to deal with emergencies and to ensure the nation's security.[82] Although no one could argue with this position in the abstract, particularly in an age of global terrorism, the problem is that presidents can sometimes be too anxious to act forcefully in response to what they perceive as security threats. The framers of the Constitution gave Congress, and not the president, the power to make war precisely because they feared that presidents might be altogether too willing to commit the nation to armed conflicts. "The strongest passions and most dangerous weakness of the human breast," wrote James Madison, "ambition, avarice, vanity, the honorable or venial love of fame, are all in a conspiracy [within the executive branch] against the desire and duty of peace. Hence it has grown into an axiom that the executive is the department of power most distinguished by its propensity to war."[83]

But if the president is too anxious to go to war, is Congress too reluctant to respond to emergencies? The short answer is no. It would be difficult to identify an instance of the past half century in which the nation's security was compromised because Congress refused to act, though in a number of cases, including perhaps the recent Iraq War, the president was, as Madison feared, too quick to take vigorous action. When the nation has faced actual emergencies, Congress has seldom refused to grant appropriate powers to the president. Indeed, the legislative branch has generally been too pliable, granting presidents powers to deal with emergencies of their own making, as in the case of the Gulf of Tonkin Resolution, which President Lyndon Johnson used as the legislative basis for his Vietnam war policies.

Contemporary executive power, moreover, is not held in reserve for national emergencies but is, instead, employed by presidents on a routine basis, often to implement mundane elements of their agenda that lack sufficient support in Congress to be enacted into law. Thus, President Clinton used the power of regulatory review to launch an environmental program that had been blocked in Congress. Similarly, President Bush used an executive order to place limits on stem-cell research, a decision that pleased religious conservatives but could never have mustered majorities in the House and Senate. Right or wrong, these decisions hardly involved national emergencies. In both instances, the president was simply asserting his policy preferences and using his executive powers to override or ignore those of his opponents. Thus, support of presidential power on the grounds of the superior capacity of the executive to respond to emergencies is Myth 1.

The Public Interest

A second argument often made in favor of expanded presidential power is that the president champions the national interest as opposed to the particularistic interests defended by members of Congress, party politicians, bureaucrats, and most other political actors. This notion of the president's being above party seems reminiscent of the premodern yearning for a wise and beneficent king who would brush aside the selfish claims of manipulative courtiers and rule in

82 A contemporary statement of this position is Harvey C. Mansfield, Jr., *Taming the Prince: The Ambivalence of Modern Executive Power* (New York: Free Press, 1989), chap. 1.

83 Richard Loss, ed., *The Letters of Pacificus and Helvidius* (Delmar, NY: Scholars Facsimiles and Reprints, 1976), pp. 91–92.

the best interests of all his subjects. Perhaps such kings existed from time to time, but the behavior of the kingly stratum as a whole does not inspire much confidence in the notion that powerful executives are a good antidote to factional selfishness and rent-seeking special interests.

Presidents, to be sure, are unitary actors. As such they may find it more difficult than members of Congress to escape responsibility for their conduct or, through inaction, to become free riders on the efforts of others. To this extent, the presidentialist argument might have some merit. Empirically, however, presidents do not appear much less likely than senators and representatives to set aside personal concerns in favor of some abstract public good. Presidents often enough seem to promote programs designed mainly to reward important political backers and contributors even when such programs clearly do not serve the larger public interest. What public interest was served by President Clinton's decision to pardon the fugitive financier Marc Rich? Why did President Bush block stem-cell research even though such work is important to maintaining America's technological edge? In both instances, personal or political calculations appear to have outweighed presidential concern for the public interest. Hence, Myth 2, with some qualifications, is superior presidential responsiveness to the public interest.

Presidential Power and Democracy

Beyond assertions of the need for a strong presidency and the allegedly superior commitment of the president to the national interest, a third argument is frequently made in support of enhanced presidential power. This is the contention that the presidency is a more democratic institution than Congress.[84] This argument has a certain surface plausibility. The president is, of course, the nation's only elected official who can claim to represent all the people. As a decision-making institution, however, the presidency is perhaps America's least democratic entity.

Presidential decision making generally takes place in private and is often shrouded in secrecy. Recent presidents have vehemently asserted that the secrecy of the processes leading up to their decisions is shielded by executive privilege. This was the Bush administration's claim when it refused to disclose information regarding the composition or deliberations of the task forces with whom Vice President Cheney met in 2001 to plan the administration's energy policies. The Supreme Court supported the administration's position on the grounds that the "energetic performance" of the executive branch's duties required protection from intrusive requests for information.[85] Successive presidents have also disciplined staffers who revealed information to Congress and worked to block legislation that would protect whistle-blowers. Not only are the deliberations leading up to presidential decisions often removed from the public domain, but even the decisions themselves are sometimes not revealed to the public or even to Congress. Many so-called national security directives issued by presidents

84 Grant McConnell, *The Modern Presidency* (New York: St. Martin's, 1976). See also Steven Calabresi, "Some Normative Arguments for the Unitary Executive," 48 *Arkansas Law Review* 23 (1995), p. 58.

85 *U.S. v. U.S. District Court of the District of Columbia*, 124 S.Ct. 1391 (2004).

in recent years have been used to initiate secret missions by intelligence and defense agencies.[86] For many years, too, presidents have signed secret executive agreements with other governments obligating the United States to various forms of action without congressional knowledge, much less approval.

Arguably, the Congress is inherently a more democratic decision-making institution than the presidency. To exert influence, competing factions in Congress must maintain active and ongoing relationships with important groups and forces in civil society. For members of Congress, constituency mobilization and political power are closely connected. Journalists may cluck their tongues at the "senator from Boeing" or the "congressman from the UAW." But ties to these and a host of other key constituency forces help members of Congress exercise influence on Capitol Hill and strengthen the Congress as a collective body vis-à-vis the executive branch. Today, indeed, Congress must sometimes mobilize constituency pressure just to compel the president to implement its decisions. One of Congress's weaknesses as an institution is that it must depend on the executive to carry out and enforce most of its dictates. As we saw when we discussed presidential signing statements, presidents are increasingly wont to claim that they are not required to implement decisions with which they disagree.

Presidents, of course, can also mobilize supporters and interests. Indeed, some presidents, such as Andrew Jackson and Franklin Delano Roosevelt, worked to expand the scope of political participation in order to overwhelm their political opponents at the polls and in the national legislature. When it comes to the routines of governance, however, presidents usually prefer processes that limit political debate and social mobilization. In an open political struggle, involving contestation among many interests and forces, presidents may win or they may lose. But where decisions are made discreetly if not covertly, in the corridors and offices of the White House with minimal external intervention, then surely the president will prevail. And unlike Congress, the president does not have to rely on an agency outside his sphere of control to implement his decisions. To a far greater extent, presidents control bureaucrats and soldiers and contractors and mercenaries. They view the involvement of other political actors as more likely to hinder their plans than to help them govern. For these reasons, where possible, presidents seek to develop institutions and procedures that restrict the number and range of participants in decision making and limit rather than expand the scope of political debate. These observations would seem entirely inconsistent with the idea that the presidency is somehow a more democratic institution than the Congress. Institutions matter a great deal, and the claim that the presidency is the more democratic branch is Myth 3.

For Further Reading

Cameron, Charles M. *Veto Bargaining: Presidents and the Politics of Negative Power.* New York: Cambridge University Press, 2000.

86 Christopher Simpson, *National Security Directives of the Reagan and Bush Administrations* (Boulder, CO: Westview Press, 1995).

Canes-Wrone, Brandice. *Who Leads Whom? Presidents, Policy, and the Public.* Chicago: University of Chicago Press, 2006.

reader selection

Crenson, Matthew, and Benjamin Ginsberg. *Presidential Power: Unchecked and Unbalanced.* New York: Norton, 2007.

Deering, Christopher, and Forrest Maltzman. "The Politics of Executive Orders: Legislative Constraints on Presidential Power," *Political Research Quarterly* 52 (1999): 767–83.

Howell, William G. *Power without Persuasion: The Politics of Direct Presidential Action.* Princeton, NJ: Princeton University Press, 2003.

reader selection

Krutz, Glen, and Jeffrey Peake. *Presidential-Congressional Governance and the Rise of Executive Agreements.* Ann Arbor: University of Michigan Press, 2009.

Lowi, Theodore J. *The Personal President: Power Invested, Promise Unfulfilled.* Ithaca, NY: Cornell University Press, 1985.

Milkis, Sidney M. *The President and the Parties: The Transformation of the American Party System since the New Deal.* New York: Oxford University Press, 1993.

Nelson, Michael, ed. *The Presidency and the Political System.* 8th ed. Washington, DC: Congressional Quarterly Press, 2005.

Neustadt, Richard E. *Presidential Power and the Modern Presidents: The Politics of Leadership from Roosevelt to Reagan.* 1960. Rev. ed. New York: Free Press, 1990.

reader selection

Pfiffner, James P. *The Modern Presidency.* 4th ed. Belmont, CA: Wadsworth, 2005.

Skowronek, Stephen. *The Politics Presidents Make: Leadership from John Adams to Bill Clinton.* Cambridge, MA: Harvard University Press, 1997.

Yoo, John. *The Powers of War and Peace.* Chicago: University of Chicago Press, 2005.

Visit **wwnorton.com/studyspace/** to access free review materials such as:

- Vocabulary Flashcards of All Key Terms
- Chapter Review Quizzes
- Complete Study Outlines

reader selection

Highlighted selections are included in *Readings in American Politics: Analysis and Perspectives*, Second Edition.

8

PART 1 X 3 4

INSTITUTIONS

The Executive Branch: Bureaucracy in a Democracy

Chapter Outline

- Why Bureaucracy?
- How Is the Executive Branch Organized?
- The Problem of Bureaucratic Control
- How Can Bureaucracy Be Reduced?
- Conclusion

The bureaucracy is the administrative heart and soul of government. It is where the rubber meets the road—where the policies formulated, refined, and passed into law by elected officials are interpreted, implemented, and ultimately delivered to a nation's citizens. Government touches the life of the ordinary citizen most directly in his or her interactions with bureaucratic agents—at the Department of Motor Vehicles when obtaining a driver's license; in filing one's income tax return with the Internal Revenue Service; at the recruiting center when enlisting in one of the armed services; at the Board of Elections when registering to vote. We examine the federal bureaucracy in this chapter both as an organizational setting within which policies are interpreted and implemented and as a venue in which politicians pursue their own (and sometimes the public's) interests.

As an organizational setting, a bureaucracy is something created by elected politicians. These politicians seek to coordinate governmental effort in order to accomplish public purposes (and private objectives) as well as to solve collective action problems. Sometimes bureaucracies are created in the face of a pressing need, indeed at times of crisis. Consider the case of the Department of Homeland Security (DHS).

On March 1, 2003, 22 federal agencies with responsibilities for combating international terrorism in the United States were combined in the Department of Homeland Security (see Table 8.1). By all accounts, this event marked the most dramatic reform of the federal bureaucracy since the establishment of the Department of Defense in 1947. The story begins with the catastrophic events of September 11, 2001. Both Republicans and Democrats realized that the public was going to demand some ongoing response to the terrorist threat (beyond the immediate military response in Afghanistan).[1] A congressional investigation

1 John W. Kingdon calls events that limit and focus our political options "windows of political opportunity." See his *Agendas, Alternatives, and Public Policies* (Boston: Little, Brown, 1984).

quickly revealed that serious security lapses and a lack of coordination among the various agencies with responsibility for domestic and foreign intelligence had occurred during the administrations of both President Bill Clinton and President George W. Bush. Both political parties might be blamed if the government did not respond aggressively enough to the terrorist threat. Furthermore, the major alternative solution—the creation of a homeland-security "czar"—was tried and proved inadequate. In the end, there seemed to be no alternative available to the president and members of Congress. The path to a cabinet-level agency was clear.

Whatever the initial stimulation or inspiration for the creation of a new bureaucracy, such an entity does not drop fully formed from the heavens. It is actively shaped by politicians who come at the problem from a variety of perspectives and must hammer out an agreement (often involving bargaining and compromise) about the size, shape, and authority of the new entity. DHS was an amalgam of 22 major units previously housed in 7 cabinet departments and several other independent entities. They were stitched together through intense negotiations between President Bush's White House and legislators on Capitol Hill. Bureaucracies, thus, are administrative in purpose but are born through a political process. Their features are designed by politicians who appreciate, as in our institution principle, that the institutional powers with which they endow a bureaucracy have consequences for the kinds of decisions subsequently made.

CORE OF THE ANALYSIS

Bureaucratic institutions are created by Congress to achieve policy goals.

By implementing the laws and policies passed by elected officials, bureaucrats can be seen as agents of Congress and the presidency. As in any principal-agent relationship, the agent (the bureaucracy) is delegated authority and has a certain amount of leeway for independent action.

Despite the efforts of elected officials (the principals) to check departments and agencies (the agents), bureaucrats have their own goals and thus exercise their own influence on policy.

Although controling the growth of bureaucracy has been a concern in American politics, most Americans benefit in some way from government programs and thus are reluctant to cut back on specific programs.

Table 8.1

THE SHAPE OF A DOMESTIC SECURITY DEPARTMENT

DEPARTMENT OF HOMELAND SECURITY	AGENCIES AND DEPARTMENTS NOW PART OF THE MAIN DIVISIONS OF THE DHS	PREVIOUSLY RESPONSIBLE AGENCY OR DEPARTMENT
Border and Transportation Security Directorate	U.S. Citizenship and Immigration Services	Treasury
	Immigration and Naturalization Service*	Justice
	Federal Protective Service†	
	Transportation Security Administration	Transportation
	Federal Law Enforcement Training Center	Treasury
	Animal and Plant Health Inspection Service*	Agriculture
	Office for Domestic Preparedness	Justice
Emergency Preparedness and Response Directorate	Federal Emergency Management Agency‡	Health and Human Services
	Strategic National Stockpile and the National Disaster Medical System	
	Nuclear Incident Response Team	Energy
	Domestic Emergency Support Teams	Justice
	National Domestic Preparedness Office	FBI
Science and Technology Directorate	CBRN (Chemical, Biological, Radiological and Nuclear) Countermeasures Programs	Energy
	Environmental Measurements Laboratory	Energy
	National BW (Biological Warfare) Defense Analysis Center	Defense
	Plum Island Animal Disease Center	Agriculture
Information Analysis and Infrastructure Protection Directorate§	Federal Computer Incident Response Center	General Services Administration
	National Communications System	Defense
	National Infrastructure Protection Center	FBI
	Energy Security and Assurance Program	Energy
Secret Service		Treasury
Coast Guard		Transportation

*Only partially under the aegis of DHS; some functions remain elsewhere.
†New.
‡Previously independent.
§Established to analyze information provided by the CIA, the FBI, the Defense Intelligence Agency, the National Security Agency, and other agencies.
SOURCE: Department of Homeland Security, "History: Who Became Part of the Department?" www.dhs.gov/xabout/history/editorial_0133.sht.

Bureaucracies are also venues in which bureaucratic actors pursue public and private purposes. Bureaucrats are politicians who make decisions, form coalitions, engage in bargaining; in short, they bring private preferences and values to the table as they engage in various administrative processes—just as our rationality principle suggests. We should no more think of them as automatons or cogs in some giant wheel than we do legislative, executive, or judicial politicians. The private hopes and aspirations they bring to this setting interact with the institutional features with which their bureaucracy has been endowed to produce policies, outcomes, and decisions. And these, as the policy principle tells us, will reflect both the private interests of bureaucratic politicians and the institutional ways in which they conduct their business.

In our focus on the federal bureaucracy—the administrative structure that on a day-by-day basis is the American government—we first define and describe bureaucracy as a social and political phenomenon. Second, we look in detail at American bureaucracy in action by examining the government's major administrative agencies, their role in the governmental process, and their political behavior.

WHY BUREAUCRACY?

Bureaucracies touch nearly every aspect of daily life. Government bureaucracies implement the decisions made by the political process. Bureaucracies are full of routine because routine ensures that services are delivered regularly and that each agency fulfills its mandate. For this reason, students often conclude that bureaucracy is mechanical, routinized, and just plain boring. But that is a mistake. Bureaucracy is not just about collecting garbage, training police, or mailing Social Security checks. It is all these things for sure, but it is much more besides. Mainly, it is a reflection of political deals consummated by elected politicians, turf wars among government agents and private-sector suppliers and contractors, policy-delivery successes and failures in the eyes of the public, and to complete the circle, reactions to these by the very same elected officials who cut the deals in the first place. It is politics through and through.

Public bureaucracies are powerful because legislatures and chief executives—and, indeed, the people—delegate to them vast power to make sure a particular job is done, enabling the rest of us to be freer to pursue our private ends. The public sentiments that emerged after September 11 revealed this underlying appreciation of public bureaucracies. When faced with the challenge of making air travel safe again, the public strongly supported giving the federal government responsibility for airport security even though this meant increasing the size of the federal bureaucracy in order to make the security screeners federal workers. The former House majority whip Tom DeLay sought to forestall this growth in the federal government, declaring that "the last thing we can afford to do is erect a new bureaucracy that is unaccountable and unable to protect the

American public."[2] But the antibureaucratic language that had been so effective before September 11 no longer resonated with a fearful public. Instead, there was a widespread belief that a public bureaucracy would provide more effective protection than the cost-conscious private companies that had been charged with airport security in the past.

We can shed some systematic light on public attitudes toward government bureaucracy by examining one of the standard questions posed in election years by the American National Election Studies (ANES). As part of its survey of the American public, the ANES asks a range of questions, among which is "Do you think that people in the government waste a lot of money we pay in taxes, waste some of it, or don't waste very much of it?" Although not perfect for eliciting from the public a nuanced assessment of bureaucratic performance, the question allows respondents to register a blunt evaluation. Results from the past several decades are given in Figure 8.1.

Figure 8.1

THE PUBLIC THINKS THERE IS A LOT OF WASTE IN GOVERNMENT

ANALYZING THE EVIDENCE

Survey respondents were asked the following question: "Do you think that people in the government waste a lot of money we pay in taxes, waste some of it, or don't waste very much of it?" What do you think? Is the public justified in its belief that the government wastes a lot of money?

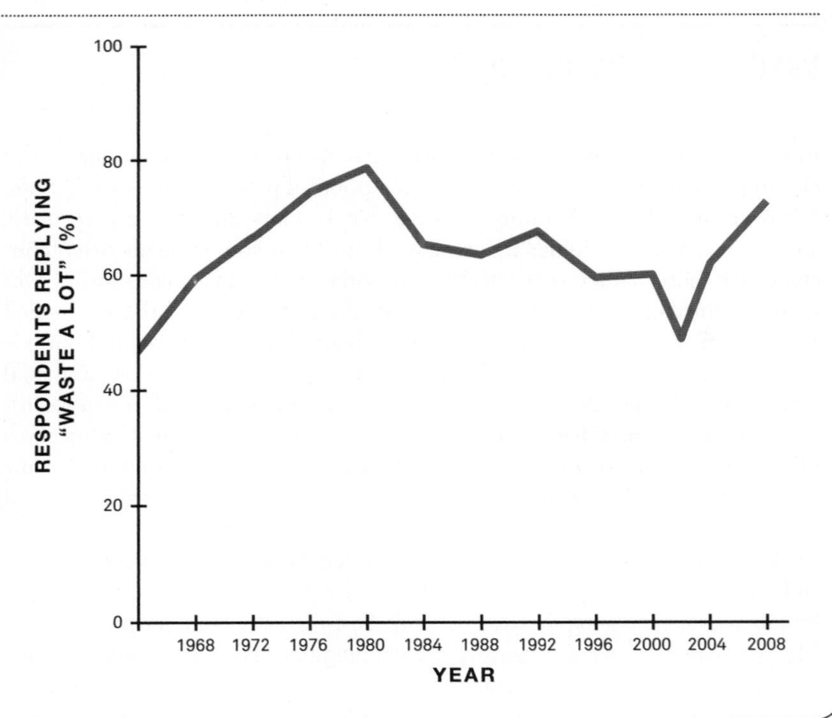

SOURCE: American National Election Studies, Cumulative Data File, 1958–2008, www.electionstudies.org/nesguide/toptable/tab5a_3.htm (accessed 12/7/11).

2 Janet Hook, "U.S. Strikes Back: Political Landscape; GOP Bypasses the Bipartisan Truce," *Los Angeles Times*, October 14, 2001, p. A8.

Public unhappiness with bureaucratic inefficiency grew during the 1960s and 1970s and became one of Ronald Reagan's campaign themes in the 1980 election. In recent decades, this unhappiness has declined somewhat from a high of nearly 80 percent of the survey respondents believing government "wastes a lot" in 1980. This opinion held steady near the low 60 percent range between 1984 and 2000. There was a significant downward tick in 2002, just after September 11. But whatever honeymoon there might have been after the terrorist attacks, it appears that the public remains increasingly cynical about bureaucratic performance. The poor response of the Federal Emergency Management Agency (FEMA)—part of DHS—to the Hurricane Katrina crisis in the fall of 2005, and domestic terrorist incidents later in the decade that seem to have evaded early detection, contributed to further cynicism.

Bureaucratic Organization Enhances Efficiency

Despite this tendency to criticize bureaucracy, most Americans recognize that maintaining order in a large society is impossible without some sort of large governmental apparatus, staffed by professionals with some expertise in public administration. Bureaucracy refers to the actual offices, tasks, and principles of organization that are employed in the most formal and sustained administration. The core of bureaucracy is the division of labor. The key to bureaucratic effectiveness is the coordination of experts performing complex tasks. If each job is specialized to gain efficiencies, then each worker must depend on the output of other workers, and that dependence requires careful allocation of jobs and resources. Inevitably bureaucracies become hierarchical, often approximating a pyramid in form. At the base of the organization are workers with the fewest skills and specializations; one supervisor can deal with a relatively large number of these workers. At the next level of the organization, where there are more highly specialized workers, the supervision and coordination of work involves fewer workers per supervisor. Toward the top of the organization, a very small number of high-level executives engages in the "management" of the organization, meaning the organization and reorganization of all the tasks and functions, plus the allocation of the appropriate supplies and the distribution of the output of the organization to the market (if it is a private-sector organization) or to the public.

 **bureaucracy**

The complex structure of offices, tasks, rules, and principles of organization that are employed by all large-scale institutions to coordinate the work of their personnel

Bureaucracies Allow Governments to Operate

Bureaucracy, when used pejoratively, conjures up images of endless paperwork, red tape, and lazy, uncaring employees. But bureaucracy in fact represents a rather spectacular human achievement. By dividing up tasks, matching tasks to a labor force that develops appropriately specialized skills, routinizing procedure, and providing the incentive structure and oversight arrangements to get large numbers of people to operate in a coordinated, purposeful fashion, bureaucracies accomplish tasks and missions in a manner that would otherwise be unimaginable. The provision of an array of "government goods" as broad as the defense of people, property, and national borders or as narrow as a subsidy to a wheat farmer, a beef rancher, or a manufacturer of specialty steel requires organization, routines, standards, and at the end of the day, the authority that allows for someone to cut a check and put it in the mail. Bureaucracies are created to do these things. Although there are mistakes and miscalculations, a bureaucracy reflects instrumental thinking about how to accomplish particular tasks; it is the rationality principle at work. No large organization would be larger than the sum of its parts, and many would be smaller, without bureaucratizing its activities.

Bureaucracy also consolidates a range of complementary programs and insulates them from the predatory ambitions of out-of-sympathy political forces. Nothing in this world is permanent, but bureaucracies come close. By creating clienteles—in the legislature, the world of interest groups, and public opinion—a bureaucracy establishes a coalition of supporters, some of whom will fight to the end to keep it in place. It is a well-known rule of thumb that everyone in the political world cares deeply and intensely about a subset of policies and the agencies that produce them and opposes other policies and agencies, but not with nearly the same passion. Opponents, to succeed, must clear many hurdles, while proponents, to maintain the status quo, must marshal their forces only at a few veto points. In the final analysis, opponents typically meet obstacle after obstacle and eventually give up their uphill battles and concentrate on protecting and expanding what they care most deeply about. In a complex political system like that of the United States, it is much easier to do the latter. Politicians appreciate this fact of life. Consequently, both opponents and proponents of a particular set of governmental activities wage the fiercest battles at the time programs are enacted and a bureaucracy is created. Once created, these organizations assume a status of relative permanence.

This raises an interesting dilemma that we only flag here, because we will develop it more systematically in the next section. In principle, bureaucratic agents are "servants" of elected politicians. They are charged with implementing statutes and policies produced by their "masters," the elected politicians in the White House and on Capitol Hill. But the relative permanence enjoyed by bureaucracy is a form of insulation—servants have discretion and masters are limited in their ability to control them. Elected officials who might want to steer a bureaucracy in a different direction often find the obstacles substantial. Only those with intense concern for the jurisdiction of a bureaucracy are likely to persist in their efforts to guide it; others have more important fish to fry in different bureaucratic jurisdictions. Thus bureaucratic agents are most affected by legislators with extraordinary interest in the bureaucratic mission. Even among these, rational legislators in support of the bureaucratic mission are likely to dominate, because those in opposition succumb to the obstacles and move their attention elsewhere.

So in response to the question of how bureaucracy makes government possible, there is an efficiency part to the answer and a credibility part. The creation of a bureau is a way to deliver government goods efficiently, and it is a device by which to tie one's hands, thereby providing a credible commitment to the long-term existence of a policy.

Bureaucrats Fulfill Important Roles

Bureaucracy conveys to most people a picture of hundreds of office workers shuffling millions of pieces of paper. There is a lot of truth in that image, but we have to look more closely at what papers are being shuffled and why.

Bureaucrats Implement Laws. Bureaucrats, whether in public or in private organizations, communicate with each other to coordinate all the specializations within their organization. This coordination is necessary to carry out the primary task of bureaucracy, which is implementation—that is, implementing the objectives of the organization as laid down by its board of directors (if a private company) or by law (if a public agency). In government, the "bosses" are ultimately the legislature and the elected chief executive. As we saw in Chapter 1, in a principal-agent relationship it is the principal who stipulates what he or she wants done, relying on appropriate incentives and other control mechanisms to secure the agent's compliance with his or her wishes. Thus we can argue that legislative principals establish bureaucratic agents—in departments, bureaus, agencies, institutes, and commissions of the federal government—to implement the policies promulgated by Congress and the president.

implementation

The efforts of departments and agencies to translate laws into specific bureaucratic routines

Bureaucrats Make and Enforce Rules. When the bosses—Congress, in particular, when it is making the law—are clear in their instructions to bureaucrats, implementation is a fairly straightforward process. Bureaucrats translate the law into specific routines for each employee of an agency. But what happens to routine administrative implementation when there are several bosses who disagree as to what the instructions ought to be? The agent of multiple principals who disagree among themselves often finds himself or herself in a bind. The agent must chart a delicate course, seeking to do the best he or she can and trying not to offend any of the bosses too much. This requires yet another job for the bureaucrats: interpretation. Interpretation is a form of implementation in that the bureaucrats have to carry out what they believe to be the intentions of their superiors. But when bureaucrats have to interpret a law before implementing it, they are in effect engaging in lawmaking.[3] Congress

3 When bureaucrats engage in interpretation, the result is what political scientists call bureaucratic drift. Bureaucratic drift occurs because, as we've suggested, the "bosses" (in Congress) and the agents (within the bureaucracy) don't always share the same purposes. Bureaucrats also have their own agendas to fulfill. A vast body of political science literature focuses on the relationship between Congress and the bureaucracy. For a review, see Kenneth A. Shepsle. *Analyzing Politics: Rationality, Behavior, and Institutions*, 2nd ed. (New York: Norton, 2010), pp. 420–40.

often deliberately delegates to an administrative agency the responsibility of lawmaking. Members of Congress often conclude that some area of industry needs regulating or some area of the environment needs protection, but they are unwilling or unable to specify just how that should be done. In such situations, Congress delegates to the appropriate agency a broad authority within which the bureaucrats have to make law, through the procedures of rule making and administrative adjudication.

rule making 

A quasi-legislative administrative process that produces regulations by government agencies

administrative adjudication 

The application rules and precedents to specific cases to settle disputes with regulated parties

Rule making is essentially the same as legislation; in fact, it is often referred to as quasi-legislation. The rules issued by government agencies provide more detailed and specific indications of what a policy will actually mean. For example, the Forest Service is charged with making policies that govern the use of national forests. Just before President Clinton left office, the agency issued rules that banned new road building and development in the forests. This was a goal long sought by environmentalists and conservationists. In 2005, the Forest Service relaxed the rules, allowing states to make proposals for building new roads within the national forests. Just as the timber industry opposed the Clinton rule banning road building, environmentalists have challenged the new ruling and have sued the Forest Service in federal court for violating clean-water and endangered-species legislation.

New rules proposed by an agency take effect only after a period of public comment. Reaction from the people or businesses that are subject to the rules may cause an agency to modify the rules they first issue. The rule-making process is thus a highly political one. Once rules are approved, they are published in the *Federal Register* and have the force of law.[4]

Bureaucrats Settle Disputes. Administrative adjudication is very similar to what the judiciary ordinarily does: apply rules and precedents to specific cases to settle disputes. In administrative adjudication, the agency charges the person or business suspected of violating the law. The ruling in an adjudication dispute applies only to the specific case being considered. Many regulatory agencies use administrative adjudication to make decisions about specific products or practices. For example, product recalls are often the result of adjudication. To take another example, the National Labor Relations Board (NLRB) has used case-by-case administrative adjudication in a great many instances. One large class of cases involves union certification. Groups of workers seek the right to vote on the formation of a union or the right to affiliate with an existing union as their bargaining agent and are opposed by their employers, who assert that relevant provisions of labor law do not apply. The NLRB takes testimony case by case, considers evidence, and makes determinations for one side or the other, acting essentially like a court.

In sum, bureaucrats in government do essentially the same things that bureaucrats in large private organizations do. But because of the authoritative, coercive

4 The *Federal Register* is the daily journal of the U.S. government. It is published every day by the Government Printing Office and contains publications and notices of government agencies.

nature of government, far more constraints are imposed on public bureaucrats than on private bureaucrats, even when their jobs are the same. Public bureaucrats are required to maintain a far more thorough paper trail. They are also subject to a great deal more access by the public—newspaper reporters, for example, have access to public bureaucrats. And public access has been vastly facilitated in the past half century; the adoption of the Freedom of Information Act (FOIA) in 1966 gave ordinary citizens the right of access to agency files and agency data so that they might determine whether those files (and data) contain derogatory information about them and learn what the agency is doing in general.

Finally, citizens are given opportunities to participate in the decision-making processes of public agencies. This kind of access is limited by time, money, and expertise, but it occupies a great deal of the time of mid-level and senior public bureaucrats. Such public exposure and access serve a purpose, but they also cut down significantly on the efficiency of public bureaucrats. Thus lower levels of efficiency in public agencies can be attributed at least in part to the political, judicial, legal, and publicity restraints put on public bureaucrats.

Politics

We have provided two main answers to the question "Why bureaucracy?": (1) Bureaucracies enhance efficiency, and (2) they are the instruments of policy implementation. We would be remiss if we didn't include a third important answer: legislatures find it valuable to delegate.

In principle, the legislature could make all bureaucratic decisions itself, writing very detailed legislation each year, dotting every *i* and crossing every *t*. In some jurisdictions—tax policy, for example—this is in fact done. Tax policy is promulgated in significant detail by the House Ways and Means Committee, the Senate Finance Committee, and the Joint Committee on Taxation. The Internal Revenue Service, the administrative agency charged with implementation, engages in relatively less discretionary activity than many other regulatory and administrative agencies. But it is the exception.

The norm is for statutory authority to be delegated to the bureaucracy, sometimes with specificity but often in relatively vague terms. The bureaucracy is expected to fill in the gaps. This, however, is not a blank check to exercise unconstrained discretion. The bureaucracy is expected to be guided by legislative intent, and it will be held to account by the legislature's oversight of bureaucratic performance. The latter is monitored by the staffs of relevant legislative committees, which also serve as repositories for complaints from affected parties.[5] Poor performance or the exercise of discretion inconsistent with the

5 See Mathew D. McCubbins and Thomas Schwartz, "Congressional Oversight Overlooked: Police Patrols versus Fire Alarms," *American Journal of Political Science* 28 (1984): 165–79.

preferences of important legislators invites sanctions ranging from the brow-beating of senior bureaucrats to the trimming of budgets and the clipping of authority.

The delegation relationship will be revisited later in this chapter. For now, simply note that over and above the more conventional reasons for bureaucracy, politicians find it convenient to delegate many of the nuts-and-bolts decisions to bureaucratic agents. We will take up the reasons shortly.

HOW IS THE EXECUTIVE BRANCH ORGANIZED?

Cabinet departments, agencies, and bureaus are the operating parts of the bureaucratic whole. These parts can be separated into four general types: (1) cabinet departments; (2) independent agencies; (3) government corporations; and (4) independent regulatory commissions.

Although Figure 8.2 is an organizational chart of the Department of Agriculture, any other department could have been used as an illustration. At the top is the head of the department, called the secretary of the department. Below the department head and his or her deputy are several top administrators, such as the general counsel and the chief financial officer, whose responsibilities cut across the various departmental functions and provide the secretary with the ability to manage the entire organization. Of equal status are the undersecretaries and assistant secretaries, each of whom has management responsibilities for a group of operating agencies, which are arranged vertically below each of the undersecretaries.

The next tier, generally called the bureau level, is the highest level of responsibility for specialized programs. The names of these bureau-level agencies are often very well known to the public: the Forest Service and the Food Safety and Inspection Service are two examples. Sometimes they are officially called bureaus, as in the FBI, which is a bureau in the Department of Justice. Nevertheless, *bureau* is also the generic term for this level of administrative agency. Within the bureaus, there are divisions, offices, services, and units—sometimes designating agencies of the same status, sometimes designating agencies of lesser status.

Not all government agencies are part of cabinet departments. A second type of agency, the independent agency, is set up by Congress outside the departmental structure altogether, even though the president appoints and directs the heads of these types of agencies. Independent agencies usually have broad powers to provide public services that are either too expensive or too important to be left to private initiatives. Some examples of independent agencies are the National Aeronautics and Space Administration (NASA), the Central Intelligence Agency (CIA), and the Environmental Protection Agency (EPA). Government corporations are a third type of government agency but are more like private businesses

Figure 8.2

ORGANIZATIONAL CHART OF THE DEPARTMENT OF AGRICULTURE

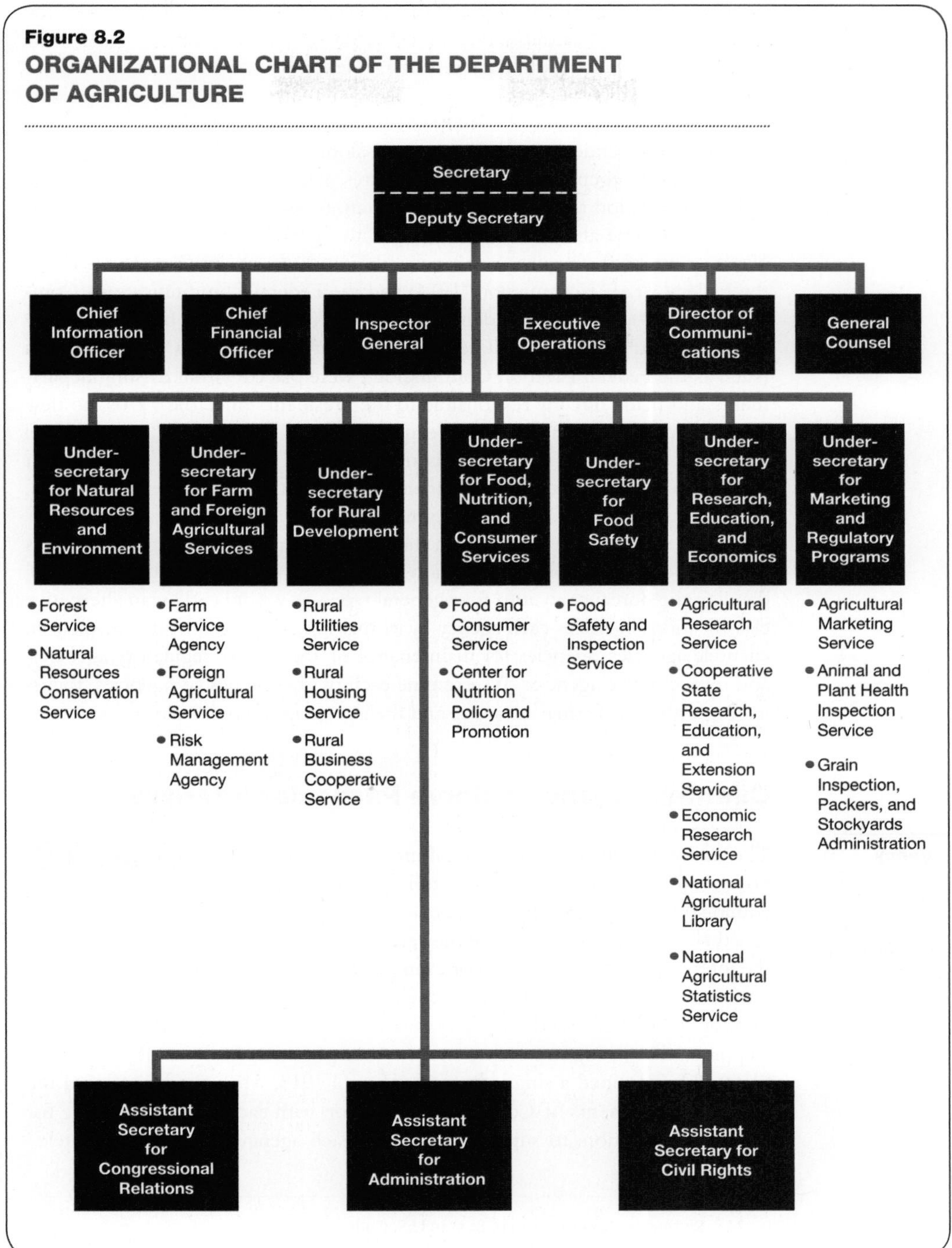

SOURCE: U.S. Department of Agriculture, www.usda.gov/img/content/org_chart_enlarged.jpg.

performing and charging for a market service, such as delivering the mail (the U.S. Postal Service) or transporting railroad passengers (Amtrak).

Yet a fourth type of agency is the independent regulatory commission, given broad discretion to make rules. The first regulatory agencies established by Congress, beginning with the Interstate Commerce Commission in 1887, were set up as independent regulatory commissions because Congress recognized that regulatory agencies are mini-legislatures, whose rules and rulings are the same as legislation and legislative interpretation but require the kind of expertise and full-time attention that is beyond the capacity of Congress. Until the 1960s, most of the regulatory agencies that were set up by Congress, such as the Federal Trade Commission (1914) and the Federal Communications Commission (1934), were independent regulatory commissions. But beginning in the late 1960s and early 1970s, all new regulatory programs, with a few exceptions (such as the Federal Election Commission), were placed within existing departments and made directly responsible to the president. Since the 1970s, no new major regulatory programs have been established, independent or otherwise. However, during the financial crisis of 2008–09, Congress and the president formulated new regulatory arrangements involving the Federal Reserve System, the Federal Deposit Insurance Corporation, the Treasury, and related agencies.

There are too many agencies in the executive branch to identify, much less to describe, so a simple classification of agencies will be helpful. Instead of dividing the bureaucracy into four general types, as we did earlier, an alternative classification organizes each agency by its mission, as defined by its jurisdiction: clientele agencies, agencies for maintenance of the Union, regulatory agencies, and redistributive agencies. We examine each of these types of agencies, focusing on both their formal structure and their place in the political process.

Clientele Agencies Serve Particular Interests

clientele agency 

A department or bureau of government whose mission is to promote, serve, or represent a particular interest

The entire Department of Agriculture is an example of a clientele agency. So are the Departments of the Interior, Labor, and Commerce. Although all administrative agencies have clienteles, certain agencies are singled out and called clientele agencies because they are directed by law to foster and promote the interests of their clientele. For example, the Department of Commerce and Labor was founded in 1903 as a single department "to foster, promote, and develop the foreign and domestic commerce, the mining, the manufacturing, the shipping, and fishing industries, and the transportation facilities of the United States."[6] It remained a single department until 1913, when the law created the separate departments of Commerce and Labor, with each statute providing for the same obligation: to support and foster each agency's respective clientele.[7]

6 *U.S. Statutes at Large* 32 (1903): 825; 15 U.S. Code 1501.

7 For a detailed account of the creation of the Department of Commerce and Labor and its division into separate departments, see Theodore J. Lowi, *The End of Liberalism: The Second Republic of the United States,* 2nd ed. (New York: Norton, 1979), pp. 78–84.

The Department of Agriculture serves the many farming interests that, taken together, are one of the largest economic sectors of the United States.

Most clientele agencies locate a relatively large proportion of their total personnel in field offices dealing directly with their clientele. The Extension Service of the Department of Agriculture is among the most familiar, with its numerous local "extension agents" who consult with farmers on farm productivity. These same agencies also seek to foster the interests of their clientele by providing "functional representation"—that is, they try to learn what their clients' interests and needs are and then operate almost as a lobby in Washington on their behalf. In addition to the Departments of Agriculture, the Interior, Labor, and Commerce, other clientele agencies include five of the newest cabinet departments: Housing and Urban Development (HUD), created in 1965; Transportation (DOT), created in 1966; Energy (DOE), created in 1977; Education (ED), created in 1979; and Health and Human Services (HHS), created in 1979.[8]

Agencies for the Maintenance of the Union Keep the Government Going

The Constitution entrusts many of the vital functions of public order, such as the police, to the state governments. But some agencies vital to maintaining national bonds do exist in the national government, and they can be grouped into three categories: (1) agencies for managing the sources of government revenue; (2) agencies for controlling conduct defined as a threat to internal national security; and (3) agencies for defending American security from external threats. The most powerful departments in these three areas are Treasury, Justice, Defense, State, and Homeland Security.

Revenue Agencies. The Internal Revenue Service (IRS) is the most important revenue agency. The IRS is also one of the federal government's largest bureaucracies. Over 100,000 employees are spread throughout 4 regions, 63 districts, 10 service centers, and hundreds of local offices. In 2006, more than 130 million individual tax returns were filed. In that same year, the IRS collected nearly $2.2 trillion in taxes from individuals and corporations.

Agencies for Internal Security. As long as the country is not in a state of insurrection, most of the task of maintaining the Union takes the form of legal work, and the main responsibility for that lies with the Department of Justice. It is indeed a luxury, and rare in the world, when national unity can be maintained by routines of civil law rather than imposed by military force. The largest and most important agency in the Justice Department is the Criminal Division, which is responsible for enforcing all the federal criminal laws except a few

8 Until 1979, the Department of Education and the Department of Health and Human Services were joined in a single department, Health, Education, and Welfare (HEW), which was established by Congress in 1953.

specifically assigned to other divisions. Criminal litigation is actually conducted by the U.S. attorneys. A presidentially appointed U.S. attorney is assigned to each federal judicial district, and he or she supervises the work of assistant U.S. attorneys. The work or jurisdictions of the Antitrust and Civil Rights Divisions are described by their official names. Although it looms so very large in American folklore, the FBI is simply another bureau of the Department of Justice. The FBI handles no litigation but instead serves as the information-gathering agency for all the other divisions.

In 2002, Congress created the Department of Homeland Security (DHS) to coordinate the nation's defense against the threat of terrorism. The new department is responsible for a number of tasks, including protecting commercial airlines from would-be hijackers. Most visible to the traveling public are the employees of the Transportation Security Administration (TSA). Consisting of 50,000 security officers and employees protecting airports, rail and bus depots, and staffing security screening operations, TSA is the largest unit of the DHS.

Agencies for External National Security. Two departments occupy center stage here, State and Defense. A few key agencies outside State and Defense also have external national-security functions. They are treated in this chapter only as bureaucratic phenomena and as examples of the political problems relevant to administration.

Although diplomacy is generally considered the primary task of the State Department, diplomatic missions make up only one of its organizational dimensions. The State Department is also composed of geographic, or regional, bureaus concerned with all problems within the defined regions of the world; "functional" bureaus, which handle such things as economic and business affairs, intelligence, and research; and international organizations and bureaus of internal affairs, which handle such areas as security, finance and management, and legal issues.

Despite the importance of the State Department in foreign affairs, fewer than 20 percent of all U.S. government employees working abroad are directly under its authority. By far the largest number of career government professionals working abroad are under the authority of the Defense Department.

The creation of the Department of Defense by legislation enacted between 1947 and 1949 was an effort to unify the two historic military departments, the War Department and the Navy Department, and integrate them into a new department, the Air Force Department. Real unification did not occur, however. Instead, the Defense Department added more pluralism to national security.

America's primary political problem with its military has not been the historic one of how to keep the military out of the politics of governing, a problem that has plagued so many countries in Europe and Latin America. The American military problem is instead the more mundane politics of the pork barrel. President Clinton's long list of proposed military-base closings, a major part of his budget-cutting drive for 1993, caused a firestorm of opposition even in his own party, with some of the opposition coming from members of Congress who otherwise prominently favored significant reductions in the Pentagon budget. Emphasis on jobs rather than strategy and policy means pork-barrel use of the military for political purposes. This is a classic way for a bureaucracy to defend itself politically in a democracy. It is the distributive tendency, in which the bureaucracy ensures political support among elected officials by making sure to distribute things—military bases, contracts, facilities, and jobs—to the states and districts that elected the legislators.

Regulatory Agencies Guide Individual Conduct

As we saw in Chapter 3, our national government did not even begin to get involved in the regulation of economic and social affairs until the late nineteenth century. Until then, regulation was strictly a state and local affair. The federal regulatory agencies are, as a result, relatively new, most dating from the 1930s. But they have come to be extensive and important. In this section, we look at these regulatory agencies as an administrative phenomenon, with its attendant politics.

regulatory agency

A department, bureau, or independent agency whose primary mission is to eliminate or restrict certain behaviors defined as negative in themselves or negative in their consequences

The United States has many regulatory agencies. Some of these are bureaus within departments, such as the Food and Drug Administration (FDA) in the Department of Health and Human Services, and the Occupational Safety and Health Administration (OSHA) in the Department of Labor. Other regulatory agencies are independent regulatory commissions—for example, the Federal Trade Commission (FTC). But whether departmental or independent, an agency or commission is regulatory if Congress delegates to it relatively broad powers over a sector of the economy or a type of commercial activity and authorizes it to make rules governing the conduct of people and businesses within that jurisdiction. Rules made by regulatory agencies have the force and effect of legislation; indeed, the rules they make are referred to as administrative legislation. And when these agencies make decisions or orders settling disputes between parties or between the government and a party, they are acting like courts.

administrative legislation

Rules made by regulatory agencies and commissions

Because regulatory agencies exercise a tremendous amount of influence over the economy and because their rules are a form of legislation, Congress was at first loath to turn them over to the executive branch as ordinary agencies under the control of the president. Consequently, most of the important regulatory programs were delegated to independent commissions with direct responsibility to Congress rather than to the White House. This is the basis of the 1930s reference to them as the "headless fourth branch."[9] With the rise of presidential government, most recent presidents have supported more regulatory programs but have successfully opposed the expansion of regulatory independence. The 1960s and 1970s witnessed the adoption of an unprecedented number of new regulatory programs but only four new independent commissions.

9 *Final Report of the President's Committee on Administrative Management* (Washington, DC: Government Printing Office, 1937). The term *headless fourth branch* was invented by a member of the committee staff, the Cornell University government professor Robert Cushman.

Agencies of Redistribution Implement Fiscal or Monetary and Welfare Policies

Welfare agencies and fiscal or monetary agencies are responsible for the transfer of hundreds of billions of dollars annually between the public and the private spheres, and through such transfers these agencies influence how people and corporations spend and invest trillions of dollars annually. We call them agencies of redistribution because they influence the amount of money in the economy and because they directly influence who has money, who has credit, and whether people will want to invest or save their money rather than spend it.

fiscal policy

Policies that use spending and taxing to accomplish policy purposes

monetary policy 

Policies that control the supply of money, the price of money (interest rate), and the availability of credit

Fiscal and Monetary Agencies. Governmental activity affecting or relating to money may be partitioned into fiscal and monetary policy. Fiscal policy includes taxing and spending activities. Monetary policy focuses on banks, credit, and currency.

Administration of fiscal policy is primarily performed in the Treasury Department. It is no contradiction to include the Treasury both here and with the agencies for maintenance of the Union. This duplication indicates (1) that the Treasury is a complex department, performing more than one function of government; and (2) that traditional controls have had to be adapted to modern economic conditions and new technologies.

Today, in addition to administering and policing income tax and other tax collections, the Treasury is responsible for managing the enormous federal debt. The Treasury Department also prints the currency that we use, but currency is only a tiny proportion of the entire money economy. Most of the trillions of dollars used in the transactions that make up the private and public sectors of the American economy exist on printed accounts and computers, not in currency.

Federal Reserve System (the Fed) 

Consisting of 12 Federal Reserve districts, the Fed facilitates exchanges of cash, checks, and credit; it regulates member banks; and it deploys monetary policies to fight inflation and deflation

Another important fiscal agency (although for technical reasons it is called an agency of monetary policy) is the Federal Reserve System, headed by the Federal Reserve Board. The Federal Reserve System (the Fed) has authority over the credit rates and lending activities of the nation's most important banks. Established by Congress in 1913, the Fed is responsible for adjusting the supply of money to both the needs of banks in the different regions and the commerce and industry in each. The Fed helps shift money from where there is too much to where there is too little. It also ensures that banks do not overextend themselves by adopting lending policies that are too liberal. The basis for this responsibility is the fear that if there is a sudden economic scare, a run on a few banks might be contagious and cause another terrible crash like the one in 1929. The Federal Reserve Board sits at the top of a pyramid of 12 district Federal Reserve Banks, which are "bankers' banks," serving the monetary needs of the hundreds of member banks in the national bank system. The subprime mortgage crisis of 2008 and 2009, which resulted after banks and other lenders provided home mortgages that proved unusually risky and led to home foreclosures, reflected gaps and loopholes in the regulation of the banking sector.

Welfare Agencies. No single government agency is responsible for all the programs making up the "welfare state." The largest agency in the field is the Social Security Administration (SSA), which manages the social insurance aspects of Social Security and Supplemental Security Income (SSI). As the baby-boom generation ages, a growing bloc of voters (and their children) have become concerned about the solvency of this system. It is a live political issue that has figured prominently in presidential election campaigns for the past quarter century. Many argue that without some adjustments in benefit schedules, taxes, or retirement age, the present population will begin drawing down the enormous amount of funds in the Social Security Trust Fund in two decades and exhaust it in 40 years.

Agencies in the Department of Health and Human Services administer Temporary Assistance to Needy Families (TANF) and Medicaid, and the Department of Agriculture is responsible for the Food Stamp Program. With the exception of Social Security, these are *means-tested* programs, requiring applicants to demonstrate that their total annual cash earnings fall below an officially defined poverty line. These public-assistance programs create a large administrative burden. In August 1996, virtually all of the means-tested public-assistance programs were legally abolished as national programs and "devolved" to the states (see also Chapter 3).

THE PROBLEM OF BUREAUCRATIC CONTROL

Two centuries, millions of employees, and trillions of dollars after the Founding, we must return to James Madison's observation that "you must first enable the government to control the governed; and in the next place oblige it to control itself."[10] Today the problem is the same, but the form has changed. The problem today is the challenge of keeping the government bureaucracy accountable to elected political authorities.

Bureaucrats Have Their Own Motivational Considerations

The economist William Niskanen proposed that we regard a bureau or department of government as analogous to a division of a private firm and conceive of the bureaucrat just as we would the manager who runs that division.[11] In

10 Alexander Hamilton, James Madison, and John Jay, *The Federalist Papers*, Clinton L. Rossiter, ed. (New York: New American Library, 1961), no. 51.

11 William A. Niskanen, Jr., *Bureaucracy and Representative Government* (Chicago: Aldine, 1971).

particular, Niskanen stipulated that the behavior of a bureau chief or department head be thought of as following the rationality principle. In this view the bureaucrat is a rational maximizer of his or her budget (just as the private-sector counterpart is a maximizer of his or her division's profits).

There are quite a number of motivational bases on which bureaucratic budget maximizing might be justified. A cynical (though some would say realistic) basis for budget maximizing is that the bureaucrat's own compensation is often tied to the size of his or her budget. Not only might bureaus with large budgets have higher-salaried executives with more elaborate fringe benefits but there also may be enhanced opportunities for career advancement, travel, a poshly appointed office, possibly even a chauffeur-driven limousine.

A second, related motivation for large budgets is nonmaterial personal gratification. An individual understandably enjoys the prestige and respect that comes from running a major enterprise. You can't take these things to the bank or put them on your family's dinner table, but your sense of esteem and your stature are surely buoyed by the conspicuous fact that your bureau or division has a large budget. That you are also boss of a large number of subordinates, made possible by a large bureau budget, is another aspect of this sort of ego gratification.

But personal salary, "on-the-job consumption," and power tripping are not the only forces driving a bureaucrat toward gaining as large a budget as possible. Some bureaucrats, perhaps most, actually *care* about their mission.[12] They initially choose to go into public safety, or the military, or health care, or social work, or education—as police officers, soldiers, hospital managers, social workers, and teachers, respectively—because they believe in the importance of helping people in their community. As they rise through the ranks of a public bureaucracy and assume management responsibilities, they take this mission orientation with them. Thus as chief of detectives in a big-city police department, as head of procurement in the air force, as director of nursing services in a public hospital, as supervisor of the social work division in a county welfare department, or as assistant superintendent of a town school system, individuals try to secure as large a budget as they can to succeed in achieving the mission to which they have devoted their professional lives.

Whether for cynical, self-serving motives or for the noblest of public purposes, it is entirely plausible that individual bureaucrats seek to persuade others (typically legislators or taxpayers) to provide them with as many resources as possible. Indeed, it is sometimes difficult to distinguish the saint from the sinner because each sincerely argues that he or she needs more to do more. This is one

12 John Brehm and Scott Gates, *Working, Shirking, and Sabotage: Bureaucratic Response to a Democratic Public* (Ann Arbor: University of Michigan Press, 1997). For detailed insight about the motivations for government service combining the personal and the patriotic, consider the case of Henry Paulson who became George W. Bush's Treasury secretary. Paulson's story is described well in Andrew Ross Sorkin, *Too Big to Fail* (New York: Viking, 2009), chap. 2.

nice feature of the rationality principle in general, and Niskanen's assumption of budget maximizing in particular: it doesn't really matter *why* a bureaucrat is interested in a big budget; what matters is simply that he or she prefers more resources to fewer.

This does not mean that the legislature, which controls the bureau's budget, has to fork over whatever the bureau requests. Critics of Niskanen's budget-maximizing theory call into question precisely this assumption about the passivity of the legislature. The legislature, the only customer of the bureau's product, in essence tells the bureau how much it is willing to pay for various levels of the bureau's product; the bureau then figures out how much it can extract from the legislature and, according to Niskanen, goes for the maximum. The critics suggest that this is akin to a customer walking onto a used-car lot and telling the salesman the most he or she is willing to spend for each vehicle.[13]

In a representative democracy, it may be difficult for the legislature to keep silent about its valuation of the bureau's product. The bureau, at any rate, can do some research to judge the preferences of various legislators. For example, the bureau can draw inferences about the importance of its product for a legislator from the characteristics of the legislator's constituency. But legislators can do research, too. Indeed, we suggested in Chapter 6 that the collection, evaluation, and dissemination of information—in this case information about bureaucratic supply—are precisely the things in which specialized legislative committees engage. Committees hold hearings, request documentation on production, assign investigatory staff to various research tasks, and query bureau personnel on the veracity of their data and their use of the lowest-cost technologies (making it more difficult for the bureau to disguise on-the-job consumption). After the fact, the committees engage in oversight, making sure that what the legislature was told at the time when authorization and appropriations were voted actually holds in practice. In short, the legislature can be much more proactive than the Niskanen budget-maximizing theory gives it credit for. And in the real world, the legislature is more proactive, as we see later in this chapter. This doesn't mean budget maximizing is an implausible hypothesis about bureau motivations; it simply means that bureaus don't always get (all of) what they want.

Before leaving motivational considerations, we should remark that budget maximizing is not the only objective that bureaucrats pursue. It needs to be emphasized and reemphasized that career civil servants and high-level political appointees are *politicians.* They spend their professional lives pursuing political goals, bargaining, forming alliances and coalitions, solving cooperation and collective action problems, making policy decisions, operating within and interfacing with political institutions—in short, doing what other politicians do.

13 This and other related points are drawn from Gary J. Miller and Terry M. Moe, "Bureaucrats, Legislators, and the Size of Government," *American Political Science Review* 77, no. 2 (June 1983): 297–323.

They do not have elections to win, but even elections affect their conditions of employment by determining the composition of the legislature and the partisan and ideological complexion of the chief executive. Bureaucrats are politicians beholden to other politicians for authority and resources. They are servants of many masters.

As politicians subject to the oversight and authority of others, bureaucrats must make contingency plans. They must be strategic and forward thinking. Whichever party wins control of the House or the Senate, whichever candidate wins the presidency, whoever becomes chair of the legislative committee with authorization or appropriation responsibility over their agency, life will go on and bureau chiefs will have to adjust to the prevailing political winds. To protect and expand authority and resources, bureaucratic politicians seek, in the form of autonomy and discretion, insurance against political change. They don't always succeed in acquiring this freedom, but they do try to insulate themselves from changes in the broader political world.[14] So bureaucratic motivations include budget-maximizing behavior, to be sure, but bureaucrats also seek the autonomy to weather changes in the political atmosphere and the discretion and flexibility to achieve their goals.

Control of the Bureaucracy Is a Principal-Agent Problem

As we have mentioned already, bureaucrats can be understood as the agents of elected officials (the principals). In any principal-agent relationship, two broad categories of control mechanisms enable a principal to guard against opportunistic or incompetent agent behavior. They can be illustrated by a homeowner (the principal) who seeks out a contractor (the agent) to remodel a kitchen. The first category is employed before the fact and depends on the reputation an agent possesses. One guards against selecting an incompetent or corrupt agent by relying on various methods for authenticating the promises made by the agent. These include advice from people you trust (your neighbors who just had their kitchen remodeled), certification by various official boards (an association of kitchen contractors), letters of recommendation and other testimonials, credentials (specialized training programs), and interviews. Before-the-fact protection relies on the assumption that an agent's reputation is a valuable asset that he or she does not want to depreciate.

The second class of control mechanisms operates after the fact. Payment may be made contingent on completion of various tasks by specific dates, so

14 **For an expanded view of bureaucratic autonomy and insulation with historical application to the U.S. Department of Agriculture and the Post Office, see Daniel P. Carpenter, *The Forging of Bureaucratic Autonomy: Reputations, Networks, and Policy Innovation in Executive Agencies, 1862–1928* (Princeton, NJ: Princeton University Press, 2001).**

that it may be withheld for nonperformance. Alternatively, financial incentives (for example, bonuses) for early or on-time completion may be part of the arrangement. The agent may be required to post a bond that would be forfeited for lack of performance. An inspection process, after the work is completed, may lead to financial penalties, bonuses, or possibly even legal action. Of course, the principal can always seek legal relief for breach of contract, either in the form of an injunction stipulating that the agent comply or in the form of an order demanding that the agent pay damages.

How does the principal-agent problem apply to the president's and Congress's control of the bureaucracy?

Suppose the legislation that created the EPA required that after 10 years new legislation be passed renewing its existence and mandate. The issue facing the House, the Senate, and the president in their consideration of renewal involves how much authority to give this agency and how much money to permit it to spend. Suppose the House is conservative on environmental issues and prefers limited authority and a limited budget. The Senate wants the agency to have wide-ranging authority but is prepared to give it only slightly more resources than the House is (because of its concern with the budget deficit). The president is happy to split the difference between House and Senate on the matter of authority but feels beholden to environmental types and is thus prepared to shower the EPA with resources. Bureaucrats in the EPA want more authority than even the Senate is prepared to grant and more resources than even the president is willing to grant. Eventually relevant majorities in the House and the Senate (including the support of relevant committees) and the president agree on a policy reflecting a compromise among their various points of view.

The bureaucrats are not particularly pleased with this compromise because it gives them considerably less authority and funding than they had hoped for. If they flout the wishes of their principals and implement a policy exactly to their liking, they risk the unified wrath of the House, the Senate, and the president. Undoubtedly the politicians would react with new legislation (and they would also presumably find other political appointees and career bureaucrats at the EPA to replace the current bureaucratic leadership). If, however, the EPA implements some policy located between its own preferences and the preferences of its principals, it might be able to get away with it.

Thus we have a principal-agent relationship in which a political principal—a collective principal consisting of the president and coalitions in the House and Senate—formulates policy and creates an implementation agent to execute its details. The agent, however, has policy preferences of its own and, unless subjected to further controls, will inevitably implement a policy that drifts toward its ideal.

A variety of controls might conceivably restrict this bureaucratic drift. Indeed, legislative scholars often point to congressional hearings in which bureaucrats may be publicly humiliated; annual appropriations decisions that may be used to punish out-of-control bureaus; and watchdog agents, such as the Government Accountability Office, that may be used to monitor and scrutinize

bureaucratic drift

The oft-observed phenomenon of bureaucratic implementation that produces policy more to the liking of the bureaucracy than faithful to the original intention of the legislation that created it, but without triggering a political reaction from elected officials

the bureau's performance. But these all come after the fact and may be only partially credible threats to the agency.[15]

Before-the-Fact Controls. The most powerful before-the-fact political weapon is the appointment process. The adroit control of the political stance of a given bureau by the president and Congress, through their joint powers of nomination and confirmation (especially if they can arrange for appointees who closely share the political consensus on policy), is a self-enforcing mechanism for ensuring reliable agent performance.

A second powerful before-the-fact weapon, following from the institution principle, is procedural controls. The general rules and regulations that direct the manner in which federal agencies conduct their affairs are contained in the Administrative Procedure Act. This act is almost always the boilerplate of legislation creating and renewing federal agencies. It is not uncommon, however, for an agency's procedures to be tailored to suit particular circumstances.

Coalitional Drift as a Collective Action Problem. Not only do politicians want the legislative deals that they strike to be faithfully implemented by the bureaucracy, but they also want those deals to endure. This is especially problematic in American political life, with its shifting alignments and absence of permanent political cleavages. Today's coalition transforms itself overnight. Opponents today are partners tomorrow, and vice versa. A victory today, even one implemented in a favorable manner by the bureaucracy, may unravel tomorrow. What is to be done?

To some extent, legislators are disinclined to undo legislation. If a coalition votes for handsome subsidies to grain farmers, say, it is very hard to reverse this policy without the gatekeeping and agenda-setting assistance of members on the House and Senate Agriculture Committees, yet their members undoubtedly participated in the initial deal and are unlikely to turn against it. But even these structural units are unstable; old politicians depart, and new ones are enlisted. For example, the 2010 elections, giving Republicans majority control of the House in the 112th Congress, has provided them with opportunities to overturn legislation passed in the Democratic-dominated 111th Congress. High on their hit list is the 2010 health care legislation.

coalitional drift

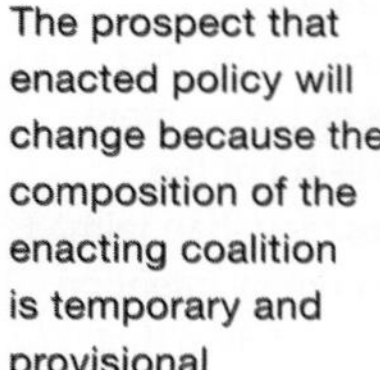
The prospect that enacted policy will change because the composition of the enacting coalition is temporary and provisional

In short, legislatively formulated and bureaucratically implemented output is subject to coalitional drift.[16] To prevent shifting coalitional patterns among

15 For the classic statement that, despite before-the-fact and after-the-fact tools available to the political principals, the bureau-agent will "drift" in policy implementation toward its own preferences, see Mathew D. McCubbins, Roger G. Noll, and Barry R. Weingast, "Structure and Process; Politics and Policy: Administrative Arrangements and the Political Control of Agencies," *Virginia Law Review* 75 (1989): 431–82.

16 This idea, offered as a supplement to the analysis of bureaucratic drift, is found in Murray J. Horn and Kenneth A. Shepsle, "Administrative Process and Organizational Form as Legislative Responses to Agency Costs," *Virginia Law Review* 75 (1989): 499–509. It is further elaborated in Kenneth A. Shepsle, "Bureaucratic Drift, Coalitional Drift, and Time Consistency," *Journal of Law, Economics, and Organization* 8 (1992): 111–8.

politicians from endangering carefully fashioned policies, one thing the legislature might do is insulate the bureaucracy and its implementation activities from legislative interventions. If an enacting coalition makes it difficult for its *own* members to intervene in implementation, then it also makes it difficult for enemies of the policy to disrupt the flow of bureaucratic output. This political insulation can be provided by giving bureaucratic agencies long lives, their political heads long terms of office and wide-ranging administrative authority, and other political appointees overlapping terms of office and secure sources of revenue. This insulation comes at a price, however. The civil servants and political appointees of bureaus insulated from political overseers are thereby empowered to pursue independent courses of action. Protection from coalitional drift comes at the price of an increased potential for bureaucratic drift. It is one of the great trade-offs in the field of intergovernmental relations.

The President, as Chief Executive, Can Direct Agencies

In 1937, President Franklin Delano Roosevelt's Committee on Administrative Management gave official sanction to an idea that had been growing increasingly urgent: "The president needs help." The national government had grown rapidly during the preceding 25 years, but the structures and procedures necessary to manage the burgeoning executive branch had not yet been established. The response to the call for help for the president initially took the form of three management policies: (1) all communications and decisions that related to executive policy decisions must pass through the White House; (2) to cope with such a flow, the White House must have an adequate staff of specialists in research, analysis, legislative and legal writing, and public affairs; and (3) the White House must have additional staff to follow through on presidential decisions—to ensure that those decisions are made, communicated to Congress, and carried out by the appropriate agency.

Establishing a management capacity for the presidency began in earnest with Roosevelt, but it did not stop there. The story of the modern presidency can be told largely as a series of responses to the plea for managerial help. Indeed, each expansion of the national government into new policies and programs in the twentieth century was accompanied by a parallel expansion of the president's management authority. This pattern began even before Roosevelt's presidency, with the policy innovations of President Woodrow Wilson between 1913 and 1920. Congress responded to Wilson's policies with the 1921 Budget and Accounting Act, which conferred on the White House agenda-setting power over budgeting. The president, in his annual budget message, transmits comprehensive budgetary recommendations to Congress. Because Congress retains ultimate legislative authority, a president's proposals are sometimes said to be dead on arrival on Capitol Hill. Nevertheless, the power to frame deliberations is potent and constitutes an important management tool. Each successive president has continued this pattern of setting the congressional agenda, creating what we now know as the managerial presidency.

Along with the development of the managerial presidency came expectations of administrative competence. Presidents are now *expected* to be CEOs and are roundly criticized for ineptitude. For example, President Clinton was often disparaged for the way he managed his administration. (Clinton's easygoing approach led critics to liken his management style to college bull sessions.) George W. Bush was the first president with a graduate degree in business. His management strategy followed a standard business-school dictum: select skilled subordinates and delegate responsibility to them. Bush followed this model closely in his appointment of highly experienced officials to cabinet positions. This was no guarantee of policy success as doubts emerged about the conduct of the Iraq war and the administration's mishandling of relief to New Orleans and the Gulf Coast after Hurricane Katrina. Barack Obama's administrative style fell somewhere in between his two predecessors. He selected highly talented and self-assured manager-politicans at the State (Hillary Clinton) and Defense (Robert Gates) departments. Yet he brought a "Chicago crowd" to the White House, led by chief-of-staff Rahm Emmanuel, who choreographed administrative policy from the center.

Congress Can Promote Responsible Bureaucracy through Oversight and Incentives

Congress is constitutionally essential to responsible bureaucracy because the key to governmental responsibility is legislation. When a law is passed and its intent is clear, then the president knows what to "faithfully execute," and the responsible agency understands what is expected of it. In our modern age, legislatures rarely make laws directly for citizens; most laws are really instructions to bureaucrats and their agencies. But when Congress enacts vague legislation, agencies must rely on their own interpretations. The president and the federal courts step in to tell them what the legislation intended. And so do intensely interested organized groups. But when everybody—from the president to the courts to interest groups—gets involved in the interpretation of legislative intent, to whom is the agency responsible?

oversight

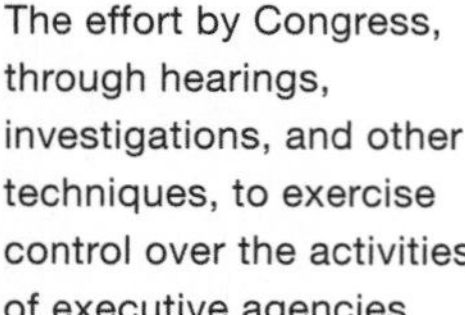

The effort by Congress, through hearings, investigations, and other techniques, to exercise control over the activities of executive agencies

The answer lies in the process of oversight. The more legislative power Congress has delegated to the executive bureaucracy, the more it has sought to get back into the game through committee and subcommittee oversight of the agencies. The standing committee system in Congress is well suited for oversight, inasmuch as most of the congressional committees and subcommittees are organized with jurisdictions roughly parallel to one or more executive departments or agencies. Appropriations committees as well as authorization committees have oversight powers, as do their respective subcommittees. In addition to these, there is a committee on government operations in both the House and the Senate, each with oversight powers not limited by departmental jurisdiction.

The best indication of Congress's oversight efforts is the holding of public hearings, before which bureaucrats and other witnesses are summoned to discuss and defend agency budgets and decisions.

However, often the most effective and the most influential control over bureaucratic accountability is the power of the purse—the ability of the House and Senate committees and subcommittees on appropriations to look at agency performance through the microscope of the annual appropriations process. This process makes bureaucrats attentive to Congress, especially members of the relevant authorizing committee and appropriations subcommittee, because they know that Congress has a chance each year to reduce their authority or funding.[17] This may be another explanation for why there may be some downsizing but almost no terminations of federal agencies.

Oversight can also be carried out by individual members of Congress. Such inquiries addressed to bureaucrats are considered standard congressional "casework" and can turn up significant questions of public responsibility even when the motive is only to meet the demand of an individual constituent. Oversight also very often takes place through communications between congressional staff and agency staff. Congressional staff has grown tremendously since the Legislative Reorganization Act of 1946, and the legislative staff, especially the staff of the committees, is just as professionalized and specialized as the staff of an executive agency. In addition, Congress has created for itself three quite large agencies whose obligations are to engage in constant research on problems taking place in the executive branch: the Government Accountability Office, the Congressional Research Service, and the Congressional Budget Office. Each is designed to give Congress information independent of the information it can get through hearings and other communications directly with the executive branch.[18]

Congressional Oversight: Abdication or Strategic Delegation?

Congress often grants the executive-branch bureaucracies discretion in determining certain features of a policy during the implementation phase. Although the complexities of governing a modern industrialized democracy make the granting of discretion necessary, some argue that Congress not only gives

17 See Aaron Wildavsky, *The New Politics of the Budgetary Process*, 2nd ed. (New York: HarperCollins, 1992), pp. 15–16.

18 Until 1983, there was still another official tool of legislative oversight, the legislative veto. Each executive agency was obliged to submit to Congress proposed decisions or rules. These were to lie before both houses for 30 to 60 days; then, if Congress took no explicit action by a one-house or two-house resolution to veto a proposed measure, it became law. The legislative veto was declared unconstitutional by the Supreme Court in 1983 on the grounds that it violated the separation of powers because the resolutions Congress passed to exercise its veto were not subject to a presidential veto, as required by the Constitution. See *Immigration and Naturalization Service v. Chadha*, 462 U.S. 919 (1983). On the congressional staff more generally, see Robert H. Salisbury and Kenneth A. Shepsle, "Congressman as Enterprise," *Legislative Studies Quarterly* 6 (1981): 559–76. On the role and activities of the Government Accountability Office, see Anne Joseph O'Connell, "Auditing Politics or Political Auditing?" UC Berkeley Public Law Research Paper no. 964656 (2007), http://ssrn.com/abstract=964656 (accessed 1/19/11).

unelected bureaucrats too much discretion but also delegates too much policy-making authority to them. Congress, they say, has transferred so much power that it has created a "runaway bureaucracy" in which unelected officials accountable neither to the electorate nor to Congress make important policy decisions.[19] By enacting vague statutes that give bureaucrats broad discretion, so the argument goes, members of Congress effectively abdicate their constitutionally designated roles and effectively remove themselves from the policy-making process. Ultimately this extreme delegation has left the legislative branch weak and ineffectual and has dire consequences for the health of our democracy.

Others claim that even though Congress may possess the tools to engage in effective oversight, it fails to use them simply because we do not see Congress actively engaging in much oversight activity.[20] However, Mathew McCubbins and Thomas Schwartz argue that these critics have focused on the wrong type of oversight and have missed a type of oversight that benefits members of Congress in their bids for re-election (in accord with the rationality principle).[21] McCubbins and Schwartz distinguish between two types of oversight: police patrol and fire alarm. Under the police-patrol variety, Congress systematically initiates investigation into the activity of agencies. Under the fire-alarm variety, members of Congress do not initiate investigations but wait for adversely affected citizens or interest groups to bring bureaucratic perversions of legislative intent to the attention of the relevant congressional committee. To make sure that individuals and groups bring these violations to members' attention—to set off the fire alarm, so to speak—Congress passes laws that help individuals and groups make claims against the bureaucracy, granting them legal standing before administrative agencies and federal courts.

McCubbins and Schwartz argue that fire-alarm oversight is more efficient than the police-patrol variety, given costs and the electoral incentives of members of Congress. Why should members spend their scarce resources (mainly time) to initiate investigations without having any evidence that they will reap electoral rewards? Police-patrol oversight can waste taxpayers' dollars too, because many investigations will not turn up any evidence of violations of legislative intent. It is much more cost effective for members to conserve their resources and then claim credit for fixing the problem (and saving the day) after the fire alarms have been sounded (also see the Analyzing the Evidence section on page 318).

On the other hand, bureaucratic drift might be contained if Congress spent more of its time clarifying its legislative intent and less of its time on oversight activity. If its original intent in the law were clearer, Congress could then afford

19 Lowi, *The End of Liberalism*; and Lawrence C. Dodd and Richard L. Schott, *Congress and the Administrative State* (New York: Wiley, 1979).

20 Morris S. Ogul, *Congress Oversees the Bureaucracy: Studies in Legislative Supervision* (Pittsburgh: University of Pittsburgh Press, 1976); and Peter Woll, *American Bureaucracy*, 2nd ed. (New York: Norton, 1977).

21 McCubbins and Schwartz, "Congressional Oversight Overlooked."

to defer to presidential management to maintain bureaucratic responsibility. Bureaucrats are more responsive to clear legislative guidance than to anything else. But when Congress and the president are at odds (or coalitions within Congress are at odds), bureaucrats have an opportunity to evade responsibility by playing one side off against the other.

Policy Implications. Because the bureaucracy finds itself squarely in the middle of the separation of powers between the legislature and the executive, it often manages to elude systematic and comprehensive review and oversight. The institution principle suggests as much. Rational political actors in both branches will pay some attention to the bureaucracy, but as we have just seen, their own goals and objectives may not be well served by obsessive attention. The result is a bureaucracy that retains some discretion—partly because political actors' own specialization and expertise warrant it, but also because political arrangements permit their oversight to fall between the institutional cracks. Bureaus, in turn, perform their missions in ways that aim to maintain this kind of independence. They produce rulings, interpretations, and particular implementations of policy in order to deter after-the-fact oversight, allowing sleeping dogs (potential overseers) to lie.

Rational political adaptations to these institutional arrangements have policy consequences. In particular, bureaucrats will be extraordinarily attentive to the policy needs of those legislators who are in a position to help or harm them. Thus, states and districts represented on the House and Senate authorizing committees, as well as on the relevant appropriations subcommittees, can expect to have government largesse steered their way. Legislative lore points to instances in which, for example, a major weapons system is sustained politically by an implicit agreement between Defense Department agents and private sector contractors to ensure that subcontracts are distributed, geographically, to politically significant locations.

Repeat this pattern of deals among agency officials, powerful legislators, and private-sector special interests over many projects in many policy areas and we have a "distributive tendency" in which successful play of the political game by legislators and bureaucrats requires the wide distribution of spending. More efficient targeting of spending takes a backseat to the practical politics of making sure the "right" states and districts are taken care of. One classic example of the distributive tendency is found in the attempt by President Lyndon Johnson in the mid-1960s to focus federal assistance on those central cities in direst need of economic stimulus. His Model Cities program identified 10 cities in desperate straits. But 10 was too small a number in a political system with 50 states and 435 legislative districts. By the time Johnson's proposal had worked its way through the legislative process, the relevant bureaucratic entities had been given discretion to spread funds to many distressed cities—numbering in the hundreds when all was said and done—rather than concentrating assistance on the most desperate ones. The policy principle suggests that institutional arrangements (bicameralism and the separation of powers in this instance) combined with rational political behavior (re-election motivations of legislators and

When Does Congress Rein in the Bureaucracy?

CHAPTER 08

Contributed by
Jamie Carson
University of Georgia

Although we often think of Congress as a lawmaking body, it also carries out another important task—keeping a watchful eye on the executive branch. If Congress thinks the bureaucracy is no longer serving the public's interest as defined by the legislative branch, it can use its oversight powers to pull the agency back where it belongs. As the figure below shows, millions of employees work in the bureaucracy. How does Congress monitor all of the departments and agencies, and the vast range of executive branch activities? How does it know when agencies need to be reined in?

Scholars Mathew McCubbins and Thomas Schwartz define two types of oversight: police patrols and fire alarms. Police-patrol oversight implies that members of Congress are actively monitoring executive agencies. The goal is to catch and punish enough violators so that the rest of the bureaucracy will be discouraged from straying too far from legislative intent. However, Congress does not have the resources to monitor all agencies at once. Fire-alarm monitoring is less active when compared to police patrols. Instead, Congress sets up a series of rules and procedures that allows citizens and interest groups to keep executive agencies in check. McCubbins and Schwartz argue the fire-alarm method is more effective because, "Instead of sniffing for fires, Congress places fire-alarm boxes on street corners, builds neighborhood fire houses and sometimes dispatches its own hook-and-ladder in response to an alarm."[1]

Executive Branch Employees[2]

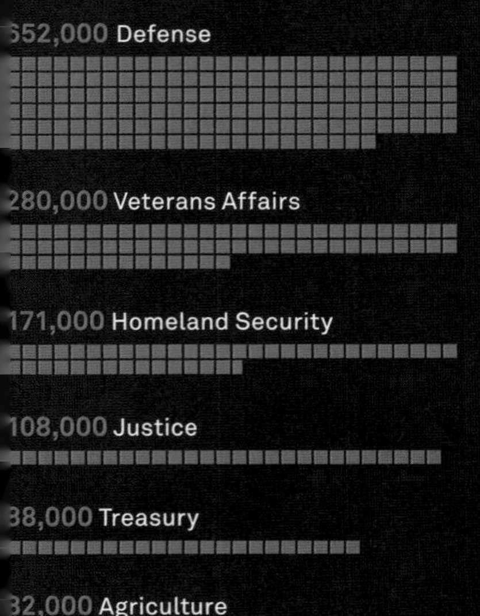

Government Efficiency and Bureaucratic Oversight Hearings

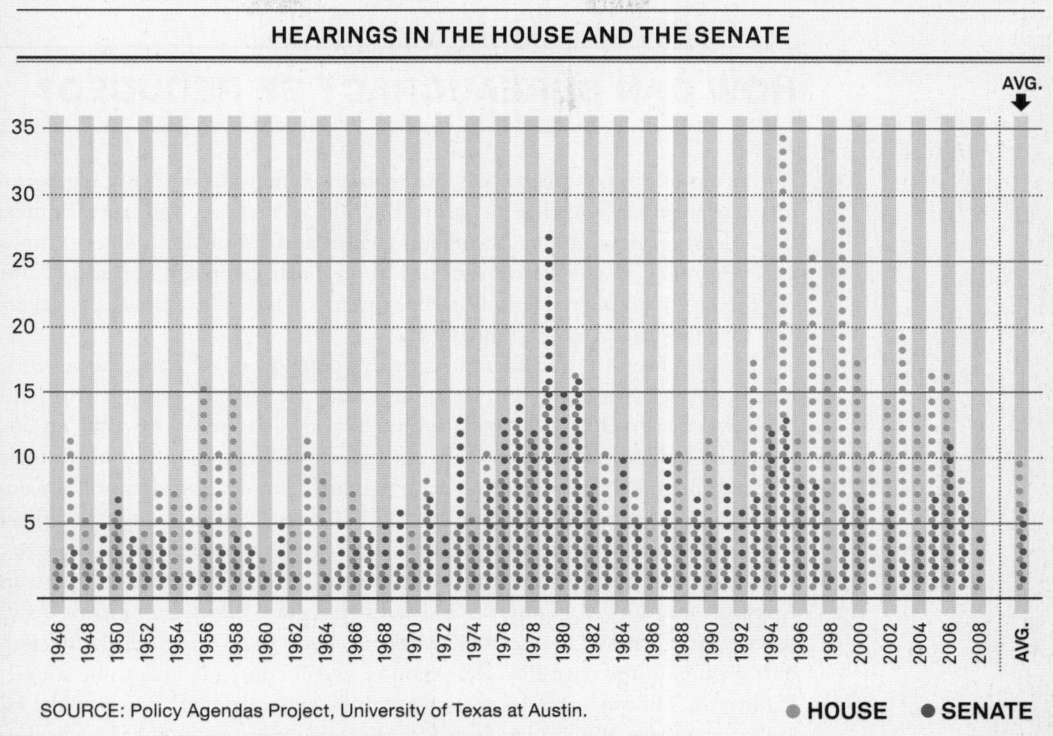

How has oversight varied over the years? The graph above depicts the number of Government Efficiency and Bureaucratic Oversight Hearings held by the House and Senate from 1946 through 2008. Two patterns stand out. First, the House holds more hearings compared to the Senate. On average, the House holds 9.9 hearings a year with only 6.2 for the Senate. Second, we see two periods where the number of hearings increased dramatically. Both chambers began to hold more hearings in the mid- to late 1970s in the wake of Watergate and Vietnam, and again following the Republican takeover of the House in 1994. Which form of monitoring seems likely to have been predominant in these periods?

1 Mathew McCubbins and Thomas Schwartz, "Congressional Oversight Overlooked: Police Patrols and Fire Alarms," *American Journal of Political Science* 28, no. 1 (1984): 165–79.

2 Bureau of Labor Statistics, U.S. Department of Labor, *Career Guide to Industries, 2010–11 Edition*, Federal Government, excluding the Postal Service, www.bls.gov/oco/cg/cgs041.html (accessed 6/22/11).

EXPLORE **FEDERAL BUREAUCRACY** FURTHER AT:

wwnorton.com/studyspace

programmatic survival instincts of bureaucrats) produce policy distortions (the wide distribution of programmatic funds to sustain programs and to avoid the risk of critical oversight).

HOW CAN BUREAUCRACY BE REDUCED?

Americans like to complain about bureaucracy. Americans don't like big government because big government means big bureaucracy, and bureaucracy means the federal service—about 2.8 million civilian and 1.4 million military employees.[22] Promises to cut the bureaucracy are popular campaign appeals; "cutting out the fat," with big reductions in the number of federal employees, is held out as a sure-fire way of cutting the deficit.

Despite fears of bureaucratic growth's getting out of hand, however, the federal service has hardly grown at all during the past 30 years; it reached its peak postwar level in 1968 with 2.9 million civilian employees plus an additional 3.6 million military personnel (a figure swollen by the war in Vietnam). The number of civilian federal executive-branch employees has since remained close to that figure. The growth of the federal service is even less imposing when placed in the context of the total workforce and compared to the size of state and local public employment, which was 19.4 million full- and part-time employees in 2009.[23] Figure 8.3 indicates that since 1950 the ratio of federal service employment to the total workforce has been fairly steady, declining only slightly in the past 25 years. Another useful comparison is to be found in Figure 8.4: Although the dollar increase in federal spending shown by the bars looks impressive, the red line indicates that even here the national government has simply kept pace with the growth of the economy. During the Clinton years, federal outlays as a percent of the size of the economy (GDP) actually declined. During the Bush years, it steadily grew (from 18.5 percent to over 20 percent). During the first four years of Obama's presidency, outlays rose to 25 percent of GDP, in large part an effect of the great recession and financial crisis (smaller GDP) and a response to it (larger outlays).

In sum, the national government is indeed very large, but the federal service has not been growing any faster than the economy or the society. The same is roughly true of the growth pattern of state and local public personnel. Our bureaucracy keeps pace with our society, despite our seeming dislike for it, because we cannot operate the control towers, the prisons, the Social Security system, and other essential elements of the state without it. And we certainly

22 U.S. Bureau of the Census, *Statistical Abstract of the United States, 2011* (Washington, DC: Government Printing Office, 2011), Tables 494 and 508.

23 U.S. Bureau of the Census, www.census.gov/govs/

Figure 8.3

EMPLOYEES IN THE FEDERAL SERVICE: TOTAL NUMBER AS A PERCENTAGE OF THE WORKFORCE

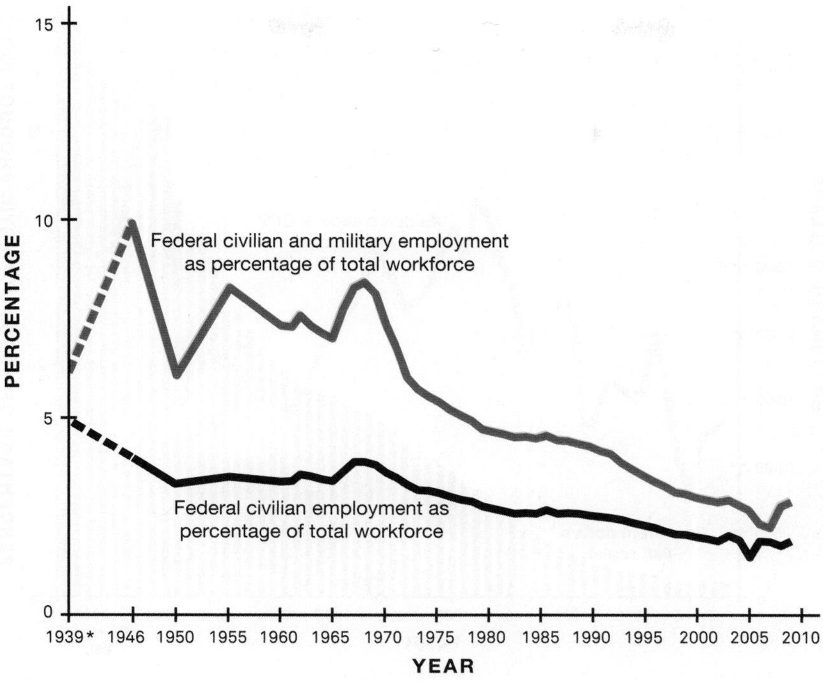

PERCENTAGE

Federal civilian and military employment as percentage of total workforce

Federal civilian employment as percentage of total workforce

1939* 1946 1950 1955 1960 1965 1970 1975 1980 1985 1990 1995 2000 2005 2010

YEAR

*Lines between 1939 and 1946 are broken because they connect the last prewar year with the first postwar year, disregarding the temporary ballooning of federal employees, especially in the military, during the war years.

NOTE: Workforce includes unemployed persons.

SOURCES: Tax Foundation, *Facts and Figures on Government Finance* (Baltimore: Johns Hopkins University Press, 1990), pp. 22, 44; Office of Management and Budget, *Budget of the U.S. Government, Fiscal Year 2009*, Table 17.5; and U.S. Bureau of Labor Statistics, "Employment Status of the Civilian Population by Sex and Age," *Labor Force Statistics from the Current Population Survey*, http://stats.bls.gov/webapps/legacy/cpsatab1.htm, table A1.

could not conduct wars in Iraq and Afghanistan without a gigantic military bureaucracy.

Nevertheless, some Americans continue to argue that bureaucracy is too big and that it should be reduced. In the 1990s, Americans seemed particularly enthusiastic about reducing the federal bureaucracy. However, following the attacks of September 11, 2001, and during the deep economic recession beginning in December 2007, popular sentiment toward an enlarged role for government softened.

Figure 8.4
ANNUAL FEDERAL OUTLAYS

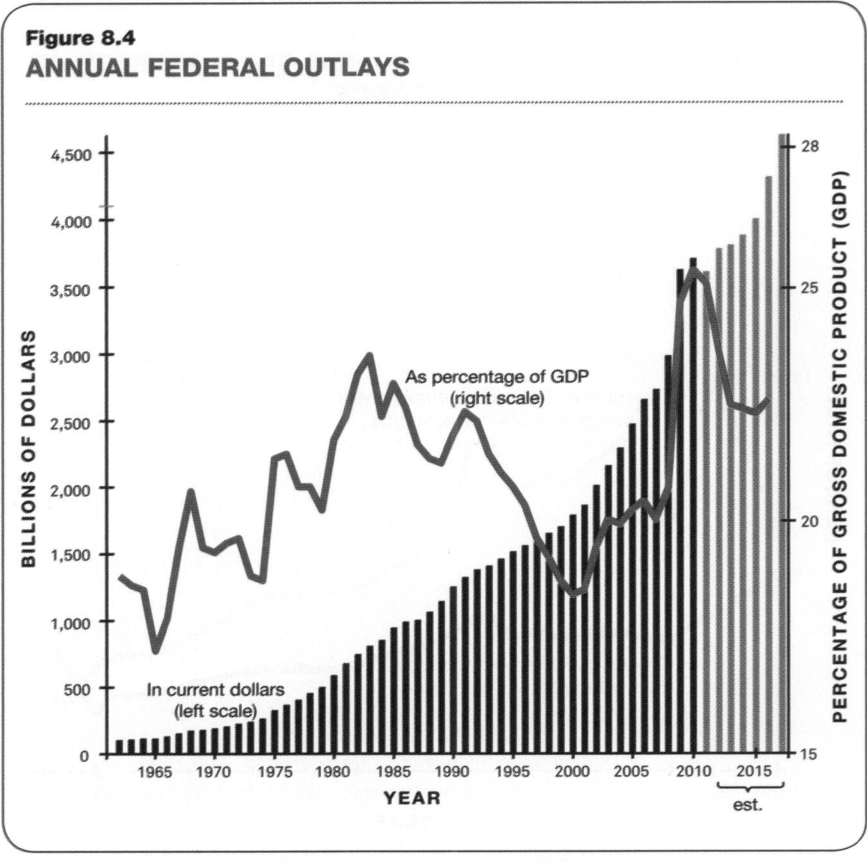

*Data for 2011–16 are estimated.

SOURCE: Office of Management and Budget, *Budget of the U.S. Government, Fiscal Year 2013*, Tables 1.1 and 1.2.

Termination

The only *certain* way to reduce the size of the bureaucracy is to eliminate programs. But most agencies have a supportive constituency—people and groups who benefit from the programs—that will fight to reinstate any cuts that are made. Termination is the only way to ensure an agency's reduction, and it is a rare occurrence.

The overall lack of success in terminating bureaucracy is a reflection of Americans' love-hate relationship with the national government. As antagonistic as Americans may be toward bureaucracy in general, they grow attached to the services rendered and protections offered by particular bureaucratic agencies—that is, they fiercely defend their favorite agencies while perceiving no inconsistency between that defense and their antagonistic attitude toward the bureaucracy in general. A good case in point was the agonizing problem of closing military bases in the wake of the end of the Cold War, when the United States no longer needed so many bases. Because every base is in some congressional member's district, it proved impossible for Congress to decide to close any of them. Consequently, between 1988 and 1990, Congress established the Defense Base Closure and Realignment Commission to decide on base closings. Even though the matter is now out of Congress's hands altogether, the process has been slow and agonizing.

Elected leaders have come to rely on a more incremental approach to downsizing the bureaucracy. They have done much by budgetary means, reducing the budgets of all agencies across the board by small percentages and cutting some poorly supported agencies by larger amounts. Yet these changes are still incremental, leaving the existence of agencies unaddressed.

An additional approach has been taken to thwart the highly unpopular regulatory agencies, which are so small (relatively) that cutting their budgets contributes virtually nothing to reducing the deficit. This approach is called deregulation, simply defined as a reduction in the number of rules promulgated by regulatory agencies. But deregulation by rule reduction is still incremental and has certainly not satisfied the hunger of the American public in general and Washington representatives in particular for a genuine reduction in the size of the bureaucracy.

deregulation

The policy of reducing or eliminating regulatory restraints on the conduct of individuals or private institutions

Devolution

An alternative to genuine reduction in the size of the bureaucracy is devolution—downsizing the federal bureaucracy by delegating the implementation of programs to state and local governments. Indirect evidence for this is seen in Figure 8.5, which shows the increase in state and local government employment against a backdrop of flat or declining federal employment. This evidence suggests a growing share of governmental actions taking place on the state and local levels.

devolution

The policy of removing a program from one level of government by deregulating it or passing it down to a lower level, for example, from the national government to the state and local governments

Devolution often alters the pattern of who benefits most from government programs. In the early 1990s, a major devolution in transportation policy sought to open up decisions about transportation to a new set of interests. Since the 1920s, transportation policy had been dominated by road-building interests in the federal and state governments. Many advocates for cities and many environmentalists believed that the emphasis on road building hurt cities and harmed the environment. The 1992 reform, initiated by environmentalists, put more power into the hands of metropolitan planning organizations and lifted many federal restrictions on how the money should be spent. Reformers hoped that these changes would open up the decision-making process so that those advocating alternatives to road building, such as mass transit, bike paths, and walkways, would have more influence over how federal transportation dollars

Figure 8.5
GOVERNMENT EMPLOYMENT

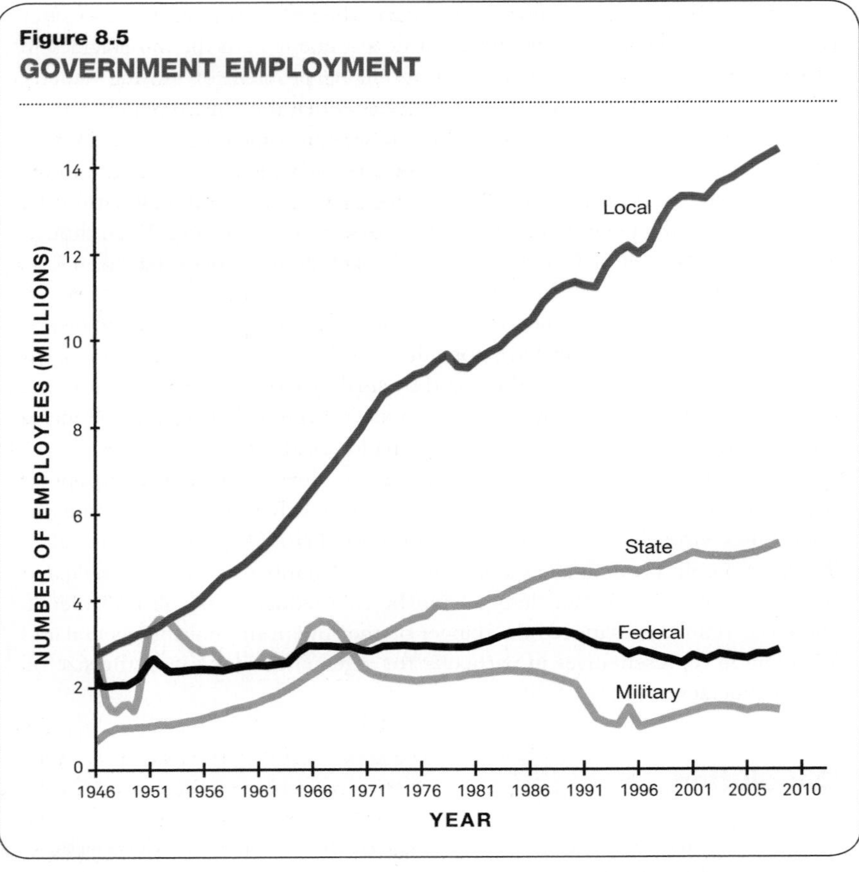

NOTE: Federal government employment figures include civilians only. Military employment figures include only active-duty personnel.

SOURCE: U.S. Bureau of the Census, *Statistical Abstract of the United States 2011* (Washington, DC: Government Printing Office, 2011), Tables 459 and 509.

were spent. Although the pace of change has been slow, devolution has indeed brought new voices to decisions about transportation spending, and alternatives to highways have received increasing attention.

Often the central aim of devolution is to provide more efficient and more flexible government services. Yet by its very nature, devolution entails variation across the states. In some states, government services may improve as a consequence of devolution. In other states, services may deteriorate as the states use devolution as an opportunity to cut spending and reduce services. This has been the pattern in the implementation of the welfare reform passed in 1996, the most significant devolution of federal social programs in many decades. Some states, such as Wisconsin, have used the flexibility of the reform to design innovative programs that respond to clients' needs; other states, such as Idaho, have virtually dismantled their welfare programs. Because the legislation placed a five-year lifetime limit on receiving welfare, the states will take on an even greater role in the future as existing clients lose their eligibility for federal benefits. Welfare reform has been praised by many for reducing welfare rolls and responding to the public desire that welfare be a temporary program. At the same time, it has placed more low-income women and their children at risk of being left with no form of assistance at all.

This variation is the dilemma that devolution poses. Up to a point, variation can be considered one of the virtues of federalism. But in a democracy dangers are inherent in large variations in the provision of services and benefits.

Privatization

Privatization, another downsizing option, may seem like a synonym for termination, but that is true only at the extreme. Most of what is called privatization is not termination at all but the provision of government goods and services by private contractors under direct government supervision. Except for top-secret strategic materials, virtually all of the production of military hardware, from boats to bullets, is done on a privatized basis by private contractors. Billions of dollars of research services are bought under contract by governments; these private contractors are universities as well as ordinary industrial corporations and private think tanks. Privatization simply means that a public purpose is provided under contract by a private company.[24] But such programs are still very much government programs; they are paid for by government and supervised by government. Privatization downsizes the government only in that the workers providing the service are no longer counted as part of the government bureaucracy.

 **privatization**

The act of moving all or part of a program from the public sector to the private sector

The central aim of privatization is to reduce the cost of government. When private contractors can perform a task as well as a government but for less money, taxpayers win. Government workers are generally unionized and, therefore, receive good pay and generous benefits. Private-sector workers are less likely to be unionized, and private firms often provide lower pay and fewer benefits. For this reason, public-sector unions have been one of the strongest voices arguing against privatization. Other critics of privatization observe that private firms may not be more efficient or less costly than government. This is especially likely when there is little competition among private firms and public bureaucracies are not granted a fair chance to bid in the contracting competition.

24 A more general term is *outsourcing*. Privatization is outsourcing to the private sector. Devolution is outsourcing to a lower level of government. A third example is the opposite of devolution, as when a small community contracts with a county for, say, police services.

When private firms have a monopoly on service provision, they may be more expensive than government.

There are important questions about how private contractors can be held accountable. As one analyst of Pentagon spending put it, "The Pentagon is supposed to be representing the taxpayer and the public interest—its national security. So it's really important to have transparency, to be able to see these competitions and hold people accountable."[25] As security has become the nation's paramount concern, new worries about privatization have surfaced. Some Pentagon officials fear that too many tasks vital to national security may have already been contracted out and that national security might best be served by limiting privatization.

The new demands of domestic security have altered the thrust of bureaucratic reform. The emphasis on reducing the size of government that was so prominent during the previous two decades is gone. Instead, there is an acceptance of the idea that the federal government will grow as needed to ensure the safety of American citizens. The administration's security effort, focusing the entire federal bureaucracy on a single central mission, will require unprecedented levels of coordination among federal agencies. Despite the strong agreement on the goal of fighting terrorism, the effort to streamline the bureaucracy by focusing on a single purpose is likely to face considerable obstacles along the way. Reform of public bureaucracies is always complex because strong constituencies may attempt to block changes that they believe will harm them. Initiatives that aim to improve coordination among agencies can easily provoke political disputes if the proposed changes threaten to alter the access of groups to the bureaucracy. And groups that oppose bureaucratic changes can appeal to Congress to intervene on their behalf.

CONCLUSION

Bureaucracy is one of humanity's most significant inventions. It is an institutional arrangement that allows for division and specialization of labor, harnesses expertise, and coordinates collective action for social, political, and economic purposes. It enables governments to exist and perform. In this chapter, we have focused on what public bureaucracies do, how they are organized at the national level in the United States, and how they are controlled (or not) by elected politicians.

25 Ellen Nakashima, "Defense Balks at Contract Goals: Essential Services Should Not Be Privatized, Pentagon Tells OMB," *Washington Post*, January 30, 2002, p. A21.

At a theoretical level, public bureaucracy is the concrete expression of rational, purposeful, political action. Elected politicians have goals—as broad as defending the realm, maintaining public health and safety, or promoting economic growth; as narrow as securing a post office for Possum Hollow, Pennsylvania, or an exit off the interstate highway for Springfield, Massachusetts. Bureaucracy is the instrument by which political objectives, established by elected legislators and executives, are transformed from ideas, concepts, and intentions into the actual "bricks and mortar" of implemented policies.

At a practical level, this transformation depends upon the motivations of bureaucratic agents and the institutional machinery created when a bureaucratic entity is formed or reformed. Elected politicians engage in institutional design in creating agencies. They have their greatest impact at this point. Once an agency is up and running, elected officials only imperfectly control their bureaucratic agents. Institutional arrangements, and simple human nature, provide a certain amount of insulation to agencies, enabling bureaucrats to march to their own drummers, at least some of the time. Of course, bureaucrats are not entirely free agents. But control is a constant and recurring problem for elected officials.

The policy principle suggests that the combination of bureaucratic arrangements and individual motivations produce evident patterns in policy. Because of its insulation, an agency's policies, once underway, are difficult to reverse. Insulation thwarts only but the most intensely expressed interventions in the affairs of an agency. This has the benefit of commitment—interested parties are reassured about the continued provision of a bureaucratic product or service. The farmer can rely on his subsidy check; the senior citizen can count on her monthly Social Security stipend; truckers and other motorists can be secure in the expectation that the interstate highways will be there for them.

But it has distributive costs. Bureaucrats will be most attentive to the most intense interested parties. As a consequence, policies will come to be skewed in particular ways. The efficiency gains that come from the expertise and coordinating services of bureaucracy are thus dissipated by these political pressures. For example, highway funds will find their way disproportionately to the states and districts of legislators who sit on the public works authorizing and appropriating committees. For the last quarter century, until 2009, Alaska was a major beneficiary of infrastructure expenditures precisely because one of its senators (Ted Stevens) and its lone representative (Don Young) were powerhouses in their respective legislative chambers.

In describing the federal bureaucracy in this chapter, we hope we have made clear the ways in which rationality, institutional ways of doing things, and the resulting policy outputs are a consequence of the way in which agencies straddle the divide produced by the separation of powers. Attuned partly to the executive and partly to the legislature, bureaucratic agents tread a careful line between their several masters, protected in part by the natural insulation associated with bureaucracy but vulnerable to intense political pressure. Politics is at the very heart of these organizations and the policies they produce.

For Further Reading

Aberbach, Joel, and Bert A. Rockman. *In the Web of Politics: Three Decades of the U.S. Federal Executive*. Washington, DC: Brookings Institution, 2000.

Besley, Timothy. *Principled Agents? Motivations and Incentives in Politics*. Oxford, UK: Oxford University Press, 2006.

Brehm, John, and Scott Gates. *Working, Shirking, and Sabotage: Bureaucratic Response to a Democratic Public*. Ann Arbor: University of Michigan Press, 1997.

Downs, Anthony. *Inside Bureaucracy*. Boston: Little, Brown, 1966.

Esman, Milton J. *Government Works: Why Americans Need the Feds*. Ithaca, NY: Cornell University Press, 2000.

Fiorina, Morris P. "Legislative Choice of Regulatory Forms: Legal Process or Administrative Process." *Public Choice* 39 (1982): 33–66.

Goodsell, Charles. *The Case for Bureaucracy*. 4th ed. Washington, DC: Congressional Quarterly Press, 2003.

Heclo, Hugh. *On Thinking Institutionally*. Boulder, CO: Paradigm, 2007.

Huber, John, and Charles Shipan. *Deliberate Discretion? The Institutional Foundations of Bureaucratic Autonomy*. New York: Cambridge University Press, 2002.

Kerwin, Cornelius M. *Rulemaking*. 3rd ed. Washington, DC: Congressional Quarterly Press, 2003.

Kettl, Donald F., and James Fesler. *The Politics of the Administrative Process*. 3rd ed. Washington, DC: Brookings Institution, 2005.

Light, Paul C. *The True Size of Government*. Washington, DC: Brookings Institution, 1999.

McCubbins, Mathew, Roger Noll, and Barry Weingast. "Structure and Process; Politics and Policy: Administrative Arrangements and the Political Control of Agencies." *Virginia Law Review* 75 (1989): 431–82.

reader selection

McCubbins, Mathew, and Thomas Schwartz. "Congressional Oversight Overlooked: Police Patrols versus Fire Alarms." *American Journal of Political Science* 28 (1984): 165–79.

Meier, Kenneth J., and John Bohte. *Politics and the Bureaucracy.* 5th ed. Belmont, CA: Wadsworth, 2006.

Seidman, Harold. *Politics, Position, and Power: The Dynamics of Federal Organization.* 5th ed. New York: Oxford University Press, 1998.

Wilson, James Q. *Bureaucracy: What Government Agencies Do and Why They Do It.* New York: Basic Books, 1989.

reader selection

Visit **wwnorton.com/studyspace/** to access free review materials such as:

- ➜ Vocabulary Flashcards of All Key Terms
- ➜ Chapter Review Quizzes
- ➜ Complete Study Outlines

reader selection

Highlighted selections are included in *Readings in American Politics: Analysis and Perspectives*, Second Edition.

9

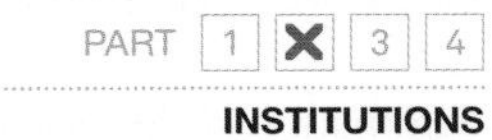

INSTITUTIONS

The Federal Courts

Chapter Outline

- The Judicial Process
- The Organization of the Court System
- How Courts Work as Political Institutions
- The Power of Judicial Review
- The Supreme Court in Action
- Judicial Decision Making
- The Expanding Power of the Judiciary

Courts serve an essential and ancient function. When disputes arise, those involved need an impartial arbiter to help settle the matter. When laws must be enforced, justice requires an impartial judge to determine guilt and innocence and, if the accused is found guilty, the appropriate punishment. And when questions arise about the meaning of those laws, we rely on the wisdom of judges to interpret what Congress meant and how that meaning applies in a given circumstance. It is not possible, or even wise, to pass a law to cover every contingency. Thus, nearly every nation today has established a system of courts to satisfy the need for an arbiter and interpreter.

Perhaps the most significant and distinctive feature of the American judiciary is its independence. The Constitution of the United States, as it was written and as it has evolved over time, set up the courts as a separate entity from the legislature, the executive, and the states, and insulated it from electoral politics. As we see in this chapter, four important features of the institutions of the American judiciary ensure a powerful, independent court system. First, the Constitution establishes the federal courts as a separate branch of government from Congress and the president. Second, authority among the courts is hierarchical, with federal courts able to overturn state courts, and the U.S. Supreme Court as the ultimate authority. Third, the U.S. Supreme Court and other federal courts of appeals can strike down actions of Congress, the president, or the states if the judges deem those acts to be violations of the Constitution. This authority to find government actions unconstitutional is the power of *judicial review*. And fourth, federal judges are appointed for life. Federal judges are not subject to the pressures of running for re-election and need not be highly responsive to changes in public opinion.[1]

1 However, judges in many state and local courts are elected.

An independent judiciary has been one of the most successful institutions of our government. It has settled constitutional crises, when Congress and the president are at odds. It has guaranteed that no person is above the law, even members of Congress and the president. It has helped ensure that all people, even noncitizens, enjoy the equal protection of the laws. It has made it possible for small businesses, large corporations, and workers to engage in economic activities and agreements, knowing that their rights will be protected. It has ensured that the democratic branches of government operate in a democratic manner and that every citizen's vote counts equally in the selection of the legislature. The cumulative effect of an independent judiciary has been a stable, successful democracy and economy.

On its face, granting judges lifetime appointments and the power to strike down acts of Congress might seem like the foundation for tyrannical rule by courts. The sources and nature of judicial power in American government are, however, quite subtle and even democratic. Courts lack Congress's power of the purse or the president's ability to move troops or to order other branches of the executive to act or the bureaucracy's power to police. Courts are also passive

CORE OF THE ANALYSIS

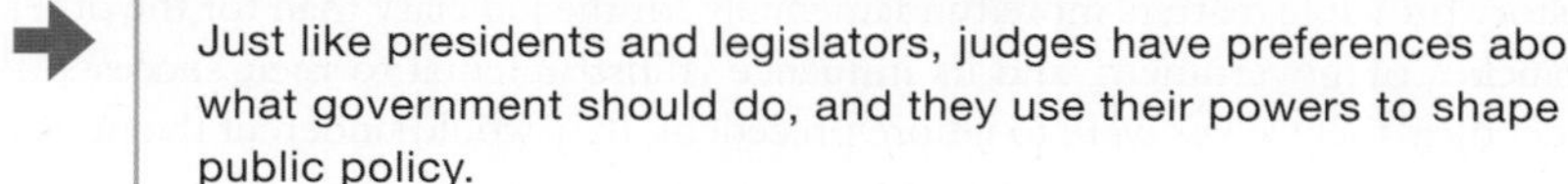

- Just like presidents and legislators, judges have preferences about what government should do, and they use their powers to shape public policy.
- Judicial decisions are highly constrained by the past, in the form of common law and precedents, but every decision also contributes to the evolution of the law.
- The courts maintain their independence from the legislature and executive because federal judges are appointed for life and not elected. Independence allows the courts to act as a check on the democratically chosen branches of government.
- Courts can block or overturn political decisions of the legislature or executive if those decisions violate the Constitution or conflict with other laws, a power called judicial review.
- However, the courts are also constrained by the checks and balances built into the institutional setting within which they operate.

and must wait for people to file lawsuits in order to make any decisions or issue any decree.

The real power of the courts emanates from their ability to interpret the meaning of the laws in a way that society accepts. Courts are powerful to the extent that the people and groups involved accept the decrees that judges issue. In nearly all cases, judges' edicts are ultimately accepted. However, if people ignored the decrees of judges in local courts or if Congress routinely passed legislation contradicting the Supreme Court, the judicial function in our society would vanish. Herein lies the ability of the judiciary not just to interpret but to make law. The decree of any one judge in any single case may not seem very important, but each decision or settlement in a court is an act of lawmaking, a function as important as the passage of a statute by the legislature. Any one decision may serve as a precedent or guide for deciding a future case, and the accumulation of many such decisions, accepted by common practice, eventually becomes the norm.

Common law consists of all past agreements that we accept when we reach any decision. A contract for a real estate sale, for example, consists of many pages of language pertaining to the possible contingencies that might arise, what would happen in each case, and who would bear responsibility. Each clause has been developed through past legal decisions accumulated over centuries, indeed millennia, dating back in some instances to ancient Rome. The Supreme Court is similarly constrained by decisions that it has made in the past. When a majority of justices have issued an opinion interpreting the law a particular way, that opinion has the standing of precedent and constrains future courts. The history principle matters more fundamentally for the judiciary than for the other branches of government, and its influence is instrumental to their success. If the judges themselves were to ignore precedent, they would undercut the power of the courts and their own authority.

Precedents limit the power of the independent judiciary, but the past does not render the courts impotent. In any decision, a judge is both constrained by the past and contributes to the future meaning of the law. Usually, the influence of the courts on American politics is incremental and difficult to discern. At times, however, courts have made sweeping changes in the country's law and politics. With industrialization in the late nineteenth century came new ideas about the enforcement of contracts that dominated the thinking of the courts. The New Deal eventually won the support of the Supreme Court and with that a new acceptance of the role of government in the economy and society. During the 1950s and 1960s, the Supreme Court confronted lingering problems of race relations, religious freedoms, birth control and the sexual revolution, police powers, and legislative redistricting. Today, the courts must deal with new questions, many of which stem from rapid changes in information and biological technologies. Who owns your DNA? Do you have a right to privacy when you send an e-mail? As in the past, our society will call on the courts to settle cases that raise such questions, and how the courts address these issues will shape the meaning of the law and the definition of fundamental rights, such as the right to property and privacy.

The place of the judiciary in the American system of government points to a basic lesson about the courts in the United States and throughout the world: they are fundamentally political. Just like presidents and legislators, judges have preferences about what the government should do, and they use their powers to interpret, apply, and review laws to shape public policy. Judges are also constrained by the institutional setting within which they operate. They are mindful that others in the political process may try to alter or undo a court's rulings.

In this chapter, we examine the judicial process first, including the types of cases that the federal courts consider and the types of laws with which they deal. Second, we assess the organization and structure of the federal court system and explain how judges are appointed to the courts. Third, we analyze courts as political institutions and consider their roles in the political system. Fourth, we consider judicial review and how it makes the Supreme Court a lawmaking body. Fifth, we examine the flow of cases through the courts and various influences on the Supreme Court's decisions. Finally, we analyze the process of judicial decision making and the power of the federal courts in the American political process, looking in particular at the growth of judicial power in the United States.

THE JUDICIAL PROCESS

Many centuries ago a court was the place where a sovereign ruled—where a king and his entourage governed. Judging—settling disputes between citizens—was part of governing. Over time the function of settling disputes was slowly separated from the king and the king's court and made into a separate institution of government. Courts have taken over from kings the power to settle controversies by hearing the facts on both sides and deciding which side possesses the greater merit. But because judges are not kings, they must have a basis for their authority. That basis in the United States is the Constitution and the law. Courts decide cases by applying the relevant law or principle to the facts. This approach of applying relevant law lends authority derived from past law and past social compacts. It also provides a basis for continuing judicial independence, as common law and past precedents evolve on their own, often separate from the legislation passed by Congress and the executive. What then are these systems of rules that the judiciary has developed? What are the organizations and institutions of the judiciary, and how do they help carry out the complex function of the administration and interpretation of the law?

Court cases in the United States proceed under two broad categories of law: criminal and civil. One form of civil law, public law, is so important that we consider it as a separate category (Table 9.1).

Cases of criminal law are those in which the government charges an individual with violating a statute that has been enacted to protect the public health, safety, morals, or welfare. In criminal cases, the government is always the plaintiff (the party that brings charges) and alleges that a criminal violation has been

 **criminal law**

The branch of law that deals with disputes or actions involving criminal penalties (as opposed to civil law)

Table 9.1
TYPES OF LAWS AND DISPUTES

TYPE OF LAW	TYPE OF CASE OR DISPUTE	FORM OF CITATION
Criminal law	Cases arising out of actions that violate laws protecting the health, safety, and morals of the community. The government is always the plaintiff.	*U.S. (or state) v. Jones, Jones v. U.S. (or state)* if Jones lost and is appealing
Civil law	Law involving disputes between citizens or between a government and a citizen where no crime is alleged. Two general types are contract law and tort law. Contract cases are disputes that arise over voluntary actions. Tort cases are disputes that arise out of obligations inherent in social life. Negligence and slander are examples of torts.	*Smith v. Jones, New York v. Jones, U.S. v. Jones, Jones v. New York*
Public law	All cases in which the powers of government or the rights of citizens are involved. The government is the defendant. Constitutional law involves judicial review of the basis of a government's action in relation to specific clauses of the Constitution as interpreted in Supreme Court cases. Administrative law involves disputes over the statutory authority, jurisdiction, or procedures of administrative agencies.	*Jones v. U.S. (or state), In re Jones Smith v. Jones* if a license or statute is at issue in their private dispute

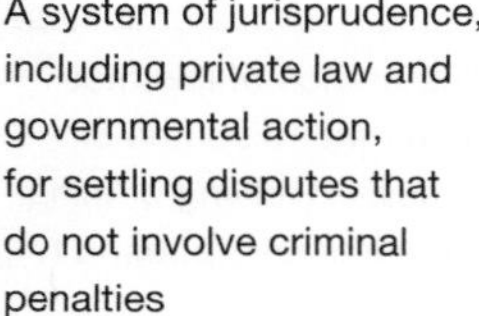

civil law

A system of jurisprudence, including private law and governmental action, for settling disputes that do not involve criminal penalties

committed by a named defendant. Most criminal cases arise in state and municipal courts and involve matters ranging from traffic offenses to robbery and murder. Although the great bulk of criminal law is still a state matter, a large and growing body of federal criminal law deals with such matters as tax evasion, mail fraud, and the sale of narcotics. Defendants found guilty of criminal violations may be fined or sent to prison.

Cases of civil law involve disputes between individuals or between individuals and the government where no criminal violation is charged. Unlike criminal cases, the losers in civil cases cannot be fined or sent to prison, although they may be required to pay monetary damages for their actions. In a civil case, the one who brings a complaint is the plaintiff and the one against whom the complaint is brought is the defendant. The two most common types of civil cases involve contracts and torts. In a typical contract case, an individual or corporation charges that it has suffered because of another's violation of a specific agreement between the two. For example, the Smith Manufacturing Corporation may charge that Jones Distributors failed to honor an agreement to deliver raw materials at a specified time, causing Smith to lose business. Smith asks the court to order Jones to compensate it for the damage allegedly suffered. In a typical tort case, one individual charges that he or she has been injured by another's negligence or malfeasance. Medical malpractice suits are one example of tort cases.

In deciding cases, courts apply statutes (laws) and legal precedents (prior decisions). State and federal statutes often govern the conditions under which contracts are and are not legally binding. Jones Distributors might argue that it was not obliged to fulfill its contract with the Smith Corporation because actions by Smith—the failure to make promised payments—constituted fraud under state law. Attorneys for a physician being sued for malpractice, on the other hand, may search for prior instances in which courts ruled that actions similar to those of their client did not constitute negligence. Such precedents are applied under the doctrine of *stare decisis*, a Latin phrase meaning "let the decision stand."

precedents

Prior cases whose principles are used by judges as the bases for their decisions in present cases

stare decisis

Literally, "let the decision stand." The doctrine whereby a previous decision by a court applies as a precedent in similar cases until that decision is overruled

A case becomes a matter of a third category, public law, when a plaintiff or defendant in a civil or criminal case seeks to show that his or her case involves the powers of government or the rights of citizens as defined under the Constitution or by statute. One major form of public law is constitutional law, under which a court will examine the government's actions to see if they conform to the Constitution as it has been interpreted by the judiciary. Thus what began as an ordinary criminal case may enter the realm of public law if a defendant claims that his or her constitutional rights were violated by the police. Another important arena of public law is administrative law, which involves disputes over the jurisdiction, procedures, or authority of administrative agencies. Under this type of law, civil litigation between an individual and the government may become a matter of public law if the individual asserts that the government is violating a statute or abusing its power under the Constitution. For example, landowners have asserted that federal and state restrictions on land use constitute violations of the Fifth Amendment's restrictions on the government's ability to confiscate private property. Recently the Supreme Court has been very sympathetic to such claims, which effectively transform an ordinary civil dispute into a major issue of public law.

public law

Cases involving the action of public agencies or officials

Most of the Supreme Court cases we examine in this chapter involve judgments concerning the constitutional or statutory basis of the actions of government agencies. As we see, in this arena of public law Court decisions can have significant consequences for American politics and society.

THE ORGANIZATION OF THE COURT SYSTEM

Types of Courts

trial court

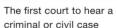

The first court to hear a criminal or civil case

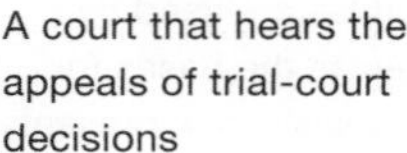

court of appeals (or appellate court)

A court that hears the appeals of trial-court decisions

supreme court

The highest court in a particular state or in the United States. This court primarily serves an appellate function

In the United States, systems of courts have been established both by the federal government and by the governments of the individual states. Both systems have several levels, as shown in Figure 9.1. Nearly 99 percent of all court cases in the United States are heard in state courts. The overwhelming majority of criminal cases, for example, involve violations of state laws prohibiting such actions as murder, robbery, fraud, theft, and assault. If such a case is brought to trial, it will be heard in a state trial court in front of a judge and sometimes a jury, who will determine whether the defendant violated state law. If the defendant is convicted, he or she may appeal the conviction to a higher court, such as a state court of appeals, and from there to a state's supreme court. Similarly, in civil cases, most litigation is brought in the courts established by the state in which the activity in question took place. For example, a patient bringing suit against a physician for malpractice would file the suit in the appropriate court in the state where the alleged malpractice occurred. The judge hearing the case would apply state law and state precedent to the matter at hand. (It should be noted that in

Figure 9.1
THE U.S. COURT SYSTEM

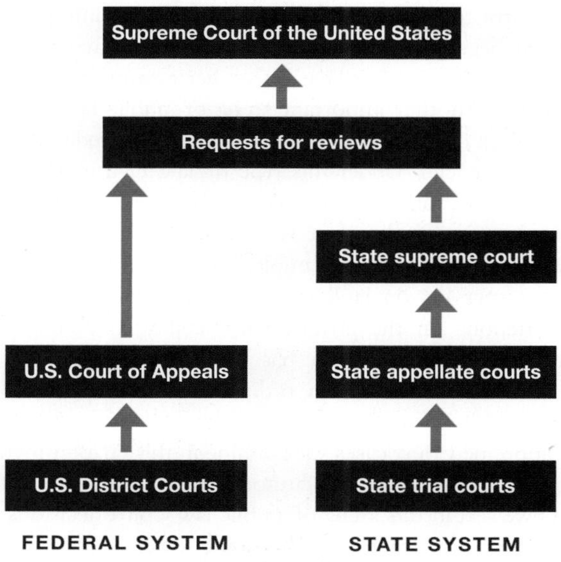

Supreme Court of the United States
Requests for reviews
State supreme court
U.S. Court of Appeals
State appellate courts
U.S. District Courts
State trial courts
FEDERAL SYSTEM
STATE SYSTEM

both criminal and civil matters, most cases are settled before trial through negotiated agreements between the parties. In criminal cases, these agreements are called plea bargains. Such bargains may affect the severity of the charge and/or the severity of the sentence.)

In addition, the U.S. military operates its own court system under the Uniform Code of Military Justice, which governs the behavior of men and women in the armed services. On rare occasions, the government has constituted special military tribunals to hear cases deemed inappropriate for the civil courts. Such tribunals tried Nazi saboteurs apprehended in the United States during World War II. More recently, President George W. Bush ordered the creation of military tribunals to try individuals suspected of acts of terrorism against the United States.

Federal Jurisdiction

Cases are heard in the federal courts if they involve federal laws, treaties with other nations, or the U.S. Constitution; these areas are the official jurisdiction of the federal courts. In addition, any case in which the U.S. government is a party is heard in the federal courts. If, for example, an individual is charged with violating a federal criminal statute, such as evading the payment of income taxes, charges would be brought before a federal judge by a federal prosecutor. Civil cases involving the citizens of more than one state and in which more than $75,000 is at stake may be heard in either the federal or the state courts, usually depending on the preference of the plaintiff.

 **jurisdiction**

The domain over which an institution or member of an institution has authority

But even if a matter belongs in federal court, how do we know which federal court should exercise jurisdiction over the case? The answer to this seemingly simple question is somewhat complex. The jurisdiction of each federal court is derived from the U.S. Constitution and federal statutes. Article III of the Constitution gives the Supreme Court appellate jurisdiction in all federal cases and original jurisdiction in cases involving foreign ambassadors and issues in which a state is a party. Article III assigns original jurisdiction in all other federal cases to the lower courts that Congress was authorized to establish. Over the years, as Congress enacted statutes creating the federal judicial system, it specified the jurisdiction of each type of court it established. For the most part, Congress has assigned jurisdictions on the basis of geography. The nation is currently, by statute, divided into 94 judicial districts, including one court for each of three U.S. territories: Guam, the U.S. Virgin Islands, and the Northern Marianas. Each of the 94 U.S. district courts exercises jurisdiction over federal cases arising within its territorial domain. The judicial districts are, in turn, organized into 11 regional circuits and the District of Columbia circuit (Figure 9.2). Each circuit court exercises appellate jurisdiction over cases heard by the district courts within its region.

Geography is not the only basis for federal court jurisdiction. Congress has also established several specialized courts that have nationwide original jurisdiction in certain types of cases. These include the U.S. Court of International Trade, created to deal with trade and customs issues, and the U.S. Court of Federal Claims, which handles damage suits against the United States. Congress has,

Figure 9.2
GEOGRAPHIC BOUNDARIES OF U.S. COURTS OF APPEALS

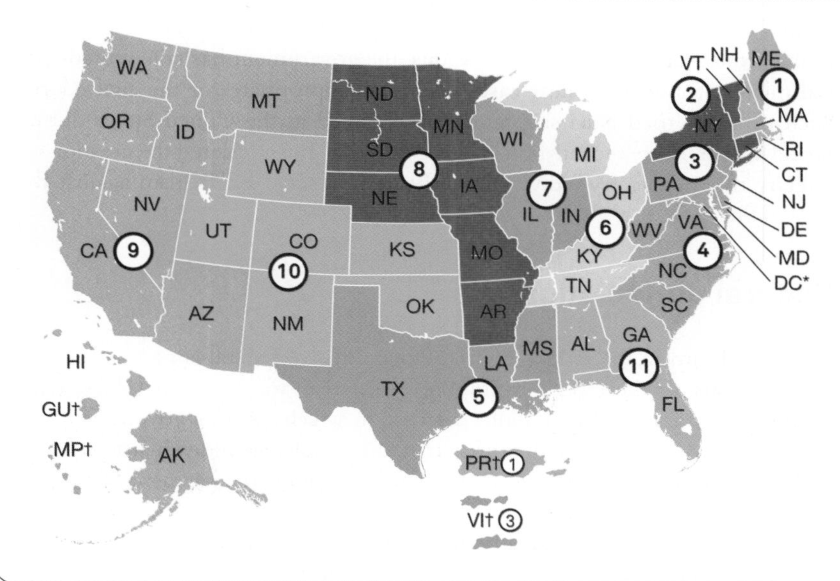

* The District of Columbia has its own circuit, called the D.C. Circuit.
† U.S. Postal Service abbreviations for Guam (GU), Northern Mariana Islands (MP), Puerto Rico (PR), and the U.S. Virgin Islands (VI).
SOURCE: Administrative Office of the U.S. Courts, www.uscourts.gov/images/CircuitMap.pdf.

in addition, established a court with nationwide appellate jurisdiction. This is the U.S. Court of Appeals for the Federal Circuit, which hears appeals involving patent law and those arising from the decisions of the trade and claims courts. Other federal courts assigned specialized jurisdictions by Congress include the U.S. Court of Appeals for Veterans Claims, which exercises exclusive jurisdiction over cases involving veterans' claims, and the U.S. Court of Appeals for the Armed Forces, which deals with questions of law arising from trials by court martial.

With the exception of the claims court and the Court of Appeals for the Federal Circuit, these specialized courts were created not in accordance with Article III of the Constitution but by Congress on the basis of the powers the legislature exercises under Article I. Article III was designed to protect judges from political pressure by granting them life tenure and prohibiting reduction of their salaries while they serve. The judges of Article I courts, by contrast, are appointed by the president for fixed terms of 15 years and are not protected by the Constitution from salary reduction. As a result, these so-called legislative courts are generally viewed as less independent than the courts established under Article III of the Constitution. The three territorial courts were also established under Article I, and their judges are appointed for 10-year terms.

The appellate jurisdiction of the federal courts also extends to cases originating in the state courts. In both civil and criminal cases, a decision of the highest state court can be appealed to the U.S. Supreme Court by raising a federal issue. Appellants might assert, for example, that they were denied the right to counsel or otherwise deprived of the due process guaranteed by the federal Constitution, or they might assert that important issues of federal law were at stake in the case. The U.S. Supreme Court is not obligated to accept such appeals and will accept them only if it believes that the matter has considerable national significance. (We return to this topic later in this chapter.) In addition, in criminal cases defendants who have been convicted in a state court may request a writ of *habeas corpus* from a federal district court. Sometimes known as the Great Writ, *habeas corpus* is a court order to the authorities to release a prisoner deemed to be held in violation of his or her legal rights. In 1867, its distrust of southern courts led Congress to authorize federal district judges to issue such writs to prisoners they believed had been deprived of their constitutional rights in state court. Generally speaking, state defendants seeking a federal writ of *habeas corpus* must show that they have exhausted all available state remedies and raise issues not previously raised in their state appeals. Federal courts of appeals and, ultimately, the U.S. Supreme Court have appellate jurisdiction over federal district court *habeas* decisions.

due process

The guarantee that no citizen may be subjected to arbitrary action by national or state government

writ of *habeas corpus*

A court order demanding that an individual in custody be brought into court and shown the cause for detention. *Habeas corpus* is guaranteed by the Constitution and can be suspended only in cases of rebellion or invasion

Over the past three decades, the caseload of the federal courts has nearly quadrupled, to more than 350,000 cases a year. This has come about because Congress has greatly expanded the number of federal crimes, particularly in the realm of drug possession and sale. Behavior that was once exclusively a state criminal matter has, to some extent, come within the reach of federal law. In 1999, Chief Justice William Rehnquist criticized Congress for federalizing too many offenses and intruding unnecessarily into areas that should be handled by the states.[2] About 80 percent of federal cases end in the district courts, and the remainder are appealed to the circuit courts. In recent years, moreover, approximately 2,000 circuit court decisions per year were appealed to the Supreme Court. Most of the cases filed with the Supreme Court are dismissed without a ruling on their merits. The Court has broad latitude to decide what cases it will hear and generally listens only to those it deems to raise the most important issues. Thus in recent years, fewer than 90 cases per year were given full-dress Supreme Court review (the nine justices actually sitting en banc—in full court—and hearing lawyers argue the case).[3]

Even seemingly unimportant events can raise fundamental questions of law, such as when the First Amendment protects speech. The case of *Morse v. Frederick*, although not the most serious matter facing the nation, exemplifies the appellate process at work in the United States. On January 24, 2002, the

2 Roberto Suro, "Rehnquist: Too Many Offenses Are Becoming Federal Crimes," *Washington Post*, January 1, 1999, p. A2.

3 Administrative Office of the U.S. Courts, 2006, www.uscourts.gov/adminoff.html.

Olympic torch relay passed through Juneau, Alaska, on its way to Salt Lake City and the winter games. The parade, to be carried on local television, passed immediately in front of Juneau-Douglas High School. The high school's principal Deborah Morse, decided to allow staff and students to cheer on the relay as it paraded down the street in front of the high school. As the torch relay passed by the school, Joseph Frederick, a senior, and several of his friends unfurled a 14-foot banner that read *BONG HiTS 4 JESUS*. Principal Morse promptly confiscated the banner and later suspended Frederick for 10 days for promoting illegal drug use at a school-sponsored event. Frederick appealed his suspension to the Juneau School Committee. The expression "BongHits4Jesus," he argued, did not advocate drug use. It was a meaningless phrase that merely attracted the attention of the television cameras. The school committee was not sympathetic.

Frederick felt that his right to free speech under the First Amendment had been violated. He went to court. The federal district court ruled that the school committee had qualified immunity from the First Amendment. Frederick pushed his appeal onward and won. The Ninth Circuit Court of Appeals ruled that "a school cannot censor or punish students' speech merely because the students advocate a position contrary to government policy." The school committee did not let the matter end there. It appealed the circuit court's ruling to the U.S. Supreme Court. The Court agreed to hear the case because it raised significant legal questions about the reach of the First Amendment. Citing a 1969 school speech decision involving antiwar protests, a majority of the justices ruled in favor of Principal Morse and the school committee. "Schools may reasonably take steps to safeguard those entrusted to their care from speech that can reasonably be regarded as encouraging illegal drug use," Chief Justice Roberts wrote for the majority.[4]

Although the federal courts hear only a small fraction of all the civil and criminal cases decided each year in the United States, their decisions are extremely important. (See Table 9.2.) It is in the federal courts that the Constitution and federal laws that govern all Americans are interpreted and their meaning and significance established. Moreover, it is in the federal courts that the powers and limitations of the increasingly powerful national government are tested. Finally, through their power to review the decisions of the state courts, it is ultimately the federal courts that dominate the American judicial system.

Federal Trial Courts

The federal district courts are trial courts of general jurisdiction, and their cases are, in form, indistinguishable from cases in the state trial courts.

There are 89 district courts in the 50 states, one each in the District of Columbia and Puerto Rico, and one in each of the three U.S. territories. There are 663 district judgeships. District judges are assigned to district courts according to the workload; the busiest of these courts may have as many as

4 *Mouse v. Frederick*, 551 U.S. 393 (2007).

Table 9.2

LANDMARK SUPREME COURT CASES

Not all cases and decisions are equally important. Landmark cases are decisions that revolutionize an area of law and announce new legal standards or have far-reaching political consequences.
Marbury v. Madison (1804). The Court declared part of the Judiciary Act unconstitutional, establishing judicial review.
McCulloch v. Maryland (1819). The Supreme Court justified the "implied powers" of the government under the Constitution, enabling Congress and the president to assert their authority beyond those activities explicitly mentioned in the Constitution.
Gibbons v. Ogden (1824). This decision establishes the supremacy of the federal government over the states in the regulation of commerce so as to create uniform business law.
Dred Scott v. Sandford (1857). The Court declared that people of African origin brought to the United States as part of the slave trade were not given the rights of citizenship under the Constitution and could, therefore, claim none of the rights and privileges that the Constitution provides.
Plessy v. Ferguson (1896). The Court interpreted the post–Civil War amendments to the Constitution in such a way as to allow segregation, so long as facilities were "separate but equal."
Lochner v. New York (1905). The Court established a general right to enter freely into contracts as part of business, including the right to purchase and sell labor. The decision made it more difficult for unions to form.
Schenck v. United States (1919). The Court declared that the right to free speech does not extend to words that are "used in such circumstances and are of such a nature as to create a clear and present danger."
Korematsu v. United States (1944). The Court allowed the United States government to intern Japanese-Americans in concentration camps during World War II as a safeguard against insurrection or spying.
Brown v. Board of Education (1954). The Court ruled that separate educational facilities could not be equal, overturning *Plessy*, and ordering an end to segregation "with all deliberate speed."

(Continued)

Table 9.2
(Continued)

Mapp v. Ohio (1961). The Court ruled that all evidence obtained by searches and seizures in violation of the federal Constitution is inadmissible in a court of law.
Baker v. Carr (1962). The justices established that the Court had the authority to hear cases involving legislative districting, even though that is a "political matter," ultimately guaranteeing equal representation in the state legislatures and the U.S. House of Representatives.
Griswold v. Connecticut (1965). The Court struck down a Connecticut law prohibiting counseling on the use of contraceptives and declared that the Bill of Rights implied a right to privacy.
Roe v. Wade (1973). The Court held that a mother may abort her baby for any reason up to the point that the fetus becomes "viable" and that any law passed by a state or Congress inconsistent with this holding violated the right to privacy and the right to enter freely into contracts.
Kelo v. City of New London (2005). The Court upheld the power of local government to seize property for economic development.
Boumediene v. Bush (2008). The Court declared that foreign terrorism suspects have the constitutional right to challenge their detention (using the writ of *habeas corpus*) at the Guantánamo Bay naval base in U.S. courts, even though the detainees are not citizens.

28 judges. Only one judge is assigned to each case, except where statutes provide for three-judge courts to deal with special issues. The routines and procedures of the federal district courts are essentially the same as those of the lower state courts except that federal procedural requirements tend to be stricter. States, for example, do not have to provide a grand jury, a 12-member trial jury, or a unanimous jury verdict. Federal courts must provide all these things. As we saw earlier, in addition to the district courts, cases are handled by several specialized courts, including the U.S. Tax Court, the Court of Federal Claims, and the Court of International Trade.

Federal Appellate Courts

Roughly 20 percent of all lower-court cases, along with appeals of some federal agency decisions, are subsequently reviewed by a federal appeals court. As already noted, the country is divided into 12 judicial circuits, each with a U.S. Court of Appeals. Every state and the District of Columbia are assigned to the circuit in the continental United States that is closest to it. A thirteenth appellate court, the U.S. Court of Appeals for the Federal Circuit, is defined by subject matter (patent law and decisions of trade and claims courts) rather than geographic jurisdiction.

Except for cases selected for review by the Supreme Court, decisions made by the appeals courts are final. Because of this finality, certain safeguards have been built into the system. The most important is the provision of more than one judge for every appeals case. Each court of appeals has from 3 to 28 permanent judgeships, depending on the workload of the circuit. Although normally three judges hear appealed cases, in some instances a larger number of judges sit together en banc. Another safeguard is provided by the assignment of a Supreme Court justice as the circuit justice for each of the 12 circuits. The circuit justice deals with requests for special action by the Supreme Court. The most frequent and best-known action of circuit justices is that of reviewing requests for stays of execution when the full Court is unable to do so—mainly during the summer, when the Court is in recess.

The Supreme Court

The Supreme Court is America's highest court. Article III of the Constitution vests "the judicial Power of the United States" in the Supreme Court, and this court is supreme in fact as well as form. The Supreme Court is made up of a chief justice and eight associate justices. The chief justice presides over the Court's public sessions and conferences. In the Court's actual deliberations and decisions, however, the chief justice has no more authority than his colleagues. Each justice casts one vote. The chief justice, though, is always the first to speak and the last to vote when the justices deliberate. In addition, if the chief justice has voted with the majority, he decides which of the justices will write the formal opinion for the Court. To some extent, the influence of the chief justice is a function of his leadership ability. Some chief justices, such as Earl Warren, have been able to lead the court in a new direction. In other instances, a forceful associate justice, such as Felix Frankfurter, is the dominant figure on the Court.

 **chief justice**

The justice on the Supreme Court who presides over the Court's public sessions

The Constitution does not specify the number of justices that should sit on the Supreme Court; Congress has the authority to change the Court's size. In the early nineteenth century, there were six Supreme Court justices; later there were seven. Congress set the number of justices at nine in 1869, and the Court has remained that size ever since. In 1937, President Franklin Delano Roosevelt, infuriated by several Supreme Court decisions that struck down New Deal programs, asked Congress to enlarge the Court so that he could add sympathetic justices to the bench. Although Congress balked at Roosevelt's "Court-packing" plan, the Court gave in to Roosevelt's pressure and began to take a more favorable view of his policy initiatives. The president, in turn, dropped his efforts to enlarge the Court. The Court's surrender to Roosevelt came to be known as "the switch in time that saved nine."[5]

5 For an alternative view, see David R. Mayhew, "Supermajority Rule in the Senate," *PS: Political Science and Politics* 36 (2003): 31–36.

How Judges Are Appointed

The president appoints federal judges. Nominees are typically prominent or politically active members of the legal profession. Many federal judges previously served as state court judges or state or local prosecutors; some were prominent attorneys; others were highly regarded law professors. Supreme Court justice Thurgood Marshall was the chief counsel for the NAACP and argued *Brown v. Board of Education* before the Court. Felix Frankfurter was a prominent law professor at Harvard University and adviser to Franklin Delano Roosevelt. Still others were prominent elected officials. Prior experience as a judge is not necessary, either for appointment or ultimately success. Many of the greatest Supreme Court justices, including John Marshall, William Rehnquist, Louis Brandeis, Earl Warren, William O. Douglas, Harlan Fiske Stone, Robert Jackson, Felix Frankfurter, Joseph Storey, and Roger Taney, had no prior experience as judges. They were political and intellectual leaders in the country. John Marshall, the longest serving chief justice, was John Adams's secretary of state. Roger Taney, who delivered the *Dred Scott* opinion in 1858, was a trusted adviser of Andrew Jackson and served as attorney general and secretary of treasury. Earl Warren was governor of California. Elena Kagan, appointed in 2010, was dean of Harvard Law School and Barack Obama's first solicitor general.

In general, presidents endeavor to appoint judges who possess legal experience and good character and whose partisan and ideological views are similar to theirs. During the presidencies of Richard Nixon, Ronald Reagan, George H. W. Bush, and George W. Bush, most federal judicial appointees were conservative Republicans. Bill Clinton's appointees to the federal bench, on the other hand, tended to be liberal Democrats. Following the example of Jimmy Carter, Clinton also made a major effort to appoint women and African Americans to the federal courts. Nearly half his nominees were drawn from these groups. George W. Bush made a strong effort to appoint Hispanics to the federal bench.

The Constitution calls on the Senate to "advise and consent" to federal judicial nominations. This power gives the upper chamber of the Congress an important check on the president's influence over the judiciary. Before the president formally nominates a candidate for a federal district judgeship, the senators from the nominee's state must indicate that they support him or her. This is an informal but seldom violated practice called senatorial courtesy. If one or both senators from a prospective nominee's home state belong to the president's political party, the president will almost invariably consult them and secure their blessing for the nomination. Because the president's party in the Senate will rarely support a nominee opposed by a home-state senator from their ranks, this arrangement gives these senators virtual veto power over appointments to the federal bench in their own states. Senators often see this power to grant their support as a way to reward important allies and contributors in their states. If the state has no senator from the president's party, the governor or members of the state's House delegation may make suggestions.

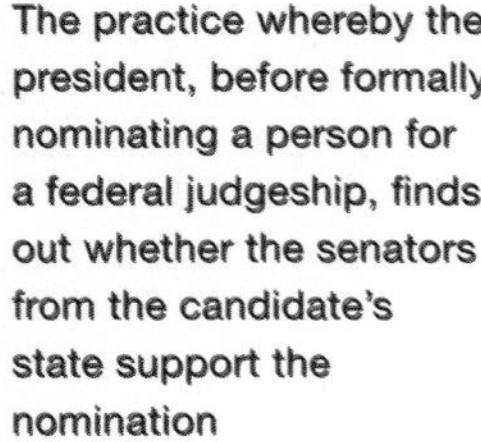

senatorial courtesy

The practice whereby the president, before formally nominating a person for a federal judgeship, finds out whether the senators from the candidate's state support the nomination

Once the president has formally nominated an individual, the appointment must be considered by the Senate Judiciary Committee and confirmed by a majority vote in the full Senate. The politics and rules of the Senate determine the fate of a president's judicial nominees and influence the types of people the president selects for judicial positions. Like any piece of legislation, approval of a nomination must be given by the relevant committee and brought to the floor of the Senate, and to be successful, the nomination must receive a majority of votes. What is more, because this takes place in the Senate, there is always the risk of a filibuster, and cloture of debate requires three-fifths of the senators present. (See Chapter 6 for discussion of these procedures.) The composition of the Senate Judiciary Committee as well as the Senate as a whole, then, is critical in determining whether a particular nominee will succeed.

Before the 1950s, the Senate Judiciary Committee rarely questioned nominees on their judicial views. Instead, committee inquiries would focus exclusively on qualifications. This norm changed in 1954, however. When President Eisenhower nominated John Marshall Harlan II to succeed Robert Jackson on the Supreme Court. The Senate did not act on his nomination, and Eisenhower had to nominate him a second time. The chairman of the Senate Judiciary Committee, Senator James Eastland of Mississippi, and several other southern Democratic senators delayed any hearings fearing that Harlan would support school integration and that he would further strengthen the Court's efforts to desegregate the South. When the committee finally did hold hearings, the senators grilled the normally reticent Harlan about his views on *Plessy v. Ferguson* and other judicial opinions. Every Supreme Court nominee since Harlan has been questioned about his or her views by the Judiciary Committee.

Since the mid-1950s, then, judicial appointments have become increasingly partisan and, ultimately, ideological. Today, the Judiciary Committee of the Senate subjects nominees for the federal judiciary to lengthy questioning about a wide range of issues, from gun rights to abortion to federal power under the commerce clause. Senators' support for or opposition to specific nominees turns on the individual's ideological and judicial views as much as qualifications. And, for their part, presidents nominate individuals who share their own political philosophy. Presidents Ronald Reagan and George H. W. Bush, for example, appointed five justices whom they believed to have conservative perspectives: Sandra Day O'Connor, Antonin Scalia, Anthony Kennedy, David Souter, and Clarence Thomas. Reagan also elevated William Rehnquist to the position of chief justice. Reagan and George H. W. Bush sought appointees who believed in reducing government intervention in the economy and supported the moral positions taken by the Republican Party in recent years, particularly opposition to abortion. However, not all the Reagan and Bush appointees fulfilled their sponsors' expectations. David Souter, for example, appointed by President George H. W. Bush, was attacked by conservatives as a turncoat for his decisions on school prayer and abortion rights. Nevertheless, through their appointments, Reagan and George H. W. Bush were able to create a far more conservative Supreme Court. For his part, President Clinton endeavored to appoint liberal justices. He named Ruth Bader Ginsburg and Stephen Breyer to the Court, hoping to counteract the influence of the Reagan and Bush appointees.

Table 9.3

SUPREME COURT JUSTICES, 2012

NAME	YEAR OF BIRTH	PRIOR EXPERIENCE	APPOINTED BY	YEAR OF APPOINTMENT
John G. Roberts, Jr., *Chief Justice*	**1955**	Federal judge	G. W. Bush	**2005**
Antonin Scalia	**1936**	Federal judge	Reagan	**1986**
Anthony M. Kennedy	**1936**	Federal judge	Reagan	**1988**
Clarence Thomas	**1948**	Federal judge	G. H. W. Bush	**1991**
Ruth Bader Ginsburg	**1933**	Federal judge	Clinton	**1993**
Stephen G. Breyer	**1938**	Federal judge	Clinton	**1994**
Samuel A. Alito, Jr.	**1950**	Federal judge	G. W. Bush	**2006**
Sonia Sotomayor	**1954**	Federal judge	Obama	**2009**
Elena Kagan	**1960**	Solicitor General	Obama	**2010**

In 2005, President George W. Bush was given an opportunity to put his own stamp on the Supreme Court after Justice O'Connor announced her decision to retire and Chief Justice Rehnquist died. Bush quickly nominated the federal appeals court judge John Roberts, initially to replace O'Connor and then as chief justice after Rehnquist's death. Roberts, a moderate conservative with an impressive legal record, provoked some Democratic opposition but was confirmed without much difficulty. Bush's next nominee, though, sparked an intense battle within the president's own party. To the surprise of most observers, the president named a long-time associate, White House counsel Harriet Miers, to replace O'Connor. Many Republicans viewed Miers as merely a Bush crony who lacked judicial qualifications and was insufficiently supportive of conservative causes. Opposition to Miers within the Republican Party was so intense that Democrats remained gleefully silent as the president was forced to allow her to withdraw her name from consideration. In the wake of the Miers debacle, President Bush turned to a more conventional nominee, the federal appeals court judge Samuel Alito, who pleased conservative Republicans. Democrats and liberal political forces attempted to block the nomination but ultimately failed, and

Alito was confirmed in February 2006. Barack Obama's nominations of Sonia Sotomayor and Elena Kagan to the Court were easily approved, despite Republican criticisms, thanks to a strong Democratic majority in the Senate (Table 9.3).

These struggles over judicial appointments reflect the growing intensity of partisanship in the United States today. They also indicate how much importance competing political forces attach to Supreme Court appointments. Because the contending forces see the outcome as critical, they are willing to engage in a fierce struggle when Supreme Court appointments are at stake.

The increasing role of partisanship or ideology in the nomination process creates a potential danger for the court system. Courts, as we said at the outset, derive much of their authority from their position of political independence, as nonpartisan arbiters in our society. The politics of appointments, which have grown increasingly focused on ideology, risks tainting judges and the judicial process as little more than extensions of the political views of the people who nominated them. Fortunately, the individuals appointed to the federal judiciary tend to have a strong independent sense of themselves and their mission. Throughout the history of the federal courts we find instances of judges who have frustrated the presidents who appointed them.

HOW COURTS WORK AS POLITICAL INSTITUTIONS

Judges are central players in important political institutions, and this role makes them politicians. To understand what animates judicial behavior, we need to place the judge or justice in context by considering the role of the courts in the political system more generally. In doing so, we emphasize the role of the courts as dispute resolvers, coordinators, and interpreters of rules.

Dispute Resolution

Much productive activity occurs in a modern society because its members do not have to devote substantial resources to protecting themselves and their property or monitoring compliance with agreements. For any potential violation of person or property or defection from an agreement, all parties know in advance that an aggrieved party may take an alleged violator to court. The court, in turn, is a venue in which the facts of a case are established, punishment is meted out to violators, and compensation awarded to victims. An employee, for example, may sue his or her employer for allegedly violating the terms of a privately negotiated employment contract. Or a consumer may sue a producer for violating the terms of a product warranty. The court, then, is an institution that engages in fact-finding and judgment. It provides the service of dispute resolution. In criminal cases, the "aggrieved party" is not only the victim of the crime but also the entire society whose laws have been violated.

Coordination

Dispute resolution occurs after the fact—that is, after a dispute has occurred. We may also think of courts and judges as before-the-fact coordination mechanisms inasmuch as the anticipation of legal consequences allows private parties to form rational expectations and thereby coordinate their actions in advance of possible disputes. A prospective embezzler, estimating the odds of getting caught, prosecuted, and subsequently punished, may think twice about cheating his partner. Conversely, the legal system can work as an incentive: two acquaintances, for example, may confidently entertain the possibility of going into business together, knowing that the sword of justice hangs over their collaboration.

In this sense, the court system is as important for what it doesn't do as for what it does. The system of courts and law coordinates private behavior by providing incentives and disincentives for specific actions. To the extent that these work, there are fewer disputes to resolve and thus less after-the-fact dispute resolution for courts and judges to engage in.

Rule Interpretation

Dispute resolution and coordination affect private behavior and the daily lives of ordinary citizens tremendously. Judges, however, are not entirely free agents. In matching the facts of a specific case to judicial principles and statutory guidelines, judges must engage in interpretive activity: they must determine what particular statutes or judicial principles mean, which of them fit the facts of a particular case, and then, having determined this, ascertain the disposition of the case at hand. Does the statute of 1927 regulating the electronic transmission of radio waves apply to television, cellular phones, ship-to-shore radios, fax machines, and e-mail? Does the law governing the transportation of dangerous substances, passed in 1937, apply to nuclear fuels, infected animals, and artificially created biological hazards? Often the enacting legislative body has not been entirely clear about the scope of the legislation it passed.

Interpreting the rules is probably the single most important activity in which higher courts engage. This is because the court system is hierarchical in the sense that judgments by higher courts constrain the discretion of judges in lower courts. If the Supreme Court rules that nuclear fuels are covered by the 1937 law on transporting dangerous substances, then lower courts must render subsequent judgments in a manner consistent with this ruling.

As we see in the following section, courts and judges engage not only in statutory interpretation but in constitutional interpretation as well. Here they interpret the provisions of the U.S. Constitution, determining their scope and content. In determining, for example, whether the act of Congress regulating the transportation of dangerous substances from one state to another is constitutional, the justices of the Supreme Court might invoke the commerce clause of the Constitution (allowing the federal government to regulate interstate commerce) to justify the constitutionality of the act. On the other hand, a Supreme

Court majority might also rule that a shipment of spent fuel rods from a nuclear reactor in Kansas City to a nuclear-waste facility outside St. Louis is not covered by this law because the shipment took place entirely within the boundaries of a single state and thus did not constitute interstate commerce.

In short, judges and justices are continually engaged in elaborating, embellishing, even rewriting the rules by which private and public life are organized. However, judicial interpretation—elaboration, embellishment, and "redrafting"—of statutes is naturally subject to review. Statutory interpretation, even if it is conducted by the highest court in the land, is exposed to legislative review. If Congress is unhappy with a specific statutory interpretation, then it may amend the legislation so as to overcome the Court's objection or even reverse its ruling. In January 2005, for example, the Supreme Court struck down the mandatory-sentencing rules enacted by Congress in 1984.[6] The rules severely limited judicial discretion in the realm of sentencing and had long been resented by the bench. Members of Congress vowed to reinstate the guidelines through new legislation. Senator Jeff Sessions (R-Ala.) said, "The challenge will be to . . . re-create the guidelines in a way that will meet the court's test."[7] Of course, if the court makes a constitutional ruling, Congress cannot then abrogate that ruling through new legislation. Congress would need to commence the process of constitutional amendment to overturn a constitutional interpretation with which it disagreed.

THE POWER OF JUDICIAL REVIEW

The phrase judicial review refers to the power of the judiciary to examine and, if necessary, invalidate actions undertaken by the legislative and executive branches. The phrase is sometimes also used to describe the scrutiny that appellate courts give to the actions of trial courts, but strictly speaking, that is an improper usage. A higher court's examination of a lower court's decisions might be called appellate review, but it is not judicial review (Figure 9.3).

judicial review

The power of the courts to declare actions of the legislative and executive branches invalid or unconstitutional. The Supreme Court asserted this power in *Marbury v. Madison* (1803)

The development of judicial review, which is not expressed explicitly in the Constitution, is one of the most powerful expressions of the independent judiciary. In countries without an independent judiciary and without judicial review, the parliament or the executive is the ultimate authority. In English law, for example, the parliament is sovereign. Judicial review exists only in scrutinizing the administration of the laws. An individual cannot challenge an act of Parliament in the courts and ask that the courts void that law as a violation of the constitution. But in the U.S. system of government the process of judicial review has taken root and is an essential means by which the judiciary checks the legislature and executive.

6 *United States v. Booker*, 543 U.S. 220 (2005).

7 Quoted in Carl Hulse and Adam Liptak, "New Fight over Controlling Punishments Is Widely Seen," *New York Times*, January 13, 2005, p. A27.

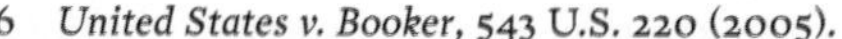

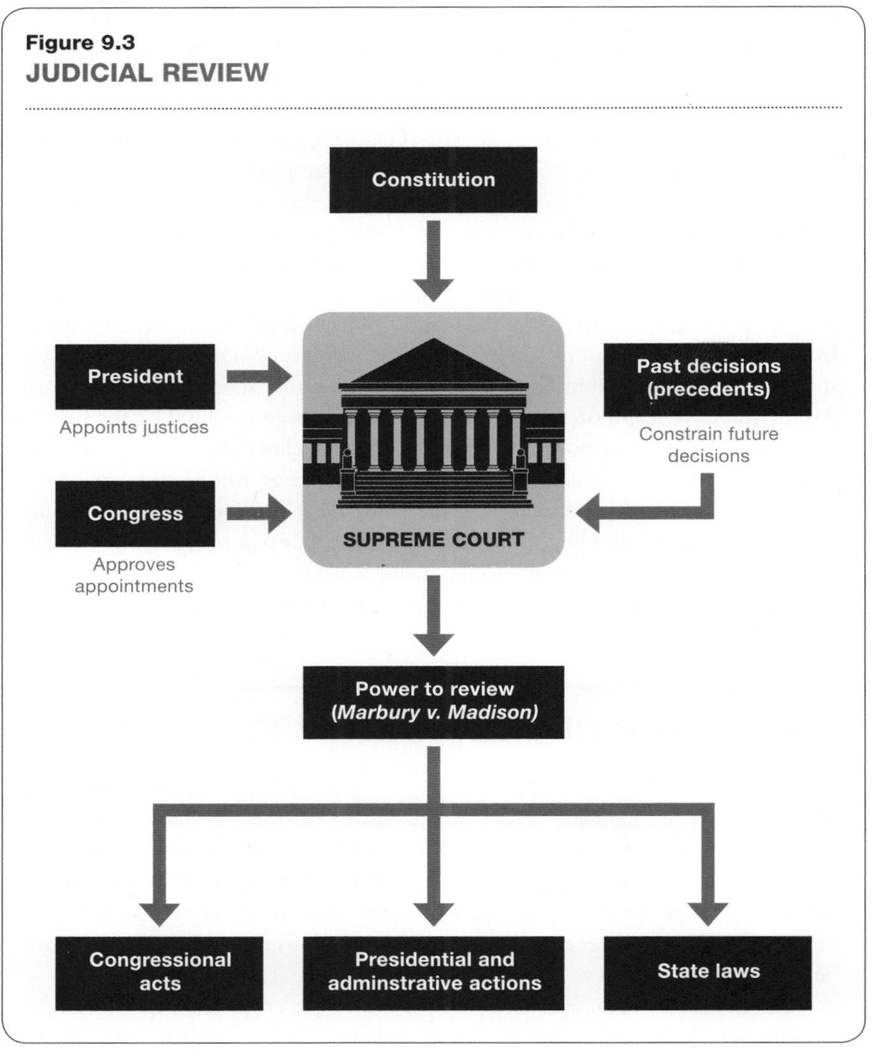

Judicial Review of Acts of Congress

Because the Constitution does not give the Supreme Court the power of judicial review of congressional enactments, the Court's exercise of it may be seen as something of a usurpation. Among the proposals debated at the Constitutional Convention was one to create a council composed of the president and the judiciary that would share the veto power over legislation. Another proposal was to route all legislation through both the Court and the president; overruling a veto by either one would have required a two-thirds vote of the House and the Senate. Those and other proposals were rejected by the delegates, and no further effort was made to give the Supreme Court review power over the other branches. This does not prove that the framers of the Constitution opposed judicial review, but it does indicate that "if they intended to provide for it in the Constitution, they did so in a most obscure fashion."[8]

Disputes over the intentions of the framers were settled in 1803 in the case of *Marbury v. Madison*.[9] In that case, William Marbury sued Secretary of State James Madison for Madison's failure to complete Marbury's appointment to a lower judgeship that had been initiated by the outgoing administration of President John Adams. Quite apart from the details of the case, Chief Justice John Marshall, speaking on behalf of the Court, used the case to declare a portion of a law unconstitutional. In effect, he stated that although the substance of Marbury's request was not unreasonable, the Court's jurisdiction in the matter was based on a section of the Judiciary Act of 1789, which the Court declared unconstitutional.

Although Congress and the president have often been at odds with the Court, its legal power to review acts of Congress has not been seriously questioned since 1803. One reason is that judicial power has been accepted as natural, if not intended. Another reason is that during the early years of the Republic, the Supreme Court was careful to use its power sparingly, striking down only two pieces of legislation during the first 75 years of its history. One of these decisions was the 1857 *Dred Scott* ruling, which invalidated the Missouri Compromise and helped precipitate the Civil War. In *Dred Scott v. Sandford*, Chief Justice Roger Taney wrote in the Court's majority opinion that the fact that a slave, Dred Scott, had been transported to a free state (Illinois) and a free territory (Wisconsin) before returning to the slave state of Missouri did not alter the fact that he was property.[10] This ruling had the effect of invalidating a portion of the Missouri Compromise of 1820, thus permitting slavery in all the country's territories. In recent years, with the power of judicial review securely accepted, the Court has been more willing to use it. Between 1986 and 2007, the Supreme Court struck down more than 36 acts of Congress.

Judicial Review of State Actions

The power of the Supreme Court to review state legislation or other state action and to determine its constitutionality is neither granted by the Constitution nor inherent in the federal system. But the logic of the supremacy clause of Article VI of the Constitution—which declares the Constitution and laws made under its authority to be the supreme law of the land—is very strong. Furthermore, in the Judiciary Act of 1789, Congress conferred on the Supreme Court the power

supremacy clause

A clause of Article VI of the Constitution that states that all laws passed by the national government and all treaties are the supreme laws of the land and superior to all laws adopted by any state or any subdivision

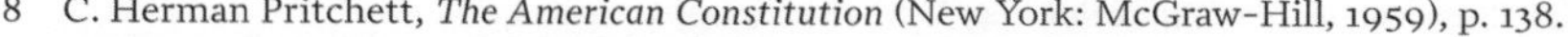

8 C. Herman Pritchett, *The American Constitution* (New York: McGraw-Hill, 1959), p. 138.

9 *Marbury v. Madison*, 1 Cranch 137 (1803).

10 *Dred Scott v. Sandford*, 60 U.S. 393 (1857).

to reverse state constitutions and laws whenever they are clearly in conflict with the U.S. Constitution, federal laws, or treaties.[11] This power gives the Supreme Court jurisdiction over all of the millions of cases handled by American courts each year.

The civil rights area abounds with examples of state laws that were overturned because the statutes violated the guarantees of due process and equal protection contained in the Fourteenth Amendment to the Constitution. For example, in the 1954 case of *Brown v. Board of Education*, the Court overturned statutes in Kansas, South Carolina, Virginia, and Delaware that either required or permitted segregated public schools, on the basis that such statutes denied black schoolchildren equal protection of the law.[12] In 1967 in *Loving v. Virginia*, the Court invalidated a Virginia statute prohibiting interracial marriages.[13] State statutes in other areas are equally subject to challenge. In *Griswold v. Connecticut*, the Court invalidated a Connecticut statute prohibiting the general distribution of contraceptives to married couples, on the basis that the statute violated the couples' right to marital privacy.[14]

Judicial Review of Federal Agency Actions

Although Congress makes the law, as we saw in Chapters 6 and 8, Congress can hardly administer the thousands of programs it has enacted and must delegate power to the president and to a huge bureaucracy to achieve its purposes. For example, if Congress wishes to improve air quality, it cannot possibly anticipate all the conditions and circumstances that may arise over the years with respect to its general goal. Inevitably Congress must delegate to the executive substantial discretionary power to make judgments about the best ways to bring about improved air quality in the face of changing circumstances. Thus, over time, almost any congressional program will result in thousands and thousands of pages of administrative regulations developed by executive agencies nominally seeking to implement the will of Congress.

The issue of delegation of power has led to a number of court decisions over the past two centuries, generally involving the question of the scope of the delegation. Courts have also been called on to decide whether the rules and regulations adopted by federal agencies are consistent with Congress's express or implied intent.

As presidential power expanded during the New Deal era, one measure of increased congressional subordination to the executive was the enactment of laws that contained few if any principles limiting executive discretion. Congress

11 This review power was affirmed by the Supreme Court in *Martin v. Hunter's Lessee*, 14 U.S. 304 (1816).

12 *Brown v. Board of Education*, 347 U.S. 483 (1954).

13 *Loving v. Virginia*, 388 U.S. 1 (1967).

14 *Griswold v. Connecticut*, 381 U.S. 479 (1965).

enacted legislation, often at the president's behest, that gave the executive virtually unfettered authority to address a particular concern. For example, the Emergency Price Control Act of 1942 authorized the executive to set "fair and equitable" prices without offering any indication of what those terms might mean. Although the Court initially challenged these delegations of power to the president during the New Deal, a confrontation with President Franklin Delano Roosevelt caused the Court to retreat from its position. Perhaps as a result, no congressional delegation of power to the president has been struck down as impermissibly broad since then. In the last two decades in particular, the Supreme Court has found that as long as federal agencies developed rules and regulations "based upon a permissible construction" or "reasonable interpretation" of Congress's statute, the judiciary would accept the views of the executive branch.[15] Generally the courts give considerable deference to administrative agencies as long as those agencies have engaged in a formal rule-making process and can show that they have carried out the conditions prescribed by the various statutes governing agency rule making. These statutes include the 1946 Administrative Procedure Act, which requires agencies to notify parties affected by proposed rules and to allow them ample time to comment on such rules before they go into effect.

Judicial Review and Presidential Power

The federal courts are also called on to review the actions of the president. As we saw in Chapter 7, presidents have increasingly made use of unilateral executive powers rather than relying on congressional legislation to achieve their objectives. On many occasions, presidential orders and actions have been challenged in the federal courts by members of Congress and by individuals and groups opposing the president's policies. In recent years, assertions of presidential power in such realms as foreign policy, war and emergency powers, legislative power, and administrative authority have, more often than not, been upheld by the federal bench. Indeed, the federal judiciary has sometimes taken extraordinary presidential claims that were made for limited and temporary purposes and rationalized them—that is, the Court has converted them into routine and permanent instruments of presidential government. Take, for example, Richard Nixon's sweeping claims of executive privilege. In *United States v. Nixon*, the Court, to be sure, rejected the president's refusal to turn over tape recordings to congressional investigators. For the first time, though, the justices recognized the validity of the principle of executive privilege and discussed the situations in which such claims might be appropriate.[16] This judicial recognition of executive privilege encouraged Presidents Bill Clinton and George W. Bush to base broad

15 *Cookman Realty Group, Inc. v. West Virginia Division of Environmental Protection*, no. 30116 (W. Va. S. Ct. App. 2002).

16 *United States v. Nixon*, 418 U.S. 683 (1974).

claims on that principle during their terms in office.[17] Executive privilege has even been invoked to protect the deliberations of the vice president from congressional scrutiny, in the case of Dick Cheney's consultations with representatives of the energy industry.

This pattern of judicial deference to presidential authority is also manifest in the Supreme Court's recent decisions regarding President Bush's war on terrorism. In June 2004, the Supreme Court ruled on three cases involving the president's antiterrorism initiatives and claims of executive power and in two of them appeared to place some limits on presidential authority. Although the Court's decisions were widely hailed as reining in the executive branch, they fell far short of stopping presidential power in its tracks.

Perhaps the most important of these cases was *Hamdi v. Rumsfeld*.[18] In June 2004, the Supreme Court ruled that Yaser Esam Hamdi was entitled to a lawyer and "a fair opportunity to rebut the government's factual assertions." However, the Supreme Court affirmed that the president possessed the authority to declare a U.S. citizen an enemy combatant and order that such an individual be held in federal detention. Several of the justices intimated that once designated an enemy combatant, a U.S. citizen might be tried before a military tribunal, with the normal presumption of innocence suspended. In 2006, in *Hamdan v. Rumsfeld*, the Court ruled that the military commissions established to try enemy combatants and other detainees violated both the Uniform Code of Military Justice and the Geneva Conventions.[19]

Thus the Supreme Court did assert that presidential actions were subject to judicial scrutiny and placed some constraints on the president's power. But at the same time, the Court affirmed the president's single most important claim: the unilateral power to declare individuals, including U.S. citizens, "enemy combatants" who could be detained by federal authorities under adverse legal circumstances.

Judicial Review and Lawmaking

Much of the work of the courts involves the application of statutes to a particular case at hand. Over the centuries, however, judges have developed a body of rules and principles of interpretation that are not grounded in specific statutes. This body of judge-made law is called common law.

The appellate courts are in another realm. Their rulings can be considered laws, but they are laws governing only the behavior of the judiciary. They

17 On Clinton, see Jonathan Turley, "Paradise Lost: The Clinton Administration and the Erosion of Executive Privilege," *Maryland Law Review* 60 (2001): 295. On Bush, see Jeffrey P. Carlin, "*Walker v. Cheney*: Politics, Posturing, and Executive Privilege," *Southern California Law Review* 76 (November 2002): 235.

18 *Hamdi v. Rumsfeld*, 542 U.S. 507 (2004).

19 *Hamdan v. Rumsfeld*, 548 U.S. 557 (2006).

influence citizens' conduct only because, in the words of Justice Oliver Wendell Holmes, Jr. (who served on the Supreme Court from 1902 to 1932), lawyers make "prophecies of what the courts will do in fact."[20]

The written opinion of an appellate court is about halfway between common law and statutory law. It is judge made and draws heavily on the precedents of previous cases. In that it tries to articulate the rule of law controlling the case in question and future cases like it, it is like a statute. But a statute addresses itself to the future conduct of citizens, whereas a written opinion addresses itself mainly to the willingness or ability of courts in the future to take cases and render favorable opinions.

An example may help clarify the distinction. In *Gideon v. Wainwright*, the Supreme Court ordered a new trial for Clarence Earl Gideon, an indigent defendant, because he had been denied the right to legal counsel. This ruling said to all trial judges and prosecutors that henceforth they would be wasting their time if they cut corners in the trials of indigent defendants.[21] The Court was thereby predicting what it would and would not do in future cases of this sort. It also invited thousands of prisoners to appeal their convictions.

Many areas of civil law have been constructed in the same way—by judicial messages to other judges, some of which are codified eventually in legislative enactments. It has become "the law," for example, that employers are liable for injuries in the workplace without regard to negligence. But the law in this instance is simply a series of messages to lawyers that they should advise their corporate clients not to appeal injury decisions.

In the realm of criminal law, almost all the dramatic changes in the treatment of criminals and persons accused of crimes have been made by the appellate courts, especially the Supreme Court. The Supreme Court brought about a veritable revolution in the criminal process with three cases over less than five years. The first, *Gideon v. Wainwright*, in 1963, was just discussed. The second, *Escobedo v. Illinois*, in 1964, gave suspects the right to remain silent and the right to have counsel present during questioning.[22] But the decision left confusion that allowed differing decisions to be made by lower courts. In the third case, *Miranda v. Arizona*, in 1966, the Supreme Court cleared up the confusion by setting forth what is known as the Miranda rule: arrested people have the right to remain silent, the right to be informed that anything they say can be held against them, and the right to counsel before and during police interrogation.[23]

One of the most significant changes brought about by the Supreme Court was the revolution in legislative representation unleashed by the 1962 case of *Baker v. Carr*.[24] In this landmark case, the Supreme Court held that it could no longer avoid reviewing complaints about the apportionment of seats in state

20 Oliver Wendell Holmes, Jr., "The Path of the Law," *Harvard Law Review* 10 (1897): 457.

21 *Gideon v. Wainwright*, 372 U.S. 335 (1963).

22 *Escobedo v. Illinois*, 378 U.S. 478 (1964).

23 *Miranda v. Arizona*, 384 U.S. 436 (1966).

24 *Baker v. Carr*, 369 U.S. 186 (1962).

legislatures. Following that decision, the federal courts went on to force reapportionment of all state, county, and local legislatures in the country.

As these various cases illustrate, the appellate courts are intimately involved in creating and interpreting laws. Many experts on court history and constitutional law criticize the federal appellate courts for being too willing to introduce radical change, even when the experts agree with the general direction of the changes. Often they are troubled by the willingness of the courts (especially the Supreme Court) to jump into such cases prematurely—before the constitutional issues have been fully clarified by decisions of district and appeals courts in many related cases in various parts of the country.[25] But from the perspective of the appellate judiciary, and especially the Supreme Court, the situation is one of choosing between the lesser of two evils: they must take the cases as they come and then weigh the risks of opening new options against the risks of embracing the status quo.

THE SUPREME COURT IN ACTION

The Supreme Court sits at the pinnacle of the U.S. judiciary. It is the only court expressly mentioned in the Constitution, and it is one of the most distinctive political bodies created by the U.S. system. The Supreme Court is often the focal point for understanding the judiciary both because of its special constitutional status but also because it embodies the many principles of the American court system—its independence, its durability, the collective nature of court decision making, and the delicate balance that judges strike between historical precedent and new interpretation. The Supreme Court plays a vital role in the government as it is part of the structure of checks and balances that prevents the legislative and executive branches from abusing their power. The Court also operates as an institution unto itself. It has its own internal rules for decision making, its own version of the policy principle discussed in Chapter 1.

How Cases Reach the Supreme Court

Given the millions of disputes that arise every year, the job of the Supreme Court would be impossible if it were not able to control the flow of cases and its own caseload. The Supreme Court has original jurisdiction in a limited variety of cases defined by the Constitution. Original jurisdiction includes: (1) cases between the United States and one of the 50 states; (2) cases between two or

25 See Philip B. Kurland, *Politics, the Constitution, and the Warren Court* (Chicago: University of Chicago Press, 1970).

more states; (3) cases involving foreign ambassadors or other ministers; and (4) cases brought by one state against citizens of another state or against a foreign country. The most important of these cases are disputes between states over land, water, or old debts. Generally the Supreme Court deals with these cases by appointing a "special master," usually a retired judge, to hear the case and present a report. The Supreme Court then allows the states involved in the dispute to present arguments for or against the master's opinion.[26]

Rules of Access. Over the years, the courts have developed specific rules that govern which cases within their jurisdiction they will and will not hear. Thus the Court is an institution very much in control of its own agenda, which, according to the institution principle, gives it a great deal of independence to follow the preferences of its members. To have access to the courts, cases must meet certain criteria that are initially applied by the trial court but may be reconsidered by appellate courts. These rules of access can be broken down into three major categories: case or controversy, standing, and mootness.

Both Article III of the Constitution and past Supreme Court decisions define judicial power as extending only to "cases and controversies." This means that the case before a court must be an actual controversy, not a hypothetical one, with two truly adversarial parties. The courts have interpreted this language to mean that they do not have the power to render advisory opinions to legislatures or agencies about the constitutionality of proposed laws or regulations. Furthermore, even after a law is enacted, the courts will generally refuse to consider its constitutionality until it is actually applied.

Parties to a case must also have standing—that is, they must show that they have a substantial stake in the outcome of the case. The traditional requirement for standing has been that one must show injury to oneself; that injury can be personal, economic, or even aesthetic, for example. In order for a group or class of people to have standing (as in class-action suits), each member must show specific injury. This means that a general interest in the environment, for instance, does not provide a group with a sufficient basis for standing.

standing

The right of an individual or an organization to initiate a court case

The third criterion in determining whether the Supreme Court will hear a case is mootness. In theory, this requirement disqualifies cases that are brought too late—after the relevant facts have changed or the problem has been resolved by other means. The criterion of mootness, however, is subject to the discretion of the courts, which have begun to relax the rules pertaining to this criterion, particularly in cases in which a situation that has been resolved is likely to come up again. In the abortion case of *Roe v. Wade*, for example, the Supreme Court rejected the lower court's argument that because the pregnancy had already come to term, the case was moot. The Court agreed to hear the case because no pregnancy was likely to outlast the lengthy appeals process.

mootness

A criterion used by courts to avoid hearing cases that no longer require resolution

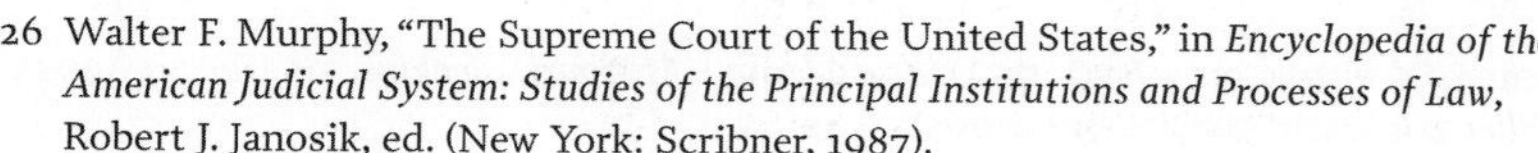
26 Walter F. Murphy, "The Supreme Court of the United States," in *Encyclopedia of the American Judicial System: Studies of the Principal Institutions and Processes of Law*, Robert J. Janosik, ed. (New York: Scribner, 1987).

Putting aside the formal criteria, the Supreme Court is most likely to accept cases that involve conflicting decisions by the federal circuit courts, cases that present important questions of civil rights or civil liberties, and cases in which the federal government is the appellant.[27] Ultimately, however, the question of which cases are accepted can come down to the preferences and priorities of the justices. If a number of justices believe that the Court should intervene in a particular area of policy or politics, they are likely to look for a case or cases that will be vehicles for judicial intervention. For many years, for example, the Court was not interested in considering challenges to affirmative action or other programs designed to provide particular benefits to minorities. In recent years, however, several of the Court's more conservative justices have been eager to push back the limits of affirmative action and racial preference and have therefore accepted a number of cases that would allow them to do so. In 1995, the Court's decisions in *Adarand Constructors v. Pena*, *Missouri v. Jenkins*, and *Miller v. Johnson* placed new restrictions on federal affirmative action programs, school desegregation efforts, and attempts to increase minority representation in Congress through the creation of "minority districts" (see Chapter 11).[28] Similarly, the Court has taken on some social issues that it and other branches of the federal government have long avoided, such as gun control. Laws regulating gun ownership and licensing have been left to the states. Inconsistencies across states' gun laws have fueled debate at the national level between those activists who want strict, national regulation of gun ownership and those who want minimal regulations. The heart of the debate is the Second Amendment to the Constitution and the meaning of the "right to bear arms." The Supreme Court has heard several cases dealing with the Second Amendment, including the 1939 case of *United States v. Miller*.[29] In 2003, six residents of the District of Columbia sued in federal district court to challenge a D.C. law banning residents from owing handguns. The federal district court dismissed the lawsuit, and the plaintiffs appealed to the U.S. Court of Appeals, which reversed the district court in a 2-to-1 vote, declaring the District of Columbia's gun law unconstitutional. In 2008, the Supreme Court ruled that the district could require Heller and the other plaintiffs to register their handguns and obtain licenses to carry handguns, but that the plaintiffs clearly had a right to have handguns. In 2010, the Court went further in *McDonald v. Chicago*, ruling that the Second Amendment right to "bear arms" applied to the states.

writ of *certiorari*

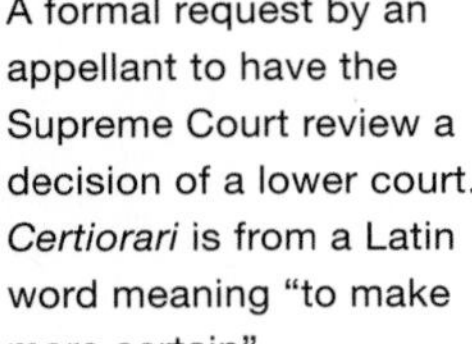

A formal request by an appellant to have the Supreme Court review a decision of a lower court. *Certiorari* is from a Latin word meaning "to make more certain"

Most cases reach the Supreme Court through a writ of *certiorari* (Figure 9.4). *Certiorari* is an order to a lower court to deliver the records of a particular case to be reviewed for legal errors. The term is sometimes shortened to *cert*, and cases deemed to merit *certiorari* are referred to as *certworthy*. An individual who loses in

27 Gregory A. Caldeira and John R. Wright, "Organized Interests and Agenda Setting in the U.S. Supreme Court," *American Political Science Review* 82, no. 4 (December 1988): 1109–27.

28 *Adarand Constructors v. Pena*, 115 U.S. 200 (1995); *Missouri v. Jenkins*, 515 U.S. 70 (1995); *Miller v. Johnson*, 515 U.S. 900 (1995).

29 *United States v. Miller*, 307 U.S. 134 (1939).

Figure 9.4

REACHING THE SUPREME COURT THROUGH *CERTIORARI*

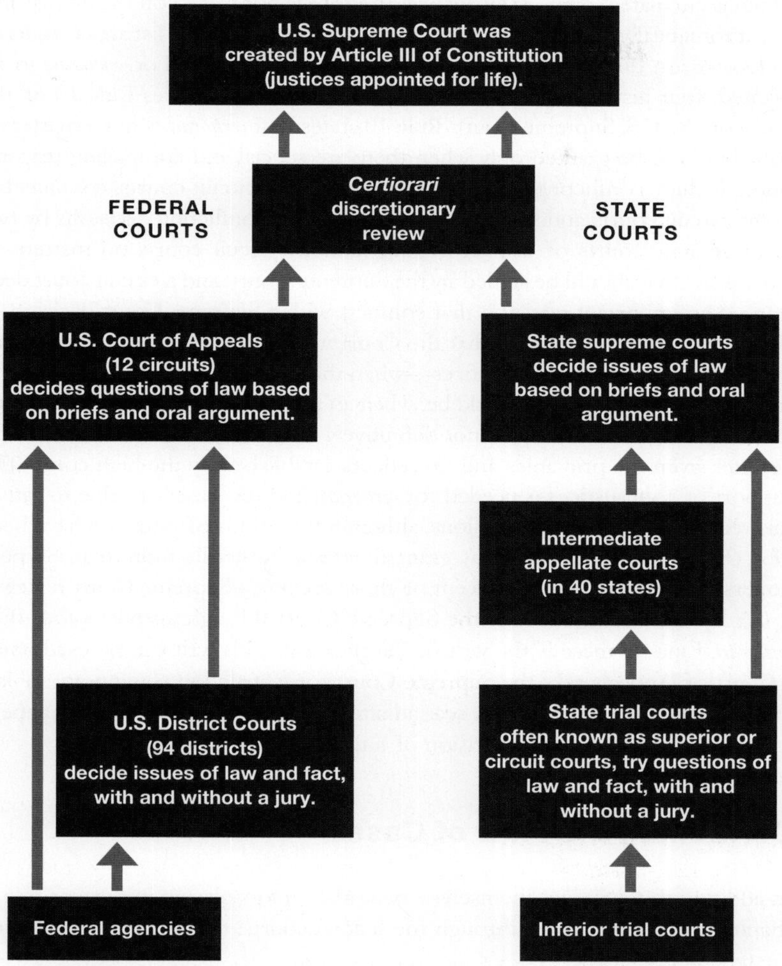

a lower federal court or a state court and wants the Supreme Court to review the decision has 90 days to file a petition for a writ of *certiorari* with the clerk of the Supreme Court. There are two types of petitions: paid petitions and petitions *in forma pauperis* ("in the form of a pauper"). The former requires the payment of filing fees, submission of a certain number of copies, and compliance with a variety of other rules. For *in forma pauperis* petitions, which are usually filed by prison inmates, the Court waives the fees and most other requirements.

Since 1972, most of the justices have participated in a "*certiorari* pool" in which their law clerks work together to evaluate the petitions. Each petition is reviewed by one clerk, who writes a memo summarizing the facts and issues and making a recommendation for all the justices participating in the pool. Clerks for the other justices add their comments to the memo. After the justices have reviewed the memos, any one of them may place any case on the discuss list, which is circulated by the chief justice. If a case is not placed on the discuss list, it is automatically denied *certiorari*. Cases placed on the discuss list are considered and voted on during the justices' closed-door conference. For *certiorari* to be granted, four justices must be convinced that the case satisfies Rule 10 of the Rules of the U.S. Supreme Court. Rule 10 states that *certiorari* is not a matter of right but is to be granted only when there are special and compelling reasons. These include conflicting decisions by two or more circuit courts, conflicts between circuit courts and state courts of last resort, conflicting decisions by two or more state courts of last resort, decisions by circuit courts on matters of federal law that should be settled by the Supreme Court, and a circuit court decision on an important question that conflicts with a Supreme Court decision. It should be clear from this list that the Court will usually take action under only the most compelling circumstances—when there are conflicts among the lower courts about what the law should be, when an important legal question has been raised in the lower courts and not definitively answered, or when a lower court deviates from the principles and precedents established by the high court. The support of four justices is needed for *certiorari*, and few cases are able to satisfy this requirement. In recent sessions, although thousands of petitions have been filed (Figure 9.5), the Court has granted *certiorari* to hardly more than 80 petitioners each year—about 1 percent of those seeking a Supreme Court review.

A handful of cases reach the Supreme Court through avenues other than *certiorari*. One of these is the writ of certification. This writ can be used when a Court of Appeals asks the Supreme Court for instructions on a point of law that has never been decided. A second alternative avenue is the writ of appeal, which is used to appeal the decision of a three-judge district court.

Controlling the Flow of Cases

In addition to the judges themselves, two other actors play an important role in shaping the flow of cases through the federal courts: the solicitor general and the federal law clerks.

The Solicitor General. If any single person has greater influence than the individual justices over the work of the Supreme Court, it is the solicitor general of the United States. The solicitor general is third in status in the Justice Department (below the attorney general and the deputy attorney general), but he or she is the top government lawyer in virtually all cases before the appellate courts in which the government is a party. Although others can regulate the flow of cases, the solicitor general has the greatest control, with no review of his or her actions by any higher authority in the executive branch. More than half the Supreme Court's total workload consists of cases under the direct charge of the solicitor general.

Figure 9.5
CASES FILED IN THE U.S. SUPREME COURT

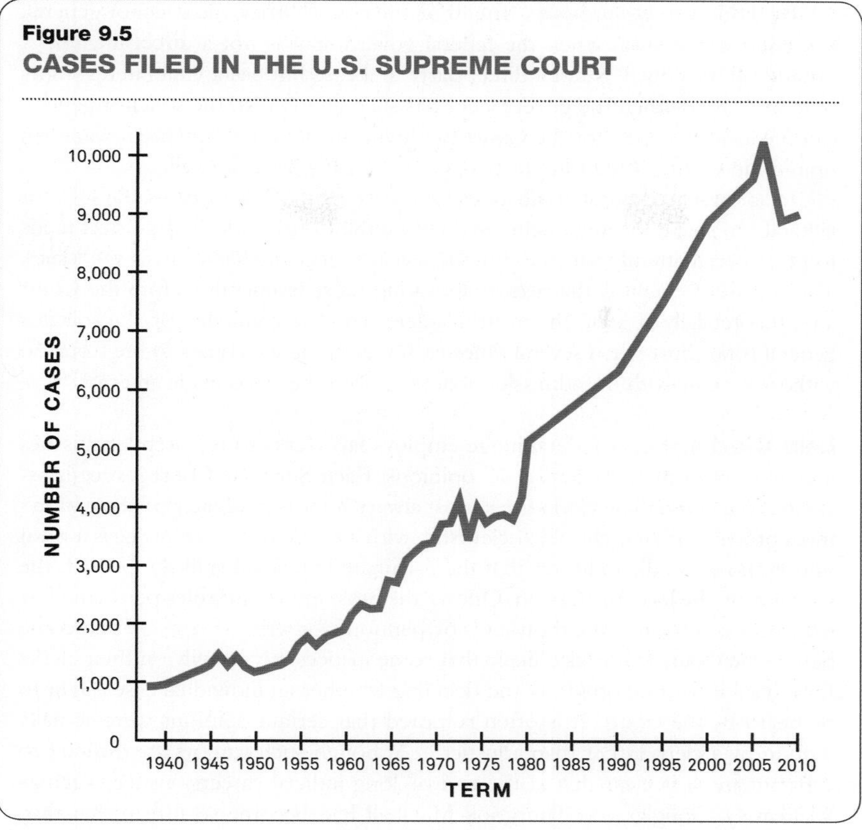

SOURCES: Years 1938–69: successive volumes of U.S. Bureau of the Census, *Statistical Abstract of the United States* (Washington, DC: Government Printing Office); 1970–79: Office of the Clerk of the Supreme Court; 1980–2010: U.S. Census Bureau, *The 2012 Statistical Abstract*, Table 331, www.census.gov/prod/2011pubs/12statab/law.pd (accessed 12/8/12).

The solicitor general exercises especially strong influence by screening cases long before they approach the Supreme Court; indeed, the justices rely on the solicitor general to "screen out undeserving litigation and furnish them with an agenda to hear government cases that deserve serious consideration."[30] Typically, more requests for appeals are rejected than are accepted by the solicitor general. Agency heads may lobby the president or otherwise try to circumvent the solicitor general, and a few of the independent agencies have a statutory right to make direct appeals, but without the solicitor general's support these are seldom reviewed by the Court.

30 Robert Scigliano, *The Supreme Court and the Presidency* (New York: Free Press, 1971), p. 162. For an interesting critique of the solicitor general's role during the Reagan administration, see Lincoln Caplan, "Annals of the Law," *New Yorker*, August 17, 1987, pp. 30–62.

amicus curiae

"Friend of the court," an individual or group who is not party to a lawsuit but seeks to assist the court in reaching a decision by presenting an additional brief

By writing an *amicus curiae* ("friend of the court") brief, the solicitor general, can enter a case even when the federal government is not a direct litigant. A "friend of the court" is not a direct party to a case but has a vital interest in its outcome. Thus when the government has such an interest, the solicitor general can file as *amicus curiae*, or the Court can invite such a brief because it wants an opinion in writing. Other interested parties may file briefs as well.

In addition to exercising substantial control over the flow of cases, the solicitor general can shape the arguments used before the Court. Indeed, the Court tends to give special attention to the way the solicitor general characterizes the issues. The solicitor general is the person appearing most frequently before the Court and, theoretically at least, the most disinterested. The credibility of the solicitor general is not hurt when several times each year he or she comes to the Court to withdraw a case with the admission that the government has made an error.[31]

Law Clerks. Every federal judge employs law clerks to research legal issues and assist with the preparation of opinions. Each Supreme Court justice is assigned four clerks. The clerks are almost always honors graduates of the nation's most prestigious law schools. A clerkship with a Supreme Court justice is a great honor and generally indicates that the fortunate individual is likely to reach the very top of the legal profession. One of the most important roles performed by the clerks is screening the thousands of petitions for writs of *certiorari* that come before the Court.[32] It is also likely that some justices rely heavily on their clerks for advice in writing opinions and deciding whether an individual case ought to be heard by the Court. It is often rumored that certain opinions were actually written by a clerk rather than a justice.[33] Although such rumors are difficult to substantiate, it is clear that at the end of long judicial careers, justices such as William O. Douglas and Thurgood Marshall had become so infirm that they were compelled to rely on the judgments of their law clerks.

The Supreme Court's Procedures

brief 

A written document in which an attorney explains—using case precedents—why the Court should rule in favor of his or her client

The Preparation. The Supreme Court's decision to accept a case is the beginning of what can be a lengthy and complex process (Figure 9.6). First, the attorneys on both sides must prepare briefs—written documents in which

31 On the strategic and informational role played by the solicitor general, see Kevin McGuire, "Explaining Executive Success in the U.S. Supreme Court," *Political Research Quarterly* 51 (1998): 505–26. Also see Michael Bailey, Brian Kamoie, and Forrest Maltzman, "Signals from the Tenth Justice: The Political Role of the Solicitor General in Supreme Court Decision Making," *American Journal of Political Science* 49 (2005): 72–85.

32 H. W. Perry, Jr., *Deciding to Decide: Agenda Setting in the United States Supreme Court* (Cambridge, MA.: Harvard University Press, 1991).

33 Edward Lazarus, *Closed Chambers: The First Eyewitness Account of the Struggles inside the Supreme Court* (New York: Times Books, 1998).

Figure 9.6
THE SUPREME COURT'S DECISION-MAKING PROCESS

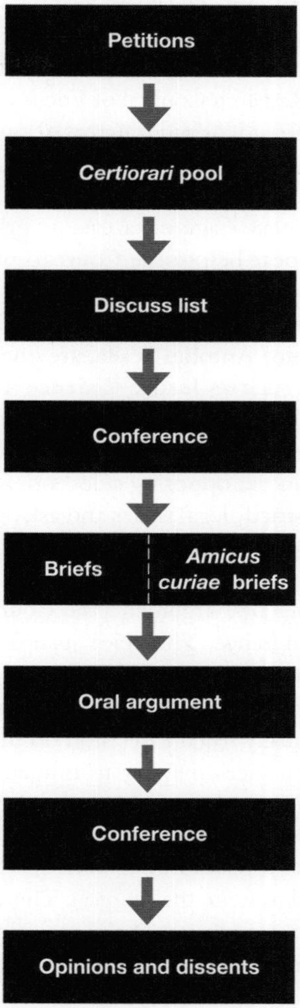

the attorneys explain why the Court should rule in favor of their client. The document filed by the individual bringing the case is called the petitioner's brief. It summarizes the facts of the case and presents the legal basis on which the Supreme Court is being asked to overturn the lower court's decision. The document filed by the side that prevailed in the lower court is called the respondent's brief. It explains why the Supreme Court should affirm the lower court's verdict. The petitioners then file a brief answering and attempting to refute the points made in the respondent's brief. This document is called the petitioner's reply brief. Briefs are filled with references to precedents specifically chosen to show that other courts have frequently ruled in the same way that the Supreme Court is being asked to rule.

As the attorneys prepare their briefs, they often ask sympathetic interest groups for their help by means of *amicus curiae* briefs. In a case involving separation of church and state, for example, liberal groups such as the American Civil Liberties Union (ACLU) and People for the American Way are likely to be asked to file *amicus* briefs in support of strict separation, whereas conservative religious groups, the Family Research Council or Focus on the Family, for example, are likely to file *amicus briefs* advocating increased public support for religious ideas. Often dozens of briefs will be filed on each side of a major case.

oral argument

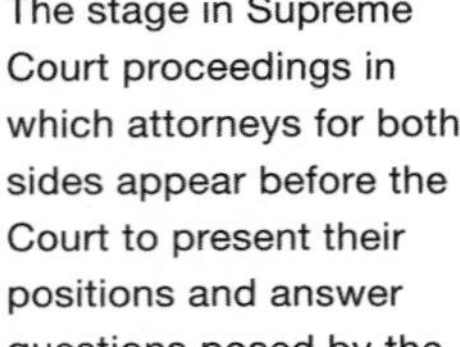

The stage in Supreme Court proceedings in which attorneys for both sides appear before the Court to present their positions and answer questions posed by the justices

Oral Argument. The next stage of a case is oral argument, in which attorneys for both sides appear before the Court to present their positions and answer the justices' questions. Each attorney has only a half hour to present his or her case, and this time includes interruptions for questions. Certain members of the Court, such as Justice Antonin Scalia, are known to interrupt attorneys dozens of times. Others, such as Justice Clarence Thomas, seldom ask questions. Oral argument can be very important to the outcome of a case. It allows justices to understand better the heart of a case and raise questions that might not have been addressed in the opposing sides' briefs. It is not uncommon for justices to go beyond the strictly legal issues and ask opposing counsel to discuss the implications of the case for the Court and the nation at large.[34]

The Conference. After oral argument, the Court discusses the case in its Wednesday or Friday conference. The chief justice presides over the conference and speaks first; the other justices follow in order of seniority. The Court's conferences are secret, and no outsiders are permitted to attend. The justices discuss the case and eventually reach a decision on the basis of a majority vote. As the case is discussed, justices may try to influence or change each other's opinions. At times, this may result in compromise decisions.

opinion

The written explanation of the Supreme Court's decision in a particular case

Opinion Writing. After a decision has been reached, one of the members of the majority is assigned to write the opinion. This assignment is made by the chief justice or the most senior justice in the majority if the chief justice is on the losing side. The assignment of the opinion can make a significant difference to the interpretation of a decision, as its wording and emphasis can have important implications for future litigation. Thus in assigning an opinion, the justices must give serious thought to the impression the case will make on lawyers and the public, as well as to the probability that one justice's opinion will be more widely accepted than another's.[35]

34 On the consequences of oral argument for decision making, see Timothy R. Johnson, Paul J. Wahlbeck, and James F. Spriggs II, "The Influence of Oral Arguments on the U.S. Supreme Court," *American Political Science Review* 100, no. 1 (February 2006): 99–113.

35 For this and other strategic aspects of the Court's process, see Forrest Maltzman, James F. Spriggs II, and Paul J. Wahlbeck, *Crafting Law on the Supreme Court: The Collegial Game* (New York: Cambridge University Press, 2001).

One of the more dramatic instances of this tactical consideration occurred in 1944, when Chief Justice Harlan Fiske Stone chose Justice Felix Frankfurter to write the opinion in the "white primary" case *Smith v. Allwright*, which overturned the southern practice of prohibiting black participation in primaries. The day after Stone made the assignment, Justice Robert Jackson wrote a letter to Stone arguing that Frankfurter, a foreign-born Jew from New England, would not win over the South with his opinion, regardless of his brilliance. Stone accepted the advice and substituted Justice Stanley F. Reed, an American-born Protestant from Kentucky and a southern Democrat in good standing.[36]

Once the majority opinion is drafted, it is circulated to the other justices. Some members of the majority may agree with both the outcome and the rationale but wish to emphasize or highlight a particular point and so draft a concurring opinion, called a regular concurrence. In other instances, one or more justices may agree with the majority but disagree with the rationale presented in the majority opinion. Then the justices may draft a special concurrence, explaining their disagreements with the majority. The pattern of opinions that emerge on a case ultimately depends on bargaining among the justices, as suggested by the collective action principle.

Dissent. Justices who disagree with the majority decision of the Court may choose to publicize the character of their disagreement in the form of a dissenting opinion. The dissenting opinion is generally assigned by the senior justice among the dissenters. Dissents can be used to express irritation with an outcome or to signal to defeated political forces in the nation that their position is supported by at least some members of the Court. Ironically, the most dependable way an individual justice can exercise a direct and clear influence on the Court is to write a dissent. Because there is no need to please a majority, dissenting opinions can be more eloquent and less guarded than majority opinions. The current Supreme Court often produces 5–4 decisions, with dissenters writing long and detailed opinions that, they hope, will help them convince a swing justice to join their side on the next round of cases dealing with a similar topic. Thus, for example, Justice David Souter wrote a 34-page dissent in a 2002 case upholding the use of government-funded school vouchers to pay for parochial school tuition. Souter called the decision "a dramatic departure from basic Establishment Clause principle" and went on to say that he hoped it would be reconsidered by a future court.[37]

dissenting opinion

A decision written by a justice who voted with the minority opinion in a particular case, in which the justice fully explains the reasoning behind his or her opinion

Dissent plays a special role in the work and impact of the Court because it amounts to an appeal to lawyers all over the country to keep bringing cases of the sort at issue. Therefore, an effective dissent influences the flow of cases through the Court as well as the arguments that lawyers will make in later cases.

These rules of collective decision making shape how the Supreme Court addresses cases. But they are just the structure within which judges operate. The

36 *Smith v. Allwright*, 321 U.S. 649 (1944).

37 Warren Richey, "Dissenting Opinions as a Window on Future Rulings," *Christian Science Monitor*, July 1, 2002, p. 1.

rules tell us something about the nature of judicial authority—it is restrained and cautious, it is incremental and rational. But the rules, in the end, tell us little about how judges will deal with the great political and social questions of the day. The same basic appellate system yielded both *Plessy v. Ferguson* and *Brown v. Board of Education*. How the courts ultimately decide matters of law depends ultimately on the views and beliefs of those in the judiciary and the nature of the problems they must address and on the relationship of the courts to the other branches of government.

JUDICIAL DECISION MAKING

The judiciary is conservative in its procedures, but its effect on society can be radical. That effect depends on a variety of influences, two of which stand out above the rest. The first is the individual members of the Supreme Court, their attitudes and goals, and their relationships with each other. The second is the other branches of government, particularly Congress.

The Supreme Court Justices

The Supreme Court explains its decisions in terms of law and precedent. But although law and precedent do have an effect on the Court's deliberations and eventual decisions, it is the Supreme Court that decides what laws mean and what importance precedents will have. Throughout its history, the Court has shaped and reshaped the law. If any individual judges in the country influence the federal judiciary, the Supreme Court justices are the ones who do.

From the 1950s to the 1980s, the Supreme Court took an activist role in such areas as civil rights, civil liberties, abortion, voting rights, and police procedures. For example, the Supreme Court was more responsible than any other governmental institution for breaking down America's system of racial segregation. The Supreme Court virtually prohibited states from interfering with the right of a woman to seek an abortion and sharply curtailed state restrictions on voting rights. And it was the Supreme Court that placed restrictions on the behavior of local police and prosecutors in criminal cases. But since the early 1980s, resignations, deaths, and new appointments have led to many shifts in the mix of philosophies and ideologies represented on the Court. In a series of decisions between 1989 and 2001, the conservative justices who had been appointed by Ronald Reagan and George H. W. Bush were able to swing the Court to a more conservative position on civil rights, affirmative action, abortion rights, property rights, criminal procedure, voting rights, desegregation, and the power of the national government.

The importance of ideology was very clear during the Court's 2000–01 term. In important decisions, the Court's most conservative justices—Scalia,

Thomas, and Rehnquist, usually joined by Kennedy—generally voted as a bloc.[38] Indeed, Scalia and Thomas voted together in 99 percent of all cases. At the same time, the Court's most liberal justices—Breyer, Ginsburg, Souter, and Stevens—also generally formed a bloc, with Ginsburg and Breyer and Ginsburg and Souter voting together 94 percent of the time.[39] Justice O'Connor, a moderate conservative, was the swing vote in many important cases.[40] This ideological division led to a number of important 5–4 decisions. In the Florida election case, *Bush v. Gore*, Justice O'Connor joined with the conservative bloc to give Bush a 5–4 victory. Indeed, more than 33 percent of all the cases heard by the Court in its 2000–01 term were decided by a 5–4 vote. In the Court's 2003–04 term, 8 of the 14 most important cases were also decided by a 5–4 margin.

However, precisely because the Court was so evenly split during this period, the conservative bloc did not always prevail. On some issues Justice O'Connor or Justice Kennedy sided with the liberal camp, producing a 5–4 and, sometimes, a 6–3 victory for the liberals. In the 2003 case of *Missouri v. Seibert*, for example, Justice Kennedy joined a 5–4 majority to strengthen Miranda rights.[41] Similarly, in *McConnell v. Federal Election Commission*, Justice O'Connor joined the liberal bloc to uphold the validity of the Bipartisan Campaign Reform Act.[42] On abortion, women's rights, and affirmative action, Justice O'Connor often joined the liberal bloc. With the departure of O'Connor and her replacement by Alito in 2006, many anticipated a series of new 5–4 decisions favoring the conservatives under new chief justice John Roberts.[43] In 2007, for example, the Court upheld the Partial Birth Abortion Ban Act—a law favored by conservatives—by a 5–4 majority.

However, the Court's policy influence comes not from the "horse race" results often trumpeted by the media but from the written opinions providing the constitutional or statutory rationale for policy in the future. These opinions establish the guidelines that govern how federal courts must decide similar cases in the future. The departure of Justice O'Connor shifted the center of the Court (the part that proves pivotal in formulating opinions) to Justice Kennedy, who by many measures does not significantly differ from O'Connor in his jurisprudence. The Court's policies may have drifted

38 Linda Greenhouse, "In Year of Florida Vote, Supreme Court Also Did Much Other Work," *New York Times*, July 2, 2001, p. A12.

39 Charles Lane, "Laying Down the Law," *Washington Post*, July 1, 2001, p. A6.

40 For an insightful discussion about identifying the swing justice on the Court, see Andrew D. Martin, Kevin M. Quinn, and Lee Epstein, "The Median Justice on the U.S. Supreme Court," *North Carolina Law Review* 83 (2005): 1275–1322.

41 *Missouri v. Seibert*, 542 U.S. 600 (2004).

42 *McConnell v. Federal Election Commission*, 540 U.S. 93 (2003).

43 Adam Liptak, "Entrances and Exits: The New 5-to-4 Supreme Court," *New York Times*, April 22, 2007.

rightward since O'Connor's departure, but only from O'Connor's position to Kennedy's, not nearly so dramatic a difference as that between O'Connor and Alito.[44]

Activism and Restraint. One element of judicial philosophy is the issue of activism versus restraint. Over the years, some justices have believed that courts should interpret the Constitution according to the stated intentions of its framers and defer to the views of Congress when interpreting federal statutes. Justice Felix Frankfurter, for example, advocated judicial deference to legislative bodies and avoidance of the "political thicket," in which the Court would entangle itself by deciding questions that were essentially political rather than legal in character. Advocates of judicial restraint are sometimes called strict constructionists because they look strictly to the words of the Constitution in interpreting its meaning.

judicial restraint 

The judicial philosophy whose adherents refuse to go beyond the text of the Constitution in interpreting its meaning

The alternative to restraint is judicial activism. Activist judges such as Chief Justice Earl Warren believe that the Court should go beyond the words of the Constitution or a statute to consider the broader societal implications of its decisions. Activist judges sometimes strike out in new directions, promulgating new interpretations or inventing new legal and constitutional concepts when they believe them to be socially desirable. For example, Justice Harry Blackmun's opinion in *Roe v. Wade* was based on a constitutional right to privacy that is not found in the words of the Constitution but was, rather, based on the Court's prior decision in *Griswold v. Connecticut.* Blackmun and the other members of the majority in the *Roe* case argued that the right to privacy is implied by other constitutional provisions. In this instance of judicial activism, the Court knew the result it wanted to achieve and was not afraid to make the law conform to the desired outcome.

judicial activism 

The judicial philosophy that posits that the Court should see beyond the text of the Constitution or a statute to consider broader societal implications for its decisions

Political Ideology. The second component of judicial philosophy is political ideology. The liberal or conservative attitudes of justices play an important role in their decisions.[45] (See the Analyzing the Evidence section on page 370.) The philosophy of activism versus restraint is sometimes a smoke screen for political ideology. In the past, liberal judges have been activists, willing to use the law to achieve social and political change, whereas conservatives have been associated with judicial restraint. Conservative politicians often castigate "liberal activist" judges and call for the appointment of conservative jurists who will refrain from reinterpreting the law. It is interesting, however, that in recent years some conservative justices who have long called for restraint have become activists in seeking to undo some of the work of liberal jurists over the past three decades. To be sure, some liberal jurists are activists and some conservatives have been advocates of restraint, but the relationship is by no means one to one. Indeed, the Rehnquist Court, dominated by

44 For a development of this argument, see David W. Rohde and Kenneth A. Shepsle, "Advising and Consenting in the 60-Vote Senate: Strategic Appointments to the Supreme Court," *Journal of Politics* 69, no. 3 (August 2007): 664–77.

45 C. Herman Pritchett, *The Roosevelt Court: A Study in Judicial Politics and Values* (New York: Macmillan, 1948); Jeffrey A. Segal and Harold J. Spaeth, *The Supreme Court and the Attitudinal Model* (New York: Cambridge University Press, 1993); and by the same authors, *The Supreme Court and Attitudinal Model Revisited* (New York: Cambridge

conservatives, was among the most activist Supreme Courts in American history, striking out in new directions in areas such as federalism and election law.

In our discussion of congressional politics in Chapter 6, we described legislators as policy oriented. In conceiving of judges as legislators in robes, we are effectively claiming that judges, like other politicians, have policy preferences that they seek to implement. The Analyzing the Evidence section in this chapter looks at ideology in the Court.

Other Institutions of Government

Congress. At both the national and the state level in the United States, courts and judges are players in the policy game because of the separation of powers. Essentially this means that the legislative branch formulates policy (defined constitutionally and institutionally by a legislative process), the executive branch implements policy (according to well-defined administrative procedures and subject to initial approval by the president or the legislative override of his veto), and the courts, when asked, rule on the faithfulness of the legislated and executed policy, either to the substance of the statute or to the Constitution itself. The courts, that is, may strike down an administrative action either because it exceeds the authority granted in the relevant statute (statutory rationale) or because the statute itself exceeds the authority granted the legislature by the Constitution (constitutional rationale).

If the Court declares the administrative agent's act as outside the permissible bounds, the Court's majority opinion can effectively declare whatever policy it wishes. If the legislature is unhappy with this judicial action, then it may either recraft the legislation (if the rationale for striking it down was statutory)[46] or initiate a constitutional amendment that would enable the stricken policy to pass constitutional muster (if the rationale for originally striking it down was constitutional).

In reaching their decisions, Supreme Court justices must anticipate Congress's response. As a result, judges will not always vote according to their true preferences because doing so may provoke Congress to enact legislation that moves the policy further from what the judges prefer. By voting for a lesser preference, the justices can get something they prefer to the status quo without provoking congressional action to overturn their decision. The most famous example of this phenomenon is the "switch in time that saved nine," when two justices voted in favor of New Deal legislation, the constitutionality of which they doubted, in an effort to diminish congressional support for President Franklin Delano Roosevelt's plan to "pack" the Court by increasing the number of justices. In short, the interactions between the Court and Congress are part of a complex strategic game.[47]

46 William N. Eskridge, Jr., "Overriding Supreme Court Statutory Interpretation Decisions," *Yale Law Journal* 101 (1991): 331–55.

47 A full strategic analysis of the maneuvering among legislative, executive, and judicial branches in the separation-of-powers arrangement choreographed by the U.S. Constitution may be found in William N. Eskridge, Jr., and John Ferejohn, "The Article I, Section 7, Game," *Georgetown Law Review* 80 (1992): 523–65. The entire issue of this , journal is devoted to the theme of strategic behavior in American institutional politics.

ANALYZING THE EVIDENCE

Ideological Voting on the Supreme Court

CHAPTER 09

Contributed by
Andrew D. Martin
Washington University in St. Louis
& **Kevin M. Quinn**
UC Berkeley School of Law

Do the political preferences of Supreme Court justices influence their behavior? The starting point for the analysis of the behavior of Supreme Court justices is to look at their votes.[1] For non-unanimous cases, we can compute agreement scores—the fraction of cases in which a pair of justices vote the same way. We display these agreement scores for the Court's 2009 term in the first figure below. If you examine this figure, you will see that two groups of justices emerge. Within each group, the justices agree with one another a lot, around 70 percent of the time. Voting is more structured than we would expect by chance.

One way to represent that structure is by arranging the justices on a line as in the diagram below to the right.[2] Justices who agree a lot should be close to one another; justices who disagree a lot should be far apart.

Does the fact that there are patterns of agreement mean that the justices are deciding based on political ideology? Not necessarily. These patterns are consistent with ideological decision making, but other things might explain the patterns as well. However, when we read the cases and see who wins or loses, there is a great deal of support for the idea that political ideology influences how justices vote.[3]

Agreement Scores for the 2009 Term

	Stevens	Sotomayor	Breyer	Ginsburg	Kennedy	Roberts	Alito	Scalia	Thomas
Stevens	1	.7	.65	.6	.48	.37	.29	.3	.24
Sotomayor	.7	1	.76	.78	.54	.53	.39	.41	.35
Breyer	.65	.76	1	.76	.51	.48	.43	.33	.35
Ginsburg	.6	.78	.76	1	.6	.57	.52	.38	.4
Kennedy	.48	.54	.51	.6	1	.78	.73	.66	.52
Roberts	.37	.53	.48	.57	.78	1	.75	.78	.71
Alito	.29	.39	.43	.52	.73	.75	1	.69	.71
Scalia	.3	.41	.33	.38	.66	.78	.69	1	.82
Thomas	.24	.35	.35	.4	.52	.71	.71	.82	1

< 0.4 · 0.4–0.55 · 0.56–0.69 · 0.7–0.99

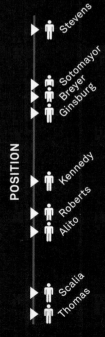

POSITION
Stevens
Sotomayor
Breyer
Ginsburg
Kennedy
Roberts
Alito
Scalia
Thomas

The figure to the left contains the agreement scores for the 2009 term of the U.S. Supreme Court for all non-unanimous cases. These scores are the proportion of cases when each justice agreed with every other justice. Two justices who always disagreed with one another would get a zero; two justices that always agreed would get a one. Red indicates low agreement scores; green indicates high agreement scores. The policy dimension at the right of the figure is one that best represents the patterns in the agreement scores.

0 = Justices always disagreed
1 = Justices always agreed

This type of analysis can be done for any court, but it becomes more difficult if we are interested in comparing justices across time instead of during just one term. What if we are interested in whether the Supreme Court is becoming more ideologically polarized over time? Or whether individual justices have become more liberal or conservative? Martin-Quinn scores based on a statistical model of voting on the Court help solve this problem.[4]

A number of interesting patterns emerge. Consider the case of Justice Harry Blackmun, who often claimed, "I haven't changed; it's the Court that changed under me."[5] The figure below shows that Justice Blackmun's position did in fact change ideologically over the course of his career. This evidence is consistent with some clear changes in Justice Blackmun's behavior, especially in the area of the death penalty.

We can also look at patterns in the positions of chief justices. While the chief's vote counts just the same as the other justices, he or she plays an important role in organizing the court. Justice Rehnquist was the most conservative justice on the court when he arrived in 1971, but as the figure below shows, after he was elevated in 1986 he, too, drifted more toward the middle. This is what we would expect to see of a justice who was working strategically to build coalitions, as any good chief would.

Ideological Trajectories of Selected Justices

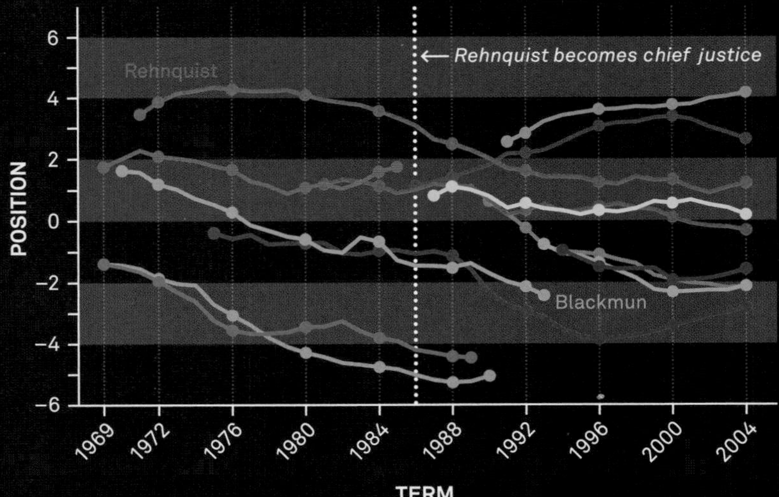

JUSTICES

- Blackmun
- Brennan
- Breyer
- Burger
- Ginsburg
- Kennedy
- Marshall
- O'Connor
- Rehnquist
- Scalia
- Souter
- Stevens
- Thomas

This figure shows the Martin-Quinn score for selected justices serving in the Burger (1969–86) and Rehnquist Courts (1986–2004). Each line represents the trajectory of each justice on the ideological dimension.

1 C. Herman Pritchett, *The Roosevelt Court: A Study in Judicial Politics and Values, 1937–1947* (New York: MacMillan Co., 1948).

2 Glendon A. Schubert, *The Judicial Mind: The Attitudes and Ideologies of Supreme Court Justices, 1946–1963* (Evanston, IL: Northwestern University Press, 1965).

3 Jeffry A. Segal and Harold J. Spaeth, *The Supreme Court and the Attitudinal Model* (New York: Cambridge University Press, 1993).

4 Andrew D. Martin and Kevin M. Quinn, "Dynamic Ideal Point Estimation via Markov Chain Monte Carlo for the U.S. Supreme Court, 1953–1999." *Political Analysis*, 10, no. 2, (2002): 134–53, http://mqscores.wustl.edu (accessed 10/18/11).

5 Linda Greenhouse, *Becoming Justice Blackmun* (New York: Times Books, 2005).

EXPLORE **IDEOLOGY AND THE COURTS** FURTHER AT: **wwnorton.com/studyspace**

The President. The president's most direct influence on the Court is the power to nominate justices. Presidents typically nominate judges who they believe are close to their policy preferences and close enough to the preferences of a majority of senators, who must confirm the nomination.

Yet the efforts by presidents to reshape the federal judiciary are not always successful. Often in American history, judges have surprised and disappointed the presidents who named them to the bench. Justice Souter, for example, was far less conservative than President George H. W. Bush and the Republicans who supported Souter's appointment in 1990 thought he would be. Likewise, Justices O'Connor and Kennedy disappointed conservatives by opposing limitations on abortion.

Nevertheless, with a combined total of 12 years in office, Reagan and Bush were able to exercise a good deal of influence on the composition of the federal district and appellate courts. By the end of Bush's term, he and Reagan together had appointed nearly half of all the federal judges. Thus, whatever impact Reagan and Bush ultimately had on the Supreme Court, their federal appointments have certainly had a continuing influence on the temperament and behavior of the district and circuit courts. President Clinton promised to appoint more liberal jurists to the district and appellate courts and to increase the number of women and minorities serving on the federal bench. During his first two years in office, Clinton held to this promise (Figure 9.7). A large number of judicial vacancies remained unfilled, however, when the Republicans took control of Congress at the end of 1994.

During President George W. Bush's first term in office, Senate Democrats fought a pitched battle with the White House to block judicial nominees they deemed too conservative. Ten of Bush's nominees to the circuit courts were blocked by Democratic filibusters, though Bush infuriated Democrats by giving two of them, Charles Pickering, Sr., and William Pryor, temporary recess appointments. Democrats had hoped to block Bush's nominees until the 2004 elections and then see a Democratic president chosen. After Bush's re-election, however, the battle resumed, and Republicans threatened to change the Senate rules to prevent a continuation of the Democrats' filibuster. As noted earlier, this threat, known as the nuclear option, was ultimately shelved by the Republicans. The 2006 and 2008 elections changed the political landscape around judicial appointments further. Democrats gained control of the Senate in 2006, which meant that the Senate Judiciary Committee became majority Democratic. As a result, any Bush appointments to the federal bench had to satisfy the Democrats. The 2008 election saw the addition of eight more Democrats to close debate and end filibusters of Barack Obama's judicial appointments. After the 2010 election, Republicans again used the filibuster to stop or slow appointments. One high-profile nominee, Goodwin Lin, withdrew his nomination to the Ninth Circuit Court of Appeals in 2011, after a year-and-a-half wait.

The Implementation of Supreme Court Decisions

The president and the rest of the executive branch, along with Congress, the states, the lower courts, and a variety of private organizations and individuals

Figure 9.7

DIVERSITY OF FEDERAL DISTRICT COURT APPOINTEES

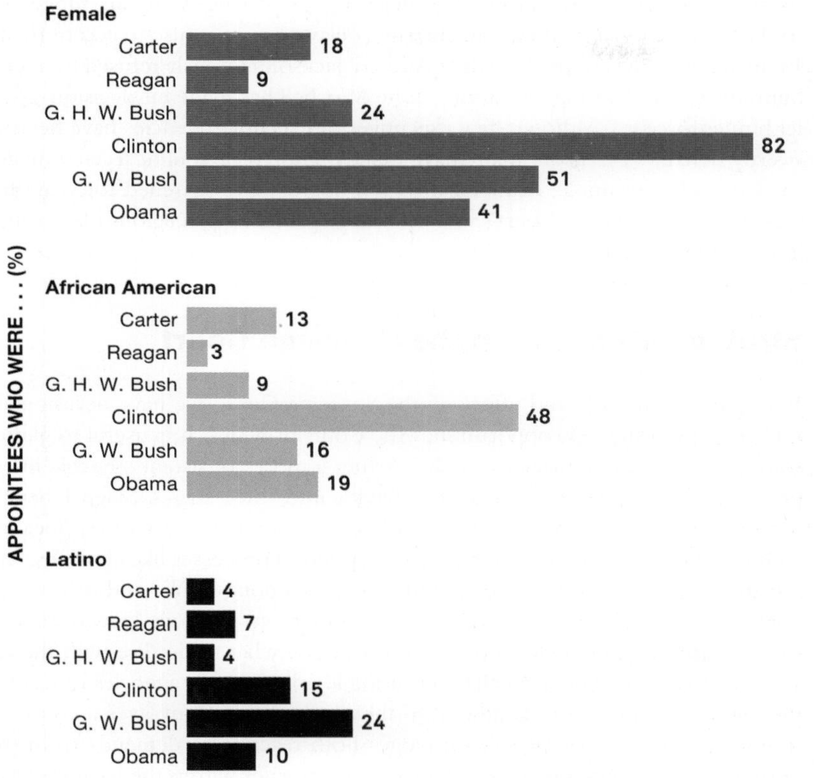

APPOINTEES WHO WERE . . . (%)

Female

Carter 18
Reagan 9
G. H. W. Bush 24
Clinton 82
G. W. Bush 51
Obama 41

African American

Carter 13
Reagan 3
G. H. W. Bush 9
Clinton 48
G. W. Bush 16
Obama 19

Latino

Carter 4
Reagan 7
G. H. W. Bush 4
Clinton 15
G. W. Bush 24
Obama 10

SOURCE: The Federal Judicial Center, Diversity on the Bench, www.fjc.gov/history/home.nsf/page/judges_diversity.html (accessed 9/14/11).

also play key roles in the implementation of Supreme Court decisions. Once the high court has made a decision, a variety of other government agencies must put it into effect. The lower courts must understand and apply to new cases the principles asserted by the Supreme Court. The executive branch must enforce the Court's decision. State legislators and governors must implement the decision in their own jurisdictions. And often individuals and organizations must take action in the courts and in the political arena to demand that the Supreme Court's verdicts be fully implemented. At each of these stages, opposition on the part of the revelant actors may delay full national implementation of a Supreme Court decision, sometimes for years.

For example, if lower-court judges strongly disagree with a Supreme Court decision, they may use a variety of tactics to avoid fully implementing it. Lower-court judges may, for example, avoid applying the case by disposing of similar cases on technical or procedural grounds. Similarly, they may apply the case as narrowly as possible or declare that some portion of the Court's opinion was merely "dicta"—useful as guidance but not binding.

As for executive agencies, most Supreme Court decisions must be implemented by federal, state, and local agencies. If these agencies are unsympathetic to the Court's decision, they may obstruct, delay, or even refuse to accept them. In the nineteenth century, President Andrew Jackson famously refused to obey a Supreme Court decision, declaring, "John Marshall has made his decision. Now let him enforce it." Although few executives or executive agencies have been as overtly defiant as Jackson, many have quietly ignored or sought to circumvent the Court. For example, many local school boards have searched for years for ways to circumvent the Court's various rulings prohibiting religious observance in the public schools.

Strategic Behavior in the Supreme Court

In describing the role and effect of the Supreme Court, we have occasionally referred to the strategic opportunities the Court provides. It is useful to gather some of them in one place to stitch together a more consistent strategic interpretation. Let's divide this strategic behavior into three stages. Stage 1 begins with a period of "normal" politics—in (local or national) legislatures, (local or national) executive and regulatory agencies, political processes like elections, and the stuff of everyday life involving interactions among public and private entities (citizens, corporations, nonprofits, voluntary associations, governments). Conflict arises, and interested parties must decide what to do: live with the results, pursue normal political channels using legislatures and agencies to resolve the conflict, or move the conflict into the courts. Stage 2 involves a court responding to its environment, with judges both reacting to demands from the outside and fashioning their own behavioral strategies within the legal process. Stage 3 involves what happens once a court renders a decision and how the actors in stages 1 and 2 anticipate the decision and adjust their behavior to its expectations. Although our discussion could be developed for all courts, we will focus on the Supreme Court. Indeed, we will narrow things even further by devoting the bulk of our remarks to the internal strategic environment of the Supreme Court at stage 2, when it both reacts to developments that have preceded its being drawn into a conflict (stage 1) and anticipates what will happen if it responds in a particular manner (stage 3).

Stage 1. Assume that a conflict has arisen and appeals have been made through normal channels. Administrative and regulatory agencies, for example, often have well-defined procedures for appealing a ruling within the agency, with the opportunity of a subsequent appeal to a court always being available. Dissatisfied with the outcome, one of the parties moves the dispute to the courts, and at some point in the process the option of appeal to the Supreme Court is available. The aggrieved party has a decision to make. It is a calculated, strategic decision in three respects.

First, an appeal will consume resources that might otherwise be redeployed and used for different purposes. A prospective appellant must weigh an appeal against this "opportunity cost." The Sierra Club, for example, might use resources to appeal a lower-court decision on environmental protection to the Supreme Court or, alternatively, devote some of those same resources to lobbying Congress on other issues.

Second, a high-court appeal sometimes competes with alternative political moves. An interest group such as the Sierra Club that lost its lower-court appeals might find it more sensible to lobby Congress for a change in the National Environmental Policy Act to ameliorate the condition addressed in the legal proceedings.

Third, all options are uncertain propositions whose resolution stretches out over time. Regarding uncertainty, a prospective appellant must recognize that the probability of successfully getting to the Court is slim, and even if it succeeds in obtaining *certiorari*, it may not win on the merits of its case. Regarding the time dimension, even if the appellant wins, the process may take years, making the delayed victory bittersweet. Ultimately these strategic calculations revolve around what an appellant can expect in pursuing an appeal—that is, what might happen in stages 2 and 3.[48]

Stage 2. As we have already noted, thousands of cases are appealed to the Supreme Court. The decision to appeal from a lower federal or state court is consummated in a petition for a writ of *certiorari*. The nine justices of the Supreme Court (or, more accurately, their clerks) must sort through these petitions and, according to the rule of four, build their docket each session: a case is added to the docket if four justices vote to include it. The Court, in short, has the power to create its own agenda. Appellants for each session are competing with about 10,000 others to claim one of fewer than 100 slots.

rule of four

The rule that *certiorari* will be granted only if four justices vote in favor of the petition

In building their docket for the current session of the Court, how do justices think about the available options? They support some cases undoubtedly out of a strong belief that an area is ripe for constitutional clarification. They support others out of an interest in the development of legal principles in a particular area of the law—criminal rights, privacy, First Amendment, abortion, affirmative action, federal-state relations, and so on—or in the belief that contradictory decisions in lower courts need to be sorted out. They may oppose certain appeals because they believe a particular case will not provide a sufficiently clear-cut basis for clarifying a legal issue. That is, even though a case might attract the interest of a justice on substantive grounds or might be perceived by a justice as containing procedural errors that could lead to a reversal, he or she might not

48 There are subtleties to the strategies of appellants. They may seek an appeal to the Supreme Court, for example, as a bluff to induce the winner in the lower court to accommodate in advance some of their preferences—in effect, to settle out of court. Why might the lower-court winners be induced to accommodate the losers? There are at least two reasons: first, to avoid the exorbitant costs of fighting an appeal to the Supreme Court and, second, to avoid the prospect that their victory in the lower court may be reversed.

support *certiorari* because of a strategic calculation that it is not a particularly good vehicle or that it would be prudent to wait until a better vehicle comes up through the appeals process in a subsequent session.[49]

Once a case is included on the docket and oral arguments have been delivered by the attorneys for the litigants and *amicus curiae* briefs filed by other interested parties, the case becomes the subject of two decisions.[50] The first takes place after it is discussed by the justices in one of the regularly scheduled conferences during the Court's term. When discussion has concluded and all attempts at persuasion have come to an end, there is a vote on the merits—a vote in favor of the appeal or against it. In principle, this vote affects only the parties to the case, either affirming or reversing the lower-court decision.

It is the second decision that has a wider bearing. Having decided one way or the other, the justices must determine whether there is agreement on the reasons for their decision. The most senior justice on the winning side—the chief justice if he is in this group—assigns a colleague to write the majority opinion or keeps it for himself to write. This is a highly strategic decision because the Court's impact over and above its effect on the contesting parties depends on the reasons it gives for the decision at hand. The reasons of a Court majority set legal precedent for similar cases in the future, thus influencing litigation in lower courts. If the majority cannot agree among themselves on why they decided as they did, there is no binding effect on other comparable cases. Drafting an opinion that can attract the signatures of at least five justices is therefore of pivotal significance. A justice on the winning side who stakes out an extreme position relative to the others is unlikely to be able to draft such an opinion, so moderate members of the Court usually do the heavy lifting of opinion drafting for especially controversial cases. Of course, in some cases a majority may agree on the merits of a case but are unable to come to a consensus on the reasons. In such cases, there will be no majority opinion, though each justice is free to write his or her own opinion (possibly cosigned by others), either supporting or dissenting from the decision on the merits, giving his or her particular reasons. These opinions have no binding effect on future lower-court cases but may still serve a strategic signaling role, conveying to the lower courts and the legal community where a justice stands on the issues involved in the case at hand.[51]

Stage 3. The Supreme Court is not an island unto itself. It is the top rung of one branch in a separation-of-powers system. Its decisions are not automatically implemented; it must depend on executive agencies for implementation and on

49 An excellent discussion of this facet of Supreme Court decision making is found in Perry, *Deciding to Decide*.

50 On the strategic decisions of *amicus* groups, see Thomas Hansford, "Information Provision, Organizational Constraints, and the Decision to Submit an *Amicus Brief* in a U.S. Supreme Court Case," *Political Research Quarterly* 57 (2004): 219–30.

51 For an insightful discussion of the strategic elements influencing how the senior justice in the winning coalitions assigns opinion writing, see David W. Rohde, "Policy Goals, Strategic Choice, and Majority Opinion Assignments in the U.S. Supreme Court," *Midwest Journal of Political Science* 16 (1972): 652–82.

lower courts for enforcement of its dicta. In fact, it ultimately depends on the willingness of others, especially ordinary citizens, to conform to its rulings. In some instances, the Court may worry about resistance. Throughout the 1940s and 1950s, for example, there were concerns that issues relating to integration would meet with popular disapproval and defiance in the South. Indeed, in the famous *Brown* decision desegregating public schools in 1954, Chief Justice Earl Warren worried about precisely this. When he wrote the majority opinion for the Court, he strategically softened some of its language in order to attract the signatures of all nine justices. The 9–0 decision and opinion were a signal to a potentially defiant South that the Court was united and that it would take a very long time (the time needed to replace at least five justices) before there would be any prospect of reversal—that is, resistance would not pay off in the near or medium term.

In addition to compliance, enforcement, and resistance, the Court must also worry about reversal. On a decision taken by the Court on a statutory issue—for example, on whether an existing law covers a particular situation—majorities in both houses of Congress and the president may pass a new statute reversing the Court's interpretation. If, for example, the Court rules that the Radio Act of 1927 does not cover transmissions by cellular phones and Congress and the president think otherwise, then Congress may pass legislation, and the president may sign it into law, amending the Radio Act of 1927 to allow for its provisions to govern the regulation of cell phones. The Court may well say "what the law is" (to quote Justice Oliver Wendell Holmes), but Congress and the president are free to change the law.[52]

For decisions taken by the Court on constitutional (as opposed to statutory) grounds, no mere revision of existing law is sufficient to reverse the Court; an amendment to the Constitution is required. President George W. Bush, for example, gave his blessing to efforts to amend the Constitution to reverse the *Roe v. Wade* decision permitting a woman to choose an abortion in the first two trimesters of her pregnancy.

In the long run, the Supreme Court is the final legal authority on whether governmental and interpersonal practices satisfy statutory or constitutional scrutiny. But as Yogi Berra put it, "It ain't over till it's over." The other branches of government must be taken into account as justices vote on cases and write legal opinions; the justices are not free agents. Hence strategic calculation can never be far from their thinking.

THE EXPANDING POWER OF THE JUDICIARY

Over the past 50 years, the place of the judiciary in American politics and society has changed dramatically. Demand for legal solutions has increased, and the reach of the judiciary has expanded. Some now call for reining in the

52 On the strategic interaction among Court, Congress, and the President, see Eskridge and Ferejohn, "The Article I, Section 7, Game."

power of the courts and discretion of judges in areas ranging from criminal law and sentencing to property rights to liability and torts. How our society deals with these issues will shape the nature of the judiciary—its independence and effectiveness—over the generations to come. All indications now are that even the most conservative justices are reluctant to relinquish their newfound power, authority that, once asserted, has become accepted and thus established.

Let us summarize what we have learned so far: judges enjoy great latitude because they are not subject to electoral pressures. Judges and justices, more than any other politicians in America, can pursue their own goals and preferences concerning what is right, their own ideologies. They are, however, constrained—by institutional rules governing access to the courts, by other courts, by Congress and the president, by their lack of enforcement powers, and, most important, by the past in the form of precedent and common law. For much of its history, the federal judiciary acted very cautiously. The Supreme Court rarely challenged Congress or the president. The justices instead tended to legitimate laws passed by Congress and the actions of the president. The scope of the Court's decisions were limited only to those individuals granted access to the courts.

Two judicial revolutions have expanded the power and reach of the federal judiciary in the decades since World War II. The first of these revolutions brought about the liberalization of a wide range of public policies in the United States. As we saw in Chapters 4 and 5, in policy areas—including school desegregation, legislative apportionment, and criminal procedure, as well as obscenity, abortion, and voting rights—the Supreme Court was at the forefront of a series of sweeping changes in the role of the U.S. government and, ultimately, the character of American society. The Court put many of these issues before the public long before Congress or the president were prepared to act. At the same time that the courts forged these policy innovations, they were bringing about a second, less visible revolution. During the 1960s and 1970s, the Supreme Court and other federal courts began a series of institutional changes in judicial procedures that had major consequences by fundamentally expanding the power of the courts in the United States. First, the federal courts liberalized the concept of standing to permit almost any group seeking to challenge the actions of an administrative agency to bring its case before the federal bench. In 1971, for example, the Supreme Court ruled that public interest groups could invoke the National Environmental Policy Act to challenge the actions of federal agencies by claiming that the agencies' activities might have adverse environmental consequences.[53] Congress helped make it even easier for groups dissatisfied with government policies to bring their cases to the courts by adopting Title 42, Section 1988, of the U.S. Code, which permits the practice of "fee shifting." Section 1988 allows citizens who successfully bring a suit against a public official for violating their constitutional rights to collect their attorneys' fees and costs from the government. Thus Section 1988 encourages individuals and groups to bring their problems to the courts rather than to Congress or the executive

53 *Citizens to Preserve Overton Park v. Volpe,* 401 U.S. 402 (1971).

branch. These changes have given the courts a far greater role in the administrative process than ever before.

In a second institutional change, the federal courts broadened the scope of relief to permit themselves to act on behalf of broad categories or classes of persons in "class-action" cases, rather than just on behalf of individuals.[54] A class-action suit is a procedural device that permits a large number of persons with common interests to join together under a representative party to bring or defend a lawsuit. In 1999, for example, a consortium of several dozen law firms filed a class-action suit against firearms manufacturers on behalf of victims of gun violence. Claims could ultimately amount to billions of dollars. Some of the same law firms had been involved earlier in the decade in a massive class-action suit against cigarette manufacturers on behalf of victims of tobacco-related illnesses. This suit eventually led to a settlement in which the tobacco companies agreed to pay out several billion dollars. The beneficiaries of the settlement included the treasuries of all 50 states, which received compensation for costs allegedly borne by the states in treating illnesses caused by tobacco use. Of course, the attorneys who brought the case also received an enormous settlement, splitting more than $1 billion. Continuing litigation against tobacco firms remains to be resolved.

 **class-action suit**

A lawsuit in which a large number of persons with common interests join together under a representative party to bring or defend a lawsuit, as when hundreds of workers join together to sue a company

In the third major judicial change, the federal courts began to employ so-called structural remedies, in effect retaining jurisdiction of cases until a court's mandate had been implemented to its satisfaction.[55] The best-known of these instances was the effort by federal judge W. Arthur Garrity to operate the Boston school system from his bench to ensure its desegregation. Between 1974 and 1985, Judge Garrity issued 14 decisions relating to different aspects of the Boston school desegregation plan that had been developed under his authority and put into effect under his supervision.[56]

Through these three judicial mechanisms, the federal courts paved the way for an unprecedented expansion of national judicial power. In essence, liberalization of the rules of standing and expansion of the scope of judicial relief drew the federal courts to link with important social interests and classes. The introduction of structural remedies enhanced the courts' ability to serve these constituencies. Thus during the 1960s and 1970s the power of the federal courts expanded in the same way the power of the executive expanded during the 1930s: through links with constituencies—such as groups advocating civil rights, consumers' rights, gay rights, women's rights, and environmental issues—that staunchly defended the Supreme Court in its battles with Congress, the executive, or other interest groups.

During the 1980s and 1990s, the Reagan and Bush administrations sought to end the relationship between the Court and liberal political forces. Conservative judges appointed by these Republican presidents modified the Court's position

54 See "Developments in the Law—Class Actions," *Harvard Law Review* 89 (1976): 1318.

55 See Donald L. Horowitz, *The Courts and Social Policy* (Washington, DC: Brookings Institution, 1977).

56 *Morgan v. McDonough*, 540 F. 2nd 527 (1 Cir., 1976); *cert.* denied 429 U.S. 1042 (1977).

in areas such as abortion, affirmative action, and judicial procedure, though not so completely as some conservative writers and politicians had hoped. Within a one-week window in 2003, for example, the Supreme Court affirmed the validity of affirmative action, reaffirmed abortion rights, strengthened gay rights, offered new protection to individuals facing the death penalty, and issued a ruling in favor of a congressional apportionment plan that dispersed minority voters across several districts—a practice that appeared to favor the Democrats.[57] The Court hadn't changed, rather it had made these decisions based on the justices' interpretations of precedent and law, not simply personal belief.

The current Court has not been conservative in another sense. It has not been eager to surrender the expanded powers carved out by earlier Courts, especially in areas that assert the power of the national government over the states. Indeed, the opponents to the U.S. Constitution (the Antifederalists in Chapter 2) feared the assertion of the national interest over the states through the independent judiciary. Over two centuries of U.S. history, the reach and authority of the federal judiciary has expanded greatly, and the judiciary has emerged as a powerful arm of our national politics. Whatever their policy beliefs or partisan orientations, judges and justices understand the newfound importance of the courts among the three branches of American government and act not just to interpret and apply the law but also to maintain the power of the courts.

For Further Reading

Abraham, Henry J. *The Judicial Process: An Introductory Analysis of the Courts of the United States, England, and France.* 7th ed. New York: Oxford University Press, 1998.

Baum, Lawrence. *The Puzzle of Judicial Behavior.* Ann Arbor: University of Michigan Press, 1997.

Bickel, Alexander M. *The Least Dangerous Branch: The Supreme Court at the Bar of Politics.* Indianapolis, IN: Bobbs-Merrill, 1962.

Epstein, Lee, and Jack Knight. *The Choices Justices Make.* Washington, DC: Congressional Quarterly Press, 1998.

Kahn, Ronald. *The Supreme Court and Constitutional Theory, 1953–1993.* Lawrence: University Press of Kansas, 1994.

reader selection *Marbury v. Madison*, 5 U.S. (1 Cranch) 137, 1803.

57 David Van Drehle, "Court That Liberals Savage Proves to Be Less of a Target," *Washington Post*, June 29, 2003, p. A18.

O'Brien, David M. *Storm Center: The Supreme Court in American Politics.* 7th ed. New York: Norton, 2005.

Perry, H. W., Jr. *Deciding to Decide: Agenda Setting in the United States Supreme Court.* Cambridge, MA: Harvard University Press, 1991.

Rosenberg, Gerald. *The Hollow Hope: Can Courts Bring About Social Change?* Chicago: University of Chicago Press, 2008.

reader selection

Segal, Jeffrey A., and Harold J. Spaeth. *The Supreme Court and the Attitudinal Model Revisited.* New York: Cambridge University Press, 2002.

Silverstein, Mark. *Judicious Choices: The New Politics of Supreme Court Confirmations.* New York: Norton, 1994.

Toobin, Jeffrey. *The Nine: Inside the Secret World of the Supreme Court.* New York: Knopf, 2008.

Whittington, Keith. *Political Foundations of Judicial Supremacy: The President, the Supreme Court, and Constitutional Leadership in U.S. History.* Princeton, NJ: Princeton University Press, 2008.

Visit **wwnorton.com/studyspace/** to access free review materials such as:

- Vocabulary Flashcards of All Key Terms
- Chapter Review Quizzes
- Complete Study Outlines

reader selection

Highlighted selections are included in *Readings in American Politics: Analysis and Perspectives*, Second Edition.

PART 1 2 X 4

DEMOCRATIC POLITICS

10

Public Opinion

Chapter Outline

Public support is the coin of the realm in Washington politics. Popular presidents succeed; unpopular presidents struggle. A president who has the backing of a large majority of the public gains leverage in dealing with Congress and the bureaucracy, but a president who lacks public support often meets resistance from members of Congress, even those in his own party. President George W. Bush described a president's popularity as political capital, an asset that must be spent wisely on a few well-chosen issues.[1]

Members of Congress are perhaps even more attuned than the president to the ups and downs of public opinion. Representatives in the U.S. House must run for re-election every two years, a very short election cycle. They cannot afford to make many unpopular decisions for fear of being punished by their constituents in the next election. A saying among members of Congress goes, "It's okay to be on the losing side of a vote, but you don't want to be on the wrong side." That is, they worry about going against their constituents' preferences. Members of Congress and party leaders pay close attention to various indicators of public sentiment, including polls, visits to their districts or home states, and letters, phone calls, and e-mails from constituents.

Even the courts are not immune to the influence of public opinion. Courts lack the power to enforce their decisions; they depend on the compliance of those affected and the cooperation of Congress, the president, and political leaders in the states. That cooperation is not always forthcoming. As we saw in Chapter 5, *Brown v. Board of Education*, perhaps the most important court

1 Chris Suellentrop, "America's New Political Capital," *Slate*, November 30, 2004, www.slate.com/id/2110256/ (accessed 3/18/09). Also see Richard Neustadt, *Presidential Power and the Modern Presidents*, 4th ed. (New York: Free Press, 1990), and Brandice Canes-Wrone, *Who Leads Whom? Presidents, Policy, and the Public* (Chicago: University of Chicago Press, 2006).

decision of the twentieth century, met with immediate opposition in the southern states. In 1963, Governor George Wallace of Alabama stood on the statehouse steps and declared his firm opposition to the Supreme Court's edict that the states desegregate "with all deliberate speed." Desegregation occurred slowly, often in the face of violent protests. Only after public opinion turned in support of equal rights for all races did Congress and the president act, accelerating the pace of desegregation.[2]

Aside from particular government decisions, public opinion is also the standard by which we judge democracy in America. Ideally, representative democracy approximates what the nation as a whole would choose to do were all 300 million Americans to consider a given matter. Congress and the president are supposed to act as the public's agents, enacting laws that a clear majority of the public wants and rejecting laws that fail to achieve widespread support. Also ideally, representative democracy in the United States enacts laws that benefit society and that respond to changes in public sentiment, with the constraint that the laws not violate the freedoms and rights guaranteed in the Bill of Rights. If the norms of society shift strongly in one direction for a period of time, so too should the laws of the land. The nature and origins of public opinion are among the central concerns of modern political science precisely because democratic government is supposed to reflect the will of the people.

CORE OF THE ANALYSIS

There are a wide range of interests at stake in any question that the government must decide, as well as differing preferences, beliefs, and opinions about what ought to be done.

Public opinion is the aggregation of individuals' views. It expresses the range of attitudes and beliefs and on which side of any question a majority of people fall.

Politicians follow public opinion as part of the representative process. They take signals from polls and other indicators of public sentiment to gauge whether a particular decision might affect their prospects at the next election.

Politicians, interest groups, the media, and others try to shape public opinion by influencing what issues are debated, what alternatives are offered, and what information is presented.

2 Gerald Rosenberg, *The Hollow Hope* (Chicago: University of Chicago Press, 1991).

The rationality principle and, specifically, the idea that members of the public have goals and preferences can help us understand the role of public opinion in American politics. What does it mean when large majorities support or oppose the president? How can we measure what the majority of people want the government to do on important issues such as taxation, military intervention, or social problems? Do individuals know enough to make decisions about the direction of the government or public policies? The rationality behind democratic government is a key element in democracy. The translation of people's preferences into electoral decisions and public policies also depends on institutions, problems of collective action, and history. These factors will be emphasized in later chapters on elections, interest groups, political parties, and the media. Public opinion operates through these various institutions to determine who serves in government, what problems government must address, and the principles and values that shape public policy.

In conceiving how democracy works, democratic theory and civics lessons often present a highly idealized notion of democratic citizens. It is assumed that people follow all the important issues of the day closely, are well informed about the decisions of their representatives, understand the consequences of their actions, and participate in public debate, elections, and even in public decision making. There is ample evidence that individuals fall far short of this ideal. Some people do not like the choices they are presented with in American politics and opt out altogether. Studies have suggested that the typical American may not know enough or have strong enough beliefs to make reasoned decisions about many political issues, especially where foreign policy is involved. Some research has even cast doubt on whether individuals know what they want and whether they have consistent preferences when it comes to politics. And some political leaders have exploited these inconsistencies and weaknesses to accomplish objectives not in line with the true preferences of the majority.[3]

The prospect that political leaders can readily manipulate the public presents a lingering and difficult problem. Do Americans in fact know enough to sustain democracy? Or are they easily led and misled? Are Americans sufficiently active and involved? Or do we need greater political participation in the United States? Throughout this chapter and those that follow, we encourage you to keep these questions in mind. The United States continually grapples with these difficult problems. They motivate radical critiques of the failings of American politics and efforts at political reform, ranging from campaign finance to media regulation to election administration. A tacit assumption about the public lies behind most of the legal decisions and electoral laws governing the United States—the view that America is a wide-open democracy. Our system of government does not presume that people must have a minimum level of competence or literacy to participate, or even that they must participate at all. Rather, public opinion is the expression of what people prefer and believe, of their wants and experiences. Although a better informed and more engaged public may be ideal, not all citizens are highly educated and engaged.

3 William Riker, *The Art of Political Manipulation* (New Haven, CT: Yale University Press, 1986).

WHAT IS PUBLIC OPINION?

 **public opinion**

Citizens' attitudes about political issues, leaders, institutions, and events

Public opinion may be understood on two levels—aggregate and individual. The term public opinion itself refers to an aggregate—the public—and commonly the public is treated as if it were a thinking, rational organism. It is not. Rather, public opinion reflects the accumulation of millions of individuals' expressions of their opinions, attitudes, and choices.

There are many different procedures for aggregating individual opinion, including voting, town meetings, protests, and other forms of political participation, as well as public opinion polls. The aggregate expression of the choices that people make or the opinions they offer is rarely unanimous; instead, public opinion is usually shorthand for what most people want or think—in other words, majority rule.

Aggregate opinion may not always appear rational, but there is power in numbers. The basic idea behind democracy holds that the sum of many millions of votes produces a better outcome than the decision of a small number of people. This idea is brilliantly expressed in the Jury Theorem. The Marquis de Condorcet, a French political philosopher, argued that the majority of a jury would more likely reach the right decision in a trial than would a single individual who heard the same evidence. Every individual would like to make the right decision, but there is some chance that an individual will make a mistake. Adding up the private judgments of many separate individuals, however, reduces the probability of a mistake. A majority of a jury of 12 people, then, is less likely to reach the wrong decision than a single individual. And according to this idea, 130 million voters are even more likely to produce the right verdict.[4] Democracy works, as Condorcet observed, because aggregating opinions collects the knowledge widely held in society.

This idea has been rediscovered at the beginning of the twenty-first century, as new information technology has expanded the opportunities and the possibility for millions of people to express their opinions on virtually any matter. Firms such as Amazon.com collect such information and aggregate the millions of decisions made by consumers to figure out who is likely to buy particular products. There is wisdom in masses, a lesson borne out in markets and democracy.[5]

4 Marquis de Condorcet, "Essai sur l'application de l'analyse à la probabilité des décisions rendues à la pluralité des voix," http://gallica.bnf.fr/ark:/12148/bpt6k417181 (accessed 3/24/09). Condorcet also argued that democracy has a weakness in that it need not always produce a definite majority-rule winner and may be manipulated by a clever agenda setter. This idea was rediscovered in the middle of the twentieth century by the Nobel Prize–winning economist Kenneth Arrow in *Social Choice and Individual Values* (New York: Wiley, 1963).

5 See Cass Sunstein, *Infotopia: How Many Minds Produce Knowledge* (Oxford, UK: Oxford University Press, 2006).

Public opinion can also be understood at the level of individuals. Votes cast during elections, answers to surveys, letters and e-mails to members of Congress, and other ways that people communicate their opinions reflect how individuals think and behave politically. Aggregate public opinion, after all, is the collection of these many expressions. The meaning of individual political opinions depends on three factors: (1) the individual's underlying preferences (what he or she wants); (2) his or her beliefs about the current circumstances and the consequences of different courses of action; and (3) the choices presented. A person will make a given political choice among the options presented, say, in an election or on a survey, because he or she wants a certain outcome (such as higher income or better education for one's own children) and because he or she believes that a given political option is the best approach among the alternatives offered. The choices offered in any situation are usually few in number—Democrat or Republican, a proposed bill versus the status quo, vote yes or vote no, get involved or stay at home. The significance of the individual's actions depends on why he or she chooses one of the alternatives.

Preferences and Beliefs

Preferences and beliefs are quite complex. Preferences reflect what people want, such as material goods and money, and also people's values, such as justice and morality. For example, income is often taken as the basis for political preferences. People want higher income, and they prefer government policies that will increase their income. Other things being equal, people want lower taxes and more spending on programs that benefit them directly. But it is also the case that moral values, shaped by religion and family and social conscience, influence the way Americans behave. Some observers argue that because of the collective nature of political choices, values matter even more in politics than narrow self-interest, and that politicians can win by emphasizing values, rather than narrow self-interest.[6] These two factors—economic self-interest and social or moral values—are viewed as the basis for people's preferences in the political or public arena.

Preferences are also characterized by their intensity—how much individuals want a certain outcome or care about a given issue. It is virtually impossible to compare intensity of preferences directly, to say that one person wants something twice as much as someone else. But it is obvious from behavior that some people do have stronger or more intense preferences than others. Those who have strong opinions and attitudes are more likely to express their views and take political action than those who do not. It is also clear that people differ in the strength of their preferences about different issues. Public opinion polls reveal that some people care more about some issues or problems, such as taxes, while others care more about other issues, such as abortion.

Beliefs reflect what people know and how they understand the world and the consequences of their actions. An individual who has developed considerable

6 Benjamin Wattenberg, *Values Matter Most* (New York: Simon & Schuster, 1995).

expertise about a topic usually has clearer beliefs about that subject. He or she will have more certainty about the choices involved and the consequences of different actions. However, strong beliefs about politics are not necessarily based only on fact. Often in politics, one encounters people who have strong convictions about a specific issue that are based on the intensity of their general political views. When the facts don't fit their theories, they may ignore fact and stick with their theory. Thus, Democrats and Republicans may observe the same event, such as a political debate, and come to completely opposite conclusions about who won. And public figures may, in the face of strong scientific evidence, reject the science if it does not favor their own political position. As in other aspects of life, people often find it easier to stick to their political beliefs than to change their minds.

Choices

Whether and how individuals' preferences and beliefs are expressed depends, ultimately, on a third component of opinion and that is the choice offered. We never really observe an individual's preferences and beliefs. Rather we only observe how they respond to a given situation or issue and the alternatives presented. In a public opinion survey, respondents answer the questions put to them, which usually reflect important issues at a given time. In elections, we chose among a relatively small set of choices: the candidates or parties. Those candidates themselves have taken stands on many different issues—taxes, spending, national defense, welfare, abortion, and so on. However, we can not mix and match the different positions. If one candidate is low tax and anti-abortion and another is high tax and pro-abortion, then the only choices are between those two clusters of policies. If a voter wants low taxes and is pro-abortion, there is no candidate who reflects the cluster of policies (or perhaps ideology) that the voter prefers. A wider set of candidates might yield someone who reflects the voter's ideology, but it is not in fact an option in the election.

Not only might some ideological positions not be reflected in the choices offered, some issues may not be on the political agenda. Throughout the 1930s and 1940s, the national Democratic leadership did its best to keep race relations out of the Democratic Party platform in order to keep southern Democrats in the party. Such an issue is called latent. Because the issue is not on the agenda there is no opportunity for people to express their preferences on it. In 1948, then-mayor Hubert Humphrey of Minneapolis proposed a plank to the Democratic Party's national platform calling for desegregation. Senator Strom Thurmond and other southern politicians, unhappy with the change in the racial platform of the party, left the Democrats. Thurmond himself ran for president that year as the Dixiecrat candidate against Harry Truman and Thomas Dewey. Not only did race rise from a latent national issue for the parties, but it became an active electoral choice in the form of the Dixiecrat Party.

Some latent issues never rise even to the level of public discourse. Race in the 1930s and 1940s, although off the national agenda, was nonetheless an issue on which most people had well-formed opinions. Some issues are so thoroughly removed from public debate that many people today would have a hard time formulating a clear opinion because they simply have not thought much about the matter. The process through which issues are vetted and debated publicly, then, is also an essential part of the formulation and expression of public opinion. Americans had debated the question of race relations for centuries by the 1948 election, and they continue to debate the matter today. Other fundamental issues lurk beneath the surface but have received little public debate. Other countries, such as Spain and Canada, have recently had to grapple with questions of separatism—whether Quebec should remain in Canada or how much independence ought Catalonia, the Basque Region, and Galicia have in Spain. One might imagine similar independence movements in the United States, but they have not surfaced since the 1870s; nor has there been serious discussion on the topic. Also, one might imagine significant constitutional reform, such as the creation of a unicameral legislature (as in Nebraska) at the national level. Some states have considered it, but there has been no serious national discussion. Were separatism or unicameralism put on a public opinion poll today it seems likely that most people would have no clear opinion. That is not to say that public opinion could not form on these matters. On latent issues such as these, coherent public opinion likely does not exist or if it does it takes the form of knee jerk reactions—"of course we shouldn't get rid of the U.S. Senate." After extensive debate on such matters, people would eventually discover where their preferences lay, but before that discourse occurs on most latent issues many people would have a hard time expressing what they want government to do.

The choices offered to people in elections, polls, town meetings, and other venues shape how preferences and beliefs are expressed in democratic politics. Public opinion, then, is never the pure expression of preferences but rather revealed preference, the choices people make among a given set of issues and alternatives available. In this chapter we examine the basis for individuals' preferences and the origins of their beliefs, as well as aggregate public opinion.

Variety of Opinion

The term *public opinion* is often bandied about in a way that suggests that all people are of the same mind, that there is national consensus on the matter. As we've noted, that is rarely the case. The term *public opinion* is really a shorthand description of the variety of opinion in society on a given question. What percentage are for a given bill in Congress and what percentage are against? What percentage support the president and what percentage oppose him? What percentage favor declaring war and what percentage do not?

Americans do hold common views on questions vital to governance and society. There is consensus on the legitimacy of the Constitution of the United States and trust in the rule of law, the principle that no one is above the law. There is consensus that we are a democratic society and that the outcomes of elections, whether a person likes the winners or not, determine who governs. These commonly held opinions and values are essential to maintaining a well-functioning democracy in the United States. They ensure peaceful transitions of government after each election and respect for laws produced by a legitimately chosen government.

There is also wide agreement on fundamental political values, such as equality of opportunity, liberty, and democracy.[7] Nearly all Americans agree that all people should have equal rights, regardless of race, gender, or social standing. Americans hold a common commitment to freedom. People who live in the United States are free to live where they want, travel where they want, work where they want, say what they want, and practice whatever religion they wish, including no religion at all. And Americans have an undying belief in democracy, that whenever possible public officials should be chosen by majority vote.[8] It makes sense to think of the American public as having a single opinion on these elemental questions.

On most matters that come before the government, however, the public does not hold a single view. Usually, opinions are divided between those who support the government or a proposed action and those who do not. Politicians are still attuned to public opinion when it is divided, but what matters most are the balance and direction of opinion. What do the majority of constituents want? Which way is opinion trending? Is it possible to find a popular middle ground?

People express their views to those in power in a variety of ways. Constituents contact their members of Congress directly through letters, phone calls, e-mails, and even personal visits to the representatives' offices. Most questions before Congress elicit little reaction from the public, but some questions start a maelstrom of objections. During the fall of 2008, Congress considered a $700 billion bailout of financial institutions. The volume of e-mail related to this bill was so great that at one point the House of Representatives had to limit incoming e-mail to keep its computers from crashing.[9]

People also express their opinions more publicly, through blogs, letters to newspapers and op-ed pieces, and conversations with others. They express their support for candidates with lawn signs and bumper stickers; by working on campaigns; by giving money to candidates, groups, and party organizations; and, most simply, by voting.

Such expressions of opinions and preferences are not always easy to interpret. If a constituent votes against a member of Congress, did the voter do so because of a controversial decision that the legislator made in Congress or because the voter decided to vote against all politicians from the legislator's party? Or for some other reason?

Political scientists and political consultants try to provide more refined and structured descriptions of public opinion using surveys. On any important issue,

7 See Louis Hartz, *The Liberal Tradition in America: An Interpretation of American Political Thought since the Revolution* (New York: Harcourt, Brace, 1955).

8 For a discussion of political beliefs of Americans, see Everett Carl Ladd, *The American Ideology* (Storrs, CT: Roper Center, 1994).

9 Jordy Yeager, "House Limits Constituent E-mail to Prevent Crash," *The Hill*, September 30, 2008, http://thehill.com/leading-the-news/house-limits-constituent-e-mails-to-prevent-crash-2008-09-30.html (accessed 3/24/09).

the government may pursue different policies. Public opinion on a given issue can be thought of as the distribution of opinion across the different options. Likewise, public opinion may represent the division of support for a leader or party. We try to gauge where majority support lies and how intensely or firmly citizens across the spectrum hold their views. More and more, politicians rely on opinion polls to anticipate the effects of their decisions, to identify opportunities, and to develop ways to blunt the objections to controversial decisions. Answering a survey, then, can also be a form of political action, because it may influence political decisions.

For political scientists and other researchers, the challenge is to ask questions that allow people to express their preferences and that capture how people think about important issues at that moment. It is a good exercise for any student to try their hand at writing a survey. The typical public opinion survey over the phone lasts about 5 to 10 minutes, and each question takes about 15 seconds to ask and answer. That means that a typical survey consists of 20 to 40 questions that capture a broad set of current issues and events as well as demographic characteristics of people. (It is a good exercise to try to write your own survey on a topic of interest.) Each question, then, must be asked efficiently. It must try to summarize the issue at stake in few words and capture the full range of possible or likely answers in a reasonably small set of options.

For instance, the debate over the legality of abortion quickly sorted into two polar positions in the 1970s—pro-life and pro-choice. Survey research has since measured the percentage of the public that identifies as pro-life or as pro-choice. As this issue has evolved over time, however, it has become clear that those are not the only possible policies that the government could pursue, and survey researchers have developed more refined questions to ascertain the conditions under which people would and would not allow abortion. Would a respondent allow abortion for teenagers if parents did not consent? What about cases of rape or incest? What if the pregnancy endangered the life of the mother? Such refinements have allowed for a more nuanced expression of public preference on this issue, and they have led Congress to make public policies that are more attuned to the public's preferences. Congress stopped Medicaid funding for abortions in the 1980s and passed a ban on late-term or "partial birth" abortions, both of which were opposed by large majorities. But Congress has not approved highly restrictive laws, even though they have been introduced frequently.[10] Public opinion, then, should not be thought of as a single-minded view or consensus on a given matter, but as a range of options. Social scientists call this a variable, and social scientists and political strategists try to gauge the frequency of support for each option or side in a public debate and determine where the majority's favor lies.

Much of the science of public opinion research concerns the appropriate way to ask questions. If a question is too vague or confusing or doesn't offer

10 Throughout the 1980s and 1990s, Representative Henry Hyde of Illinois regularly introduced an amendment to appropriations and other bills to ban abortion in the United States. The Hyde Amendment, as it came to be called, was never passed.

the opinion that the survey respondent would have said, the respondent will skip the question or perhaps answer the question in a confused way. Researchers have also learned that the framing of questions need to be balanced. Leading questions will prompt respondents to give answers that fit with the bias of the question, because many people try to answer questions in ways that they think the surveyor would like them to. The challenge is to discover ways of asking questions that allow people to express their own views, without the questions getting in the way.

Opinions themselves take a variety of forms, depending on what is at issue. It is helpful to keep in mind a few common examples in thinking about this subject.

Evaluations of Those in Government and Other Institutions. Survey researchers use a variety of questions to gauge support for or opposition to the government. They ask about approval of the job that the president is doing, approval of the job that Congress is doing, approval of individual members of Congress, and approval of the job the Supreme Court is doing. At elections, those who vote express their support for and opposition to members of government directly through their votes. In other disciplines, similar questions are asked about social and economic institutions and leaders.

Assessments of Public Policies. Do you support or oppose a given policy? Do you think a problem is important or not? What do you think is the most important problem that the government should address? How people answer such questions depends on the choices that are presented and immediate circumstances. Views on specific issues may follow the same patterns as general political orientations, if they directly affect partisan groups or derive from ongoing political debates between parties or ideological groups. For instance, a bill that would alter wages for public employees affects unions directly and thus touches a core constituency of the Democratic Party. So, we might find that Democrats are more likely to view this issue in a certain way.

Assessments of Current Circumstances. Is the economy performing well or poorly? Is crime high or low? Is the country headed in the right direction? Such questions might seem to have objective answers, but often there are differences of opinion about the state of the economy and other aspects of our society, depending on each individual's own experiences and what he or she has read or heard through the media.

Political Orientations. The two most important indicators of individuals' general political orientations are party identification and ideology. Do you consider yourself a Democrat, a Republican, of another party, or of no party in particular? Do you consider yourself liberal, moderate, or conservative? These concepts capture general political orientations that are usually quite stable. Researchers have shown that party identifications predict voting preferences very well and correlate strongly with evaluations of those in office. Party identification often acts as a filter for information, a tinted lens that colors the way people view the world and interpret any piece of information. Immediately after an election, members and supporters of the winning party express much greater optimism about the economy, about global affairs, and even about their own personal finances. Often a Democrat and a Republican will offer markedly different views on a presidential debate, with the Democrat concluding that the Democratic candidate clearly won and the Republican concluding that the Republican candidate was victorious.

Political scientists characterize the variation in public opinion by measuring the percentage of people who choose each particular option or variable. Often a bar chart in which the height of each bar is the percentage of people choosing each outcome of a variable represents the distribution of public opinion. Typically, we care about which option receives the most support or the support of a majority. In elections, for example, counties and states tally the votes received by each candidate. The candidate with the largest number of votes (not necessarily a majority) wins. Nationwide in 2012, Barack Obama received 51 percent of all votes cast (a total of 65,387,700 votes), Mitt Romney received 47 percent of all votes cast (60,724,464 votes), and all other candidates combined received 2 percent of votes cast (2,244,213 votes). Obama's share of the vote was slightly lower in 2012 than in 2008, in which he won the largest share for a Democratic presidential candidate since Lyndon Johnson in 1964. Social scientists, journalists, and even politicians view the size of the winner's vote margin as an indication of the breadth and intensity of the support for the winner.

Opinion data, such as the information gathered in surveys, provide an even more subtle and varied measure of public attitudes and political orientations. Consider ideology (which we discuss in more detail later in this chapter). According to Gallup poll results reported in January 2012, shortly before Obama's victory, 40 percent of Americans described themselves as conservative, 35 percent as moderate, and 21 percent as liberal. Another 4 percent do not think of themselves in these terms.[11] For an indicator such as ideology, then, no single camp has a clear majority, but we can say that self-described conservatives outnumber self-described liberals.[12]

One particularly important debate about public opinion today concerns ideological polarization. Pundits and other observers have often argued that the public is deeply divided into very conservative and very liberal groups, with relatively few people in the middle. Observers assume that this view of "two Americas" holds true for questions about ideology and across a wide range of issues, such as taxation, health care, education, and foreign affairs. The political

11 Lydia Saad, "Conservatives Remain the Largest Ideological Group in the U.S.," January 12, 2012, www.gallup.com/poll/152021/conservatives-remain-largest-ideological-group.aspx (accessed 11/20/12).

12 As an exercise, we recommend: (1) writing down several concepts of interest (such as ideology, partisanship, policy preferences on taxes or abortion); (2) finding surveys that have measured public opinion on those topics (for example, at the Roper Center or the Pew Research Center on People and the Press); and (3) making a bar chart showing the percent of people who chose each category for a given question.

scientists Morris Fiorina, Jeremy Pope, and Samuel Abrams tackled this alleged polarization in their 2004 book *Culture War? The Myth of a Polarized America.* Fiorina and his coauthors made simple bar charts to describe the distribution of public opinion in the United States. Rather than a deep divide, they found that on most issues Americans are centrists, meaning either moderate or leaning somewhat to the right or left. This finding has important implications about the ability to reach consensus in public debate. It also raises an even more elusive puzzle. Although most Americans are centrist, most representatives in Congress vote either on the very liberal end of the spectrum or on the very conservative end. The public, then, is not polarized, but Congress is. It is worth pausing to consider why this is the case. Political scientists have suggested that it is the nature of the debate in Washington and the choices put before Congress, or that it is due to the organization of parties in Congress or to the election process—who votes and who doesn't, primary elections, and campaign contributors. The debate over this question has yet to come to a definitive resolution; as yet a convincing answer has not been found.[13]

Just as we do not think of public opinion as consensus, nor do we think of the public as monolithic. From the start, American society was conceived to be a large, heterogeneous nation. The guarantees of freedom of religion, the press, and association in the Bill of Rights were meant to protect this diversity of opinion and belief. Indeed, one of the problems the Founders faced was how to maintain a stable democracy in a large society. James Madison famously wrote that "expanding the sphere" of the United States would make it less likely for any single group to achieve a stable majority capable of riding roughshod over other groups. A large heterogeneous nation, then, would cure the "mischief of faction."

Madison's vision of diverse opinions and beliefs has indeed come to pass. American society is a hodgepodge of different ethnic and racial groups; Americans differ greatly in educational attainment, income, and religion. The U.S. Census, conducted every 10 years, measures variations in housing, family, employment, and other demographic characteristics. The Census Bureau also conducts monthly surveys on everything from communication to employment to voting. These data provide a rich picture of the diversity and complexity of American society. For example, 15 percent of Americans claim Hispanic ethnicity, 13 percent are black or African American, 5 percent are Asian, 1 percent are Native American, and 74 percent identify themselves as white. One person of every eight living in the United States today was not born here. Although the large majority of Americans

13 For five different views, see Morris Fiorina et al., *Culture War?* 2nd ed. (New York: Pearson, Longman, 2005); Nolan McCarty et al., *Polarization in America*: The Dance of Ideology and Unequal Riches (Princeton, NJ: Princeton University Press, 2007); Gary Jacobson, *A Divider, Not a Uniter: George W. Bush, the American People, the 2006 Election, and Beyond* (White Plains, NY: Longman, 2007); Alan Abramowitz, "Constraint, Ideology, and Polarization in the American Electorate," paper presented at the annual meeting of the American Political Science Association, August 30, 2007; and Stephen Ansolabehere et al., "Purple America," *Journal of Economic Perspectives* 20, no. 2 (Spring 2006): 97–118.

identify with some form of Christianity and most of those are Protestant, the single largest sect is Roman Catholicism. Slightly more than 25 percent of adults in the United States have a college degree; 15 percent did not complete high school. America is one of the richest nations on earth, but approximately 1 in 10 Americans still lives in poverty. The most populous region of the country is the South, with approximately 35 percent of the people. American society can be divided in many other ways. The picture that emerges from the census data is indeed one of a heterogeneous society.[14] In describing and understanding the attitudes, opinions, needs, and wants of the American public, we must be mindful of the fact that the public itself is fractured into many subgroups and interests.[15]

ORIGINS OF PUBLIC OPINION

To understand the meaning and origins of the public's opinions, we must have some sense of the basis for individuals' preferences and beliefs. An individual's opinions are the products of his or her personality, social characteristics, and interests. They mirror who a person is, what she wants, and the manner in which she is embedded in a family and community, and the broader economy and society. But opinions are also shaped by institutional, political, and governmental forces that make it more likely that an individual will hold some beliefs and less likely that he will hold others.

Self-Interest

Individuals' preferences about politics and public policy are rooted partly in self-interest. Laws and other governmental actions directly affect people's interests—their disposable income, the quality of public services and goods, and personal safety, to give just a few examples. It is not surprising, then, that when people express their political opinions, they react to the effects that government actions have had on them personally.

Economic interests are perhaps the most salient preferences when it comes to people's opinions. Government policies, ranging from export and import rules to regulations to spending and taxes, directly affect individual Americans'

---

14 *The Statistical Abstract of the United States.*

15 As an exercise, we recommend consulting the *Statistical Abstract of the United States* and constructing bar charts (distributions) for the following demographic variables: (1) household incomes; (2) residency (urban, suburban, and rural); (3) region; (4) race; and (5) religion. Note the largest category for each variable. For income, calculate the level of income such that half of the people have income below that level and half have income above it (the median).

personal well-being. Taxes reduce disposable income. The average American family has income of $64,000 before taxes and $50,000 after taxes. Those taxes, of course, pay for government programs like Social Security and Medicare, national defense, and other goods. Not all families and individuals are taxed equally; nor do all benefit equally from government programs. Very low-income families pay little or no taxes because they cannot afford to, and they are net-recipients of government assistance. Middle-income families are also direct and indirect beneficiaries of government programs, such as public education for children.

Government regulations also affect people's economic self-interests. Government rules aim to protect people from potentially harmful pollutants; they preserve the value of neighbors' property, protect consumers from potential harm, and even create the property rights necessary to maintain a well-functioning market economy. But they also limit how people use their property and may raise the cost of operating a business.

Governments also act as a source of insurance. The Federal Deposit Insurance Corporation insures bank accounts against possible risk of failure by the bank where consumers have checking, savings, or other accounts. The government offers income assistance to those in short-run unemployment and disability insurance for those permanently unable to work. Such programs guard the average American against economic risks.

And the government is directly involved in the labor market. Twenty-one million people, 14 percent of the U.S. civilian labor force, work for federal, state, or local governments; another 1 million people are in the armed services. Government spending comprises a substantial share of the national economy (though less than in most other nations). In the United States federal government expenditures account for 20 percent of gross domestic product (GDP).[16] Virtually every American has an interest in the government's role in the nation's economy and strong preferences about tax rates and expenditure priorities. Public opinion about taxes and spending reflect these preferences. Given the enormous influence of the federal government in the economy, assessments of the president and the party in power often correspond to how well the nation's economy performs.

Individuals' attitudes toward government reflect other forms of self-interest as well. Laws affect families, the status of civic and religious organizations, and neighborhoods. Zoning laws and urban redevelopment programs shape the nature of neighborhoods, including the mix of commercial and residential housing and the density of low-income housing in an area. Tax laws treat nonprofits, such as universities, religious organizations, and social clubs, differently from for-profit companies, making it easier for nonprofit organizations to exist. Family law affects how easy it is for families to stay together, what happens when they break down, and what rights and responsibilities parents have.

16 The gross domestic product consists of the value of all goods and services produced in the United States. It is one measure of the nation's income.

Individuals have a personal stake in decisions bearing on their own communities and families. Proposed changes in such laws bring immediate reaction from those affected.

Values

Much of what individuals want from their government is rooted in values concerning what is right or wrong, or in other words, our philosophies about morality, justice, and ethics. Most of us have values systems—principles of right and wrong that we can apply to new problems and circumstances. Such values systems originate in many places—families, religion, education, groups, and so forth—and they shape what we want. Views of right and wrong are deeply seated and often determine our preferences in particular circumstances. Individuals will often act in ways that defy their economic self-interest because such behavior is guided by their values. For example, many religions call for their adherents to tithe—to give some fraction of their income to those less well off. Such behavior runs strictly against economic self-interest, but it is nonetheless rational behavior to the extent that it is consistent with the individual's values.

Tithing is an example of economic justice. Values of what is right and wrong may determine an individual's preferences about how government and society distributes or redistributes income. Americans generally adhere to a belief in equal opportunity. So long as all people have an equal opportunity, an equal chance to excel, we will have a just society. That idea has driven our society to try to root out discrimination in employment, housing, and education. It has also led us to create a universal public education system. In some states, such as New Hampshire, Ohio, and California, courts have invoked this principle of equality to insist that the states try to equalize public school expenditures per pupil across districts.

Values also shape our notions of what is a crime and what is a suitable punishment. One of the most morally laden debates in American history is the debate over capital punishment. Does the government have the right to take the life of an individual, even if that individual has taken the life of someone else? An ancient sense of justice seems to call for exactly that: an eye for an eye. Other ideas of morality speak against capital punishment. And our values about government and its appropriate powers say that people must be protected against arbitrary and capricious acts of government. The death penalty is irreversible and the possibility of a governmental error has led some to claim that the government can never have the power to take the life of an individual. In 1972, the U.S. Supreme Court ruled just that in *Furman v. Georgia*, though it validated the death penalty in certain cases four years later.[17]

Our values also reflect established social norms of our community, analogous to common law. What, for example, is marriage? One might argue that marriage is an economic convenience, as defined by laws that tie taxes and

17 *Furman v. Georgia* 408 U.S. 238 (1972).

inheritance to marital status. Most people, however, express more basic ideas of marriage, and those principles dictate whether they think that gay marriages ought to be allowed. Such norms change over time. For example, a century ago interracial marriages were deemed unacceptable by most in American society, and most states adopted laws designed to prevent interracial marriage. Some of these laws have survived to this day, and have become the center of the controversy over gay marriage. Indeed, it was a challenge to just such a law in Massachusetts, the case of *Goodridge v. Department of Public Health*, that ultimately allowed the state's Supreme Judicial Council to allow gay marriage in the state in May 2004.[18]

Principles and values guide our notions of what we want government to do. When government acts contrary to our values, the hurt we feel can be as intense as if our pecuniary interests were at stake. Values, however, often conflict with one another. Many of us struggle with knowing what is right and wrong in various circumstances because a given law or policy touches on different values and in conflicting ways. A question like capital punishment evokes our notions of how much power government ought to have over individuals, even criminals, and our fundamental ideas of justice and vengeance. At a societal level, conflicting values are particularly difficult to resolve. Unlike situations involving economic interests, it is hard to bargain over our differences when the differences strike at fundamental principles of right and wrong.

By the same token, there are many values that unite us. Probably no nation and certainly no democracy could survive if its citizens did not share some fundamental beliefs. If Americans had few common values or perspectives, it would be very difficult for them to reach agreement on particular issues. Over the past half century, political philosophers and political scientists have reflected on what those values are and settled on three important precepts. Americans almost universally agree with: (1) the democracy principle (that majority rule is a good decision rule); (2) the importance of equal opportunity; and (3) the idea that that government is best which governs least.

Identities

A third source of political preferences are our identities. How do we consider ourselves? Do we think of ourselves as being of a particular race or religion? Do we identify strongly with a given place? What language or languages do we speak? People use race, religion, place, language, and many other characteristics to describe and define themselves. These descriptors tap fundamental psychological attachments that go beyond self-interest and values, though they are often reinforced by our interests and values. Identities have real effects on our sense of happiness and well-being and therefore affect our preferences.

One of the most salient political identities in the United States is political party. The authors of *The American Voter* characterize party identification as

18 *Goodridge v. Department of Public Health* 798 N.E. 2d 941 (Mass. 2003).

a stable psychological attachment usually developed in childhood and carried throughout one's adult life. Party identifications are, of course, shaped by interests and values as well as by current events, but partisanship also has deep roots in family, local culture, and other factors that shape identities. It is common, for example, for people to rely on their partisan identities in filtering information. Partisan identifiers who watch presidential debates overwhelmingly think their candidate won the debate, regardless of what actually transpired. Party also has its own unique hold on our voting behavior. Even after taking into account self-interests, moral values, and other identities, partisanship continues to be one of the best predictors of how someone will vote. (See the discussion of party voting in Chapters 11 and 12.)

An ingenious study showing how identity matters to people's preferences was conducted by Alan Gerber and Gregory Huber of Yale University. They studied consumption behavior of people following elections and found that people who identified strongly with a particular party and whose party won the election spent much more on durable consumer goods, such as washing machines and other appliances, than did people whose candidates did not win or people who did not identify strongly with a party. Behavioral economists and social psychologists have documented other such phenomena, such as the effect of sports teams' victories on feelings of happiness.[19]

People who hold a specific identity often express strong affinity for others of the same identity. You might vote for someone of the same national background or ethnicity quite apart from, or in spite of, the sorts of laws that politician promises to enact. Political scientists call this preference for like types of people "descriptive representation." The preference for people of the same identity is an important subject in the area of race and elections. The Voting Rights Act tries to protect African Americans, Hispanics, and other racial and ethnic groups against discriminatory electoral practices that prevent those voters from electing their preferred candidates. Since the Voting Rights Act was passed in 1965, the percentage of members of Congress who are African American and Hispanic has increased from 0 to about 15 to 20 percent. Race, gender, social class, and place—all create strong identities that shape voting behavior.

Social Origins of Preferences

Identities, values, and even interests are not hard wired in our psyche nor do most people arrive at these bases for their preferences through quiet, philosophical contemplation. Rather, our preferences are developed through our upbringing as children, through our schooling and religion, through our interactions with friends and family, through our coworkers and our experiences in the world. Even our most basic instincts related to survival and comfort are expressed in

19 Alan Gerber and Gregory Huber, "Partisanship and Economic Behavior," *American Political Science Review* 103 (2009): 407–26.

reaction to circumstances. In other words, our preferences are formed socially, a process called political socialization.

political socialization

The induction of individuals into the political culture; the process of learning the underlying beliefs and values on which the political system is based

There are at least four components to political socialization. The first is information, or what you know. Information is critical to the formulation of beliefs, as many of our basic beliefs concern how we think the world works. Information can also lead us to develop preferences. For example, when we read the news online or in a newspaper, listen to the radio, watch TV, and talk to friends, we learn basic facts about the world and from those we infer what's important or salient, which determines the intensity of our preferences.

The second is education, or how to think. High school civics courses teach students the basics of government—how to vote, the organization of the government, and so forth. But they also present students with choices and challenge students to express their ideas and beliefs. One of the great puzzles about American society is why it is that better educated people tend to hold values that embrace more strongly the protection of civil liberties. Learning is certainly not limited to schools. We learn how to think about politics and government at home, in church, and when reading newspapers or Web sites. All are arenas where we learn values and principles and how to apply them to politics and other domains.

The third component of socialization is context. The context in which we live creates opportunities and incentives that shape our behavior and our preferences. If we live in a community where we often encounter people of many different economic backgrounds and racial groups, we come to develop a greater awareness of the circumstances of different sorts of people. People in such highly integrated communities are thought to develop values distinct from those who live in socially homogeneous cultures. Someone who lives their entire life in a wealthy suburb probably has little idea and awareness of what life for someone living on minimum wage is really like. Social structure is another example. Some societies are very hierarchical and where you are in the hierarchy determines what you want. The hierarchy itself is an institution and, as such, creates incentives or constraints on how people can achieve what they want, but the social context can also instill in an individual new values, including a desire to maintain the hierarchy itself.

A fourth, and perhaps most important, factor is social pressure. Others influence who we are and what we think. We all grew up and live in social groups—families, networks of friends, schools, companies, and so on. The influence is sometimes overt, such as when a group tries to coerce someone to vote for a certain candidate. But most often the influence of social groups over us is subtle. We respect authority figures, such as our parents or religious leaders, and we readily take on the beliefs and values of those individuals as our own.

Some of the most famous social science research has examined the influence of authority figures and of ones position within a group on behaviors. Professor Stanley Milgram designed a compelling set of experiments in which an authority figure (an expert) instructed individuals (subjects) to administer shocks to a third person (the learner). Subjects were told that this study tested a novel educational approach in which wrong answers were punished with a small electrical shock, and they were instructed to administer a shock to the learner for each wrong answer he gave. The learner was in fact a professional actor who pretended to have received a shock, as no shocks were actually administered. What Milgram really wanted to understand was whether average Americans would inflict high, even lethal, levels of electrical shocks simply because an authority figure told them to. Most social psychologists at the time (the 1960s) thought the typical American would resist such pressures, but a majority of the subjects in Milgram's studies willingly applied extremely high and sometimes lethal electrical shocks to the learner. These studies, now known as the Milgram experiments, demonstrated convincingly the power that social pressure, especially that coming from authority, has on what we believe and how we behave.

This is not to say that social pressure is bad. It is through the social structure of families, schools, churches, and the media that our society transfers values from one generation to the next. These institutions are, no doubt, the routes by which our belief in the American system of government, in democracy itself, is conveyed.

In contemporary America, some elements of the socialization process tend to produce differences in outlook, whereas others promote similarities. For many generations there were only three national television networks, and their evening news programs were quite similar. During these times, the media tended to report similarly on many different topics, and the mass media were viewed as a source of social and political consensus. Today, the news media are more fractured, the audiences have segmented, and the new media environment is often thought to contribute to discord and dissensus.

Political socialization is a complex process. It pervades our lives from the time we are infants, and the components of socialization—information, education, context, and pressure—interact with one another. Education systems often rely on hierarchies (context) and social pressure from peers and teachers to perform (pressure). And there are many politically important agents of socialization including the family, organized religion, membership in social groups, education, the media, and current events themselves. Although these factors cannot fully explain the development of any one individual's political outlook, let us consider the ways in which they tend to influence most people.

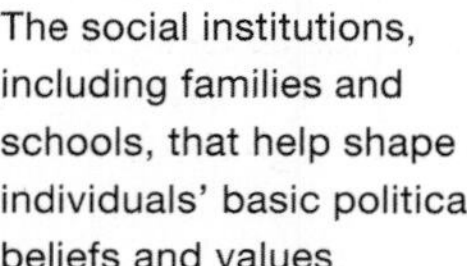

The social institutions, including families and schools, that help shape individuals' basic political beliefs and values

The Family. Most people acquire their initial orientation to politics from their families. Although relatively few parents spend much time teaching their children about politics, political conversations occur in many households, and children tend to absorb the political views of their parents and other caregivers, perhaps without realizing it. Studies have suggested, for example, that party preferences are initially acquired at home. Children raised in households in which the primary caregivers are Democrats tend to become Democrats themselves, whereas children raised in homes where their caregivers are Republicans tend to favor the Republican Party.[20] Similarly, children reared in politically liberal

20 See Angus Campbell, Philip E. Converse, Warren E. Miller, and Donald E. Stokes, *The American Voter* (New York: Wiley, 1960), p. 147. Psychological attachments to political parties, called party identification, are discussed in Chapter 12.

households are more likely than not to develop a liberal outlook, whereas children raised in politically conservative settings are likely to see the world through conservative lenses. Obviously, not all children absorb their parents' political views. For instance, two of the four children of Ronald Reagan, a conservative Republican president, rejected their parents' conservative values. The late president's son Ron supported the Democrat John Kerry in the 2004 presidential race and Barack Obama in the 2008 presidential race. Moreover, even those children whose views are initially shaped by parental values may change their minds as they mature and experience political life for themselves. Nevertheless, the family is an important initial source of political orientation for everyone.

Education. Education is a uniquely important influence on an individual's political beliefs and preferences (Table 10.1). In some respects, of course, schooling is a great equalizer. Governments use public education to try to teach all children a common set of civic values. It is mainly in school that Americans acquire their basic belief in liberty, equality, and democracy. In history classes, students are taught that the Founders fought for the principle

Table 10.1

EDUCATION AND PUBLIC OPINION

	LEVEL OF EDUCATION (% AGREEING)			
ISSUES	**GRADE SCHOOL**	**HIGH SCHOOL**	**SOME COLLEGE**	**COLLEGE GRADUATE**
Women and men should have equal roles	73	82	90	90
Abortion should never be permitted.	27	17	12	9
The government should adopt national health insurance.	66	58	50	49
Helping to bring democracy to other nations is very important	36	37	21	12
Government should see to fair treatment in jobs for African Americans.	80	58	54	60
Government should provide fewer services to reduce government spending	10	18	21	25

SOURCE: American National Election Studies 2008 data, Center for Political Studies, University of Michigan, www.electionstudies.org.

ANALYZING THE EVIDENCE

What factors might explain the relationship between education and opinion? Some commentators believe that many college courses have a liberal political orientation. Do you agree? How have your college courses affected your opinions on social and political issues?

of liberty. Through participation in class elections and student government, students are taught the virtues of democracy. In the course of studying such topics as the Constitution, the Civil War, and the civil rights movement, students are taught the importance of equality. These lessons are repeated at every grade level in a variety of contexts. No wonder they are such an important element in Americans' beliefs.

At the same time, however, differences in educational attainment are strongly associated with differences in political outlook. In particular, those who attend college are often exposed to philosophies and modes of thought that will forever distinguish them from their friends and neighbors who do not pursue college diplomas. Table 10.1 outlines some general differences of opinion that are found between college graduates and other Americans. One of the major differences is in levels of political participation. College graduates vote, write letters to the editor, join campaigns, take part in protests, and generally make their voices heard.

Social Groups. Social groups are another important source of divergent political orientations and values. Social groups include those to which individuals belong involuntarily—gender and race, for example—as well as those to which people belong voluntarily—such as political parties, labor unions, religious organizations, and educational and occupational associations. Some social groups have both voluntary and involuntary attributes.

Membership in social groups has strong and distinctive effects on the political values and beliefs of individuals. A clear example arises upon comparing whites and African Americans. In surveys conducted by the Pew Research Center, clear majorities of whites supported the ideas that government should do more to guarantee food and shelter (62 percent) and generally help the needy (55 percent). Much larger majorities of blacks expressed support for the guarantee of food and shelter (80 percent) and the provision of help for the needy (72 percent).[21] Other issues show similar patterns, reflecting the differences in experience, background, and interests between blacks and whites in America (Figure 10.1).

More striking still, race seems to affect how other factors, like income and education, shape preferences. Among whites, there is a definite correlation between conservatism and income. Higher-income whites tend to support more conservative policies and are more likely to identify with the Republican Party, while lower-income whites tend to favor more liberal economic policies and align with the Democratic Party. Nearly all African Americans, on the other hand, side with the Democrats and support liberal economic policies, regardless of income. Why are high-income African Americans not as supportive of Republicans as their white counterparts? There are many other such instances, including differences across religious groups, between men and women, and

21 Pew Research Center for the People and the Press, "The Black and White of Public Opinion," October 31, 2005, http://people-press.org/commentary/?analysisid=121 (accessed 3/24/09).

Figure 10.1

DISAGREEMENT AMONG BLACKS AND WHITES

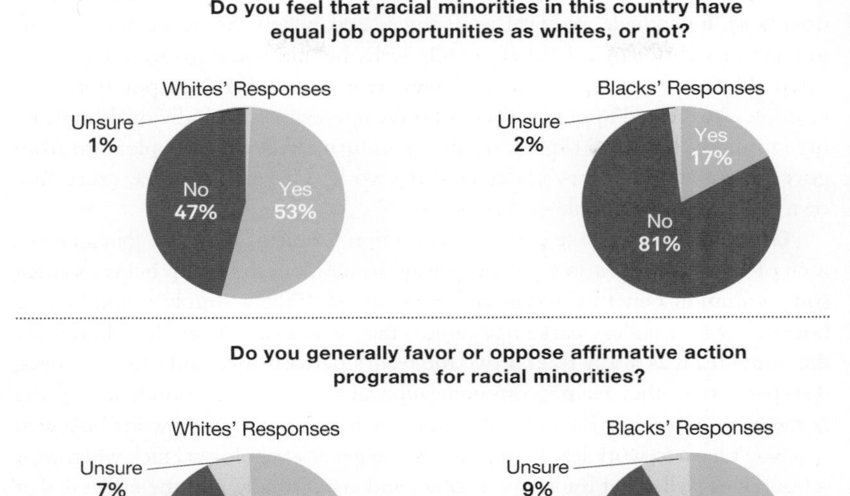

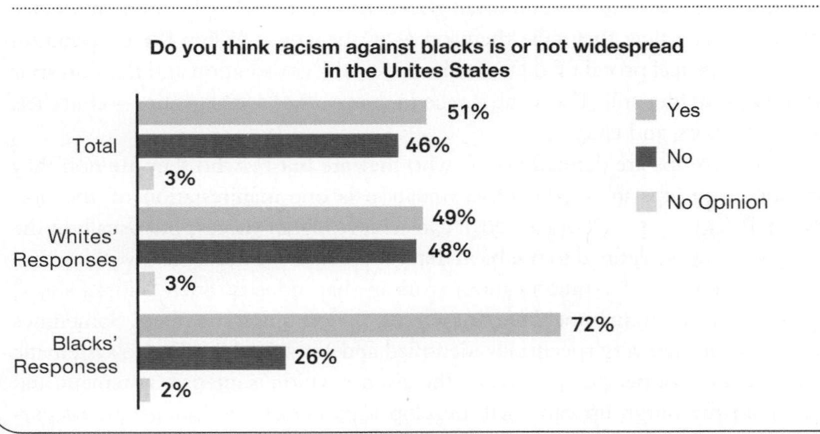

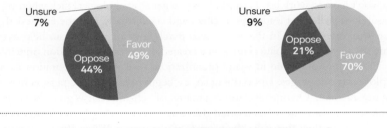

SOURCES: Gallup polls, June 8–25, 2006, June 12–15, 2003, and October 16–19, 2009, gallup.com.

ANALYZING THE EVIDENCE

Although America's system of legally mandated racial segregation ended nearly half a century ago, its effects continue to linger. In contemporary America, blacks and whites have different perspectives on race relations. Do you think that black-white differences have increased or decreased in the past few decades? Are these differences of opinion important?

between young and old. Some of these differences may be traced to self-interest, but most cannot. The explanations for differences in opinions and voting behaviors among social groups surely has something to do with the nature of such groups in American society.

Social psychology of groups offers a rich and fertile way to understand the origins of individuals' political preferences and beliefs. Some degree of self-interest or of ideological belief usually lurks behind social groups. These are often the reason groups form to begin with. Unions and corporations, for example, are created to pursue the economic interests of the individuals in those organizations, but these organizations can in turn affect what people want from government and how they understand the world. Groups, however, exert their own influence over people's preferences.

Groups help overcome the collective action problem. When we join a group, each of us usually does so for some private benefit, but the group helps us attain some common benefit through collective action. Take a simple example. The home crowd at a college basketball game is the "sixth man." They cheer loudly for the home team as a way to improve the team's performance and often it works, disrupting the other team's communication and raising the confidence of the home team. Why cheer? Your grades won't be better; your tuition won't be lower; you won't have to work less hard. Rather, you get a psychological kick when your school does well. That leads you to cheer and cheer loudly, and the effect is that your team does better. In this way, social psychology of groups can help overcome the obstacles to political influence created by the collective action principle.

The same holds true in many organizations. We join a corporation as an employee to gain wages. Upon doing so, we begin to take on the perspective of that organization. On one level this is a matter of self-interest: as goes the corporation so goes our wages. But it often goes much deeper. People often internalize the collective value; they take them on as if their own. When the corporation does well, we feel proud of the contribution to the corporation and that can spur us to work harder still. The same is true in many other social groups—churches, schools, towns, and cities.

Some groups are defined not by who they are but by who they are not; they are the outgroups in society. Discrimination is one manifestation of the outgroup. If a group is well organized, it can achieve higher success but usually at the expense of those defined to not be in that group. In some industries, workers who are not members of a union cannot work in that industry. Such "closed shop" rules benefit union members but at the cost of non-union members. Sometimes the outgroups are very specifically identified and ostracized, leading to systematic discrimination or persecution. When the discrimination is intense, systematic and long-held the outgroup can itself develop a particular psychology. Social psychologist James Sidanius expresses this as a social dominance relationship and argues that more numerous groups in all societies systematically discriminate against less numerous groups. The less numerous groups develop a common identity, and they come to see their own situation in the treatment of others of their group. Writing about the particular psychology of African Americans in the United States, Professor Michael Dawson calls this the "linked fate" of African Americans. It has been found in many other societies as well, such as Albanians in

Table 10.2
CHANGING PARTISAN DIVISION IN THE LATINO COMMUNITY

	2004		2008	
BACKGROUND	**DEM. (%)**	**REP. (%)**	**DEM. (%)**	**REP. (%)**
Cuban	17	52	53	20
Mexican	47	18	50	18
Puerto Rican	50	17	61	11

SOURCE: Mark Hugo Lopez and Susan Minushkin, "2008 National Survey of Latinos: Hispanic Voter Attitudes," Pew Hispanic Center Report, July 24, 2008, http://pewhispanic.org/files/reports/90.pdf (accessed 4/30/09).

ANALYZING THE EVIDENCE

Members of America's Latino community share a linguistic heritage, but they are not politically homogeneous. What factors might account for these differences? Why might so many Cuban Americans have changed their party allegiance between 2004 and 2008?

Italy. Discrimination then is the collective bad against which the identity of all in a given group must act. Even high-income African Americans will, thus, be led by the collective needs and identities of their group to support policies that are likely to help large numbers of low-income or underemployed African Americans.

Social groups can further affect public opinion through communication, shaping the flow of information and even creating ways to exert social pressure. Social groups develop communication networks and accumulate resources in order to inform their members and others about the choices they face and how to get involved. A labor union, for instance, can inform its members of an upcoming election and identify which candidates the union endorses. This does not mean that the members will vote according to the unions' preferences but it does make it easier for the members to do so by providing the information that the members need to vote in the interests of the union. In this way, the social group can help to overcome the collective action problems that its members face.

Groups such as unions, corporations, and other associations often pool their resources to conduct political campaigns. Groups give funds directly to candidates and parties to help the candidates they support to win elections. The groups also conduct their own advertising campaigns on specific issues or on behalf of candidates. For example, corporations, environmental groups, labor unions, and other organizations spent $147 million in 2010 in their efforts to persuade the public to vote either yes or no on nine separate propositions. The most controversial was Proposition 23, which would have repealed the state of California's new cap on emission of greenhouse gases. These campaigns tried to influence the beliefs and preferences of all Californians, even those who were not employed by one of the corporations or dues-paying members of one of the environmental groups.

The importance of social groups in understanding public opinion is borne out in differences in public opinion across groups in our society. We have seen that there are deep differences between African Americans and whites. Latinos are another major American subgroup with distinctive opinions on some public issues (Table 10.2). A 2012 survey by the Pew Hispanic Center found that

Table 10.3
SHOULD SAME-SEX MARRIAGE BE LEGALIZED?

RELIGIOUS GROUP	IN FAVOR (%)	OPPOSED (%)
White evangelical Protestant	14	81
White nonevangelical Protestant	43	47
White non-Hispanic Catholic	41	49
Black Protestant	15	79
Secular	60	30

SOURCE: Pew Research Center for the People and the Press, "A Stable Majority: Most Americans Still Oppose Same-Sex Marriage," April 1, 2008, http://pewforum.org/docs/?DocID=290 (accessed 3/24/09).

education is the top concern of Hispanic voters, whereas the economy ranked highest among white non-Hispanic voters.[22] There are also often differences within social groups tied to specific issues or generational changes. Among Latinos, Cuban Americans have long been disproportionately Republican, while those of Mexican, Puerto Rican, and Central American descent identify more often as Democrats. That difference traces to the Cuban Americans relationship with their homeland and the longstanding differences between the Republicans and Democrats over Cuba. Interestingly, that difference had largely vanished by 2008; surveys during the presidential campaign found that Cuban Americans are now nearly as Democratic as other Hispanic groups.

In recent years, contending political forces have placed a number of religious and moral issues on the national political agenda. The Republican Party, in particular, has emphasized its support for traditional "family values" and its opposition to abortion, same-sex marriage, and other practices opposed by conservative religious leaders. It is not surprising that public opinion on these issues differs along religious lines, with evangelical Protestants being most supportive of traditional values and respondents identifying themselves as "secular" manifesting the least support for them. For example, Table 10.3 shows how different religious groups view same-sex marriage.

Men and women express differing political opinions as well. Women tend to be less militaristic than men on issues of war and peace, more likely than men to favor measures to protect the environment, and more supportive than men of government social and health-care programs (Table 10.4). Perhaps because of these differences on issues, women are more likely than men to vote for

22 Mark Lopez and Ana Gonzalez-Barrera, "Latino Voters Support Obama by 3-to-1 Margin, But Are Less Certain Than Others About Voting," Pew Hispanic Center, October 11, 2012, www.pewhispanic.org/2012/10/11/latino-voters-support-obama-by-3-1-ratio-but-are-less-certain-than-others-about-voting/ (accessed 12/8/12).

Table 10.4

DISAGREEMENTS AMONG MEN AND WOMEN ON ISSUES OF WAR AND PEACE

	APPROVE OF ACTION (%)	
GOVERNMENT ACTION	**MEN**	**WOMEN**
Going to war against Iraq (2003)	66	50
Brokering a cease-fire in Yugoslavia instead of using NATO air strikes (1999)	44	51
Ending the ban on homosexuals in the military (1993)	34	51
Engaging in a military operation against a Somali warlord (1993)	72	60
Going to war against Iraq (1991)	72	53

SOURCES: Gallup polls, 1991,1993, and 1999; *Washington Post*, 2003.

Democratic candidates, whereas men have become increasingly supportive of Republicans.[23] This tendency for men's and women's opinions to differ is called the gender gap. Perhaps surprisingly, the gender gap has virtually vanished on the abortion issue. An August 2006 Pew Research Center poll indicated that men and women are nearly identical—52 percent versus 51 percent—on the issue of allowing abortion in general or on a limited basis, and 46 percent of both men and women believe abortion should always or almost always be illegal.[24]

 **gender gap**

A distinctive pattern of voting behavior reflecting the differences in views between women and men

As we see in Chapter 12, political party membership can be another factor affecting political orientation. Partisans tend to rely on party leaders and spokespersons for cues on the appropriate position to take on major political issues. In recent years, congressional redistricting and partisan realignment in the South have reduced the number of conservative Democrats and all but eliminated liberal Republicans from Congress and positions of prominence in the party. As a result, the leadership of the Republican Party has become increasingly conservative and that of the Democratic Party has become more

23 For data, see Center for American Women and Politics, Eagleton Institute of Politics, Rutgers, State University of New Jersey, www.cawp.rutgers.edu/fast_facts/voters/turnout.php (accessed 4/30/09).

24 Pew Research Center for the People and the Press, "Pragmatic Americans Liberal and Conservative on Social Issues: Most Want Middle Ground on Abortion," August 3, 2006, http://people-press.org/report/283/pragmatic-americans-liberal-and-conservative-on-social-issues (accessed 3/24/09).

and more liberal. These changes in the positions of party leaders have been reflected in the views of party adherents and sympathizers in the general public on some issues. The war in Iraq offers a dramatic example of such polarization. Nine months into the war, a large majority of Democrats opposed the war and supported withdrawal. A large majority of Republicans supported the war and continued efforts to stabilize the situation. In April 2008, a Gallup survey asked, "If you had to choose, which do you think is better for the U.S., to keep a significant number of troops in Iraq until the situation there gets better, even if that takes many years, or to set a timetable for removing troops from Iraq and to stick to that timetable regardless of what is going on in Iraq?" Eighty-one percent of Democrats chose a timetable for withdrawal, compared with 32 percent of Republicans. Sixty-five percent of Republicans favored continued engagement, compared with 15 percent of Democrats.[25]

It is worth noting again that, like the other agents of socialization, group membership can never fully explain a given individual's political views. Group membership is conducive to particular outlooks, but it is not determinative. It is also worth pointing out, in line with the rationality principle, that objective interests, though not always determinative, exert a strong influence on opinions and behavior—hence the small numbers of black Republicans or of socialist businesspeople.

Political Conditions. A fourth set of factors shaping political orientation and values has to do with the conditions under which individuals and groups are recruited into and involved in political life—that is, the circumstances in which an individual comes of age politically. Although political beliefs are influenced by family background and group membership, the precise content and character of these views is, to a large extent, determined by political circumstances. For example, many Americans who came of political age during the Great Depression and World War II developed an intense loyalty to President Franklin Delano Roosevelt and became permanently attached to his Democratic Party. In a similar vein, the Vietnam War and the social upheavals of the 1960s produced lasting divisions among Americans of the baby-boom generation. Indeed, arguments over Vietnam persisted into the 2004 presidential election, some 30 years after American troops left Southeast Asia. Perhaps the September 11 terrorist attacks and ongoing threats to America's security will have a lasting impact on the political orientation of contemporary Americans.

In a similar vein, the views held by members of a particular group can shift drastically over time as political circumstances change. For example, white southerners were staunch members of the Democratic Party from the Civil War through the 1960s. As members of this political group, they became key supporters of liberal New Deal and post–New Deal social programs that greatly expanded the size and power of the national government. Since the 1960s, however, southern whites have shifted in large numbers to the Republican Party. Now they provide a major base of support for efforts to scale back social

---

25 Jeffrey M. Jones, "Iraq War Attitudes Politically Polarized," *Gallup News*, April 8, 2008, www.gallup.com/poll/106309/Iraq-War-Attitudes-Politically-Polarized.aspx (accessed 3/24/09).

programs and sharply reduce the size and power of the national government. The South's move from the Democratic to the Republican camp took place because of white southern opposition to the Democratic Party's racial policies and because of determined Republican efforts to win white southern support. It was not a change in the character of white southerners but a change in the political circumstances in which they found themselves that induced this major shift in political allegiances and outlook in the South. The moral of this story is that a group's views cannot be inferred simply from the character of the group. College students are not inherently radical or inherently conservative. Jews are not inherently liberal. Southerners are not inherently conservative. Men are not inherently militaristic. Any group's political outlooks and orientations are shaped by the political circumstances in which the group finds itself, and those outlooks can change as circumstances change. Quite probably, the generation of American students now coming of political age will have a very different view of the use of American military power than members of a generation who reached political consciousness during the 1960s, when opposition to the Vietnam War and military conscription were important political phenomena.

Political Ideology

As we have seen, people's beliefs about government can vary widely. But for some individuals the set of underlying orientations, ideas, and beliefs through which they understand and interpret politics fits together in a political ideology.

In America today, people often describe themselves as liberals or conservatives. Liberalism and conservatism are political ideologies that include beliefs about the role of government, ideas about public policies, and notions about which groups in society should properly exercise power. In earlier times, these terms were defined somewhat differently. As recently as the nineteenth century, a liberal was an individual who favored freedom from state control, whereas a conservative was someone who supported the use of governmental power and favored continuation of the influence of the church and the aristocracy in national life.

Today, in the United States, the term liberal has come to imply support for political and social reform; extensive government intervention in the economy; the expansion of federal social services; more vigorous efforts on behalf of the poor, minorities, and women; and greater concern for consumers and the environment. In social and cultural areas, liberals generally support abortion rights and oppose state involvement with religious institutions and religious expression. In international affairs, liberal positions usually include support for arms control, opposition to the development and testing of nuclear weapons, support for aid to poor nations, opposition to the use of American troops to influence the domestic affairs of developing nations, and support for international organizations such as the United Nations. Of course, liberalism is not monolithic. For example, among individuals who view themselves as liberal, many support American military intervention when it is tied to a humanitarian purpose, as in the case of America's military action in Kosovo in 1998–99. Most liberals initially supported President

 **liberal**

A liberal today generally supports political and social reform; extensive government intervention in the economy; the expansion of federal social services; more vigorous efforts on behalf of the poor, minorities, and women; and greater concern for consumers and the environment

George W. Bush's war on terrorism even when some of the president's actions seemed to curtail civil liberties.

conservative 

Today this term refers to those who generally support the social and economic status quo and are suspicious of efforts to introduce new political formulas and economic arrangements. Many conservatives also believe that a large and powerful government poses a threat to citizens' freedoms

By contrast, the term conservative today is used to describe those who generally support the social and economic status quo and are suspicious of efforts to introduce new political formulas and economic arrangements. Conservatives believe strongly that a large and powerful government poses a threat to citizens' freedom. Thus in the domestic arena conservatives generally oppose the expansion of governmental activity, asserting that solutions to social and economic problems can be developed in the private sector. Conservatives in particular oppose efforts to impose government regulation on business, pointing out that such regulation is frequently economically inefficient and costly and can ultimately lower the entire nation's standard of living. As for social and cultural positions, many conservatives oppose abortion and support school prayer. In international affairs, conservatism has come to mean support for the maintenance of American military power. Like liberalism, conservatism is far from a monolithic ideology. Some conservatives support many government social programs. George W. Bush, a Republican, called himself a compassionate conservative to indicate that he favored programs that assist the poor and the needy. Other conservatives oppose efforts to outlaw abortion, arguing that government intrusion in this area is as misguided as government intervention in the economy. The real political world is far too complex to be seen in terms of a simple struggle between liberals and conservatives.

There are many other ideologies beside liberal and conservative. Some people seek to expand liberty above all other principles and wish to minimize government intervention in the economy and society. Such a position is sometimes called libertarian. Other ideologies seek a particular outcome, such as environmental protection. Such a stance may emphasize certain issues, such as economic growth, and deemphasize other issues, such as abortion. Communism and fascism are ideologies that involve government control of all aspects of the economy and society. These ideologies dominated politics in many European countries from the 1920s through the 1940s. Political discourse in the United States, however, has revolved around the division between liberals and conservatives for most of the last century.

Liberal and conservative differences manifest themselves in a variety of contexts. For example, the liberal approach to increasing airline safety in October 2001 was to create a workforce of federal employees who would screen and inspect passengers' luggage. The conservative approach was to call for better training of current employees and better supervision of private-sector screeners. To some extent, contemporary liberalism and conservatism can be seen as blends of the fundamental American political values of liberty and equality. For liberals, equality is often the most important of the core values. Liberals are willing to tolerate government intervention in such areas as college admissions and business decisions to help remedy high levels of race, class, or gender inequality. For conservatives, on the other hand, liberty is the core value. Conservatives oppose most efforts by the government, however well intentioned, to intrude into private life or the marketplace. This simple formula for distinguishing liberalism and conservatism is of course not always accurate because political ideologies seldom lend themselves to neat or logical characterizations. Conservatives, for example, are sometimes more tolerant of, and liberals more resistant to, government intervention in social policy realms involving the family, marriage, homosexuality, and abortion.

Often political observers search for logical connections among the various positions identified with liberalism or conservatism, and they are disappointed or puzzled when they are unable to find a set of coherent philosophical principles that define and unite the several elements of either set of beliefs. On the liberal side, for example, what is the logical connection between opposition to U.S. government intervention in the affairs of foreign nations and calls for greater intervention in America's economy and society? On the conservative side, what is the logical relationship between opposition to government regulation of business and support for a ban on abortion?

Frequently, the relationships among the various elements of liberalism or the several aspects of conservatism are political rather than logical. One underlying basis of liberal views is that all or most of them are criticisms of or attacks on the foreign and domestic policies and cultural values of the business and commercial strata that have been prominent in the United States for more than a century. In some measure, the tenets of contemporary conservatism are this elite's defense of its positions against its enemies, who include organized labor, minority groups, and some intellectuals and professionals. Thus liberals attack business and commercial elites by advocating more government regulation, including consumer protection and environmental regulation; opposition to weapons programs; and support for expensive social programs. Conservatives counterattack by asserting that government regulation of the economy is ruinous and that military weapons are needed in a changing world.

Of course, it is important to note that many people who call themselves liberals or conservatives accept only part of the liberal or conservative ideology. Although it appears that Americans have adopted a more conservative outlook on some issues, their views in other areas have remained largely unchanged or have even become more liberal in recent years. Thus many individuals who are liberal on social issues are conservative on economic issues. There is certainly nothing illogical about these mixed positions. They simply indicate the relatively open and fluid character of American political debate.

PUBLIC OPINION AND POLITICAL KNOWLEDGE

As they read newspapers, listen to the radio, watch television, and chat with their friends and associates, citizens are constantly confronted by new political events, issues, and personalities. Often they will be asked what they think about a particular issue or whether they plan to support a particular candidate. Indeed, in our democracy we expect every citizen to have views about the major problems of the day as well as opinions about who should be entrusted with the nation's leadership.

Some Americans know quite a bit about politics, and many have general views and hold opinions on several issues. Few Americans, though, devote sufficient time, energy, or attention to politics to really understand or evaluate the myriad issues with which they are bombarded on a regular basis. Since the advent of polling in the 1930s, studies have repeatedly shown that the average American knows little about current events or even basic facts of American government.[26]

Low levels of information lead to instability and incoherence in people's responses to surveys. Professor Philip Converse, in one of the most widely cited pieces of social science research, noted that most people do not seem to have clear opinions on important issues. The answers they give to a question one year correlated poorly to the answers they gave to the same question two years later, and the answers across issues did not seem to form a consistent pattern or system of belief. The incoherence of respondents' opinions was traceable to their level of education. Better educated people gave more coherent answers and more stable answers over time. This research led social scientists to argue that people are in fact not capable of expressing meaningful opinions on issues because of their low levels of information or cognitive ability.

Converse's views have represented an important pole in the debate over public knowledge and democracy. More recent research, including new analyses of Converse's own data have shown a markedly different picture. It is not that people are incapable of reasoning, but that surveys are not perfect instruments for measuring what people know and how they think. Vague or difficult questions, it turns out, explain much of the apparent incoherence that Converse's respondents expressed. When the data were reanalyzed and subsequent studies were conducted, researchers found much more stability in people's preferences from year to year and much more coherence from issue to issue. Even people who have less than a high school education or did not know many common facts about the government still have fairly coherent and stable preferences.[27] It was the survey, not the people that failed the test.

Even still, there is something compelling to Converse's account. Large numbers of people do not seem to know many facts about politics and government that one might reasonably expect of voters. Why do people seem to know so little, and what might be the consequence of low levels of information about current events and political institutions for the long-run health of democracy?

Ignorance is probably an inevitable fact of political life. Attending to the day-to-day goings on in Washington or the state capital or city council is costly; it means spending time at the very least, and often money as well, to collect, organize, and digest political information.[28] Balanced against this cost to an

---

26 Philip E. Converse, "The Nature of Belief Systems in Mass Publics," in *Ideology and Discontent,* David E. Apter, ed. (New York: Free Press, 1964).

27 See Christopher Achen, "Mass Political Attitudes and the Survey Response," *American Political Science Review* 69 (1975), p. 1281, and Stephen Ansolabehere, Jonathan Rodden, and James M. Snyder, Jr., "The Strength of Issues," *American Political Science Review* 102 (2008), pp. 215–32.

28 Anthony Downs, *An Economic Theory of Democracy* (New York: Harper & Row, 1957).

individual is the very low probability that he or she will, on the basis of this costly information, take an action that would not otherwise have been taken and that such a departure in behavior would make a beneficial difference to him or her and that such a difference, if it existed, would exceed the cost of acquiring the information in the first place. Because individuals anticipate that informed actions that they take will rarely make much difference and that the costs of informing oneself are often not trivial, it may be rational to remain ignorant. In other words, the rationality principle suggests that many people should more profitably devote their personal resources—particularly their time—to more narrowly personal matters. This idea is in turn suggested by the collective action principle, in which the bearing of burdens—such as the cost of becoming informed—is not likely to have much impact in a mass political setting. A more moderate version of "rational" ignorance recognizes that some kinds of information are inexpensive to acquire, such as sound bites from the evening news, or can be pleasant, such as reading the front page of the newspaper while drinking a cup of coffee. In such cases, an individual may become partially informed, but usually not in detail.

Precisely because becoming truly knowledgeable about politics requires a substantial investment of time and energy, many Americans seek to acquire political information and to make political decisions on the cheap, using shortcuts, labels, and stereotypes, rather than following current events closely. One "inexpensive" way to become informed is to take cues from trusted others—the local minister, the television commentator or newspaper editorialist, an interest-group leader, friends, and relatives.[29] Sometimes the cue giver is distrusted, in which case the cue leads the receiver in the opposite direction. For example, if a liberal is told that a Republican president is backing a major overhaul of the Social Security system, he or she will probably not read thousands of pages of economic projections before exhibiting suspicion of the president's efforts. Along the same lines, a common shortcut for political evaluation and decision making is to assess new issues and events through the lenses of one's general beliefs and orientation. Thus if a conservative learns of a plan to expand federal social programs, he or she might express opposition to the endeavor without carefully pondering the specifics of the proposal.

Neither of these shortcuts is entirely reliable, however. Taking cues from others may lead individuals to accept positions that they would not support if they had more information. And general ideological orientations are usually poor guides to decision making in concrete instances. For one thing, especially when applied to discrete issues, most individuals' beliefs turn out to be filled with contradictions. For example, what position should a liberal take on immigration? Should a liberal favor keeping America's borders open to poor people from all over the world, or should he or she be concerned that America's open borders

29 For a discussion of the role of information in democratic politics, see Arthur Lupia and Mathew D. McCubbins, *The Democratic Dilemma: Can Citizens Learn What They Need to Know?* (New York: Cambridge University Press, 1998).

create a pool of surplus labor that permits giant corporations to drive down the wages of poor American workers? Many other issues defy easy ideological characterization. What should liberals think of new drug licensing procedures? How should conservatives view America's military actions in Libya or Afghanistan? Each of these policies combines a mix of issues and is too complex to lend itself to simple ideological interpretation.

Although understandable and perhaps inevitable, widespread inattentiveness to politics weakens American democracy in two ways. First, those who lack political information or resort to inadequate shortcuts to acquire and assess information cannot effectively defend their political interests and can easily become victims or losers in political struggles. Second, the presence of large numbers of politically inattentive or ignorant individuals means that the political process can be more easily manipulated by the various institutions and forces that seek to shape public opinion.

As to the first of these problems, in our democracy millions of ordinary citizens take part in political life, at least to the extent of voting in national elections. Those with little knowledge of the election's issues, candidates, or procedures can find themselves acting against their own preferences and interests. One example is U.S. tax policy. Over the past several decades, the United States has substantially reduced the rate of taxation for its wealthiest citizens.[30] Tax cuts signed into law by President Bush in 2001 and mostly maintained throughout the decade provided a tax break mainly for the top 1 percent of the nation's wage earners, and further tax cuts proposed by the president offered additional benefits to this privileged stratum. It is surprising, however, that polling data show that millions of middle-class and lower-middle-class Americans who did not stand to benefit from the president's tax cuts seemed to favor them nonetheless. The explanation for this odd state of affairs appears to be a lack of political knowledge. Millions of individuals who were unlikely to derive much advantage from President Bush's tax policy thought they would. The political scientist Larry Bartels has called this phenomenon "misplaced self-interest."[31] Upper-bracket taxpayers, who are usually served by an army of financial advisers, are unlikely to suffer from this problem. Knowledge may not always translate into political power, but lack of knowledge is almost certain to translate into political weakness. And according to the policy principle, the lack of knowledge and concomitant political weakness mean policy disappointment. Campaigns and other forums for public discourse can change public attitudes on issues by altering the nature of the choices or informing the public about the effects of policies. For example, during the

30 One of the most detailed analyses of the distribution of the tax burden in advanced industrial democracies in the past half century is Thomas Piketty and Emmanuel Saez, "How Progressive Is the U.S. Federal Tax System? Historical and International Perspectives," working paper 12404, National Bureau of Economic Research, 2006, www.nber.org/papers/w12404 (accessed 3/25/09).

31 Larry M. Bartels, "Homer Gets a Tax Cut: Inequality and Public Policy in the American Mind," *Perspectives on Politics* 3 (2005): 15–31.

2008 presidential election campaign, Barack Obama seized on the tax issue at a time when the economy was worsening and people's economic prospects looked bleak. Then-candidate Obama promised to raise taxes on the incomes of those making more than $300,000 per year, a pledge that proved highly popular. In this way, Obama shifted the discourse away from taxes on inheritance and other assets that people hold and to the incomes of the top 1 percent of earners. The Democratic campaign used advertisements, debates, and other public events to remind voters that his proposal would increase taxes for only a small percentage of the population. The Analyzing the Evidence section on the following page looks at how public opinion on taxes has shifted over time.

Although political ignorance is troubling, it does not render democratic politics impossible. Quite the contrary. As we suggested earlier, democratic theorists since the Marquis de Condorcet have understood that aggregation counteracts the effects of political ignorance. When people do not know fully their interests they will make mistakes. Fortunately, those mistakes usually look like "random" errors, and individuals' opinions and choices are aggregated, in surveys or elections, those errors seem to average out. In this sense, aggregate public opinion can appear more stable and clearer than individuals' opinions.[32] In addition, public policy (as we discuss in later chapters) is fairly responsive to shifts in public opinion. Professor James Stimson has provided a comprehensive assessment of the link between aggregate public opinion and public policy. His research tracks public opinion on a wide variety of issues from the 1950s to the present. When aggregate public opinion has shifted left, as in the 1960s, or right, as in the 1980s, public policy has generally followed suit. Although it is hard to know whether public policy exactly equaled what a majority of people wanted in each policy area, the high level of responsiveness of policy outcomes to changes in aggregate opinion suggests that the political system follows the general sense of aggregate opinion, or what Stimson calls the policy mood. This result, he argues, strongly suggests that "the magic of aggregation" provides a corrective for low levels of knowledge that the typical citizen has.

SHAPING OPINION: POLITICAL LEADERS, PRIVATE GROUPS, AND THE MEDIA

The fact that many Americans are inattentive to politics and lack even basic political information renders public opinion and the political process more easily susceptible to manipulation. Although direct efforts to influence opinion don't always succeed, three forces play especially important roles in shaping opinion. These are the government, private groups, and the news media.

32 James Stimson, Robert Erikson, and Michael MacKuen, *The Macro Polity* (Cambridge, UK: Cambridge University Press, 1998).

ANALYZING THE EVIDENCE

Public Opinion and Taxes

CHAPTER 10

Contributed by
Andrea Campbell
Massachusetts Institute of Technology

Nobody likes to pay taxes. The United States was founded in part due to disputes over taxes. Talk of taxes dominates political campaigns. Americans simply hate taxes, right?

While the answer appears to be "yes" today, that wasn't always the case. Both the importance of taxes to politics and American dislike of taxes were lower during the 1950s and 1960s than during the period from the 1970s to the present. How do we know this? And what caused the change after the 1960s?

Mentions of Taxes in Presidential Nomination Speeches

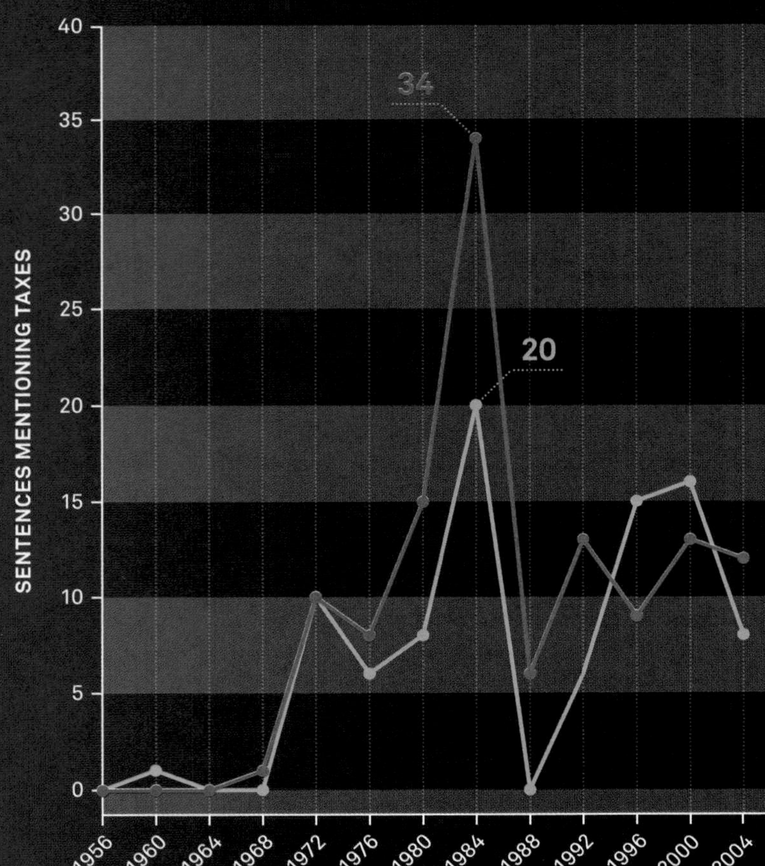

One measure of the centrality of taxes in political campaigns is the number of times the topic is mentioned in presidential nomination acceptance speeches. These data show that the word *taxes* barely passed the lips of the major-party nominees until after the 1960s. The numbers on the vertical axis represent the number of sentences mentioning taxes in nomination acceptance speeches.

Republicans
Democrats

Taxes and the Public's Perception of the Parties

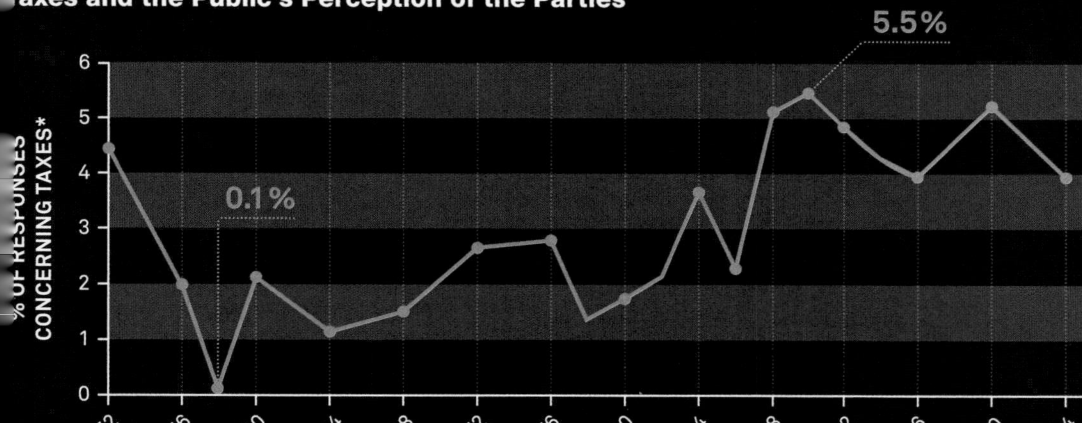

* Note: Figure shows percentage of all likes and dislikes of the Democratic and Republican parties that concern taxes.
SOURCE: American National Election Studies Cumulative File.

In earlier decades, taxes weren't very important to members of the public, either. The American National Election Study has asked respondents what they like and dislike about each of the political parties at least every four years since 1952. Here the vertical axis shows the percentages of all "likes" and "dislikes" (for Republicans and Democrats combined) that concern taxes.

So what changed after the 1960s? Why did taxes become more important to the public? What encouraged politicians to campaign on tax issues? Political scientists don't have a definitive answer, but there are a number of plausible explanations.[1] One factor could be the increasing effective costs of taxes. During the 1950s and 1960s, per capita taxes increased rapidly, but real wages grew even faster, so the impact of taxes was muted. But during the 1970s, oil shocks, a worldwide economic slowdown, and high inflation meant that taxes took a bigger bite.

Another possible explanation is that with the Great Society policies of the 1960s, white Americans in particular came to resent the use of their tax dollars for welfare and other means-tested policies they believed they would never benefit from themselves.[2] The salience of taxes may also have been fueled by institutional changes within Congress. Reforms that opened up committee hearings and involved a broader number of legislators in the tax policy-making process paved the way for tax politics as public spectacle. Finally, tax revolts in some states in the 1970s demonstrated to politicians the expediency of taxes as a political issue.[3] Entrepreneurial politicians, particularly in the Republican Party, strove to keep taxes on the public agenda.

It is likely that all of these factors contributed to the heightening of taxes as a political issue. And given the current budget deficit, growing national debt, and mismatch between projected revenues and likely spending on Social Security, Medicare, and Medicaid over the long term, taxes will likely be high on the political agenda for some time to come.

EXPLORE
PUBLIC OPINION ON MAJOR ISSUES
FURTHER AT:
wwnorton.com/studyspace

1 Discussion adapted from Andrea Louise Campbell, *How Americans Think about Taxes* (Princeton, NJ: Princeton University Press, 2009).

2 Thomas Edsall and Mary Edsall, *Chain Reaction* (New York: Norton, 1992).

Government and the Shaping of Public Opinion

All governments attempt, to a greater or lesser extent, to influence, manipulate, or manage their citizens' beliefs. But the extent to which public opinion is affected by government public relations efforts is probably limited. The government—despite its size and power—is only one source of information in the United States. Very often government claims are disputed by the media and interest groups, and at times by opposing forces within the government itself. Often, too, government efforts to manipulate public opinion backfire when the public is made aware of the government's tactics. Thus in 1971 the government's efforts to build popular support for the Vietnam War were hurt when CBS News aired its documentary "The Selling of the Pentagon," which purported to reveal the extent and character of government efforts to sway popular sentiment. In this documentary, CBS demonstrated the techniques, including planted news stories and faked film footage, that the government had used to misrepresent its activities in Vietnam. These revelations, of course, undermined popular trust in government claims.

A hallmark of the administration of President Bill Clinton was the steady use of election-campaign-type techniques to bolster popular enthusiasm for White House initiatives. The president established a political "war room" similar to the one that operated in his campaign headquarters. In the presidential version, representatives from all cabinet departments met daily to discuss and coordinate the president's public relations efforts. Many of the same consultants and pollsters who directed the successful Clinton campaign were also employed in the selling of the president's programs.[33]

After he assumed office in 2001, George W. Bush asserted that political leaders should base their programs on their own conception of the public interest, not on the polls. This did not mean that Bush ignored public opinion, however. He relied on the pollster Jan van Lohuizen to conduct a low-key operation, sufficiently removed from the limelight to allow the president to renounce polling while continuing to make use of survey data.[34] At the same time, the Bush White House developed an extensive public relations program, led initially by the former presidential aide Karen Hughes, to bolster popular support for the president's policies. Hughes, working with the conservative TV personality Mary Matalin, coordinated White House efforts to maintain popular support for the administration's war against terrorism. These efforts included presidential speeches, media appearances by administration officials, numerous press conferences, and thousands of press releases presenting the administration's views.[35] The White House also made a substantial effort to sway opinion in foreign

33 Gerald F. Seib and Michael K. Frisby, "Selling Sacrifice," *Wall Street Journal*, February 5, 1993, p. 1.

34 Joshua Green, "The Other War Room," *Washington Monthly*, April 2002.

35 Peter Marks, "Adept in Politics and Advertising, Four Women Shape a Campaign," *New York Times*, November 11, 2001, p. B6.

countries, even sending officials to present the administration's views on television networks serving the Arab world.

Not all political media strategies work. President Obama, attempting to maintain the political momentum from his 2008 election campaign, attempted to use social media to keep up the same buzz about his legislative agenda as his campaign enjoyed. He brought Macon Philips, who developed the campaign's social media strategy, into the White House team to organize the effort. The White House maintains a newsy Web site, a blog, a YouTube channel, a Facebook page, and a Twitter account. But many have criticized the low level of actual engagement with people. Each of these new media is being used like the old media—to talk at people rather than with them, to disseminate information to the press rather than respond to reporters' questions. Indeed, many White House reporters feel that the Obama press office is less accessible than its predecessors.[36]

Private Groups and the Shaping of Public Opinion

We have already seen how the government tries to shape public opinion. But the ideas that become prominent in political life are also developed and spread by important economic and political groups searching for issues that will advance their causes. Rational political entrepreneurs pursue strategies that—in an application of the collective action principle—give the groups they lead a decided advantage in the political arena in comparison with latent, unorganized groups. In some instances, in the hope of bringing others over to their side, private groups espouse values they truly believe in. Take, for example, the campaign against so-called partial birth abortion, which resulted in the Partial Birth Abortion Ban Act of 2003. Proponents of the act believed that prohibiting particular sorts of abortions would be a first step toward eliminating all abortions, something they view as a moral imperative.[37] In other cases, however, groups will promote principles designed mainly to further hidden agendas of political and economic interests. One famous example is the campaign against cheap imported handguns—the so-called Saturday-night specials—that was covertly financed by the domestic manufacturers of more expensive firearms. The campaign's organizers claimed that cheap handguns pose a grave risk to the public and should be outlawed. The real goal, though, was not safeguarding the public but protecting the economic well-being of the domestic gun industry. A more recent example is the campaign against the alleged "sweatshop" practices of some American companies manufacturing their products in third world countries. This campaign is mainly financed by U.S. labor unions seeking to protect

36 Michael Calderone, "White House News Strategy Causes Concerns about Access," February 15, 2011, http://news.yahoo.com/s/yblog_thecutline/20110215/bs_yblog_thecutline/white-house-media-strategy-causes-concerns-about-access (accessed 8/22/11).

37 Cynthia Gorney, "Gambling with Abortion," *Harper's Magazine*, November 2004, pp. 33–46.

their members' jobs by discouraging American firms from manufacturing their products abroad.[38]

Typically, ideas are marketed most effectively by groups with access to financial resources, public or private institutional support, and sufficient skill or education to select, develop, and draft ideas that will attract interest and support. Thus the development and promotion of conservative themes and ideas in recent years have been greatly facilitated by the millions of dollars that conservative corporations and business organizations such as the U.S. Chamber of Commerce and the Public Affairs Council spend each year on public information and what is now called in corporate circles "issues management." In addition, conservative business leaders have contributed millions of dollars to such conservative institutions as the Heritage Foundation, the Hoover Institution, and the American Enterprise Institute.[39] Many of the ideas that helped those on the right influence political debate were first developed and articulated by scholars associated with institutions such as these.

Although they do not usually have access to financial assets that match those available to their conservative opponents, liberal intellectuals and professionals have ample organizational skills, access to the media, and practice in creating, communicating, and using ideas. During the past three decades, the chief vehicle through which liberal intellectuals and professionals have advanced their ideas has been the "public interest group," an institution that relies heavily on voluntary contributions of time, effort, and interest on the part of its members. Through groups such as Common Cause, the National Organization for Women, the Sierra Club, Friends of the Earth, and Physicians for Social Responsibility, intellectuals and professionals have been able to use their organizational skills and educational resources to develop and promote ideas.[40] Often research conducted at universities and liberal "think tanks" such as the Brookings Institution provides the ideas on which liberal politicians rely. For example, the welfare reform plan introduced by the Clinton administration in 1994 originated with the work of Harvard professor David Ellwood. Ellwood's academic research led him to the conclusion that the nation's welfare system would be improved if services to the poor were expanded in scope but limited in duration. His idea was adopted by the 1992 Clinton presidential campaign, which was searching for a position on welfare that would appeal to both liberal and conservative Democrats. The Ellwood plan seemed perfect: It promised liberals an immediate expansion of welfare benefits, yet it held out to conservatives the idea that welfare recipients would receive benefits for only a limited time. The Clinton welfare reform plan even borrowed phrases from Ellwood's book *Poor Support*.[41]

38 David P. Baron and Daniel Diermeier, "Strategic Activism and Nonmarket Strategy," *Journal of Economics and Management Strategy* (2006).

39 See David Vogel, "The Power of Business in America: A Reappraisal," *British Journal of Political Science* 13 (1983): 19–44.

40 See David Vogel, "The Public Interest Movement and the American Reform Tradition," *Political Science Quarterly* 96 (Winter 1980): 607–27.

41 Jason DeParle, "The Clinton Welfare Bill Begins Trek in Congress," *New York Times*, July 15, 1994, p. 1.

Academics pervaded the Bush and Obama administrations. Secretary of State Condoleezza Rice was a professor of political science at Stanford University and Professor Gregory Mankiw was chairman of the Council of Economic Advisors under Bush. The ideas behind Obama's social networking and grassroots organizing campaign came from, among others, Marshall Ganz, a labor organizer who teaches organizing and leadership at Harvard's Kennedy School of Government, and the Obama administration drew widely on the academic community in putting together its administration, from law professors (such as Elena Kagan, Obama's first solicitor general) to Christina Romer (a Berkeley economics professor and chair of the Council of Economic Advisers) to Lawrence Summers (Harvard economics professor and former Harvard president and director of the White House National Economic Council). All brought with them new ideas and drew on the enormous expertise in their own fields.

The Media and Public Opinion

The communications media are among the most powerful forces operating in the marketplace of ideas. Most Americans say that their primary source of information about public affairs is news media—newspapers, broadcast and cable news, radio, and Internet news providers. The alternative sources of political information are direct contact with politics, information provided by groups, and information conveyed by other individuals, such as family members or coworkers. Certainly few people actually go to Washington to find out what's going on in American politics, and the broad access people have to media outlets dwarfs the number of households that receive direct mail from organizations and elected officials. Personal conversation is also an important source for information, but people tend to avoid controversial topics. For example, at work or school, sports and weather are much safer topics for casual conversation than politics.

The mass media, as the term suggests, can be thought of as mediators. They are the conduits through which information flows. Through newspapers, radio and television, magazines, and the Internet we can learn about what's going on in our world and in our government. Providing this opportunity to learn about the world and politics is the most important way the media contribute to public opinion.

People rely on the media, rather than other sources of information, to find out what's going on in politics and public affairs because it is easy to do so. Media outlets are ubiquitous. More households in the United States have television than have indoor plumbing. Radio penetration is nearly as universal. Nearly every community has a newspaper, with 1,500 daily newspapers published throughout the United States. The number of news programs and the availability of news has also expanded tremendously in recent decades. In the 1960s there were only three television news outlets—CBS, NBC, and ABC. They aired evening and nightly news programs and allowed a half-hour slot for news from local affiliates. The rise of cable television in the 1980s brought a 24-hour news station, CNN; expanded news programming through the Public Broadcasting System (PBS); and a network devoted exclusively to broadcasting proceedings of Congress and government agencies, C-SPAN. Important competitors to the big three networks emerged, including Fox and the Spanish-language networks Univision and Telemundo. Today there is no shortage of televised news programming available at all hours.[42]

Technological innovations continue to push change in political communication in the United States. Today, more than 75 percent of Americans have Internet access.[43] To put that in historical perspective, Internet penetration in the United States today is comparable to television penetration in the late 1950s. This technology, then, has yet to reach its full power and potential. Nevertheless, the rise of the Internet has already opened the flow of communication further. Conventional media have moved much of their content online, provided for free. Internet users can gain access not only to U.S. media but also to media from around the world. The Internet has also changed the traditional media, leading to the development of interactive graphics and reader forums. We have also witnessed the rise of new forms of communications, most notably Web logs ("blogs" for short), which provide a platform for anyone to have their say. Several Web sites, such as Google News and realclearpolitics.com, are clearinghouses for traditional media, newswire stories, and blogs. This new, highly competitive media environment has put increased financial pressures on the traditional media, and it has radically changed the flow and nature of communication in the United States and the availability of information to the public. In Chapter 14, we discuss the media as a democratic institution at greater length. Our concern here is the media's role in how people learn about politics and public affairs.

Learning through mass media occurs both actively and passively. Active learning occurs when people search for a particular type of program or a particular type of information. If you turn on the nightly news to find out what has happened in national and international affairs, you are engaged in actively learning. If you search the Web for information about your member of Congress, you are engaged in active learning. Passive learning may be just as important. Many entertainment programs discuss current affairs and issues, such as social issues or an election. When that occurs, learning takes a passive form. You watch the program for entertainment but gain information about politics. One study of information gain among voters found that people learned as much from Oprah as from the evening news.[44] Political advertising is perhaps the most common form of passive information. During the last month of national political campaigns, it is not uncommon to see three or four political advertisements during one commercial break in a primetime television program.

Mass media are our primary source for information about current affairs. They influence how Americans understand politics not just through the volume of information available but also through what is presented and how. Editors,

---

42 See Stephen Ansolabehere, Roy Behr, and Shanto Iyengar, *The Media Game* (New York: Macmillan, 1993).

43 These figures are tracked regularly by the Pew Internet and American Life Project, www.pewinternet.org/Static-Pages/Trend-Data/Whos-Online.aspx (accessed 7/14/11).

44 See Matthew Baum, *Soft News Goes to War* (Princeton, NJ: Princeton University Press, 2006).

reporters, and others involved in preparing the content of the news must ultimately decide what topics to cover, what facts to include, and whom to interview. Journalists usually try to present issues fairly, but it is difficult, perhaps impossible, to be perfectly objective. C-SPAN takes an unusual approach. It sets up a camera at an event and simply records what occurs; it adds no commentary and does not edit the material. Just the facts. However, even that approach necessarily involves some slant, depending on what events C-SPAN decides to cover. By choosing to cover some events and not others, it sends a message about what, in its view, is important.

What the media cover and how news is presented and interpreted can affect public opinion. Psychologists have identified two potential pathways through which media coverage shapes what people think. First, the news sets the public's agenda. Through this agenda-setting effect, the media cues people to think about some issues rather than others; it makes some considerations more salient than others. Suppose, for example, that the local news covers crime to the exclusion of all else. When someone who watches the local news regularly thinks about the mayoral election, crime is more likely to be his or her primary consideration, compared with someone who does not watch the local news. Psychologists call this priming.

agenda-setting effect

The power to bring attention to particular issues and problems

priming

A process of preparing the public to take a particular view of an event or a political actor

Second, news coverage of an issue frames the way the issue is defined. News coverage of crime, to continue the example, may include a report on every murder that happens in a large city. Such coverage would likely make it seem that murder occurs very often and is much more common than it actually is. This in turn might heighten viewers' sense of insecurity or threat, leading to an exaggerated sense of risk of violent crime and increased support for tough police practices.[45] Framing refers to the media's power to influence how events and issues are interpreted.

framing

The power of the media to influence how events and issues are interpreted

Priming and framing are often viewed as twin evils. One can distract us from other important problems, and the other can make us think about an issue or a politician in a biased way. The cumulative effects of priming and framing on public opinion depend ultimately on the variety of issues covered and the diversity of perspectives represented. That, after all, is the idea behind the guarantee of a free press in the First Amendment to the Constitution. Free and open communication media allow the greatest likelihood that people will learn about important issues, that they will gain the information they need to distinguish good ideas from bad ones, and that they will learn which political leaders and parties can best represent their interests.

In this regard, the most significant framing effects take the form of the balance in the information available to people. Those in politics—elected officials, candidates, leaders of organized groups—work hard to influence what the news covers. A competitive political environment usually translates into a robust flow of information. However, some political environments are not very competitive, where only one view gets expressed and only one view is reflected in the media. Congressional elections are a case in point. Incumbent politicians today are able to

45 The seminal work on priming and framing in public policy and politics is Shanto Iyengar and Donald Kinder, *News That Matters* (Chicago: University of Chicago Press, 1987).

raise much more money than their challengers (an advantage of about $3 to $1). As a result, House elections often have a gross imbalance in the amount of advertising and news coverage between the two campaigns, that of the incumbent member of Congress and that of the challenger. This will likely affect public opinion, because voters hear the incumbent's views and message more often than the challenger's.

A further example of an imbalance in news coverage arises with the president and Congress. Presidential press conferences and events receive much more coverage than the press events of the leaders of the House or Senate. This gives the president the upper hand in setting the public agenda through the media, because members of the public are more likely to hear the president's arguments for a particular policy. That opportunity and power, of course, must be used wisely. A president who pursues an ill-advised policy can easily squander the advantage that is gained from disproportionate attention from the media. If a policy fails, the president's media advantage can be short lived. President Clinton, for example, used his 1993 State of the Union address to introduce an initiative to pass national health insurance. That initiative got bogged down in Congress, was challenged by the insurance industry in a nationwide advertising campaign, and failed, contributing to the Democrats' loss of Congress in 1994. In 2002, President George W. Bush convinced the nation that Iraq was developing weapons of mass destruction and the United States needed to topple the regime of Saddam Hussein immediately. The invasion occurred and Hussein's regime quickly fell, but large caches of chemical and nuclear weapons were never found, and the United States remained in Iraq for the better part of a decade. The backlash against these policies cost the Republicans support among the public, contributing to their loss of control of Congress in the 2006 election, and ultimately the presidency in 2008. The power of the president is the power to persuade, but control of information for political aims is a power to be used with caution.

Today, it is easy to learn about public affairs and to hear different opinions—even when we don't want to. The rise of cable television and the Internet has weakened the old media outlets, such as ABC, CBS, and NBC, and the newspaper industry. But, it is widely conjectured, the new media have facilitated learning and muted some of the biases that may emerge through priming and framing. No one voice or perspective dominates our multifaceted media environment and competitive political system. And biases in the media often reflect not the lack of outlets or restrictive editorial control but, rather, failures of political competition.

MEASURING PUBLIC OPINION

A century ago, American political leaders gauged public opinion by people's applause and the size of crowds at meetings. This direct exposure to the people's views did not necessarily produce accurate knowledge of public opinion. It did, however, give political leaders confidence in their public support—and therefore confidence in their ability to govern by consent.

Abraham Lincoln and Stephen Douglas debated each other seven times in the summer and autumn of 1858, two years before they became presidential nominees. Their debates took place before audiences in parched cornfields and courthouse squares. A century later most presidential debates, although seen by millions, take place before a few reporters and technicians in television studios that might as well be on the moon. The public's response cannot be experienced firsthand. This distance between leaders and followers is one of the agonizing problems of modern democracy. The media provide information to millions of people, but they are not yet so efficient at providing leaders with feedback from the public. Is government by consent possible when the scale of communication is so large and impersonal? To compensate for the decline in their ability to experience public opinion for themselves, leaders have turned to science, in particular the science of opinion polling.

It is no secret that politicians and public officials make extensive use of public-opinion polls to help them decide whether to run for office, what policies to support, how to vote on important legislation, and what types of appeals to make in their campaigns. President Lyndon Johnson was famous for carrying the latest Gallup and Roper poll results in his pocket, and it is widely believed that he began to withdraw from politics because the polls reported losses in public support. All recent presidents and other major political figures have worked closely with polls and pollsters.

public-opinion poll

The scientific instrument for measuring public opinion

Constructing Public Opinion from Surveys

The population in which pollsters are interested is usually quite large, such as all adults or all voters in the United States. To conduct their polls, survey researchers first identify the relevant population and choose a sample of the total population. The selection of this sample is important. Above all, it must be representative: the views of those in the sample must accurately and proportionately reflect the views of the whole. To a large extent, the validity of the poll's results depends on the sampling procedure used.

sample

A small group selected by researchers to represent the most important characteristics of an entire population

Sampling Techniques and Selection Bias. The most common techniques for choosing such a sample are probability sampling and random digit dialing. In the case of probability sampling, the pollster begins with a list of the population to be surveyed. This list is called the sampling frame. After each member of the population has been assigned a number, a table of random numbers or a computerized random selection process is used to pick those members of the population to be surveyed.

probability sampling

A method used by pollsters to select a representative sample in which every individual in the population has an equal probability of being selected as a respondent

It is important to emphasize, first, that a sample selected in this manner produces a subset of the population that is representative of the population—it is a microcosm, so to speak. It is also important to point out that whatever is learned about this representative sample can also be attributed to the larger population with a high level of assurance. Random sampling helps ensure that the way in which people were chosen for the study is not related to characteristics of the individuals, such as their level of education.

This technique for constructing a sample is appropriate when the entire population can be identified. For example, all students registered at Texas colleges and universities can be identified from college records, and a sample of them can easily be drawn. When the pollster is interested in a national sample of Americans, however, this technique is not feasible, because no complete list of Americans exists.[46]

Exit polls conducted during national elections use areas to construct their sample. The polling organization randomly selects a set of precincts (voting stations) within each state throughout the nation. In most states, the organizations will select between 50 and 150 such locations. The polling organization trains individuals to conduct the exit poll on election day and deploys those individuals to the voting stations. The pollster approaches people as they leave the voting area and persuades them to fill out the exit poll questionnaire. To guard against biases, the pollster is instructed how many people to choose and which people to approach, such as every seventh person. As the day progresses the pollsters tally the results of the exit poll and report them to the organization, which tallies those figures and distributes them to the media outlets that use them on election night.

random digit dialing

A poll in which respondents are selected at random from a list of 10-digit telephone numbers, with every effort made to avoid bias in the construction of the sample

For the typical public-opinion poll today, national samples are usually drawn using a technique called random digit dialing—in which a computerized random-number generator produces a list of as many 10-digit numbers as the pollster deems necessary. As with exit polls, the pollster is trained how to interview people and record responses. Because there are biases in who answers the phone in a given home, pollsters randomly choose an adult in the house, such as the "oldest female adult," "oldest male adult," "youngest adult male" and so forth. Given that more than 95 percent of American households have telephones, this technique provides very good coverage of all households in the United States. Randomization—of which household is chosen and of which person is to be interviewed in each household—helps guard against potential biases.

In recent years, however, problems have arisen with the traditional phone poll. With the growth in cell phone use and the enactment of "do-not-call" legislation to discourage telemarketers, random digit dialing has become less reliable. Computerized methods of random digit dialing have difficulty reaching households that are registered on the do-not-call list or that only have cell phones. As a result traditional methods of sampling will underrepresent these segments of the population, and they happen to be younger. In addition, random digit dialing will overrepresent households with several phone lines, which tend to be higher income and better educated households. These are problems that create biases in surveys. In addition, some people are simply more willing to talk to pollsters. If pollsters could be certain that those who responded to their surveys simply reflected the views of those who refused to respond, there would be no problem. Some studies suggest, however, that the views of respondents and nonrespondents can differ, especially along social-class lines. Middle- and upper-middle-class individuals are more likely to be willing to respond to surveys

46 Herbert Asher, *Polling and the Public* (Washington, DC: Congressional Quarterly Press, 2001), p. 64.

than their working-class counterparts.[47] The experience with cell phones and random digit dialing phone polls points to a general feature of public-opinion research. It is driven by the ways that people communicate in our society. Innovations in technology and the spread of new modes of communication create problems for establishing research methods, as we have seen in the case with cell phones. They also create opportunities. These new methods often offer much cheaper ways to contact people and conduct research, but their newness usually means that not everyone uses these modes of communication equally. The challenge for capturing the potential of new technologies is to figure out how to reach as broad a segment of the population using these methods and how to ensure the representativeness of the resulting samples.

Over the past 10 years a new set of firms have emerged that conduct survey research over the Internet. They use a variety of techniques to enlist people into their surveys, such as pop-up ads on websites. However, not everyone uses the Internet and people respond to pop-ups differently. To correct for such issues, Internet survey firms try different ways of reaching different audiences over the Internet and different sorts of appeals to potential respondents. After they have collected survey responses, Internet survey firms (indeed all polling firms) further adjust their data to correct for segments of the population that they over- or underrepresent.

Although these technical aspects of how surveys are constructed may seem obscure, the importance of sampling was brought home early in the history of political polling. A 1936 *Literary Digest* poll predicted that the Republican presidential candidate, Alf Landon, would defeat the Democrat, Franklin Delano Roosevelt, in that year's election. The election, of course, ended in a Roosevelt landslide. The main problem with the survey was what is called selection bias in drawing the sample. The pollsters had relied on telephone directories and automobile registration rosters to produce a sampling frame. During the Great Depression, however, only wealthy Americans owned telephones and automobiles. Thus the millions of working-class Americans who constituted Roosevelt's principal base of support were excluded from the sample.

selection bias

A polling error in which the sample is not representative of the population being studied, so that some opinions are over- or underrepresented

A more recent instance of polling error caused by selection bias occurred during the 1998 Minnesota gubernatorial election. A poll conducted by the *Minneapolis Star Tribune* just six weeks before the election showed the former professional wrestler Jesse Ventura running a distant third to the Democratic candidate, Hubert Humphrey III (who seemed to have the support of 49 percent of the electorate) and the Republican, Norm Coleman (whose support stood at 29 percent). Only 10 percent of those polled said they were planning to vote for Ventura. On election day, Ventura outpolled both Humphrey and Coleman. Analysis of exit poll data showed why the pre-election polls had been so wrong. In an effort to be accurate, pre-election pollsters' predictions often take account of the likelihood that respondents will actually vote. They do this by polling only people who have voted in the past or by correcting for past frequency of voting. The *Star Tribune* poll was conducted only among individuals who had voted in the previous election.

47 John Goyder, Keith Warriner, and Susan Miller, "Evaluating Socio-economic Status Bias in Survey Nonresponse," *Journal of Official Statistics* 18, no. 1 (2002): 1–11.

Ventura, however, brought to the polls not only individuals who had not voted in the last election but also many people who had never voted before in their lives. Approximately 12 percent of Minnesota's voters in 1998 said they came to the polls only because Ventura was on the ballot. This surge in turnout was facilitated by the fact that Minnesota permits same-day voter registration. Thus the pollsters were wrong because Ventura changed the composition of the electorate.[48] Polling organizations are ever mindful of these fateful stories. Their business depends on producing accurate representations of the American public's opinions and behavior.

Sample Size. The degree of reliability in polling is also a function of sample size. For polls of citizens of the United States, the typical size of a sample ranges from 450 to 1,500 respondents. This number reflects a trade-off between cost and degree of precision desired. A larger and hence more costly sample size is associated with greater precision in making generalizations to the full population than is a smaller sample size.

The chance that the sample used does not accurately represent the population from which it is drawn is called the sampling error, or *margin of error*. The sampling error measures the range of possibilities for a particular characteristic of a population based on the estimate of that characteristic in the sample drawn. The margin of error acknowledges that any given sample may not be perfectly representative of the full population. A typical survey of 1,500 respondents, for example, will have a sampling error of approximately 3 percent. When a pre-election poll indicates that 51 percent of voters surveyed favor the Republican candidate and 49 percent support the Democratic candidate, the outcome is in fact too close to call because it is within the margin of error of the survey. A figure of 51 percent means that between 54 and 48 percent of voters in the population favor the Republicans, whereas a figure of 49 percent indicates that between 52 and 46 percent of all voters support the Democrats. Thus in this example, any outcome ranging from a 54-to-46 Republican victory to a 48-to-52 Republican loss is consistent with the survey evidence. The precision of the poll in this case does not permit a clear prediction of a winner.

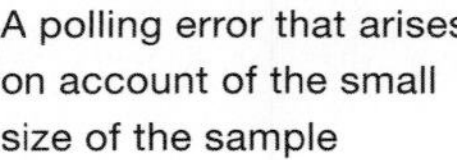

A polling error that arises on account of the small size of the sample

Table 10.5 shows how accurate two of the major national polling organizations have been in predicting the outcome of presidential elections. In the 2000, 2004, and the 2012 presidential elections, for example, in light of a 3 percent margin of error, the polls predicted a "dead heat." The most accurate pollster in recent years has been Nate Silver at the *New York Times*. Silver predicted the national outcome and state-by-state outcomes.[49]

48 Carl Cannon, "A Pox on Both Our Parties," in *The Enduring Debate: Classic and Contemporary Readings in American Politics*, 2nd ed., David T. Canon, Anne Khademian, and Kenneth R. Mayor, eds. (New York: Norton, 2000), p. 389.

49 For a recent paper on the difficulties with polls, especially in trying to assess the preferences of specific subgroups in the population, see David Leal, Matt Barreto, Jongho Lee, and Rodolfo O. de la Garza, "The Latino Vote in the 2004 Election," *PS: Political Science and Politics* 38 (January 2005): 41–9.

Table 10.5

TWO POLLSTERS AND THEIR RECORDS

YEAR	PRESIDENTIAL CANDIDATES	HARRIS	GALLUP	ACTUAL OUTCOME
2012	Romney Obama	NA*	50% 49	47% 51
2008	McCain Obama	44 50	43 51	46 53
2004	Bush G. W Kerry Nader	49 48 1	49 49 1	51 48 0
2000	Bush G.W. Gore Nader	47 47 5	48 46 4	48 49 3
1996	Clinton Dole Perot	51 39 9	52 41 7	49 41 8
1992	Clinton Bush G. H. W. Perot	44 38 17	44 37 14	43 38 19
1988	Bush G. H. W. Dukakis	51 47	53 42	54 46
1984	Reagan Mondale	56 44	59 41	59 41
1980	Reagan Carter Anderson	48 43	47 44 8	51 41
1976	Carter Ford	48 45	48 49	51 48
1972	Nixon McGovern	59 35	62 38	61 38
1968	Nixon Humphrey Wallace	40 43 13	43 42 15	43 43 14

(Continued)

ANALYZING THE EVIDENCE

Since their poor showing in 1948, the major pollsters have been close to the mark in every national presidential election. In 2000, though, neither Gallup nor Harris accurately predicted the outcome. From what you have learned about polling, what were some of the possible sources of error in these two national polls?

Table 10.5
(Continued)

YEAR	PRESIDENTIAL CANDIDATES	HARRIS	GALLUP	ACTUAL OUTCOME
1960	Kennedy Nixon	49 41	51 49	50 49
1956	Eisenhower Stevenson	NA*	60 41	58 42
1952	Eisenhower Stevenson	47 42	51 49	55 44
1948	Truman Dewey	NA*	44.5 49.5	49.6 45.1

*Not asked
NOTE: Figures are percentages. All except those for 1948 are rounded.
SOURCE: Data from the Harris survey and the Gallup poll, Chicago Tribune–New York News Syndicate, various press releases, 1964–2008. Courtesy of Louis Harris & Associates and the Gallup Organization.

measurement error 

The failure to identify the true distribution of opinion within a population because of errors such as ambiguous or poorly worded questions

Survey Design. Even with reliable sample procedures, surveys may fail to reflect the true distribution of opinion within a target population. One frequent source of measurement error is the wording of survey questions. The precise words used in a question can have an enormous effect on the answers a survey elicits. The validity of survey results can also be adversely affected by poorly formatted questions, a faulty ordering of questions, inappropriate vocabulary, ambiguous questions, or questions with built-in biases. Often seemingly minor differences in the wording of a question can convey vastly different meanings to respondents and thus produce quite different response patterns (Figure 10.2). For example, for many years the University of Chicago's National Opinion Research Center has asked respondents whether they think the federal government is spending too much, too little, or about the right amount of money on "assistance for the poor." Answering the question posed this way, about two-thirds of all respondents seem to believe that the government is spending too little. However, the same survey also asks whether the government spends too much, too little, or about the right amount for "welfare." When the word welfare is substituted for assistance for the poor, about half of all respondents indicate that too much money is being spent.[50]

50 Michael R. Kagay and Janet Elder, "Numbers Are No Problem for Pollsters, Words Are," *New York Times*, August 9, 1992, p. E6.

Figure 10.2
IT DEPENDS ON HOW YOU ASK

THE QUESTION
President Clinton has proposed setting aside approximately two-thirds of an expected budget surplus to fix the Social Security system. What do you think the leaders in Washington should do with the remainder of the surplus?

Variation 1:
Should the money be used for a tax cut, or should it be used to fund new government programs?

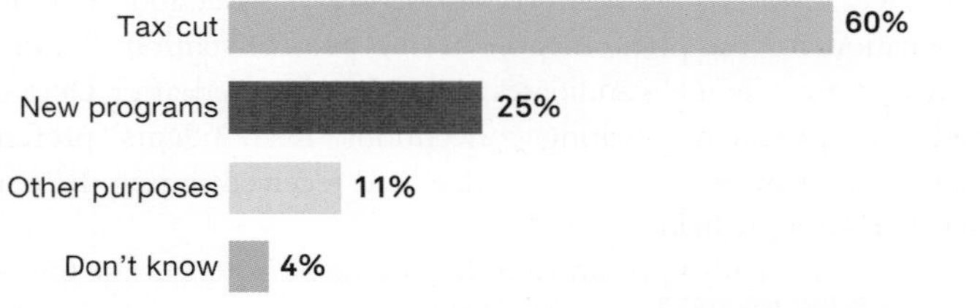

Variation 2:
Should the money be used for a tax cut or should it be spent on programs for education, the environment, health care, crime fighting, and military defense?

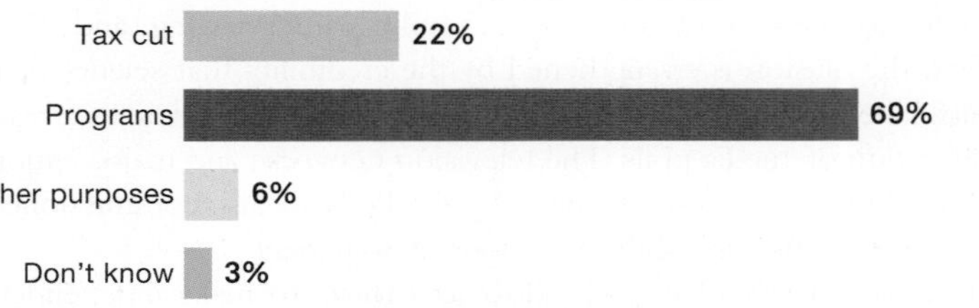

ANALYZING THE EVIDENCE

The public's desire for tax cuts can be hard to measure. Pollsters asking what should be done with the nation's budget surplus got different results, depending on the specifics of the question. What differences in the two versions of the question do you think account for the different answers?

SOURCE: Pew Research Center for the People and the Press, reported in the *New York Times*, January 30, 2000.

Push Polling. In recent years, another form of bias has been introduced into surveys by the use of a technique called push polling. This technique involves asking a respondent a loaded question about a political candidate, with the question designed to elicit the response sought by the pollster and, simultaneously, to shape the respondent's perception of the candidate in question. For example, during the 1996 New Hampshire presidential primary, push pollsters employed by the campaign of one of Lamar Alexander's rivals called thousands of voters to ask, "If you knew that Lamar Alexander had raised taxes six times in Tennessee, would you be less inclined or more inclined to support him?"[51] More than 100

push polling
A polling technique in which the questions are designed to shape the respondent's opinion

51 Donn Tibbetts, "Draft Bill Requires Notice of Push Polling," *Manchester Union Leader*, October 3, 1996, p. A6.

consulting firms across the nation now specialize in push polling, which is not a conventional use of legitimate survey methods and has been condemned by the American Association for Public Opinion Researchers.[52] Calling push polling the "political equivalent of a drive-by shooting," Representative Joe Barton (R-Tex.) launched a congressional investigation into the practice.[53] Push polls may be one reason why Americans are becoming increasingly skeptical of the practice of polling and increasingly unwilling to answers pollsters' questions.[54]

Illusion of Salience. In the early days of a political campaign, when voters are asked which candidates they do or do not support, the answer they give often has little significance because the choice is not yet important to them. Their preferences may change many times before the election. This is part of the explanation for the phenomenon of the postconvention "bounce" in the popularity of presidential candidates, which is observed after Democratic and Republican national nominating conventions. Respondents' preferences reflected the amount of attention a candidate had received during the conventions rather than strongly held views.

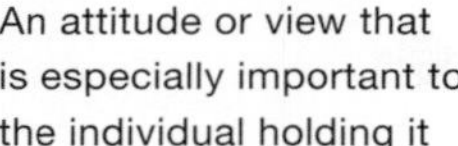

salient interest

An attitude or view that is especially important to the individual holding it

illusion of salience

The impression conveyed by polls that something is important to the public when it actually is not

The issues that are truly uppermost in the minds of voters at the time of an election, called salient interests, are often difficult to forecast very far in advance. These are interests that are of more than ordinary concern to respondents in a survey or to voters in the electorate. Politicians, social scientists, journalists, or pollsters who assume that something is important to the public when in fact it is not are creating an illusion of salience. This illusion can be created and fostered by polls despite careful controls in sampling, interviewing, and data analysis. In fact, the illusion is strengthened by the credibility that science gives survey results. The problem of salience has become especially acute as a result of the proliferation of media polls. The television networks and major national newspapers all make heavy use of opinion polls. Polls are also commissioned by local television stations and local and regional newspapers.

On the positive side, polls allow journalists to make independent assessments of political realities, assessments not influenced by the partisan claims of politicians. At the same time, however, media polls can allow journalists to make news when none exists. Polling diminishes journalists' dependence on news makers. A poll commissioned by a news agency can provide the basis for a good story even when candidates, politicians, and other news makers are not engaging in especially newsworthy activities. Thus on days when little or nothing is taking place in a political campaign, poll results, especially apparent changes in candidates' popularity margins, can provide exciting news. Several times during the 2008 presidential campaign, for example, small changes in the relative

52 See "AAPOR Statement on "'Push' Polls," www.aapor.org/aaporstatementonpushpolls?s=push%20polling (accessed 3/25/09).

53 Amy Keller, "Subcommittee Launches Investigation of Push Polls," *Roll Call*, October 3, 1996, p. 1.

54 For a discussion of the growing difficulty of persuading people to respond to surveys, see John Brehm, *Phantom Respondents* (Ann Arbor: University of Michigan Press, 1993).

standing of the Democratic and Republican candidates produced banner headlines around the country. Stories about what the candidates actually did or said often took second place to reporting the "horse race."

Because rapid and dramatic shifts in candidates' margins tend to take place when voters' preferences are least fully formed, it is interesting that horse-race news is most likely to make the headlines when it is least significant. In other words, media interest in poll results is inversely related to the salience of voters' opinions and the significance of the polls' findings. However, by influencing perceptions, especially those of major contributors, media polls can influence political realities.

Bandwagon Effect. One of the most noted polling problems is the bandwagon effect, which occurs when polling results influence people to support the candidate marked as the probable victor. Some scholars argue that the bandwagon effect can be offset by an "underdog effect," in favor of the candidate who is trailing in the polls.[55] However, a candidate who demonstrates a lead in the polls usually finds it considerably easier to raise campaign funds than does a candidate whose poll standing is low. With these additional funds, poll leaders can often afford to pay for television time and other campaign activities that will cement their advantage.

 **bandwagon effect**

A shift in electoral support to the candidate whom public-opinion polls report as the front-runner

HOW DOES PUBLIC OPINION INFLUENCE GOVERNMENT POLICY?

One of the fundamental notions on which the U.S. government was founded was that "the public" should not be trusted when it comes to governing. The framers designed institutions that, although democratic, somewhat insulated governmental decision making from popular pressure. For example, the indirect election of senators and presidents was supposed to prevent the government from being too dependent on the vagaries of public opinion.

Research from the 1950s and 1960s indicates that the framers' concerns were well founded. Individual-level survey analysis reveals that the respondents lacked fundamental political knowledge and had ill-formed opinions about government and public policy.[56] Their answers seemed nothing more than "doorstep opinions"—opinions given off the top of the head. When an individual was asked the same questions at different times, he or she often gave different answers. The dramatic and unpredictable changes seemed to imply that the public was indeed unreliable as a guide for political decisions. However, the political scientists Benjamin Page and Robert Shapiro take issue with the notion that

55 See Michael Traugott, "The Impact of Media Polls on the Public," in *Media Polls in American Politics*, Thomas E. Mann and Gary Orren, eds. (Washington, DC: Brookings Institution, 1992), pp. 125–49.

56 Campbell et al., *The American Voter*; Converse, "The Nature of Belief Systems."

the public should not be trusted when it comes to policy making.[57] They contend that public opinion at the aggregate level is coherent and stable and that it moves in a predictable fashion in response to changing political, economic, and social circumstances.

How is this possible, given what previous studies have found? Page and Shapiro hypothesize that the individual-level responses are plagued by various types of errors that make people's opinions seem incoherent and unstable. When a large number of individual-level responses to survey questions are added up to produce an aggregate public opinion, the errors, or "noise," in the individual responses, if more or less random, will cancel each other out, revealing a collective opinion that is stable, coherent, and meaningful. From their results, Page and Shapiro concluded that the general public can indeed be trusted when it comes to governing.

In democratic nations, leaders should pay heed to public opinion, and most evidence suggests that they do. In many instances, public policy and public opinion do not coincide, but in general the government's actions are consistent with citizens' preferences. One study, for example, found that between 1935 and 1979, in about two-thirds of all cases significant changes in public opinion were followed within one year by changes in government policy consistent with the shift in the popular mood.[58] Other studies have come to similar conclusions about public opinion and government policy at the state level.[59] Do these results imply that elected leaders merely pander to public opinion? The answer is no.

A recent study on the role that public opinion played during the failed attempt to enact health care reform in the early days of the Clinton presidency found that public opinion polls had very little influence on individual members of Congress, who used these polls first to justify positions they had already adopted and then to shape public thinking on the issue. In other words, opinion and policy were related because policy makers shaped opinion to support paths they already planned to take. This pattern is consistent with the opinion-manipulation efforts we examined earlier in this chapter. However, the study also found that congressional party leaders based their health care legislation strategies on their concerns about the effects of public opinion on the electoral fortunes of individual members of Congress. Leaders' concerns about public opinion thus help explain why the congressional policy-making process follows public opinion even though individual members of Congress do not.[60] The salience of health care has remained high for more than a decade since the failure of Clinton's effort. President Bush's prescription drug plan for senior citizens came about in response to public concerns

57 Benjamin I. Page and Robert Y. Shapiro, *The Rational Public: Fifty Years of Trends in Americans' Policy Preferences* (Chicago: University of Chicago Press, 1992).

58 Benjamin I. Page and Robert Y. Shapiro, "Effects of Public Opinion on Policy," *American Political Science Review* 77, no. 1 (March 1983): 175–90.

59 Robert S. Erikson, Gerald C. Wright, and John P. McIver, *Statehouse Democracy: Public Opinion and Policy in the American States* (New York: Cambridge University Press, 1993).

60 Lawrence R. Jacobs, Eric D. Lawrence, Robert Y. Shapiro, and Steven S. Smith, "Congressional Leadership of Public Opinion," *Political Science Quarterly* 113 (Spring 1998): 21–41.

about rising prescription-drug costs. Even after Barack Obama and a Democratic Congress succeeded in passing health care legislation in 2010, many Americans remained concerned about the issue, and some Republicans promised to revisit the new legislation (or even repeal it) if they gained a majority in Congress.

There are always areas of disagreement between opinion and policy. For example, the majority of Americans favored stricter government control of handguns for years before Congress adopted the modest restrictions on firearms purchases embodied in the 1994 Brady gun control bill and the amendment of the 1968 Omnibus Crime Control and Safe Streets Act. Similarly, most Americans, blacks as well as whites, oppose school busing to achieve racial balance, yet such busing continues to be used in many parts of the nation. Most Americans are also far less concerned with the rights of the accused than the federal courts seem to be. And most Americans oppose U.S. military intervention in other nations' affairs, yet such intervention continues to take place and often wins public approval after the fact.

Several factors can contribute to a lack of consistency between opinion and government policy. First, the nominal majority on a particular issue may not be as intensely committed to its preference as the adherents of the minority viewpoint. An intensely committed minority may often be more willing to commit its time, energy, efforts, and resources to the affirmation of its opinions than an apathetic majority, even if it is large. In the case of firearms, for example, although the proponents of gun control are in the majority by a wide margin, most do not regard the issue as being of critical importance to themselves and are not willing to commit much effort to advancing their cause. The opponents of gun control, by contrast, are intensely committed, well organized, and well financed and as a result are usually able to carry the day. In accordance with the institution principle, the collective action principle, and the policy principle, intense commitment, organization, and financial resources are potent assets in the legislature, the executive bureaucracy, and the courts.

A second important reason why public policy and public opinion may not coincide has to do with the character and structure of the American system of government. The framers of the Constitution, as we saw in Chapter 2, sought to create a system of government that was based on popular consent but did not invariably and automatically translate shifting popular sentiments into public policies. As a result, the American governmental process includes arrangements such as an appointed judiciary that can produce policy decisions that may run contrary to prevailing popular sentiment—at least for a time.

Perhaps the inconsistencies between opinion and policy could be resolved if we made broader use of a mechanism currently employed by a number of states: the ballot initiative. This procedure allows propositions to be placed on the ballot and voted into law by the electorate, bypassing most of the normal machinery of representative government. In recent years, several important propositions sponsored by business and conservative groups have been enacted.[61] For example, California's Proposition 209, approved by the state's

61 David Broder, *Democracy Derailed: Initiative Campaigns and the Power of Money* (New York: Harcourt, 2000).

voters in 1996, prohibited state and local government agencies in California from using race or gender preferences in hiring, contracting, or university admissions decisions. Responding to conservatives' success, liberal groups launched a number of ballot initiatives in 2000. In Washington State, for example, voters were asked to consider propositions sponsored by teachers unions that would have required annual cost-of-living raises for teachers and more than $1.8 billion in additional state spending over the next six years.[62]

Initiatives such as these seem to provide the public with an opportunity to express its will. During the 2006 and 2008 elections, propositions on social issues—gay marriage, stem-cell research, immigration—were on the ballot in many states, bypassing stalled efforts of the normal political process. In 2012, voters in numerous states were asked to decide on the constitutionality of same-sex marriage, on the eligibility of "undocumented" immigrants who had been raised in the United States to attend college at in-state tuition rates, on the legalization of marijuana, and on a variety of state budget and tax matters. The problem, however, is that government by initiative offers little opportunity for reflection and compromise. Voters are presented with a proposition, usually sponsored by a special interest group, and are asked to take it or leave it. Perhaps the true will of the people lies somewhere between the positions taken by the various interest groups. For example, California voters might have wanted affirmative action programs to be modified but not scrapped altogether, as Proposition 209 mandated. In a representative assembly, as opposed to a referendum campaign, a compromise position might have been achieved that would have been more satisfactory to all the residents of the state. This capacity for compromise is one reason the Founders strongly favored representative government rather than direct democracy.[63]

When all is said and done, however, the actions of the American government do not remain out of line with popular sentiment for long. A major reason for this is, of course, the electoral process. Nonetheless, we should not forget that the close relationship between government and opinion in America may also be in part a result of the government's success in molding opinion.

CONCLUSION

Representative democracy was a novel form of government when the United States created its Constitution. Behind this radical system lies one central idea—that the government reflects the will of the people. People have the opportunity

62 Robert Tomsho, "Liberals Take a Cue from Conservatives: This Election, the Left Tries to Make Policy with Ballot Initiatives," *Wall Street Journal*, November 6, 2000, p. A12.

63 For the classic treatment of take-it-or-leave-it referendums and initiatives, see Thomas Romer and Howard Rosenthal, "Political Resource Allocation, Controlled Agendas, and the Status Quo," *Public Choice* 33 (1978): 27–44.

to express their preferences through elections, public meetings and organizations, and free expression and debate. Public deliberations and public choices, it is conjectured, aggregate individuals' preferences and opinions to form the collective "will of the people" that would guide those in office. This chapter has explored the meaning of this idea today.

We no longer speak of the people of the United States as if they were an organic whole with a coherent will. Rather we characterize the "people" as the aggregation of individuals' preferences about the choices presented to them—in a phrase, public opinion. The individual is the foundation of public opinion. Politicians assume that individuals will pursue and express their own preferences and beliefs. They will act in ways to protect and expand their own property and wealth: They will express their own ideologies and ideals about what is right; they will pursue their own happiness and not sacrifice their own interests for those of the state or the community. When then vote, attend meetings, talk to others, or otherwise engage in democratic politics, people are free to say what they want, meet with whomever they want, and do what they want, so long as they don't harm others. The aggregation of all those activities and actions expresses the public's opinion.

The succeeding chapters will consider how public opinion manifests itself through different institutions of democracy—elections, parties, organized interests, and communications media. As we discuss these institutions, it will be useful to keep in mind how we have described public opinion in this chapter. Specifically, every individual has his or her own preferences and own beliefs about the right policy or action to pursue. On any particular question or issue, individuals face a range of choices or options. Expressing their preferences, individuals choose the options that best reflect their preferences as to the outcomes and their beliefs about what is the best way to achieve those outcomes. On many issues, social scientists describe the range of people's preferences along a single dimension, such as ideology (from very liberal to very conservative) or partisanship (from strongly Democratic to strongly Republican). On general economic indicators, such as income, most people in the United States have what may be described as middle-class incomes; a significant percentage are poor, and a very small percentage are wealthy. Preferences about social spending and taxation often reflect these economic differences. On matters of ideology or public policy, social scientists gauge the percentage of people adhering to each of the many possible views. Most people in the United States hold fairly centrist or moderate views on most questions. The tilt, depending on the issue and the choices offered, is slightly right of center or slightly left of center. Neither right nor left nor center, however, commands an outright majority of public support in the United States on any issue of importance. Anyone adhering to one of these views must reach out beyond his or her particular ideological slant in order to find a coalition large enough to capture the support of a majority.

Democracy in this free and open society is complicated further by the heterogeneity of American society. The nation's political institutions tolerate all manner of religious and political beliefs and all manner of social and economic relations, and the United States has long been a refuge for those from other countries seeking religious or political asylum or just a better way of life. As a result the United States is one of the most diverse societies in the world, with freedom to practice every major religion, with all manner of political and social organizations, and with great concentrations of wealth and poverty. This would seem to be a recipe not for consensus but for disagreement and conflict, even civil conflict.

The open society in the United States, however, has worked for over two centuries, and it works because its members have a strong common commitment to democracy itself. Americans, in essence, agree to disagree. We agree that it is best to have a heterogeneous society and to tolerate many different opinions. We value liberty and restrain the government from imposing itself on how people think or express themselves politically. We further agree to allow the institutions of democracy to help us reach collective decisions about who should govern and how they should govern.

The next four chapters examine those institutions in detail. How do elections facilitate the choice of and control over the government? How do political parties simplify choices and compete in the political domain? How do people mobilize their interests to allow for the expression of interests in a more concerted way than just voting? And finally, how do the media help us overcome collective action problems and allow us to learn from each other, communicate with each other, and find consensus?

For Further Reading

Althaus, Scott. *Collective Preferences and Democratic Politics.* New York: Cambridge University Press, 2003.

Ansolabehere, Stephen, Jonathan Rodden, and James M. Snyder, Jr. "Purple America." *Journal of Economic Perspectives* 20, no. 2 (Spring 2006): 97–118.

reader selection

Bartels, Larry. *Unequal Democracy: The Political Economy of the New Gilded Age.* Princeton, NJ: Princeton University Press, 2008.

Berinsky, Adam. *In Time of War: Understanding Public Opinion from World War II to Iraq.* Chicago: University of Chicago Press, 2009.

Erikson, Robert S., and Kent L. Tedin. *American Public Opinion: Its Origins, Content, and Impact.* 6th ed. New York: Longman, 2001.

Fiorina, Morris, Samuel Abrams, and Jeremy Pope. *Culture War?* 2nd ed. New York: Pearson, Longman, 2005.

Frank, Thomas. *What's the Matter with Kansas?* New York: Macmillan, 2004.

Ginsberg, Benjamin. *The Captive Public: How Mass Opinion Promotes State Power.* New York: Basic Books, 1986.

Jacobson, Gary. *A Divider, Not a Uniter: George W. Bush, the American People, the 2006 Election, and Beyond.* White Plains, NY: Longman, 2007.

Key, V. O. *Public Opinion and American Democracy.* New York: Knopf, 1961.

Lee, Taeku. *Mobilizing Public Opinion.* Chicago: University of Chicago Press, 2002.

Lupia, Arthur, and Matthew D. McCubbins. *The Democratic Dilemma: Can Citizens Learn What They Need to Know?* New York: Cambridge University Press, 1998. **reader selection**

McCarty, Nolan, Keith Poole, and Howard Rosenthal. *Polarized America: The Dance of Ideology and Unequal Riches.* Princeton, NJ: Princeton University Press, 2007. **reader selection**

Page, Benjamin I., and Robert Y. Shapiro. *The Rational Public: Fifty Years of Trends in Americans' Policy Preferences.* Chicago: University of Chicago Press, 1992.

Stimson, James A. *Public Opinion in America: Moods, Cycles, and Swings.* 2nd ed. Boulder, CO: Westview Press, 1998.

Zaller, John R. *The Nature and Origins of Mass Opinion.* New York: Cambridge University Press, 1992. **reader selection**

Visit wwnorton.com/studyspace/ to access free review materials such as:

- Vocabulary Flashcards of All Key Terms
- Chapter Review Quizzes
- Complete Study Outlines

reader selection

Highlighted selections are included in *Readings in American Politics: Analysis and Perspectives*, Second Edition.

11

PART 1 2 3 4

DEMOCRATIC POLITICS

Elections

Chapter Outline

The most profound expression of an individual's political preferences is the vote. It is a blunt but effective instrument for controlling the government. Citizens usually cannot decide directly what laws are enacted, what the tax or interest rates will be, or whether to declare war. Citizens can affirm a commitment to stay the course or to change their government when they think a new direction is needed. It is our way of reining in government and ensuring that elected officials remain attentive to public preferences. Elections have proved a remarkably successful method of bringing about continual renewal of government through peaceful means.

Frequent, regular elections are the hallmark of democracy. And the United States embraces this idea to a greater extent than any other democracy. America has elections very frequently, with great regularity, and for all manner of governments. Voters in the United States elect the president, governors, and other executive officers every four years,[1] federal and state legislators every two years, and thousands of local mayors, councilors, and commissioners with similar frequency. All told there are over 88,000 governments at the federal, state, and local levels in the United States, nearly all of them run by elected bodies.[2] In a typical election, a voter may choose candidates for a dozen different offices, as well as deciding bond issues and other local questions put before the voters.

Why do elections work? How is it that elections generally create a government and policies that reflect and respond to the preferences of the public? The

1 Vermont and New Hampshire elect their governors every two years.

2 One federal government, 50 state governments, over 3,000 county governments, about 36,000 municipal and town governments, about 13,500 school districts, and over 35,000 special districts (for example, water or utility). www.census.gov/govs/www/cog2007.html (accessed 3/26/09).

simple idea behind democracy is that there is power, and perhaps even wisdom, in numbers. Voting allows each of us to express our preferences, and election procedures aggregate those votes into a legitimate collective choice. Election laws determine how votes are counted and translate into a government—who wins seats in the legislature, who is elected to the executive, or how much is spent on schools in a municipality.

Elections in the United States work by choosing who will govern, not what they should do or what the laws should be. We do not have direct democracy in federal elections, although many states and municipalities allow voting on bonds and a small number of laws. For the most part, elections are, to put the matter in terms we first considered in Chapter 1, occasions when multiple principals—the citizens—choose political agents to act on their behalf.

Two problems immediately arise for the principals (the citizens). First, are we selecting the best people for the job? This is a problem of adverse selection and stems from hidden information. We want to choose the people who have the necessary competence to write legislation or who have our interests at heart. Second, once elected, do the politicians do the job as we wish them to? This is

 **adverse selection**

The problem of incomplete information—of choosing alternatives without fully knowing the details of available options

CORE OF THE ANALYSIS

 The United States holds frequent elections as a means of keeping politicians close to the preferences of a majority of the people.

 The United States uses a system of plurality rule in which the candidate with the most votes wins the electoral district. Plurality rule creates a strong pressure toward two-party politics and makes it difficult for third parties to succeed.

 Plurality rule also shapes the incentives facing candidates and parties. It creates strong pressure on the parties or candidates to take more centrist policies so as to appeal to the median voter among the electorate as a whole.

 Most voters develop strong attachments to political parties, based on agreement on policy, social pressure, or upbringing. Those who identify with a party vote with that party nearly all of the time.

 Campaigns try to mobilize their candidate's supporters and persuade undecided voters. In the process, they provide information that helps solve some of the informational problems inherent in representative democracy.

moral hazard 

The problem of not knowing all aspects of the actions taken by an agent (nominally on behalf of the principal but potentially at the principal's expense)

a problem of moral hazard and stems from hidden actions. Once selected, representatives cannot easily be monitored. Political leaders necessarily engage in many acts that do not attract public attention, such as making deals with other politicians to build a winning coalition for a particular bill. In these situations, we need to make sure that the decisions the politicians make are the ones we want them to make. However, voters cannot know everything about candidates for office or about politicians' actions once they are elected. In fact, the incentives to be highly knowledgeable are minimal. In a nation of 170 million registered voters or even a district of 700,000 voters, surely one's own ballot is unlikely to make a difference in the outcome and the cost of making a mistake is nil. Why, then, go to great lengths to find out the details of the candidates' backgrounds and personalities or to learn about the goings-on in Congress?

Voters use the simplest rules to solve these problems. Politicians caught in scandals are usually voted out of office. Voters usually take economic downturns as evidence of mismanagement of economic policy, and they vote against the incumbent president's party, as occurred in 2008 and 2010. They will also reward a party for economic good times and express their desire to continue with current economic policies, as occurred in 2004. One need not know the details about the inner workings of government to hold politicians accountable for large-scale malfeasance. But how do we hold politicians accountable for the details of legislation?

Ultimately, elections work through competition. The public relies on competition among politicians, the parties, interest groups, and the media to inform them. This chapter focuses on the politicians; later chapters go into greater detail about the parties, interest groups, and the media.

In the United States politicians are central. Rival politicians or teams of politicians (parties) seek to hold elective office—we can consider that their primary motivation. They try to formulate positions on important policies that appeal to the greatest number of voters; they develop personal appeals; they advertise their own ability to do the job at hand, their honesty and strength of character, and their fidelity to the public. Likewise, politicians draw attention to the failings of their rivals. Candidates and parties use advertisements, press conferences, speeches, and other modes of reaching the public to highlight policy decisions made by their opponents that are out of step with the wishes of a majority of voters, and they expose scandalous behavior and play up political gaffes. Politicians themselves, then, bear much of the cost of informing the public about their own performance and ideas and those of their opponents. Competition, then, creates strong incentives for those vying for office to reveal information to the electorate.

Competition alone does not cure all. Proponents of electoral reform criticize many features of U.S. election laws, including the campaign finance system, redistricting procedures, the lack of third parties, and the relatively low levels of voter turnout. In this chapter, we look at how the institutional features of American elections shape the way citizens' goals and preferences are reflected in their government and how voters decide among the candidates and questions put before them on the ballot. Democracy is a work in progress. Americans constantly tinker with the rules to try to make it a better system.

INSTITUTIONS OF ELECTIONS

Elections don't just happen. They are not spontaneous affairs but formal institutions for making collective decisions. As in Congress, the executive branch, and the courts, rules (institutions) determine the operations of elections—who is allowed to vote, how votes are cast and counted, and how we determine who wins office. Election rules consist of a mix of state and federal laws, legal decisions, and local administrative practices. Federal laws regulate the time of congressional and presidential elections, the qualifications for office, the allocation of seats, the structure of electoral districts, and the qualifications and rights of voters. State laws determine a wider range of factors, including how votes are cast and counted, the procedures for registering voters, candidate qualifications for all elected officials other than members of Congress and the president, the procedures for nominating candidates and getting on the ballot, the operations of the parties, and the conduct of all state and local elections. The responsibility for making all of this go smoothly on Election Day falls, in turn, on the roughly 5,000 local election offices in counties and municipalities. Workers in local election offices manage the registration lists, prepare the ballots and voting machinery, set up polling places, recruit and train poll workers, and tally and certify the votes. And at the polling places on Election Day the poll workers, roughly 1 million volunteers across the country, administer the election.

The laws and procedures governing elections have important consequences. They can skew the electorate toward one interest or another; they can create barriers to some sorts of political organizations; and they can create a legislature that reflects the diversity in the population or one that has a clear majority.

Four features of U.S. election laws deserve particular emphasis.

- First, *who*. The United States provides for universal adult suffrage—all citizens over the age of 18 have the right to vote.[3]
- Second, *how*. Americans vote in secret and choose among candidates for particular office using a form of the ballot called the "Australian ballot."
- Third, *where*. The United States selects almost all elected offices through single-member districts that have equal populations—one person, one vote.
- Fourth, *what* it takes to win. For most offices in the United States, the candidate who wins the most votes among all of those competing for a given seat wins the election.

We consider each matter and its consequences in turn. In short, we will see that in the United States these rules create a two-party system that broadly encompasses the entire adult population but that exaggerates the political power of the

3 In addition, there is the restriction that those currently serving sentences for felonies cannot vote; some states prohibit ex-felons from voting.

majority. Other features of American election laws and procedures, including rules governing campaign expenditures and fund-raising, party nominations, and ballot access, further shape political competition in the United States.

Also notable are rules that the United States does not have. Federal and state laws do not limit the amount of television and other forms of advertising, total campaign spending, the activities of groups and parties on behalf of candidates, or how the media cover the campaigns. Most other countries limit the use of television or forbid it altogether, restrict how candidates can campaign and how much they can spend, and tightly regulate the activities of organized interest groups. Compared with other countries, then, the United States has a relatively unregulated electoral system that allows candidates to run on their own, separate from the parties, and allows candidates to spend relatively freely on media and other aspects of their campaigns. We turn to these campaign activities in the next section, especially as they bear on the important question of voter learning through campaigns. The features of election law considered here regulate the nature of the electorate and the choices that voters face.

The rules governing elections are not static. The features of American electoral institutions have evolved over time through legislation, court decisions, administrative rulings of agencies, and public agitation for electoral reform. The nation has gradually converged on our present system of universal suffrage with secret voting and to the use of single-member districts with plurality rule. The future will likely bring further innovations in voting and elections. With waves of immigration, new communication technologies, and other changes reshaping society, the institutions of democracy must change as well. Perhaps the most dramatic changes under way involve the rise of "convenience voting"—voting by mail or voting early at a polling center or town hall. In 1972, approximately 5 percent of all votes nationwide were cast in absentia; in 2012, approximately one-third of all votes were absentee or early ballots. The states of Oregon and Washington vote entirely by mail. A few states, such as New Jersy, accept absentee ballots by e-mail, which is particularly convenient for military personnel. The rise of these new modes of voting presents new questions about secrecy and about the form of the ballot; it provides new opportunities for reform and modes of voting (such as instant runoff voting). Such changes rarely come about through carefully planned federal legislation. Rather, new election institutions will emerge out of the experiences and experiments of local election officials and state laws.

Who Votes: Electoral Composition

Over the course of American history the electorate has expanded greatly. At the beginning of the nineteenth century, America was unusually democratic compared with the rest of the world because the United States provided for universal suffrage for all adult white male citizens and in some cities even noncitizens. In contrast, during the nineteenth century, property qualifications restricted the electorate in European nations in a manner acceptable to the aristocracy and other ruling classes. In France before 1848, to cite just one example, limiting the suffrage to property owners restricted the electorate to just 240,000 out of 7 million men over age 21.[4] No women were allowed to vote at this time. During the same era, other nations manipulated the electorate's composition by assigning unequal weights to different classes of voters. The 1831 Belgian constitution, for example, assigned individuals anywhere from one to three votes, depending on their property holdings, education, and social position. Even in the American context there were significant restrictions on the size of the electorate, especially on the basis of race and gender. In the southern states, blacks were not allowed to vote before the Civil War. The passage of the Fifteenth Amendment in 1870 gave blacks voting rights, but in the late nineteenth century, southern states passed "Jim Crow" laws establishing literacy tests, poll taxes, and all-white primaries. Local election officials administered these laws in ways that kept the large majority of blacks from voting. One by one, these institutions were struck down by the courts as violations of the Constitution and finally forbidden by the Voting Rights Act of 1965 and the Twenty-third Amendment. Gender qualifications excluded an even larger segment of the population. In most states, women were not allowed to vote until 1920, following the passage of the Nineteenth Amendment. The most recent expansion of the franchise came in 1971, when Congress decided to lower the voting age from 21 to 18 with the passage of the Twenty-sixth Amendment. If eighteen-year-olds could be drafted to serve their country in the military, it was argued, they deserved the full privileges of citizenship, including the right to vote.

Voting in the United States is treated as a right, not a requirement. Some countries, such as Australia and Germany, have compulsory voting: all eligible voters are required to vote or pay a modest fine. These societies treat electoral participation as a necessity. Americans view voting somewhat differently. Like most other activities in our society, voting is voluntary. If we do not feel strongly about government, we do not have to participate. If we want to send a message of dissatisfaction, one way to do so is to not vote. Of course, if no one voted, it would be a disaster for American democracy; it would signal the end of Americans' commitment to their form of government. When large numbers of people do participate in the collective decision making of the country at each election, it is evidence of a robust democracy. Governments at all levels in the United States also have so many elections that voters may not feel the need to participate in all elections all the time in order to weigh in on the activities of government. And there are many other ways that we can participate in electoral politics, such as blogging and speaking with others, joining organizations, and giving money. Compared with other nations, the United States is one of the best examples of participatory democracy in the world.[5]

---

4 Stein Rokkan, *Citizens, Elections, Parties: Approaches to the Comparative Study of the Process of Development* (New York: David McKay, 1970), p. 149. Also see Daron Acemoglu and James A. Robinson, "Why Did the West Extend the Franchise?" *Quarterly Journal of Economics* 115 (2000): 1167–99.

5 Sidney Verba, Kay Schlozman, and Henry Brady, *Voice and Equality: Civic Volunteerism in America* (Cambridge, MA: Harvard University Press, 1995).

ANALYZING THE EVIDENCE

The United States trails many democracies in the rate at which citizens vote. Are Americans simply more apathetic about politics, or do institutional features in the United States produce greater obstacles to participation?

Figure 11.1

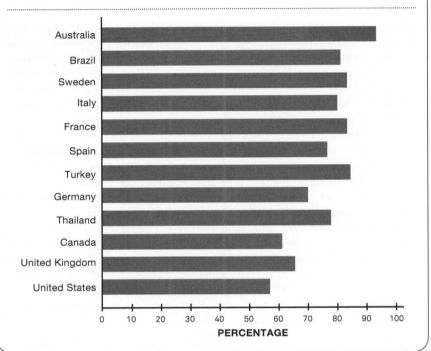

VOTER TURNOUT AROUND THE WORLD

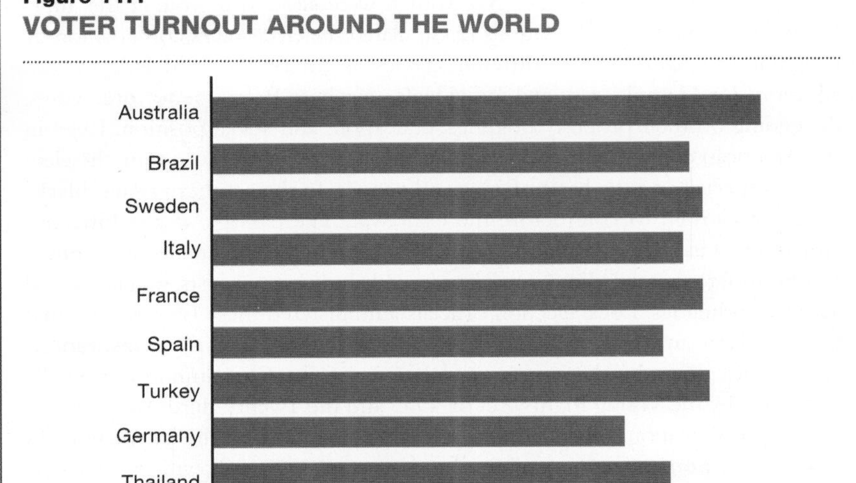

NOTE: Turnout as a percentage of voting-age population in the most recent national presidential or parliamentary election as of 2011.
SOURCE: International Institute of Democracy and Electoral Assistance, www.idea.int/vt/ (accessed 8/29/11).

That said, levels of voter participation in the latter half of the twentieth century were quite low in the United States as compared with those of other Western democracies (Figure 11.1).[6] Indeed, voter participation in presidential elections in the United States barely averaged 50 percent (Figure 11.2). Turnout in the 2000 presidential election was 51 percent of voting-age Americans; in 2012, it was approximately 54 percent. During the nineteenth century, by contrast, voter turnout in the United States was extremely high, considerably higher than it is today (Figure 11.2).[7]

6 See Walter Dean Burnham, "The Changing Shape of the American Political Universe," *American Political Science Review* 59, no. 1 (March 1965): 7–28. It should be noted that other democracies, such as India and Switzerland, have even lower turnout rates, as do some of the new democracies in eastern Europe.

7 See statistics of the U.S. Bureau of the Census and the Federal Election Commission. For voting statistics for 1960 to 2004, see "National Voter Turnout in Federal Elections: 1960–2004," at www.infoplease.com/ipa/A0781453.html (accessed 3/26/09).

Figure 11.2
VOTER TURNOUT IN U.S. PRESIDENTIAL ELECTIONS

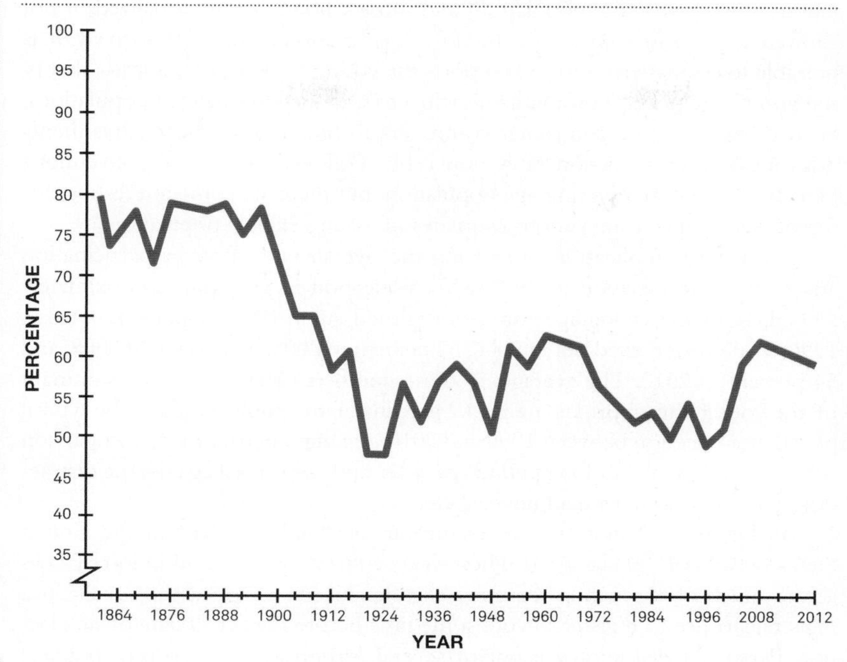

NOTE: Data reflect the population of eligible voters; the percentage of the voting-age population that voted would be smaller.
SOURCES: For 1860–1928, U.S. Bureau of the Census, Historical Statistics of the United States, Colonial Times to 1970, www.census.gov/prod/www/abs/statab.html (accessed 3/26/09); pt. 2, p. 1071; for 1932–92, U.S. Bureau of the Census, Statistical Abstract of the United States, 1993 (Washington, DC: Government Printing Office, 1993), p. 284; for 1996–2008, Federal Election Commission data.

ANALYZING THE EVIDENCE

Voter turnout for American presidential elections was significantly higher in the nineteenth century than in the twentieth. What institutional change caused the sharp decline in turnout between 1890 and 1910? Why did this change have such a dramatic effect? Did it have any positive outcomes?

An important caveat about the quantitative measure of turnout is in order. When a turnout rate of 54 percent is reported, we may ask, 54 percent of what? A turnout rate is a ratio comparing the number of people who voted to some baseline population. The first part of this ratio is relatively uncontroversial—it is the number of individuals who present themselves at polling stations or submit absentee ballots. Not all states report such figures in their certified tally of the vote. In fact, 11 states do not report total turnout, and researchers must substitute the total votes for all candidates for the presidency or another office on the top of the ballot. So, for example, if an individual voter in one of these states does not cast a vote for president but does turn out to vote on other questions on the ballot, this voter might not be counted in the total turnout. However, since nearly all voters who turn out do vote on the races at the top of the ticket, counting those totals is a reasonably accurate substitute for official turnout records. The appropriate baseline in the turnout ratio is more difficult to define. Conventionally, turnout is calculated as a percentage of the voting-age population. This understates turnout, because it includes some noncitizens (about 3 percent of the population) and those who are institutionalized or not allowed to vote in some states because they are ex-felons. Alternatively, it is possible to estimate from census reports the voting-eligible population—that is, the voting-age population minus noncitizens and institutionalized populations. Such calculations are somewhat controversial, but making these adjustments does increase participation rates noticeably. Following the usual conventions here, we focus on the voting-age population, but there are some interesting differences in trends using various estimates of voting-eligible population.[8]

A further complication in gauging the overall rate of voter participation arises from the variation in turnout from election to election. Approximately 55 percent of the voting-age population turned out in 1992; 50 percent voted in 1996; 51 percent turned out in 2000; 55 percent in 2004; 57 percent in 2008; and 54 percent in 2012. The average of these numbers offers a succinct summary of the voting rate: approximately 53.7 percent of the public voted in the typical presidential election between 1990 and 2010. Averages permit ready comparison across nations and over long periods of time, and help guard against the distraction that might arise with an unusual election.

As Figure 11.2 indicates, voter turnout declined markedly in the United States between 1890 and 1910. These years coincide with the adoption of laws across much of the nation requiring eligible citizens to appear personally at a registrar's office to register to vote some time before the actual date of an election. Personal registration was one of several "progressive" reforms of political practices initiated at the beginning of the twentieth century. The ostensible purpose of registration was to discourage fraud and corruption. But to many progressive reformers, corruption was a code word, referring to the type of politics practiced in the large cities, where political parties had organized immigrant and ethnic populations. Reformers not only objected to the corruption that surely was a facet of party politics in this period but also opposed the growing political power of urban populations and their leaders.

Personal registration imposed a new burden on potential voters and altered the format of American elections. Under the registration systems adopted after 1890, it became the duty of individual voters to secure their own eligibility. This duty could prove to be a significant burden for potential voters for a number of reasons. First, during a personal appearance before the registrar, individuals seeking to vote were (and are) required to furnish proof of identity, residence, and citizenship. Although the inconvenience of registration varied from state to state, usually voters could register only during business hours on weekdays. Many potential voters could not afford to lose a day's pay in order to register. Second, voters were usually required to register well before the next election, in some states up to several months earlier. Third, because most personal

8 Michael McDonald and Samuel Popkin, "The Myth of the Vanishing Voter," *American Political Science Review* 95 (December 2001): 963–74.

registration laws required a periodic purge of the election rolls, ostensibly to keep them up-to-date, voters often had to re-register to maintain their eligibility. Thus, although personal registration requirements helped diminish the widespread electoral corruption that accompanied a completely open voting process, they also made it much more difficult for citizens to participate in the electoral process. Rational citizens with busy lives might well be expected to forgo political participation as its complications and costs increase.

Registration requirements depress the participation of those with little education and low income in particular, because registration requires a greater degree of political involvement and interest than does the act of voting itself. To vote, a person need only be concerned with the particular election campaign at hand. Yet requiring individuals to register before a coming election forces them to make a decision to participate on the basis of an abstract interest in the electoral process rather than a simple concern with a specific campaign. Such an abstract interest in electoral politics is largely a product of education. Those with relatively little education may become interested in political events once the stimuli of a particular campaign become salient, but by that time it may be too late to register. As a result, personal registration requirements not only diminish the size of the electorate but also tend to create an electorate that is, in the aggregate, less representative of the voting-age population. The electorate is better educated, has a higher income and social status, and includes fewer African Americans and other minorities than the citizenry as a whole (Figure 11.3).

Over the years, voter registration restrictions have been modified somewhat to make registration easier. In 1993, for example, Congress approved and President Bill Clinton signed the "motor voter" bill to ease voter registration by allowing individuals to register when they applied for driver's licenses, as well as in public-assistance and military-recruitment offices.[9] In many jurisdictions, casting a vote automatically registers the voter for the next election. In Europe, there is typically no registration burden on the individual voter; voter registration is handled automatically by the government. This is one reason that voter turnout rates in Europe are higher than those in the United States.

Another factor explaining low rates of voter turnout in the United States is the relative weakness of the American party system. During the nineteenth century, American political party machines employed hundreds of thousands of workers to organize and mobilize voters and bring them to the polls. The result was an extremely high rate of turnout, typically more than 90 percent of eligible voters.[10] But political party machines began to decline in strength in the early twentieth century and by now have largely disappeared. Without party workers to encourage them to go to the polls and even take them there if necessary, many eligible voters will not participate. In the absence of strong parties, participation rates drop the most among poorer and less-educated citizens. Because

9 Helen Dewar, "'Motor Voter' Agreement Is Reached," *Washington Post*, April 28, 1993, p. A6.

10 Erik W. Austin and Jerome M. Clubb, *Political Facts of the United States since 1789* (New York: Columbia University Press, 1986), pp. 378–79.

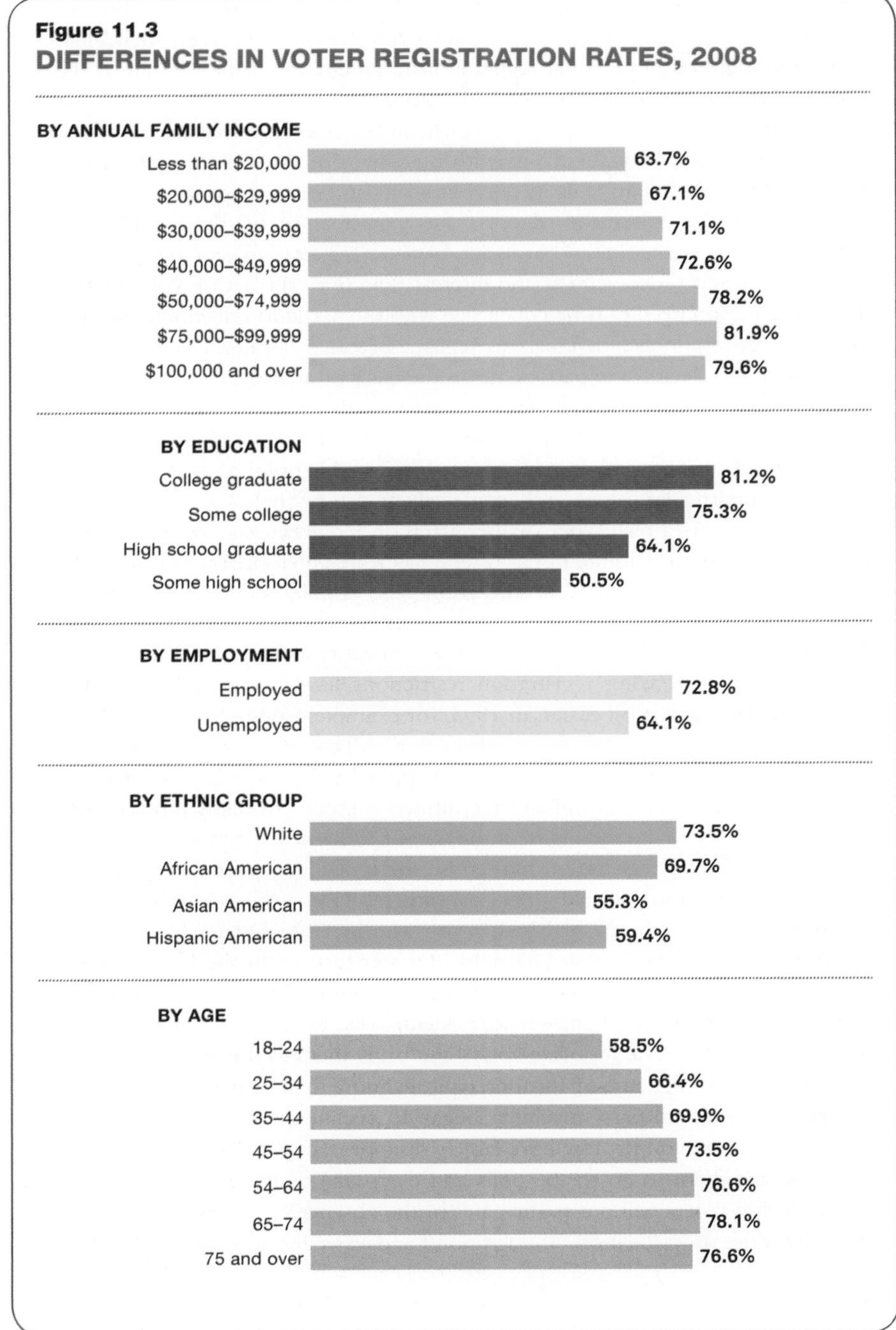

SOURCE: U.S. Bureau of the Census, Population Division, Education and Social Stratification Branch, "Voting and Registration in the Election of November 2008," May 2010, www.census.gov/hhes/www/socdem/voting/index.html (accessed 8/29/11).

of the absence of strong political parties, the American electorate is smaller and skewed more toward the middle class than toward the population of all those potentially eligible to vote.[11]

If registration systems create a hurdle to voting, they also facilitate the voting process. Registration systems contain a fairly reliable list of all people who are interested in voting. Local election offices and campaigns use the registration lists to communicate with voters about when, where, and how to vote. Campaigns also use these lists to prepare grassroots organizing efforts and direct-mail campaigns.

Registration lists serve another very important purpose: they enable local election offices to format ballots, set up precincts, and determine which voters should vote in which place. Any given area contains many overlapping election jurisdictions, creating many different combinations of unique sets of offices. For example, one voter might reside in Congressional District 1, State Senate District 7, State Representative District 3, City Council District 1, and so forth. Variations in district boundaries may mean that a few blocks away, another voter lives in Congressional District 2, State Senate District 4, State Representative District 12, City Council District 6, and so forth. Although they live in the same city, these voters live in very different sets of political districts and must vote on different ballots. The first voter is not supposed to vote in Congressional District 2, for instance. Registration lists have become vitally important in sorting out where people should vote. Using the definitions of the boundaries, local election offices determine how many distinct ballots they must prepare. Each distinct ballot is assigned to a precinct: to avoid confusion there is only one ballot constellation per precinct. The local election office then uses the registration list to assign individuals to precincts and to communicate to the voter exactly where he or she is supposed to vote. Without this means of assigning voters to precincts and communicating to voters, there would be considerable confusion and practical difficulty running elections on Election Day.

Efforts to get rid of or reform registration requirements must confront this very practical problem. Some states, such as Minnesota and Wisconsin, allow registration at the polls on Election Day (called same-day registration or Election Day registration). These states have noticeably higher turnout but also must recruit additional poll workers to handle the new registrants in the precincts. Other states, such as Colorado, are trying to get rid of traditional precincts and have experimented with vote centers. Electronic voting equipment now makes it possible to program many different ballots on a single machine. The voter need only key in his or her address to get the appropriate ballot and vote. Such machines enable people to vote anywhere and lessen the need for lists to assign voters to precincts. Innovations such as these may lead ultimately to an election system that does not require or rely heavily on registration before Election Day, but even these mechanisms still require the voter to register at some point.

11 In the 2008 election, both parties devoted considerable resources to targeting potential new voters, helping them register, and mobilizing them on Election Day. Elevated turnout in the election reflects this effort.

Wherever these innovations in voting may lead in the long term, the United States today relies heavily on registration to run elections, even though it creates a hurdle to voting.

With the exception of registration requirements, contemporary governments generally do not limit the composition of their electorate. Instead, they allow all adults to vote in an effort to make the government as responsive as possible to the needs and interests of the population as a whole.

How Americans Vote: The Ballot

The way Americans cast their votes reflects some of our most cherished precepts about voting rights. Most people today view voting as a private matter. They may tell others how they voted or choose not to tell them, but that is their prerogative. Polling places provide privacy for voters and keep an individual's vote secret. In some respects, the secret ballot seems incongruous with voting, because elections are a very public matter. Indeed, for the first century of the Republic, voting was conducted in the open. However, public voting led to vote buying and voter intimidation. American history is full of lore involving urban party workers paying poor voters for their support or intimidating members of the opposing party to keep them from voting. The secret ballot became widespread at the end of the nineteenth century in response to such corrupt practices.

The secret ballot has important implications for how people see themselves as voters. The secret ballot is a strong assertion of the individual. When a person votes, the law treats that person as an autonomous individual. The vote is meant to reflect the individual's own mind—what the individual knows about the choices and what his or her own preferences are about government—not the influences of others. In contrast, when voting is public, the choices individuals make reflect the group as well as their own thinking. American elections still have vestiges of public voting, in town meetings in New England states and at party nominating caucuses, such as in Iowa, Colorado, and Minnesota.

Attend a caucus or town hall meeting and you will appreciate the difference between these events and voting in the seclusion of a voting booth. Town meetings and caucuses often exhibit what social psychologists call groupthink, the tendency of the pack to follow particular individuals or to reflect a public conversation rather than each individual's private information. Public voting also demands more of the individual—more time and more attention to the decision-making process. Attending a caucus, for example, is an all-evening affair. As a result, public voting tends to draw in a much smaller and more committed electorate. These two methods can lead to radically different results. A good example comes from the Democratic nominating process in Texas during the 2008 election. Primary elections determine how many delegates to the party's national convention are allotted to each candidate. The Texas Democratic Party allocates one-half of its delegates through a primary election involving secret ballots and the other half through caucuses. Primary voting runs throughout the day; the caucuses begin in the evening immediately after polls close. In 2008, Hillary Rodham Clinton won a decisive victory over Barack

Obama in the primary voting in Texas, but Barack Obama won the caucuses by an equally large margin, offsetting the primary results entirely. Caucuses, however, are the exception. Almost all votes in the United States are cast by secret ballot.

With the secret ballot came another innovation, the Australian ballot. The Australian ballot lists the names of all candidates running for a given office and allows the voter to select any candidate for any office. This way of offering choices to voters was first introduced in Australia in 1851, and in the United States today it is universal. Before the 1880s Americans voted in different ways. Some voted in public meetings; others voted on paper ballots printed by the political parties or by slates of candidates distributed to the voters. Voters chose which ballot they wished to submit—a Republican ballot, a Democratic ballot, a Populist ballot, a Greenback ballot, and so forth. The ballots were often printed on different-colored paper so that voters could distinguish among them—and so that the local party workers could observe who cast which ballots. With party ballots, voters could not choose candidates from different parties for different offices; they had to vote the party line.

 **Australian ballot**

An electoral format that presents the names of all the candidates for any given office on the same ballot. Introduced at the end of the eighteenth century, the Australian ballot replaced the partisan ballot and facilitated split-ticket voting

In a 10-year period from 1885 to 1895, nearly every state adopted the Australian ballot, and with it the secret ballot. This new form of voting came about in an era of administrative reform in government throughout the United States. County governments took on the job of formatting and printing ballots, and the conduct of elections became an administrative task of government rather than a political activity of the parties. The move toward this new way of casting votes also reflected the efforts of the state governments to break the hold of local political organizations. All ballots are identical under the Australian form, making it difficult to observe who votes for which party. More importantly, voters could choose any candidate for any office, breaking the hold of parties over the vote. The introduction of the Australian ballot gave rise to the phenomenon of split-ticket voting, in which some voters select candidates from different parties for different offices.[12]

The secret and Australian ballot creates the opportunity for voters to choose candidates as well as parties and, as we discuss in more depth later, created a necessary condition for the rise of the personal vote and the incumbency advantage in American electoral politics. (See the discussion of the incumbency advantage in Congress in Chapter 6.) The party ballot made it impossible to choose particular candidates without voting for an entire list of candidates nominated by a party or slate. Voters could not split their tickets, choosing, say, one party's nominee for president and another party's nominee for the House of Representatives. If a voter liked the candidate for the House seat, but disliked the party's candidate for president, she would have to choose between sacrificing her choice for the House seat to bring about a new administration or voting for an unappealing presidential candidate in order to support her preferred candidate for the House. In the absence of a real possibility of split-ticket voting, the electorate could express a desire for change only as a vote against all candidates

12 Jerold G. Rusk, "The Effect of the Australian Ballot Reform on Split Ticket Voting, 1876–1908," *American Political Science Review* 64, no. 4 (December 1970): 1220–38.

of the party in power. When the electorate voted to oust those in power at the national level, the election would sweep into power the opposing party or slate at the state and local levels as well. As a result, elections in the United States before 1896 were highly partisan affairs, often producing wholesale changes in control of government at all levels. The Australian ballot allows voters to cast a more sophisticated ballot that reflects both to the performance of individual officeholders and assessments of the political parties as a whole.

The possibility of split-ticket voting created greater fragmentation in the control of government in the United States. With the party ballot, an insurgent party could more readily be swept to power at all levels of government in a given election. A strong national tide toward one of the parties in the presidential election, resulting in a landslide victory, would change not just the presidency but also political control of every state and locality that gave a majority of its votes to that presidential candidate's party. The party ballot thus reinforced the effect of elections on party control of government and public policy. In contrast, because the Australian ballot permitted voters to choose for each office separately, it lessened the likelihood that the electorate would sweep an entirely new administration into power. Thus, ticket splitting led to increasingly divided control of government as well as the rise of personal voting.

Where: Electoral Districts

Elected officials in the United States represent places as well as people. Today, the president, representatives, senators, governors, and many other state officers, state legislators, and most local officers are elected by the people through geographic areas called electoral districts. Generally speaking, the United States employs single-member districts with equal populations. This means that the U.S. House of Representatives, the state legislatures, and almost all local governments have their own districts and elect one representative per district, and all of the districts for a given legislative body must have equal populations.

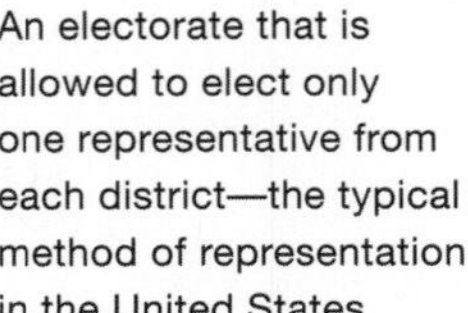

single-member district

An electorate that is allowed to elect only one representative from each district—the typical method of representation in the United States

Elections for the U.S. Senate and the presidency are the odd cases. In the U.S. Senate, the states are the districts. Senate districts, then, have multiple members and unequal populations. In presidential elections, every state is allocated votes in the electoral college equal to the number of U.S. senators (two) plus the number of House members. The states are the districts, and each state chooses all of its electors, who commit to casting their votes for a certain candidate in the electoral college, in a statewide vote.[13] Within the political parties, the nomination process in most states allocates delegates to the parties' national conventions on the basis of House districts, and thus population. However, some states choose their delegates on a statewide basis, with all districts selecting multiple delegates to the party conventions.

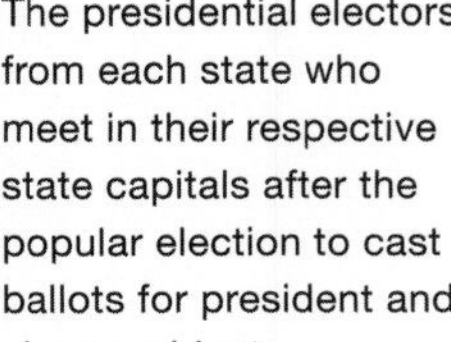

electoral college

The presidential electors from each state who meet in their respective state capitals after the popular election to cast ballots for president and vice president

The system of single-member districts with equal populations was not part of the Founders' original design. Rather, it evolved over nearly two centuries,

13 The exceptions are Maine and Nebraska, which choose the House electors in individual House districts and the Senate electors in a statewide vote.

from 1790 to 1970. Article II of the Constitution designed the House to represent the people, with the number of seats elected by each state allocated on the basis of population following each decennial census, and the Senate to represent the states. The Constitution originally specified that the state legislatures would choose the U.S. senators, with each state choosing two senators to staggered six-year terms. That system was jettisoned in 1913 with the adoption of the Seventeenth Amendment, providing for direct election of senators.

The Constitution said nothing about the election of individual House members or electors to the electoral college. That task fell to the states, and in early times the states used many different electoral systems for choosing their House delegations. Most of the early state laws adopted single-member districts. The states divided their territory into as many districts as they had House seats, and each district elected one member. Some states created multimember districts, in which a district would elect more than one legislator. This was common in urban counties and cities, where the population exceeded the number required for two or more districts, but the legislature did not want to draw district boundaries. And some states elected all their House members in a single, statewide election (called an at-large election). An even greater hodgepodge of election procedures applied to the state legislatures and local councils.[14]

Congress tried to bring order to the election of House members with the 1842 Apportionment Act. Following the sixth decennial census (of 1840), Congress had to pass a new apportionment bill to assign House seats to the states. Through an amendment from Representative John Campbell of South Carolina, the act included an additional requirement on districts:

> [I]n every case where a State is entitled to more than one Representative, the number to which each State shall be entitled under this apportionment shall be elected by districts, composed of contiguous territory, equal in number to the number of Representatives to which said State may be entitled; no one district electing more than one Representative.[15]

Most states complied with this provision, even though it placed a new responsibility on the states of creating appropriate districts, especially around urban areas. Some states, however, insisted on using at-large and multimember districts up to the 1960s. Finally, in the 1967 Apportionment Act, Congress forbade the use of anything but single-member districts.

A second important change in the nature of political districts in the United States occurred at that time as well. In a series of decisions beginning with *Baker v. Carr* in 1962, the U.S. Supreme Court ruled that all federal and state legislative districts must have equal populations: one person, one vote. That simple aphorism today rings as the very definition of democracy, but before 1962 state legislative districts often had highly unequal populations, which

14 For a history of districting politics, see Stephen Ansolabehere and James Snyder, Jr., *The End of Inequality: One Person, One Vote and the Transformation of American Politics* (New York: Norton, 2008).

15 Congressional Globe, 27th Cong., 2d sess., 1842, 11, Part 1:471, 348.

meant that some votes in effect counted more than others. In the California state senate, Los Angeles County elected as many seats as Alpine County, even though Los Angeles had almost 500 times as many people. As a result, voters in Alpine County had greater representation (500 times greater) relative to their population than did voters in Los Angeles County. Similar inequities reigned in every state legislature, producing a pattern of overrepresentation of rural areas and underrepresentation of most urban areas and, especially, suburban counties. In most states these inequalities arose from neglect. Most state constitutions require redistricting to keep district populations equal, but as urban populations grew, especially in the first half of the twentieth century, those in power realized that redistricting might jeopardize their own re-election. As a result, the legislatures chose to do nothing. With each successive decade, representation in the United States became more unequal, and there seemed to be no way to force the state legislatures to act. Finally, the U.S. Supreme Court ruled, in a series of important cases, that unequal representation violated the Fourteenth Amendment's guarantee of equal protection under the law. By 1971, nearly every legislative district in the United States elected one representative, and the populations of the districts for each legislative chamber were equal. Lawsuits brought by civil rights groups in the 1980s forced school districts and city councils to adopt single-member districts as well. Single-member districts with equal populations have become the rule in the United States, from city councils and school districts to the House of Representatives.[16]

The U.S. Senate and the electoral college remain the two great exceptions to the requirements of single-member districts with equal populations. The apportionment of Senate seats to states makes that chamber inherently unequal. California's 35 million people have the same number of senators as Wyoming's 500,000 people. The allocation of electoral college votes creates a population inequity in presidential elections, with larger states selecting fewer electors per capita than smaller states. In the 1960s, the Supreme Court let stand the unequal district populations in the Senate and the electoral college, because the representation of states in the Senate is specified in the Constitution. The reason lies in the politics of the Constitutional Convention (see Chapter 2). That convention consisted of delegations of states, each of which held equal numbers of votes under the Articles of Confederation. In order to create a House of Representatives based on population, the large states had to strike a deal with the smaller states. That deal, the Connecticut Compromise, created the U.S. Senate to balance representation of people with representation of places and led to a clause in Article V of the Constitution that guarantees equal representation of the states in the Senate.

Nonetheless, the Senate and the electoral college share the salient feature of elections for the House and other elections in the use of districts to select representatives. All elections in the United States and all elected officials are tied to geographically based constituencies rather than to the national electorate as a whole. This is certainly true for the House and Senate. It applies also

16 The story of this transformation is told in Ansolabehere and Snyder, *The End of Inequality*.

to presidential elections, in which candidates focus on winning key states in the electoral college rather than on winning a majority of the popular vote.

Electoral districts have an important political consequence: the use of districts tends to magnify the power of the majority. In a system like that of the United States with two parties and single-member districts, the party that wins a majority of the vote nationwide tends to win a disproportionate share of the seats. In 2010, Republicans won 53.5 percent of the two-party vote nationwide for the U.S. House, but 55.6 percent of the seats. As an empirical matter, in the United States, when the election is a tie, the parties win equal shares of the vote, and for every 1 percent of the vote above 50 percent a party gains an additional 2 percent of the seats. This pattern has been observed in data on U.S. House elections over the last 60 years. In 2012, however, Democrats and Republicans finished in a virtual tie for popular votes cast for the two parties in House races, but the GOP won 54 percent of the seats. This anomaly was in part the result of the Republican advantage in redrawing district boundaries. These boundaries are drawn by the state legislatures, and in 2010 the GOP won control of a majority of these bodies. Candidate recruitment, retirements, and reapportionment also played a role. The electoral college tends to magnify the vote majority even more dramatically. Barack Obama won 51 percent of the vote nationwide in 2012, but he captured 61 percent of the electoral college delegates. Electoral districts, then, create a strong tendency toward majority rule.

This magnifying effect has been a particular problem for smaller parties and minority groups. Just as districts magnify the seats won by the majority party, they shrink the representation of small parties. If a party wins 5 percent of the vote nationwide, it is difficult for it to win any seats or electoral college delegates unless the support for that party is highly concentrated in a particular geographic area. The most successful third party in recent U.S. history was the Reform Party, started by Ross Perot in 1992. Perot won 19 percent of the presidential vote nationwide that year, a very strong third place throughout the country, but he won no electoral college delegates.

The majoritarian tendency of districts makes it very difficult for racial minorities to gain representation. Blacks and Hispanics constitute roughly a quarter of the population. Districts crafted without regard to race would spread the minority vote across many districts, making it unlikely that those groups would be a sufficiently large segment in any one district to elect proportionate numbers of blacks or Hispanics to the legislature. This problem, compounded by the historic discrimination against blacks and Hispanics, led Congress to amend the Voting Rights Act in 1982 to provide for the creation of legislative districts with sufficient numbers of black and Hispanic voters to elect House members representative of those groups. This law has been interpreted and implemented to mean that the state legislatures must create many districts, called majority-minority districts, containing majorities of black or Hispanic people. As we discuss later, that provision has proved controversial, but the Voting Rights Act has been renewed repeatedly by Congress and has withstood legal challenges. It is a direct reaction against the majoritarian pressures created by districts.

House districts and state legislative districts are not static. In order to comply with the dictum of equal population representation, they must be remade every

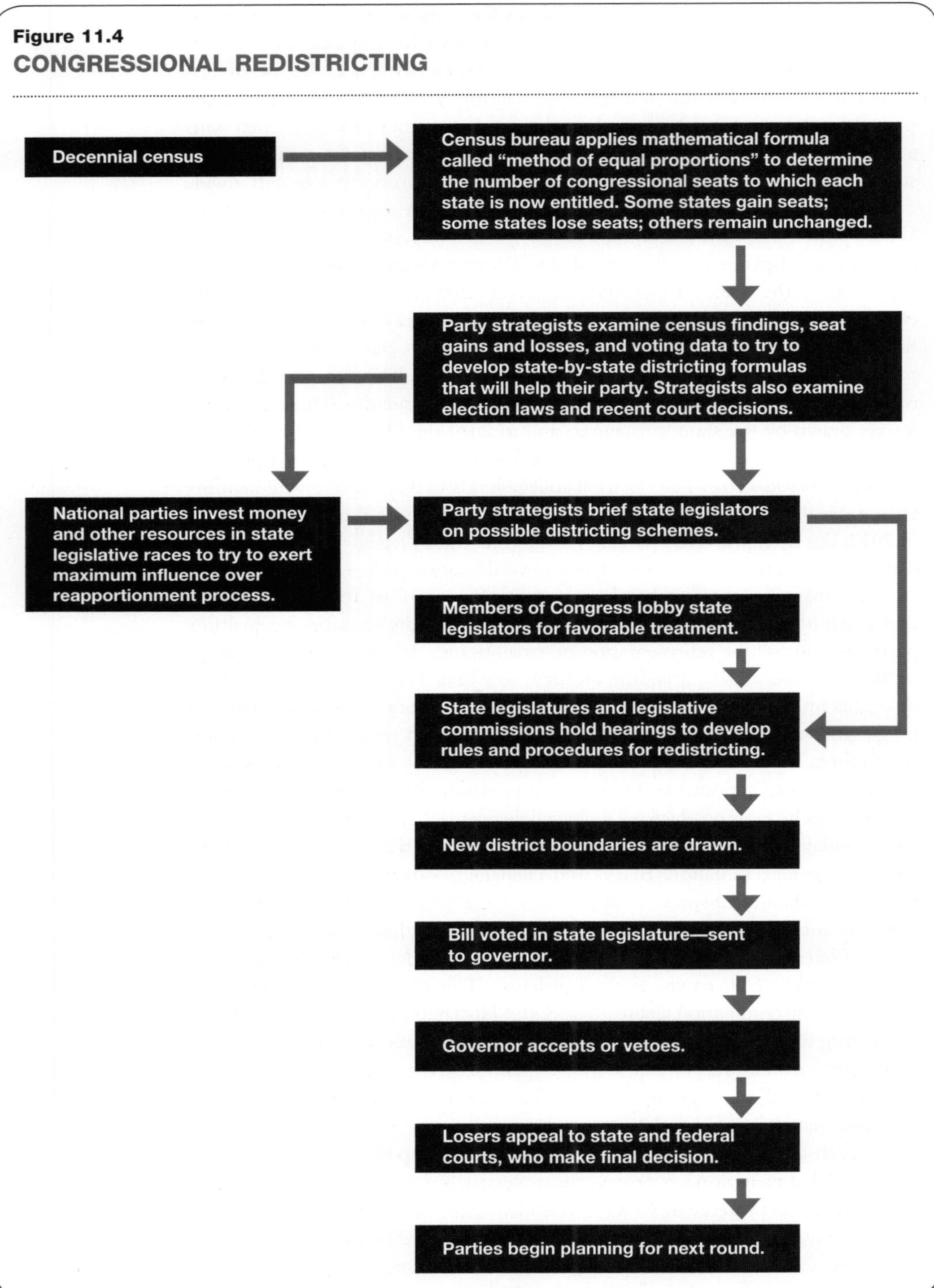
Figure 11.4
CONGRESSIONAL REDISTRICTING
Decennial census
Census bureau applies mathematical formula called "method of equal proportions" to determine the number of congressional seats to which each state is now entitled. Some states gain seats; some states lose seats; others remain unchanged.
Party strategists examine census findings, seat gains and losses, and voting data to try to develop state-by-state districting formulas that will help their party. Strategists also examine election laws and recent court decisions.
National parties invest money and other resources in state legislative races to try to exert maximum influence over reapportionment process.
Party strategists brief state legislators on possible districting schemes.
Members of Congress lobby state legislators for favorable treatment.
State legislatures and legislative commissions hold hearings to develop rules and procedures for redistricting.
New district boundaries are drawn.
Bill voted in state legislature—sent to governor.
Governor accepts or vetoes.
Losers appeal to state and federal courts, who make final decision.
Parties begin planning for next round.

decade. Responsibility for drawing new district boundaries rests, in most states, with the state legislatures and the governors, with the supervision of the courts and sometimes with the consultation of commissions (Figure 11.4). Every 10 years, the U.S. census updates the official population figures of the states to a fine level of geographical detail. The politicians, their staffs, party consultants, and others with a stake in the outcome use the census data to craft a new district map; ultimately, the legislatures must pass and the governors must sign a law defining new U.S. House and state legislative districts. This job is forced on the legislatures by their constitutions and by the courts. As the history of unequal representation suggests, most legislatures would, if left to their own devices, leave the existing boundaries in place. Periodic redistricting, although it corrects one problem, invites another. Those in charge of redistricting may try to manipulate the new map to increase the likelihood of a particular outcome. This problem arose with some of the earliest congressional district maps. A particularly egregious map of the 1812 Massachusetts House districts drawn with the imprimatur of Governor Elbridge Gerry prompted an editorial writer in the *Boston Gazette* to dub a very strangely shaped district the "Gerry-Mander." The term stuck, and gerrymandering refers broadly to any attempt at creating electoral districts for political advantage.

gerrymandering

The apportionment of voters in districts in such a way as to give unfair advantage to one political party

It is easy to draw an intentionally unfair electoral map, especially with the sophisticated software and data on local voting patterns that are available today. To facilitate districting, the Census Bureau divides the nation into very small geographic areas, called census blocks, that typically contain a few dozen people. U.S. House districts contain over 700,000 people. Political mapmakers combine various local areas, down to census blocks, to construct legislative districts. Those seeking political advantage try to make as many districts as possible that contain a majority of their own voters, maximizing the number of seats won for a given division of the vote. There are constraints on political cartography: the district populations must be equal, and all parts of the district must touch (be contiguous). Even with those constraints, the number of possible maps that could be drawn for any one state's legislative districts is extremely large.[17] The Analyzing the Evidence unit on page 460 shows how this works, using a hypothetical state to explain some basic strategies that politicians might implement to influence elections through the manipulation of district lines, as well as a real-world example of how redistricting affects election outcomes.

Political scientists examine the fairness of plans by assessing quantitatively the features of any given districting plan. Such measures are widely used by state legislatures, commissions, and courts in assessing districting plans. Of central importance is the notion of bias. In a hypothetical election where the vote is divided equally between the two major parties, what share of seats do we expect each party to win? An unbiased or fair districting plan would give both parties half of the seats in this hypothetical election. To gauge the magnitude of the bias, political scientists then simulate such hypothetical elections among a state's electorate under a given districting plan. A bias of, say, 5 points means that when

17 For definitions of these units, see Bureau of the Census, Geographic Area Reference Manual, www.census.gov/geo/www/garm.html (accessed 3/27/09).

The Electoral Impact of Congressional Redistricting

District boundaries can have subtle but significant effects on the partisan division of a legislature. If a party can control the districting process, it may be able to craft the lines in such a way that the party wins more seats for the same number of Republican and Democratic votes.

Drawing District Lines

SCENARIO 1

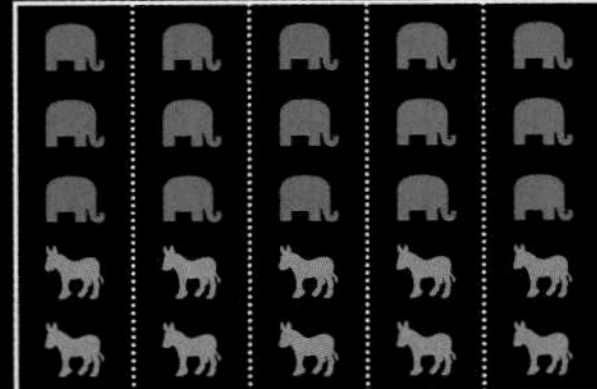

SCENARIO 2

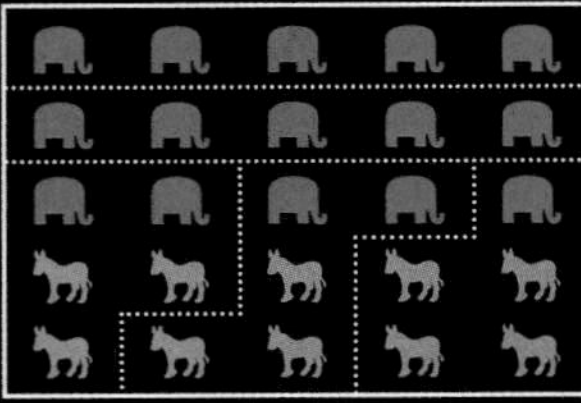

Consider a hypothetical state where Republicans represent 60 percent of voters and Democrats represent the remaining 40 percent of voters. As a result of population changes during the preceding decade, this state now has five congressional districts. A state legislature controlled by a Republican majority could draw congressional districts in such a way that Republicans are 60 percent of voters in each seat and expected to win every seat.

Now suppose that the Democrats are in control of the state legislature. With the same distribution of voters in the state, they could draw the districts to favor the Democrats as much as possible (with Democratic voters dominating three of the districts).

U.S. House Districts, Texas, 2011

PLAN C185

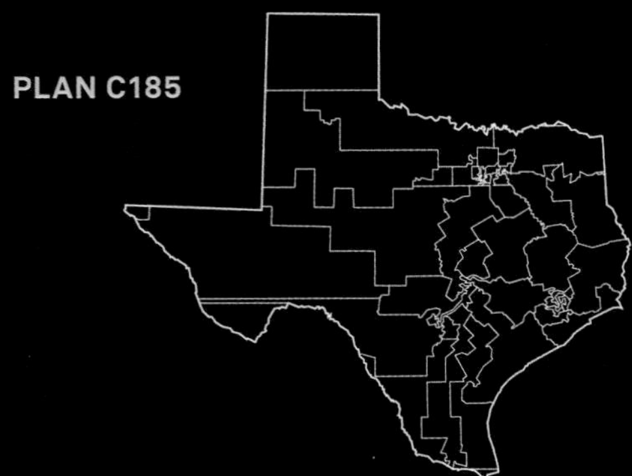

Consider a real-world example. Reapportionment following the 2010 census allotted Texas four new districts, and the shifting demographics of the state required considerable redrawing of the congressional district lines. The Democrats and Republicans in the Texas state legislature each proposed new district plans. The Republican-controlled legislature passed the Republican plan (Plan C185), and Republican governor Rick Perry signed that plan into law.

In a state of 25 million people, comparing different districting plans is more complicated than in our simple models, but comparing the Republican plan (C185) and the main Democratic plan (C166) in Texas revealed a significant difference. Political scientists started by calculating each party's share of the two-party vote in statewide and federal elections over the decade from 2002 to 2010: the average was 42.3 percent Democratic and 57.7 percent Republican. This average is called the normal vote. Using the normal vote as the measure of the Democratic and Republican strength in each area, Democrats comprise 42.3 percent of the electorate, and they are the majority in 27.8 percent of districts (10 seats) and Republicans the majority in 72.2 percent of districts (26 seats).

Political scientists analyzing this case also estimated the bias toward one party or the other. Imagine a hypothetical election in which the two parties divide the votes in the entire state 50–50. To calculate the bias of the new Texas districting plan, we add 7.7 percentage points (the difference between 50 percent and the Democratic normal vote of 42.3 percent) to the Democractic vote share in each congressional district under the plan. This will give us the expected outcome for each district in an election where each party wins 50 percent of the vote statewide. Then, calculate the percentage of districts where the Democrats' share of the vote exceeded the Republicans' share of the votes and the percentage where the Republicans' share of the votes exceeded the Democrats' share. The difference between the seat share in this hypothetical election and 50 percent is the partisan bias of the plan.

Expected Share of Seats: Democrats

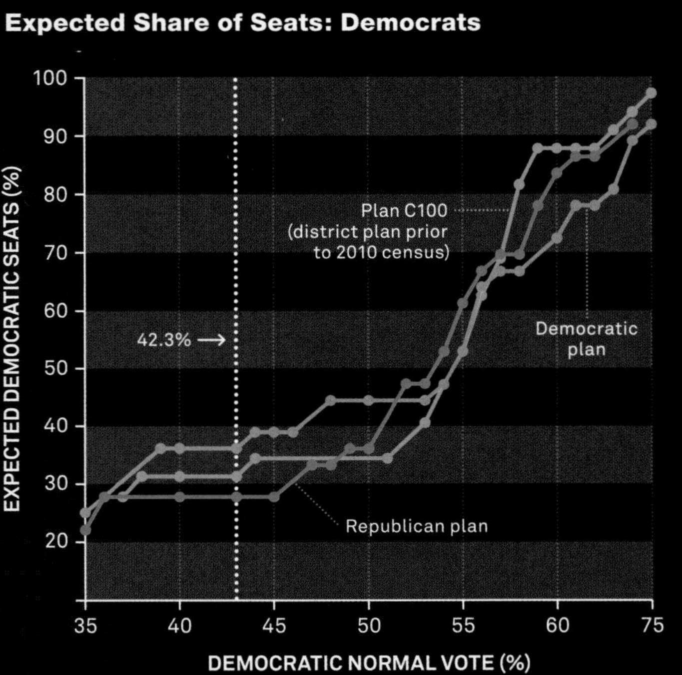

SOURCE: Texas Legislative Council, http://www.tlc.state.tx.us/redist/redist.html (accessed 10/31/11) and author's calculations.

The graph shows the expected Democratic share of Texas U.S. House seats won at 42.3 percent and for percentages of the statewide vote above and below that average, including at the 50 percent point. We can see the partisan biases of each plan in the graph by looking at the expected Democratic seat share at 50 percent of the vote. The plan passed into law (the red line) has a 13-point bias: Under Texas's new districts, Democrats are expected to win 37 percent of seats if they win half of the vote statewide (the difference between 37 and 50 is the partisan bias). Under the Democrats' own plan (the blue line), the bias is just 5 points.

EXPLORE **ELECTORAL DISTRICTS** FURTHER AT: **wwnorton.com/studyspace**

the two parties split the vote evenly, one of the parties wins 55 percent of the seats and the other 45 percent. With each round of districting, experts weigh in with their assessments of the bias in the plans. Those who want fair elections will try to achieve no bias. Those who want to gain the upper hand try to inject bias into elections with a cleverly constructed map.

Empirical study of U.S. House and state legislative elections has documented several very important patterns in the bias of electoral districts. First, bias has declined greatly over the past half century. In 1960, the typical state legislative electoral map had approximately a 10- to 12-point bias in favor of one of the parties (depending on who drew the map). That means that around 1960, a dead-even election would actually produce a large majority for one of the parties in the legislature. Second, bias has declined substantially over time. In the 1990s and 2000s, the bias in the average state legislative district map was approximately 5 points, still substantial but much lower than in the past.[18] Since the 1960s, frequent redistricting and court oversight has forced state legislatures to create districting plans that treat both parties more fairly. Interestingly, this is one of the benefits of divided party control of the legislature and executive (see Chapter 7). When the legislature and executive are controlled by the same party, the legislature can create a map heavily biased toward that party, and the governor will likely sign it. However, when the legislature and executive are controlled by different parties, then the legislature might face a veto from the governor and must create districts that will be acceptable to the other party.[19]

Politicians can use gerrymandering to dilute the strength not only of a party but also of a group. Until recently, many state legislatures employed gerrymandering to dilute the strength of racial minorities. One of the more common strategies involved redrawing congressional district boundaries in such a way as to divide and disperse a black population that would have constituted a majority within the original district. This form of gerrymandering, sometimes called cracking, was used in Mississippi during the 1960s and 1970s to prevent the election of a black candidate to Congress. Historically, the black population of Mississippi was clustered in the western half of the state along the Mississippi River Delta. From 1882 until 1966, the Delta constituted one congressional district. Although blacks were a clear majority within this district, discrimination against them in voter registration and at the polls guaranteed the continual election of white congressmen. With the passage of the Voting Rights Act in 1965, this district would almost surely be won by a black candidate or one favored by the black majority. To prevent that from happening, the Mississippi state legislature drew new House districts in 1965 in order to minimize the voting power of the black population. Rather than a majority of a single district that encompassed the Delta, the black population was split across three districts and constituted

18 See Ansolabehere and Snyder, *The End of Inequality*, chap. 11.

19 See Gary King and Robert X. Browning, "Democratic Representation and Partisan Bias in Congressional Elections," *American Political Science Review* 81, no. 4 (December 1987): 1252–73.

a majority in none. Mississippi's gerrymandering scheme was preserved in the state's redistricting plans in 1972 and 1982 and helped prevent the election of any black representative until 1986, when Mike Espy became the first African American since Reconstruction to represent Mississippi in Congress.

Continuing controversies about the legislatures' involvement in drawing their own districts have raised deep concerns about the fairness of the process. Many states have created commissions to draw plans or appointed "special masters" to draw the maps. It has proved difficult to find a satisfactory reform. Perhaps the most unusual and creative attempt to engage the issue is that proposed by Ohio Secretary of State Jennifer Brunner. Working with the League of Women Voters of Ohio, Common Cause, and state representatives Joan Lawrence and Dan Stewart, the Ohio secretary of state created a public contest in 2009 to develop the best districting plan—the Ohio Redistricting Competition. The purpose of the competition was not to produce a new districting law but to show how "a robust public conversation about the process can occur, leading to the development of the best possible redistricting recommendations for consideration by the Ohio General Assembly."[20] This was a way to inform the legislature and courts about what the public wanted in the districting plans and to produce a blueprint to guide those who would draw the official maps.

The Ohio experiment was just the beginning in an important transformation in districting. In 2011, the Public Mapping Project, led by Professor Michael McDonald and Harvard researcher Micah Altman, conducted similar contests in a dozen states. And, independent software developer David Bradlee developed Dave's Redistricting App, a powerful tool that is easy to use and free.[21] The districting process has for two centuries has been closed off to the public, to interest groups, even to members of the minority party within the legislature. New developments in GIS software and provision of census data now make it possible for anyone to draw credible district maps. These resources have made it especially easy for groups who have strong interests in the legislative process, such as racial or ethnic groups, unions, and corporations, to develop their own plans and to engage with the legislature and advocate for their interests. Perhaps more important still, readily available software and data have made it possible for the courts to scrutinize the process more closely by examining analyses of the partisan and social consequences of plans and even by appointing special masters to draw plans when the legislature has failed to create a plan up to legal standards.

What It Takes to Win: Plurality Rule

The fourth prominent feature of U.S. electoral law is the criterion for winning. Americans often embrace majority rule as a defining characteristic of democracy. However, that is not quite right. The real standard is plurality rule. The

plurality rule

A type of electoral system in which victory goes to the individual who gets the most votes in an election, but not necessarily a majority of the votes cast

20 www.ohioredistricting.org (accessed 5/1/09). Sponsored by the Ohio Secretary of State (accessed 8/31/11).

21 Dave's Redistricting, http://gardow.com/davebradlee/redistricting (accessed 8/31/11); Public Mapping Project, www.publicmapping.org (accessed 8/31/11).

candidate who receives the most votes in the relevant district or constituency wins the election, even if that candidate doesn't receive a majority of votes. Suppose, for example, three parties nominate candidates for a seat and divide the vote such that one wins 34 percent and the other two each receive 33 percent of the vote. Under plurality rule, the candidate with 34 percent wins the seat, even though she did not win a majority of votes (more than 50 percent). There are different types of plurality systems. The system currently used in the United States combines plurality rule with single-member districts and is called *first past the post*. The electoral college is a plurality system in which the candidate who receives the most votes wins all of the delegates: winner take all.[22] Some states set an even higher standard and require a candidate to receive at least 50 percent of all votes in order to win. This is majority rule. Louisiana and Georgia, for instance, require a candidate to receive an outright majority in an election in order to be declared the winner. If no candidate receives a majority in an election, a runoff election is held about one month later between the two candidates who received the most votes in the first round. Other systems also use plurality- and majority-rule criteria. For instance, some city councils still have multimember districts. The top vote getters win the seats. If there are, say, seven seats to fill, the seven candidates who win the most votes each win a seat.

majority rule

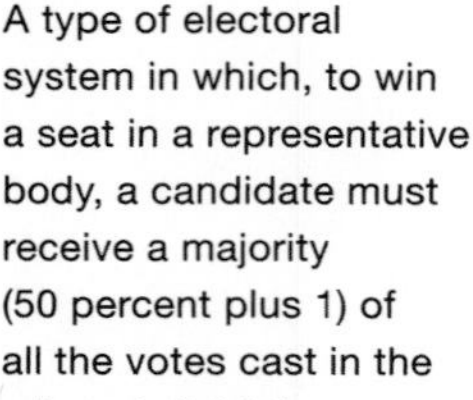

A type of electoral system in which, to win a seat in a representative body, a candidate must receive a majority (50 percent plus 1) of all the votes cast in the relevant district

Plurality rule is often criticized for yielding electoral results that do not reflect the public's preferences. The votes for the losing candidates seem wasted, because they do not translate directly into representation. Indeed, as the example of the three-candidate race above suggests, it is possible that a majority of voters wanted someone other than the winner. In the aggregate, plurality rule with single-member districts tends to inflate the share of seats won by the largest party and deflate the others' shares. A striking example of the effects comes from Great Britain. In 2005, the British Labour Party won 35 percent of the vote and 55 percent of the seats; the Conservatives finished second, with 31 percent of the vote and 31 percent of the seats; the Liberal Democrats garnered 22 percent of the popular vote, but won just 8 percent of the seats. The distribution of voters across districts determines the shares of all seats won by each party. A particularly egregious gerrymander might bias the results heavily against one party and cause further deviations of election results from proportionality. Nevertheless, plurality rule offers certain advantages. It gives voters the ability to choose individuals to represent them personally, not just political parties, and it picks a definite winner without the need for runoff elections.

Among the democracies of the world, the main alternative to plurality rule is proportional representation, also called PR for short. Under proportional representation, competing parties win legislative seats in proportion to their share of the popular vote. For example, if three parties running for seats in the legislature divide the vote such that one wins 34 percent and the other two receive

proportional representation (PR)

A multiple-member-district system that allows each political party representation in proportion to its percentage of the vote

22 Over the centuries, many systems for voting and determining electoral outcomes have been devised. For an excellent analysis of voting systems and a complete classification see Gary Cox, *Making Votes Count* (New York: Cambridge University Press, 1997).

33 percent of the vote, the first party receives 34 percent of the seats and the other two receive 33 percent of the seats.

PR is used rarely in the United States. The most substantial elections in which it is employed are the Democratic presidential primary elections. During the 1988 primary season, Jesse Jackson routinely won 20 percent of the vote in the primaries but ended up with only about 5 percent of the delegates. To make the Democratic National Convention and the party more representative of its disparate voting groups, Jackson negotiated with other party leaders to change the delegate allocation rules so that delegates within congressional districts would be assigned on a proportional basis. If a district elects five delegates, a candidate wins a delegate if the candidate receives at least 20 percent of the vote in the district, two delegates if the candidate wins at least 40 percent of the vote, and so forth. Prior to this rule change the Democratic Party awarded all delegates from a given congressional district to the candidate who won a plurality of the vote. Like any districted system with plurality rule, this created a strong majoritarian tendency.

Plurality rule in single-member districts has a very important consequence. It is the reason for two-party politics in the United States. Around the world, countries with plurality rule in single-member districts have far fewer political parties than other nations. Typically, elections under plurality rule boil down to just two major parties that routinely compete for power, with one of them winning a majority of legislative seats outright. Proportional representation systems, on the other hand, tend to have many more than two parties. Rarely does a single party win a majority of seats. Governments form as coalitions of many different parties. The political scientist Maurice Duverger described that pattern in a pathbreaking book, *Party Politics*, first published in 1951. Duverger formalized his law of politics quite simply: Plurality rule creates two-party politics; proportional representation encourages more than two parties.

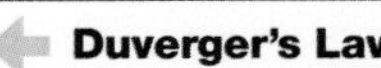

Duverger's Law

Law of politics, formalized by Maurice Duverger, stating that plurality-rule electoral systems will tend to have two political parties

The rationale behind Duverger's Law has two components, the strategic behavior of politicians and the behavior of voters. Consider, first, how politicians would think about the prospects of forming a new party. Suppose that there already are two parties, a center-right party and a center-left party. A politician from the far right, for example, might be unhappy that the parties do not represent the ideals he espouses. He wants a far-right policy most, a center-right policy less, and least of all a center-left policy. One solution for the far-right politician is to leave the center-right party and form a far-right party. The problem with doing that is that it helps the center-left party. A far-right party in this circumstance splits the vote of those on the right without affecting the vote for the center-left party. Under plurality rule, the center-left party would almost certainly win, an outcome that the far-right politician likes even less. Thus, politicians on the extremes cannot gain by forming a new party. A politician with a centrist orientation also cannot win the election if the center-right and center-left parties are not too extreme. The center-right party would win all votes of voters on the right and on the center-right. The same is true for the center-left party. That would leave only a small segment of true centrists for a potential centrist party. Hence, if the current parties are not too extreme, there is no incentive for a third party to enter a two-party system when plurality rule is the criterion for winning.

Voters follow a similar logic. They do not want to waste their votes. If voters understand that the extremist party or candidate cannot win, they will vote for the more moderate alternative. Although second best for extremist voters, the moderate has a better chance of winning. This logic leads the extremist voters to choose the moderate party or candidate in order to have a better chance of selecting a candidate more to their liking. Extremist parties and candidates, then, have little incentive to enter a race, and when they do they usually attract few votes.

Such sophisticated voting occurs often in U.S. primary elections. John McCain was significantly more moderate than Mike Huckabee and Mitt Romney in the 2008 Republican presidential primaries, and he was more moderate than the typical Republican voter. Nevertheless, he won the nomination easily because many Republicans understood that McCain represented their best chance in the general election.

Proportional representation (PR), in contrast, creates an incentive for more parties and candidates to enter, because they will win seats in proportion to their support among the national electorate. PR systems often have a multitude of parties, none of which represents a decisive majority. Elections in PR systems rarely decide which party will lead the government and often lead to coalition governments, because no one party wins enough seats to govern. In the Democratic Party, proportional representation has the further effect of stretching out the nominating season. If a candidate wins a plurality of 40 percent of the vote in a state's Democratic primary, he or she wins roughly 40 percent of the delegates. As a result, it takes many more victories in the Democratic primaries to accumulate sufficient delegates to lock the nomination. In 2008, the Democratic primaries came very close to being indecisive, which would have meant a convention at which neither Obama nor Clinton controlled a majority of delegates. Plurality rule and winner take all on the Republican side means that even when there are many candidates, as in 2012, the primary elections are decided rather quickly. Mitt Romney won only about 40 percent of the vote in the early primary elections, but by the end of April, he had captured enough delegates to force his opponents to concede the race.

How votes are cast and counted, and what it takes to win a seat, then, have very substantial consequences for American politics. Plurality rule with single-member districts creates strong pressures toward two-party politics and majority rule in the legislature.

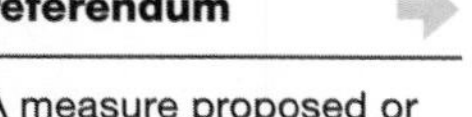

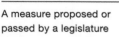

referendum

A measure proposed or passed by a legislature that is referred to the vote of the electorate for approval or rejection

Direct Democracy: The Referendum and the Recall

In addition to voting for candidates, 24 states also provide for referendum voting. The referendum process allows citizens to vote directly on proposed laws or other governmental actions. In recent years, voters in several states have voted to set limits on tax rates, block state and local spending proposals, and prohibit social services for illegal immigrants. Although it involves voting, a referendum is not an election. The election is an institution of representative government. Through an election, voters choose officials to act for them. The referendum process, by contrast, is an institution of direct democracy; it allows voters to govern directly without intervention by government officials. The validity of referendum results, however, are subject to judicial action. If a court finds that a referendum outcome violates the state or national constitution, it can overturn the result. This happened in the case of a 1995 California referendum curtailing social services to illegal aliens.[23] It should be emphasized that the issues that emerge as referendum subjects are usually of the "hot-button" variety. It is not clear that these often emotional issues, which require deliberation and reflection, are best dealt with by direct democracy. In other words, referendum issues are often adversely selected.

Twenty-four states also permit various forms of the initiative. Whereas the referendum process described above allows citizens to affirm or reject a policy produced by legislative action, the initiative provides citizens with a way forward in the face of legislative inaction. This is done by placing a policy proposal (legislation or a state constitutional amendment) on the ballot to be approved or rejected by the electorate. To have a place on the ballot, a petition must be accompanied by a minimum number of voters' signatures—a requirement that varies from state to state—that have been certified by the state's secretary of state.

initiative

A process by which citizens may petition to place a policy proposal on the ballot for public vote

The initiative is also vulnerable to adverse selection. Ballot propositions involve policies that the state legislature cannot (or does not want to) resolve. Like referendum issues, these are often highly emotional and, consequently, not always well suited to resolution in the electoral arena. One of the "virtues" of the initiative is that it may force action. That is, leaders in the legislature may induce recalcitrant legislators to move on controversial issues by using as a threat the possibility that a worse outcome will result from inaction.[24]

Legal provisions for recall elections exist in 18 states. The recall is an electoral device that was introduced by early-twentieth-century Populists to allow voters to remove governors and other state officials from office before the expiration of their term. Federal officials such as the president and members of Congress are not subject to recall. Generally speaking, a recall effort begins with a petition campaign. For example, in California—the site of a tumultuous recall battle in 2003—if 12 percent of those who voted in the last general election sign petitions demanding a special recall election, one must be scheduled by the state board of elections. Such petition campaigns are relatively common, but most fail to garner enough signatures to bring the matter to a statewide vote. In California in 2003, however, a conservative Republican member of Congress, Darrell Issa, led a successful effort to recall Governor Gray Davis, a Democrat. Voters were unhappy about the state's economy and dissatisfied with Davis's

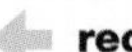
recall

The removal of a public official by popular vote

23 *League of United Latin American Citizens v. Wilson*, 908 F. Supp. 755 (C.D. Calif., 1995).

24 This point is developed in Morton Bennedsen and Sven Feldmann, "Lobbying Legislatures," *Journal of Political Economy* 110 (2002): 919–46.

performance: they blamed him for the state's $38 billion budget deficit. Issa and his followers were able to secure enough signatures to force a vote, and in October 2003 Davis became the second governor in American history to be recalled by his state's electorate (the first was North Dakota governor Lynn Frazier, who was recalled in 1921). Under California law, voters in a special recall election are also asked to choose a replacement for the official whom they dismiss. In 2003 Californians elected the movie star Arnold Schwarzenegger to be their governor. Although critics charged that the Davis recall had been a "political circus," the campaign had the effect of greatly increasing voter interest and involvement in the political process. More than 400,000 new voters registered in California in 2003, many drawn into the political arena by the opportunity to participate in the recall campaign.

The referendum, initiative, and recall all entail shifts in agenda-setting power. The referendum gives an impassioned electoral majority the opportunity to reverse legislation that displeases it, thus affecting the initial strategic calculations of institutional agenda setters (who want to get as much of what they want without its being subsequently reversed). The initiative has a similar effect on institutional agenda setters, but here it inclines them toward action rather than inaction. Combining the two, an institutional agenda setter is caught on the two horns of an institutional dilemma: Do I act, risking a reversal via referendum, or do I maintain the status quo, risking an overturn via initiative? The recall complements both of these choices, keeping institutional agenda setters on their toes to avoid being ousted. As the institution principle implies, these arrangements do not just provide citizens with governance tools. They also affect the strategic calculations of institutional politicians—legislators and governors.

HOW VOTERS DECIDE

An election expresses the preferences of millions of individuals about whom they want as their representatives and leaders. Electoral rules and laws—the institutional side of elections—impose order on that process, but ultimately, elections are a reflection of the people, the aggregation of many millions of individuals' expressions of their preferences about politics.

The voter's decision can be understood as really two linked decisions: whether to vote and for whom to vote. Social scientists have examined both facets of the electoral decision by studying election returns, survey data, and experiments conducted in laboratories as well as field experiments conducted during actual elections. Out of generations of research into these questions, a broad picture emerges of how voters decide. First, the decision to vote or not to vote correlates very strongly with the social characteristics of individuals, especially age and education, but it also depends on the electoral choices and context. An individual who does not know anything about the candidates or dislikes all of the choices is unlikely to vote. Second, which candidates or party voters choose depends primarily on three factors: partisan loyalties, issues, and candidate characteristics. Partisan loyalties have been found to be the strongest single predictor of the vote, though party attachments also reflect issues and experience with candidates. Party, issues, and candidates act together to shape vote choice.

Voters and Nonvoters

As we saw earlier in the chapter, turnout in modern American presidential elections ranges from 50 to 60 percent of the voting-age population. The Census Bureau's Current Population Survey provides the most comprehensive and trusted data about the demographics of voting. According to that survey, 65 percent of adults were registered voters in 2008, and 58 percent of adults voted that year. Excluding noncitizens, who are ineligible to vote in federal elections, 71 percent of the adult citizen population is registered, and 64 percent of citizens of voting age turned out in 2008, the highest level of participation in a presidential contest since 1960.

Even in a year of such high turnout, almost 40 percent of those who could have voted did not. Why do so many people not vote? This phenomenon has long puzzled social scientists and motivated reformers. A general explanation is elusive, but what social scientists do know about this phenomenon is that a few demographic characteristics routinely prove to be strong predictors of who votes. The most important of these characteristics are age, education, and residential mobility. Other factors, such as gender, income, and race also matter, but to a much smaller degree. According to the 2008 Current Population Survey, 49 percent of those under age 30 voted that year, fully 15 points below the population average. By comparison, 71 percent of those over 65 years of age voted. The difference between these groups was 24 percentage points, and the effect of age on voting surely translated into an electoral difference. The interests of retirees are much more likely to receive attention by the government than are the interests of those in college or just entering the labor force.

Education shows similarly large differences. Those without a high school degree voted at half the rate of those with a college education. More than three in four people with a college education voted, and the rate was 83 percent among those with a professional degree. In contrast, slightly fewer than 40 percent of those without a high school diploma voted, and 55 percent of those with only a high school degree voted. Finally, consider residency and mobility. Only 57 percent of people who lived in their current residence less than a year report voting, compared with 78 percent of people who lived in their residence at least five years. Those who own their home or apartment vote at a 68 percent rate, but only 52 percent of those who rent vote.[25] Politicians listen to those who vote, and those who vote are disproportionately older, better educated, and more rooted in their communities.

25 The most reliable source of information about the demographics of voting is the Current Population Survey, conducted by the Census Bureau. For these and other statistics see Kelly Holder, "Voting and Registration in the Election of November 2004," March 2006, www.census.gov/prod/2006pubs/p20-556.pdf (accessed 3/27/09).

One important concern is whether differences in voting reflect electoral institutions. Election laws have historically had a large effect on the size and character of the electorate, especially laws preventing racial discrimination at polling places (in 1965) and expanding the suffrage to women (in 1920). Those interested in encouraging greater participation today have focused on voter registration requirements, which are thought to create an unnecessary hurdle and thus to depress turnout. The decision to vote itself consists of two steps: registration and turnout. In 2008, 90 percent of those who reported that they registered said they voted. Weakening registration requirements may increase participation. One approach to minimizing such requirements is Election Day registration. As of 2011, seven states allow people to register on Election Day at the polls or at a government office. The three states with the longest experience with same-day registration—Minnesota, Wisconsin, and Maine—do have higher turnout than most other states, and most studies suggest that in a typical state adopting such a law would increase turnout by about 3 to 5 percent.[26]

Demographics and laws are only part of what accounts for voting and nonvoting. The choices presented to the voters are also quite important. The problem is not that many people have a hard time making up their minds but that many people do not feel engaged by current elections or dislike politics altogether. People who are disinterested, "too busy to vote," or do not like the candidates tend not to vote. The Census Bureau survey asks registered nonvoters why they did not vote. The top four reasons are "too busy," "sick or disabled," "not interested," and "did not like the choices."

Not voting may also stem partly from a sense that the election does not hinge on how any individual votes. There are, however, strong differences across demographic groups in their voting rates, and these might have political consequences. One hypothetical to consider is, what if everyone voted? In some specific domains, universal voting would certainly alter government policy. Increasing the voting rate of younger cohorts would probably affect government policy on Social Security, for instance. But would 100 percent turnout lead the country to elect a different person for president or put a different party in control of Congress? Interestingly, the answer seems to be no. Voters and nonvoters, for all of their demographic and political differences, hold fairly similar partisan views, ideological orientations, and preferences about the candidates.[27] Voters are somewhat more conservative and more Republican than nonvoters, as a result of the higher income levels and higher home ownership incidence of voters, but the median voter would be only slightly more liberal if everyone voted.

---

26 The classic study in this area is Raymond Wolfinger and Steven Rosenstone, *Who Votes?* (New Haven, CT: Yale University Press, 1978). See also Steven Rosenstone and John Mark Hansen, *Participation, Mobilization and American Democracy* (New York: Macmillan, 1993).

27 See for instance Sidney Verba, Kay Schlozman, and Henry Brady, *Voice and Equlity* (Cambridge, MA: Harvard University Press, 1995).

Partisan Loyalty

The single strongest predictor of how a person will vote is that individual's attachment to a political party. The American National Election Study (ANES), exit polls, and media polls have found that even in times of great political change in the United States, the overwhelming majority of Americans identifies with one of the two major political parties and votes almost entirely in accordance with that identity. Survey researchers ascertain party identification with simple questions along the following lines: Generally speaking, do you consider yourself to be a Democrat, a Republican, an Independent, or what?[28] Survey researchers further classify people by asking of those who choose a party whether they identify strongly or weakly with that party, and by asking independents whether they lean toward one party or another.

party identification

An individual's attachment to a particular political party, which might be based on issues or ideology, past experience, or upbringing

Over the past three decades party identifications have broken evenly between the Democrats and Republicans. Figure 12.2, in the next chapter on political parties, shows the historical fluctuations in party identifications. From the 1930s to the 1970s, Democratic identifiers outnumbered Republican identifiers, sometimes by a sizable margin. In the 1980s, the parties reached parity in identifications, especially because younger Americans at that time identified very heavily with the Republican Party. The balance in party identifications remained fairly stable through 2000, even though from 1992 to 2004 those aged 18 to 25 chose the Democrats by a sizable margin. From 2002 through the summer of 2009, Democrats steadily gained in overall party identification and Republicans lost ground, because of generational changes and the backlash against the Iraq War. By July 2009, 50 percent of Americans identified as Democrats or leaned toward the Democratic Party, while 42 percent of Americans identified as Republicans or leaned toward the Republican Party.[29] Since the summer of 2009, however, the partisan battles over health care and other legislative initiatives, the continuing wars in Iraq and Afghanistan, and unemployment ranging from 8 to 10 percent have dragged down public support for the Democrats. Today, public support for the parties is evenly split, approximately 45 to 45, with some variation depending on sampling. Interestingly, over a 50-year period there has been little change in the percentage of people calling themselves independents and leaning toward neither party. Only 10 to 15 percent consider themselves pure independents.[30]

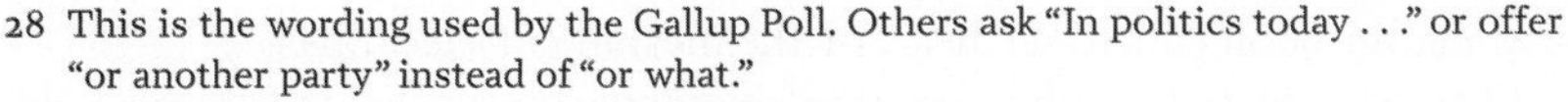

28 This is the wording used by the Gallup Poll. Others ask "In politics today . . ." or offer "or another party" instead of "or what."

29 Jeffrey M. Jones, "More Independents Lean GOP; Smallest Gap since '05," September 30, 2009, www.gallup.com/poll/123362/independents-lean-gop-party-gap-smallest-since-05.aspx (accessed 8/30/11).

30 Marc Hetherington, "Resurgent Mass Partisanship: The Role of Elite Polarization," *American Political Science Review* 95, no. 3 (September 2001): 619–31. Pew Research Center for the People and the Press, "Obama Leads McCain 52% to 46% in Campaign's Final Days," November 2, 2008, http://pewresearch.org/pubs/1020/pew-final-pre-election-poll (accessed 3/31/09).

Party identifications capture the voters' predisposition toward their party's candidates. Many of these predispositions are rooted in public policies, such as the parties' positions on taxes or civil rights. Those longstanding policy positions lead to divisions in party identifications and voting patterns among different demographic groups. Large majorities of African Americans and Hispanics, for example, identify and vote with the Democratic Party. Since 1980 there has been a clear gender gap in voting. Women tend to identify more and vote more with the Democrats than men do. In 1980, Ronald Reagan won 55 percent of the vote of men and 47 percent of the vote of women. That gap was novel in 1980, but it has persisted, averaging 7 percentage points over the past three decades. In 2012, Barack Obama received 55 percent of the vote of women, but only 45 percent of the vote among men. That difference is not as large as the difference across racial groups, but it is significant because women now comprise a majority of voters. It is a subject of considerable debate as to why the gender gap arose in the late 1970s and early 1980s and why it has persisted. Is it due to the parties' policies on abortion, or on some other issue, such as equal pay or divorce law or defense policy? Is it due to the types of candidates nominated? Or is there some deeper cultural difference between the parties that sustains it?

Although specific features of the choices and context matter as well, party identifications express how the voter would likely vote in a "neutral" election. Party identifications are extremely good predictors of voting behavior in less prominent elections, such as for state legislatures or lower-level statewide offices, about which voters may know relatively little. Even in presidential elections, with their extensive advertising and very thorough news coverage, party predispositions predict individual voting behavior. Figure 11.5 displays the percentages of Democratic identifiers, Republican identifiers, and self-described independents who voted for Mitt Romney, Barack Obama, or someone else in 2012. Approximately 92 percent of party identifiers voted for their own party's standard bearer. Independents (including independents who lean toward either party) broke 50 to 45 for Romney. The 2012 election was typical in that partisan loyalty is usually in the range of 90 percent, while the independent vote is usually divided fairly evenly between the two major party candidates.

Since the discovery of its importance in the 1950s, party identification has raised deeper questions about its origins and meaning. There are three distinct views about what party identification is. They are not necessarily exclusive of each other, but they point to very different understandings of the nature of party identification and its effect on elections.[31] Debate over the meaning of party identification cuts to the heart of the meaning of elections.

First, party identification is a psychological attachment that individuals hold, often throughout their adulthood, to one of the parties. Individuals learn as children and adolescents from parents, other adults, and even peers about politics, and as part of that socialization they develop attachments to a party, not

31 For an excellent treatment of the meanings of party identification and analysis of the implications of different theories, see Donald Green, Bradley Palmquist, and Eric Schickler, *Partisan Hearts and Minds* (New Haven, CT: Yale University Press, 2003).

Figure 11.5
THE EFFECT OF PARTY IDENTIFICATION ON THE VOTE FOR PRESIDENT, 2012

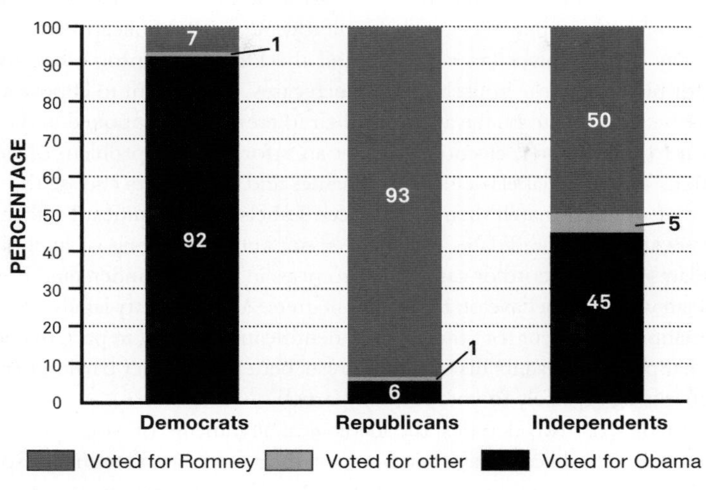

unlike religion and community. Party identifications continue to form into early adulthood. The first few presidential elections that an individual experiences as an adult are thought to have particularly profound influence on that individual's understanding of the parties and politics. And as different cohorts come into politics, their experiences carry forward throughout their lives. Those who were 18 to 24 years old in 1984, for example, identify overwhelmingly with the Republican Party, because those elections marked the triumph of Ronald Reagan's presidency and political philosophy, the rise of a revitalized Republican Party, and the beginning of the end of the Cold War. Those 18 to 24 years old in 2008, on the other hand, identify disproportionately with the Democratic Party, because the Obama campaign galvanized young voters around a new vision for the future. However it is developed, an individual's psychological affinity for a party makes that person want that party to win and want to support that party, even when he or she disagrees with the party on important policies or disapproves of the party's nominees for office.

Of course, the Democratic and Republican parties are quite different entities today than they were 40 years ago or 80 years ago. On matters of race relations, for example, the Democratic Party has moved over the past century from supporting segregation to spearheading civil rights. The Republican Party, once a bastion of economic protectionism, now champions free trade. However strong generational transmission of party identifications may be, the dissonance between identities and issues must surely weaken the pull of party, which suggests a second theory of party. This second idea is that party identification reflects underlying ideologies of voters and policy positions of parties. Parties in government, as we discussed in Chapter 6, are meaningful organizations for producing public policies.

The relatively high degree of party loyalty in Congress and other branches of government means that voters can reasonably anticipate how politicians will act in office. Citizens identify with parties that pursue public policies more to their liking. For example, a union worker will feel a stronger attachment to the Democratic Party because the Democrats have historically protected union interests. A high-income earner may feel a strong pull toward the Republican Party because that party pushes lower taxes overall, and the Democrats promote higher tax rates for higher-income households. In such cases, voters want to choose a party, not just a candidate, to be the agent for their interests. As mentioned in the introduction to this chapter, elections present an informational problem of adverse selection. The party labels act as brand names and help voters choose the candidates that will best match their preferences. Labels carry significant information to voters about the candidates. Voters need not know the details of an individual candidate's voting record or campaign promises in order to understand how that politician will likely behave on important matters. As such, party labels provide an informational short cut for voters. Party identification means, in part, that a voter feels that party represents his or her interests better than other parties; hence, an identifier is highly likely to vote for that party.[32]

Over the past two decades, the ideological alignments of voters and parties have shifted. Republicans have lost many of their moderate identifiers, especially in the Northeast, and conservative Southerners, who a generation ago would have called themselves Democrats, now overwhelmingly identify with the Republican Party. This shift reflects long-term changes in the ideological orientations of the parties at the elite level and thus their brand names. The 1994 election was critically important in establishing a new label for the Republicans, because that election swept into office large numbers of Republican members of Congress in the South and eliminated much of the conservative wing of the Democratic Party. The parties, then, became more distinctive, presenting a much clearer choice to voters.[33]

Not all people fit neatly into one ideological camp or another. Some people do not think about politics in ideological or policy terms. Others are indifferent to the parties ideologically. A significant portion of Americans consider themselves to be centrists and feel that the Democrats are somewhat too liberal and the Republicans somewhat too conservative. They may turn one way or the other, but they do not have a strong affinity for either party. Other people feel pulled in different directions by different issues and concerns. A union member who strongly opposes abortion, for example, is drawn to the Democrats' labor policies and the Republicans' abortion policies. Campaigns target such cross-pressured voters, who are often pivotal in elections.[34]

---

32 For a detailed assessment of the political use of information-economizing devices such as party labels, see Arthur Lupia and Mathew D. McCubbins, *The Democratic Dilemma: Can Citizens Learn What They Need To Know?* (New York: Cambridge University Press, 1998).

33 See Hetherington, "Resurgent Mass Partisanship."

34 For a more in-depth discussion of independent voters, policy indifference, and cross pressure, see Sunshine Hillygus and Todd Shields, *The Persuadable Voter: Wedge Issues in Presidential Campaigns* (Princeton, NJ: Princeton University Press, 2008).

A third explanation is that party identification reflects experiences with political leaders and representatives, especially the presidents from each of the parties. As the political scientist Morris Fiorina put it, party identifications are running tallies of experience. Americans hold their presidents, and to a lesser extent Congress, accountable for the economic performance of the country and success in foreign affairs. A bad economy or a disastrous military intervention will lead voters to disapprove of the president and to lower their assessment of the president's party's ability to govern. Parties are, by this account, teams seeking to run the government. They consist of policy experts, managers, and leaders who will conduct foreign policy, economic policy, and domestic policies (such as environmental protection and health care). When things go well, voters infer that the incumbent party has a good approach to running national affairs, but when things go badly, they learn that the party lacks the people needed to run the government competently or the approach needed to produce economic prosperity, international peace, and other outcomes desired by the public. With each successive presidency and their experience of it, individuals update their beliefs about which party is better able to govern.

Psychological attachments, ideological affinities, and past experiences add up to form an individual's current party identification. But party is not the only factor in voting. Some partisans do defect, especially in elections when voters are dissatisfied with the incumbent party or are especially drawn to a particular candidate. In 2008, for instance, significant defections occurred down the ticket. In the 2008 Virginia Senate election, two ex-governors squared off against one another, the Democrat Mark Warner against the Republican Jim Gilmore. In a state where the Democratic presidential nominee, Barack Obama, won just 8 percent of the votes of Republican Party identifiers, Mark Warner received 25 percent of the vote of Republican identifiers. The issues at stake and the characteristics of the candidates overrode party attachments for large numbers of Republican identifiers and drew large numbers of independents and Republicans to Warner. We consider next how issues and candidates shape voting behavior.

Issues

Issues and policy preferences constitute a second factor influencing voters' decisions. Voting on issues and policies cuts to the core of our understanding of democratic accountability and electoral control over government. A simple, idealized account of issue voting goes as follows. Governments make policies and laws on a variety of issues that affect the public. Voters who disagree with those policies and laws on principle or who think those policies have failed will vote against those who made the decisions. Voters who support the policies or like the outcomes that government has produced will support the incumbent legislatures or party. It is important to note that policies are not taken as constants or fixed attributes of the candidates or parties. Rather, politicians choose what kinds of laws to enact and what kinds of administrative actions to take with the express aim of attracting electoral support. Voters, as we discussed in the

 **issue voting**

An individual's propensity to select candidates or parties based on the extent to which the individual agrees with one candidate more than others on specific issues

previous chapter, have preferences about what policies the government pursues or what outcomes result, and they choose the candidates and parties that produce the best results or most preferred laws. Even party identifications, as we have noted, reflect the policy preferences of the voters and the policies pursued by the parties and candidates.

prospective voting

Voting based on the imagined future performance of a candidate

retrospective voting

Voting based on the past performance of a candidate

Voters' choice of issues usually involves a mix of their judgments about the past behavior of competing parties and candidates and their hopes and fears about candidates' future behavior. Political scientists call choices that focus on future behavior prospective voting and those based on past performance retrospective voting. To some extent, whether prospective or retrospective evaluation is more important in a particular election depends on the strategies of the competing candidates. Candidates always endeavor to define the issues of an election in terms that will serve their interests. Incumbents running during a period of prosperity will seek to take credit for the economy's happy state and define the election as revolving around their record of success. This strategy encourages voters to make retrospective judgments. By contrast, an insurgent running during a period of economic uncertainty will tell voters it is time for a change and ask them to make prospective judgments. Thus Barack Obama focused on the need for change in 2008, but the White House has repeatedly stressed the need to stay the course in 2010 and 2012.

Not all issues, however, are alike. There are, as discussed in the previous chapter, different sorts of issues and dimensions to politics, such as economic concerns, moral questions, and foreign affairs. Voters may hold different views on each. Some voters might favor low taxes and no government restrictions on abortion (a libertarian perspective), while others want low taxes and a prohibition on abortion; still others may see a need for high taxes and no restrictions on abortion; and so on. And voters differ according to how important they judge each issue to be. Some voters weigh economics more heavily; others give the greatest weight to social issues. According to a survey of registered voters conducted in September 2012, 87 percent viewed the economy as "very important" to their vote, more than for any other issue. Jobs followed closely at 83 percent, with 74 saying health care was very important and 69 saying education was very important. Among respondents who said they favored Mitt Romney, the economy was the most-cited very important issue (93 percent), followed by jobs (87 percent), the budget deficit (82 percent), and taxes (70 percent). Among respondents favoring Obama, education was the most-cited very important issue (84 percent), followed by the economy (83 percent), healthcare (82 percent), and jobs (81 percent).

spatial issue

An issue for which a range of possible options or policies can be ordered, say, from liberal to conservative or from most expensive to least expensive

Issues differ politically in another important respect, and that is the extent to which the policy principle is invoked. Broadly speaking, issues may be distinguished as spatial issues and valence issues. Spatial issues are issues on which voters have preferences over what policy is pursued. On many issues voters have beliefs about which policies will lead to the best outcomes, or they have moral convictions that lead them to value the means, not just the ends. Valence issues are issues on which voters do not care about the means (the policy) only the ends (the outcome). Voters care about having peaceful and prosperous lives, quite apart from how they are achieved.

Spatial Issues. Many issues are characterized by a range of different policies and conflicting preferences over policies and outcomes. We call these spatial preferences because the choices can be mapped along a continuum or line, such as tax rates or size of government. Minimum wages offer an excellent example. Low-wage workers and unions favor minimum wages because they benefit from them. Low-wage workers will earn higher wages, and union members expect all wages to be pushed up with the minimum wage. Employers and investors tend not to like the minimum wage because it increases labor costs and reduces profit margins. Abortion rights provide another often-discussed example of a spatial issue. At one extreme are those who defend the legality of abortion under all circumstances; at the other extreme are those who want to ban the procedure under all circumstances. Between those two poles lie a range of policy alternatives, from putting some restrictions on access, such as parental consent or consultation with a medical professional, to regulations on the time during pregnancy and procedures used, to allowing the practice only when the life of the mother is threatened. Public-opinion research (as discussed in Chapter 10) has demonstrated that public preferences are distributed across such policy options, with many people favoring a moderate approach of placing some restrictions on the practice. Minimum-wage laws and abortion laws exemplify the features of spatial issues—a range of policy options and a lack of consensus on the right policy.

Politicians compete for voters by pursuing particular policies that they think will attract the most voters. During the 2008 presidential race, Obama railed against the failed missions in Iraq and Afghanistan and promised a different approach to those conflicts; he criticized the administration's handling of the economy and financial crisis and promised greater regulation of the financial industry; and he promised energy policy that would develop green jobs and health care reforms that would provide universal coverage. His opponent John McCain had inherited many of the issues and positions of the incumbent administration, especially the war on terrorism and the wars in Iraq and Afghanistan. Even though he was not tied to the administration, McCain inherited some of the blame for the economy simply because he was a Republican and would be expected to pursue policies similar to those of the Bush administration. On health care, McCain and Obama proposed very different policies, with McCain wanting to leave things as they were. On energy, the two candidates had somewhat similar policies aimed at reducing carbon emissions, though McCain sought to do so through an aggressive expansion of nuclear power.

Voters made judgments based on a head-to-head comparison of many of these issues and the overall ideologies of these candidates. Likewise, the 2010 midterm elections reflected assessments of the Obama administration's economic policies and handling of particular issue areas, especially health care. Throughout 2009 and 2010 the alternative to the administration policies came not from a competing candidate but from the Republican leadership in Congress. The Republicans steadfastly opposed numerous bills proposed by the Obama administration, especially the economic stimulus package, financial regulations, an increase in the minimum wage, extension of the State Children's Health Insurance Program, energy legislation, and, most importantly, Obama's health care bill. The last of these pieces of legislation became a rallying point for the

Republicans. During the 2012 presidential election, Republican candidate Mitt Romney campaigned against Obama's health care legislation and the president's handling of the national economy, promising to repeal Obamacare and to create programs that would increase employment and restore prosperity. Romney pointed to his record as an entrepreneur as evidence of his credibility on economic matters. Obama replied that Romney had a record of sending jobs abroad and showing disdain for ordinary American workers. Romney and Obama also debated the appropriate role of government, with Romney preferring free market approaches and Obama maintaining that government services were essential to society.

Spatial voting is one way that voters solve the adverse selection problem. They choose politicians who promise to enact certain policies that the voters support and who have a track record of voting in ways that are consistent with the voter's preferences. To solve adverse selection, choose someone who is like you. Spatial voting also helps correct for moral hazard. Voters can choose to vote against politicians with whom they disagree. Recent research on congressional roll-call voting suggests that this is a strong factor in U.S. House elections and accounts for a significant portion of party identification.[35]

The ability of voters to make choices on the basis of issue or policy preferences is diminished, however, if competing candidates do not differ substantially or do not focus their campaigns on policy matters. Very often candidates deliberately take the safe course and emphasize topics that will not be offensive to any voters. Thus candidates often trumpet their support for more police to appear tough on crime or their support for ethics laws to appear anticorruption. Although it may be perfectly reasonable for candidates to take the safe course, this strategy means that voters would not face policy choices because the candidates would offer the same policies. This often occurs in primary elections, where the candidates within a party are often difficult to distinguish on policies or ideologies.

median-voter theorem

A proposition predicting that when policy options can be arrayed along a single dimension, majority rule will pick the policy most preferred by the voter whose ideal policy is to the left of half of the voters and to the right of exactly half of the voters. See Chapter 6 for further discussion

When voters engage in issue voting, competition between two candidates has the effect of pushing the candidates' issue positions toward the middle of the distribution of voters' preferences. This is known as the median-voter theorem, made famous by Duncan Black and Anthony Downs.[36] (Chapter 6 discussed the median-voter theorem in the context of congressional committees.) To see the logic of this claim in the context of elections, imagine a series of possible stances on a policy issue as points along a line, stretching from 0 to 100 (Figure 11.6). A voter is represented by an "ideal" policy and preferences, which decline as policy moves away from this ideal. Thus voters in group 1 prefer policy X_1 most, and their preference declines as the policy moves to the left or right of X_1. Voters whose ideal policy lies between, say, 0 and 25 are said to be liberal on this policy (groups 1 and 2), those whose ideal lies between 75 and 100 are conservative (groups 4 and 5), and those whose favorite policy

35 See Stephen Ansolabehere and Philip Jones, "Constituents' Responses to Congressional Roll-Call Voting," *American Journal of Political Science* 54 (July 2010): 583–97.

36 See Duncan Black, *The Theory of Committees and Elections*, 2nd ed. (Boston: Kluwer, 1998), and Anthony Downs, *An Economic Theory of Democracy* (New York: Harper & Row, 1957). A general, accessible treatment of this subject is found in Shepsle and Bonchek, *Analyzing Politics*, chap. 5.

Figure 11.6
THE MEDIAN-VOTER THEOREM

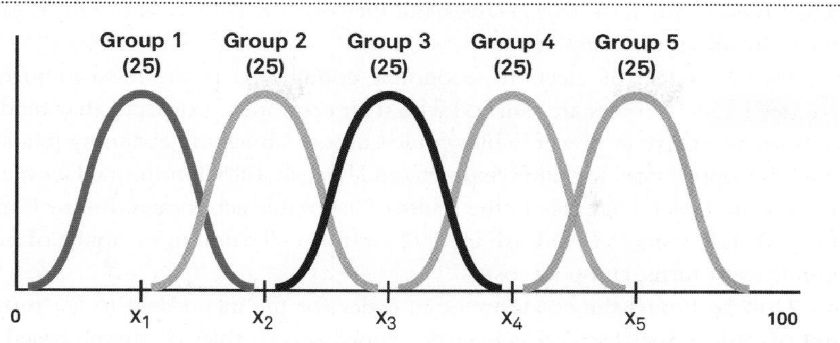

is between 25 and 75 are moderate (group 3). An issue voter cares only about issue positions, not partisan loyalty or candidates' characteristics, and would, therefore, vote for the candidate whose announced policy is closest to his or her own most preferred policy.

Consider now an electorate of 125 voters evenly distributed among the five groups shown in Figure 11.6.[37] The middle group contains the median voter because half or more of this electorate has an ideal policy at or to the left of X_3 (groups 1, 2, and 3), and half or more has an ideal policy at or to the right of X_3 (groups 3, 4, and 5). Group 3 is in the driver's seat, as the following reasoning suggests. If a candidate announces X_3 as his policy—the most preferred alternative of the median voter—and if his opponent picks any point to the right, then the median voter and all those with ideal policies to the left of the median voter's (groups 1–3) will support the first candidate. They constitute a majority, by definition of the median, so this candidate will win. Suppose instead that the opponent chose as her policy some point to the left of the median ideal policy. Then the median voter and all those with ideal policies to the right of the median voter's (groups 3–5) will support the first candidate—and he wins, again. In short, the median-voter theorem says that the candidate whose policy position is closest to the ideal policy of the median voter will defeat the other candidate in a majority contest. We can conclude from this brief analysis that issue voting encourages candidate convergence (in which both candidates move to cozy up to the position of the median voter). Even when voters are not exclusively issue voters, two-candidate competition still encourages a tendency toward convergence, although it may not fully run its course.[38]

37 For the sake of this illustration, 25 voters have been included in each group. This argument holds true with any distribution of voters among the groups.

38 This convergence will also be a moderating force as candidates move toward what they believe will appeal to voters in the middle. But if the middle of the voter distribution of preferences tilts toward the right or the left, it may not be very moderate. If X_3, for example, were barely to the left of X_4, then the median voter would be fairly right wing rather than in the middle of the issue dimension.

Valence Issues. Some issues lack conflict: all people want the same outcome. All people want less crime, more prosperity and less poverty, less inflation, better health, peace, and security. They may have different beliefs about what to do to attain those objectives, but they don't really care about the means; they care about the outcome.

valence issue 

An issue or aspect of a choice for which all voters prefer a higher value, in contrast to a spatial issue. For example, voters prefer their politicians to be honest, and honesty is a valence issue

In the context of elections, economic conditions are the most important valence issue. If voters are satisfied with their economic prospects, they tend to support the party in power, while voters' unease about the economy tends to favor the opposition. Richard Nixon, Ronald Reagan, Bill Clinton, and George W. Bush won re-election easily in the midst of favorable economies. Jimmy Carter in 1980 and George H. W. Bush in 1992 ran for re-election in the midst of economic downturns, and both lost.

How bad must the economy be in order for the incumbent to get turned out of office? Social scientists have developed several rules of thumb based on historical correlations between economic performance and the vote. A common sort of empirical analysis uses economic growth (annual percentage changes in gross domestic product) to predict the vote. The idea is that large numbers of voters decide to vote against the incumbent party in bad times and with the incumbent party in good times. Every individual may have a different sense of the economy, but adding up the 100 million or so votes will aggregate every individual's experiences and reflect roughly what is going on in the economy and how the economy affects his or her voting. Although the fit between economic growth and votes for the incumbent party is hardly perfect, correlation is sufficient to allow statistically minded political scientists to make forecasts. Roughly speaking, every additional 1 percent growth in GDP corresponds to a 1 percentage point increase in the incumbent president's party's vote.[39]

Another approach relies on the Consumer Confidence Index, which has been calculated over the past quarter century by the Conference Board, a business research group. The Consumer Confidence Index is based on a public opinion survey that administers a simple battery of questions about people's sense of the economy in their area and their expectations over the coming months. It has proven a fairly accurate predictor of presidential outcomes. It would appear that a generally rosy view, indicated by a score greater than 100, augurs well for the party in power. An index score of less than 100, suggesting that voters are pessimistic about the economy's trend, suggests that incumbents should worry about their job prospects (Figure 11.7). In 2012, the index was only 72.2, but it had been rising steadily for the past several months.

Economic voting is one way that voters solve the moral hazard problems inherent in representative democracy. They cannot monitor every policy that the government initiates. They do, however, have a rudimentary way to hold the government accountable—staying the course when times are good, and voting for change when the economy sours.

39 Perhaps the most comprehensive study of the responsiveness of elections to fluctuations in the U.S. economy is Robert Erikson, Michael MacKuen, and James Stimson, *The Macro-Polity* (New York: Cambridge University Press, 2002).

Figure 11.7
CONSUMER CONFIDENCE AND PRESIDENTIAL ELECTIONS

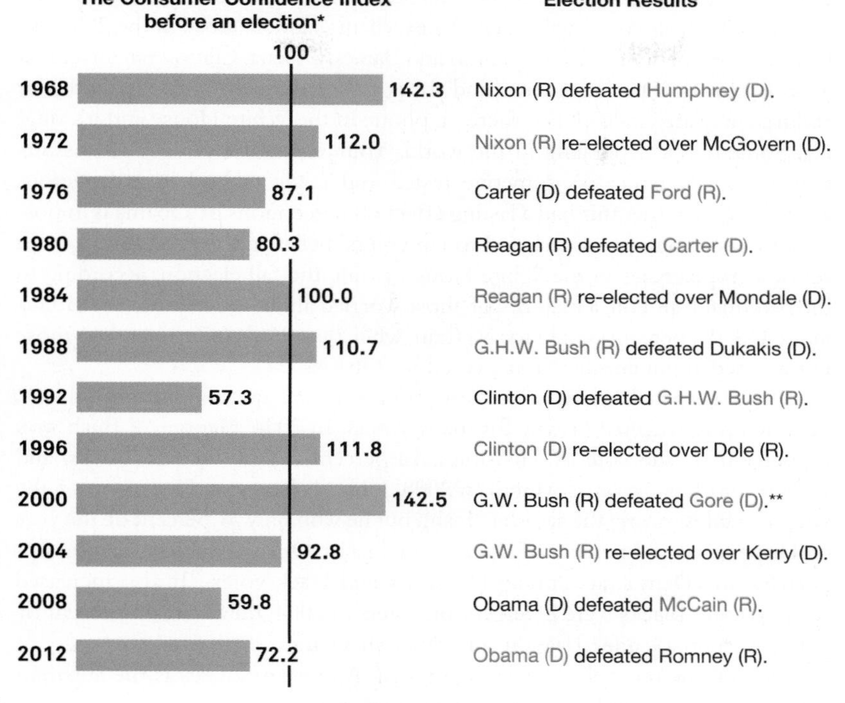

The Consumer Confidence Index before an election*
Election Results
100
1968
142.3
Nixon (R) defeated Humphrey (D).
1972
112.0
Nixon (R) re-elected over McGovern (D).
1976
87.1
Carter (D) defeated Ford (R).
1980
80.3
Reagan (R) defeated Carter (D).
1984
100.0
Reagan (R) re-elected over Mondale (D).
1988
110.7
G.H.W. Bush (R) defeated Dukakis (D).
1992
57.3
Clinton (D) defeated G.H.W. Bush (R).
1996
111.8
Clinton (D) re-elected over Dole (R).
2000
142.5
G.W. Bush (R) defeated Gore (D).**
2004
92.8
G.W. Bush (R) re-elected over Kerry (D).
2008
59.8
Obama (D) defeated McCain (R).
2012
72.2
Obama (D) defeated Romney (R).

*Figures for 1968, 1972, and 1976 are for October; from 1980 on, they are for September.
**Gore won the popular vote, but Bush was elected by the electoral college.
NOTE: The candidate representing the incumbent party appears in red.
SOURCE: *Bloomberg Markets*.

Candidate Characteristics

Candidates' personal attributes always influence voters' decisions. The more important characteristics that affect voters' choices are race, ethnicity, religion, gender, geography, and social background. In general, voters prefer candidates who are closer to themselves in terms of these categories. Voters presume that such candidates are likely to have views close to their own. Moreover, they may be proud to see someone of their background in a position of leadership. This is why politicians often seek to "balance the ticket" by including members of as many important groups as possible.

Just as a candidate's personal characteristics may attract some voters, so they may repel others. Many voters are prejudiced against candidates of certain ethnic, racial, or religious groups. And for many years, voters were reluctant to support the political candidacy of women, although this tendency appears to be changing.

Voters also pay attention to candidates' personality characteristics, such as their "competence," "honesty," and "vigor." Voters want these skills and attributes because the politicians who have them are more likely to produce good outcomes, such as laws that work, fair and honest administration of government, and ability to address crises. Candidates will emphasize certain qualities that they think all voters will value. An excellent example arose in the 2008 primary election between Hillary Clinton and Barack Obama. Clinton ran an ad that intended to show her experience and ability to solve crises. "It's 3 A.M. and your children are safely asleep. But there's a phone in the White House and it's ringing. Something's happening in the world. Your vote will decide who answers that call. . . . Whether it's someone tested and ready to lead in a dangerous world. . . ." Whether this had a lasting effect on perceptions of Obama is impossible to know, but it was designed to tap voters' belief in the need for a certain set of competencies in the White House. Come the fall election, according to the National Exit Poll, a majority of those worried about another terrorist attack in the U.S. (54 percent) voted for McCain, while two-thirds (67 percent) of those not worried about another attack voted for Obama.

Other personal characteristics of candidates are quite important as well. Obama's race weighed heavily for many voters. In 2004, George W. Bush won 43 percent of the vote of Hispanics, 12 percent of the vote of blacks, and 58 percent of the vote of whites. In 2008, John McCain won 55 percent of the vote of whites (nearly the same as Bush), but he won only 31 percent of the vote of Hispanics and 4 percent of the vote of blacks. Obama's race raised the support for the Democrats among Hispanics and black voters. It also increased their turnout. Blacks were 8 percent of voters in 2004; they were 13 percent of voters in 2008. Gender, religion, and other characteristics also matter.

One of the most distinctive features of American politics is the apparent advantage that incumbents have, as we saw in Chapter 6. Beginning around 1970, political scientists noted a peculiar change overtaking electoral politics, especially in congressional elections. Incumbents were winning re-election at higher rates than in previous generations and by wider margins. Closer examination of the election results revealed that this phenomenon appeared due to incumbency itself. As a simple natural experiment, Professor Robert Erikson compared the same politician running for election not as an incumbent and as an incumbent. In the first sort of election, the politician ran for a seat left vacant by an incumbent's retirement or against an incumbent and won. In the second sort of election, the politician had just won the previous election and had to defend the seat in the next election as a "sophomore." Erikson called the increase in the politician's vote share from the first election to the second the "sophomore surge." It is the increase in the vote attributable solely to the fact that the politician ran as an incumbent rather than as a non-incumbent. Erikson found an incumbency effect of approximately 5 percentage points around 1970. If the party division of the vote in a congressional district without an incumbent is, say, 50–50, then in a race where one candidate is the incumbent, that same district would vote for the incumbent with 55 percent to 45 percent.

Since Erikson documented it in 1970, the incumbency advantage has grown both in magnitude and in importance in U.S. elections. Incumbency advantages in House elections grew rapidly beginning in the mid-1950s, when they were worth only 1 to 2 percentage points, to 5 or 6 percentage points by the end of the 1960s. They have continued to inch upward, reaching as high as 15 points in the mid-1980s. Today, almost every elective office at the state and federal level exhibits an incumbency advantage. Those advantages have ranged from about 5 percent in state legislative elections to 10 percent for U.S. House, U.S. Senate, and governor. A 10 percent incumbency advantage is a massive electoral edge. It turns a 50–50 seat into a safe seat. It turns a competitive race into a blowout for the incumbent.[40]

Why the incumbency advantage has emerged and grown remains something of a puzzle. Redistricting is almost certainly not the explanation: incumbency effects are as large in gubernatorial elections, where there are no districts, as in House elections. It is thought that about half of the incumbency advantage reflects the activities of the legislator in office; it is the result of voters rewarding incumbents for their performance. The other half of the incumbency advantage evidently reflects not the incumbents but their opponents.[41] The typical challenger in U.S. elections may not have the personal appeal of the typical incumbent; after all, the typical incumbent has already won office once. Moreover, challengers usually lack the experience and resources that the incumbent has for running a campaign. This is critical. The ability to communicate with the voters can give a politician the edge in close elections.

Although party, issues, and candidate characteristics are perhaps the three most important factors shaping voting decisions, there is much debate among political scientists as to the relative importance of each. Problems of measurement and the limitations of research methods have made it exceedingly difficult to parse the relative importance of these factors in voters' thinking. Recent scholarship suggests that they have roughly equal weight in explaining the division of the vote in national elections.[42] Part of the difficulty in understanding their importance is that the extent to which these factors matter depends on the information levels of the electorate. In the absence of much information, most voters rely almost exclusively on party cues. A highly informed electorate relies more heavily on issues and candidate characteristics.[43]

40 See Stephen Ansolabehere and James M. Snyder, Jr., "The Incumbency Advantage in U.S. Elections: An Analysis of State and Federal Offices, 1942–2000," *Election Law Journal* 1 (2002): 315–38.

41 The partitioning of the incumbency effect into officeholder advantages and challenger qualities begins with the important work of Gary Jacobson. See, for example, his text, *The Politics of Congressional Elections*, 7th ed. (White Plains, NY: Longman, 2008). Estimating exactly what fraction of the incumbency effect is due to officeholder benefits is tricky. See Stephen Ansolabehere, James M. Snyder, Jr., and Charles H. Stewart III, "Old Voters, New Voters, and the Personal Vote: Using Redistricting to Measure the Incumbency Advantage," *American Journal of Political Science* 44, no. 1 (January 2000): 17–34.

42 See Stephen Ansolabehere, Jonathan Rodden, and James M. Snyder, Jr., "Issue Voting," *American Political Science Review* (May 2008).

43 The classic study showing this is Philip Converse, "The Nature of Belief Systems in Mass Publics," in *Ideology and Discontent*, David Apter, ed. (New York: Free Press, 1964).

CAMPAIGNS: MONEY, MEDIA, AND GRASS ROOTS

American political campaigns are freewheeling events with few restrictions on what candidates may say or do. Candidates in hotly contested House and Senate races spend millions of dollars to advertise on television and radio, as well as direct mail and door-to-door canvassing. Those seeking office are in a race to become as well known and as well liked as possible and to get more of their supporters to vote. Federal laws limit how much an individual or organization may give to a candidate, but with the exception of the presidential campaigns, place no restrictions on how much a candidate or party committee may spend.

Adding to the freewheeling nature of campaigns is their organizational structure. Most political campaigns are temporary organizations. They form for the sole purpose of winning the coming elections and disband shortly afterward. To be sure, political parties in the United States have a set of permanent, professional campaign organizations that raise money, strategize, recruit candidates, and distribute resources. These are, on the Republican side, the Republican National Committee, the National Republican Senatorial Committee, and the National Republican Congressional Committee. On the Democratic side are the Democratic National Committee, the Democratic Senatorial Campaign Committee, and the Democratic Congressional Campaign Committee. They account for roughly one-third of the money in politics and have considerable expertise. But most campaigns are formed by and around individual candidates, who often put up the initial cash to get the campaign rolling and rely heavily on family and friends as volunteers. Thousands of such organizations are at work during an election. The two presidential campaigns operate 50 different state-level operations, with other campaigns competing for 34 Senate seats, 435 House seats, dozens of gubernatorial and other statewide offices, and thousands of state legislative seats. There is relatively little coordination among these myriad campaigns, though they all simultaneously work toward the same end—persuading as many people as possible to vote for their candidate on Election Day.

All campaigns, big and small, face similar challenges—how to bring people in, how to raise money, how to coordinate activities, what messages to run, and how to communicate with the public. There is no single best way to run a campaign. There are many tried-and-true approaches, especially building up a campaign from many local connections, from the grass roots. Candidates have to meet as many people as possible and get their friends and their friends' friends to support them. In-person campaigning becomes increasingly difficult in larger constituencies. Candidates continually experiment with new ways of communicating with the public and new ways of organizing in order to more efficiently reach large segments of the electorate. In the 1920s, radio advertising eclipsed handbills and door-to-door canvassing, as broadcasting captured economies of scale. In the 1960s, television began to eclipse radio. In the 1980s and 1990s, cable television and innovations in marketing (especially phone polling and focus groups) allowed candidates to target very specific demographic groups through the media. The great innovation of the Obama campaign was to meld Internet networking tools with old-style organizing methods to develop a massive communications and fund-raising network, what came to be called a "netroots" campaign.

However they are organized, campaigns play an essential role in American democracy. They are the opportunity for the politicians to present themselves to the public to explain who they are, what they have accomplished, and what they will do in office. Television advertisements, get-out-the-vote activities, direct mail, and the like provide voters with factual information about the personal characteristics and ideologies of the candidates, about the meaning of the party labels, and about what issues distinguish the politicians.

Campaigns are also a time when the foibles and failures of those in office may be revealed. Challengers must make the case that a new direction is needed, and that case rests on showing that the incumbent is the wrong person to represent the constituency (a case of adverse selection) or has failed to do the job as constituents wanted (a case of moral hazard). Incumbents, for their part, try to appeal to voters on the basis of their ideological fit with their constituents and their performance in office. It has become an assumption of American elections and election law that candidates and parties will mount competitive campaigns to win office. They will spend millions, even billions of dollars, to persuade people to vote and how to vote. And because of those efforts voters will understand better the choices they face in the elections. In short, campaigns inform voters, and they do so through competition.

In addition to being costly, American political campaigns are long, often spanning years. Campaigns for the presidency officially launch a year and a half to two years in advance of Election Day. Serious campaigns for the U.S. House of Representatives begin at least a year ahead of the general election date and often span the better part of two years. To use the term of the Federal Election Commission, an election is a two-year "cycle," not a single day or even the period between Labor Day and Election Day loosely referred to as "the general election."

The long campaigns in the United States are due in large part to the effort required to mount a campaign. There are roughly 310 million people in the United States, and the voting-age population exceeds 240 million people. Communicating with all of those people is an expensive and time-consuming enterprise. A simple calculation reveals the challenge. Suppose you ran for president of the United States. Sending one piece of mail to each household in the United States would cost approximately $100 million dollars. That is probably the minimum imaginable campaign effort. How long would it take to raise $100 million and mobilize such an effort to communicate with the American people? In the 2012 election cycle, Barack Obama spent close to $700 million raised from individual contributions, while Mitt Romney spent close to $450 million. The Democratic and Republican national party operations spent another $665 million on the presidential contest. Candidates and party organizations spent approximately $1.8 billion on House and Senate races. Perhaps another $1 billion was spent by groups and individuals seeking to influence the presidential or congressional races but acting independently of the campaigns. The Supreme Court's *Citizens United* decision declared such spending to be a form of free speech not subject to federal limits. The grand spending total for 2012 came to $4.7 billion. It takes extensive operations to reach out to so many people and to raise such vast sums. Simply putting such an organization in place takes months. Even a congressional campaign takes considerable time to cultivate. The average U.S. House campaign raised and spent approximately $1,153,000 in 2012, with the lion's share of that money coming from hundreds of individual donors. Once a campaign has enough money to initiate operations, it begins to communicate with the voters, often starting small by attending meetings with various groups. A successful campaign builds on early successes, bringing in more supporters and volunteers and culminating with intensive advertising campaigns in the final months or weeks before Election Day. Every campaign for Congress or president is built by the individual candidates and their close friends and associates from the ground up. The personal style of political campaigning that Americans have come to appreciate reflects an enormous investment of time and resources. Incumbent members of Congress have particular advantages in campaign fund-raising. They have already been tested; they have their campaign organizations in place; they have connections in their constituencies as well as in Washington, D.C. The average U.S. House incumbent in 2012 spent $1.7 million, to the $595,000 spent by the typical challenger. Partly as a result of this financial advantage, only 40 House incumbents lost their seats (13 in the primaries, 27 in the general election).

The campaign season is further extended by the election calendar. American elections proceed in two steps: the party primary elections and the general election. General elections for federal offices are set by the U.S. Constitution to take place on the first Tuesday after the first Monday in November. The first presidential caucuses and primaries come early in January and last through the beginning of June. State and congressional primaries do not follow the same calendar, but most occur in the spring and early summer, with a handful of some states waiting to hold their nominating elections until September of the election year. The immediate result of this year-long calendar of elections is to stretch the campaigns over the entire election year.

American electoral campaigns contrast starkly with those in other democracies, such as Germany, France, Japan, and even the United Kingdom. Parliamentary systems have short campaigns. Once the government calls for an election, the campaign proceeds for a few months, and an election is held. The years-long gestation of an American election is unheard of and even considered unseemly in most other democracies. Most democracies also limit candidates' campaign expenditures and fund-raising activities, constraining the ability of individual politicians to develop personal campaign organizations and appeals. Money and other resources in other democracies flow through party organizations, often with little government oversight. Most democracies also regulate how candidates and parties campaign. Very few countries permit television advertising, phone banks, or door-to-door canvassing. Posters and billboards are commonplace in other democracies, as are public campaign forums. These restrictions on campaign communications make the campaigns themselves less important and make media coverage of the parties, the candidates, and the government more prominent. And however much leaders, candidates, and parties try to shape news coverage, they cannot control it.

The expense, duration, and chaos of American campaigns have prompted many efforts at reform, including attempts to limit campaign spending, shorten the campaign season, and restrict what candidates and organizations can say in advertisements. The most sweeping campaign reforms came in 1971, when Congress passed the Federal Elections Campaign Act (FECA). It limited the amounts that a single individual could contribute to a candidate or party to $1,000 per election for individuals and $5,000 for organizations (these limits have since been increased, as Table 11.1 indicates). It further regulated how business firms, unions, and other organizations could give money, prohibiting donations directly from the organization's treasury and requiring the establishment of a separate, segregated fund—a political action committee (PAC for short). It established public funding for presidential campaigns and tied those funds to expenditure limits. And it set up the Federal Election Commission (FEC) to oversee public disclosure of information and to enforce the laws.[44] Congress has amended the act several times, most importantly in the Bipartisan Campaign Reform Act of 2002 (BCRA, also called the McCain-Feingold Act, after senators John McCain and Russell Feingold, its primary sponsors in the Senate). The McCain-Feingold Act prohibited unlimited party spending (called soft money) and banned certain sorts of political attack advertisements from interest groups in the last weeks of a campaign. See Table 11.1 for rules governing campaign finance in federal elections.

political action committee (PAC)

A private group that raises and distributes funds for use in election campaigns

FECA also established public funding for presidential campaigns. If a candidate agrees to abide by spending limits, that candidate's campaign is eligible for matching funds in primary elections and full public funding in the general election. Until 2000, nearly all candidates bought into the system. George W. Bush chose to fund his 2000 primary election campaign outside this system and spent $500 million to win the Republican nomination. Barack Obama and Hillary Clinton ignored the public financing system in their 2008 primary contest, and Obama opted out of the public system in the general election as well, allowing him to spend several hundred million more dollars than the Republican nominee, John McCain. In 2012, neither Obama nor the Republican candidates for president used public funding.

FECA originally went much farther than the law that survives today. Congress originally passed mandatory caps on spending by House and Senate candidates and prohibited organizations from running their own independent campaigns on behalf of or in opposition to a candidate (and not coordinated with any candidate). James Buckley, a candidate for U.S. Senate in New York, challenged the law, arguing that the restrictions on spending and contributions

44 The FEC's Web site is an excellent resource for those interested in U.S. campaign finance (www.fec.gov).

Table 11.1

FEDERAL CAMPAIGN FINANCE REGULATION

THE RULES FOR CAMPAIGN CONTRIBUTIONS			
Who	**may contribute . . .**	**to . . .**	**if . . .**
Individuals	up to $2,300	a candidate	they are contributing to a single candidate in a single election
Individuals	up to $28,500	a national party committee	
Individuals	up to $5,000	a PAC	
PACs	up to $5,000	a candidate	they contribute to the campaigns of at least five candidates
Individuals and PACs	unlimited funds	a 527 committee	the funds are used for issue advocacy and the 527 committee's efforts are not coordinated with any political campaign
Individuals and PACs	up to $10,000	a state party committee	the money is used for voter registration and get-out-the-vote efforts
Individuals and PACs	unlimited funds	an independent expenditure committee (super PAC)	the money is used for political ads advocating for or against candidates and the committee's efforts are not coordinated with any political campaign

Table 11.1
(Continued)

THE RULES FOR CAMPAIGN ADVERTISING		
Who	**may not finance . . .**	**if . . .**
Unions, corporations, and nonprofit organizations	broadcast issue ads mentioning federal candidates	they occur within 60 days of a general election or 30 days of a primary
THE RULES FOR PRESIDENTIAL PRIMARIES AND ELECTIONS		
Candidates . . .	**may receive . . .**	**if . . .**
In primaries	federal matching funds, dollar for dollar, up to $5 million	they raise at least $5,000 in each of 20 states in contributions of $250 or less
In general elections	full federal funding (but may spend no more than their federal funding)	they belong to a major party (minor-party candidates may receive partial funding)
In any election	money from independent groups (PACs and 527 committees)	the groups' efforts are not tied directly to the official campaign
IMPORTANT DEFINITIONS FOR CAMPAIGN FINANCE REGULATION		

- Political action committee (PAC): Private group that raises and distributes funds for use in election campaigns
- 527 committee: Tax-exempt organization that engages in political activities, often through unlimited "soft-money" contributions. The committee is not restricted by current law on campaign finance, thus exploiting a loophole in the Internal Revenue Service code
- 501(c)4: Not-for-profit group that may engage in unlimited political spending so long as amount spent does not exceed 50 percent of its budget. Unlike the 527s, 501(c)4s are not required to disclose contributor and recipient information
- Independent expenditure committee: Organization that may engage in unlimited political spending to run advertising for and against candidates so long as their efforts are not coordinated with those of the candidates
- Federal matching funds: Federal funds that match, dollar for dollar, all individual contributions of $250 or less received by a candidate. To qualify, the candidate must raise at least $5,000 in individual contributions of $250 or less in each of 20 states
- Federal Election Commission: The commission that oversees campaign finance practices in the United States

limited his rights to free speech and that FEC had excessive administrative power. In the 1976 landmark case *Buckley v. Valeo*, the U.S. Supreme Court agreed in part.[45] The Court ruled that "money is speech," but the government also has a compelling interest in protecting elections from corrupt practices, such as bribery through large campaign donations. The justices declared the limits on spending unconstitutional because they violated free speech rights of candidates and groups. However, the need to protect the integrity of the electoral process led the justices to leave contribution limits in place. The presidential public-funding system was also validated because it is voluntary. Candidates can opt into the system, but they are not required to; hence, there is no violation of free speech. What survived *Buckley* is a system in which candidates, groups, and parties may spend as much as they like to win office, but donations must come in small amounts. In an expensive election, campaigns must accumulate their resources from large numbers of individuals and groups. This is a more democratic process of campaign finance, but it increases the effort and time needed to construct a campaign.

The Supreme Court's decision in *Buckley*, though highly controversial, rests on an essential truth of American democracy and elections. The First Amendment right to free speech amounts to a "profound national commitment to the principle that debate on public issues should be uninhibited, robust, and wide-open."[46] "In a republic where the people are sovereign," the Court continued, "the ability of the citizenry to make informed choices among candidates for office is essential, for the identities of those who are elected will inevitably shape the course that we follow as a nation. . . . It can hardly be doubted that the constitutional guarantee has its fullest and most urgent application precisely to the conduct of campaigns for political office."[47] Without competitive political campaigns, voters would lack the information to make electoral decisions. Most of us might not even know when or how to vote; we would certainly lack basic information about the choices before us.

In 2010, the Supreme Court reinforced its reasoning in *Buckley v. Valeo* in the case *Citizens United v. FEC*.[48] In *Citizens United* the justices ruled that the BCRA of 2002 had erred in imposing restrictions on independent spending by corporations. It overturned key components of the BCRA and reversed its ruling in the case that had upheld BCRA, *McConnell v. FEC*.[49] The majority opinion struck down limits on independent expenditures from corporate treasuries but kept in place limits on direct contributions from corporations and other organizations to candidates. The majority opinion went further than past

45 *Buckley v. Valeo*, 424 U.S. 1 (1976).

46 The majority opinion in *Buckley* quotes an earlier landmark case, *New York Times Co. v. Sullivan*, 376 U.S. 254 (1964).

47 *Buckley v. Valeo*, 424 U.S. 1 (1976).

48 *Citizens United v. FEC*, 558 U.S. 08-205 (2010).

49 *McConnell v. FEC*, 540 U.S. 93 (2003).

decisions, however, in solidifying corporations' right to free political speech, on par with the right to free speech of individuals. This opinion has raised fears of a surge in corporate campaign advertising, but its main immediate result was reinforcing the doctrine and principles laid out in the Court's decision in *Buckley*. *Citizens United* and other recent cases concern independent spending. Recent court decisions have left standing and even reinforced the system of direct contributions.

In this way, campaigns address the information problems discussed at the beginning of this chapter. In mass elections, individual voters have little incentive or opportunity to find information about the many candidates and ballot measures at issue. This situation creates an opportunity for candidates and parties. Through advertising, get-out-the-vote activities, and other campaign efforts, politicians try to shape the electorate and the outcome of the election. Candidates and parties bear much of the responsibility and costs for gathering and disseminating electoral information and for creating an informed electorate. Through their campaigns, parties and candidates present voters with the information they need to make a decision come Election Day—what the candidates and parties have done and what they promise to do, who they are, and which person is right for the job and the challenges the country faces.

Elections, of course, fail to serve this important function when competition is weak or lacking all together. At times in our history, there have been prolonged outages of electoral competition. Perhaps the most infamous example took the form of Democratic dominance in the South from the 1890s through 1960s—a political arrangement termed the Solid South. During this period, election laws were employed to exclude blacks and many poor whites from primary elections, and Republicans comprised a relatively small part of the electorate. As a result, Democrats won nearly every House seat, Senate seat, and gubernatorial race in the South from the end of Reconstruction through the passage of the Voting Rights Act in 1965. In some southern states, Democrats won every state legislative seat. Electoral competition, to the extent that it existed, resided only in the Democratic primary, and then only half of all seats saw competition. Shifting political alignments in the South during the 1960s and 1970s brought a rapid rise in Republican fortunes in the South and with that the benefits of electoral competition.

Today, some observers fear that the incumbency advantage stifles electoral competition. As we noted in the previous section, incumbents enjoy a sizable electoral advantage, a bonus of roughly 10 percentage points. Some of that advantage reflects the voters' reward of the incumbents' performance in office, but some of it may also reflect an imbalance in campaign politics. That imbalance is most obvious in campaign funds. The average House challenger in 2012 raised and spent approximately $595,000; the typical incumbent raised and spent more than three times as much, approximately $1.7 million. To put matters another way, incumbents could spend roughly $2.42 per voting-age person in the district; the typical challenger could spend only $0.85 per voting-age person. Incumbents' funding advantages allow them to communicate more extensively with constituents than their opponents.

THE 2012 ELECTION

In the fall of 2012, more than 128 million Americans went to the polls to select a president, members of Congress, governors, and numerous other officials. Voters re-elected Barack Obama to the presidency and confirmed the Democratic Party's control of the Senate and the Republican Party's majority in the House of Representatives. Obama won 65 million votes, roughly 51 percent, while his Republican challenger, Mitt Romney, received about 61 million votes, or 47 percent. Though the president's margin of victory was about 5 percentage points less than in 2008, it was enough to give him 332 electoral votes, 62 more than the 270 needed to win a majority in the electoral college. The president's margin of victory was built on a coalition of women, working-class voters, and minority voters in several key battleground states. Despite the billions of dollars spent by candidates and the hoopla of the campaign, the 2012 election was decided more by demographic realities than political rhetoric.

Generally speaking, incumbent presidents have a substantial advantage when they seek re-election to a second term. During the course of American history, incumbent presidents standing for re-election have won about 70 percent of the time. Despite this advantage of incumbency, the re-election of President Obama in 2012 was never a foregone conclusion. Although Obama

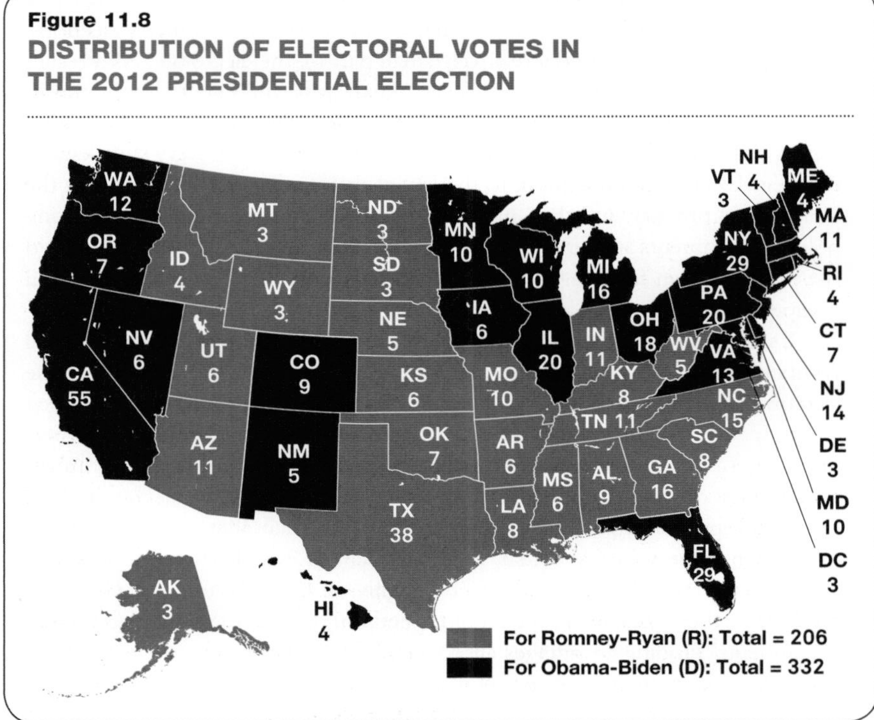

Figure 11.8
DISTRIBUTION OF ELECTORAL VOTES IN THE 2012 PRESIDENTIAL ELECTION

scored major legislative successes early in his first term, these accomplishments, especially the Affordable Care Act, were controversial. To make matters worse, unemployment remained high throughout Obama's first four years. The combination of controversial legislation and a weak economic record made the incumbent vulnerable coming into the 2012 election season.

In his 2008 campaign, Obama energized legions of young supporters who saw in the senator from Illinois a charismatic and energetic politician who would pursue a progressive social agenda and bring an end to America's wars in the Middle East. Many liberal voters had also been eager to elect America's first black president and thus make a break with the nation's long and unhappy history of racial oppression and discrimination. Once in office, Obama was keen to make good on his promise of change. He worked to bring an end to the war in Iraq and to wind down the war in Afghanistan, partly in order to shift the nation's spending priorities from the military to domestic social needs. In the realm of domestic policy, between 2008 and 2010, with both chambers of Congress controlled by the Democrats, the president succeeded in passing a $700 billion economic stimulus bill, a law that guaranteed equal pay for women, new financial regulations, and an extensive overhaul of the nation's health care laws. President Obama also appointed two women to the United States Supreme Court. The Affordable Care Act, which came to be known as "Obamacare," became a flashpoint for the 2010 and 2012 elections. The law sought to make access to health care universal: it required individuals without insurance to purchase insurance, it required businesses to provide insurance, it set up insurance pools to allow those without care to purchase inexpensive insurance, it required states to extend their Medicaid coverage, and it forbid insurance companies from excluding people from coverage for pre-existing conditions.

These successes came at a cost. The president appeared to push aggressively a liberal legislative agenda, and the opportunity for a corrective came at the 2010 midterm election. It is often the case that the president's party loses some seats in the midterm elections, but in 2010 the Democrats lost a whopping 60 seats and ceded control of the House to the Republicans. A majority of Americans opposed Obamacare. They saw it as a costly government takeover of a major industry and an unwarranted intrusion into the lives of all Americans. Many people also saw financial reform and economic stimulus as policies that would impose too much regulation or create mounting debt problems. The backlash against Obama's early legislative successes took the form of a loose but broad conservative movement called the Tea Party, whose organizations sponsored rallies and protests and recruited candidates to run for office. Against this background of dissatisfaction and dissent, Republican challengers in 2010 defeated numerous Democratic members of Congress and left the president with a Republican House of Representatives that vowed to block any new presidential initiatives. Over the next two years, the president and Congress engaged in acrimonious battles over the federal budget and the federal government's borrowing power (the debt limit) that twice brought the U.S. government to the brink of financial ruin before last-minute compromises temporarily averted disaster.

All the while, the nation's economy, which had been battered by recession in 2007 and 2008, showed only tepid signs of recovery throughout Obama's first four years in office. For much of the president's first term, unemployment remained in the uncomfortably high 8 to 9 percent range, with hundreds of thousands of recent college graduates finding themselves unemployed or underemployed; the housing market was weak; and a number of major financial institutions seemed to totter on the edge of failure. As a result, President Obama's re-election hardly seemed assured. However, the Republicans needed to find a candidate who could defeat the president and appeal to the various factions of their party.

Political Parties in 2012: Unity and Division

The American political landscape experienced a national realignment of political forces in the 1960s and 1970s, as we will discuss in Chapter 12. Over time, the Democrats became a much more liberal party and the Republicans a much more conservative political force. This ideological realignment of the two parties is one reason that partisan struggles in Congress—and between Congress and the White House when party control of the two branches is divided—have become especially intense in recent years.

The growing ideological split between the two parties has not meant that each party is ideologically uniform, however. Rather, disputes among the various liberal groups within the Democratic Party and among the disparate conservative groups in the GOP have also been quite heated. In 2012, the divisions among the Democrats were relatively inconsequential for the simple reason that the party's presidential nominee was a given. Like it or not, all the party's factions had to line up behind President Obama, or risk losing the White House altogether. The divisions in the GOP, however, did matter, and the Republican nomination battle took place among candidates representing different factions within the party. Former Massachusetts governor and successful financier Mitt Romney spoke for the party's fiscal conservatives, who feel excessive taxation and regulation are the major issues facing the country. Former Pennsylvania senator Rick Santorum and Minnesota congresswoman Michele Bachmann were the champions of the social conservatives, who seek to end abortion and prevent same-sex marriage. Former House Speaker Newt Gingrich represented neoconservatives who favor a robust military policy, and former Texas congressman Ron Paul spoke for the libertarians and isolationists. Several other candidates, who lacked significant bases of support, including business executive Herman Cain, Texas governor Rick Perry, former Utah governor and ambassador Jon Huntsman, former New Mexico governor Gary Johnson, and former Minnesota governor Tim Pawlenty, sought to stake out positions that might attract supporters if the front runners faltered.

Between May 2011 and February 2012, Republican hopefuls engaged in a series of televised debates where each argued that he or she would be best able to defeat the Democrats. The candidates were generally polite to one another and saved their criticisms for Obama and the Democrats. Gradually, candidates who found themselves unable to attract much support dropped out of the race, and by February 2012, only four remained: Gingrich, Paul, Romney, and Santorum. Over the next several months, these four candidates faced one another in a series of Republican primaries and caucuses, competing for the votes of 2,286 Republican convention delegates, with 1,144 needed to win the nomination.

From the beginning, Romney's superior organization and financial base made him the front-runner. The GOP's social and religious conservatives, though, were unenthusiastic about the former Massachusetts governor. Some saw him as a liberal in Republican clothing while others, particularly evangelical Protestants, were unhappy about the idea of a member of the Mormon faith leading the party. These groups gave their support to Rick Santorum, who eventually carried 11 states and more than 20 percent of the primary vote. By April 2012, though, Romney had clearly won the delegate votes needed for the nomination, and Santorum suspended his campaign.

Having won the Republican nomination, Romney moved to reassure the party's social conservatives that he was worthy of their enthusiastic support in the general election. One of the biggest challenges facing candidates is motivating putative supporters to actually *vote* come Election Day. Conservatives would not jump to the Obama camp, but anything less than enthusiastic participation in the campaign by social conservatives would doom the GOP's ticket. Accordingly, Romney endorsed a party platform that would appeal to this group. Its provisions included a constitutional amendment to ban abortion; elimination of government-funded family planning programs, with the exception of abstinence-only education; and a program of detention for "dangerous" aliens. Other provisions included repealing the Affordable Care Act and reducing taxes. As icing on the conservative cake, Romney chose as his vice-presidential running mate Congressman Paul Ryan of Wisconsin. Ryan had vigorously opposed Democratic fiscal and social policies and was enthusiastically supported by the GOP's social and fiscal conservatives.

The General Election

U.S. presidential elections are shaped by fundamental forces: the economy, foreign conflicts, the underlying partisanship and composition of the electorate, and the approval rating of the incumbent president. The election in 2012 proved to be no exception. But the fundamentals in 2012 pointed in conflicting directions. Barack Obama was a fairly popular incumbent who boasted significant foreign policy successes; however, he also had to defend a record of four years of slow economic growth and, in some parts of the country, economic stagnation. No president has been re-elected with an unemployment rate exceeding 8 percent, but no president with an approval rating of 50 percent has failed to win re-election. Political scientists' and economists' forecasts based on these fundamentals predicted a very tight election, with a slight edge to the president. The average of many forecasting models predicted that President Obama would win 50.3 percent of the vote, but there was considerable uncertainty associated with that forecast.

In recent years, the bedrock base of GOP support has consisted of reasonably affluent, educated, middle-aged, middle-class white men living in suburban and rural areas. The Democrats, on the other hand, have been able to rely upon the votes of a majority of women, less affluent Americans, urban residents, younger voters, African Americans, and, increasingly, Hispanic voters. While there are certainly poor Republicans and affluent Democrats, this split approaches a classic division between the "have mores" and "have lesses." Mitt Romney alluded to this division when he said, in what he thought to be a closed-door meeting with Republican donors, that 47 percent of Americans paid few taxes, depended on government handouts, and would never vote for him. When news of Romney's comments leaked, Republicans sought to contain the damage but did not necessarily dispute the accuracy of Romney's analysis.

The division of the electorate into "have mores" and "have lesses" also dictated a major struggle in the campaign. In a number of states, Republican governors and legislatures enacted voter ID laws requiring prospective voters to present valid, government-issued photo identification cards at the polls. Republicans said such laws were needed to prevent fraudulent voting. The GOP's calculus, though, was that less-educated and minority voters (who tend to vote Democratic) were less likely to be able to produce valid ID at the polls and would thus be barred from voting. Two dozen states enacted voter ID laws, and though Democrats mounted court challenges, many of these laws were in effect on Election Day.

Table 11.2A

CONGRESSIONAL ELECTION RESULTS, 1994–2012

HOUSE OF REPRESENTATIVES					
YEAR	TURNOUT	PARTY RATIO	SEAT SHIFT	DEMOCRATS RE-ELECTED	REPUBLICANS RE-ELECTED
1994	41.1%	204 D, 230 R	+54 R	89.3%	99.4%
1996	51.7	207 D, 227 R	+3 D	98.3	91.4
1998	38.1	211 D, 223 R	+4 D	99.5	97.2
2000	54.2	212 D, 222 R	+1 D	98.0	97.5
2002	39.5	205 D, 229 R	+8 R	97.4	97.5
2004	60.3	201 D, 232 R	+3 R	97.4	99.0
2006	40.2	233 D, 202 R	+30 D	100	89.6
2008	61.0	257 D, 178 R	+24 D	97.9	92.1
2010	37.8	193 D, 242 R	+64 R	78.8	98.7
2012	54	201 D, 234 R	+8 D	89	90

SOURCE: Michael McDonald, United States Election Project, http://elections.gmu.edu/2010_vote_forecasts.html (accessed 11/4/2010).

While America, of course, consists of 50 states, presidential elections are usually fought in only a handful of "battleground" states. This is so because some states are solidly Republican (sometimes called the red states) while others are solidly Democratic (known as the blue states). The states of the Deep South and mountain West, for example, are so securely in the Republican camp that Democratic presidential candidates hardly bother to campaign there. Most of the states of the Northeast and West Coast, on the other hand, are heavily committed to the Democrats and receive little attention from the GOP. In 2012 opinion polls indicated that only 8 of the 50 states were actually toss-ups. These were Colorado, Florida, Iowa, Nevada, New Hampshire, Ohio, Virginia, and Wisconsin. A handful of other states, including Michigan, Minnesota, New Mexico, and Pennsylvania were seen as leaning toward Obama, while Arizona, Indiana, and North Carolina were viewed as leaning toward Romney. The remaining 35 states seemed to be solidly in either the Democratic or the Republican camp.

Table 11.2B

(Continued)

SENATE					
YEAR	TURNOUT	PARTY RATIO	SEAT SHIFT	DEMOCRATS RE-ELECTED	REPUBLICANS RE-ELECTED
1994	41.1%	47 D, 53 R	+10 R	87.5%	80.0%
1996	51.7	45 D, 55 R	–	100	85.7
1998	38.1	45 D, 55 R	–	92.3	87.5
2000	54.2	50 D, 50 R	+5 D	93.3	64.3
2000	39.5	48 D, 51 R	+1 R	83.3	93.3
2004	60.3	44 D, 55 R	+4 R	92.9	100
2006	40.2	50 D, 49 R	+6 D	100	57.1
2008	61.0	59 D, 41 R	+8 D	100	66.7
2010	37.8	53 D, 47 R	+6 R	76.9	100
2012	54	55 D*, 45 R	+2 D	100	71

* Includes 2 Independents expected to caucus with the Democrats.

Thus, the 2012 presidential race was waged in 8 to 10 battleground states. Here the Obama and Romney campaigns and their various supporters matched each other dollar for dollar in an unprecedented amount of political advertising. All told, Team Obama and allied groups spent over $400 million on televised advertising across the United States, and Team Romney and allied groups spent almost $500 million on television advertising. Nearly all of it was concentrated in the battleground states. In places like Las Vegas, Nevada; Denver, Colorado; Columbus, Ohio; and Charlotte, North Carolina, the campaigns bought over 30,000 TV ads. In places like Los Angeles, California, and New York, New York, they bought none. While voters in many states would hardly have reason to notice the presidential contest, voters in the battleground states could hardly turn on their television sets or answer their phones without being urged to support Obama or Romney.

The Debates

The candidates faced each other in one major set of national forums: three nationally televised presidential debates along with the one vice-presidential debate. The first presidential debate, which was watched by 67 million people, was more remarkable for style than substance. In terms of substance, the candidates discussed the economy, the federal deficit, Social Security, and the Affordable Care Act, with Romney criticizing Obama's record and the president defending his accomplishments. Though both candidates made mistakes and factual errors, both seemed to possess a thorough knowledge of the details of major American domestic policies. In terms of style, however, Obama and Romney differed sharply. Governor Romney seemed alert and aggressive, making points assertively and methodically as he accused the president of increasing the nation's debt, failing to bolster the economy, and undermining the private sector in favor of government-run programs. The president, for his part, appeared disengaged and listless. In the wake of the first debate, the national polls, which had consistently shown Obama with a slim lead over his Republican opponent, now suggested that the race was neck and neck. Republicans were elated and Democrats dismayed by the debate and its results.

The president improved his performance in the next two debates and was generally judged to have been the winner, as was Vice President Biden in his confrontation with Republican vice-presidential candidate Paul Ryan. However, in the 34 states that allowed early voting in 2012, hundreds of thousands of voters had cast their ballots after the first debate but before the other debates. With the damage done, Obama had two weeks after the debates to slow his opponent's growing momentum.

Obama responded by redoubling his efforts in battleground states, with speeches and campaign commercials labeling Romney a multimillionaire who was out of touch with ordinary Americans and who sent American jobs overseas. The Obama campaign argued that Romney had favored allowing Detroit to go bankrupt, despite the potential loss of hundreds of thousands of jobs. These efforts succeeded in shoring up Obama's support among working-class Americans. According to exit polls, the president won 63 percent of the votes of those whose family incomes were less than $30,000 per year and 57 percent of those

Table 11.3

2008 AND 2012 EXIT POLLS, BY DEMOGRAPHICS

	2008			2012		
	PERCENTAGE OF VOTERS WHO WERE	PERCENTAGE OF GROUP VOTING		PERCENTAGE OF VOTERS WHO WERE	PERCENTAGE OF GROUP VOTING	
		D	R		D	R
GENDER						
Male	47	49	48	47	45	52
Female	53	56	43	53	55	44
AGE						
18–29	18	66	32	19	60	37
30–44	29	52	46	27	52	45
45–64	37	50	49	38	47	51
65+	16	45	53	16	44	56
PARTY						
Democrat	38	89	10	38	92	7
Republican	28	9	90	32	6	93
Independent or something else	34	52	44	29	45	50

(Continued)

Table 11.3
(Continued)

	2008			2012		
	PERCENTAGE OF VOTERS WHO WERE	PERCENTAGE OF GROUP VOTING		PERCENTAGE OF VOTERS WHO WERE	PERCENTAGE OF GROUP VOTING	
		D	R		D	R
RACE						
White	74	43	55	72	39	59
Black	13	95	4	13	93	6
Hispanic	9	67	31	10	71	27
Asian	2	62	35	3	73	26
INCOME						
Under $50,000	38	60	38	41	60	38
$50,000–100,000	36	49	49	31	46	52
More than $100,000	26	49	49	28	44	54

Source: "Exit Polls 2012," *The Washington Post*, www.washingtonpost.com/wp-srv/special/politics/2012-exit-polls/table.html (accessed 11/28/12).

who earned between $30,000 and $49,000 per year. Among more affluent voters, by contrast, Romney was the winner, taking 52 percent of the votes of those who earned between $50,000 and $100,000 per year and about 54 percent of the votes of those whose annual family incomes exceeded $100,000.

The Obama campaign also redoubled its efforts among women voters. In recent years, women have tended to give a majority of their votes to the Democrats, producing a so-called gender gap in the electoral arena. Democratic ads reminded women that it was the Democratic Party that supported such issues as equal pay. Foolish remarks on rape and abortion by GOP senatorial candidates in Indiana and Missouri were highlighted by the Democrats to underscore

Republican insensitivity to women. On Election Day, 55 percent of women voters supported Obama, while Obama received the votes of only 45 percent of America's men. That is a gender gap or difference of 10 percentage points (see Table 11.3). This is one of the largest gaps between men and women ever measured; it was up 3 points from 2008, and it was bad news for Romney because women comprise about 53 percent of the voters, while men comprise about 47 percent.

Finally, Obama campaign workers were determined to ensure high levels of turnout among minority voters, who potentially could be decisive in several battleground states. African American voters were a loyal Democratic constituency and could be counted upon to turn out for the president. But the Democrats had been making enormous efforts to bring Asian and, especially, Latino voters into their camp, too. Latinos are the most rapidly growing group in the American population and were responsible for about 10 percent of the votes cast in 2012. The Democratic Party had made a major effort to court Latinos on such issues as immigration and, in 2012, Democrats had pushed for ballot initiatives in a number of states that offered undocumented young Latinos who had been raised in the United States the opportunity to attend public colleges at the in-state tuition rate. This strategy proved extremely successful. Not only did Obama capture 93 percent of the African American vote, but he also won approximately 71 percent of the Latino vote across the country. While African Americans usually vote at a very high rate for Democrats, Obama had a particularly strong showing among Hispanics. Four years earlier, Obama won 67 percent of the Latino vote, and in 2004 Democrat John Kerry won only 54 percent of the Latino vote. Among whites, by contrast, Romney received 58 percent of the vote.

Taken together, working-class voters, women, and minority constituents gave Obama the votes he needed for victory. Astonishingly, President Obama carried the eight toss-up battleground states, and in each one, exit polls suggested that the critical margin was provided by low-income groups, minorities, and women.

Looking toward the Future

As they surveyed the results, Republicans consoled themselves that 2012 had not been a complete disaster. To be sure, in Senate races, Democrats increased their majority by a net gain of two, from 51 to 53 seats. In addition, two Independents promised to work with the Democrats in the Senate, effectively making the Democrats' margin 55 to 45 seats. Nevertheless, the GOP had successfully defended its bastion in the House of Representatives. In House races, the Republicans lost a net of eight seats, and maintained their majority, albeit with a somewhat smaller margin. After machine recounts in several very close elections, Republicans had won 234 seats to the Democrats 201. Republicans also picked up one gubernatorial seat, North Carolina, that had previously been held by a Democrat. (See Tables 11.2A and 11.2B.)

The 2012 House results provided a silver lining to an otherwise difficult night for Republican candidates. The loss of the presidential election and the Democrats' surprising gains in the Senate led many Republicans to question whether their party must change, reaching out to women, to Latinos and Asians, and to other groups that seem to have been driven further away from the GOP during the 2012 election. Not only did Republicans struggle to win the support of these groups, but these groups are a growing portion of the electorate. If the GOP remained merely the party of affluent white men, particularly as the U.S. population became less white, demographics would doom it to the status of a permanent minority. Thus, if it hoped to become a party capable of winning majorities in 2016 and beyond, the GOP would need to find a way to broaden its appeal to women and to racial and ethnic minorities, especially Hispanics.

CONCLUSION: ELECTIONS AND ACCOUNTABILITY

Elections should stir wonder in even the most jaded person. In an election, no one person matters much, and each person acts in apparent isolation, indeed secrecy. The individual voter's decisions reflect diverse experiences, opinions, and preferences about government and public policy. And the millions of votes cumulate into an expression of whom the majority wants to have as its representatives in state government, in Congress, and in the presidency.

The design of the institutions of American elections facilitate majority rule. Single-member districts and plurality rule create strong pressures toward a two-party system and majoritarianism. Even in elections in which one party wins a plurality but not a majority, that party typically wins an outright majority of legislative seats. The election itself, then, determines the government. Other systems often produce multiparty outcomes, resulting in a period of negotiation and coalition formation among the parties in order to determine who will govern.

The significance of elections derives not so much from the laws as from the preferences of voters. Voting behavior depends in no small part on habit and the tendency to vote for a given party as a matter of ingrained personal identity. If that were all there is to voting behavior, then it is not clear that elections would provide a meaningful way of governing. Elections would be reduced to little more than a sporting event, in which people merely rooted for their own team. Voters' preferences are as strongly rooted in the issues at hand as in the choices themselves, the candidates. Voting decisions reflect individuals' assessments about whether it makes sense to keep public policies on the same track or to change direction, whether those in office have done a good job and deserve to be re-elected, or whether they have failed and it is time for new representation. The aggregation of all voters' preferences responds collectively to fluctuations in the economy, to differences in the ideological and policy orientations of the parties, and to the personal abilities of the candidates.

For Further Reading

reader selection

Ansolabehere, Stephen, and James M. Snyder, Jr. *The End of Inequality: One Person, One Vote and the Transformation of American Politics*. New York: Norton, 2008.

Brady, David W. *Critical Elections and Congressional Policy Making.* Palo Alto, CA: Stanford University Press, 1988.

Carmines, Edward G., and James A. Stimson. *Issue Evolution: Race and the Transformation of American Politics.* Princeton, NJ: Princeton University Press, 1989.

Conway, M. Margaret. *Political Participation in the United States.* 3rd ed. Washington, DC: CQ Press, 2000.

Fowler, Linda L. *Candidates, Congress, and the American Democracy.* Ann Arbor: University of Michigan Press, 1994.

Gelman, Andrew, et al. *Red State, Blue State, Rich State, Poor State: Why Americans Vote the Way They Do.* Princeton, NJ: Princeton University Press, 2008.

Ginsberg, Benjamin, and Martin Shefter. *Politics by Other Means: Politicians, Prosecutors, and the Press from Watergate to Whitewater.* 3rd ed. New York: Norton, 2002.

Green, Donald, and Alan Gerber. *Get Out the Vote: How to Increase Voter Turnout.* Washington, DC: Brookings Institution, 2004.

Jacobson, Gary. *The Politics of Congressional Elections,* 7th Edition. White Plains, NY: Longman, 2009.

McCarty, Nolan, Keith Poole, and Howard Rosenthal. *Polarized America: The Dance of Ideology and Unequal Riches.* Cambridge, MA: MIT Press, 2006.

Morton, Rebecca B. *Analyzing Elections.* New York: Norton, 2006.

Reichley, A. James, ed. *Elections American Style.* Washington, DC: Brookings Institution, 1987.

Rosenstone, Steven, and John Mark Hansen. *Participation, Mobilization, and Democracy in America.* New York: Macmillan, 1993. **reader selection**

Witt, Linda, Karen M. Paget, and Glenna Matthews. *Running as a Woman: Gender and Power in American Politics.* New York: Free Press, 1994.

Visit **wwnorton.com/studyspace/** to access free review materials such as:

- Vocabulary Flashcards of All Key Terms
- Chapter Review Quizzes
- Complete Study Outlines

reader selection

Highlighted selections are included in *Readings in American Politics: Analysis and Perspectives*, Second Edition.

12

PART 1 2 X 4

DEMOCRATIC POLITICS

Political Parties

Chapter Outline

- Why Do Political Parties Form?
- What Functions Do Parties Perform?
- Parties and the Electorate
- Parties as Institutions
- Party Systems

Political parties are defined as teams of politicians, activists, and voters whose goal is to win control of government. They do so by recruiting and nominating candidates to run for office; by accumulating the resources needed to run political campaigns, especially manpower and money; and by pursuing a policy agenda that can appeal to large numbers of voters and secure electoral majorities. As we saw in Chapter 6, once in office, parties organize the legislature and attempt to put their stamp on the laws passed by Congress and the president. Their potential political power is immense.

The prospect of "party rule" has long made Americans suspicious of these organizations. Indeed, the separation of powers into different branches was meant to blunt any attempts by a "faction" or party to gain control of government, as might more readily occur in a parliament.[1] Divided government, in which one party controls the presidency and the other has a majority in at least one chamber of the legislature, has been the norm in American national and state politics, especially over the past 50 years. In some elections, as in 1980, one party wins a landslide victory for the presidency but still fails to capture control of Congress. And, in some midterm elections, as in 1994, 2006, and 2010, the public decides to give control of Congress to the party opposing the president in order to rein in the executive. Our political system intentionally makes it difficult for any party or organized interest to gain complete control of American government, and when one does, unified government is often short lived. Separation of powers and divided government have not, however, put the parties out of business. Quite the contrary.

The Democratic and Republican parties remain essential to the day-to-day operation of the legislature and the conduct of elections. It is difficult to imagine

1 James Madison famously made this argument in *Federalist* 51 during the campaign to ratify the Constitution of the United States.

how candidates would emerge and how individuals would vote without political parties to organize the electoral system. Our inability to conceive of democracy without parties is not a failure of our imaginations or an accident of American history. Rather, it reflects a law of democratic politics. Parties form to solve key problems of rationality and collective action in a democracy. They are not unlike businesses providing a service that consumers need. Parties offer clear choices to voters, lowering the costs of collecting information about the candidates and making it easier for voters to hold government accountable. Parties also ease the transition from elections to government. They bear the costs of bringing together representatives of disparate constituencies into coherent coalitions that can act collectively in government. Thus, parties link elections to governing. Throughout this chapter we highlight some of the general functions of parties in any democracy, but we are especially attentive to party politics in the United States.

The simplest observation about American parties is also perhaps the most important: the United States has just two major parties, the Democrats and the

CORE OF THE ANALYSIS

Political parties are teams of politicians, activists, and interest groups organized to win control of government.

The United States has a two-party system, in which Democrats and Republicans compete for most offices. This two-party system is a consequence of the form of government (presidential-congressional as opposed to parliamentary) and election laws, especially the use of single-member legislative districts.

Parties offer distinctive views about how government ought to operate and what laws ought to be enacted and policies implemented, and they often serve distinct interests and communities.

Parties help solve an important informational problem for voters. By offering distinctive "brands," the parties simplify the choices that voters must make and reduce the costs of gathering information about how to vote.

The legislative and executive branches of the U.S. government are organized by the parties, with the party that won a majority of seats controlling most of the key positions and levers of power, especially congressional committees, the congressional agenda, and the appointment of agency heads.

Republicans. The American two-party system is impressive in its durability and flexibility. Sustained third parties have not been able to compete with the Democrats and Republicans since the 1850s. The Democratic and Republican parties have, for the past 150 years, elected every president and nearly every member of Congress and governor and state legislator in the United States. Occasionally, a governor or legislator decides to run as a third-party candidate, but those independent candidacies usually fail unless the person eventually attaches him- or herself to one of the parties. When a faction breaks from one of the parties, as occurred with the Progressive Republicans in the 1920s and the Southern Democrats in 1948 and again in 1968, those factions eventually return to the fold or move into the other party. The parties have shifted their regional bases of support, with Democrats moving from a southern base to a northern one and the Republicans' base moving from the Northeast and Midwest increasingly to the South. And the two major parties have adapted to radical changes in the ideologies and social structure of American society.

The institutions of a two-party system, combined with majority rule, mean that the choice between the parties translates into the choice of government. Whichever party wins a majority of seats in House or Senate elections wins control of that chamber. Whichever party wins a majority of electoral votes wins the presidency. At election time, we choose between those who are in power and those who would like to be; those who are on the side of the president or the ruling coalition in the legislature, and those opposed to them. Choosing to change the government means voting against the party that currently holds the presidency and Congress.

In contrast, most parliamentary systems, especially those who allocate seats to parties based on the proportion of votes won nationwide, have more than two parties. In such systems, no party regularly wins a majority, and governments consist of coalitions of several parties. It is difficult to anticipate which coalitions might form, and it is hard to assign blame to any one party in a coalition government. There is a great simplicity in having a two-party system.

The Democratic and Republican parties have proved remarkably adept at accommodating diverse sets of interests and ideas while still presenting distinctive visions for governing. They each capture a range of ideological views while keeping successful third parties at bay. This situation arises in large measure because of the electoral and governmental institutions of the United States and the strategic skills of the party leaders. The opportunity for a third party to enter the races and win large numbers of congressional seats or the presidency is very limited.

The French political scientist Maurice Duverger laid out the reason for this state of affairs in his classic book *Political Parties*. Duvenger relied on both the institution principle and the rationality principle. As we discussed briefly in Chapter 11, any third-party movement that attempts to enter the American party system would likely fail to win, or worse, improve the electoral fortunes of the party it most opposes. Also, any voter would not want to waste votes on a losing cause. Hence, the number of successful parties is two.

U.S. government institutions and electoral rules create strong pressures to maintain just two parties, distinctive in their plans for governing but expansive in the interests and ideas that they encompass. This simplifies politics inside governing institutions, because one party will have a majority and control that institution (the presidency or one or both chambers of Congress). It also simplifies vote choice, because voters can readily sort into one of the two major party camps or use the party labels to figure out the most effective way to vote.

Parties, however, are not benevolent. They don't solve these problems simply to make democracy work. Those in the party recognize that these problems represent opportunities to secure elected office, to influence public policy, even to make a profit. For the politicians inside these organizations, the parties provide a clear path to office through the nominating system and to power through the party organization. For its activists, the party is a potential way to pull the policies of government in a direction more favorable to the party's views. For interest groups that sustain the parties, the parties offer the potential benefits of being closer to power and influencing what government does. At times, the influence of activists, party leaders, organized interests, and local bosses becomes too great. Regulations on campaign contributions and government contracting, sunshine laws and federal advisory rules, even civil-service reforms have all come about through efforts to prevent party bosses and interest groups from taking advantage of their power. Party organizations have been weakened by these reforms, but they have invariably found new resources to draw on. As a result, American history has witnessed eras of very strong party organization and periods of relative party weakness.

Today, American politics is characterized by relatively strong party organizations and disciplined legislative parties. They offer the American voter meaningful electoral choices and a simple strategy for changing the direction of government.

WHY DO POLITICAL PARTIES FORM?

Political parties, like interest groups, are organizations seeking influence over government. Ordinarily, they can be distinguished from interest groups on the basis of their orientation. A party seeks to control the entire government by electing its members to office, thereby controlling the government's personnel. Interest groups, through campaign contributions and other forms of electoral assistance, are also concerned with electing politicians—in particular, those who are inclined in their policy direction. But interest groups ordinarily do not sponsor candidates directly, and between elections they usually accept government and its personnel as givens and try to influence government policies through them. They are benefit seekers, whereas parties are composed mainly of office seekers.[2]

political party

An organized group that attempts to influence government by electing its members to office

Political parties organize because of three problems with which politicians and other political activists must cope. The first is the problem of collective action. This is chiefly an outgrowth of elections in which a candidate for office

2 This distinction is from John H. Aldrich, *Why Parties? The Origin and Transformation of Party Politics in America* (Chicago: University of Chicago Press, 1995).

must attract campaign funds, assemble a group of activists and workers, mobilize prospective voters, and persuade them to vote for him or her. Collective action is also a problem inside government, where kindred spirits in a legislature must arrange for, and then engage in, cooperation. The second problem for which parties are sometimes the solution is that of collective choice of policy.[3] The give-and-take within a legislature and between the legislature and the executive can make or break policy success and subsequent electoral success. The third problem follows from the fact that fellow politicians, like members of any organization, seek success simultaneously for the organization and for themselves. This problem of ambition can undermine the collective aspirations of fellow partisans unless astutely managed. We briefly examine each of these problems below.

To Facilitate Collective Action in the Electoral Process

Political parties as we know them today developed along with the expansion of suffrage and can be understood only in the context of elections. Parties and elections are so intertwined that American parties actually take their structure from the electoral process. The shape of party organization in the United States has followed a simple rule: for every district where an election is held, there should be some kind of party unit. These units provide the brand name, the resources (both human and financial), the "buzz," and the link to the larger national organization, which all help the party's candidates arouse interest in their candidacy, stimulate commitment, and ultimately overcome the free riding that diminishes turnout in general elections.

Party organization also enables and encourages electoral competition by groups. The Republican Party has long been the party of business interests (among other groups), especially small business and peak associations (organizations of organizations) such as the Chamber of Commerce and the National Association of Manufacturers. Since the 1930s, women have gravitated to the Democratic Party. Often, groups with significant numbers but lacking substantial economic and institutional resources find their voice in the party system. Women's organizations worked closely with the Progressive faction inside the Republican Party in the 1900s and 1910s in the struggle to gain the right to vote for women. By the 1970s, changing social issues and changed strategies by the parties led many newer womens' groups, such as the National Organization of Women, to align with the Democratic Party. Throughout American history, immigrant

3 A slight variation on this theme is emphasized by Gary W. Cox and Mathew D. McCubbins in *Legislative Leviathan: Party Government in the House* (Berkeley: University of California Press, 1993). They suggest that parties in the legislature are electoral machines whose purpose is to preserve and enhance party reputation, thereby giving meaning to the party labels when elections are contested. By keeping order within their ranks, parties make certain that individual actions by members do not discredit the party label. This is an especially challenging task for party leaders when there is diversity within each party, as has often been the case in American political history.

groups have aligned themselves with the parties. Irish immigrants attached themselves to the Democrats, whose urban political organizations helped those immigrants find jobs and negotiate the immigration system; Italian immigrants tended toward Republicans; most Hispanic groups have gravitated to the Democrats because of the party's immigration policies; and Cubans aligned with the Republicans because that party took a harder line against the Castro regime. In the 1970s, disaffection with liberal policies concerning school prayer, funding of religious schools, abortion, and other social issues led fundamentalist church leaders to align with the Republican Party. Fundamentalist and born-again Christians became an essential and enduring part of the Republican electoral coalition that Ronald Reagan constructed leading up to the 1980 election.

The relationship between collective action by groups and party electoral strategy is clearly a two-way street. Groups that align with a party provide that party with essential electoral resources, including a reliable voting bloc, money, personnel, and even candidates. When the party they support wins, these interests gain influence over public policy. Of course there are risks as well. An organized interest may suffer if the party it supports loses the election.

To Resolve Problems of Collective Choice in Government

Political parties are also essential elements in the process of making policy. Within the government, parties are coalitions of individuals with shared or overlapping interests who, as a rule, will support each other's programs and initiatives. Even though there may be areas of disagreement within each party, a common party label in and of itself gives party members a reason to cooperate. Because they are permanent coalitions, parties greatly facilitate the policy-making process. If alliances had to be formed from scratch for each legislative proposal, the business of government would slow to a crawl or halt altogether. Parties create a basis for coalition and thus sharply reduce the time, energy, and effort needed to advance a legislative proposal. For example, in January 1998, when President Bill Clinton considered a series of new policy initiatives, he met first with the House and Senate leaders of the Democratic Party. Although some congressional Democrats disagreed with the president's approach to a number of issues, all felt they had a stake in cooperating with Clinton in order to burnish the party's image in preparation for the next round of national elections. Without the support of a party, the president would be compelled to undertake the daunting and probably impossible task of forming a completely new coalition for every policy proposal—a virtually impossible task.

Sometimes party cohesion breaks down because of fundamental conflict between the public philosophy of the party and the need for action on a crucial issue. In September 2008, facing a collapse of the financial industry, President George W. Bush proposed a $700 billion intervention to unlock frozen credit markets. The government needed to act quickly. Democratic leaders in the House twisted enough arms to produce a sizable majority of Democratic votes in favor of the Republican president's plan. The competing presidential nominees, Barack Obama and John McCain, called for colleagues in their respective parties to back the bill. But Republican leadership in the House failed to produce enough Republican votes to pass the measure. Those voting against the bill argued that the plan would increase the size of government, that it rewarded irresponsible investors, and that it violated the free-market principles that lie at the heart of the Republican policy agenda. The failure of the president and his party to come to agreement on this plan in advance doomed the president's proposal. The following day the Dow Jones Industrial Index dropped 777 points, losing almost one-tenth of its value.[4]

To Deal with the Problem of Ambition

Parties are important vehicles that enable individual politicians to achieve their ambitions. The very "brand names" they provide are often a significant electoral asset. Moreover, once their candidates are elected, parties provide these politicians, who share principles, causes, and constituencies, with a basis for coordination, common cause, cooperation, and joint enterprise. But individual ambition, sometimes in the background but often in the foreground, constantly threatens to undermine any bases for cooperation. Political parties, by regulating career advancement, providing for the orderly resolution of ambitious competition, and attending to the post-career care of elected and appointed party officials, do much to rescue coordination and cooperation and permit fellow partisans to pursue common causes where feasible. Simple devices such as primaries, for example, provide a context in which clashing electoral ambitions can be resolved. Representative partisan bodies, like the Democratic Committee on Committees in the House (with comparable bodies for the Republicans and for both parties in the Senate), resolve competing claims for power positions. In short, politics consists not of foot soldiers walking in lockstep but, rather, of ambitious and autonomous individuals seeking power. The unchecked and unregulated burnishing of individual careers is a formula for chaos and destructive competition in which the dividends of cooperation are rarely reaped. Political parties constitute organizations of relatively kindred spirits who try to capture some of those dividends by providing a structure in which ambition is not suppressed altogether but is not so destructive either.

WHAT FUNCTIONS DO PARTIES PERFORM?

Parties are mainly involved in nominations and elections—providing the candidates for office, getting out the vote, and facilitating mass electoral choice. That is, they help solve the problems of collective action and ambition to which we

4 Carl Hulse and David M. Herszenhorn, "Defiant House Rejects Huge Bailout; Next Step Is Uncertain," *New York Times*, September 29, 2008, www.nytimes.com/2008/09/30/business/30cong.html (accessed 4/3/09).

alluded earlier. They also influence the institutions of government—providing leadership as well as organization of the various congressional committees and activities on the floor in each chamber. That is, they help solve the problem of collective choice concerning institutional arrangements and policy formulation that we also noted earlier.

Recruiting Candidates

One of the most important but least noticed party activities is the recruitment of candidates for local, state, and national office. Each election year, candidates must be found for thousands of state and local offices as well as for congressional seats. Where an incumbent is not running for re-election, party leaders attempt to identify strong candidates and interest them in entering the campaign. One reason for the great success of the Democrats in the 2006 midterm elections was the heightened role played by their campaign committees in the House and Senate and, especially, the active recruitment of new candidates by the chairs of the Democratic congressional and senatorial campaign committees.[5] The Democrats were able to recruit well-qualified candidates and to provide them with campaign resources. In 2010, the Republicans worked to emulate the Democratic example.

An ideal candidate will have an unblemished record and the capacity to raise enough money to mount a serious campaign. Party leaders are usually not willing to provide financial backing to candidates who are unable to raise substantial funds on their own. For a House seat, this can mean several hundred thousand dollars; for a Senate seat, a serious candidate must be able to raise several million dollars. Often party leaders have difficulty finding attractive candidates and persuading them to run. In recent years, party leaders in several states have reported that many potential congressional candidates declined the opportunity to run for office, saying they were reluctant to leave their homes and families for the hectic life of a member of Congress. Candidate recruitment has become particularly difficult in an era when political campaigns often involve mudslinging and candidates must assume that their personal lives will be intensely scrutinized in the press.[6]

Nominating Candidates

Article I, Section 4, of the Constitution makes only a few provisions for elections. It delegates to the states the power to set the "Times, Places and Manner of holding Elections," even those for U.S. senators and representatives. It

---

5 See Adam Nagourney, "Eyeing '08: Democrats Nurse Freshmen at Risk," *New York Times*, December 22, 2006.

6 For an excellent analysis of the parties' role in recruitment, see Paul S. Herrnson, *Congressional Elections: Campaigning at Home and in Washington* (Washington, DC: Congressional Quarterly Press, 1995).

does, however, reserve to Congress the power to make such laws if it chooses to do so. The Constitution has been amended from time to time to expand the right to participate in elections. Congress has also occasionally passed laws regulating elections, congressional districting, and campaign practices. But the Constitution and the laws are almost completely silent on nominations, setting only citizenship and age requirements for candidates. The president must be at least thirty-five years of age, a natural-born citizen, and a resident of the United States for 14 years. A senator must be at least thirty, a U.S. citizen for at least nine years, and a resident of the state he or she represents. A member of the House must be at least twenty-five, a U.S. citizen for seven years, and a resident of the state he or she represents.

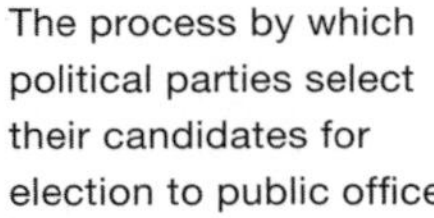

nomination

The process by which political parties select their candidates for election to public office

Nomination is the process by which a party selects a single candidate to run for each elective office. Nomination is the parties' most serious and difficult business. The nominating process can precede the election by many months (Figure 12.1), as it does when the many candidates for the presidency are eliminated from consideration through a grueling series of debates and state primaries until there is only one survivor in each party—that party's nominee.

Nomination by Convention. A nominating convention is a formal caucus bound by a number of rules that govern participation and nominating procedures. Conventions are meetings of delegates elected by party members from the relevant county (a county convention) or state (a state convention). Delegates to each party's national convention (which nominates the party's presidential candidate) are chosen by party members on a state-by-state basis; there is no single national delegate selection process.

Nomination by Primary Election. In primary elections, party members select the party's nominees directly rather than selecting convention delegates who then select the nominees. Primaries are far from perfect replacements for conventions because it is rare that more than 25 percent of the enrolled voters participate. Nevertheless, they have replaced conventions as the dominant method of nomination.[7] At the present time, only a small number of states, including Connecticut, Delaware, and Utah, provide for state conventions to nominate candidates for statewide offices, and even those states also use primaries whenever a substantial minority of delegates has voted for one of the defeated aspirants.

Generally speaking, candidates chosen in primary elections tend to be more aggressive and more ambitious individuals, whereas those selected by party conventions are more likely to have mastered the arts of compromise and collegiality. The shift from party conventions to primary elections for the nomination of presidential candidates is one reason contemporary presidents tend to be more ambitious and, indeed, more driven than their nineteenth-century predecessors.

7 For a discussion of some of the effects of primary elections, see Peter F. Galderisi and Benjamin Ginsberg, "Primary Elections and the Evanescence of Third Party Activity in the United States," in *Do Elections Matter?* Benjamin Ginsberg and Alan Stone, eds. (Armonk, NY: Sharpe, 1986), pp. 115–30.

Figure 12.1
TYPES OF NOMINATING PROCESSES

TRADITIONAL ROUTE	PRIMARY ROUTE	INDEPENDENT ROUTE
Declaration for party's support: informal designation is the result of a following among committee members and delegates.	Formal designation: petition is filed, with a minimum number of signatures, as provided by law.	Self-declaration or support by small "independent" party.
↑	↑	↑
Convention or caucus: Delegates vote for candidates or party.	Primary election: Enrolled voters choose by secret ballot among two or more designated candidates.	Petition is filed, with a minimum number of signatures, as provided by law.
↑	↑	↑
Results are reported to county board of elections and the secretary of state. Ballots are printed and election is administered at government expense.		

Party conventions tend to choose candidates who can get along, whereas primary elections tend to favor politicians with the energy and enterprise to mount a public campaign.[8] Thus there is a "selection" effect that results from the particular institutional arrangement a state employs. Institutions matter in this case because they encourage or discourage particular types of candidates, as the institution principle suggests.

Primary elections fall mainly into two categories—closed and open. In a closed primary, participation is limited to individuals who have previously declared their affiliation by registering with the party. In an open primary, individuals declare their party affiliation on the day of the primary election. To do so, they simply go to the polling place and ask for the ballot of a particular party. The open primary allows each voter to consider candidates and issues before deciding whether to participate and in which party's contest to participate. Open primaries, therefore, are less conducive to strong political parties. But in either case, primaries are more open than conventions or caucuses to new issues and new types of candidates.

 **closed primary**

A primary election in which voters can participate in the nomination of only those candidates of the party in which they have been enrolled for a period of time before primary day

 **open primary**

A primary election in which voters can choose on the day of the primary which party to enroll in to select candidates for the general election

8 Matthew Crenson and Benjamin Ginsberg, *Presidential Power: Unchecked and Unbalanced* (New York: Norton, 2007).

Getting Out the Vote

The election period begins immediately after the nominations. Historically, this has been a time of glory for the political parties, whose popular base of support is fully displayed. All the paraphernalia of party committees and all the committee members are activated in the form of local party workforces.

The first step in the electoral process involves voter registration. This aspect of the process takes place all year round. There was a time when party workers were responsible for virtually all of this kind of electoral activity, but they have been supplemented (and in many states virtually displaced) by civic groups such as the League of Women Voters, unions, and chambers of commerce.

Those who have registered have to decide on Election Day whether to go to the polling place, stand in line, and vote for the various candidates and referendums on the ballot. Political parties, candidates, and campaigning can make a big difference in persuading eligible voters to vote. Because it is costly for voters to participate in elections and because many of the benefits that winning parties bestow are public goods (that is, parties cannot exclude any individual from enjoying them), people will often free ride by enjoying the benefits without incurring the costs of electing the party that provided the benefits. This is the free-rider problem (see Chapter 1), and parties are important because they help overcome it by mobilizing the voters to support the candidates.

In recent years, not-for-profit groups such as America Votes, MoveOn, and Rock the Vote have registered and mobilized large numbers of people to vote and raised millions of dollars to devote to election organizing and advertising. These groups have legions of workers, often volunteers, and have proved especially effective at using new technologies like e-mail and social media to build networks of supporters and communicate through those networks. They are the "netroots" organizations of politics. To comply with federal election and tax law, these groups must maintain their independence from the political parties, although they have the same objectives as the parties and work very hard to elect politicians from the party they support. Such organizations act as shadow appendages of the two parties, with some groups mobilizing Democratic supporters and others mobilizing Republicans. They have proved vitally important in every campaign since 2004.

Facilitating Mass Electoral Choice

Parties make the electoral choice much easier. It is often argued that we should vote for the best person regardless of party affiliation. But on any general-election ballot, there are likely to be only two or three candidacies for which the characteristics and policy positions of the candidates are well-known to the voters. Without party labels, voters would be constantly confronted by a bewildering array of new faces and new choices and might have considerable difficulty making informed decisions. Without a doubt, their own party identifications and candidates' party affiliations help voters make reasonable choices.

Parties lower the information costs of participating by providing a recognizable "brand name." Without knowing a great deal about a candidate for office, voters can infer from party labels how the candidate will likely behave once elected. Individuals know about the parties through their past experience with those parties in state and federal office and from the actions of prominent political leaders from both parties. In the United States, the Democratic Party is associated with a commitment to more extensive government regulation of the economy and a larger public sector; the Republican Party favors a limited government role in the economy and reduced government spending paired with tax reductions. The Democrats favor aggressive protection of civil rights and a secular approach to religion in public life. The Republicans want to ban abortion and favor government participation in expanding the role of religious organizations in civil society. The parties' positions on the economy were cemented in the 1930s, and their division over civil society emerged during the 1960s and 1970s. The Democratic positions are loosely labeled liberal and those of the Republicans conservative.

Most Americans personally identify with one of the two parties. When asked in surveys whether they think of themselves as Democrats, as Republicans, or neither, large majorities pick one of the two major parties. When voting, those who identify with a party are extremely likely to vote with that party (usually about 90 percent of the time). For these individuals, party simplifies the electoral decision. Except in rare circumstances, they vote with their team.

Even those who do not identify with one of the major parties derive value from the party labels. Nonpartisan voters are more conflicted about which party or candidate best represents their interests and ideals. But it would be the height of folly to try to learn about every politician running for every office. A voter would spend an enormous amount of time tracking down the information about dozens of different people. And if the entire electorate behaved this way, the advertising costs to politicians would be tremendous.

Party labels simplify the decision making of nonpartisan voters by reducing the choice to an evaluation of two competing policy positions or of the evaluation of the performance of those in office. The independent voter may ask, which of the two parties will better represent my ideals and interests? The voter will choose the party that offers the best option today. Or the voter may ask, am I better off now than four years ago? If not, he or she will vote against the president's party up and down the ballot. If yes, he or she will vote to keep the president and his party in power. Whichever strategy the independent voter uses, parties are essential for simplifying what is otherwise a bewildering choice.

For all voters, partisans and independents alike, the parties make it easier to hold government accountable. People can vote against the party in power in bad times and for the party in power in good times. They can vote against the party in power if that party enacts very unpopular or irresponsible legislation. Thus political parties solve one of the most important collective action problems facing American democracy, the problem of collective responsibility. If every politician ran on his or her own, without regard to other candidates or districts or what was happening in the nation at large, each race for legislator or executive would become an isolated event. In such a setting it would be exceedingly difficult for voters to send a message to the government that they want government to go in a different direction. Parties, then, lend coherence to government and meaning to elections.[9]

The content of the labels is sustained because like-minded people sort themselves into the respective organizations. People who broadly share the principles espoused by a party and who wish to participate on a high level in politics will attend party meetings, run for leadership positions in local and state party organizations, attend state and national conventions, and even run for elected office. Surveys of those who attend national conventions as delegates and of candidates for the U.S. House find that Democratic candidates' personal views on the economy and social issues are quite liberal and that Republican candidates hold very conservative personal views on these matters.[10] Each party, then, draws on a distinct pool for activists and candidates. Each successive election reinforces the existing division between the parties.

Influencing National Government

The ultimate test of the party system is its relationship to and influence on the institutions of government and the policy-making process. Thus it is important to examine the party system in relation to Congress and the president.

Parties and Policy. One of the most familiar observations about American politics is that the two major parties are "big tents." They position themselves to bring in as many groups and ideas as possible. The parties make such broad coalitions as a matter of strategy, much as businesses purchase other companies to expand their market share. Positioning themselves as broad coalitions prevents effective national third parties from emerging and guarantees that the Democrats and Republicans vie for control of Congress.

The coalitions that come together in the Democratic and Republican parties shape the parties' platforms on public policy. The political coalitions that party leaders assemble determine what interests and social groups align with the parties and also what sorts of issues can emerge. The Democratic Party today embraces a philosophy of active government intervention in the economy, based on the premise that regulation is necessary to ensure orderly economic growth, to prevent the emergence of monopolies, and to address certain costs of economic activity, such as pollution. In addition, the Democratic Party pushes for aggressive expansion and protection of civil rights, especially for women and racial minorities. The Republican Party espouses a philosophy of laissez-faire economics and a minimal government role in the economy. The coalition that Ronald Reagan built in the late 1970s paired this vision of

9 Morris Fiorina, "The Decline of Collective Responsibility in American Politics," *Daedalus* 109, no. 3 (Summer 1980): 25–45.

10 Comprehensive studies of delegates were conducted by Walter J. Stone and Ronald B. Rapoport from 1980 through 1996. See Ronald B. Rapoport and Walter J. Stone, *Three's A Crowd: The Dynamic of Third Parties, Ross Perot, and Republican Resurgence* (Ann Arbor: University of Michigan Press, 1999). Surveys of candidates find similar sorting.

limited government intervention in the economy with an expanded role for religion in society and strong opposition to immigration, affirmative action, and abortion.

To many European observers, the American parties appear as odd amalgams of contradictory ideas. Liberalism, as it developed as a political philosophy in Europe, naturally pairs laissez-faire economics with liberal views on civil rights. Conservatism, which maintains a respect for social and political order, would speak for a stronger role for social organizations in society, especially religions; a greater respect for existing social hierarchies, most notably social classes and higher-educated elites; and government power in the economy. The American parties, partly because of their histories, have scrambled these traditional views and developed their own political philosophies. In the Republican Party today, laissez-faire economics goes hand in hand with conservative views on civil rights and religion in society. In the Democratic Party today, liberal views on civil rights are tied to an expansive view of government in the economy. The American parties have mixed and matched different ideas as new issues have emerged and as leaders within the parties have seized opportunities. The New Deal coalition that President Franklin Delano Roosevelt assembled consisted of Progressive Republicans, who favored greater economic regulation; old-line Democrats, especially in the South; and urban political machines in northern and Midwestern cities. This peculiar coalition gave rise to the political philosophy and public policies pursued under the New Deal. It also constrained what Roosevelt could do on some issues. Most important, he could not push for expanding civil rights for blacks without losing the support of southerners. The meaning of Democratic liberalism in the United States, then, was very much a function of the history of the parties.

Even though American liberalism and conservatism do not coincide neatly with their European counterparts, they still represent distinct views about how government ought to act, and they appeal to distinctly different core constituencies. The Democratic Party at the national level seeks to unite organized labor, the poor, members of racial minorities, and liberal upper-middle-class professionals. The Republicans, by contrast, appeal to business, upper-middle- and upper-class groups in the private sector, and social conservatives. Often party leaders will seek to develop issues that they hope will add new groups to their party's constituent base. During the 1980s, for example, under the leadership of President Reagan, the Republicans devised a series of "social issues," including support for school prayer, opposition to abortion, and opposition to affirmative action, designed to cultivate the support of white southerners. This effort was extremely successful in increasing Republican strength in the once solidly Democratic South. In the 1990s, under the leadership of President Clinton, who called himself a "new Democrat," the Democratic Party sought to develop social programs designed to solidify the party's base among working-class and poor voters and somewhat conservative economic programs aimed at attracting the votes of middle- and upper-middle-class voters.

As these examples suggest, parties do not always support policies because they are favored by their constituents. Instead, party leaders can play the role of policy entrepreneurs, seeking ideas and programs that will expand their party's base of support while eroding that of the opposition. In recent years, for example, leaders of both major political parties have sought to develop ideas and programs they hoped would appeal to America's most rapidly growing electoral bloc: Latino voters. Thus President George W. Bush recommended a number of proposals designed to help Latinos secure U.S. residence and employment. Democrats, for their part, have proposed education and social service programs designed to appeal to the needs of Latino immigrants. Both parties promoted their ideas extensively within the Latino community in the 2004 presidential campaign, and although the Democrats won more Latino votes in 2004, each party claimed to be satisfied with its long-term strategy for building Latino support. The 2006 election campaign, however, produced much more one-sided results. A hard-line view on immigration, especially from Latin America, put Republicans at a competitive disadvantage. Democratic support among Latinos rose dramatically in the midterm elections, and several prominent Republican incumbents in the Southwest lost their seats as a result. The 2008 and 2012 elections saw a continuation of this pattern. Exit polls revealed that Democrats won 66 percent and 71 percent of the Hispanic vote, respectively, a huge swing from 2004, and Hispanics continued their steady rise as a percentage of all voters. In 2000, one out of five voters was Hispanic or black; in 2012, one out of four voters was Hispanic or black. It is one of the essential characteristics of party politics in America that a party's programs and policies often lead, rather than follow, public opinion. Like their counterparts in the business world, party leaders seek to identify and develop "products" (programs and policies) that will appeal to the public. The public, of course, has the ultimate voice. With its votes, it decides whether or not to "buy" the new policy offerings.

Through members elected to office, both parties have made efforts to translate their general goals into concrete policies. Republicans, for example, implemented tax cuts, increased defense spending, cut social spending, and enacted restrictions on abortion during the 1980s and 1990s. Democrats were able to defend consumer and environmental programs against Republican attacks and sought to expand domestic social programs in the late 1990s. During his two terms in office, President George W. Bush sought substantial cuts in federal taxes, "privatization" of the Social Security system, and a larger role for Republican-allied faith-based organizations in the administration of federal social programs. In the context of the nation's campaign against terrorism, Bush sought to shift America's defense posture from an emphasis on deterrence to a doctrine of preemptive strikes against perceived threats.

The Parties and Congress. The two major political parties have a profound influence on the organization and day-to-day operation of Congress. The speaker of the House, perhaps the most powerful person in Congress, is essentially a party office. All the members of the House take part in the election of the Speaker, but the actual selection is made by the majority party. When the majority party caucus presents a nominee to the entire House, its choice is invariably ratified in a straight party-line vote.

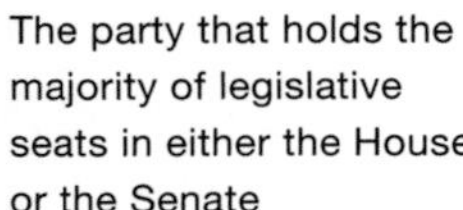

majority party

The party that holds the majority of legislative seats in either the House or the Senate

The committee system of both houses of Congress is also organized by the parties. Although the rules organizing committees and the rules defining the jurisdiction of each committee are adopted like ordinary legislation by the whole membership, all other features of the committees are shaped by the party leadership and caucuses. For example, each party is assigned a quota of members for each committee, depending on the percentage of total seats held by the party. On the rare occasions when an independent or third-party candidate is elected, the leaders of the two parties must agree against whose quota this member's committee assignments will count. Presumably, the member will not be able to serve on any committee until the question of quota is settled.[11] As we saw in Chapter 6, the assignment of individual members to congressional committees is a party decision. Each party has a committee on committees to make such decisions. Whether to grant permission to transfer to another committee is also a party decision. Moreover, who advances up the committee ladder toward the chair is a party decision. Since the late nineteenth century, most advancements have been automatic, based on the length of continuous service on the committee. This seniority system has survived only because of the support of the two parties, and each party can depart from it by a simple vote. During the 1970s, both parties reinstituted the practice of reviewing each chairmanship, voting anew every two years on whether each chair would be continued. In 2001, Republicans lived up to their 1995 pledge to limit House committee chairs to three terms. Existing chairs were forced to step down but were generally replaced by the next most senior Republican member of each committee. (Even after they were reduced to minority status in the 2006 elections, Republicans stuck to this policy. Republican chairs in the 109th Congress who had served three terms were not permitted to serve as ranking minority member in the 110th Congress.)

President and Party. The presidency is, in many ways, the focal point of the party system in the United States. As we saw earlier, the president carries the mantle of leader of his or her party, and the electoral fortunes of the parties rise and fall with the success of the president. During midterm congressional elections, when the president is not on the ballot, voters hold the president's party accountable for current problems. When the economy does poorly, Americans will punish the party of the president, even when the opposing party controls Congress.

The president of the United States also relies heavily on fellow party members in organizing the executive and passing legislation. Unlike parliamentary governments, such as in the United Kingdom, the heads of executive departments are not sitting members of the legislature. With few exceptions, heads of the executive departments and other key presidential appointments are people loyal to the president and his political party. Most are politicians who have served as governors of states or members of Congress or are close advisors who have worked with the president on political campaigns or in offices the president previously held. For example, of President Obama's original 15 Cabinet secretaries, there were 8 former governors or members of Congress, 2 former managers of

11 Scott A. Frisch and Sean Q. Kelly, *Committee Assignment Politics in the U.S. House of Representatives* (Norman: University of Oklahoma Press, 2006).

large municipal agencies, 2 former military leaders, 1 former banker, 1 former judge, and 1 physicist. They are people he trusts to make sound policy decisions and political strategies, and that trust usually is held inside party circles.

The president and White House staff also work closely with congressional party leaders to shepherd legislation through Congress. As discussed in Chapter 7, when the president's party controls both chambers of Congress, there is the opportunity to get the large majority of the president's legislative agenda passed. The president cannot introduce legislation, but must rely on members of Congress to do so. (There are a few exceptions such as nominations and treaties.) Nearly all of the president's legislative initiatives are proposed as bills by fellow party members in the U.S. House and Senate. And, the leadership of the president's party helps to negotiate with individual members of Congress to construct a majority behind a White House sponsored bill. Sometimes the president will reach out to individual legislators to try to persuade the member of Congress to support a particular bill.

The president's ability to prevail in Congress depends strongly on which party controls the House and Senate. When the president's party enjoys majorities in the House and Senate, the president's legislative agenda succeeds most of the time. A typical president will win in excess of 80 percent of the time on bills if his or her party controls the House and Senate. Barack Obama, during his first year in office, had the highest degree of support for a president since World War II, with a majority of Congress supporting his position 96 percent of the time.[12] When another party controls at least one chamber of Congress, however, the White House has a much more difficult time getting new laws passed. During the first six years of his presidency, with majorities in the House and Senate, George W. Bush won majority support in Congress 81 percent of the time, but in 2007 and 2008, a majority of Congress supported the positions taken by President George W. Bush only 23 percent of the time, a record low in the post war period.

PARTIES AND THE ELECTORATE

party identification 

An individual voter's psychological ties to one party or another

Political parties are more than just organizations and leaders; they are made up of millions of rank-and-file members. As we saw in Chapter 11's discussion of elections, individual voters tend to develop party identification with one of the political parties. Party identification partly reflects a psychological attachment developed in childhood or adolescence and carried throughout life. Party identification also has a rational component, rooted in evaluations of the performance of the parties in government, the policies they will pursue, and an individual's interest and ideology.[13] Voters generally form attachments to parties that reflect

12 Don Gonyea, "CQ: Obama's Winning Streak on Hill Unprecedented," NPR, January 11, 2010, www.npr.org/templates/story/story.php?storyId=122436116.

their views and interests. Once those attachments are formed, however, they are likely to persist and even be handed down to children unless some very strong factors convince individuals that their party is no longer an appropriate object of their affections. In some sense, party identification is similar to brand loyalty in the marketplace: consumers choose a brand of automobile for its appearance or mechanical characteristics and stick with it out of loyalty, habit, and unwillingness to reexamine their choices constantly, but they may eventually switch if the old brand no longer serves their interests.

Although the strength of partisan ties in the United States seems to have declined in the 1960s and 1970s, most Americans continue to identify with either the Republican Party or the Democratic Party (Figure 12.2). The Analyzing the Evidence unit in this chapter takes a closer look at how political scientists study trends in partisanship. Party identification gives citizens a stake in election outcomes that goes beyond the race at hand. This is why strong party identifiers

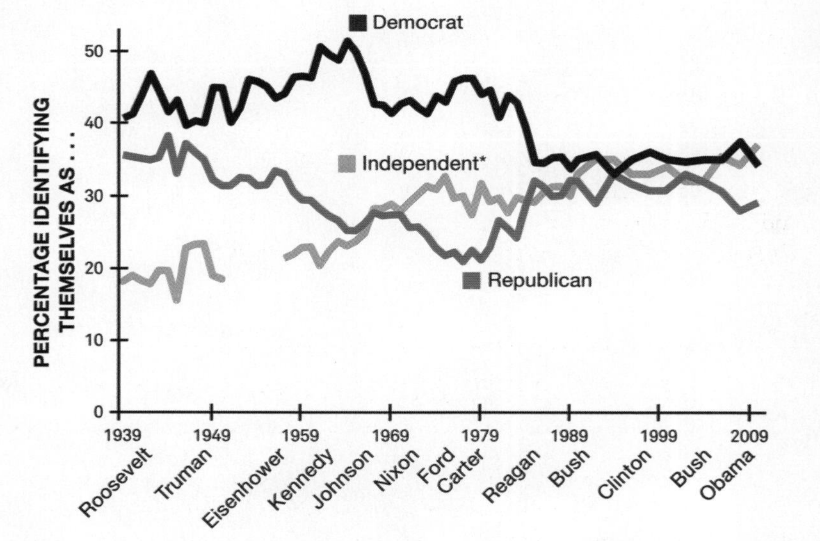

ANALYZING THE EVIDENCE

In 1952, Democrats outnumbered Republicans significantly. Today, the two parties appear to have nearly equal numbers of loyalists. What factors might account for this partisan transformation?

SOURCES: Pew Research Center for the People & the Press, "Party Identification Trend," http://people-press.org/party-identification-trend (accessed 7/1/09); "Trend in Party Identification," September 23, 2010, people-press.org/http://people-press.org/files/legacy-pdf/658.pdf (accessed 9/16/11).

13 For what is perhaps still the best discussion of the bases of party identification, see Arthur S. Goldberg, "Social Determinism and Rationality as Bases of Party Identification," *American Political Science Review* 63, no. 1 (March 1969): 5–25. For a more recent article weighing in on economic versus social determinants of party attachments, see Larry M. Bartels, "What's the Matter with What's the Matter with Kansas?" *Quarterly Journal of Political Science* 1 (2006): 201–26.

How Stable Is Party Identification?

An individual's identification with a political party is thought to be extremely stable over time. Yet, as we saw in Figure 12.2, large changes in party identifications occurred in the mid-1960s and the early 1980s, and between 2004 and 2008. If individuals' party attachments are stable, why do the aggregate percentages of people who identify with one party or the other vary so much?

Two distinct arguments are often proposed to explain this puzzle: (1) Generational replacement may account for the change, assuming individual party identifications don't change much, but the composition of the electorate changes as new generations emerge and older generations fade. (2) Conversion of individuals from one party to another might contribute to the aggregate trends; that is, party identification in individuals may be less stable than political scientists have thought. Data related to the most recent shift, between 2004 and 2008, provide some insight into these arguments.

Transitions from 2006 to 2008

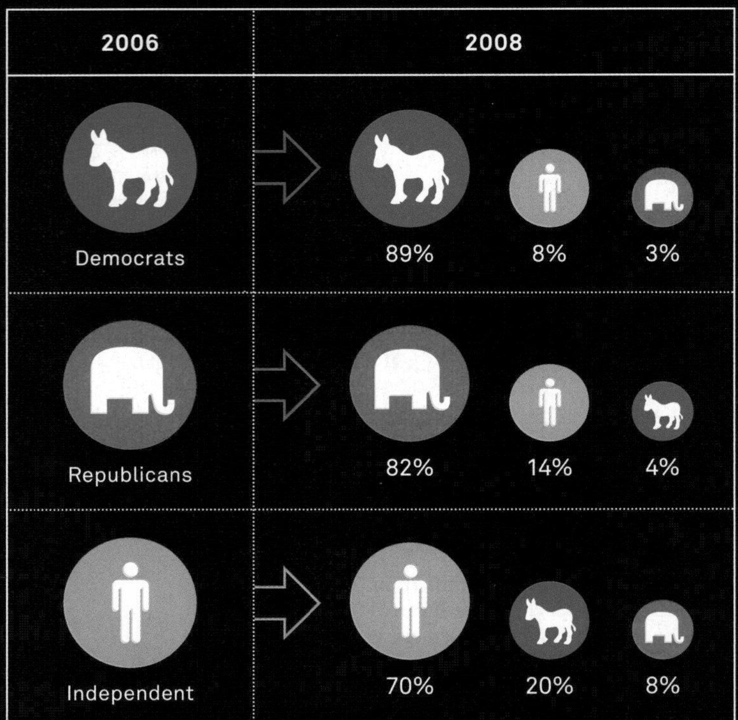

To measure how frequently people converted from one party to another, we can analyze the results of an annual survey of the same 2,000 people in 2006, 2007, and 2008[1]—a period that overlaps with the significant shift in party identifications in 2004–08. The percentages in each row show the loyalty and defection rates of those people who identified with each party in 2006. We see that the partisans are quite loyal overall, and most of the defections that occur are to the Independent category, with Republicans becoming Independents at a much higher rate than Democrats. And Independents are the source of the uptick in Democratic identifications.

Cohort Party ID, 1956–2008

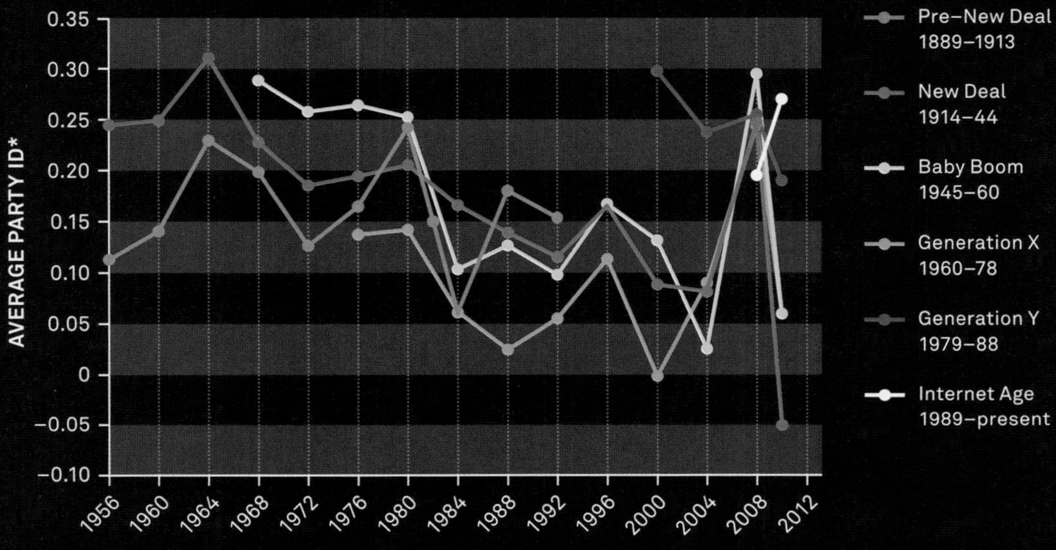

* Average party ID: Democrats = 1, Independents = 0, Republicans = –1

Can the decline in Republican identification in 2004–08 be explained by newer, more Democratic generations replacing older Republican generations? Using survey data from each national election,[2] political scientists have measured the party identification in each generation, in this case as the percent Democratic minus the percent Republican. In the graph, a higher value on the vertical axis signifies more Democrats. The graph reveals that there are generational differences—for example, the New Deal generation is consistently among the more Democratic, while Gen Xers are consistently among the more Republican—but also shows that all the generations tend to move in the Democratic or Republican direction at the same times. This suggests that generational differences may not fully explain aggregate shifts in party identification.

Analysis of these data indicates that the changes in overall party identification in 2004–08, when the Democrats gained 8 percentage points over the Republicans (see Figure 12.2), are due largely to conversion. Imagine if each generation's party identification had remained the same as it was in 2004 and only the composition of the electorate changed, with the New Deal generation shrinking somewhat and more of Gen Y and the Internet generation entering the electorate. In this case, aggregate party identification would have barely changed between 2004 and 2008. Clearly, conversions within generational cohorts occurred, and those conversions explain the aggregate shift toward the Democrats.

EXPLORE
PARTY IDENTIFICATIONS
FURTHER AT:
wwnorton.com/studyspace

1 Cooperative Congressional Election Study surveys.

2 American National Election Study and Cooperative Congressional Election Study surveys.

party activist 

A partisan who contributes time, energy, and effort to support a party and its candidates

(that is, people who identify strongly with one party) are more likely than other Americans to go to the polls and, of course, are more likely than others to support the party with which they identify. Party activists are drawn from the ranks of the strong identifiers. Activists are those who not only vote but also contribute their time, energy, and effort to party affairs. Activists ring doorbells, stuff envelopes, attend meetings, and contribute money to the party cause. No party could succeed without the thousands of volunteers who undertake the mundane tasks needed to keep the organization going. It is worth noting that attachment to a party does not guarantee voting for that party's candidates, though it does reflect a tendency. Strong identifiers do so almost always, and weak identifiers do most of the time.

Group Affiliations

The Democratic and Republican parties are America's only national parties. They are the only political organizations that draw support from most regions of the country and from Americans of every racial, economic, religious, and ethnic group. The two parties do not draw equal support from members of every social stratum, however. When we refer to the Democratic or Republican coalition, we mean the groups that generally support one or the other party. In the United States today, a variety of group characteristics are associated with party identification. These include race and ethnicity, gender, religion, class, ideology, and region.

Race and Ethnicity. Since the 1930s and Franklin Delano Roosevelt's New Deal, African Americans have been overwhelmingly Democratic in their party identification. More than 90 percent of African Americans describe themselves as Democrats and support Democratic candidates in national, state, and local elections. Approximately 25 percent of the Democratic Party's support in presidential races comes from African American voters.

Latino and Hispanic voters consist of people whose ancestors came from many different countries, with disparate political orientations. Mexican Americans are the single largest group. They have historically aligned with the Democratic Party, as have Puerto Ricans and Central Americans. Historically, Cuban Americans have voted heavily and identified as Republican. Over the past five years, however, Cubans have exhibited a rapid shift toward the Democratic Party. This trend appears to reflect generational differences, as younger Cuban Americans look to be as Democratic as other Hispanic and Latino groups. Asian Americans tend to be divided as well. Japanese, Chinese, Filipino, and Korean communities have been long established in the United States and have influential business communities. Higher-income Asians tend to be as Republican as higher-income whites. It is not clear whether newer Asian immigrant groups, such as the Hmong, the Vietnamese, Thais, and Indians, will follow the same trajectory as the Japanese and Chinese communities.

Gender. Women are somewhat more likely to support Democrats, and men are somewhat more likely to support Republicans, in surveys of party identification and voting. This difference is known as the gender gap. It is somewhat new in American politics. Early studies of the women's vote in the 1920s, shortly after the extension of the franchise, found little difference in voting behavior between men and women. If anything, women tended to be slightly more Republican, and they more strongly favored the prohibition of alcohol than men did. The modern gender gap emerged full fledged in the 1980 presidential election and has ranged from a difference of 4 percentage points in how men and women voted in 1992 to a high of 11 percentage points in 1996. In the 2012 election, Barack Obama won 55 percent of the women's vote and 45 percent of the men's vote, a ten-point gap.[14]

 **gender gap**

A distinctive pattern of voting behavior reflecting the differences in views between women and men

Religion. Jews are among the Democratic Party's most loyal constituent groups and have been since the New Deal. Nearly 90 percent of all Jewish Americans describe themselves as Democrats, although the percentage is declining among younger Jews. Catholics were once a strongly pro-Democratic group as well but have been shifting toward the Republican Party since the 1970s, when the Republicans began to focus on abortion and other social issues deemed important to Catholics. Protestants are more likely to identify with the Republicans than with the Democrats. Protestant fundamentalists, in particular, have been drawn to the Republicans' conservative stands on social issues, such as school prayer and abortion. The importance of religious conservatives to the Republican Party became quite evident in 2001. After his victory in the 2000 election, George W. Bush announced that his administration would seek to award federal grants and contracts to religious groups. By using so-called faith-based groups as federal contractors, Bush was seeking to reward religious conservatives for their loyalty to the Republican Party and to ensure that they would have a continuing stake in Republican success.

Class. Upper-income Americans are considerably more likely to affiliate with the Republicans, whereas lower-income Americans are far more likely to identify with the Democrats. This divide reflects the differences between the two parties on economic issues. In general, the Republicans support cutting taxes and social spending—positions that reflect the interests of the wealthy. The Democrats, however, favor increased social spending, even if this requires increasing taxes—a position consistent with the interests of less-affluent Americans. One important exception to this principle is that relatively affluent individuals who work in the public sector or such related institutions as foundations and universities also tend to affiliate with the Democrats. Such individuals are likely to appreciate the Democratic Party's support for an expanded role of government and high levels of public spending. White voters with less than a college education (a measure of class) have become less strongly affiliated with the

14 Susan Carroll, *Women and American Politics: New Questions, New Directions* (Oxford: Oxford University Press, 2003).

Democrats over time, but this trend is restricted almost entirely to the South. (Outside the South, voters with less than a college education have declined in their support of Democratic presidential candidates by only 1 percentage point in the last 50 years.)[15]

Ideology. Ideology and party identification are very closely linked. Most individuals who describe themselves as conservatives identify with the Republican Party, whereas most who call themselves liberals support the Democrats. This division has increased in recent years as the two parties have taken very different positions on social and economic issues. Before the 1970s, when party differences were more blurred, it was not uncommon to find Democratic conservatives and Republican liberals. Both of these species are rare today. The Voting Rights Act of 1965 was a watershed event in American politics. Over the next two decades, African American voting in the South grew dramatically, and Republicans began offering southern whites alternatives to the Democratic Party. One consequence is that each party became clearer ideologically, leaving little room for conservative Democrats or moderate Republicans.

Region. Between the Civil War and the 1960s, the "Solid South" was a Democratic bastion. Today much of the South has become solidly Republican, as have much of the West and Southwest. The area of greatest Democratic Party strength is the Northeast. The Midwest is a battleground, more or less evenly divided between the two parties.

The explanations for these regional variations are complex. Southern Republicanism has come about because conservative white southerners identify the Democratic Party with the civil rights movement and liberal positions on abortion, school prayer, and other social issues. Republican strength in the South and the West is related to the weakness of organized labor in these regions, as well as to the dependence of the two regions on military programs supported by the Republicans. Democratic strength in the Northeast is a function of the continuing influence of organized labor in the large cities of this region, as well as the region's large population of minority and elderly voters, who benefit from Democratic social programs. In the 2006 and 2008 elections, one of the biggest shifts toward the Democrats occurred in the Rocky Mountain West, where Democrats unexpectedly won a number of congressional races and governorships. This trend reflects in part the shift in the population to this region, including in particular people who value the environment and demand public services.

Age. Age is another factor associated with partisanship. At the present time, individuals younger than fifty are fairly evenly divided between Democrats and Republicans, whereas those older than fifty are much more likely to be Democrats. There is nothing about a particular numerical age that leads to a particular party loyalty. Instead, individuals from the same age cohort are likely to have experienced a similar set of events during the period when they formed their

15 Andrew Gelman et al., *Red State, Blue State, Rich State, Poor State: Why Americans Vote the Way They Do* (Princeton, NJ: Princeton University Press, 2008).

Figure 12.3

PARTY IDENTIFICATION BY SOCIAL GROUPS, 2012

	Republican	Independent	Democrat
SEX			
Men	29%	38%	29%
Women	27%	29%	40%
AGE			
18–29	23%	38%	36%
30–49	27%	38%	32%
50–64	29%	31%	36%
65 and over	34%	26%	36%
RACE AND RELIGION			
White Evangelical Protestant	52%	27%	17%
White Mainline Protestant	34%	35%	28%
Jewish	19%	28%	49%
Unaffiliated	13%	45%	39%
RACE OR ETHNICITY			
White, non-Hispanic	34%	35%	28%
Black, non-Hispanic	5%	16%	76%
Hispanic	16%	37%	42%
EDUCATION			
High school graduate or less	28%	32%	36%
Some college	30%	33%	33%
College graduate	29%	36%	32%
Postgraduate degree	25%	35%	39%
INCOME			
Less than $20,000	20%	34%	42%
$20,000–29,999	23%	34%	40%
$30,000–49,999	29%	34%	35%
$50,000–74,999	31%	33%	33%
More than $75,000	31%	34%	32%
IDEOLOGY			
Conservative	51%	28%	18%
Moderate	18%	42%	36%
Liberal	5%	29%	64%

NOTE: Percents do not add to 100 because the category "Other/don't know" is omitted. In this survey, this category was always between 2–5 percent of respondents.

SOURCE: Pew Research Center for the People and the Press, "A Closer Look at the Parties in 2012," August 23, 2012, www.people-press.org/2012/08/23/a-closer-look-at-the-parties-in-2012/ (accessed 12/10/12).

party loyalties. Thus Americans between the ages of fifty and sixty-four came of political age during the Cold War, the Vietnam War, and the civil rights movement, and those older than sixty-five are the product of the Great Depression and World War II. Apparently among voters whose initial perceptions of politics were shaped during these periods, more responded favorably to the role played by the Democrats than to the actions of the Republicans. It is interesting that among the youngest group of Americans, a group that came of age during an era of political scandals that tainted both parties, the majority describe themselves as independents.

Figure 12.3 indicates the relationship between party identification and a number of social criteria. Race, religion, and income seem to have the greatest influence on Americans' party affiliations. None of these social characteristics is inevitably linked to partisan identification, however. There are union Republicans and business Democrats, black nonchurchgoing Republicans and white born-again Democrats, Democrats in Utah, and Republicans in Rhode Island. The general party identifications just discussed are broad tendencies that both reflect and reinforce the issue and policy positions the two parties take in the national and local political arenas.

PARTIES AS INSTITUTIONS

Political parties in the United States today are not tightly disciplined, hierarchical organizations. Indeed, they never have been. Rather, the American parties consist of extensive networks of politicians, interest groups, activists and donors, consultants, and, ultimately, voters. Some of these pieces of the parties, such as the party caucuses in Congress, seem to have more influence over the policies and political strategies pursued by the parties. All of these different political players shape the ability of the party to influence what government does. Party campaign finance committees may, for example, work with the congressional caucus to maximize the party's appeal to donors. National party leaders must work with state and local party officials and activists to try to coordinate the many campaign activities in presidential and congressional elections. If parties are such wide-flung networks, how do they make decisions about their most momentous decisions, nominating candidates for offices and choosing a policy or ideological platform? Such decisions are made at every level of government in party committees, conventions, and primary elections, and it is through these institutions that the parties truly come together to make collective decisions.

Contemporary Party Organizations

In the United States, party organizations exist at virtually every level of government (Figure 12.4). These organizations are usually committees made up of a number of active party members. State law and party rules prescribe how such

Figure 12.4
HOW AMERICAN PARTIES ARE ORGANIZED

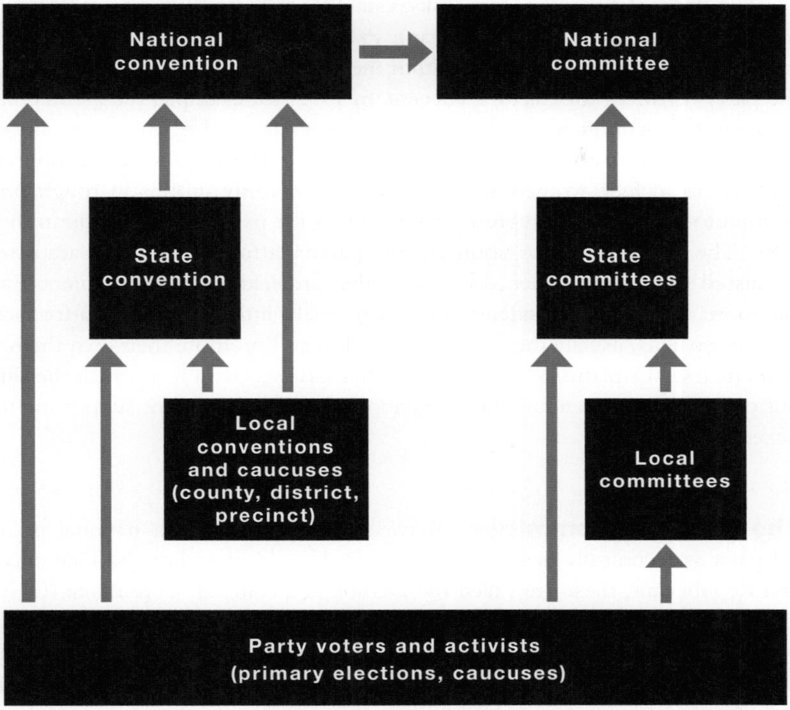

National convention

National committee

State convention

State committees

Local conventions and caucuses (county, district, precinct)

Local committees

Party voters and activists (primary elections, caucuses)

committees are constituted. Usually, committee members are elected at a local party meeting—called a political caucus—or as part of the regular primary election. The best-known examples of these committees are at the national level: the Democratic National Committee and the Republican National Committee.

 **political caucus**

A normally closed meeting of a political or legislative group to select candidates, plan strategy, or make decisions regarding legislative matters

The National Convention. At the national level, the party's most important institution is the national convention. The convention is attended by delegates from each of the states; as a group, they nominate the party's presidential and vice-presidential candidates, draft the party's campaign platform for the presidential race, and approve changes in the rules and regulations governing party procedures. Before World War II, presidential nominations occupied most of the time, energy, and effort expended at the national convention. The nomination process required days of negotiation and compromise among state party leaders and often required many ballots before a nominee was selected. In recent years, however, presidential candidates have essentially nominated themselves by winning enough delegate support in primary elections to win the official nomination on the first ballot. The convention itself has played little or no role in selecting the candidates.

The convention's other two tasks, establishing the party's rules and establishing its platform, remain important. Party rules can determine the relative influence of competing factions within the party and can increase or decrease the party's chances for electoral success. In 1972, for example, the Democratic National Convention adopted a new set of rules favored by the party's liberal wing, according to which state delegations to the Democratic convention are required to include women and members of minority groups in rough proportion to those groups' representation among the party's membership in their state. The convention also approves the party platform. Platforms are often dismissed as platitude-laden documents that are seldom read by voters. Furthermore, the parties' presidential candidates make little use of the platforms in their campaigns; usually they prefer to develop and promote their own themes. Nonetheless, the platform should be understood as a "treaty" in which the various party factions attending the convention state their terms for supporting the ticket.

The National Committee. Between conventions, each national political party is technically headed by its national committee. For the Democrats and Republicans, these are called the Democratic National Committee (DNC) and the Republican National Committee (RNC), respectively. These national committees raise campaign funds, head off factional disputes within the party, and endeavor to enhance the party's media image. Since 1972, the size of staff and the amount of money raised have increased substantially for both national committees. The actual work of each committee is overseen by its chairperson. Other committee members are generally major party contributors or fund-raisers and serve in a largely ceremonial capacity.

For the party that controls the White House, the national committee chair is appointed by the president. Typically, this means that that party's national committee becomes little more than an adjunct to the White House staff. For a first-term president, the committee devotes the bulk of its energy to the reelection campaign. The national committee chair of the party that is not in control of the White House is selected by the committee itself and usually takes a broader view of the party's needs, raising money and performing other activities on behalf of the party's members in Congress and in the state legislatures. In 2006, the DNC was headed by Howard Dean, whose failed but impressive presidential bid in 2004 launched him onto the national scene. Dean crafted a 50-state strategy for the 2006 midterm elections in an effort to build party strength and recruit quality candidates in all 50 states. Barack Obama's 2008 and 2012 presidential campaigns capitalized on Dean's 50-state strategy. Obama developed extensive grassroots organizations in every state, which registered many new Democratic voters in traditionally Republican areas, a change that will likely benefit the Democrats for years to come.

Congressional Campaign Committees. Each party forms House and Senate campaign committees to raise funds for the House and Senate election campaigns. The Republicans call their House and Senate committees the National Republican Campaign Committee (NRCC) and the National Republican Senatorial Committee (NRSC). The Democrats call their House and Senate committees the Democratic Congressional Campaign Committee (DCCC) and the Democratic Senatorial Campaign Committee (DSCC). These organizations also have professional staff devoted to raising and distributing funds, developing strategies, recruiting candidates, and conducting on-the-ground campaigns. These organizations, however, are accountable to the caucuses inside the House and Senate. The chairs of these committees come from within their respective chambers and rank high in the party leadership hierarchy. The current chairs are Representative Chris Van Hollen (D-Md.) and Senator Charles Schumer (D-N.Y.) on the Democratic side and Representative Tom Cole (R-Okla.) and Senator John Ensign (D-Nev.) on the Republican side. The national committees and the congressional committees are sometimes rivals. Both groups seek donations from the same pool of people but for different candidates: the national committee seeks funds primarily for the presidential race, whereas the congressional campaign committees focus on House and Senate seats.

State and Local Party Organizations. Each of the two major parties has a central committee in each state. The parties traditionally also have county committees and, in some instances, state senate district committees, judicial district committees, and in larger cities, citywide party committees and local assembly district "ward" committees as well. Congressional districts may also have party committees. Some cities also have precinct committees.[16]

State and local party organizations are very active in recruiting candidates, conducting voter registration drives, and providing financial assistance to candidates. In many respects, federal election law has given state and local party organizations new life, permitting them to spend unlimited amounts of money on "party-building" activities such as voter registration and get-out-the-vote drives. As a result, the national party organizations, which have enormous fund-raising abilities but are limited by law in the amount of money they can spend on candidates, transfer millions of dollars each year to the state and local organizations. The state and local parties, in turn, spend these funds, sometimes called soft money, to promote the candidacies of national, state, and local candidates. In this process, as local organizations have become linked financially to the national parties, American political parties have become somewhat more integrated and nationalized than ever before. At the same time, the state and local party organizations have come to control large financial resources and play important roles in elections despite the collapse of the old patronage machines.

16 Well-organized political parties—especially the famous old machines of New York, Chicago, and Boston—provided for "precinct captains" and a fairly tight group of party members around them. Precinct captains were usually members of long standing in neighborhood party clubhouses.

The Contemporary Party as Service Provider to Candidates

Party leaders have adapted parties to the modern age. Parties as organizations are more professional, better financed, and better organized than ever before.[17] Political parties have evolved into "service organizations," which, although they no longer hold a monopoly over campaigns, still provide services to candidates, without which it would be extremely difficult for them to win and hold office. For example, the national organizations of the political parties collect information, ranging from lists of likely supporters and donors in local areas to public opinion polls in states and legislative districts, and they provide this information directly to their candidates for state and federal offices. They also have teams of experienced campaign organizers and managers who provide assistance to local candidates who are in tight races but are understaffed.

Many politicians, especially congressional incumbents, are able to raise funds, attract volunteers, and win office without much help from the local party organizations. They are not beholden to party leaders for campaign support and do not feel that they must submit to party pressure in making political decisions in office. Instead, they may steer a course that represents their particular constituency, especially on important pieces of legislation. Leaders in Congress frequently find that they cannot rely on legislators from centrist states and districts on tough decisions and votes. Those legislators will want to vote with their districts in order to position themselves for the next election. Analysts refer to this pattern as a candidate-centered politics to distinguish it from a political process in which parties are the dominant forces. The problem with a candidate-centered politics is that it tends to be associated with low turnout, high levels of special-interest influence, and a lack of effective decision making. In short, many of the problems that have plagued American politics in recent years appear linked to the independence of American voters and politicians and the candidate-centered nature of American national politics.

Politicians, especially legislative politicians, have a collective action problem. Because they possess considerable independence, they are able to chart an independent political course—hence candidate-centered politics. But so, too, can their fellow partisans. The result is that the party label, on which all rely, is undermined and comes to stand for nothing. (It is thus no accident that more and more voters call themselves independents as parties have become big tents from which a cacophony of signals is emitted.) Legislative leaders, in an effort to protect the party label, provide entrepreneurial direction to their copartisans. They seek to reduce the exercise of "too much" independence because every such instance entails negative external effects on the party's reputation. Legislative leadership, in short, enables partisans to rein in each other's independence (which each is so sorely tempted to exercise). Although each politician is thus constrained (somewhat) in the fine-tuning of his or her political behavior to

17 See Aldrich, *Why Parties?*, chap. 8.

meet the needs of individual constituencies, he or she nevertheless benefits from maintaining an unblemished party label. As party delegations in Congress have become more homogeneous in recent years, party leaders have been in a better position to exercise this type of control, ultimately to the benefit of copartisans. This scenario is but another aspect of the "service-organization" conception of the modern political party.[18]

PARTY SYSTEMS

Our understanding of political parties would be incomplete if we considered only their composition and roles. America's political parties compete with each other for offices, policies, and power. The struggle between the major parties for control of government shapes the policies that the parties put forth, the coalitions of interests that they represent, and the ability of the parties, indeed the government, to respond to the demands of the time and age. In short, the fate of each party is inextricably linked to that of its major rival.

Political scientists often call the constellation of parties that are important at any given moment a nation's party system. The most obvious feature of a party system is the number of major parties competing for power. Usually the United States has had a two-party system, meaning that only two parties have a serious chance to win national elections.

There are both institutional and psychological reasons why the United States has just two parties. The American electoral system is winner take all. Whoever gets the most votes wins the congressional seat. Whoever gets the most electoral votes wins the presidency. The Democratic and Republican parties have positioned themselves as center-left and center-right parties, neither extremely liberal nor extremely conservative. The ideological positions they have chosen maintain their policy distinctiveness and still divide the electorate about equally. If, for example, a far-left party (such as the Green Party) decided to make a strong play to win the presidency, it would split votes with the Democratic Party. It would not decrease votes of the Republican Party but would divide the votes of left-leaning voters between the Democrats and the Greens, effectively guaranteeing a Republican victory. A third party that entered in the middle, on the other hand, would be squeezed between the two parties and would have no hope of gaining sufficient support to win. Understanding this situation, most third parties decide to stay out. Getting on the ballot, recruiting candidates, building an organization—all create tremendous costs. The best that the party could do would be to come in a

18 This argument is developed in great detail in Rohde, *Parties and Leaders in the Post-reform House,* and in the two books by Gary W. Cox and Mathew D. McCubbins, *Legislative Leviathan* and *Setting the Agenda: Responsible Party Government in the U.S. House of Representatives* (New York: Cambridge University Press, 2005).

distant third. Even worse, it could cause the major party it likes less to win. Voters also appear to understand this situation. A voter who would normally want to vote for the third party sees that by doing so, he or she ends up boosting the electoral prospects of the major party that he or she favors less.

The same forces are less likely to influence elections in parliamentary systems, or systems that allocate seats in the legislature to parties in proportion to their share of the national vote. In parliaments, if no party wins a majority, the smaller parties can join with larger parties in a coalition. Systems that divvy up power based on the percentage of the vote won, rather than winner take all, occasionally have to form coalitions in order to form a government. That creates an incentive for small parties to fracture off larger parties or to form de novo.

We have not always had the same two parties, and minor parties often put forward candidates. The term *party system*, refers to more than just the number of parties competing for power. It also connotes the organization of the parties, the balance of power between and within party coalitions, the parties' social and institutional bases, and the issues and policies around which party competition is organized.

Implicit in the idea of a party system is a sense of stability, of equilibrium. Voters can reliably expect that the Democrats and Republicans will be the main parties in the next election, that Democrats will tend to be ideologically liberal and Republicans ideologically conservative, that Democrats will align with unions and urban interests while Republicans will align more closely with corporations and rural areas.

That equilibrium is itself an outcome of the political system. It reflects the policies that those in office choose to pursue and the coalitions of interests that they represent. The stability of the party system in the United States does not mean that the system is static. Within each party there exists a tension between its more moderate interests and politicians and its more extreme interests and politicians. Moderates within the parties would like the parties to pursue more centrist policies, as that would increase the support of the party among more moderate voters and groups. The conflicts among the factions within the parties are worked out in state and national conventions, in the caucuses inside Congress and the state legislatures, and in primary elections. Those involved in the political struggle inside the parties, however, always have an ultimate goal to control government, to gain the upper hand in the struggle with their opposing parties. The party system reflects the balance of the political struggles within parties and the political struggles between them.

Seen from this perspective, one may appreciate both the apparent stability of the party system and its historical evolution. From year to year, the alignment between the parties changes, but only a little. As we discussed earlier, those who have the greatest influence over party policy-making are those already in office—the president and members of Congress, especially congressional leaders. They rose to power from within party ranks. They represent the core principles and ideology of the party and have relied on the primary interest groups within the party in their ascent to power. They are reluctant to embrace new principles or alter in any fundamental way the party coalitions, as such radical changes would likely harm their own political position.

The character of a nation's party system changes as the parties realign their electoral coalitions and alter their public philosophies. Such realignment sometimes comes subtly and sometimes suddenly. Today's American party system is very different from the party system of 1950, even though the Democrats and the Republicans continue to be the major competing forces (Figure 12.5). Half a century ago, the Democrats' political strength lay in the South and the Republicans in the North. Democrats favored racial desegregation in the South, and Republicans wanted protectionist trade policies and dismantling of Social Security. Over the past 60 years, gradual social and economic changes in the United States forced the parties to shift their policy orientations and to encompass different political coalitions. Political scientists have referred to this era of gradual change in the party system as a creeping realignment. One of the central issues driving the most recent realignment of the political parties was race. Democratic leaders of the 1940s, such as Harry Truman and Hubert Humphrey, pulled their party to embrace a new platform to end racial desegregation. That change in policy redefined the Democratic party and took the better part of a generation.[19]

Change has also come suddenly to the party system in the United States in response to historical events beyond the control of "political entrepreneurs." The American Civil War and the economic depressions of the 1890s and 1930s brought dramatic and lasting changes to the balance of power between the parties and to the principles and policies that the parties represent. The parties in power and their response to those events redefined their image among the electorate.

Over the course of American history, changes in political forces and alignments have produced six party systems, each with distinctive political institutions, issues, and patterns of political power and participation. Of course, some political phenomena have persisted across party systems. Conflicts over the distribution of wealth, for example, are an enduring feature of American political life. But even such phenomena manifest themselves in different ways during different political eras.

The First Party System: Federalists and Democratic-Republicans

Although George Washington and, in fact, many other leaders of the time deplored partisan politics, the two-party system emerged early in the history of the new Republic. Competition in Congress between northeastern mercantile and southern agrarian factions led Alexander Hamilton and the northeasterners

19 Edward Carmines and James Stimson, *Issue Evolution* (Princeton, NJ: Princeton University Press, 1989).

Figure 12.5

HOW THE PARTY SYSTEM EVOLVED

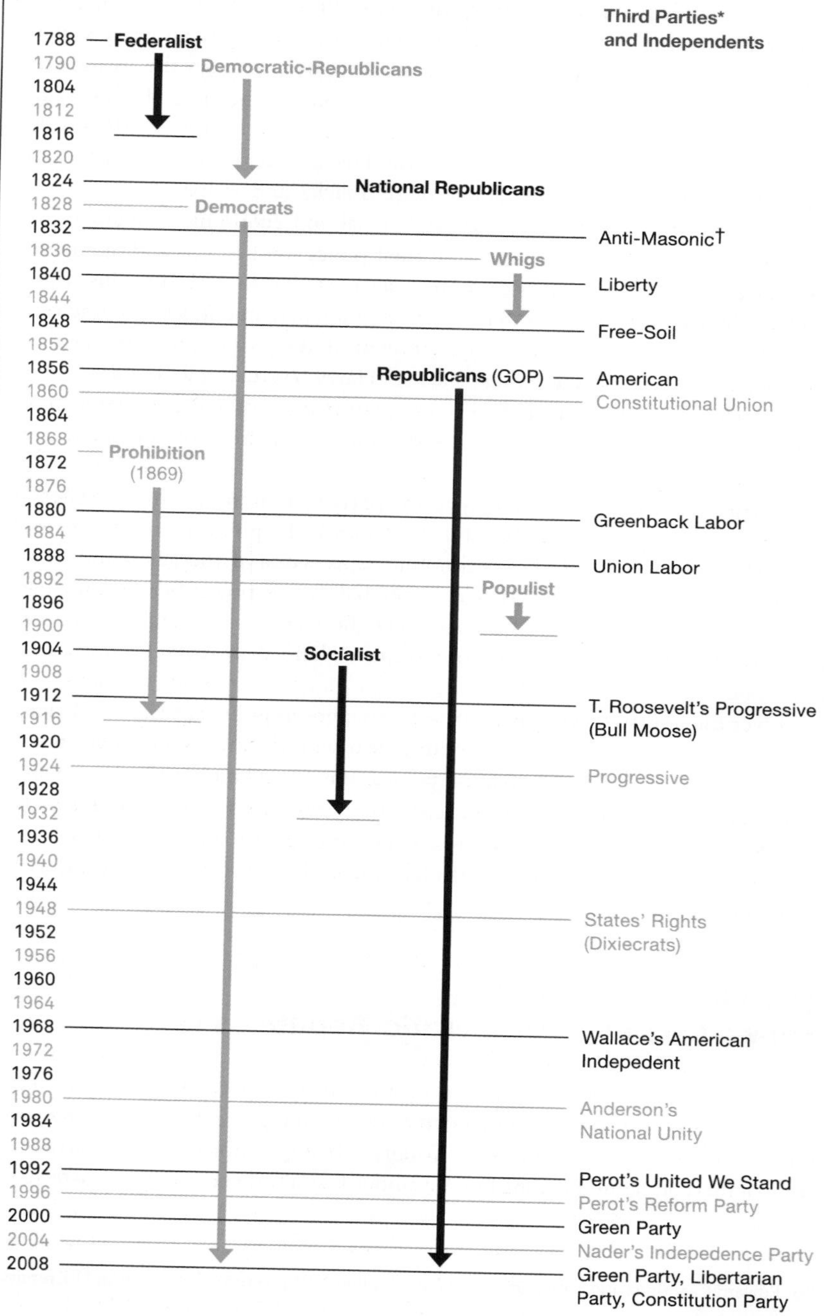

*In some cases, there was even a fourth party. Most of the parties listed here existed for only one term.
†The Anti-Masonics not only had the distinction of being the first third party but also were the first party to hold a national nominating convention and the first to announce a party platform.

to form a cohesive voting bloc within Congress. The southerners, led by Thomas Jefferson and James Madison, responded by attempting to organize a popular following to change the balance of power within Congress. When the northeasterners replied to this southern strategy, the result was the birth of America's first national parties—the Democratic-Republicans, whose primary base was in the South, and the Federalists, whose strength was greatest in the New England states. The Federalists spoke mainly for New England mercantile groups and supported protective tariffs to encourage manufacturers, the assumption of the states' Revolutionary War debts, the creation of a national bank, and resumption of commercial ties with England. The Democratic-Republicans opposed these policies, favoring instead free trade, the promotion of agrarian over commercial interests, and friendship with France.

The rationale behind the formation of both parties was primarily that they would be a means by which to institutionalize existing voting blocs in Congress around a cohesive policy agenda. Although the Federalists and the Democratic-Republicans competed in elections, their ties to the electorate were loose. In 1800, the American electorate was small, and deference was an important political factor, with voters generally expected to follow the lead of local political and religious leaders and community notables. Nominations were informal, without rules or regulations. Local party leaders would simply gather the party elites, and they would agree on the person, usually one of them, who would be the candidate. The meetings where candidates were nominated were generally called caucuses. In this era, before the introduction of the secret ballot, many voters were reluctant publicly to defy the views of influential members of their community. In this context, the Democratic-Republicans and the Federalists organized political clubs and developed newspapers and newsletters designed to mobilize elite opinion and relied on local elites to bring along their followers. In the election of 1800, Jefferson defeated the incumbent Federalist president, John Adams, and led the Democratic-Republicans to power. Over the ensuing years, the Federalists gradually weakened. The party disappeared altogether after the pro-British sympathies of some Federalist leaders during the War of 1812 led to charges that the party was guilty of treason.

The Second Party System: Democrats and Whigs

From the collapse of the Federalists until the 1830s, America had only one political party, the Democratic-Republicans. This period of one-party politics is sometimes known as the Era of Good Feeling, to indicate the absence of party competition. Throughout this period, however, there was intense factional conflict within the Democratic-Republican Party, particularly between the supporters and opponents of General Andrew Jackson, America's great military hero of the War of 1812. Jackson was one of five significant candidates for president in 1824 and won the most popular and electoral votes but a majority of neither, throwing the election into the House of Representatives. Jackson's opponents united to deny him the presidency, but Jackson won election in 1828 and again in 1832.

Jackson was greatly admired by millions of ordinary Americans living on the nation's farms and in its villages, and the Jacksonians made the most of the general's appeal to the common people by embarking on a program of suffrage expansion that would give Jackson's impecunious but numerous supporters the right to vote. To bring growing numbers of voters to the polls, the Jacksonians built political clubs and held mass rallies and parades, laying the groundwork for a new and more popular politics. Jackson's vice president and eventual successor, Martin Van Buren, was the organizational genius behind the Jacksonian movement, establishing a central party committee, state party organizations, and party newspapers. In response to widespread complaints about cliques of party leaders dominating the nominations at party caucuses and leaving no place for other party members who wanted to participate, the Jacksonians also established the state and national party conventions as the forums for nominating presidential candidates. The conventions gave control of the presidential nominating process to the new state party organizations that the Jacksonians had created and expected to control. As the political scientist John Aldrich has argued, unlike any political leader before him, Van Buren appreciated the possibilities for mass mobilization and the necessity of a well-oiled national organization to overcome free-riding and other collective action problems.[20] With a keen sense of what it took to organize a party for electoral competition, Van Buren produced institutional solutions to collective action problems, leaving as a historical legacy the blueprint for the modern mass-based political party.

The Jacksonians, whose party came to be known as the Democratic Party, were not without opponents, however, especially in the New England states. During the 1830s, groups opposing Jackson for reasons of personality and politics united to form a new political force—the Whig Party—thus giving rise to the second American party system. During the 1830s and 1840s, the Democrats and the Whigs built party organizations throughout the nation, and both sought to enlarge their bases of support by expanding the suffrage through the elimination of property restrictions and other barriers to voting—at least voting by white men. This would not be the last time that party competition paved the way for expansion of the electorate. Support for the new Whig Party was stronger in the Northeast than in the South and the West and stronger among mercantile groups than among small farmers. Hence to some extent the Whigs were the successors of the Federalists. Many, though not all, Whigs favored a national bank, a protective tariff, and federally sponsored internal improvements. The Jacksonians opposed all three policies. Yet conflict between the two parties revolved around personalities as much as policies. The Whigs were a diverse group, united more by opposition to the Democrats than by agreement on programs. In 1840, the Whigs won their first presidential election under the leadership of General William Henry Harrison, a military hero known as Old Tippecanoe. The 1840 election marked the first time in American history that two parties competed for the presidency in every state in the Union. The Whig campaign carefully avoided issues—because different party factions disagreed

20 See Aldrich, *Why Parties?*, chap. 4.

on most matters—and emphasized the personal qualities and heroism of the candidate. The Whigs also invested heavily in campaign rallies and entertainment to win the hearts, if not exactly the minds, of the voters. The 1840 campaign came to be called the hard-cider campaign to denote the then-common practice of using food and, especially, drink to elicit electoral favor.

In the late 1840s and early 1850s, conflicts over slavery produced sharp divisions within both the Whig and the Democratic parties, despite the efforts of party leaders such as Henry Clay and Stephen A. Douglas to develop sectional compromises that would bridge the widening gulf between the North and the South. By 1856, the Whig Party had all but disintegrated under the strain. The 1854 Kansas-Nebraska Act overturned the Missouri Compromise of 1820 and the Compromise of 1850, which together had hindered the expansion of slavery in the American territories. The Kansas-Nebraska Act gave each territory the right to decide whether to permit slavery. Opposition to this policy led to the formation of a number of antislavery parties, with the Republicans emerging as the strongest of the new forces.[21] They drew their membership from existing political groups—former Whigs, Know-Nothings of the American Party, free soilers, and antislavery Democrats. In 1856, the party's first presidential candidate, John C. Frémont, won one-third of the popular vote and carried 11 states.

The early Republican platforms appealed to commercial as well as antislavery interests. The Republicans favored homesteading, internal improvements, the construction of a transcontinental railroad, and protective tariffs, as well as the containment of slavery. In 1858, the Republican Party won control of the House of Representatives; in 1860, the Republican presidential candidate, Abraham Lincoln, was victorious. Lincoln's victory strengthened southern calls for secession from the Union and led, soon thereafter, to all-out civil war.

The Third Party System: Republicans and Democrats, 1860–96

During the course of the war, President Lincoln depended heavily on Republican governors and state legislatures to raise troops, provide funding, and maintain popular support for a long and bloody military conflict. The secession of the South had stripped the Democratic Party of many of its leaders and supporters, but the Democrats nevertheless remained politically competitive throughout the war and nearly won the 1864 presidential election due to war weariness on the part of the northern public. With the defeat of the Confederacy in 1865, some congressional Republicans sought to convert the South into a Republican bastion through Reconstruction, a program that enfranchised newly freed slaves while disenfranchising many white voters and disqualifying many white politicians from seeking office. Reconstruction collapsed in the 1870s as a result of divisions within the Republican Party in Congress and violent resistance to the

21 See William E. Gienapp, *The Origins of the Republican Party, 1852–1856* (New York: Oxford University Press, 1994).

program by southern whites. With the end of Reconstruction, the former Confederate states regained full membership in the Union and full control of their internal affairs. Throughout the South, African Americans were deprived of political rights, including the right to vote, despite post–Civil War constitutional guarantees to the contrary. The post–Civil War South was solidly Democratic in its political affiliation, and with a firm southern base, the national Democratic Party was able to confront the Republicans on a more or less equal basis. From the end of the Civil War to the 1890s, the Republican Party remained the party of the North, with strong business and middle-class support, while the Democratic Party was the party of the South, with support from working-class and immigrant groups in the North. Republican candidates campaigned by waving the "bloody shirt" of the Civil War and urging their supporters to "vote the way you shot." Democrats emphasized the issue of the tariff, which they claimed was ruinous to agricultural interests.

Party Machines as a Strategic Innovation. It was during the third party system that party entrepreneurs were most successful at turning party organizations into well-oiled machines. In the nineteenth and early twentieth centuries, many cities and counties, and even a few states on occasion, had such well organized parties that they were called party machines and their leaders were called bosses. Party machines depended heavily on the patronage of the spoils system, the party's power to control government jobs. Patronage worked as a selective benefit for anyone the party wished to attract to its side. With thousands of jobs to dispense to the party faithful, party bosses were able to recruit armies of political workers, who in turn mobilized millions of voters. During the height of the party machines, party and government were virtually interchangeable. Just as the creation of mass parties by Van Buren and other political entrepreneurs of the second party system solved a collective action problem, the well-oiled machines used the selective incentives of patronage and nomination to maintain their organizations and diminish free riding. Many organizational aspects of party politics, in short, involve the ingenuity of rational politicians and leaders grappling with problems of coordination and collective action, as the rationality principle and the collective action principle suggest.

party machine 

In the late nineteenth and early twentieth centuries, a local party organization that controlled local politics through patronage and the nomination process

Many critics condemned party machines as antidemocratic and corrupt. They argued that machines served the interests of powerful businesses and did not help the working people who voted for them. But one of the most notorious machine leaders in American political history, George Washington Plunkitt of New York City's Tammany Hall, considered machine politics and the spoils system to be "patriotic." Plunkitt grasped a simple, central fact about purposeful behavior and overcoming the collective action problem. To create and retain political influence and power, "you must study human nature and act accordin'." He argued with some acumen that the country was built by political parties, that the parties needed such patronage to operate and thrive, and that if patronage was withdrawn, the parties would "go to pieces." As we see shortly, Plunkitt was somewhat prescient in making this observation.

Institutional Reforms of the Progressives. As the nineteenth century gave way to the twentieth, the excessive powers and abuses of party machines and their bosses led to one of the great reform movements in American history, the so-called Progressive Era. Many Progressive reformers were undoubtedly motivated by a sincere desire to rid politics of corruption and improve the quality and efficiency of government in the United States. But simultaneously, from the perspective of middle- and upper-class Progressives and the financial, commercial, and industrial elites with whom they were often associated, the weakening or elimination of party organization would also mean that power could more readily be acquired and retained by the "best men"—that is, those with wealth, position, and education.

The list of antiparty reforms of the Progressive Era is a familiar one. As we saw in Chapter 11, the introduction of voter registration laws required eligible voters to register in person well before an election. The Australian-ballot reform took away the parties' privilege of printing and distributing ballots and thus introduced the possibility of split-ticket voting (see also Chapter 11). The introduction of nonpartisan local elections eroded grassroots party organization. The extension of "merit systems" for administrative appointments stripped party organizations of their vitally important access to patronage and thus reduced party leaders' capacity to control the nomination of candidates. These reforms obviously did not destroy political parties as entities, but taken together they did substantially weaken party organizations in the United States. After the beginning of the twentieth century, the strength of American political parties gradually diminished, and voter turnout declined precipitously. Between the two world wars, organization remained the major tool available to contending electoral forces, but in most areas of the country the "reformed" state and local parties that survived the Progressive Era gradually lost their organizational vitality and coherence and became less effective campaign tools. Although most areas of the nation continued to boast Democratic and Republican Party groupings, reform did mean the elimination of the permanent mass organizations that had been the parties' principal campaign weapons.

The Fourth Party System, 1896–1932

During the 1890s, profound and rapid social and economic changes led to the emergence of a variety of protest parties, including the Populist Party, which won the support of hundreds of thousands of voters in the South and the West. The Populists appealed mainly to small farmers but also attracted western mining interests and urban workers. In the 1892 presidential election, the Populist Party carried four states and elected governors in eight states. In 1896, the Democrats in effect adopted the Populist Party platform and nominated William Jennings Bryan, a Democratic senator with pronounced Populist sympathies, for the presidency. The Republicans nominated the conservative senator William McKinley. In the ensuing campaign, northern and midwestern business made an all-out effort to defeat what it saw as a radical threat from the Populist-Democratic alliance. When the dust settled, the Republicans had won a resounding victory.

In the nation's metropolitan regions, especially in the Northeast and upper Midwest, workers became convinced that the Populist-Democratic alliance threatened the industries that provided their jobs, while immigrants were frightened by the nativist rhetoric employed by some Populist orators and writers. The Republicans had carried the northern and midwestern states and confined the Democrats to their bastions in the South and the Far West. For the next 36 years, the Republicans were the nation's majority party, carrying 7 of 9 presidential elections and controlling both houses of Congress in 15 of 18 contests. The Republican Party of this era was very much the party of American business, advocating low taxes, high tariffs, and a minimum of government regulation. The Democrats were far too weak to offer much opposition. Southern Democrats, moreover, were more concerned with maintaining the region's autonomy on issues of race to challenge the Republicans on other fronts.

The Fifth Party System: The New Deal Coalition, 1932–68

Soon after the Republican candidate Herbert Hoover won the 1928 presidential election, the nation's economy collapsed. The Great Depression, which produced unprecedented economic hardship, stemmed from a variety of causes, but from the perspective of millions of Americans the Republican Party had not done enough to promote economic recovery. In 1932, Americans elected Franklin Delano Roosevelt and a solidly Democratic Congress. Roosevelt developed a program for economic recovery that he dubbed the New Deal, under the auspices of which the size and reach of America's national government was substantially increased. The federal government took responsibility for economic management and social welfare to an extent that was unprecedented in American history. Roosevelt designed many of his programs specifically to expand the political base of the Democratic Party. He rebuilt the party around a nucleus of unionized workers, upper-middle-class intellectuals and professionals, southern farmers, Jews, Catholics, and northern African Americans (few blacks in the South could vote) that made the Democrats the nation's majority party for 36 years. Republicans groped for a response to the New Deal but often wound up supporting popular New Deal programs such as Social Security in what was sometimes derided as "me-too" Republicanism.

The New Deal coalition was severely strained during the 1960s by conflicts over President Lyndon Johnson's Great Society initiative, civil rights, and the Vietnam War. A number of Johnson's Great Society programs, designed to fight poverty and racial discrimination, involved the empowerment of local groups that were often at odds with established city and county governments. These programs touched off battles between local Democratic political machines and the national administration that split the Democratic coalition. For its part, the struggle over civil rights initially divided northern Democrats, who supported the civil rights cause, and white southern Democrats, who defended the system of racial segregation. Subsequently, as the civil rights movement launched a northern campaign aimed at securing access to jobs and education and an end to racial discrimination in such realms as housing, northern Democrats also experienced a split, often along class lines, with blue-collar workers tending to vote Republican. The struggle over the Vietnam War further divided the Democrats, with upper-income liberal Democrats strongly opposing the Johnson administration's decision to send U.S. forces to fight in Southeast Asia. These schisms within the Democratic Party provided an opportunity for the Republican Party to return to power, which it did in 1968 under the leadership of Richard Nixon.

The Sixth Party System?

In the 1960s, conservative Republicans argued that me-tooism was a recipe for continual failure and sought to reposition the party as a genuine alternative to the Democrats. In 1964, for example, the Republican presidential candidate, Barry Goldwater, author of a book titled *The Conscience of a Conservative*, argued in favor of substantially reduced levels of taxation and spending, less government regulation of the economy, and the elimination of many federal social programs. Although Goldwater was defeated by Lyndon Johnson, the ideas he espoused continue to be major themes of the Republican Party. The Goldwater message, however, was not enough to lead Republicans to victory. As discussed in Chapter 11, it took Richard Nixon's "southern strategy" to give the Republicans the votes it needed to end Democratic dominance of the political process. Nixon appealed strongly to disaffected white southerners and, with the help of the independent candidate and former Alabama governor George Wallace, sparked the shift of voters that eventually gave the once-hated "party of Lincoln" a strong position in all the states of the former Confederacy. In the 1980s, under the leadership of Ronald Reagan, Republicans added another important group to their coalition: religious conservatives who were offended by Democratic support of abortion rights as well as alleged Democratic disdain for traditional cultural and religious values.

While Republicans built a political base with economic and social conservatives and white southerners, the Democratic Party maintained its support among unionized workers and upper-middle-class intellectuals and professionals. Democrats also appealed strongly to racial minorities. The 1965 Voting Rights Act had greatly increased the participation of black voters in the South and helped the Democratic Party retain some congressional and Senate seats in the South. And while the GOP appealed to social conservatives, the Democrats appealed strongly to Americans concerned about abortion rights, gay rights, feminism, environmentalism, and other progressive social causes. The results have been something of a draw. Democrats have won the presidency 4 out of the 11 elections since the passage of the Voting Rights Act, but held at least one chamber of Congress for most of that time. That apparent stalemate masked dramatic changes in the regional bases of the parties. Republicans surged in the south, making the southern states the foundation of their presidential and congressional victories. Those gains came at the expense of the old-line Republicans in the northeast. New England, once the bedrock of the party, had not one Republican U.S. House member after the 2008 election.

The shift of much of the South from the Democratic to the Republican camp, along with the other developments mentioned earlier, meant that each political party became ideologically more homogeneous after the 1980s. Today as we've noted before, there are few liberal Republicans or conservative Democrats. One consequence of this development is that party loyalty in Congress, which had been weak between the 1950s and the 1970s, became a more potent force. The 1990s witnessed a dramatic resurgence of party-line voting in Congress. A simple measure of party developed by Professor Stuart Rice in the 1920s and tracked by *Congressional Quarterly* since the 1950s is the party unity score. This is the percentage of bills on which a majority of a party votes against a majority of the other party. Between the 1950s and the 1970s, unity hovered around 70 percent. Since the 1980s it has regularly exceeded 90 percent.[22]

To some extent, ideology has replaced organization as the glue holding together each party's coalition. But in the long run, ideology is often an unreliable basis for party unity. Although the activists within each party grouping are united by some beliefs, ideological divisions also plague both camps. Within the Republican coalition, social conservatives are often at odds with economic conservatives, whereas among Democrats proponents of regulatory reform and economic internationalism are frequently at odds with traditional liberals, who favor big government and protecting American workers from foreign competition. The party workers of yesteryear supported the leadership almost no matter what. Today's more ideologically motivated party activists give their leaders only very conditional backing and feel free to withhold support if they disagree with the leadership's goals and plans. Because of internal divisions in the Republican Party, for example, Republican congressional leaders have adopted a strategy of avoiding votes on the many issues that might split the party.[23] The price of unity based on ideology can be the inability to act.

The ideological gap between the two parties has been exacerbated by two other factors: each party's dependence on ideologically motivated activists and the changes in the presidential nominating system that were introduced during the 1970s. As for the first of these, Democratic political candidates depend heavily on the support of liberal activists—such as feminists, environmentalists, and civil libertarians—to organize and finance their campaigns, while Republican political candidates depend equally on the support of conservative activists, including religious fundamentalists. In the nineteenth century, political activists were motivated more by party loyalty and political patronage than by programmatic concerns. Today's issue-oriented activists, by contrast, demand that politicians demonstrate strong commitments to moral principles and political causes

22 The classic statement of the connection between cohesive legislative parties and ideological homogeneity within party ranks is found in David W. Rohde, *Parties and Leaders in the Post-reform House* (Chicago: University of Chicago Press, 1991). An elaboration of this argument is presented in Cox and McCubbins, *Setting the Agenda*. See also Nolan McCarty, Keith Poole, and Howard Rosenthal, *Polarized America: The Dance of Inequality and Unequal Riches* (Cambridge, MA: MIT Press, 2006).

23 Isaiah J. Poole, "Votes Echo Electoral Themes," *Congressional Quarterly Weekly Report*, December 11, 2004, pp. 2906–8.

in exchange for their support. The demands of party activists have tended to push Democrats further to the political left and Republicans further to the political right. Often efforts by politicians to reach compromises on key issues are attacked by party activists as "sellouts," leading to stalemates on such matters as the budget and judicial appointments.

The second factor exacerbating the parties' ideological split, the changes in the presidential nominating system, took place in response to the Democratic Party's defeat in 1968. Liberal forces, guided by the so-called McGovern-Fraser Commission on party reform, succeeded in changing the rules governing Democratic presidential nominations to reduce the power of party officials and party professionals while increasing the role of issue-oriented activists. Among other changes, the new rules required national convention delegates to be chosen in primaries and caucuses rather than by each state party's central committee, as had previously been the practice in many states. Subsequently, Republican activists were able to bring about similar changes in the Republicans' rules, so that today in both parties presidential nominating processes are strongly influenced by precisely the sorts of grassroots activists who are often inclined to oppose centrist or pragmatic politicians in favor of those appearing to manifest ideological purity. As a result, elections have tended to pit liberal Democrats against conservative Republicans. Observers of post–World War II American political parties often dubbed them Tweedledum and Tweedledee, but the two parties today differ sharply on a number of social, economic, and foreign-policy issues. Compare, for example, Democratic and Republican legislative priorities at the opening of the 110th Congress, in January 2007. Republicans emphasized support of the Iraq War policy, immigration reform, and new laws to strengthen marriage and discourage abortion. The Democrats emphasized expanding social programs, protecting the jobs of unionized workers, bringing an end to operations in Iraq, and strengthening abortion rights. These competing agendas set the stage for a contentious legislative session. At the advent of the 111th Congress in 2009, the legislature was focused squarely on reviving the U.S. economy, but the parties' other priorities hadn't changed appreciably. The Republicans were willing to slow the appointment of cabinet officials for their positions on abortion and gay rights, while Democrats pushed for aggressive action on health reform, government regulation, and global warming.

American Third Parties

Although the United States is said to possess a two-party system, we have always had more than two parties. Typically, third parties in the United States have represented social and economic protests that, for one or another reason, were not given voice by the two major parties.[24] Such parties have had a good

third party

A party that organizes to compete against the two major American political parties

24 For a discussion of third parties in the United States, see Daniel A. Mazmanian, *Third Parties in Presidential Elections* (Washington, DC: Brookings Institution, 1974).

deal of influence on ideas and elections in the United States. The Populists, a party centered in the rural areas of the West and the Midwest during the late nineteenth century, and the Progressives, spokesmen for the urban middle classes in the late nineteenth and early twentieth centuries, are among the most important examples. More recently, Ross Perot, who ran in 1992 and 1996 as an independent, impressed some voters with his folksy style in the presidential debates and garnered almost 19 percent of the votes cast in the 1992 presidential election. Earlier, the independent candidate George Wallace received almost 10 percent of the vote in 1968, and John Anderson received about 5 percent in 1980.

Table 12.1 lists all the parties that offered candidates in one or more states in the presidential election of 2012. The third-party and independent candidates together polled about 2.25 million votes. They gained no electoral votes for president, and most of them disappeared immediately after the presidential election. The significance of the table is that it demonstrates the number of third parties running candidates and appealing to voters. Third-party candidacies also arise at the state and local levels. In New York, the Liberal and Conservative parties have been on the ballot for decades. In 1998, Minnesota elected a third-party governor, the former professional wrestler Jesse Ventura.

Although the Republican Party, founded as a third party in the 1850s, was the only third American political party ever to make itself permanent (by replacing the Whigs and becoming the Democrats' major competitor), other third parties have enjoyed an influence far beyond their electoral size. That is because large parts of their programs were adopted by one or both of the major parties, which sought to appeal to the voters mobilized by the new party and so expand their own electoral strength. The Democratic Party, for example, became a great deal more liberal when it adopted most of the Progressive program early in the twentieth century. Many socialists felt that President Franklin Delano Roosevelt's New Deal had adopted most of their party's program, including old-age pensions, unemployment compensation, an agricultural marketing program, and laws guaranteeing workers the right to organize into unions.

This kind of influence explains the short lives of third parties. Their causes are usually eliminated by the ability of the major parties to absorb their programs and draw their supporters into the mainstream. There are, of course, additional reasons for the short duration of most third parties. One is the typical limitation of their electoral support to one or two regions. Populist support, for example, was primarily midwestern. The 1948 Progressive Party, with Henry Wallace as its candidate, drew nearly half its votes from the state of New York. The American Independent Party polled nearly 10 million popular votes and 45 electoral votes for George Wallace in 1968—the most electoral votes ever polled by a third-party candidate. But all of Wallace's electoral votes and the majority of his popular vote came from the states of the Deep South. Americans usually assume that only the candidates nominated by one of the two major parties have any chance of winning an election. Thus a vote cast for a third-party or an independent candidate is often seen as a wasted vote. Voters who

Table 12.1

PARTIES AND CANDIDATES, 2012

CANDIDATE	PARTY	VOTE TOTAL	PERCENT OF VOTE
Barack Obama	Democratic	65,387,700	50.94%
Mitt Romney	Republican	60,724,464	47.31%
Gary Johnson	Libertarian	1,271,020	0.99%
Jill Stein	Green	465,131	0.36%
Virgil Goode	Constitution	120,683	0.09%
Roseanne Barr	Peace and Freedom	67,185	0.05%
Rocky Anderson	Justice	41,831	0.03%
Tom Hoefling	America's	40,358	0.03%
Others		238,005	0.19%
Total		128,356,377	

SOURCE: National Association of Secretaries of State, "Results for the 2012 General Election," www.nass.org/index.php?option=com_content&view=article&id=342:state-election-results-reporting&catid=928:uncategorized-elections-voting&itemid=457 (accessed 11/26/12).

ANALYZING THE EVIDENCE

Though the Democrats and the Republicans are America's dominant political forces, many minor parties nominate candidates for the presidency. Why are there so many minor parties? Why don't these parties represent much of a threat to the major parties?

would prefer a third-party candidate may feel compelled to vote for the major party candidate whom they regard as the lesser of two evils to avoid wasting their votes in a futile gesture. Third-party candidates must struggle—usually without success—to overcome the perception that they cannot win. Thus in 2004, many liberals who admired Ralph Nader nevertheless urged him not to mount an independent bid for the presidency for fear he would siphon liberal votes from the Democrats, as he had in 2000. Some former Naderites participated in efforts to keep Nader off the ballot in a number of states. Ultimately Nader did mount a presidential campaign but received 2.5 million fewer votes in 2004 than in 2000. Most of his former adherents, knowing he could not win and might prevent their second-choice candidate from winning, voted for John Kerry.

As many scholars have pointed out, third-party prospects are also hampered by America's single-member-district plurality election system. In many other nations, several individuals can be elected to represent each legislative district.

single-member district

An electorate that is allowed to elect only one representative from each district—the typical method of representation in the United States

multiple-member district

An electorate that selects several candidates at large from an entire district, with each voter given the number of votes equivalent to the number of seats to be filled

This is called a system of multiple-member districts. With this type of system, the candidates of weaker parties have a better chance of winning at least some seats. For their part, voters are less concerned about wasting ballots and usually more willing to support minor-party candidates.

Reinforcing the effects of the single-member district (as noted in Chapter 11), plurality voting rules generally have the effect of setting what could be called a high threshold for victory. To win a plurality race, candidates usually must secure many more votes than they would need under most European systems of proportional representation. For example, to win an American plurality election in a single-member district with only two candidates, a politician must win more than 50 percent of the votes cast. To win a seat in a European multimember district under proportional-representation rules, a candidate may need to win only 15 or 20 percent of the votes cast. This high threshold in American elections discourages minor parties and encourages the various political factions that might otherwise form minor parties to minimize their differences and remain within the major-party coalitions.[25]

It would nevertheless be incorrect to assert (as some scholars have maintained) that America's single-member plurality election system guarantees that only two parties will compete for power in all regions of the country. All that can be said is that American election law depresses the number of parties likely to survive over long periods of time in the United States. There is nothing magical about two.

Indeed, the single-member plurality election system can also discourage second parties. After all, if one party consistently receives a large plurality of the vote, people may eventually come to see their vote even for the second party as a wasted effort. This happened to the Republican Party in the Deep South before World War II. Of the two most successful third-party efforts of the last half century, by George Wallace in 1968 and Ross Perot in 1992, it is useful to compare the candidates' relative fates. In the last Gallup public opinion poll before the 1968 election, Hubert Humphrey, the Democrat, and Richard Nixon, the Republican, were in a near dead heat, with 43 percent and 42 percent of the vote respectively. George Wallace was the preferred choice of about 14 percent of the electorate, with some voters still undecided. In the actual balloting, Nixon barely won the popular vote, and Wallace's share shrank to less than 10 percent: Wallace lost more than one-third of his support. Fast forward to 1992, when the final Gallup poll showed the Democrat, Bill Clinton, leading the Republican, George H. W. Bush, by about five percentage points (43–38). Perot was the first preference of about 19 percent. In the final balloting, Perot got approximately that share—there was virtually no loss of support such as Wallace experienced in 1968. In each case, the third-party candidate had little chance of winning. But

25 See Maurice Duverger, *Political Parties: Their Organization and Activity in the Modern State*, trans. Barbara North and Robert North (New York: Wiley, 1954).

in the Humphrey-Nixon contest, the margin was razor thin, and many Wallace supporters, not wanting to waste their vote, opted for the lesser evil. In the Clinton-Bush race, Clinton was comfortably in the lead at the end, so Perot supporters felt less pressure to desert their favorite in order to make a difference in the contest between the two leaders. In each case, voters reflected the rationality principle in their deliberations. Indeed, there is evidence in the 2000 race between Al Gore, the Democrat, and George W. Bush, the Republican, that the third-party candidate Ralph Nader did better in those states where either Bush or Gore was nearly certain of winning, whereas his support dwindled in more closely contested states.

Conclusion: Parties and Democracy

Political parties help make democracy work. We often do not appreciate that democratic government is a contradiction in terms. Government implies policies, programs, and decisive action. Democracy, on the other hand, implies an opportunity for all citizens to participate fully in the governmental process. Full participation by everyone is inconsistent with getting things done in an efficient and timely manner. How can we balance the ideals of democracy and efficiency in government? How can we make certain that popular participation will result in a government capable of making decisions and developing needed policies? At what point should participation stop and government begin? Strong political parties are a partial antidote to the inherent contradiction between participation and governance. Strong parties can both encourage popular involvement and convert participation into effective government.

As we've seen, parties simplify the electoral process. They set the electoral agenda by laying out party platforms, broad statements of ideas and policies that the party's candidates will pursue in office. They recruit candidates, accumulate and distribute campaign resources, and they register and mobilize people to vote. Party control of the nominating process and the pressures toward two-party politics in the United States mean that most voters must decide between just two meaningful or plausible choices in any election. Parties, thus, serve as sort of an informal institution in elections and government. They structure electoral choices and manage the legislative agenda, and they serve as a bridge between elections and government.

This in turn facilitates voters' decision making. Voters can reasonably expect what sorts of policies a candidate who has a party's endorsement will represent if elected. Even before a given candidate has received the nomination, most voters have already sorted themselves into one of the two competing camps, Democratic or Republican. They know for whom they will vote before the election begins. This may seem like a gross simplification of politics. It reduces the many complex interests in our society to just two competing teams, whose policy platforms must be watered down to accommodate the many subtle differences or ideological nuances among the groups inside the party. It further reduces politics into warring factions that have little hope of finding compromise or common ground. However, what the two-party system does accomplish is that it gives meaning to the vote. It empowers the voter to say, I want to stay the course with the party in power, or, I want to go in a new direction.

For Further Reading

reader selection Aldrich, John H. *Why Parties? The Origin and Transformation of Party Politics in America.* Chicago: University of Chicago Press, 1995.

Beck, Paul Allen, and Marjorie Randon Hershey. *Party Politics in America.* 10th ed. New York: Longman, 2003.

reader selection Campbell, Angus, Philip E. Converse, Warren E. Miller, and Donald E. Stokes, *The American Voter.* Chicago: University of Chicago Press, 1980.

Chambers, William N., and Walter Dean Burnham, eds. *The American Party Systems: Stages of Political Development.* 2nd ed. New York: Oxford University Press, 1975.

Coleman, John J. *Party Decline in America: Policy, Politics, and the Fiscal State.* Princeton, NJ: Princeton University Press, 1996.

Cox, Gary W., and Mathew D. McCubbins. *Legislative Leviathan: Party Government in the House.* Berkeley: University of California Press, 1993.

———. *Setting the Agenda: Responsible Party Government in the U.S. House of Representatives.* New York: Cambridge University Press, 2005.

Hofstadter, Richard. *The Idea of a Party System: The Rise of Legitimate Opposition in the United States, 1780–1840.* Berkeley: University of California Press, 1969.

Mayhew, David. *Electoral Realignments: A Critique of an American Genre.* New Haven, CT: Yale University Press, 2007.

Rohde, David W. *Parties and Leaders in the Post-reform House.* Chicago: University of Chicago Press, 1991.

Sundquist, James L. *Dynamics of the Party System: Alignment and Realignment of Political Parties in the United States.* Washington, DC: Brookings Institution, 1983.

Wattenberg, Martin P. *The Decline of American Political Parties, 1952–1996*. Cambridge, MA: Harvard University Press, 1998.

Visit wwnorton.com/studyspace/ to access free review materials such as:

- Vocabulary Flashcards of All Key Terms
- Chapter Review Quizzes
- Complete Study Outlines

reader selection

Highlighted selections are included in *Readings in American Politics: Analysis and Perspectives*, Second Edition.

13

PART 1 2 X 4

DEMOCRATIC POLITICS

Groups and Interests

Chapter Outline

Democratic politics in the United States does not end with elections. Federal, state, and local governments provide many additional avenues through which individuals and organizations can express their preferences. People may, for example, contact elected officials, their staff, and bureaucrats directly about a particular decision or problem. They may participate in public meetings about legislation or administrative rulings; some private citizens are even selected to serve on special government commissions because of their expertise or particular concerns. People may file lawsuits to request that a government agency take a particular action or to prevent it from doing so. They may give their time and money to elect candidates to their liking. They may express their opinions in newspapers, on television and the Internet, or through other venues, and hold public protests, all without fear of persecution. Individuals, organizations, and even governments make frequent use of these many points of access. Many of these encounters with government are episodic, as when an individual contacts an agency to solve a particular problem. But a substantial amount of political activity in the United States occurs through enduring, organized efforts that bring together many individuals into collective action to seek a common goal.

Both a pull and a push drive organized political activity in the United States. The pull comes from the government's need to collect information about the impact of decisions on various constituencies or sectors of society. A responsive government needs subtle and refined information about how a decision will affect people or society or about the best way to implement a law. Legislators, judges, and bureaucrats typically do not have the time and resources to study all potential problems. Instead they rely on information from individuals and organizations to gauge the importance of a given problem and to learn about the consequences of particular decisions. The solution in American government is to allow, and indeed encourage, an open government with many points of access for competing views.

The push comes from the willingness and ability of people to contact government. Individuals and organizations bring their concerns to the government with some purpose in mind, to gain some benefit. Those benefits often take the form of simply better understanding government regulations and actions. When a commission or department issues a new regulation, firms that are potentially affected must figure out whether the regulation applies to them, how to comply if they are affected, and the exact interpretation of the regulations. Firms frequently hire representation in Washington or the state capital just to stay on top of such matters. But many of those involved in direct political action want more than information; they want to change laws and public policies to favor their particular interests. They want targeted appropriations or favorable regulatory rulings, potentially worth millions, even billions of dollars. One influential study discovered that half of the activities and efforts of businesspeople who contacted the government consisted of gathering information and half consisted of advocacy for a particular policy or action.[1]

CORE OF THE ANALYSIS

Individuals, firms, and other organizations engage in a wide variety of political activities, including contacting elected officials, attending government meetings, engaging in campaign activities, and contributing money in order to shape how those in office make and implement laws.

These activities help government solve an important problem—the problem of how to learn about what problems are important to society and how government actions might affect the society.

There is a clear orientation of interest groups toward those segments of society with better education or more economic resources, and those most directly affected by government actions, especially corporations.

Collective organization of interests is difficult, as there are strong incentives for any single individual to free ride. As a result, interests in society, especially very broad interests such as "all consumers" or "the middle class," often lack effective organizations that can express their preferences.

1 Raymond Bauer, Ithiel de Sola Pool, and Lewis Dexter, *American Business and Public Policy* (Chicago: Atherton Press, 1972).

Interest-group politics in the United States involves thousands of organizations and individuals competing for the attention of elected representatives and government officials and, once they have that attention, competing with other groups and individuals to influence particular government decisions. There are roughly 15,000 registered lobbyists in Washington, D.C., and countless more in state capitals and city governments. In the din of day-to-day politics, it can be hard to get a particular concern before Congress or the bureaucracy, and one group's "special interest" may not seem so special in comparison with the demands of many other groups. The institutions of American government further shape political outcomes that interest groups can achieve. Groups strategically seek out institutional venues they believe will be most hospitable to their goals and interests, but the system of American government often means that one must win in many different domains in order to change public policy. A group may succeed in one domain, such as a House committee, only to find itself blocked elsewhere, such as in the analogous Senate committee.

This is pluralism at work. It is messy and often disliked by the public at large, but it is an essential feature of American government. The U.S. Constitution embraces this idea fully. The more competition there is among many different interests the less likely it is that any one will triumph and the more likely it is that representatives and government officials will learn what they need to know.[2] There is always the risk, however, that organized interests will have excessive influence over the government. Regulations of lobbying and campaign contributions, as well as ethics rules in government, are designed to prevent government from serving particular interests to the detriment of the common good.

One of the most difficult and profound questions about the U.S. system of government is whether the separation of powers and free and open political competition provide sufficient safeguards against excessive influence by certain groups. How much should American governments limit what individuals and organizations say and do in order to prevent particular interests from having too much influence? In short, how should we manage the trade-off between free speech and the potential corrupting influence of groups? Other countries severely limit lobbying and campaign spending. Should the United States do so as well? Or does open political competition limit the power of special interests? The answers to these questions are continually examined and debated in American government, from city councils to the Supreme Court.

In this chapter we analyze the social basis of organizations, the problems inherent in collective action, and some solutions to these problems. We discuss the character and balance of the interests promoted through the pluralistic political system in the United States. We further examine the tremendous growth of interest groups in their number, resources, and activity in recent decades. Finally, we examine the strategies that groups use to influence politics and whether their influence in the political process has become excessive.

2 This sentiment is expressed most eloquently Alexander Hamilton, James Madison, and John Jay, *The Federalist Papers,* Clinton L. Rossiter, ed. (New York: New American Library, 1961), no. 10.

WHAT ARE THE CHARACTERISTICS OF INTEREST GROUPS?

An interest group is an organized group of individuals or organizations that makes policy-related appeals to government. Individuals form groups and engage in collective action to increase the chances that their views will be heard and their interests treated favorably by the government. Interest groups are organized to influence governmental decisions; they are sometimes referred to as lobbies.

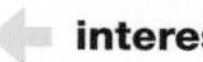

interest group

An organized group of individuals or organizations that makes policy-related appeals to government

Interest groups are sometimes confused with political action committees (see Chapter 11). The difference is that PACs focus on helping their favored candidates win elections, and interest groups focus on influencing elected officials. Another distinction we should make is that interest groups differ from political parties: interest groups tend to concern themselves primarily with the policies of government; parties tend to concern themselves primarily with the personnel of government.

Interest Groups Not Only Enhance Democracy . . .

There are an enormous number of interest groups in the United States, and millions of Americans are members of one or more groups, at least to the extent of paying dues or attending an occasional meeting. By representing the interests of such large numbers of people and encouraging political participation, organized groups can and do enhance American democracy. Organized groups educate their members about issues that affect them. Groups lobby members of Congress and the executive branch, engage in litigation, and generally represent their members' interests in the political arena. Groups mobilize their members for elections and grassroots lobbying efforts, thus encouraging participation. Interest groups also monitor government programs to make certain that they do not adversely affect their members. In all these ways, organized interests can be said to promote democratic politics.

But Also Represent the Evils of Faction

The framers of the U.S. Constitution feared the power that could be wielded by organized interests. James Madison wrote:

> The public good is disregarded in the conflict of rival [factions], . . . citizens . . . who are united and actuated by some common impulse of passion, or of interest, adverse to the rights of other citizens, or to the permanent and aggregate interests of the community.[3]

3 *The Federalist*, no. 10, p. 78

Yet the Founders believed that interest groups thrived because of freedom—the freedom, enjoyed by all Americans, to organize and express their views. To the framers, this problem presented a dilemma. If the government were given the power to regulate or in any way forbid efforts by organized interests to interfere in the political process, it would in effect have the power to suppress freedom. The solution to this dilemma was presented by Madison:

> Take in a greater variety of parties and interest [and] you make it less probable that a majority of the whole will have a common motive to invade the rights of other citizens. . . . [Hence the advantage] enjoyed by a large over a small republic.[4]

According to the Madisonian theory, a good constitution encourages multitudes of interests so that no single interest can ever tyrannize the others. The basic assumption is that competition among interests will produce balance and compromise, with all the interests regulating each other.[5] Today this Madisonian principle of regulation is called pluralism. According to pluralist theory, all interests are and should be free to compete for influence in the United States. Moreover, according to pluralist doctrine, the outcome of this competition is compromise and moderation, because no group is likely to be able to achieve any of its goals without accommodating some of the views of its many competitors.[6]

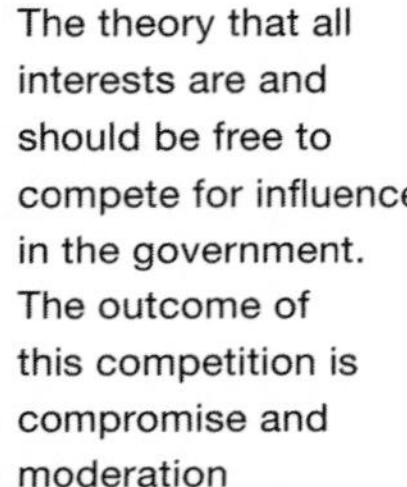
pluralism

The theory that all interests are and should be free to compete for influence in the government. The outcome of this competition is compromise and moderation

There are tens of thousands of organized groups in the United States, but the huge number of interest groups competing for influence does not mean that all interests are fully and equally represented in the American political process. The political deck is heavily stacked in favor of those interests that are able to organize and that wield substantial economic, social, and institutional resources on behalf of their cause. This means that within the universe of interest-group politics, it is political power—not some abstract conception of the public good—that is likely to prevail. Moreover, this means that interest-group politics, taken as a whole, works more to the advantage of some types of interests than others. In general, a politics in which interest groups predominate is a politics with a distinctly upper-class bias.

Organized Interests Are Predominantly Economic

When most people think about interest groups, they immediately think of groups with a direct and private economic interest in governmental actions, and, indeed, economic interest is one of the main purposes for which individuals and groups engage in political action. Interest groups are generally supported by groups of producers or manufacturers in a particular economic sector. Examples of this type of group include the National Petrochemical Refiners Association, the American Farm Bureau Federation, and the National Fed-

4 *The Federalist,* no. 10, p. 83.

5 *The Federalist,* no. 10.

6 The best statement of the pluralist view is in David B. Truman, *The Governmental Process: Political Interests and Public Opinion* (New York: Knopf, 1951), chap. 2.

eration of Independent Business, which represents small-business owners. At the same time that broadly representative groups such as these are active in Washington, specific companies—such as Disney, Shell, Microsoft, and General Motors—may be active on certain issues that are of particular concern to them.

Labor organizations, although fewer in number and more limited in their financial resources, are extremely active lobbyists. The AFL-CIO, the United Mine Workers, and the International Brotherhood of Teamsters are examples of groups that lobby on behalf of organized labor. In recent years, lobbies have arisen to further the interests of public employees, the most significant among these being the American Federation of State, County, and Municipal Employees.

Professional lobbies such as the American Bar Association and the American Medical Association have been particularly successful in furthering their interests in state and federal legislatures. Financial institutions, represented by organizations such as the American Bankers Association and America's Community Bankers, although often less visible than other lobbies, also play an important role in shaping legislative policy.

Recent decades have witnessed the growth of a powerful "public interest" lobby purporting to represent interests whose concerns are not addressed by traditional lobbies. These groups have been most visible in the consumer protection and environmental policy areas, although public interest groups cover a broad range of issues, from nuclear disarmament to civil rights to abortion. The Natural Resources Defense Council, the Union of Concerned Scientists, the National Association for the Advancement of Colored People, the Christian Coalition of America, and Common Cause are all examples of public interest groups.

The perceived need for representation on Capitol Hill has generated a public-sector lobby, including the National League of Cities, and the "research" lobby. The latter group comprises universities and think tanks, such as Harvard University, the Brookings Institution, and the American Enterprise Institute, that have an interest in obtaining government funds for research and support. Indeed, universities have expanded their lobbying efforts even as they have reduced faculty positions and course offerings and increased tuition.[7] Even with the great expansion in the number of interests, the lion's share of organizations involved in politics in Washington, D.C., and in the state capitols represent economic interests.

All Groups Require Money and Leadership, and Most Need Members

Although there are many kinds of interest groups, most share certain key organizational components. First, most groups must attract and keep members. Usually, groups appeal to members not only by promoting political goals or

7 Betsy Wagner and David Bowermaster, "B.S. Economics," *Washington Monthly* (November 1992): 19–21.

policies that they favor but also by providing them with direct economic or social benefits. Thus, for example, AARP (formerly the American Association for Retired Persons), which promotes the interests of senior citizens, at the same time offers members a variety of insurance benefits and commercial discounts. Similarly, many groups whose goals are chiefly economic or political also seek to attract members through social interaction and good fellowship. Thus the local chapters of many national groups provide their members with a congenial social environment while collecting dues that finance the national office's political efforts.

Second, every group must build a financial structure capable of sustaining an organization and funding the group's activities. Most interest groups rely on yearly membership dues and voluntary contributions from sympathizers. Many also sell members some ancillary services, such as insurance and vacation tours. Third, every group must have a leadership and decision-making structure. For some groups, this structure is very simple. For others, it can involve hundreds of local chapters that are melded into a national apparatus. Finally, most groups include an agency that actually carries out the group's tasks. This may be a research organization, a public relations office, or a lobbying office in Washington or a state capital.

Group Membership Has an Upper-Class Bias

Membership in interest groups is not randomly distributed in the population. People with higher incomes, higher levels of education, and management or professional occupations are much more likely to become members of groups than are those who occupy the lower rungs on the socioeconomic ladder.[8] Well-educated upper-income business and professional people are more likely to have the time and the money, and to have acquired through the educational process the concerns and skills, needed to play a role in a group or association. Moreover, for business and professional people, group membership may provide personal contacts and access to information that can help advance their careers. At the same time, corporate entities—businesses and trade associations—usually have ample resources to form or participate in groups that seek to advance their causes.

The result is that interest-group politics in the United States tends to have a pronounced upper-class bias. Certainly, many interest groups and political associations have a working-class or lower-class membership—labor organizations or welfare-rights organizations, for example—but the great majority of interest groups and their members are drawn from the middle and upper-middle classes. In general, the "interests" served by interest groups are the interests of society's haves. Even when interest groups take opposing positions on issues

8 Kay Lehman Schlozman and John T. Tierney, *Organized Interests and American Democracy* (New York: Harper & Row, 1986), p. 60.

and policies, the conflicting positions they espouse usually reflect divisions among upper-income strata rather than conflicts between upper and lower classes.

In general, to obtain adequate political representation, forces from the bottom rungs of the socioeconomic ladder must be organized on the massive scale associated with political parties. Parties can organize and mobilize the collective energies of large numbers of people who, as individuals, may have very limited resources. Interest groups, on the other hand, generally organize smaller numbers of the better-to-do. Thus the relative importance of political parties and interest groups in American politics has far-ranging implications for the distribution of political power in the United States. As we saw in Chapter 12, after a period of relative weakness in the 1970s, political parties have witnessed a resurgence over the past 25 years, especially in Congress. Interest groups have also become more numerous, more active, and more influential in American politics.

Groups Reflect Changes in the Political Environment

If interest groups and the concerns about them were a new phenomenon, we would not have begun this chapter with James Madison. As long as there is government, as long as government makes policies that add value or impose costs, and as long as there is liberty to organize, interest groups will abound. And if government expands, so will interest groups. For example, a spurt of growth in the national government occurred during the 1880s and 1890s, arising largely from the first government efforts at economic intervention to fight large monopolies and regulate some aspects of interstate commerce. In the latter decade, a parallel spurt of growth occurred in national interest groups, including the imposing National Association of Manufacturers and numerous other trade associations. Many groups organized around specific agricultural commodities as well. This period also marked the beginning of the expansion of trade unions as interest groups. Later, in the 1930s, interest groups with headquarters and representation in Washington began to grow significantly, concurrent with that decade's expansion of the national government.

Over the past 50 years, there has been an enormous increase both in the number of interest groups seeking to play a role in the American political process and in the extent of their opportunity to influence that process. The total number of interest groups in the United States today is not known. There are certainly tens of thousands of groups at the national, state, and local levels. One indication of the proliferation of such groups' activity is the growth over time in the number of political action committees (PACs) attempting to influence U.S. elections. PACs are how most interest group money is spent to influence elections. Nearly six times as many PACs operated in 2008 as in the 1970s (Figure 13.1). A *New York Times* report, for example, noted that during the 1970s, expanded

political action committees (PACs)

Private groups that raise and distribute funds for use in election campaigns

ANALYZING THE EVIDENCE

Since the 1970s, the number of PACs in the United States has sextupled. PACs are not the only type of interest group, but their proliferation suggests that interest-group activity has been on the rise. What factors account for the rise in interest-group activity?

Figure 13.1

PAC COUNT, 1974–2012

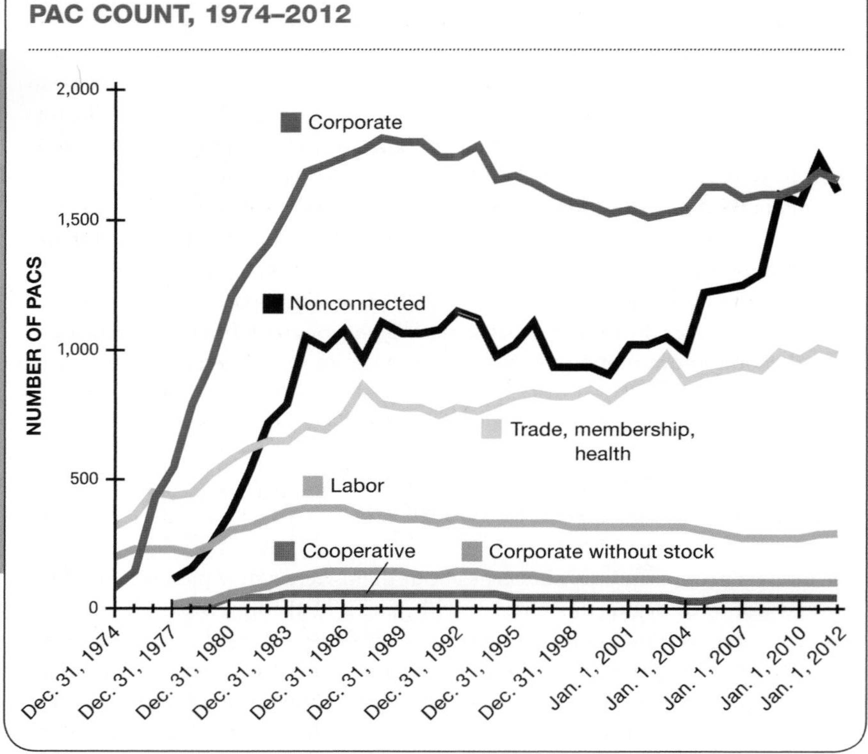

SOURCE: Federal Election Commission, "PAC Count, 1974 to present," July 2012, www.fec.gov/press/summaries/2011/2011paccount.shtml (accessed 12/10/12).

federal regulation of the automobile, oil, gas, education, and health care industries impelled each of these interests to increase substantially its efforts to influence the government's behavior. These efforts, in turn, had the effect of spurring the organization of other groups to augment or counter the activities of the first.[9] The rise of PACs exhibits one of the most common features of business political activity: businesses are reactive. They are usually drawn into politics in response to regulations, rather than to create a new program.

Similarly, federal social programs have occasionally sparked political organization and action on the part of clientele groups seeking to influence the distribution of benefits and, in turn, the organization of groups opposed to the programs or their cost. AARP, perhaps the largest membership organization in the United States, owes its emergence to the creation and expansion of Social Security and Medicare. Once older Americans had guaranteed retirement income and health insurance, they had a clear stake in protecting and even

9 John Herbers, "Special Interests Gaining Power as Voter Disillusionment Grows," *New York Times*, November 14, 1978.

expanding these benefits. AARP formed and grew in response to attempts to pare back the program.[10]

Another factor accounting for the explosion of interest-group activity in recent decades was the emergence of new social and political movements. The civil rights and antiwar movements of the 1960s and the reactions against them created a generation of upper-middle-class professionals and intellectuals who have seen themselves as a political force in opposition to the public policies and politicians associated with the nation's postwar regime. Following close on the heels of these movements came the decade-long debate over the Equal Rights Amendment, the Sagebrush Rebellion (concerning land use in the West), the nuclear disarmament movement, and the antiabortion movement. Such groups sought to make changes in social behavior and public policy, usually through civil disobedience.

Members of these movements—collectively known as the new politics movement—constructed or strengthened public interest groups such as Common Cause, the Sierra Club, the Environmental Defense Fund, Physicians for Social Responsibility, the National Organization for Women, and the various organizations formed by the consumer activist Ralph Nader. These groups were able to influence the media, Congress, and even the judiciary and enjoyed a remarkable degree of success during the late 1960s and early 1970s in securing the enactment of policies they favored. Activist groups also played a major role in promoting the enactment of environmental, consumer, and occupational health and safety legislation.

Among the factors contributing to the rise and success of public interest groups is technology. Computerized direct-mail campaigns in the 1980s were perhaps the first big innovation that allowed organizations to identify and reach out to potential members efficiently and effectively. Today, e-mail, Facebook, Twitter, and other new media have allowed public interest groups to reach hundreds of thousands of potential sympathizers and contributors. Relatively small groups can efficiently identify and mobilize their adherents throughout the nation. Individuals with perspectives that might be in a small, anonymous minority everywhere can become conscious of each other and mobilize for national political action through social networking tools that were unheard of even 30 years ago.

HOW AND WHY DO INTEREST GROUPS FORM?

Pluralist theory argues that because individuals in the United States are free to join or form groups that reflect their common interests, interest groups should easily form whenever a change in the political environment warrants their formation. If this argument is correct, groups should form roughly in proportion

10 Andrea Campbell, *How Policies Make Citizens: Senior Citizen Activism and the American Welfare State* (Princeton, NJ: Princeton University Press, 2003).

to people's interests. We should find a greater number of organizations around interests shared by a greater number of people. The evidence for this pluralist hypothesis is weak, however. In the 1980s, the political scientists Kay Schlozman and John Tierney examined interest groups that represent people's occupations and economic roles.[11] Using census data and lists of interest groups, they compared how many people in the United States have particular economic roles with how many organizations represent those roles in Washington. For example, they found that (in the mid-1980s) 4 percent of the population was looking for work, but only a handful of organizations represented the unemployed in Washington.[12] There is a considerable disparity in Washington representation across categories of individuals in the population, as Table 13.1 suggests. Schlozman and Tierney note, for example, that there are at least a dozen groups representing senior citizens, but none for the middle-aged. Although their study has not been repeated since the 1980s, a perusal of the Directory of Washington Representatives—the lobbyists' phonebook—reveals that little has changed.

The observation that groups form around some interests and not others creates a problem for the pluralist notion of democracy. If there is a bias in the sorts of groups that form, such as only wealthy groups, then political decisions may reflect the bias in who is organized and who is not. Mancur Olson's work, mentioned in Chapter 1 and discussed later in this chapter, is the most well-known challenge to the pluralists. It is in Olson's insights that we find the basis for interest-group formation.

Interest Groups Facilitate Cooperation

Groups of individuals pursuing some common interest or shared objective—maintenance of a hunting and fishing habitat, creation of a network for sharing computer software, lobbying for favorable legislation, playing a Beethoven symphony, and so on—consist of individuals who bear some cost or make some contribution on behalf of the joint goal. Each member of the Possum Hollow Rod and Gun Club may, for example, pay annual dues and devote one weekend a year to cleaning up the rivers and forests of the club-owned game preserve.

We can think of this in an analytic fashion, somewhat removed from any of these examples, as an instance of two-person cooperation writ large. Accordingly, each one of a very large number of individuals has, in the simplest situation, two options in his or her behavioral repertoire: "contribute" or "don't contribute" to achieving the jointly shared objective. If the number of contributors to the group enterprise is sufficiently large, a group goal is achieved. However, there is a twist. If the group goal is achieved, then every member of the group enjoys its benefits, whether he or she contributed to its achievement or not.

11 Schlozman and Tierney, *Organized Interests and American Democracy.*

12 Of course, the number of organizations is at best only a rough measure of the extent to which various categories of citizens are represented in the interest-group world of Washington.

Table 13.1
WHO IS REPRESENTED BY ORGANIZED INTERESTS?

ECONOMIC ROLE OF THE INDIVIDUAL	U.S. ADULTS (%)	ORGS. (%)	TYPE OF ORG. IN WASHINGTON	RATIO OF ORGS. TO ADULTS
Managerial/ administrative	7	71.0	Business association	10.10
Professional/ technical	9	17.0	Professional association	1.90
Student/ teacher	4	4.0	Educational organization	1.00
Farmworker	2	1.5	Agricultural workers' organization	0.75
Unable to work	2	0.6	Organization for the handicapped	0.30
Other nonfarm workers	41	4.0	Union	0.10
Homemaker	19	1.8	Women's organization	0.09
Retired	12	0.8	Senior citizens' organization	0.07
Looking for work	4	0.1	Unemployment organization	0.03

SOURCE: Schlozman and Tierney, *Organized Interests and American Democracy*.

ANALYZING THE EVIDENCE

What types of interests are most likely to be represented by interest groups? If interest-group politics is biased in favor of the wealthy and the powerful, should we curb group politics? What was James Madison's answer? Do you agree with Madison?

The Prisoner's Dilemma and Free Riding. Researchers often rely on the metaphor of the prisoner's dilemma when theorizing about social situations of collective action. The prisoner's dilemma is a famous hypothetical problem from game theory as it is used to discuss why people will rationally take actions that may not be optimal or in the best interests of all. This is similar to the fence-mending example in Chapter 1's discussion of bargaining failure.

In the prisoner's dilemma, two prisoners (call them A and B) are accused of jointly committing a crime. They are kept in separate interview rooms. Each prisoner is offered the same plea bargain: "Testify against the other prisoner in exchange for freedom, provided that your accomplice does not also testify against you. Remain silent, and you will possibly get the maximum sentence if

Figure 13.2
THE PRISONER'S DILEMMA

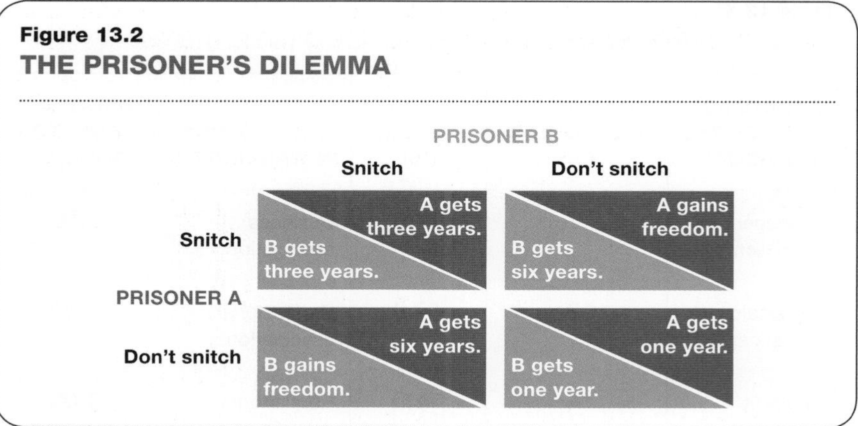

your accomplice testifies against you." Figure 13.2 displays the options Prisoner A faces along the rows and that Prisoner B faces along the columns, and in each cell are the sentences that each person receives for each combination of plea agreements. If neither "snitches," each gets one year; if both snitch each gets three years, and so on. Importantly, the outcome of the plea bargain depends on what the other person does. Before reading on, it is worth studying the table and asking what you would do if you were Prisoner A.

The prisoners face an unpleasant choice. They are self-interested, rational actors, who, given the choice between the two alternatives, will choose the one that offers the best deal. They prefer less jail time to more, and the police, understanding their motivations, have structured the choice so that each prisoner will rat on the other. Notice that in Figure 13.2, Prisoner A is better off choosing to snitch no matter what Prisoner B does. If B chooses to snitch, then A's choice to snitch gets A a three-year jail term, but a don't-snitch choice by A results in six years for A—clearly worse. On the other hand, if B chooses not to snitch, then A gets no jail time if he snitches instead of one year if he also chooses not to snitch. In short, A is always better off snitching. But this situation is symmetrical, so it follows that B is better off snitching, too. If both prisoners snitch, the prosecutor is able to convict both of them, and each serves three years. If they had both kept silent, they would have gotten only one year each. In terms of game theory (from which the prisoner's dilemma is drawn), each player has a dominant strategy—snitching is best no matter what the other player does—and this leads paradoxically to an outcome in which each player is worse off.

The prisoner's dilemma provides the insight that rational individual behavior does not always lead to the best collective results. The logic is compelling—if A appreciates the dilemma and realizes that B appreciates the dilemma, then A will still be drawn to the choice of snitching. The reasons for this are the temptation to get off scot free (if he testifies and his accomplice doesn't) and the fear of being suckered (if his accomplice testifies and he doesn't). The prisoner's dilemma carries a brilliant if troubling insight about collective decision making. People often have difficulty achieving objectives that are in the collective good because the incentive to shirk, to defect, to free ride is just too strong.

Consider the swamp-clearing example described in Chapter 1, in which each person benefits from a drained swamp even if he or she does not provide the required effort. As long as enough other people do so, any individual can ride free on the efforts of the others. This is a multiperson prisoner's dilemma because not providing effort, like snitching, is a dominant strategy, yet if everyone avails himself or herself of it, it leads to an unwanted outcome: a mosquito-infested swamp. The prospect of free riding, as we see next, is the bane of collective action.

The Logic of Collective Action. The economist Mancur Olson, writing in 1965, essentially took on the political science establishment by noting that the pluralist assumption of the time—that common interests among individuals are automatically transformed into group organization and collective action—was problematic. Individuals wishing to engage in collective action face the prisoner's dilemma. They are tempted to free ride on the efforts of others, making it exceedingly difficult to achieve outcomes that are best for all.

Olson was at his most persuasive when talking about large groups and mass collective action, such as many of the antiwar demonstrations and civil rights rallies of the 1960s. In these circumstances, the world of politics is a bit like the swamp-clearing example, where each individual has a rational strategy of not contributing. The logic of collective action makes it difficult to induce participation in and contribution to collective goals.

Olson claimed that this difficulty is most severe in large groups for three reasons. First, large groups tend to be anonymous. Each household in a city is a taxpaying unit and may share the wish to see property taxes lowered. It is difficult, however, to forge a group identity or induce households to contribute effort or activity for the cause of lower taxes on such a basis. Second, in the anonymity of the large-group context, it is especially plausible to claim that no one individual's contribution makes much difference. Should an individual citizen kill the better part of a morning writing a letter to his city council member in support of lower property taxes? Will it make much difference? If hardly anyone else writes, then the council member is unlikely to pay much heed to this one letter; on the other hand, if the council member is inundated with letters, would one more have a significant additional effect? Finally, there is the problem of enforcement. In a large group, are other group members going to punish a slacker? By definition, they cannot prevent the slacker from receiving the benefits of collective action should those benefits materialize. (Every property owner's taxes will be lowered if anyone's are.) But more to the point, in a large, anonymous group it is often hard to know who has and who has not contributed, and because there is only the most limited sort of group identity, it is hard for contributors to identify, much less take action against, slackers. As a consequence, many large groups that share common interests fail to mobilize at all—they remain latent.

This same problem plagues small groups, too, as the swamp-clearing problem in Chapter 1 reveals. But Olson argued that small groups manage to overcome the problem of collective action more frequently and to a greater extent than their larger counterparts. Small groups are more personal, and their members are therefore more vulnerable to interpersonal persuasion. In small groups, individual contributions may make a more noticeable difference, so that individuals feel that their contributions are more essential. Contributors in small groups, moreover, often know who they are and who the slackers are. Thus punishment, ranging from subtle judgmental pressure to social ostracism, is easier to effect.

Contrasting large groups that often remain latent to smaller ones, Olson called these small groups privileged, because of their advantage in overcoming the free-riding, coordination, and conflict-of-interest problems of collective action. It is for these perhaps counterintuitive reasons that small groups often prevail over, or enjoy greater privileges relative to, larger groups. These reasons, therefore, help explain why we so often see producers win out over consumers, owners of capital win out over labor, and a party's elite win out over its mass members.

informational benefits

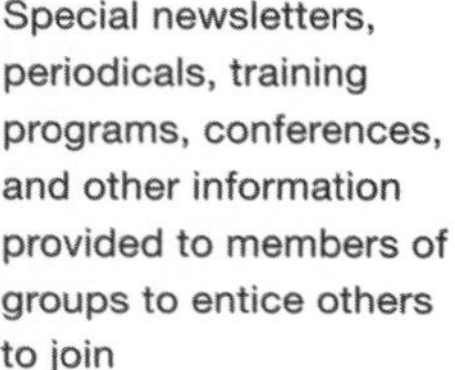
Special newsletters, periodicals, training programs, conferences, and other information provided to members of groups to entice others to join

Selective Benefits: A Solution to the Collective Action Problem

Despite the free-rider problem, interest groups offer numerous incentives to join. Most important, as Olson shrewdly noted, they make various "selective benefits" available only to group members. These benefits can be informational, material, solidary, or purposive. Table 13.2 gives some examples of the range of benefits in each of these categories.

material benefits

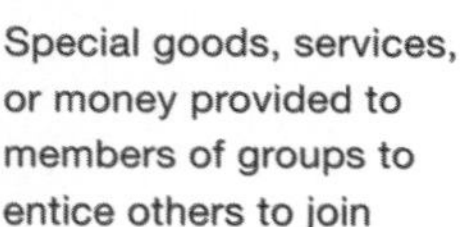
Special goods, services, or money provided to members of groups to entice others to join

Informational benefits are the most widespread and important category of selective benefits offered to group members. Information is provided through conferences, training programs, and newsletters and other periodicals sent automatically to those who have paid membership dues.

Material benefits include anything that can be measured monetarily, such as special services, goods, and even money. A broad range of material benefits can be offered by groups to attract members. These benefits often include discount purchasing, shared advertising, and perhaps most valuable of all, health and retirement insurance.

solidary benefits

Selective benefits of group membership that emphasize friendship, networking, and consciousness-raising

Another category identified in Table 13.2 is that of solidary benefits. The most notable of this class of benefits are the friendship and "networking" opportunities that membership provides. Another benefit that has been important to many nonprofit and citizens' groups is what has come to be called consciousness-raising. One example of this can be seen in the claims of many women's organizations that active participation conveys to each member of the organization an enhanced sense of her own value and a stronger ability to advance individual as well as collective civil rights.

purposive benefits

Selective benefits of group membership that emphasize the purpose and accomplishments of the group

A fourth type of benefit involves the appeal of the purpose of an interest group. The benefits of religious interest groups provide us with good examples of such purposive benefits. The Christian right is a powerful movement made up of a number of interest groups that offer virtually no material benefits to their members. The growth and the success of these groups depend on the

Table 13.2

SELECTIVE BENEFITS OF INTEREST-GROUP MEMBERSHIP

CATEGORY	BENEFITS
Informational benefits	Conferences Professional contacts Training programs Publications Coordination among organizations Research Legal help Professional codes Collective bargaining
Material benefits	Travel packages Insurance Discounts on consumer goods
Solidary benefits	Friendship Networking opportunities
Purposive benefits	Advocacy Representation before government Participation in public affairs

SOURCE: Adapted from Jack L. Walker, Jr., *Mobilizing Interest Groups in America: Patrons, Professions, and Social Movements* (Ann Arbor: University of Michigan Press, 1991), p. 86.

religious identification and affirmation of their members. Many such religiously based interest groups have arisen, especially at state and local levels, throughout American history. For example, both the abolition and the prohibition movements were driven by religious interest groups whose main attractions were nonmaterial benefits.

Ideology itself, or the sharing of a commonly developed ideology, is another important nonmaterial benefit. Many of the most successful interest groups of the past 20 years have been citizens' groups or public interest groups whose members are brought together largely around shared ideological goals, including government reform, election and campaign reform, civil rights, economic equality, "family values," or even opposition to government itself.

Political Entrepreneurs Organize and Maintain Groups

In a review of Olson's book, the economist Richard Wagner noticed that Olson's arguments about groups and politics in general, and his theory of selective incentives in particular, had very little to say about the internal workings of groups.[13] In Wagner's experience, however, groups often came into being and then were maintained in good working order, not only because of selective incentives but also because of the extraordinary efforts of specific individuals—leaders, in ordinary language, or "political entrepreneurs" in Wagner's more colorful expression.

Wagner was motivated to raise the issue of group leaders because, in his view, Olson's theory was too pessimistic. Mass organizations in the real world—labor unions, consumer associations, senior citizens' groups, environmental organizations—all exist, some persisting and prospering over long periods. Contrary to Olson's suggestions, they seem somehow to get jump-started in the real world. Wagner suggests that a special kind of theory of selective incentives is called for. Specifically, he argues that certain selective benefits may accrue to those who organize and maintain otherwise latent groups.

Senator Robert Wagner (no relation) in the 1930s and Congressman Claude Pepper in the 1970s each had private reasons—electoral incentives—to try to organize laborers and the elderly, respectively. Wagner, a Democrat from New York, had a large constituency of working men and women who would reward him by re-electing him if he bore the cost of organizing workers (or at least bore the cost of facilitating their organization). And this he did. The law that bears his name, the Wagner Act of 1935, made it much easier for unions to organize in the industrial North.[14] Likewise, Claude Pepper, a Democratic congressman with a large number of elderly constituents in his South Miami district, saw it as serving his own electoral interests to provide the initial investment of effort to organize the elderly as a political force.

In general, a political entrepreneur is someone who sees a prospective dividend from cooperation. This is another way of saying that there is a latent group that, if it were to become manifest, would enjoy the fruits of collective action. For a price, whether in votes (as in the cases of Wagner and Pepper), a percentage of the dividend, nonmaterial glory, or other perks, the entrepreneur bears the costs of organizing, expends effort to monitor individuals for slacker behavior, and sometimes even imposes punishment on slackers (such as expelling them from the group and denying them any of its selective benefits).

13 Richard Wagner, "Pressure Groups and Political Entrepreneurs," *Papers on Non-market Decision Making* 1 (1966): 161–70.

14 The Wagner Act made it possible for unions to organize by legalizing the so-called closed shop. If a worker took a job in a closed shop or plant, he or she was required to join the union there. "Do not contribute" was no longer an option, so that workers in closed shops could not free ride on the efforts made by others to improve wages and working conditions.

Thus political entrepreneurs may be thought of as complements to Olsonian selective incentives in that both provide ways of motivating groups to accomplish collective objectives. Indeed, if selective incentives resolve the paradox of collective action, then political entrepreneurs dissolve the paradox. Both are helpful and sometimes both are needed to initiate and maintain collective action. Groups that manage, perhaps on their own, to get themselves organized with a low level of activity often take the next step of creating leaders and leadership institutions to increase the activity level and the resulting cooperation dividends. Richard Wagner, in other words, took Olson's theory of selective incentives and suggested an alternative explanation, one that made room for institutional solutions to the problem of collective action.

HOW DO INTEREST GROUPS INFLUENCE POLICY?

Interest groups work to improve the probability that they and their policy interests will be heard and treated favorably by all branches and levels of the government. The quest for political influence of power takes many forms. We can roughly divide these strategies into "insider strategies" and "outsider strategies."

Insider strategies include gaining access to key decision makers and using the courts. Influencing policy through traditional political institutions, of course, requires understanding how those institutions work. A lobbyist who wishes to have Congress address a problem with legislation will try to find a sympathetic member of Congress, preferably on a committee with jurisdiction over the problem, and will work directly with the member's staff. If an organization decides to bring suit in the courts, it may want to sue in a jurisdiction where it has a good chance of getting a judge favorable to the case or where the immediate appellate courts are likely to support the case. Gaining access is not easy. Legislators and bureaucrats have little time and many requests to juggle; courts have full dockets. Interest groups themselves have limited budgets and staff. They must choose their battles well and map out the strategy most likely to succeed.

Outsider strategies include going public and using electoral tactics. Just as politicians can gain an electoral edge by informing voters, so too can groups. A well-planned public information campaign or targeted campaign activities and contributions can have as much influence as working the corridors of Congress.

Many groups employ a mix of insider and outsider strategies. For example, environmental groups such as the Sierra Club lobby members of Congress and key congressional staff members, participate in bureaucratic rule making by offering comments and suggestions to agencies on new environmental rules, and bring lawsuits under various environmental acts, such as the Endangered Species Act, which authorizes groups and citizens to come to court if they believe the act is being violated. At the same time, the Sierra Club attempts to influence public opinion through media campaigns and to influence electoral politics by supporting candidates who they believe share their environmental views and by opposing candidates who they view as foes of environmentalism.

Direct Lobbying

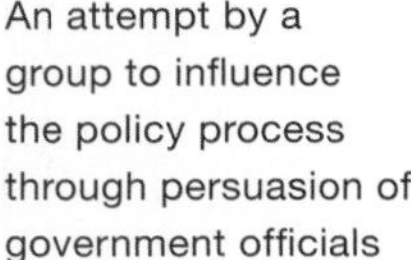

An attempt by a group to influence the policy process through persuasion of government officials

Lobbying is an attempt by a group to influence the policy process through persuasion of government officials. Most Americans tend to believe that interest groups exert their influence through direct contact with members of Congress, but lobbying encompasses a broad range of activities that groups engage in with all sorts of government officials and the public as a whole.

Organized advocacy of political interests, commonly known as lobbying, is a $3 billion-a-year industry in Washington, D.C., alone, involving 15,000 individuals, firms, and other organizations. Who is a lobbyist? The 1946 Federal Regulation of Lobbying Act defined a lobbyist as "any person who shall engage himself for pay or any consideration for the purpose of attempting to influence the passage or defeat of any legislation of the Congress of the United States." According to the 1995 Federal Lobbying Disclosure Act, any person who makes at least one lobbying contact with either the legislative or executive branch in a year, any individual who spends 20 percent of his or her time in support of such activities, or any firm that devotes 10 percent of its budget to such activities must register as a lobbyist. They must report what topics they discussed with the government, though not which particular individuals or offices they contacted. The industry that spent by far the most on lobbying over the past decade was pharmaceuticals and health products, which spent a whopping $2 billion over the course of the decade. The other "billion dollar" lobbying industries are insurance, electric utilities, business associations, computer and Internet, oil and gas, and education, with each spending at least a billion on lobbying between 1998 and 2010.[15]

The federal figures do not include campaign contributions or lobbying at the state and local levels, but the amount spent to influence state legislatures is also substantial. For example, in 2005, according to the Center for Public Integrity, lobbyists spent $240 million to influence California lawmakers, $175 million in Texas, $150 million in New York, $130 million in Pennsylvania, and more than $50 million apiece in Massachusetts and Minnesota. All told, $1.16 billion was spent in 42 states that require lobbyists to report their expenditures. The total resources devoted to lobbying at the state and federal level, then, is approximately $4 billion a year.[16]

Lobbying involves a great deal of activity on the part of someone speaking for an interest. Lobbyists badger and buttonhole legislators, administrators, and

15 Data compiled from federal reports by the Center for Responsive Politics, www.opensecrets.org/lobby/top.php?indexType=i (accessed).

16 Sarah Laskow, "State Lobbying Becomes Billion-Dollar Business," The Center for Public Integrity, December 20, 2006, www.iwatchnews.org/2006/12/20/5896/state-lobbying-becomes-billion-dollar-business (accessed 11/11/11).

committee staff members with facts about pertinent issues and facts or claims about public support of them.[17] Lobbyists can serve a useful purpose in the legislative and administrative process by providing this kind of information.

However, within each industry, there are a great many different individuals and organizations involved in government advocacy, and they usually do not speak with a common voice. Rather each advocates for and defends its own particular interests, often in conflict with other firms in the same industry. What the leading organization or peak association of an industry may advocate may be undercut by the activities of individual firms. The Entertainment Software Association, which spent roughly $3.5 million on lobbying in 2010, likely wants a different set of regulations than Microsoft or Google.

It is also worth noting that many important firms do not jump into the lobbying game, and even more refuse to give campaign contributions. Microsoft, Hewlitt-Packard, Google, Oracle, and IBM top the list of computer industry lobbyists. But Apple is nowhere to be found.

Lobbying Members of Congress. Interest groups also have substantial influence in setting the legislative agenda and in helping craft the language of legislation (Figure 13.3). Today sophisticated lobbyists win influence by providing information about policies to busy members of Congress. As one lobbyist noted, "You can't get access without knowledge. . . . I can go in to see John Dingell [chairman of the House Committee on Energy and Commerce], but if I have nothing to offer or nothing to say, he's not going to want to see me."[18]

Providing access is only one of the many services lobbyists perform. Lobbyists often testify on behalf of their clients at congressional committee and agency hearings; lobbyists sometimes help their clients identify potential allies with whom to construct coalitions; lobbyists provide research and information to government officials; lobbyists often draft proposed legislation or regulations to be introduced by friendly lawmakers; lobbyists talk to reporters, place ads in newspapers, and organize letter-writing, e-mail, and telegram campaigns. Lobbyists also play an important role in fund-raising, helping to direct clients' contributions to members of Congress and presidential candidates. In recent years, interest groups have also begun to build broader coalitions and comprehensive campaigns around particular policy issues.[19] Lobbyists, seeing an opportunity to harness the enthusiasm of political amateurs, now organize and even launch

17 For discussions of lobbying, see Jeffrey M. Berry, *Lobbying for the People: The Political Behavior of Public Interest Groups* (Princeton, NJ: Princeton University Press, 1977); and John R. Wright, *Interest Groups and Congress: Lobbying, Contributions, and Influence* (Boston: Allyn & Bacon, 1996).

18 Daniel Franklin, "Tommy Boggs and the Death of Health Care Reform," *Washington Monthly* (April 1995): 36.

19 Marie Hojnacki, "Interest Groups' Decisions to Join Alliances or Work Alone," *American Journal of Political Science* 41 (1997): 61–87; Kevin W. Hula, *Lobbying Together: Interest Group Coalitions in Legislative Politics* (Washington, DC: Georgetown University Press, 1999).

ANALYZING THE EVIDENCE

Interest groups can influence members of Congress in a variety of ways. They may seek to mobilize popular support in the form of grassroots campaigns; they may try to generate publicity favorable to their cause; they may work through congressional staffers; or they may seek to lobby the member of Congress directly. How might these various strategies work together? What pitfalls might an interest group encounter in trying to influence members of Congress?

Figure 13.3

HOW INTEREST GROUPS INFLUENCE CONGRESS

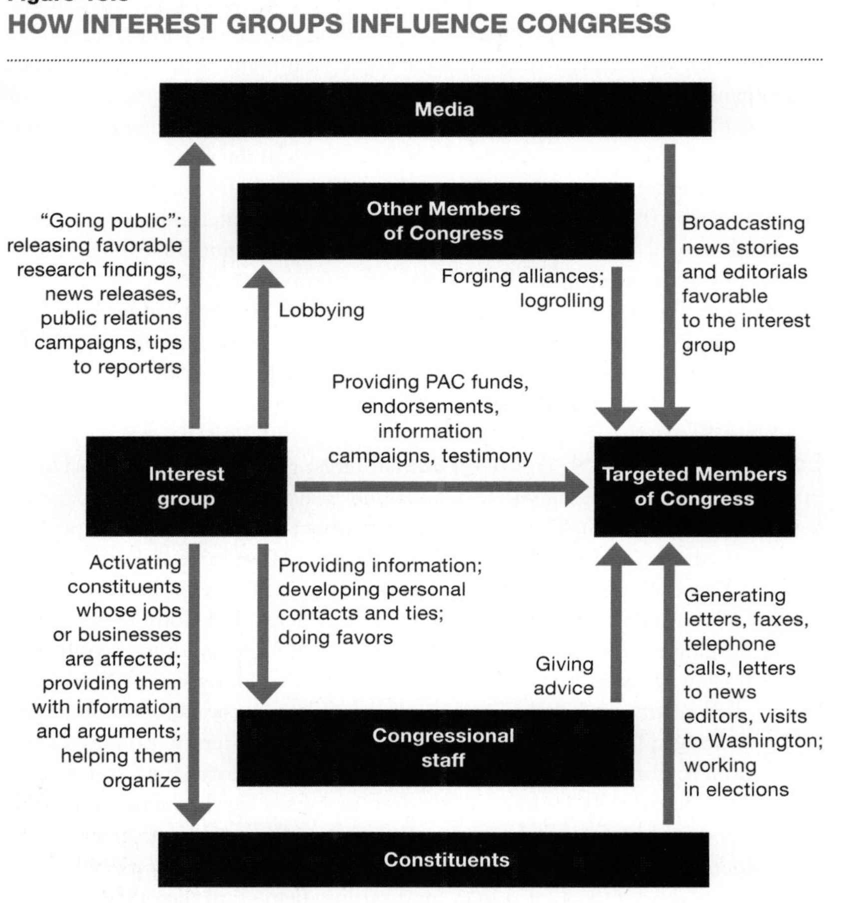

comprehensive campaigns that combine simulated grassroots activity with information and campaign funding for members of Congress.[20]

Some interest groups go still further. They develop strong ties to individual politicians or policy communities within Congress by hiring ex-staffers, ex-members of Congress, or even relatives of sitting members of Congress. The rotation of those in positions of power into lobbying jobs has become sufficiently common as to have its own term in Washington circles: revolving-door politics. The revolving door of congressional and executive staff joining the

20 An excellent example is the mobilization of corporate executives in the tax reform efforts in the mid-1980s. See Jeff Birnbaum and Alan S. Murray, *Showdown at Gucci Gulch: Lawmakers, Lobbyists, and the Unlikely Triumph of Tax Reform* (Westminster, MD; Random House, 1987).

ranks of lobbying firms is driven by the continual turnover of staff, of lobbyists, and even of the political parties in Washington. Lobbying firms must stay current and connected to Congress in order to offer the best service to their clients. This means that most of the larger lobbying firms in Washington have strong ties to both the Democrats and the Republicans on the Hill.

Lobbying the President. All these efforts and more are needed when the target of a lobbying campaign is the president of the United States. So many individuals and groups clamor for the president's time and attention that only the most skilled and well-connected members of the lobbying community can hope to influence presidential decisions. When running for president, Barack Obama laid down a bold promise to "free the executive branch from special-interest influence." No political appointee, the Obama team promised, "will be permitted to work on regulations or contracts directly and substantially related to their prior employer for two years." That promise proved exceedingly difficult to keep as many in the Obama transition team, including the nominee for Health and Human Services secretary and ex-Senate majority leader Thomas Daschle, had close ties to lobbyists or had worked for lobbying firms.[21] One of President Obama's first executive orders created an ethics standard and pledge for all executive branch appointments, and the administration imposed further restrictions on those receiving funds from the Emergency Economic Stabilization Act and the American Recovery and Reinvestment Act. Anyone wishing to receive funds from the $700 billion authorized for the economic stimulus bills had to show that they did not have conflicting interests and were not involved in lobbying the government.[22]

Lobbying the Executive Branch. Even when an interest group is very successful at getting its bill passed by Congress and signed by the president, the prospect of full and faithful implementation of that law is not guaranteed. Often a group and its allies do not pack up and go home as soon as the president turns their lobbied-for law over to the appropriate agency. On average, 40 percent of interest-group representatives regularly contact both legislative and executive branch organizations, whereas 13 percent contact only the legislative branch and 16 percent contact only the executive branch.[23]

In some respects, interest-group access to the executive branch is promoted by federal law. The Administrative Procedure Act, first enacted in 1946 and

21 Chris Frates, "Daschle Lobby Ties Bump Obama Vow," *Politico*, November 30, 2008, www.politico.com/news/stories/1108/16015.html (accessed 4/7/09); David Kirkpatrick, "In Transition, Ties to Lobbying," *New York Times*, November 15, 2008, www.nytimes.com/2008/11/15/us/politics/15transition.html (accessed 4/7/09).

22 Jacob Straus, *Lobbying the Executive Branch: Current Practices and Options for Change*. Congressional Research Service, December 6, 2010. Report 7-5700, pages 3 and 4.

23 John P. Heinz, Edward O. Laumann, Robert L. Nelson, and Robert H. Salisbury, *The Hollow Core: Private Interests in National Policy Making* (Cambridge, MA: Harvard University Press, 1993).

Interest Group Influence

CHAPTER 13

Contributed by
Beth L. Leech
Rutgers University

It is generally accepted among those who study interest groups that business and economic interests predominate. Economic interests are more likely to form organized groups, are more likely to be active, and on average spend more money and more time on political issues than do noneconomic interests like citizen groups or "public interest" groups. When we look at interest groups' involvement in the policy-making process, however, the sheer number of groups or dollars may not directly equal the amount of influence that those groups have. While numbers and dollars are important indicators of which interests are represented, it would be preferable to try to measure which groups actually were influential in politics. To address this question, the political scientist Frank Baumgartner and his colleagues interviewed 315 lobbyists and government officials about 98 randomly selected policy issues. Citizen groups were more likely to be mentioned as being important in the debates than any other type of group, despite the fact that they spent less and they made up a smaller part of the overall group population.

Why were citizen groups seen as so influential despite their relative lack of resources? It may be that those groups have important ties to constituents, granting them greater legitimacy in the eyes of members of Congress, or it could be that some members of Congress already supported the policies that the citizen groups were advocating. Whatever the reason, it is clear that citizen groups have greater voice in Washington than the dollar counts might suggest.

Types of Interest Groups Registered to Lobby

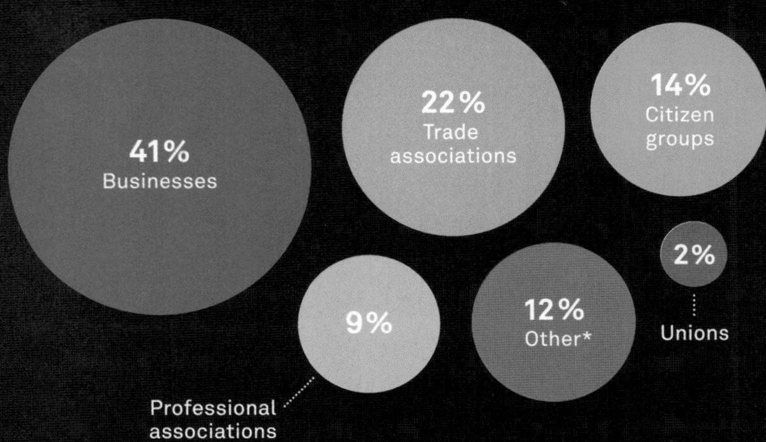

These data from the federal Lobbying Disclosure Reports show the dominance of business organizations in Washington. Businesses make up 41 percent of those registered to lobby, and trade associations, which represent groups of businesses, comprise another 22 percent. Citizen groups, professional associations, and unions make up a much smaller portion, and it is especially striking to note that unions are only 2 percent of the total.

*Includes governmental groups, think tanks, universities, and hospitals.

Average Spending on Lobbying and Campaign Contributions

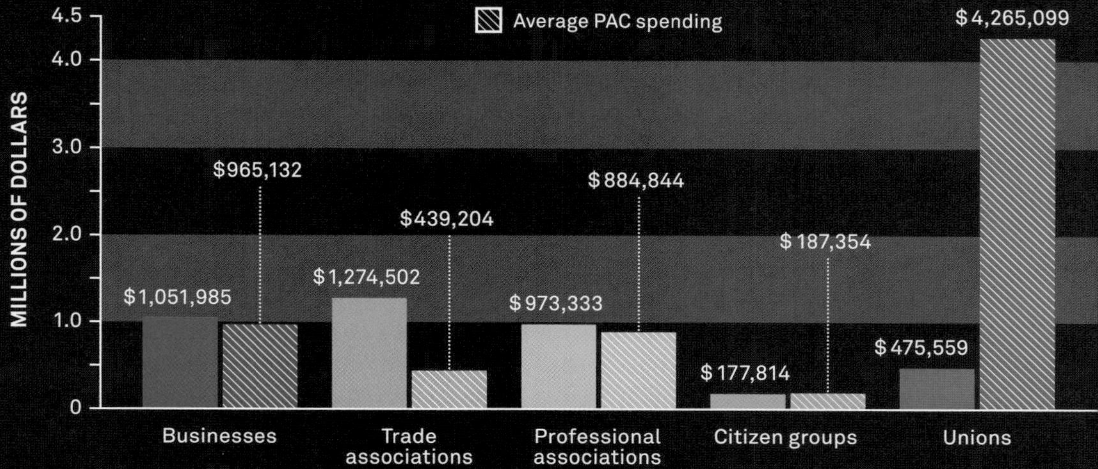

The graph above shows the average amounts spent on lobbying and campaign contributions by interest groups who played a major role in 98 randomly selected issues studied by Baumgartner et al. Citizen groups on average spent much less on lobbying and campaign contributions than other types of groups. Unions on average spent more on campaign contributions than any other type of group, but that spending is tempered by the fact that there are fewer unions.

Who Is Seen as Important in Policy Making?

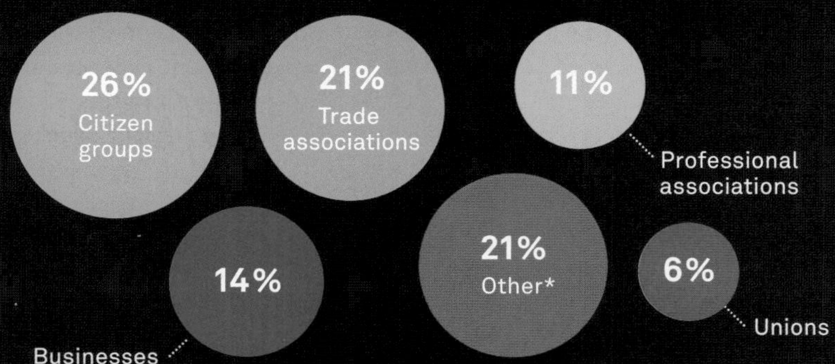

*Includes coalitions, governmental associations, and think tanks.

Although the overall population of interest groups has fewer citizen groups than business groups, as seen in the figure to the left, not all groups are equally influential. Baumgartner and his colleagues interviewed 315 lobbyists and government officials about 98 randomly selected policy issues. Citizen groups were more likely to be mentioned as being important in the debate than any other type of group. More than a quarter of the interest groups seen as being influential were citizen groups.

SOURCES:

Frank R. Baumgartner and Beth L. Leech, "Issue Niches and Policy Bandwagons: Patterns of Interest Group Involvement in National Politics," *Journal of Politics*, 63, no. 4 (2001): 1191–1213.

Frank R. Baumgartner, Jeffrey M. Berry, Marie Hojnacki, David C. Kimball, and Beth L. Leech, *Lobbying and Policy Change: Who Wins, Who Loses, and Why* (Chicago: Chicago University Press, 2009).

EXPLORE **INTEREST GROUP INFLUENCE** FURTHER AT: **wwnorton.com/studyspace**

frequently amended, requires most federal agencies to provide notice and an opportunity for comment before implementing proposed rules and regulations. So-called notice-and-comment rule making is designed to allow interests an opportunity to make their views known and participate in the implementation of federal legislation that affects them. In 1990, Congress enacted the Negotiated Rulemaking Act to encourage administrative agencies to engage in direct and open negotiations with affected interests when developing new regulations. These two pieces of legislation, which have been strongly enforced by the federal courts, have played an important role in opening the bureaucratic process to interest-group influence. Today few federal agencies would consider attempting to implement a new rule without consulting affected interests, which are known as "stakeholders."[24]

Regulations on Lobbying. As a result of the constant access to important decision makers that lobbyists seek out and require, stricter guidelines regulating the actions of lobbyists have been adopted in the last two decades. For example, as of 1993, businesses may no longer deduct from their taxes the cost of lobbying. Trade associations must report to members the proportion of their dues that goes to lobbying, and that proportion may not be reported as a business expense. The most important attempt to limit the influence of lobbyists was the 1995 Lobbying Disclosure Act, which significantly broadened the definition of people and organizations that must register as lobbyists. According to the filings under this act, almost 13,000 lobbyists were working the halls of Congress in 2010.

In 1996, Congress passed legislation limiting gifts from a single source to \$50 and no more than \$100 annually. It also banned the practice of honoraria, which had been used by special interests to supplement congressional salaries. But Congress did not limit the travel of representatives, senators, their spouses, or congressional staff members. Interest groups can pay for congressional travel as long as a trip is related to legislative business and is disclosed on congressional reports within 30 days. On these trips, meals and entertainment expenses are not limited to \$50 per event and \$100 annually. The rules of Congress allow its members to travel on corporate jets as long as they pay an amount equal to first-class airfare.

In 2007, congressional Democrats secured the enactment of a package of ethics rules designed to fulfill their 2006 campaign promise to bring an end to lobbying abuses. The new rules prohibited lobbyists from paying for most meals, trips, parties, and gifts for members of Congress. Lobbyists were also required to disclose the amounts and sources of small campaign contributions they collected from clients and "bundled" into large contributions. And interest groups were required to disclose the funds they used to rally voters to support or oppose legislative proposals. As soon as these new rules were enacted, lobbyists and politicians hurried to find ways to circumvent them, and it remains to be seen whether these reforms will have any major impact. Executive rulings and

24 For an excellent discussion of the political origins of the Administrative Procedure Act, see Martin Shapiro, "APA: Past, Present, Future," *Virginia Law Review* 72 (1986): 447–92.

memoranda issued by President Obama in 2009 have further strengthened these rules and made it much more difficult for lobbying firms to influence executive decision making either through direct lobbying or indirectly by hiring people with direct access to decision makers.

Using the Courts

Interest groups sometimes turn to the courts to augment other avenues of access. They can use the courts to affect public policy in at least three ways: (1) by bringing suit directly on behalf of the group itself; (2) by financing suits brought by individuals; and (3) by filing a companion brief as *amicus curiae* (literally, "friend of the court") to an existing court case.

Among the most significant modern illustrations of the use of the courts as a strategy for political influence are those that accompanied the "sexual revolution" of the 1960s and the emergence of the movement for women's rights. Beginning in the mid-1960s, a series of cases was brought into the federal courts in an effort to force the definition of a right to privacy in sexual matters. The effort began with a challenge to state restrictions on obtaining contraceptives for nonmedical purposes, a challenge that was effectively made in *Griswold v. Connecticut*, in which the Supreme Court held that states could neither prohibit the dissemination of information about, nor prohibit the actual use of, contraceptives by married couples. That case was soon followed by *Eisenstadt v. Baird*, in which the Court held that the states could not prohibit the use of contraceptives by single persons any more than it could prohibit their use by married couples. One year later, in the 1973 case of *Roe v. Wade*, the Court held that states could not impose an absolute ban on voluntary abortions. Each of these cases, as well as others, were part of the Court's enunciation of a constitutional doctrine of privacy.[25]

The 1973 abortion case sparked a controversy that brought conservatives to the fore on a national level. Conservative groups then made extensive use of the courts to whittle away the scope of the privacy doctrine. They obtained rulings, for example, that prohibit the use of federal funds to pay for voluntary abortions. And in 1989, right-to-life groups were able to use a strategy of litigation that significantly undermined the *Roe v. Wade* decision—namely, in the case of *Webster v. Reproductive Health Services*, which restored the right of states to place restrictions on abortion.[26]

Another extremely significant set of contemporary illustrations of the use of the courts as a strategy for political influence are those found in the history of the National Association for the Advancement of Colored People. The most important of these court cases was *Brown v. Board of Education*, in which the Supreme Court held that legal segregation of the schools was unconstitutional.[27]

25 *Griswold v. Connecticut*, 381 U.S. 479 (1965); *Eisenstadt v. Baird*, 405 U.S. 438 (1972); *Roe v. Wade*, 410 U.S. 113 (1973).

26 *Webster v. Reproductive Health Services*, 492 U.S. 490 (1989).

27 *Brown v. Board of Education*, 347 U.S. 483 (1954).

Business groups are also frequent users of the courts, because of the number of government programs that apply to them. Litigation involving large businesses is most mountainous in such areas as taxation, antitrust issues, interstate transportation, patents, and product quality and standardization. Often a business is brought to litigation against its will by virtue of initiatives taken against it by other businesses or by government agencies. But many individual businesses bring suit themselves to influence government policy. Major corporations and their trade associations pay tremendous amounts of money each year in fees to the most prestigious Washington law firms. Some of this money is expended in gaining access. A great proportion of it, however, is used to keep the best and most experienced lawyers prepared to represent the corporations in court or before administrative agencies when necessary.

The forces of the new politics movement made significant use of the courts during the 1970s and 1980s, and judicial decisions were instrumental in advancing their goals. Facilitated by changes in the rules governing access to the courts (the rules of standing are discussed in Chapter 9), the new politics agenda was clearly visible in court decisions handed down in several key policy areas. In environmental policy, new politics groups were able to force federal agencies to pay attention to environmental issues even when the agencies were not directly involved in activities related to environmental quality. By the 2000s, the courts often were the battleground on which those in the new political movements waged their fights. Perhaps the most dramatic were a string of lawsuits spanning 20 years (from 1986 to 2006) in which antiabortion protest organizations, such as Pro-Life Action Network and Operation Rescue, and the National Organization of Women repeatedly took each other to court to establish the rules governing clinic protests. Ultimately, the U.S. Supreme Court sided with the antiabortion organizations, but not before deciding three separate cases on the matter, at extremely high cost to both sides.[28]

Mobilizing Public Opinion

going public 

The act of launching a media campaign to build popular support

Organizations try to bring pressure to bear on politicians through a variety of methods designed to mobilize public opinion. This strategy is known as going public. When groups go public, they use their various resources to try to persuade large numbers of people to pay attention to their concerns. They hope that greater visibility and public support will help underline the importance of such issues to those in power. Advertising campaigns, protests, and grassroots lobbying efforts are all examples of going public. An increased use of this kind of strategy is traced to the rise of modern advertising at the beginning of the twentieth century. As early as the 1930s, political analysts distinguished between the "old lobby" of direct group representation before Congress and the "new lobby" of public-relations professionals addressing the public at large in order

28 *Scheidler v. National Organization of Women et al.*, 547 U.S. 9 (2006).

to reach Congress indirectly.[29] Going public, then, differs from other strategies that interest groups use to influence public policy. The "new lobby" techniques are designed to change the way people think, rather than just changing the actions of insiders.

One way of going public that groups often use is conventional advertising. For example, a casual scan of major newspapers, magazines, and Web sites will often reveal examples of expensive, well-designed ads by major companies and industry associations, such as those from the oil and gas, automobile, and health and pharmaceutical companies. Such ads are frequently intended to show what the firms do for the country, not merely the products they develop. Their purpose is to create and maintain a strongly positive association between the organization and the community at large in the hope that the community's favorable feelings can be drawn on as needed in specific political controversies later.

Sometimes groups advertise expressly to shift public opinion on a question. One of the most famous such advertising campaigns was run by the Health Insurance Association of America in 1993 and 1994 in opposition to President Bill Clinton's proposed national health insurance plan. These ads featured a middle-class couple, Harry and Louise (played by the actors Harry Johnson and Louise Caire Clark), sitting at their kitchen table disparaging the excessive red tape and bureaucratic problems that they would face under Clinton's plan. The Harry and Louise ads are widely attributed with turning public opinion against Clinton's plan, which never even got off the ground in Congress. A decade later, when President Barack Obama proposed an extensive overhaul of the health insurance industry in the United States, a trade group representing drug makers brought the same actors back and remade the Harry and Louise spot, but this time fully supporting the administration's plan. In the new advertisements, Harry and Louise are once again in their kitchen, and Louise pores over medical bills and forms. "Having choices we don't like," says a worried Louise, "is no choice at all." Louise concludes the ad saying "A little more cooperation, a little less politics, and we can get the job done this time."[30]

A second strategy that groups use to bring public pressure to bear on a problem is grassroots lobbying. Grassroots lobbyists use many of the same organizing methods we see in political campaigns—developing lists of supporters and urging those supporters to voice their concern with an issue and to recruit others to do so. It is common today to send direct mail that includes a draft letter that the recipient can adapt and then send to his or her representative in Congress or to send e-mails urging people to contact their member of Congress regarding a particular bill or controversy. A grassroots campaign can

---

29 Pendleton Herring, *Group Representation before Congress* (1928; repr.: New York: Russell & Russell, 1967). See also Kenneth W. Kollman, *Outside Lobbying: Public Opinion and Interests Group Strategies* (Princeton, NJ: Princeton University Press, 1998).

30 Natasha Singer, "Harry and Louise Return, With a New Message," *New York Times*, July 16, 2009, www.nytimes.com/2009/07/17/business/media/17adco.html?_r=1&ref=media (accessed 10/3/11).

cost anywhere from $40,000 to attempt to sway the votes of one or two crucial members of a committee or subcommittee to millions of dollars to mount a national effort aimed at Congress as a whole. Such grassroots campaigns are often organized around controversial, prominent appointments, especially to fill vacancies on the U.S. Supreme Court.

Grassroots lobbying campaigns have been so effective in recent years that a number of Washington consulting firms specialize in them. Firms such as Bonner and Associates, for example, will generate grassroots telephone campaigns on behalf of or in opposition to important legislative proposals.

Grassroots lobbying has become more prevalent in Washington over the last couple of decades because the adoption of congressional rules limiting gifts to members has made traditional lobbying more difficult. This circumstance makes all the more compelling the question of whether grassroots campaigning has reached an intolerable extreme. One case in particular illustrates the extremes of "Astroturf" lobbying (a play on the brand name of an artificial grass used on many sports fields). In 1992, ten giant companies in the financial services, manufacturing, and high-tech industries began a grassroots campaign and spent millions of dollars to influence a decision in Congress to limit the ability of investors to sue for fraud. Retaining an expensive consulting firm, these corporations paid for the use of specialized computer software to persuade Congress that there was "an outpouring of popular support for the proposal." Thousands of letters from individuals flooded Capitol Hill. Many of the letters were written and sent by people who sincerely believed that investor lawsuits are often frivolous and should be curtailed. But much of the mail was phony, generated by the Washington-based campaign consultants; the letters came from people who had no strong feelings, or even no opinion at all, about the issue. More and more people, including leading members of Congress, are questioning such methods, charging that these are not genuine grassroots campaigns but instead are Astroturf lobbying. Such Astroturf campaigns have increased in frequency in recent years as members of Congress grow more and more skeptical of Washington lobbyists and far more concerned about demonstrations of support for a particular issue by their constituents. But after the firms spent millions of dollars and generated thousands of letters to members of Congress in their attempt to influence legislation affecting investors' ability to sue for fraud, they came to the somber conclusion that "it's more effective to have 100 letters from your district where constituents took the time to write and understand the issue," because "Congress is sophisticated enough to know the difference."[31]

Finally, groups often organize protests as a means of bringing attention to an issue or pressure on the government. Protests, in fact, are the oldest means of going public. Those who lack other resources, such as money, contacts, and expertise, can always resort to protest as a means of making their concerns public. Indeed, the right to assembly is protected in the First Amendment of the U.S. Constitution. Protests may have many different consequences, depending

31 Jane Fritsch, "The Grass Roots, Just a Free Phone Call Away," *New York Times*, June 23, 1995, pp. A1 and A22.

on how they are managed. One basic consequence of a well-run protest is that it attracts attention. Peaceful demonstrations at city hall, the state legislature, Congress, the Supreme Court, or some other location typically involve people holding signs and chanting slogans. Passersby certainly notice, and occasionally news outlets cover the event in newspapers or on television, and the larger the protest the more likely it is to attract attention. By getting on the news, the protesters hope to attract attention to their issue and possibly raise the sympathies of others and bring them into their movement.

Organized protests also create a sense of community and common interest among those involved and raise the consciousness of people outside the protest. Civil rights protests during the 1960s brought hundreds of thousands of people to march in the nation's capitol. Newspapers and television news programs across the country carried images of Martin Luther King, Jr., and other civil rights leaders speaking to an audience that stretched from the Lincoln Memorial across the Washington Mall and surrounded the Reflecting Pool. That image wrapped the civil rights movement in the symbolism of the nation; it was not a violent confrontation between protesters and police but a peaceful plea for equal voting and civil rights. Forty years later, similar marches brought protesters for immigrants' rights to the nation's capital and to the states. In spring 2006, hundreds of thousands of people, organized mainly by Hispanic and Latino groups, as well as unions and local churches, marched in Washington, D.C., and in several state capitals to protest anti-immigration policies. That movement drew attention to immigrants' concerns in a political environment that was increasingly hostile, and it influenced the political debate over the issue. It also engaged large numbers of Hispanics and Latinos. According to the Pew Hispanic Center, one in four Hispanics in the United States participated in these protests.[32]

Finally, protests often attempt to impose costs on others by disrupting traffic or commerce, thereby forcing people to bargain with protesters. Labor strikes are a form of political action against companies, industries, or the government. Workers in a labor strike refuse to work, costing the company the revenue it would have gained from services rendered. In an industry such as automotives, the companies may have enough existing stock of cars and parts to allow for weeks or maybe months of negotiations without disrupting sales. However, in an industry such as education or the airlines, once the teachers or pilots go on strike, all service stops. On rare occasions labor organizations can instigate a general strike—all workers in the entire industry, a city, or a nation stay home from work, bringing all commerce to a stop. Such strikes have a significant effect on businesses and the larger economy and are called to remind the government and industry leaders of the political pull of labor.

Unions aren't the only groups that organize protests designed to disrupt normal activities. One impressive demonstration occurred during the winter of 1977–78. American farmers were frustrated with federal agricultural policies

---

32 Pew Hispanic Center and Pew Forum on Religion & Public Life, "Changing Faiths: Latinos and the Transformation of American Religion," 2007, http://pewhispanic.org/files/reports/75.pdf (accessed 4/7/09).

and increasing failures of family farms. The farmers' frustration culminated in the organization of a convoy of 600 tractors and other farm vehicles to Washington, D.C. The tractor procession was peaceful but highly disruptive. It snarled traffic for weeks and tore up the grass mall running between the Lincoln Memorial and the Capitol. The protest made for compelling news photographs and was covered extensively in national newsmagazines and newspapers. The farmers did not get a revision of the 1977 Farm Bill, but they did get a promise from the Federal Housing Administration (FHA) temporarily to cease seizures of land and equipment of farmers who could not repay loans.[33] Farmers' protests, teachers' strikes, and other activities disrupt government and business activity in order to force negotiation of a better deal.

Protests may spill over and become riots or even civil conflict, or they may be confronted by counterprotests. Companies affected by protests and the government have an interest in containing or breaking up demonstrations and strikes. However, the First Amendment is generally interpreted as protecting free expression through protests and strikes so long as they do not erupt into open rioting. Courts are often asked to rule on whether a protest is lawful or unlawful. For example, during George W. Bush's second inauguration, on January 20, 2005, about 250 to 300 people conducted a protest against the war in Iraq by marching through the streets of the Adams Morgan neighborhood in Washington, D.C. Police broke up the march with mass arrests. Some of the protesters sued to overturn their convictions and complained of alleged damages from police actions. The district court agreed with the protesters, reasoning that they were engaged in a peaceful protest, but had they been involved in riotous behavior, police actions may have been justified.[34]

Using Electoral Politics

In addition to attempting to influence members of Congress and other government officials, interest groups seek to use the electoral process to elect the right legislators in the first place and ensure that those who are elected will owe them a debt of gratitude for their support. To put matters into perspective, groups invest far more resources in lobbying than in electoral politics. Nevertheless, financial support and campaign activism can be important tools for organized interests.

Political Action Committees. By far, the most common electoral strategy employed by interest groups is that of giving financial support to the parties or to particular candidates. But such support can easily cross the threshold into outright bribery. Therefore, Congress has occasionally made an effort to

33 "Furious Farmers," *Time*, December 19, 1977, www.time.com/time/magazine/article/0,9171,945836,00.html (accessed 4/7/09); Marty Strange, *Family Farming: A New Economic Vision* (Lincoln: University of Nebraska Press, 1988).

34 *Carr et al. v. District of Columbia*, U.S. District Court of the District of Columbia, Civil Action, No 2006-0098, July 15, 2008, https://ecf.dcd.uscourts.gov/cgi-bin/show_public_doc?2006cv0098-69 (accessed 4/7/09).

regulate this strategy. For example, the Federal Election Campaign Act of 1971 (amended in 1974) limits campaign contributions and requires each candidate or campaign committee to provide the full name and address, occupation, and principal business of each person who contributes more than $100. The FECA requires that any organization that wishes to contribute to a candidate must do so through a "separate and segregated fund"—a political action committee. These provisions have been effective up to a point, considering the rather large number of embarrassments, indictments, resignations, and criminal convictions in the aftermath of the Watergate scandal.

The Watergate scandal itself was triggered when Republican "dirty tricksters" were caught breaking into the office of the Democratic National Committee in the Watergate apartment complex in Washington. An investigation quickly revealed numerous violations of campaign finance laws, involving millions of dollars that was passed from corporate executives to President Nixon's re-election committee. Many of these revelations were made by the famous Ervin Committee, whose official name and jurisdiction was the Senate Select Committee on Presidential Campaign Activities.

Reaction to Watergate produced further legislation on campaign finance in 1974 and 1976, but the effect has been to restrict individual rather than interest-group campaign activity. Individuals may now contribute no more than $2,300 to any candidate for federal office in any primary or general election. A political action committee, however, can contribute $5,000, provided it contributes to at least five different federal candidates each year.[35] Beyond this, the laws permit corporations, unions, and other interest groups to form PACs and pay the costs of soliciting funds from private citizens for the PACs.

Electoral spending by interest groups has increased steadily despite the campaign finance reforms that followed the Watergate scandal. Table 13.3 presents the total amounts contributed by interest groups to campaign organizations or spent on campaigns as well as the distribution of the money across House, Senate, and presidential races. Total PAC contributions continue to rise, increasing from nearly $260 million in 2000 to over $1 billion in the 2012 election cycle.

Interest groups focus their direct contributions on Congress, especially the U.S. House. Given the enormous cost of running modern political campaigns (see Chapter 12), most politicians are eager to receive PAC contributions. A typical U.S. House incumbent receives half of his or her campaign funds from interest groups. There is little evidence that interest groups buy roll call votes or other favors from members of Congress with their donations. Group donations do, however, help to keep those who are sympathetic to groups' interests and views in office.[36]

The potential influence of interest-group campaign donations over the legislature has prompted frequent calls from reformers to abolish PACs or limit their activities. The challenge is how to regulate the participation of groups without

35 Federal Election Commission, "Contribution Limits 2009–10," www.fec.gov/pages/brochures/contriblimits.shtml (accessed 4/7/09).

36 See Stephen Ansolabehere, John de Figueiredo, and James M. Snyder, Jr., "Why Is There So Little Money in U.S. Politics?" *Journal of Economic Perspectives* 17 (2006): 105–30.

Table 13.3

PAC CONTRIBUTIONS TO PRESIDENTIAL CAMPAIGNS (IN MILLIONS OF DOLLARS)

ANALYZING THE EVIDENCE

Political action committees contributed more than $1 billion to the Democratic and Republican campaign efforts in 2004. This is nearly $400,000 more than their total contributions in 2000. Why do PACs contribute so much money to political candidates? On what other sources of funding do candidates rely?

	2000	2004	2008
PAC Contributions			
All Candidates	259.8	310.5	412.8
House	193.4	225.4	301.6
Senate	51.9	63.7	79.9
President + Party	14.5	21.4	31.3
Independent Expenditures			
All	20.6	55.9	134.6
House	7.7	5.4	21.6
Senate	6.8	7.1	14.3
President	6.1	43.4	98.7
Nonfederal (Soft) Party Donations	26.4	144.5	21.8

SOURCE: Federal Election Commission, www.fec.gov

violating their members' rights to free speech and free association. In 1976, the U.S. Supreme Court weighed in on this matter in the case *Buckley v. Valeo*, which questioned the constitutionality of the 1974 Federal Elections Campaign Act.[37] In its decision to let the act stand, the majority on the Court ruled that donors' rights of expression are at stake, but that these must be weighed against the government's interest in limiting corruption, or the perception of corruption. The Court has repeatedly upheld the key tenets of its 1976 decision: (1) That money is a form of speech but (2) that speech rights must be weighed against concerns about corruption. The balance between the rights to free speech and the need to protect against corruption lie at the heart of not just campaign finance law, but how Americans think about the representation of interests in our government. We value both the right of people and organizations to say freely what they want government to do and the quality and integrity of representation provided to the people through the electoral and legislative process.

Independent Expenditures. The balance between free speech and corruption has led to a system of limitations on direct campaign contributions to candidates and parties through political action committees. For many groups, however,

37 *Buckley v. Valeo*, 424 U.S. 1 (1976).

the limits are not adequate. They would like to communicate directly with voters about the election and advocate for one candidate or party.

As we saw in chapter 11, Congress in 2002 sought to impose significant limits on independent campaign expenditures via the Bipartisan Campaign Reform Act (BCRA). BCRA restricted donations to nonfederal (e.g., state party) accounts as a necessary reform to limit corruption, and it imposed limits on the types of campaign commercials that could be aired by groups within 60 days of an election. It also raised the limits on direct campaign contributions for the first time since 1976, as inflation had seriously squeezed the value of contributions.

In 2010, the Supreme Court struck down the restrictions on independent advertising.[38] The case involved a political movie critical of then-senator and presidential candidate Hillary Clinton and created by an organization called Citizens United. The movie aired on cable television inside the blackout date for independent political advertising stipulated by the BCRA. A 5–4 majority ruled that such blackout dates imposed by BCRA restricted the rights to free speech of corporations and other associations. This decision firmly established the right of business corporations and labor unions to engage in political advocacy and opened the gates to a flood of money in the political arena.

This flood was evident during the 2012 national elections, in which independent expenditures amounted to some $1.5 billion of the nearly $6 billion spent. A significant portion of this money was raised by super PACs, which are allowed to raise unlimited amounts of money from any source—individuals, businesses, or other associations. There are some restrictions on super PACs, however: they must report donors to the Federal Election Commission, and they are not allowed to directly coordinate their activities with political candidates. However, they are allowed to advertise for and against candidates. The top two super PACs in the 2012 election were Restore Our Future and American Crossroads, both of which had a conservative bent. Together they raised over $300 million. The primary spending of all super PACs, both liberal and conservative, was on negative advertising.

Campaign Activism. Financial support is not the only way in which organized groups seek influence through the electoral process. Sometimes activism can be even more important than campaign contributions.

Perhaps the most notable instance of such activism occurs on behalf of the Democratic Party and candidates through unions. Labor unions regularly engage in massive get-out-the-vote drives during political campaigns. The largest such activities come from the Service Employees International Union (SEIU), which represents works ranging from hotel and restaurant workers to clerical staff, and the United Auto Workers (UAW). SEIU, for instance, spent in excess of $14.4 million to support Democratic candidates in 2012. Other sorts of groups routinely line up behind the Democratic and Republican campaigns. The National Rifle Association, for example, spent $9.5 million in the 2012 election cycle, and all but $7,000 was in support of Republican candidates.

38 *Citizens United v. Federal Election Commission,* 558 U.S. 08-205 (2010).

The cumulative effect of such independent campaign activism is difficult to judge. One important research initiative within political science seeks to measure systematically the marginal effectiveness of campaign contact. Professors Alan Gerber and Donald Green have developed a program of field experiments in which campaigns agree to randomly assign direct campaign activity to some neighborhoods but not others. They have been able to measure the marginal effect of an additional piece of mail, direct canvasser, or phone call. In a typical election context, it costs about $40 to get an additional voter to the polls. Professors Gerber and Green further find that campaign activism can have initially a large impact, but after six or so attempted contacts the effects of campaign contact diminish dramatically. This important empirical research has given campaigns and reformers some sense of the effectiveness of campaign activism in stimulating turnout and possibly influencing elections. Especially in low-turnout elections, such as for city council or state legislature, interest groups' get-out-the-vote activities can have very large effects on who wins, but as other money enters the scene, especially candidates' own campaign expenditures, the effects of interest groups' direct campaign activities becomes muted.[39]

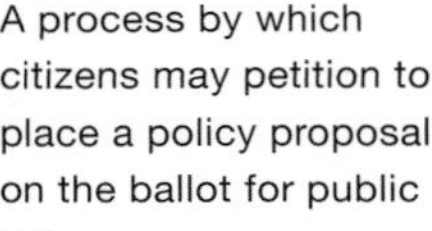

initiative

A process by which citizens may petition to place a policy proposal on the ballot for public vote

The Initiative. Another political tactic sometimes used by interest groups is sponsorship of ballot initiatives at the state level. The initiative, a device adopted by a number of states around 1900, allows proposed laws to be placed on the general election ballot and submitted directly to the state's voters. This procedure bypasses the state legislature and governor. The initiative was originally promoted by late-nineteenth-century Populists as a mechanism that allows the people to govern directly. Populists saw the initiative as an antidote to interest-group influence in the legislative process.

Ironically, many studies have suggested that most initiative campaigns today are sponsored by interest groups seeking to circumvent legislative opposition to their goals. In recent years, for example, initiative campaigns have been sponsored by the insurance industry, trial lawyers' associations, and tobacco companies. The role of interest groups in initiative campaigns should come as no surprise, since such campaigns can cost millions of dollars.

Interest Groups: Are They Effective?

Do interest groups have an effect on government and policy? A clear answer is difficult to find among the mountains of research on this question. A survey of dozens of studies of campaign contributions and legislative decision making found that in only about 1 in 10 cases was there evidence of a correlation between contributors' interests and legislators' roll-call voting.[40]

39 Donald Green and Alan Gerber, *Get Out the Vote: How to Increase Voter Turnout*, 2nd ed. (Washington DC: Brookings Institution Press, 2008).

40 Ansolabehere, deFigueiredo, and Snyder, "Why Is There So Little Money in U.S. Politics?"

Earmarks are a good case in point. Earmarks are expenditures on particular projects in specific districts or states, and they are usually included in a bill late in the legislative process to help secure enough votes for passage. Millions of dollars in earmarks are written into law every year. John de Figueiredo of UCLA and Brian Silverman of the University of Toronto examined the effectiveness of lobbyists to obtain "earmarks" for colleges and universities on whose behalf they are working.[41]

The authors discovered that lobbying had a limited impact. The more money schools spent on lobbying activities, the larger the total quantity of earmarked funds they received; however, the magnitude of the effect depended greatly on institutional factors. For most schools, every $1 spent on representation gained about $1 more on earmarks—hardly worth it. In a handful of cases, though, there appear to be exceedingly high returns. Schools in states with a senator on the Senate Appropriations Committee received $18 to $29 in earmarks for every $1 spent on lobbying. Schools in congressional districts whose representative served on the House Appropriations Committee received between $49 and $55 for every $1 spent on lobbying. Having a legislator on the relevant committee then is a precursor to having influence and explains most of the observed influence.[42]

These results suggest, as is so often the case, that institutions and politics are profoundly related. Schools without access to members of Congress in positions to help them cannot gain much from lobbying. Schools with such access still need to lobby to take advantage of the potential that representation on the Senate and House Appropriations Committees can give them. But if they do so, the potential return from lobbying is substantial.

Perhaps the largest challenge to the claim that interest-group politics drive American democracy arises when we consider how much political advocacy occurs. The usual argument about the power and influence of lobbyists and campaign contributions suggests that any dollar spent by a corporation or other organization on political activity is a dollar well spent. One can turn that thinking on its head. If it is a dollar well spent then groups should spend as much as possible on politics, and total spending on politics should reflect the value of political action to firms and organizations, relative to other sorts of investments. In other words, view the political actions of any firm—and most organizations involved in politics are firms—not as a political decision but as a business decision. What insight comes from that perspective?

Those engaged in lobbying provide a valued service for the firms that they represent by helping to shape legislation, influence administrative decisions, and advocate in court. There are, however, other investments one can make: buy new machines, purchase another company, hire additional employees. How do lobbying and campaign contributing compare with those sorts of bottom-line decisions made by firms?

41 John M. de Figueiredo and Brian S. Silverman, "Academic Earmarks and the Returns to Lobbying" working paper 9064, National Bureau of Economic Research, 2002; substantially rev., 2003, http://web.mit.edu/jdefig/www/papers/academic_earmarks.pdf (accessed 4/7/09).

42 John M. de Figueiredo and Brian S. Silverman, "Academic Earmarks and the Returns to Lobbying," *Journal of Law and Economics* 42 (October 2006): 597–626.

As a business and economic matter, the amount of money spent on political activity by firms is small. The value of goods purchased in a market is approximately equal to the amount of money someone is willing to pay for them. The total U.S. economy is valued at $15.8 trillion; government expenditures are over $5 trillion; corporate profits alone exceed $1.7 trillion. As a fraction of total government expenditures, total lobbying expenditures equal less than one-tenth of 1 percent, and lobbying is only a trace amount of the total revenue of firms' total expenses. This simple calculation suggests that the total influence of groups cannot be substantial.[43] If the returns on political investment were high, then we ought to see large firms like Microsoft, General Electric, and Wal-Mart spending much more (and getting much more) on politics.

Why isn't there more money in politics? One answer is suggested by Mancur Olson—all groups are simply free riding. But that still suggests there is an opportunity for influence for those who are engaged, and they should spend even more money to get even greater returns. The pluralist line of thinking points to a more compelling answer. The United States has a wide open political system, with many points of access and many points of influence. By allowing more political activity and discourse, no one group is able to have much influence. There is not much money in politics because the separation of powers and other features of the U. S. political system make it exceedingly difficult to have much immediate influence over the legislative and executive branches of government. The pluralist argument is wrong in asserting that all interests will find expression through political organization, but it is perhaps right that a system of divided political authority, such as in the United States, will make it exceedingly hard for particular interests to succeed in the political arena.

CONCLUSION

The institutions of American government embrace an open and democratic process in order to ensure that government is responsive to the public's preferences and needs. The Bill of Rights provides for the rights of free speech, freedom of the press, and freedom of assembly. The laws of the land have only further cemented this commitment, providing for open meetings, citizen advisory commissions, lobbying, direct contact from constituents, contributions from interested individuals and groups, an open legal system, protests, and many other routes through which individuals and groups may advocate for their interests. Through these many points of access, representatives and government officials learn how their decisions affect groups and individuals. Politics, then, becomes the arena in which these many interests compete for the attention and support of

43 See Ansolabehere, de Figueiredo, and Snyder, "Why Is There So Little Money in U.S. Politics?"

the government; sometimes they succeed in coming together to find common ground.

Such a system creates an opportunity for those who have the willingness and capacity to use their resources to represent their interests before the government. Problems of collective action and free riding prevent many latent interests from developing permanent political organizations capable of bringing concerted pressure on the government. Businesses, unions, and professional and industry associations usually have less trouble overcoming the obstacles to organization and group maintenance that many volunteer associations may face. Interest-group politics in Washington and state legislatures, consequently, tends to reflect the interests of and conflicts among those engaged in economic activity in the country.

Although firms, unions, and other organizations can solve the collective action problem, they do not necessarily succeed in the political arena. They often find politics unfamiliar, even hostile, terrain in which to pursue organizational goals. Unlike economic activity, politics involves power derived from the ability to vote on measures, to introduce legislation or rules, or to block actions from happening. Interest groups are necessarily outsiders that can do none of these things directly. Nonetheless, these organizations seek out support in the appropriate institutions, such as a court with a sympathetic judge or a subcommittee of Congress where the chairman holds views similar to those of the group. And the way to success is usually quite subtle. Often, groups succeed not by bringing pressure but by providing expertise to the government and by learning from those in office about the impact of new rules and regulations.

Over the past 30 to 40 years, interest groups have increasingly found that the best route to power is through public action and public opinion. It is not enough for a group to hire a lobbyist to advocate on its behalf in the halls of government. Real pressure may be brought to bear on politicians by shaping what others think. Through advertising, protests, and grassroots networks, interest groups have increasingly brought their issues to the attention of the public. Through public pressure, they have been able to influence politics. These new means of shaping public policy and government decision making are increasingly remote from traditional politics. Likewise, it becomes increasingly difficult for an organization to trace its influence in the political arena. Tens of thousands of organizations compete in the political sphere, alternately pursuing insider and outsider strategies, and each claiming credit for favorable policies and ducking blame for failures.

Interest-group politics at the beginning of the twenty-first century does not fit stereotypical notions clearly. There are certainly as many lobbyists as ever, but the backroom dealings of the "old lobby" are an anachronism. Interest-group politics is diffuse, spread across all branches of government and involving many different interests vying for the attention of politicians in an increasingly crowded and active interest-group ecology. Those who are organized gain the advantages of pooling resources, but an interest group's political action today constitutes only one aspect of the debate over any given political issue or decision. Other interests and voices making competing claims may very well cancel out a given organization's efforts. And the activities of all groups amount to just one facet of legislators', judges', and executives' deliberations. Those who must ultimately make political decisions and be held accountable for those decisions consider other voices as well, especially the opinions and preferences of their constituents. Perhaps a better contemporary characterization is that the organized and disorganized interests participating in politics today are really contributing to a much broader sphere of political discourse and debate. That debate takes place inside the institutions of government—Congress, courts, executives, and elections. It also takes place in another arena, the media. That forum is the final leg of our discussion of democracy in America, and to that subject we turn in the next chapter.

For Further Reading

Ainsworth, Scott. *Analyzing Interest Groups.* New York: Norton, 2002.

Alexander, Robert, ed. *The Classics of Interest Group Behavior.* New York: Wadsworth, 2005.

Ansolabehere, Stephen, John M. de Figueiredo, and James M. Snyder, Jr. "Why Is There So Little Money in U.S. Politics?" *Journal of Economic Perspectives* 17, no. 1 (Winter 2003): 105–30.

Baumgartner, Frank, Jeffrey M. Berry, Beth L. Leech, David C. Kimball, and Marie Hojnacki. *Lobbying and Policy Change: Who Wins, Who Loses, and Why.* Chicago: University of Chicago Press, 2009.

Esterling, Kevin. *The Political Economy of Expertise.* Ann Arbor: University of Michigan Press, 2004.

Galanter, Marc. "Why the 'Haves' Come Out Ahead: Spectulations on the Limits of Legal Change." *Law and Society Review* 9, no. 1 (1974): 95–160.

reader selection Kollman, Kenneth W. *Outside Lobbying: Public Opinion and Interest Group Strategies.* Princeton, NJ: Princeton University Press, 1998.

Lowi, Theodore J. *The End of Liberalism: The Second Republic of the United States.* 2nd ed. New York: Norton, 1979.

reader selection Moe, Terry M. *The Organization of Interests: Incentives and the Internal Dynamics of Political Interest Groups.* Chicago: University of Chicago Press, 1980.

Nownes, Anthony. *Total Lobbying: What Lobbyists Want and How They Try to Get It.* New York: Cambridge University Press, 2006.

reader selection Olson, Mancur, Jr. *The Logic of Collective Action: Public Goods and the Theory of Groups.* 1965. Reprinted with new preface and appendix. Cambridge, MA: Harvard University Press, 1965.

Rosenthal, Alan. *The Third House: Lobbyists and Lobbying in the States.* Washington, DC: Congressional Quarterly Press, 2001.

Rozell, Mark, Clyde Wilcox, and David Madland. *Interest Groups in American Campaigns.* Washington, DC: Congressional Quarterly Press, 2005.

Sheingate, Adam. *The Rise of the Agricultural Welfare State: Institutions and Interest Group Power in the United States, France, and Japan.* Princeton, NJ: Princeton University Press, 2003.

Strolovitch, Dara. *Affirmative Advocacy: Race, Class, and Gender in Interest Group Politics.* Chicago: University of Chicago Press, 2007.

Visit **wwnorton.com/studyspace/** to access free review materials such as:

- Vocabulary Flashcards of All Key Terms
- Chapter Review Quizzes
- Complete Study Outlines

reader selection

Highlighted selections are included in *Readings in American Politics: Analysis and Perspectives*, Second Edition.

14

PART 1 2 X 4

DEMOCRATIC POLITICS

The Media

The media make up one of the most unusual institutions of American democracy. They are not a singular institution, such as the Congress or the presidency. Rather, the media comprise an industry that exists primarily for communication and entertainment. The main business model is simple enough. Using communication technologies such as the printing press and Internet, media firms develop and distribute content—news articles, TV shows, Web sites, and the like—to attract an audience. The audience pays for access to content by purchasing subscriptions, paying cover prices and access charges, and buying computers, televisions, and radios. More significant still, other businesses, organizations, and individuals want access to that audience, and they will pay media firms to advertise their messages. Most media revenue derives from advertising, from selling access to the audience attracted by television and radio, newspapers and magazines, and the Internet.[1] And the audience is huge. Nearly every household in the United States has at least one television; three-quarters have Internet access. The typical American adult watches four hours of television a day.

Politics and public affairs are an important part of the content produced by the media. People are willing to pay for information about politics and public affairs, and politicians and organized interests are willing to pay to reach that audience through advertisements or events that will attract news coverage. Most major media outlets offer news coverage and analysis as a way to attract

1 Roughly 75 percent of newspaper revenue comes from advertising, and 20 percent from subscriptions. See Laura Houston Santhanam and Tom Rosenstiel, "Why U.S. Newspapers Suffer More Than Others," *The State of the News Media, 2011*, Pew Research Center's Project for Excellence in Journalism, http://stateofthemedia.org/2011/mobile-survey/international-newspaper-economics/ (accessed 10/3/11).

readers and listeners. The major television networks—ABC, CBS, NBC, and Fox—offer approximately six hours of news programming every day, and some media organizations are devoted exclusively to politics and public affairs. The cost of news programs to consumers is minimal, even free, and the content is presented in a widely accessible manner. In this way, the media offer most people an easy way to learn about the important actions of the government, the state of the nation, and the choices in an election.

The media, then, address one of the most important problems of democracy—how to create an informed electorate. As we discussed in Chapters 10 and 11, democratic politics assumes some awareness among the electorate about who is in power, what problems the nation faces, and what actions and policies the government has taken. The news media make information about politics and public affairs readily and widely accessible, even entertaining. Most Americans learn about government and politics not through firsthand experience but from media sources and through the lenses of those who report the news or comment on important issues and events.

CORE OF THE ANALYSIS

The primary objective of the American media is to make profits. They create and distribute content to attract an audience. They earn revenues by selling access to that audience to advertisers and by charging fees for content.

The market for news is extremely large, as most Americans rely on the media to find out about important issues, the activities of the government, and electoral choices. The centrality of the news media in informing the public makes this private industry into an important part of the public sphere.

Reporters and journalists rely on politicians, government agencies, organizations, and average people as sources of information. This provides politicians, bureaucrats, organized interests, and private citizens the opportunity to try to shape how the media portray public issues.

Rather than try to run the media as a public trust, the U.S. government takes a comparatively light hand in regulating media ownership and operation and instead relies on the marketplace to produce a robust flow of information about politics and government affairs.

The challenge for every democracy is how to foster the development of media that will allow for robust discourse and dissent. The United States, from its inception, has embraced the principle that a free press allows people to speak freely and to make reasoned electoral decisions. The First Amendment to the Constitution states that "Congress shall make no law . . . abridging the freedom of speech, or the press." Over time the Supreme Court has expanded that idea to cover all forms of communication and has interpreted that restraint to apply to all levels and branches of government, not just Congress.

A free, open, and largely unregulated media environment is the engine of American democracy. It is the great marketplace of ideas. Collectively the media present a vast range of ideas, opinions, and information and make it easily accessible to everyone. Any consumer may choose to watch, read, or listen to what he or she wants. Those media that do not attract consumers fail, whereas those that offer people what they want succeed. This system does not always provide the ideal outcome, but, at least in theory, it is considered the best way to guarantee an adequately informed public.[2] The First Amendment, wrote Judge Learned Hand at the height of World War II, "presupposes that right conclusions are more likely to be gathered out of a multitude of tongues, than through any kind of authoritative selection. To many this is, and always will be, folly; but we have staked upon it our all."[3]

An alternate view holds that journalists and owners of media firms hold a privileged and powerful position in any society, and with that privilege comes responsibilities that can only be ensured through regulation. Most countries regulate political speech by limiting advertising; they require a minimum amount of public affairs programming; and they regulate what is and is not said by reporters. Slander and libel laws apply to American journalists as do restrictions owing to national security, but there is far less regulation of reporting in the United States than in just about every other country. Most other countries underwrite or own their main broadcast media outlets, such as the Canadian or British Broadcasting Corporations. In the United States, media firms succeed or fail as businesses and rely on their ability to attract audiences and revenue, not on whether they provide a public service or good.

How and how well does the marketplace of ideas work? Is there enough competition? Today, for example, very few cities are served by more than one local newspaper. Local news monopolies may give owners, editors, and journalists excessive political power in their local markets. Or is there too much competition? The emergence of the Internet has cut into the profit margins of traditional media, forcing newspapers and television and radio companies to cut their more expensive staff, often the very reporters who produce the content on the news. Media firms, Congress, and executive agencies (especially the Federal Communications Commission) must deal with these and other complex

2 This idea is most elegantly expressed in the majority opinion in the Supreme Court case *New York Times v. Sullivan*, 376 U.S. 254 (1964).

3 *United States v. Associated Press*, 52 F. Supp. 362, 372 (D. C. S. D. N. Y. 1943).

questions over the coming decades as new communications technologies transform the media industry in the United States and the ways that people become informed about and engage in politics.

THE MEDIA AS A POLITICAL INSTITUTION

Perhaps the most salient feature of the American media—as an industry and as a political institution—is the diversity of sources, firms, and technologies. There are approximately 1,400 daily newspapers in the United States and 1,500 television stations affiliated with seven major broadcasting networks. Hundreds of weekly magazines, independent television stations, and affiliates of smaller networks are devoted to national politics. Countless Web sites stream news from sources throughout the world. These media reach every community in the United States and provide information in every language.

Types of Media

There is some order to the apparent chaos. The American media are organized into three categories—print, broadcast, and Internet. Regulations of the media follow these lines. Print media, such as newspapers and magazines, have long enjoyed strong First Amendment protections and provide a good example of the "marketplace of ideas." The technology of printing presses and digital reproduction makes it quite easy for new papers to enter local markets, and that fact has led the courts to stay the hand of those pushing for regulation of print media. Newspapers, magazines, and other print media are distributed locally through delivery services or vendors or nationally through the mail, though most are owned by national media organizations and firms.

Broadcast and cablecast media, by contrast, have historically faced technological limits that have led to restrictions on ownership, distribution, and at times content. With the advent of radio in the 1920s, the need for regulation immediately became evident. Broadcasters would vary the strength of their signal and the part of the radio-frequency spectrum over which they broadcast to find audiences and squelch other broadcasters. That behavior threatened to ruin the medium, because consumers could not reliably find the programming that they wanted. In 1927, Commerce Secretary Herbert Hoover introduced the first regulations of broadcast media, requiring every broadcaster to secure a license from the U.S. government and to agree to send its signal only over a narrow band of the spectrum (which would be allocated to that station within a certain region). The U.S. government could revoke that license for failure to comply with spectrum regulations. In the late 1940s, concern about the use of the spectrum in emerging television technology led the federal government to freeze the development of that nascent industry for four years while the Federal

Communications Commission (FCC) worked out a distribution and ownership plan. Regulation of the broadcast spectrum continues to dictate federal communications policy to this day. Because spectrum is limited, broadcasting and cablecasting firms serve a public trust and bear responsibility for their actions.[4] Of course, spectrum is not very limited. Rather, this view exhibits the history principle at work. When broadcasting and cable were developed the technology was not as good as today, and the technology limited the number of stations possible, with only some firms having access—hence, the public responsibility. Today, broadcasting and cable technology permit hundreds of channels. Nonetheless the rules developed in the 1920s persist, and those firms that have flourished under the rules fight to keep their control over the airwaves.

Since the mid-1990s, a third media sector has arisen, one driven by Internet technology. Internet technology blurs the line between the other two media sectors. It requires governance for the assignment of Web domains, but it otherwise operates as perhaps the most open and competitive of the three sectors. The Internet sector is still developing its distinctive identity as a mode of communication. For the first two decades of its existence, the traditional media dominated the Internet provision of content, as print and broadcast firms moved their content online. But since 2000 an increasingly distinctive form of Web-based political communication has emerged, including blogs and citizen journalism, which many fear is supplanting traditional media and the norms of professional journalism.[5] The 2008 election marked the true arrival of the Internet as one of the three pillars of "the media." In 2008, for the first time, more people reported that they got news from a digital platform, including websites, social networking, and mobile devices, than from newspapers. By 2012, Internet and mobile technologies had far surpassed radio and newspapers: 50 percent of the public reported that they got some of their news through the Web or a mobile device, compared with 55 percent through television and just 29 percent by newspaper with another 33 percent from radio.

Broadcast Media. Television news reaches more Americans than any other single news source. Tens of millions of individuals watch national and local news programs every day. Television news, however, covers relatively few topics and provides little depth of coverage. Television news is more like a series of newspaper headlines connected to pictures. It serves the important function of alerting viewers to issues and events but provides little else.

The 24-hour news stations such as Cable News Network (CNN) offer more detail and commentary than the networks' half-hour evening news shows.

---

4 Perhaps the best account of these developments is Erik Barnouw's excellent three-volume history *A Tower in Babel: A History of Broadcasting in the United States to 1933; The Golden Web: A History of Broadcasting in the United States, 1933 to 1953*; and *The Image Empire: A History of Broadcasting in the United States from 1953* (New York: Oxford University Press, 1966, 1968, and 1970).

5 Cass R. Sunstein, *Republic.com 2.0* (Princeton, NJ: Princeton University Press, 2007).

Table 14.1

THE TREND IN REGULAR NEWS CONSUMPTION, 1991–2010

	1991 (%)	1994 (%)	1996 (%)	1998 (%)	2000 (%)	2002 (%)	2004 (%)	2006 (%)	2008 (%)	2010 (%)	2012 (%)
Watched news on TV	68	72	59	59	56	54	60	57	57	58	55
Read a daily newspaper	56	49	50	49	47	41	42	40	34	31	29
Listened to news on radio	54	47	44	48	43	41	40	36	35	34	33
Got news online	—	—	—	—	—	—	24	23	29	34	39

SOURCE: Pew Research Center for People and the Press, "In Changing News Landscape, Even Television Is Vulnerable," September 27, 2012, www.people-press.org/2012/09/27/section-1-watching-reading-and-listening-to-the-news-3/ (accessed 12/10/12).

In 2003, at the start of the war in Iraq, CNN, Fox News, and MSNBC provided 24-hour-a-day coverage of the war, including on-the-scene reports from embedded reporters, expert commentary, and interviews with government officials. In this instance, these networks' depth of coverage rivaled that of the print media. Normally, however, CNN and the others offer more headlines than analysis, especially during their prime-time broadcasts. Nevertheless, in recent years, cable has been growing in importance as a news source (Table 14.1).

Radio news is essentially a headline service without pictures. In the short time that they devote to news (usually five minutes per hour), radio stations announce the day's major events without providing much detail. In major cities, all-news stations provide a bit more coverage of major stories, but for the most part these stations fill the day with repetition rather than detail. All-news stations such as WTOP (Washington, D.C.) and WCBS (New York City) assume that most listeners are in their cars and that, as a result, the people who constitute the audience change markedly throughout the day as they reach their destinations. Thus, rather than use their time to flesh out a given set of stories, these stations repeat the same stories each hour to present them to new listeners. In recent years, radio talk shows have become important sources of commentary and opinion. A number of conservative radio hosts, such as Rush Limbaugh, have huge audiences and have helped mobilize support for conservative political causes and candidates. Liberals have had less success in the world of talk radio and have complained that biased coverage over radio has hurt them in elections. In 2003, however, a group of wealthy liberal political activists led by Anita Drobny, a major Democratic Party donor, created Air America, a liberal talk-radio network designed to combat conservative dominance of this important medium. One executive of the new network said, "There are so many right-wing talk shows, we think it created a hole in the market you could drive a truck through." Liberals hoped their network would be entertaining as well as informative, specializing in parody and political satire.[6] In 2007, however, Air America filed for Chapter 11 bankruptcy protection and was later sold.

In recent years, much of the content of the news, especially local news, has shifted away from politics and public affairs toward "soft news"—coverage focusing on celebrities, health tips, advice to consumers, and other topics more likely to provide entertainment than enlightenment. Even a good deal of political coverage is soft. For example, articles about the Obamas' choice of their dog Bo outnumbered stories about the Iraq War by 3 to 2 during April 2009.[7]

Softer even than soft news is a category of programming sometimes called *infotainment.* This term refers to material that purports to combine information with entertainment. *The Daily Show with Jon Stewart* on Comedy Central calls itself America's "most trusted name in fake news," yet a significant fraction of people under 35 years of age report this show as one of their main sources of political information and news. The news on *The Daily Show* is not fake but a comedic twist on current events and on the media itself, especially CNN and Fox News.

Print Media. Newspapers remain an important source of news even though they are not the primary news source for most Americans. The print media are important for two reasons. First, as we see later in this chapter, the broadcast media rely on leading newspapers such as the *New York Times* and the *Washington Post* to set their news agenda. The broadcast media engage in very little actual reporting; they primarily cover stories that have been "broken," or initially reported, by the print media. For example, sensational charges that President Bill Clinton had an affair with a White House intern were reported first by the *Washington Post* and *Newsweek* before being trumpeted around the world by the broadcast media. It is only a slight exaggeration to observe that if an event is not covered in the *New York Times*, it is not likely to appear on the *CBS Evening News*. One important exception, obviously, is the case of "breaking" news, which can be carried by the broadcast media as it unfolds or soon after, whereas the print media are forced to catch up later in the day. For example, dramatic real-time videos of the collapsing World Trade Center towers were seen by tens of millions of Americans on September 11, 2001. Second, the print media provide more detailed and more complete information, offering a better context for analysis. Third, the print media are also important because they are the prime source of news for educated and influential individuals. The nation's economic, social, and political elites rely on the detailed coverage provided by the print media to inform and influence their views about important public matters. The

6 CNN.com/Inside Politics, "Liberal Radio Network Planned," February 18, 2003, www.cnn.com/2003/ALLPOLITICS/02/17/radio.politics.ap.

7 Project for Excellence in Journalism, "The Dog Days of Spring," http://journalism.org/TheDogDaysofSpring+ (accessed 5/7/09).

print media may have a smaller audience than their cousins in broadcasting, but they have an audience that matters.

Today, however, the newspaper industry is in serious economic trouble. The rise of Web sites advertising jobs, items for sale, and personal ads has dramatically reduced newspapers' revenues from traditional advertising, such as "help wanted" and personal ads. The *Rocky Mountain News* in Denver closed in 2008, and in 2009 the *Seattle Post-Intelligencer* announced it would adopt an online format only. Major newspapers serving dozens of large U.S. cities and metropolitan areas confirmed in 2008 and 2009 that they faced serious financial difficulties, including the *Philadelphia Inquirer*, the *Minneapolis Star Tribune*, the *Miami Herald*, the *Boston Globe*, and the *San Francisco Chronicle*. Each of these papers indicated that it might close entirely or shut down its print operations and issue only online editions. Such closures would leave many cities with one or possibly no daily print newspapers. It is widely believed that the troubles experienced by these papers are the beginning of a wider transformation of the print media in the United States that may leave the country with few or no print newspapers—the traditional "press"—in the future. The great unknown is whether other venues, such as the Internet, can adequately replace newspapers, especially in the provision of news about local area politics and public affairs.[8] The Analyzing the Evidence unit for this chapter explores the apparent decline of newspapers.

The possible demise of major city newspapers raises important questions. Since the beginning of the Republic, newspapers have been ingrained in the way we think about political communication. The First Amendment specifically protects a "Free Press," and legal doctrines and laws concerning political communication in the United States have evolved around the idea of a robust press serving every community. Many cities now face the prospect of no significant press, in the conventional sense. These changes will likely force a rethinking of the laws governing many aspects of political communication in this country, from campaign finance laws to obscenity standards to ownership guidelines. So far, the U.S. Supreme Court has not extended the same set of free press protections to broadcasters.[9]

This transformation of print media may change the extent to which people are informed about politics and public affairs. The media that will replace newspapers may raise the overall level of information among the mass public or create further differences between those in the know and those who decide to tune out politics. The Internet, television, radio, and other outlets that replace newspapers may reach more people with similar content, or they may segment the audience further, reducing the number of people aware of public affairs. Social science research so far suggests that the decline of newspapers is changing newsgathering behavior. Rather than rely on a single source—the daily

8 24/7 Wall Street, "The 10 Most Endangered Newspapers in America," *Time*, March 9, 2009, www.time.com/time/business/article/0,8599,1883785,00.html (accessed 5/7/09).

9 *Red Lion Broadcasting Company v. Federal Communications Commission*, 395 U.S. 367 (1969).

ANALYZING THE EVIDENCE

The End of Newspapers?

CHAPTER 14

Newspapers and the press enjoy a special place in American democracy. In the landmark case *New York Times v. Sullivan* (1963), Justice William Brennan defended the First Amendment's guarantee of freedom of the press as essential to an informed public, healthy deliberation, and democratic elections. A precipitous decline in newspaper readership in recent years, then, has caused concern among many observers and questions about the cause of the decline. Has the rise of the Internet caused the drop in newspaper readership? And what might this mean for American democracy?

Newspaper and Internet Ad Revenues

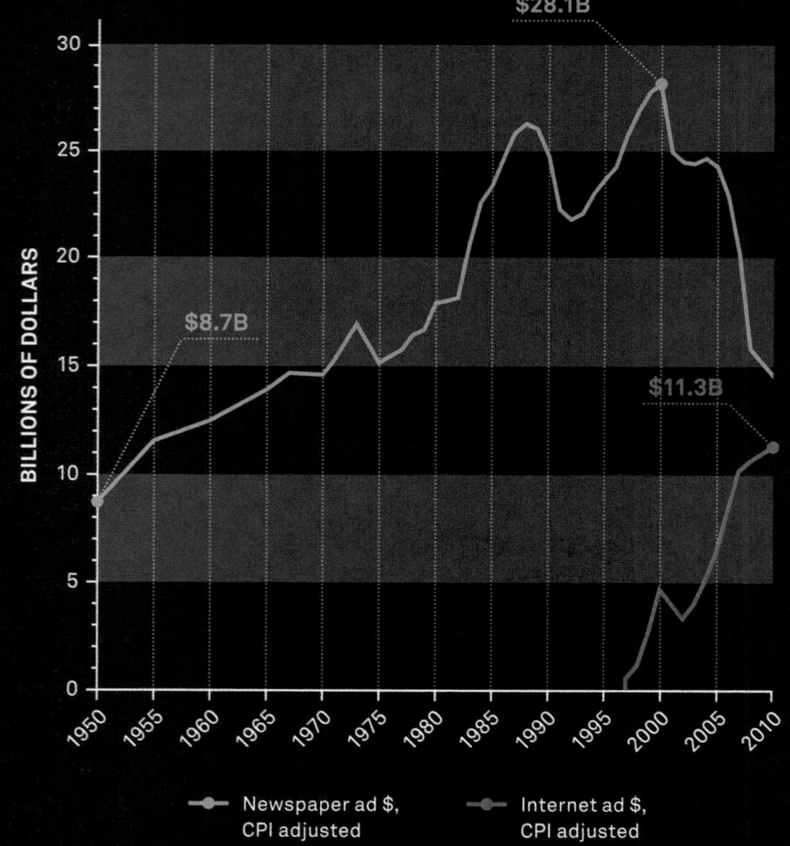

The economic difficulties of newspapers are best reflected in their balance sheets. Their main source of revenue is advertising, which accounts for about 90 percent of the revenue generated by a print newspaper. From 2000 to 2008, real revenues of newspapers declined by over $14 billion—a 50 percent decline. Over the same period, Internet advertising revenue rose by $7 billion. Advertisers, of course, are seeking the audience. The decline in ad revenues is widely seen as an indicator of eroding newspaper readership, and the pattern since 2000 suggests that the Internet is largely to blame.

Newspaper Readership

However, a longer term perspective shows that the decline in newspaper reading started long before the late 1990s, when the Internet emerged. At their peak in the 1950s, approximately 35 newspapers were sold for every 100 people in the United States. Today that figure is roughly 15 newspapers for every 100 people and falling.

Television Viewing

Although the decline of newspapers predates the increase in online advertising, the Internet does fit into a more general account of the problems facing newspapers—competition. Web sites have competed with newspapers for audience and revenue in recent years. Since the 1950s, television has competed with newspapers for the attention of the American public. Television, and, more recently, the Internet have gradually won over the newspaper audience.

OURCES:

ewspaper Readership and Revenue: Editor and Publisher, *Editor and Publisher* *ternational Yearbook* (various years).

ternet Revenue: *Internet Advertising Bureau, Internet Advertising Report, 2008 Full-Year* *esults*, www.iab.net/media/file/IAB_PwC_2008_full_year.pdf (accessed 10/24/11).

elevision Viewing: Nielsen Media Research, *NTI Annual Averages*, reported y Television Bureau of Advertising, Trends in Television (various years).

EXPLORE
MEDIA TRENDS AND POLITICS
FURTHER AT:
wwnorton.com/studyspace

paper—Americans are sampling many different sources, a practice known as "grazing" according to a recent study by the Pew Research Center. And that behavior is facilitated by the Internet.[10]

The Internet. The Internet emerged as a major form of communication in the mid-1990s. As with radio in the 1920s and television in the 1950s, over the span of a decade the Internet grew from a curiosity into one of the dominant modes of communication. Internet news providers now stand as a significant competitor to traditional media outlets. Every day tens of millions Americans scan one of many news sites on the Internet for coverage of current events. Web sites such as Craig's List have taken away one of the most important sources of revenue for newspapers—classified advertising. As classified advertising has moved online, newspapers have seen an important line of revenue dry up. At one of many recent forums on the changing media world, an editor at the *Boston Globe* said, "who knew that the problem we would face would be one of too much competition rather than too little."

In many ways, the Internet as a medium parallels newspapers, television, radio, and magazines. The main newspapers and television outlets—such as the *Wall Street Journal* and *New York Times*, Reuters and the Associated Press, CNN and Fox News—are mainstays of the Internet. All have Web sites that they use to attract audiences to their traditional media and that they use to sell advertising. The Internet, however, has revolutionized how content is provided and what content is accessible to audiences. The Internet captures the strengths of the traditional media. It combines the depth of newspaper coverage with the timeliness of television and radio, but it goes much farther. Look at the Web site of one of the traditional media outlets, such as the *New York Times* or CNN. There you will see a reproduction of the content on the newspaper or headline news from television that resembles a traditional newspaper, but there is also streaming video like a television report or audio like a radio program, and you will also find commentary from many different sources, like an opinion magazine or news journal, such as *Time* magazine.

Unlike a newspaper, which is wholly new every day, a Web site, such as for the *New York Times*, can keep important stories up for many days. Most news Web sites contain easily searchable archives of past stories, which allows persistent readers to follow the thread of the news. Many Web sites now function as aggregators, accumulating news on a given topic from many different sources. Perhaps the most powerful such aggregator is Google, whose news service accumulates and organizes information from news organizations as different as the *Wall Street Journal* and Al Jazeera, Reuters and the Associated Press, and the *Lebanon Daily Star* and *Shanghai Daily*. In addition to traditional news sites, there have emerged more specialized sites. Some focus on commentary, such as Slate; others

10 "Key News Audience Now Blend Online and Traditional Sources," Pew Research Center for the People and the Press, August 17, 2008, http://people-press.org/report/444/news-media (accesed 5/7/09).

on investigative reporting, such as the Drudge Report; others provide polling and other analytics, such as Cook Political Report; and still others offer a roundup of news, commentary, and analytics, most notably RealClearPolitics and Politico.

In many ways, the Internet most closely approximates the marketplace of ideas mentioned in this chapter's introduction. There is an unparalleled amount of information and commentary available on any one news site, let alone on one of the aggregator sites.

The Internet differs from traditional outlets in an important way: it allows people to get involved directly. Individual citizens can more easily help create the news and interpret it. Public-access television and radio has always been a source of citizen journalism, but the World Wide Web has expanded greatly the space available for news, commentary, and debate. Most news sites provide space for people to post their own photos, video, and blogs of important events. Individuals who are at the scene of a natural disaster or important political event can provide more (and sometimes even better) coverage of a story and more quickly than a reporter.

The ability to connect with others through the Internet—through e-mail, blogs, Facebook, Twitter, and other social media venues—makes the new media a two-way street. The traditional media firms can distribute information and citizens can contribute to journalism, and people can also connect with one another directly. The power of these new media is not lost on political organizers and campaigns. Political entrepreneurs within social movements and the political parties have sought to organize online advocacy groups to raise money, make their positions known through e-mail and letter campaigns, and provide support for politicians who accept their views. One of the most successful of these enterprises is MoveOn.org, founded by two liberal Silicon Valley entrepreneurs. MoveOn seeks to build electronic advocacy groups, allowing members to propose issues and strategies and then acting on behalf of those that appear to have the highest level of member support. Reflecting the importance of the Internet, two days after announcing her bid for the 2008 Democratic presidential nomination, Senator Hillary Rodham Clinton fielded questions from voters in an online chat. Speaking into a Webcam, Clinton discussed health care, energy policy, and even her favorite movies with a group of preselected voters. President Obama's Press Office developed White House Live, a service that streams video of events live and keeps an archive of past events. A typical day will have live video of two or three events, such as the president touring a natural disaster, holding a press conference, or meeting with other world leaders. As the 2012 presidential campaign unfolded, the Internet had become the medium of choice. Governor Tim Pawlenty announced his bid for the presidency on Facebook. Obama restarted his presidential campaign with an online video. And Mitt Romney kicked off his campaign with a tweet.[11]

---

11 Beth Fouhy, "Elections 2012: The Social Network, Presidential Campaign Edition," The Huffington Post, April 17, 2011, www.huffingtonpost.com/2011/04/17/elections-2012-social-media_n_850172.html (accessed 10/4/2011).

Regulation of the Broadcast and Electronic Media

In most countries, the government controls media content and owns the largest media outlets. In the United States, the government neither owns nor controls the communications networks, but it does regulate the content and ownership of the broadcast media.

The print media in the United States are essentially free from government interference. The broadcast media, on the other hand, are subject to federal regulation. American radio and television are regulated by the FCC, an independent regulatory agency established in 1934. Radio and TV stations must renew their FCC licenses every five years. Licensing provides a mechanism for allocating radio and TV frequencies in such a way as to prevent broadcasts from interfering with and garbling each other. License renewals are almost always granted automatically by the FCC. Indeed, renewal requests are now filed online.

Through regulations prohibiting obscenity, indecency, and profanity, the FCC has also sought to prohibit radio and television stations from airing explicit sexual and excretory references between 6 A.M. and 10 P.M., the hours when children are most likely to be in the audience. The FCC has enforced these rules haphazardly. Since 1990, nearly half the $5 million in fines levied by the agency have involved Howard Stern, the shock jock whose programs are built around sexually explicit material. In 2004, after another set of FCC fines, Stern's program was dropped by a major outlet, Clear Channel Communications. Stern charged that the Bush administration had singled him out for censure because of his known opposition to the president. To avoid FCC regulations, he relaunched his show on Sirius Satellite Radio in 2006.

For more than 60 years, the FCC also sought to regulate and promote competition in the broadcast industry, but in 1996 Congress passed the Telecommunications Act, a broad effort to do away with most regulations in effect since 1934. The act loosened restrictions on media ownership and allowed for telephone companies, cable television providers, and broadcasters to compete with one another for the provision of telecommunication services. Following the passage of the act, several mergers between telephone and cable companies and between different segments of the entertainment media produced an even greater concentration of media ownership.

The Telecommunications Act of 1996 also included an attempt to regulate the content of material transmitted via the Internet. This law, known as the Communications Decency Act, made it illegal to make "indecent" sexual material on the Internet accessible to anyone under 18 years of age. The act was immediately denounced by civil libertarians and brought to court as an infringement of free speech. The case reached the Supreme Court in 1997, and the act was ruled an unconstitutional infringement of the First Amendment's guarantee of freedom of speech.

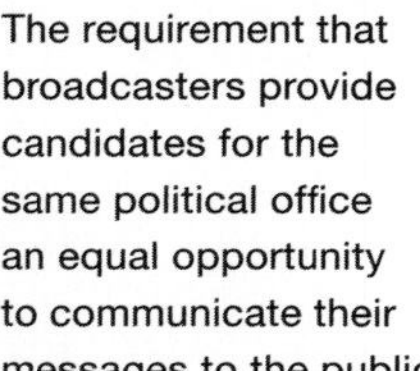
equal time rule

The requirement that broadcasters provide candidates for the same political office an equal opportunity to communicate their messages to the public

Although the government's ability to regulate the content of the electronic media on the Internet has been questioned, the federal government has used its licensing power to impose several regulations that can affect the political content of radio and TV broadcasts. The first of these is the equal time rule, under which broadcasters must provide candidates for the same political office equal opportunities to communicate their messages to the public. If, for example, a television station sells commercial time to a state's Republican gubernatorial candidate, it may not refuse to sell time to the Democratic candidate for the same position.

The second regulation affecting the content of broadcasts is the right of rebuttal, which requires that individuals be given the opportunity to respond to personal attacks. In the 1969 case of *Red Lion Broadcasting Company v. FCC*, for example, the U.S. Supreme Court upheld the FCC's determination that a radio station was required to provide a liberal author with an opportunity to respond to an attack by a conservative commentator that the station had aired.[12]

right of rebuttal

An FCC regulation giving individuals the right to have the opportunity to respond to personal attacks made on a radio or TV broadcast

For many years, a third important federal regulation was the fairness doctrine, under which broadcasters who aired programs on controversial issues were required to provide air time for opposing views. In 1985, the FCC stopped enforcing the fairness doctrine on the grounds that there were so many radio and television stations—to say nothing of newspapers and newsmagazines—that in all likelihood many different viewpoints were being presented even without the requirement that each station present all sides of an argument. Critics of this FCC decision charge that in many media markets the number of competing viewpoints is small. Nevertheless, a congressional effort to require the FCC to enforce the fairness doctrine was blocked by the administration of President Ronald Reagan in 1987, and the doctrine died.

fairness doctrine

An FCC requirement that broadcasters who air programs on controversial issues provide time for opposing views

The emergence of the Internet has presented a set of regulatory questions as well, though they have a somewhat different flavor. One of the main controversies concerns property rights and the profitability of the media industry, most famously addressed in *A&M Records v. Napster*.[13] Napster's technology allowed users to download and play any song on any computer connected to the Internet. A&M Records sued Napster to recover royalties, claiming that the record company owned those recordings. A&M Records won, leading to a series of legal decisions that make Web distribution of content similar to other forms of distribution.

An even deeper issue concerns the regulation of domains and Web servers and the setting of standards for this technology. Here the Internet breaks sharply with broadcasting and print media. The Internet emerged out of research technology developed under the auspices of the Department of Defense, largely at universities. In the mid-1990s, Tim Berners-Lee organized researchers, firms, and government agencies involved in the development of the Internet in the international World Wide Web Consortium to set standards and make other governmental decisions for the Web.[14] This form of self-regulation has been vital for the development of the technology. It is yielding new concepts of intellectual property, such as Creative Commons, and pushing this technology

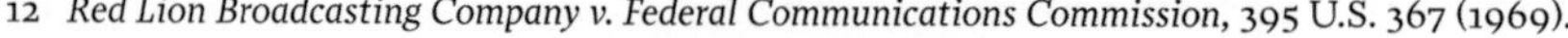

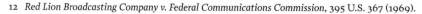

12 *Red Lion Broadcasting Company v. Federal Communications Commission*, 395 U.S. 367 (1969).

13 *A&M Records v. Napster*, 239 F.3d 104 (9th Circuit 2001).

14 Tim Berners-Lee with Mark Fischetti, *Weaving the Web: The Original Design and Ultimate Destiny of the World Wide Web by Its Inventor* (New York: HarperBusiness, 1999).

to develop in ways quite different from print media and, especially, broadcast media.[15] The philosophy behind the World Wide Web Consortium calls for much less government regulation than accompanies broadcasting but has a much more communal flavor than the philosophy of competitive markets that lies behind America's view of print media.

Freedom of the Press

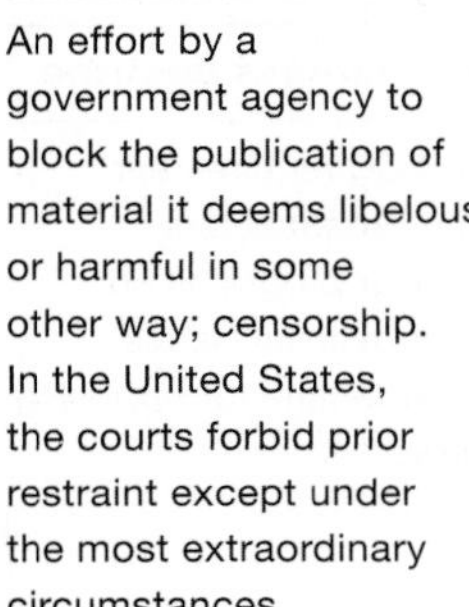

prior restraint

An effort by a government agency to block the publication of material it deems libelous or harmful in some other way; censorship. In the United States, the courts forbid prior restraint except under the most extraordinary circumstances

Unlike the broadcast media, the print media are not subject to federal regulation. Indeed, the great principle underlying the federal government's relationship with the press is the doctrine against prior restraint. Beginning with the landmark 1931 case of *Near v. Minnesota*, the U.S. Supreme Court has held that, except under the most extraordinary circumstances, the First Amendment of the Constitution prohibits government agencies from seeking to prevent newspapers or magazines from publishing whatever they wish.[16] Indeed, in the case of *New York Times v. United States*, the so-called Pentagon Papers case, the Supreme Court ruled that the government could not even block publication of secret Defense Department documents furnished to the *New York Times* by an opponent of the Vietnam War who had obtained the documents illegally.[17] In 1990, however, the Supreme Court upheld a lower-court order restraining CNN from broadcasting tapes of conversations between the former Panamanian leader Manuel Noriega and his lawyer, supposedly recorded by the U.S. government. By a vote of 7–2, the Court held that CNN could be restrained from broadcasting the tapes until the trial court in the Noriega case had listened to them and decided whether their broadcast would violate Noriega's right to a fair trial. This case would seem to weaken the no-prior-restraint doctrine. But in later decisions, the Supreme Court ruled that cable television systems were entitled to essentially the same First Amendment protections as the print media.[18]

Even though newspapers may not be restrained from publishing whatever they want, they may be subject to sanctions after the fact. Historically, newspapers have been subject to the law of libel, which provides that newspapers that print false and malicious stories can be compelled to pay damages to those they defame. In recent years, however, American courts have greatly narrowed the meaning of libel and made it extremely difficult, particularly for politicians and other public figures, to win a libel case against a newspaper. The most important case on this topic is the 1964 Supreme Court case of *New York Times v. Sullivan*, in which the Court held that to be deemed libelous, a story about a public official not only had to be untrue but also had to result from "actual malice" or

15 See http://creativecommons.org (accessed 5/7/09).

16 *Near v. Minnesota ex rel.*, 283 U.S. 697 (1931).

17 *New York Times v. United States*, 403 U.S. 713 (1971).

18 *Cable News Network v. Noriega*, 498 U.S. 976 (1990); *Turner Broadcasting v. Federal Communications Commission*, 512 U.S. 622 (1994).

"reckless disregard" for the truth.[19] In other words, the newspaper had to deliberately print false and malicious material. In practice, it is nearly impossible to prove that a paper deliberately printed false and damaging information, and as conservatives discovered in the 1980s, it is very difficult for a politician or other public figure to win a libel case. Libel suits against CBS News by General William Westmoreland and against *Time* magazine by Ariel Sharon of Israel, both financed by conservative legal foundations that hoped to embarrass the media, were defeated in court because they failed to show "actual malice." In the 1991 case of *Masson v. New Yorker Magazine*, this tradition was again affirmed by the Court's opinion that fabricated quotations attributed to a public figure were libelous only if the fabricated account "materially changed" the meaning of what the person said.[20] To all intents and purposes, the print media can publish almost anything they want about a public figure.

Organization and Ownership of the Media

The scope and breadth of the media industry in the United States are impressive: more than 2,000 television stations, approximately 1,400 daily newspapers, and more than 13,000 radio stations. There are 20 major television networks, up from just 3 in the 1970s, as well as an extensive system of public television and radio stations.

The media environment since the 1980s has opened considerably, and wholly new networks devoted to news have emerged and succeeded. CNN became a major news source in the late 1980s and gained a substantial market share during the first Gulf war in 1991. At one point, CNN was able to provide live coverage of American bombing raids on Baghdad after the major networks' correspondents had been forced to flee to bomb shelters. In the 2000s, a competitor news channel emerged: Fox News. By 2003, Fox had displaced CNN as the nation's primary cable news source, and by 2010 Fox News was the fourth most highly rated cable channel, trailing USA, TNT, and ESPN. The rise of Fox News has had important political implications because its coverage and commentators are considerably more conservative than CNN's. The emergence of Fox News also demonstrates the importance of the existence of more and varied news sources. When there are few sources of news, each is likely to appeal to the same broad national audience and, accordingly, to maintain a middle-of-the-road stance. When there are more sources, each is likely to position itself within a discrete ideological or partisan niche, increasing the diversity of viewpoints presented to listeners and viewers.

Nonetheless, there is a very real concern that these trends mask considerable concentration in the industry. The problem is most evident in the wire services, which provide a steady stream of stories and images. There is now just one

19 *New York Times v. Sullivan*, 376 U.S. 254 (1964).

20 *Masson v. New Yorker Magazine, Inc.*, 501 U.S. 496 (1991).

American wire service, the Associated Press (AP). United Press International (UPI) went bankrupt in the 1980s and has since failed to reemerge as a competitor. In Europe Reuters offers wire service and has the dominant market position similar to AP. Interestingly, CNN may make a run at offering its own competing service, especially for graphics and images.

Concentration of ownership of media outlets raises further concerns about the robustness of the marketplace of ideas. The 1996 Telecommunications Act opened the way for additional consolidation in the media industry, and a wave of mergers and consolidations has further reduced the field of independent media across the country. Since that time, among the major news networks ABC was bought by the Walt Disney Company; CBS was bought by Westinghouse and later merged with Viacom, the owner of MTV and Paramount Communications; and CNN was bought by Time Warner. NBC was owned by General Electric since from 1986 until 2011. It is now owned by Comcast. The Australian press baron Rupert Murdoch owns Fox plus a host of radio, television, and newspaper properties around the world. Murdoch's entry into the American market was of considerable importance because it required changes in U.S. laws prohibiting foreign ownership of U.S. broadcasting firms.[21] As a result of these consolidations, a relatively small number of giant corporations now control a wide swath of media holdings, including television networks, movie studios, record companies, cable channels and local cable providers, book publishers, magazines, and newspapers. This development has prompted questions about whether enough competition exists among the media to produce a diverse set of views on political and corporate matters or whether the United States has become the prisoner of media monopolies (Figure 14.1).[22]

In June 2003, the FCC announced a set of new rules that seemed to pave the way for even more concentration in the media industry. The rules mandated that the major networks could own television stations that collectively reached 45 percent of all viewers, up from 35 percent under the old rules. The new FCC rules also permitted a single company to own the leading newspaper, as well as multiple television and radio outlets, in a single market. In the largest cities, this could include a newspaper, three television stations, and as many as eight radio stations.[23] Major media companies, which had long lobbied for the right to expand their activities, welcomed the new FCC rules. Critics, however, expressed grave concern that a decision would result in a narrowing of the range of views and issues presented to the general public. Congressional opponents of the FCC's action sought to overturn the rules but were stymied by opposition from the House Republican leadership as well as a threatened presidential veto. However, a federal appeals court placed the new regulations on hold, and

21 Columbia Journalism Review provides regular updates on media ownership. See www.cjr.org/resources/index.php (accessed 9/17/11).

22 For a criticism of the increasing consolidation of the media, see the essays in Erik Barnouw et al., *Conglomerates and the Media* (New York: New Press, 1997).

23 David Lieberman, "How Will FCC's Action Affect Consumers?" *USA Today*, June 4, 2003, p. 48.

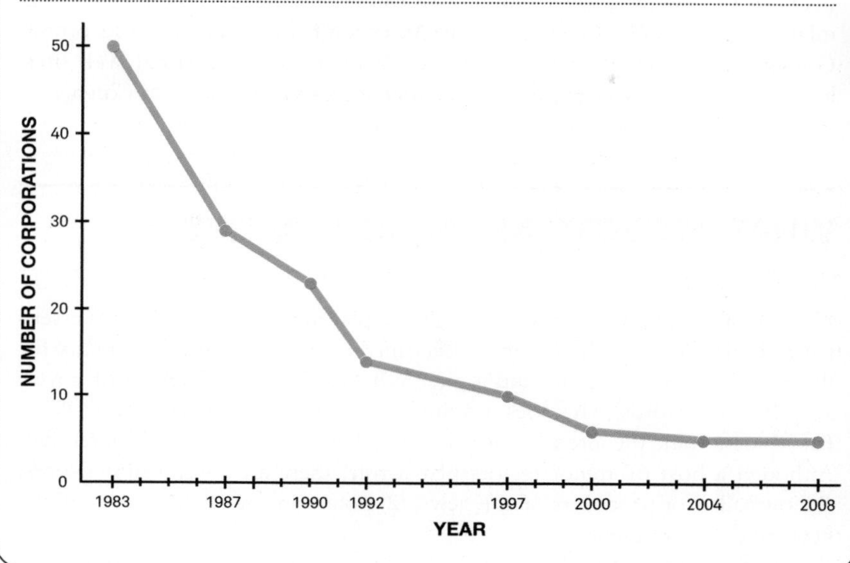

ANALYZING THE EVIDENCE

After several years of mergers and acquisitions, a small number of corporations have come to dominate the print, broadcast, cable, and Internet industries. What factors precipitated this media consolidation? What effects, if any, does media consolidation have on news reporting?

NOTE: Included are newspapers, magazines, TV and radio stations, books, music, movies, videos, wire services, and photo agencies.
SOURCE: Media Reform Information Center, www.corporations.org/media.

in January 2005 the Bush administration decided not to appeal the case to the Supreme Court. The FCC debuted new rules in 2007 to comply with the federal appeals court's ruling. The cross-ownership rule, however, might outlive the printed newspaper itself.

Distribution of news over the Internet goes against the trend toward increased concentration of media ownership. From the audience's perspective, the problem of increased concentration is that it will lead to less variety in the news and fewer voices heard. The Internet has made people less dependent on a single local newspaper to get information, however. Using Web sites that aggregate news from many different sources, a consumer can readily get many views on the same event. And people can easily search official Web sites to find out local information, such as meeting times of city councils and school committees.

One important question is whether there will become increased concentration of news distribution through the Internet as well. Google has emerged the dominant search firm. Its position allows it the power to block out certain sites and effectively censor the news. This problem arose recently with China. Google China, a subsidiary of Google, was forced by the government to censor many Web sites, especially those of dissidents. In order to maintain access to the enormous China market, Google complied, effectively blocking non-Chinese media from those users and conversely blocking Chinese media Web sites from others, including users in the United States. Eventually, Google directed traffic to those Web sites through its Hong Kong subsidiary, but the tense negotiations over access to the Web and to the Chinese market continue between Google and the Chinese government. While censorship in China might seem like a faraway problem, an American firm (Google) is at its center. Google was sufficiently powerful to negotiate access to censored Web sites, but it also had the market power to restrict access of U.S. users to China.

WHAT AFFECTS NEWS COVERAGE?

Because of the important role the media can play in national politics, it is essential to understand the factors that affect media coverage.[24] What accounts for the media's agenda of issues and topics? What explains the character of coverage? In other words, why does a politician receive good or bad press? What factors determine the interpretation, or spin, that a particular story will receive? Although a host of minor factors play a role, there are three major factors: (1) journalists or producers of the news, (2) politicians or other sources of the news, and (3) consumers.

Journalists

The character of the news is shaped by the people who produce it. The people who seek out, write, and produce the news have their own perspectives, passions, interests, and biases. Although a strong norm of objectivity and unbiasedness pervades the journalism profession, it is impossible to expect that reporters, editors, and media owners will always set aside their personal views. What motivates those who produce the news, and how do their personal beliefs and interests shape what we see and hear?

The marketplace of ideas sets out a single objective for the owners of media organizations: making a profit. Owners seek to maintain a successful business, and if their personal political beliefs endanger that business, then those beliefs will quickly be pushed aside by the internal organization in the newspaper or broadcasting station. This has not always been the case. At one time, newspaper publishers exercised a great deal of influence over their papers' news content. Publishers such as William Randolph Hearst and Joseph Pulitzer became political powers through their manipulation of news cover-

24 See the discussions in Michael Parenti, *Inventing Reality: The Politics of the Mass Media* (New York: St. Martin's Press, 1986); Herbert Gans, *Deciding What's News: A Study of CBS Evening News, NBC Nightly News, Newsweek, and Time* (New York: Vintage, 1980); and W. Lance Bennett, *News: The Politics of Illusion*, 5th ed. (New York: Longman, 2002).

age. Hearst, for example, almost single-handedly pushed the United States into war with Spain in 1898 through his newspapers' relentless coverage of the alleged brutality employed by Spain in its efforts to suppress a rebellion in Cuba, then a Spanish colony. The sinking of the American battleship *Maine* in Havana Harbor under mysterious circumstances gave Hearst the ammunition he needed to force a reluctant President William McKinley to lead the nation into war. Today, few publishers have that kind of power. The business end dominates the editorial content of papers, although a few continue to impose their interests and tastes on the news.

Individual reporters and editors have far more influence today over what is presented in the news day in and day out. They also pursue their interests and professional objectives. The goals and incentives of journalists are varied, but they often include considerations of ratings, career success and professional prestige, and political influence. For all of these reasons, journalists seek not only to report the news but also to interpret it. Journalists' goals have a good deal of influence on what is created and reported as news.

Those journalists who cover the news for the national media generally have considerable discretion or freedom to interpret stories and, as a result, have an opportunity to interject their own views and ideals into news stories. For example, some reporters' personal friendship with and respect for Franklin Delano Roosevelt and John F. Kennedy helped generate more favorable news coverage for those presidents. On the other hand, many reporters' dislike of and distrust for Richard Nixon was also communicated to the public. In the case of Ronald Reagan, the disdain that many journalists felt for the president was communicated in stories suggesting that he was often asleep or inattentive when important decisions were made.

From the perspective of the marketplace of ideas, perhaps the most troubling concern is the possibility that journalism on the whole is biased heavily in favor of one party or another or one set of ideals or another. Journalists lean decidedly to the left in their personal political beliefs. Surveys of reporters and editors at major media outlets have repeatedly found that those who produce the news are overwhelmingly liberal and Democratic. Surveys of journalists sponsored by the Pew Center for Excellence and by the Knight Foundation have found repeatedly that Democrats and liberals outnumber Republicans and conservatives by about 2 to 1 among journalists. A Knight Foundation survey conducted by Professor Dan Weaver of Indiana University found that 36 percent of journalists (across all media) identify as Democrats, while 18 percent identify as Republicans; 33 percent say that they do not identify with any party and 13 percent identify with another party.[25] The Pew survey found that most journalists identify themselves as moderates, but those who do claim an ideological orientation are decidedly more liberal than conservative. Of national reporters, 34 percent state that they are liberal and 7 percent say they are conservative, while 54 percent say they are moderates. Of local reporters, 23 percent are liberal and 12 percent are

25 Dan Weaver, *The American Journalist of the 21st Century: U.S. News People at the Dawn of a New Millennium* (Mahwah, NJ: Erlbaum, 2007).

conservative, while 61 percent say they are moderates.[26] Even among the radio talk-show hosts, Democrats outnumber Republicans by a wide margin: of 112 hosts surveyed, 39 percent had voted for the Democrat in the most recent presidential election, and only 23 percent had supported the Republican.[27] Generally speaking, reporters for major national news outlets tend to be more liberal than their local counterparts, who often profess moderate or even conservative views.

Do these political biases color the news? A classic study by Michael Robinson and Margaret Sheehan of CBS and the *New York Times* in the 1980s suggested that there was little evidence of political favoritism or bias.[28] Subsequent studies by the Pew Project for Excellence in Journalism echo that conclusion. Comparing the press coverage of the first 100 days of presidents Bill Clinton and George W. Bush, the Pew Project found nearly identical patterns of coverage. About half of printed stories were neutral toward the new presidents; a quarter were positive and a quarter negative. The same pattern arose for both presidents. Interestingly, Barack Obama received a much different welcome from the press. Using the same methodology, the Pew Project for Excellence in Journalism found that Obama's coverage was considerably more positive. Obama received positive coverage in 42 percent of stories, neutral coverage in 38 percent of stories, and negative coverage in 20 percent of stories.[29]

More subtle biases do exist, usually arising from the nature of the language used. A 2005 academic study by the political economists Timothy Groseclose and Jeffrey Milyo found that reporters use ideologically loaded terms when referring to some politicians but not others. Press reports typically mention both parties in a story, but they do so with no small degree of editorializing, using words like "radical" or "extreme conservative" to describe one politician or another. Analysis of such language revealed that most major media outlets slanted their reporting to the left, with three important exceptions. The *Wall Street Journal* and Fox News leaned to the right. Only PBS—the publicly owned and licensed network—presented balanced and evenhanded reporting of politics, government, and current events.[30]

Editorial endorsements of papers offer further evidence of political leanings of news organizations. *Editor and Publisher*, a trade journal of the media

26 Pew Center on Press and Politics, "How Journalists See Journalists," Washington, DC. 2004. www.people-press.org/http://people-press.org/files/legacy-pdf/214.pdf (accessed 9/17/11).

27 Michael Kinsley, "Bias and Baloney," *Washington Post*, November 26, 1992, p. A29; and John H. Fund, "Why Clinton Shouldn't Be Steamed at Talk Radio," *Wall Street Journal*, July 7, 1994, p. A12.

28 Michael J. Robinson and Margaret A. Sheehan, *Over the Wire and on TV: CBS and UPI in Campaign '80* (New York: Russell Sage Foundation, 1983).

29 Pew Research Center's Project for Excellence in Journalism, "Obama's First 100 Days: How the President Fared in the Press vs. Clinton and Bush," April 28, 2009, http://journalism.org/files/100%20DAYS.pdf (accessed 5/7/09).

30 Timothy Groseclose and Tom Milyo, "A Measure of Media Bias," *Quarterly Journal of Economics* 120 (2005): 1191–1237.

Figure 14.2
NEWSPAPER ENDORSEMENTS

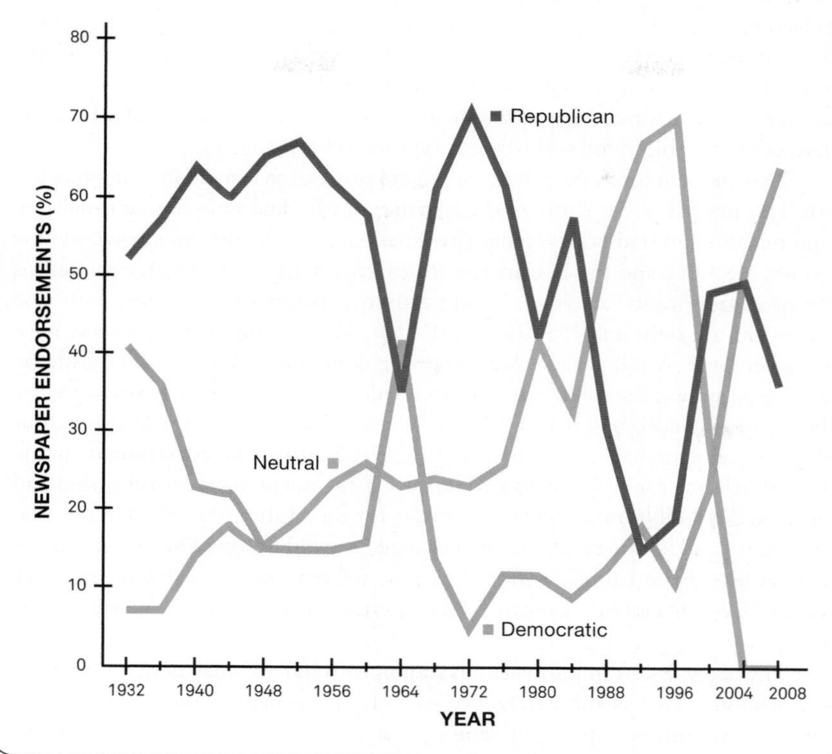

SOURCES: Harold W. Stanley and Richard G. Niemi, *Vital Statistics on American Politics, 2001–2002* (Washington, DC: CQ Press, 2001), pp. 194–5; 2004 and 2008 data from *Editor and Publisher*, www.editorandpublisher.com.

ANALYZING THE EVIDENCE

More newspapers support the Republicans, but in 2008 Obama received more editorial endorsements than McCain. Does this show a liberal or a conservative bias in the media?

business, tracks endorsements of newspapers across the United States. Before the 1960s, the editorial endorsements and political leanings of the editors of most newspapers were overwhelmingly Republican. Since the 1960s, however, newspaper endorsements for president, the U.S. Senate, the U.S. House, and statewide offices have on average balanced out between the Democrats and Republicans. George W. Bush received a solid majority (192 of 344) of endorsements in 2000; John Kerry edged Bush out in 2004; and in 2008 Barack Obama received nearly 70 percent of the endorsements over John McCain (Figure 14.2). The papers endorsing Obama had a total circulation of over 40 million people, compared with 12 million people for the papers that endorsed McCain.[31] To the

31 "Final Tally of Newspaper Endorsements—Obama Landslide at 287–159," *Editor and Publisher*, November 9, 2008, www.editorandpublisher.com.

extent that there is a partisan bias to editorials and endorsements, it is toward those already in office.[32]

Journalism, as a profession, has attempted to rise above personal motivations and biases. Most journalists adhere to strong norms of fairness and balance in reporting. They attempt to get the perspectives of both sides of a controversy. Even coverage of popular presidents still attempts to maintain balance. Indeed, one of the values of treating journalism as a profession is that doing so forces norms of behavior and ethics that help reduce political biases. But that important ethos of objectivity and fairness appears to be changing.

Two shifts in journalism are eroding the professional standards of objectivity. The first of these shifts is the blurring of the line between editorializing and reporting in traditional media. Over the past decade, the emergence of Fox News, MSNBC, and the Huffington Post have attempted to change that ethos by presenting more ideological and partisan versions of the news, with Fox News on the right and MSNBC on the left. Many traditional journalists have been tempted to follow suit. Among professional journalists much is made of the battle among the cable networks to divide the audience along partisan lines. In a widely read opinion piece, Tom Edsall, a long-time journalist with four decades of experience covering every level of American government, wrote that it was time for all journalists to throw off the norm of nonpartisanship and fairness.[33] Edsall, now a regular columnist for the Huffington Post, argues that Fox News and its large audience had changed the old norms. The gloves are off, and, at least from Edsall's corner, it is time for traditional journalists, most of whom have a liberal orientation, to take on the challenge from the conservatives directly.

The second shift in journalism is more profound and may perhaps be more far reaching. That is the emergence of citizen journalism. New technologies such as smartphones, powerful laptop computers, and the Internet now make it possible for anyone to report on events. CNN has a regular feature called i-Reporter that feeds video sent by people at events, such as natural disasters, campaigns and other political events, and political protests and rebellions. Needless to say, this is a huge threat to traditional journalism, which relies on highly trained professionals. A newspaper or television station does not need a large bureau in order to get instant recordings of events, and journalists cost money to keep on staff and to deploy to far away places such as China or Iraq. By the same token, these technologies have allowed journalism to flourish in countries with very little existing media or tight government controls on television and the press, such as those in central Africa and the Middle East.

32 Stephen Ansolabehere, Rebecca Lessem, and James M. Snyder, Jr., "The Orientation of Newspaper Endorsements 1940–2002," *Quarterly Journal of Political Science* 1, no. 4 (October 2006): 393–404, http://dx.doi.org/10.1561/100.00000009 (accessed 5/8/09).

33 Thomas Edsall, "Journalism Should Own Its Liberalism: And Then Manage It, Challenge It, and Account for It," Columbia Journalism Review, October 8, 2009, www.cjr.org/campaign_desk/journalism_should_own_its_libe.php?page=all (accessed 10/4/11).

The subtle revolution behind the rise of citizen journalism comes from the perspective of the reporter. Citizen journalism replaces the "objective reporter" with the "subjective participant." A traditional reporter from the *New York Times*, the AP, or another agency will try to get different perspectives on the same event and offer a investigative report that attempts to answer the key questions (also known as the 5 Ws) taught on day one of Journalism 101: what, who, when, where, why, and how? Citizen journalists become reporters of an event precisely because they are in the event. A protestor who sends video of a violent clash with police in Damascus or Tripoli or London is "in the event," as are a legislative staffer who Tweets about the goings on in a committee meeting or a campaign worker who texts about a rally. There is no attempt to rise above and answer the 5 Ws. The texts and videos from such communications are raw and in the moment; they are some of the most compelling journalism today. This represents a sea change in journalism. It will not replace the old style, which has been around for centuries and survived many a technological revolution. Rather, citizen journalism will augment traditional journalism and even change it somewhat. It gives traditional journalists license to also be "in the moment," in other words to be more subjective.

News Sources

News is shaped not just by who writes, edits, and distributes stories. It is also shaped by the people being covered—by politicians, public officials, CEOs of companies, experts, and other news sources whose interests and activities are actual or potential news topics. News is often described as a form of advertising. News is free media; advertising is paid. An individual, company, or interest group that wants to get attention for its perspective or to shape its public image can do so by purchasing air time, or it can do so by "creating news."

Politicians want to be seen by the public as trustworthy, energetic, caring, and generally able to discharge the public duties with which they have been or hope to be entrusted. Accordingly, most politicians will seize or, if necessary, create opportunities for media coverage they deem likely to contribute to the public image they wish to fashion. Presidents, for example, know that their speeches on important topics will be televised throughout the nation. Thus they have an opportunity to use the media to demonstrate that they possess strong leadership qualities and fully understand the problems and issues facing the nation. President George W. Bush's speech in the wake of the September 11 terrorist attacks, for example, was designed to reassure Americans and demonstrate that he was firmly in command. After natural disasters, presidents and governors frequently tour the site of the disaster. It is a way for the politician to see first hand the extent of the problem but also a chance to connect with the people affected and for the politician to show his or her ability to take command. Not doing so can be politically disastrous. Hurricane Katrina in 2005 flooded much of the Gulf Coast from Louisiana to Mississippi, including the city of New Orleans. In the days following, President George W. Bush chose not to go to the site of the disaster, and he was roundly criticized by the people affected and by commentators throughout the country for lacking empathy for the common citizen. Barack Obama, by comparison, repeatedly went to the Gulf Coast during the BP oil spill in the gulf in 2009, and he went to Joplin, Missouri, after a massive tornado that killed 140 people in May 2010.

Press events are also opportunities to set out an agenda—to state what is important and what should be done. Politicians in the United States have unique opportunities to use the media to set the public's agenda and that of Congress. Perhaps the most important such speech by the president is the State of the Union Address, which is given annually to Congress. It is televised, broadcast on radio, streamed online, and reprinted verbatim in newspapers. Governors in most states deliver a State of the State address, which receives extensive coverage in local media. During the State of the Union, presidents lay out their accomplishments and objectives, call attention to policy areas where they would like to focus attention, and introduce new legislation.

Politicians use many other techniques to develop favorable media images. Presidents, governors, and legislators often hold press conferences to announce significant events, such as the passage of legislation, military successes and failures, and changes in policy. Some politicians hold regular (weekly) press meetings. Journalists appreciate frequent and open meetings with the president or governors rather than their staff. To improve their treatment by the press, politicians cultivate their ties with or image among reporters. President John F. Kennedy sought to develop strong relationships with influential journalists. Appearances on soft news and entertainment programs allow politicians to connect with ordinary Americans and show themselves to be in touch. Bill Clinton famously tooted his saxophone on a late-night entertainment program and discussed his choice of underwear with teenage reporters on MTV. Obama has offered his picks for the NCAA basketball tournament and occasionally shot a basket for the cameras.

Beyond personalized events and speeches, the government provides a steady stream of information to the press in the form of press releases. Nearly every government agency releases a memo to the press along with the presentation of an important study. The Bureau of the Census regularly releases brief reports on the latest trends in demographics in the United States. The Bureau of Labor Statistics, the Treasury Department, and the Federal Reserve regularly release the latest figures on employment, wages, economic growth, and inflation. Medicare and the Social Security Administration regularly release reports on changes in their services. Agencies have their own constituencies, such as businesses and the elderly, and the news is tailored to those audiences. In this way, the government feeds the basic information for many specialized news venues as well as through regular press releases.

Politicians, interest groups, government officials, and other news sources employ a variety of techniques in their efforts to shape news coverage. These include news leaks, news releases, and in some instances cash payments to journalists. Although the news media are not oblivious to the efforts of sources to manipulate them, journalists and editors sometimes have a stake in allowing themselves to be manipulated. Journalists may publish leaked information in order to maintain good relations with important sources even when they know the source is pursuing his or her own political agenda. Editors and publishers have a financial stake in relying heavily on press releases even though they know the information they present is not objective. In such ways, the institutional stakes of the media may interfere with the unbiased and objective presentation of the news.

News Leaks. A news leak is the disclosure of confidential information to the news media. Leaks may emanate from a variety of sources, including whistle-blowers, lower-level officials who hope to publicize what they view as their bosses' improper activities. In 1971, for example, a minor Defense Department staffer named Daniel Ellsberg sought to discredit official justifications for America's involvement in Vietnam by leaking top-secret documents to the press. The *New York Times* and the *Washington Post* published these classified documents, the so-called Pentagon Papers, after the U.S. Supreme Court ruled that the government could not block release of the documents. In a similar vein, President George W. Bush was infuriated in 2005 when he learned that a still-unidentified source, presumed to be a whistler-blower, had leaked information concerning the president's secret orders authorizing the National Security Agency to conduct clandestine surveillance of suspected terrorists without obtaining authorization from the special federal tribunal created for that purpose. Bush ordered the Justice Department to launch a probe of the leak. In 2006, a still-unidentified source leaked to the press part of a secret intelligence summary that seemed to contradict the administration's claims of progress in the war in Iraq. The president claimed the leaked portion of the report did not accurately reflect the full report. The administration proceeded to declassify other portions of the report, which seemed to support its claims about the war. President Barack Obama pursued an even stronger line against press leaks in his administration. The Obama administration aggressively and successfully prosecuted one Defense Department worker and one FBI analyst who had leaked information to the press in 2009.

Most leaks, though, originate not with low-level whistle-blowers but rather with senior government officials and prominent politicians and political activists. Such persons often cultivate long-term relationships with journalists, to whom they regularly leak confidential information, knowing that it is likely to be published on a priority basis in a form acceptable to them. Their confidence is based on the fact that journalists are likely to regard high-level sources of confidential information as valuable assets whose favor must be retained. For example, I. Lewis "Scooter" Libby, former vice president Dick Cheney's chief of staff, was apparently such a valuable source of leaks to so many prominent journalists that his name was seldom mentioned in the newspapers despite his prominence in Washington and his importance as a decision maker.[34] And the more recipients of leaked information strive to keep their sources secret, the more difficulty other journalists will have in checking the validity of the information.

34 Michael Massing, "The Press: The Enemy Within," *New York Review of Books*, December 15, 2005, p. 36.

Through such tacit alliances with journalists, prominent figures can manipulate news coverage and secure the publication of stories that serve their purposes. The Valerie Plame affair, which was ultimately the undoing of Scooter Libby, exposed the complexities of the culture of leaks in Washington, D.C. Plame was an undercover CIA analyst who happened to be married to Joseph Wilson, a prominent career diplomat. Wilson had angered the Bush White House by making a number of statements that were critical of the president's policies in Iraq. In an apparent effort to discredit Wilson, one or more administration officials informed prominent journalists that Plame had improperly used her position to help Wilson. In so doing, these officials may have violated a federal statute prohibiting the disclosure of the identities of covert intelligence operatives. The subsequent investigation revealed that the story had been leaked to several journalists, including the *Washington Post*'s Bob Woodward, who did not use it, and the *New York Times*'s Judith Miller, who did. Miller spent several months in jail for contempt of court after initially refusing to testify before a federal grand jury looking into the leak. After Miller finally testified, Libby was charged and convicted of lying and obstruction for his role in the affair, although it later emerged that the information was actually leaked by a former State Department official, Richard Armitage. The leak in the Plame case came to light only because it might have been illegal. Thousands of other leaks each year are quietly and seamlessly incorporated into the news.

The Press Release. Also seamlessly incorporated into daily news reports each year are thousands of press releases. The press release, sometimes called a news release, is a story written by an advocate or publicist and distributed to the media in the hope that journalists will publish it under their own bylines with little or no revision. The inventor of the press release was a New York public relations consultant named Ivy Lee. In 1906, a train operated by one of Lee's clients, the Pennsylvania Railroad, was involved in a serious wreck. Lee quickly wrote a story about the accident that presented the railroad in a favorable light and distributed the account to reporters. Many papers published Lee's slanted story as their own objective account of events, and the railroad's reputation for quality and safety remained intact.

Consistent with Lee's example, today's press release presents facts and perspectives that serve an advocate's interests but is written in a way that mimics the factual news style of the paper, periodical, or television news program to which it has been sent. It is quite difficult for the audience to distinguish a well-designed press release from a news story. For example, a recent posting by PharmaWatch, a blog monitoring the pharmaceutical industry, identified an article published in the *New York Times* "Science Times" section that rehashed a news release issued by Pfizer, the giant pharmaceutical corporation. "A lawyer in New York has had to deal with what is politely referred to as 'bladder control' for as long as she can remember," the article began. "Even as a teenager she woke up at night feeling the urge to urinate but not always making it to the toilet in time." Thanks to the press release it copied, the article was able to propose a solution. "Urge incontinence is often treated with drugs like tolterodine, sold as Detrol."[35] Not surprisingly, the drug touted in this news story is sold by Pfizer.

To take another example, an article sent to thousands of newspapers by the AP was headlined "Fed Unveils Financial Education Website." Apparently written by an AP reporter, the article discussed the various ways in which a new Web site developed by the Federal Reserve could help consumers make informed decisions. The article did not mention that the information was basically a slight revision of a press release that could be found on the Federal Reserve's Web site.[36] Similarly, a *Houston Chronicle* story on teacher training claimed that students taught by teachers provided by Teach for America and other nontraditional sources performed significantly worse on standardized tests than students taught by traditionally certified instructors. The article failed to note that it was essentially a copy of a Stanford University press release touting the work of a Stanford professor who directed a traditional teacher-training program.[37] And what about the June 2005 *Los Angeles Times* story "County Homeless Number 90,000"? This article claimed, without offering an explanation, that the number of homeless individuals in Los Angeles County had quintupled since the previous year. In presenting this shocking news of the increase in homelessness, though, the reporter neglected to mention that the data came from a press release issued by the Los Angeles Homeless Services Authority (LAHSA), whose budget is tied to the number of clients it serves. For the LAHSA, more homelessness equals more money and more staff. Indeed, on its own Web site, it indicated that it had undertaken its new count of homeless individuals in part to "increase funding for homeless services in our community."[38] These should not be seen as isolated examples. According to some experts, more than 50 percent of the articles in a newspaper on any given day are based on press releases. Indeed, more than 75 percent of the journalists responding to a recent survey acknowledged using press releases for their stories.[39]

Journalists are certainly aware of the fact that the authors of press releases have their own agendas and are hardly unbiased reporters of the news. Nevertheless, the economics of publishing and broadcasting dictate that large numbers of stories will always be based on press releases. Newspapers and television stations are businesses, and for many the financial bottom line is more important

---

35 Martica Heaner, "Enduring Incontinence in Silence," *New York Times*, October 25, 2005, www.nytimes.com/2005/10/25/health/25inco.html?_r=1 (accessed 5/8/09).

36 Brian Montopoli, "Press Release Journalism," *Columbia Journalism Review Daily*, April 18, 2005.

37 Anne Linehan, "Another Example of Press Release Journalism?" BlogHouston, April 18, 2005, www.bloghouston.net/item/1048 (accessed 4/9/09).

38 "LA Times: County Homeless Population Tops Two Kazillion, No Further Reporting Required," *IndependentSources*, June 16, 2005, http://independentsources.com/2005/06/16/la-times-county-homeless-population-tops-two-kazillion-no-further-reporting-required (accessed 4/9/09).

39 Dennis L. Wilcox and Glen T. Cameron, *Public Relations: Strategy and Tactics*, 8th ed. (Boston: Allyn & Bacon, 2006), p. 357.

than journalistic integrity.[40] The use of press releases allows a newspaper or a broadcast network to present more stories without paying more staff or incurring the other costs associated with investigating and writing the news. As one newspaper executive said, the public relations people who generally write news releases are our "unpaid reporters."[41]

In recent years, the simple printed press release has been joined by the video news release, which is designed especially for television stations. The video release is a taped report, usually about 90 seconds long, the typical length of a television news story, designed to look and sound like any other broadcast news segment. In exchange for airing material that serves the interests of some advocate, the television station airing the video release is relieved of the considerable expense and bother of identifying and filming its own news story. The audience is usually unaware that the "news" it is watching is someone's canned publicity footage.

One example of a video news release was a pair of 90-second segments funded by the U.S. Department of Health and Human Services (HHS). After Congress enacted legislation adding a prescription drug benefit to the Medicare program, HHS sent a video release designed to look like a news report to local TV stations around the nation. Forty television stations aired the report without indicating that it had come from the government. A local news anchor introduced the segment by reading from a government script. Referring to the new Medicare law, the anchor read, "Reporter Karen Ryan helps sort through the details." Then, against the backdrop of film showing President Bush signing the law and the reactions of apparently grateful senior citizens, an unseen narrator, speaking like a reporter, presented the new law in a positive light: "The new law, say officials, simply offers people with Medicare ways to make their health coverage more affordable." The segment concluded with the sign-off "In Washington, I'm Karen Ryan reporting." Viewers were not told that the entire story was distributed by the government. Nor were viewers informed that Karen Ryan was not a reporter at all. She was an employee of the ad agency hired by the government to create the video release. In response to criticism, an HHS spokesperson pointed out that the same sort of video news releases had often been used by the Clinton administration and was commonly used by a number of firms and interest groups. "The use of video news releases is a common, routine practice in government and the private sector," he said. "Anyone who has questions about this practice needs to do some research on modern public information tools."[42]

Hiring Reporters. From creating phony reporters to reading make-believe news stories, it is but a small step to hiring real reporters to present sham accounts. A number of cases have come to light in recent years in which the

40 See, for example, Davis Merritt, *Knightfall: Knight Ridder and How the Erosion of Newspaper Journalism Is Putting Democracy at Risk* (New York: Amacom Books, 2005).

41 Quoted in Wilcox and Cameron, *Public Relations*, p. 357.

42 Quoted in Ben Fritz, Bryan Keefer, and Brendan Nyhan, *All the President's Spin* (New York: Touchstone Books, 2004), pp. 252–3, 357.

government or a private concern has paid journalists to write favorable accounts of its activities and efforts. Late in 2005, for example, the U.S. military acknowledged that contractors in its employ had regularly paid Iraqi newspapers to carry positive news about American efforts in that nation. The Washington-based Lincoln Group, a public-relations firm working under contract for the federal government, says it placed more than 1,000 news stories in the Arab press since 2001.[43] Iraqis reading the articles would have had no way of knowing that the material presented was produced at the behest of the American authorities.

The government's practice of hiring journalists is not limited to operations abroad. In recent years, federal agencies have paid several journalists and commentators to report favorably on government initiatives and programs in the United States. The Department of Education, for example, paid the commentator Armstrong Williams $241,000 to promote President George W. Bush's No Child Left Behind Act. Williams wrote favorably about the law in his newspaper column, commented positively about it during his cable television appearances, and urged other commentators to interview Education Secretary Roderick Paige.[44] Williams did not disclose his financial relationship with the agency whose programs he was touting. Similarly, the Department of Health and Human Services paid the syndicated columnist Maggie Gallagher $20,000 to promote the administration's views on marriage. Gallagher wrote several columns on the topic without revealing her financial relationship with the administration.

As local newspaper budgets have shrunk, some local governments have hired reporters or paid newspapers for reporters to cover local government. The Metropolitan Government of Portland, Oregon, hires a local reporter to cover goings-on in the government, including council meetings, events, and changes in policies and laws. The Los Angeles Kings hockey franchise, a Los Angeles County Supervisor, and a California trial lawyers group all hire journalists to follow their activities. The list goes on.

One group especially noted for paying writers and reporters for favorable coverage is the pharmaceutical industry. As the Detrol example suggests, many of the articles that appear in popular—and even scientific—journals reporting favorably on particular drugs are written by the drug companies themselves. In some cases, the writers are actually paid by the drug companies; in other reported instances, the writer cited in the story's byline is not the actual author of the account. Often a ghostwriter employed by a drug company writes the story while the nominal author is paid for the use of his or her name.[45]

All of these practices—hiring of reporters, press leaks, and planted news stories—offend our sensibilities about what the news is because we expect a degree of objectivity from reporters. They are our main source of information,

43 Jeff Gerth, "Military's Information War Is Vast and Often Secretive," *New York Times*, December 11, 2005, p. 1.

44 Howard Kurtz, "Administration Paid Commentator," *Washington Post*, January 8, 2005, p. 1.

45 Anna Wilde Matthews, "At Medical Journals, Writers Paid by Industry Play Big Role," *Wall Street Journal*, December 13, 2005, p. 1.

and fair and balanced reporting helps us sort out sometimes complex issues. The media also play an important watchdog role. They are there to make noise when something is amiss. That becomes increasingly difficult if the main revenues for the news come from the firm or government agency being covered. Of course, although politicians try to use the media for their purposes, reporters often have their own agenda. Often enough, hostile or merely determined journalists will break through the smoke screens thrown up by the politicians and report annoying truths.

Consumers

The print and broadcast media are businesses that, in general, seek to show a profit. This means that like any other business they must cater to the preferences of consumers. Their doing so has very important consequences for the content and character of the news media.

Catering to the Upscale Audience. In general and especially in the political realm, the print and broadcast media and the publishing industry are not only responsive to the interests of consumers generally but are also particularly responsive to the interests and views of the better-educated and more affluent segments of the audience. The preferences of these segments have a profound effect on the content and orientation of the press, radio and television programming, and books, especially in the areas of news and public affairs.[46]

Although affluent consumers do watch television programs and read periodicals whose content is designed simply to amuse or entertain, the one area that most directly appeals to the upscale audience is that of news and public affairs. The affluent—who are also typically well educated—are the core audience of newsmagazines, journals of opinion, books dealing with public affairs, serious newspapers such as the *New York Times* and the *Washington Post*, broadcast news, and evening and weekend public-affairs programming. Although other segments of the public also read newspapers and watch the television news, their level of interest in world events, national political issues, and the like is closely related to their level of education (Table 14.2). As a result, upscale Americans are overrepresented in the news and public-affairs audience. The concentration of these strata in the audience makes news, politics, and public affairs potentially very attractive topics to advertisers, publishers, radio broadcasters, and television executives.

Entire categories of events, issues, and phenomena of interest to lower-, middle-, and working-class Americans receive scant attention from the national print and broadcast media. For example, trade union news and events are discussed only in the context of major strikes or revelations of corruption. No

46 See Tom Burnes, "The Organization of Public Opinion," in *Mass Communication and Society*, James Curran, Michael Gurevitch, and Janet Woollacott, eds. (Beverly Hills, CA: Sage, 1979), pp. 44–230. See also David L. Altheide, *Creating Reality: How TV News Distorts Events* (Beverly Hills, CA: Sage, 1976).

Table 14.2
EDUCATION AND ATTENTION TO THE NEWS

	LEVEL OF ATTENTION TO HARD NEWS*		
LEVEL OF EDUCATION	**HIGH (%)**	**MEDIUM (%)**	**LOW (%)**
College graduate	36	59	6
Some college	130	59	11
High school graduate	23	59	18
Not a high school graduate	12	60	28

*People with high levels of attention to hard news follow international, national, local, and business news closely; those with low levels do not follow the news.
SOURCES: Compiled by authors from Pew Research Center for the People & the Press, "Audience Segments in a Changing News Environment," Pew Research Center Biennial News Consumption Survey, August 17, 2008, http://people-press.org/reports/pdf/444.pdf (accessed 5/8/09).

network or national periodical routinely covers labor organizations. Religious and church affairs receive little coverage unless scandal is involved. The activities of veterans', fraternal, ethnic, and patriotic organizations are also generally ignored.

The Media and Conflict. Although the media respond most to the upscale audience, groups that cannot afford the services of media consultants and issues managers can publicize their views and interests through protest. Frequently, the media are accused of encouraging conflict and even violence in response to the fact that their audiences mostly watch news for the entertainment value that conflict can provide. Clearly, conflict can be an important vehicle for attracting the attention and interest of the media and thus may provide an opportunity for media attention to groups otherwise lacking the financial or organizational resources to broadcast their views. But although conflict and protest can succeed in drawing media attention, these methods ultimately do not allow groups from the bottom of the social ladder to compete effectively in the media.

The chief problem with protest as a media technique is that, in general, the media on which the protesters depend have considerable discretion in reporting and interpreting the events they cover. For example, should the media focus on the conflict itself, rather than on the issues or concerns created by the conflict? The answer to this question is typically determined by the media, not by the protesters. Therefore, media interpretation of protest activities is more a reflection of the views of the groups and forces to which the media are responsive—which, as we have seen, are usually segments of the upper middle class—than it is a function of the wishes of the protesters themselves. It is worth noting that civil rights protesters received their most favorable media coverage when a segment of the white upper middle class saw blacks as potential political allies in the Democratic Party.

Typically, upper-middle-class protesters—student demonstrators and the like—have little difficulty securing favorable publicity for themselves and their causes. They are often more skilled than their lower-class counterparts in the techniques of media manipulation. That is, they typically have a better sense—often as a result of formal courses on the subject—of how to package messages for media consumption. For example, it is important to know what time of day a protest should occur if it is to be carried on the evening news. Similarly, the setting, definition of the issues, character of the rhetoric used, and so on all help determine whether a protest will receive favorable media coverage, unfavorable coverage, or no coverage at all. Moreover, upper-middle-class protesters can often produce their own media coverage through "underground" newspapers, college papers, student radio and television stations, and the Internet. The same resources and skills that generally allow upper-middle-class people to publicize their ideas are usually not left behind when segments of this class choose to engage in disruptive forms of political action. Note the media attention given antiwar protesters in 2003 even though polls indicated that such groups were a minor force in American politics.

CONCLUSION: MEDIA POWER AND RESPONSIBILITY

The content and character of news and public-affairs programming—what the media choose to present and how they present it—can have far-reaching political consequences. Media disclosures can greatly enhance or fatally damage the careers of public officials. Media coverage can rally support for or intensify opposition to national policies. The media choose what issues to cover and how and, as discussed in Chapter 9, set the national political agenda and frame political discourse.

The media have played a central role in shaping some of the most significant events in recent American political history. News media were critically important in the civil rights movement of the 1950s and 1960s. Television footage and photographs of civil rights marchers attacked by club-swinging police galvanized public support for the civil rights movement among northern whites and greatly increased pressure on Congress to bring an end to segregation.[47] The media were also central actors in the Watergate affair, which ultimately forced President Richard Nixon, the landslide victor in the 1972 presidential election, to resign from office in disgrace. The relentless series of investigations launched by the *Washington Post*, the *New York Times*, and the television networks led to the

47 David J. Garrow, *Protest at Selma: Martin Luther King, Jr., and the Voting Rights Act of 1965* (New Haven, CT: Yale University Press, 1978).

disclosure of various abuses of power by those in the White House, ultimately forcing Nixon to resign.[48]

Mass media have been central to every election of the past century. They cover the emergence and activities of the candidates, political debates and conventions, and election-night returns. They are the vehicles for political advertising. They even generate their own campaign news, especially by conducting public-opinion polls and reporting who is ahead and who is behind, who is gaining momentum and who is fading.

And the media go to war along with the U.S. military. Since the American Civil War, news reporting and photography have brought wars home. Graphic depictions of the atrocities in Vietnam, including the My Lai massacre, and of American war dead and wounded helped turn popular sentiment against the war, which compelled the government to negotiate an end to the conflict.[49] Video of precision bombs destroying targets in Baghdad and of the rout of Saddam Hussein's army in 1991 pushed up President George H. W. Bush's popularity and solidified his reputation as commander in chief.[50] News coverage of the Iraq War in 2003 portrayed the toppling of Saddam Hussein's statue in Baghdad, and President George W. Bush's announcement of "Mission Accomplished" at the end of combat in 2003 would later be used against the president as the military struggled for years to restore a modicum of stability in Iraq.

The tremendous power that reporters and editors sometimes wield emanates from the free hand that the press has in American politics. So long as they do not overstep the bounds of libel, journalists can (and often do) criticize the American government openly. Given the diversity of media outlets today, especially after the rise of cable television and the Internet, it is not uncommon to find defenders and critics of the government or of particular political decisions, and often those on either side of the debate argue their positions side by side. The rise of the new media has brought more voices to the fore and a broader potential debate over public policy. Wide-open debate and criticism of public officials is essential, but it sometimes exacts a social cost.

Free media are essential to democratic government. We depend on the media to investigate wrongdoing, publicize and explain governmental actions, evaluate programs and politicians, and bring to light matters that might otherwise be known only to a handful of government insiders. In short, without free and active media, popular government would be virtually impossible. Citizens would have few means of knowing or assessing the government's actions, other than the claims or pronouncements of the government itself. Moreover, without active—indeed, aggressive—media, citizens would be hard pressed to make informed choices among competing candidates at the polls. Often enough, the

48 Todd Gitlin, *The Whole World Is Watching: Mass Media in the Making and Unmaking of the New Left* (Berkeley: University of California Press, 2003).

49 Willim M. Hammond, *Reporting Vietnam: Media and Military at War* (Lawrence: University of Kansas Press, 1998).

50 Jon Krosnik and L. A. Brannon, "The Impact of the Gulf War on the Ingredients of Presidential Evaluations," *American Political Science Review* 87 (1993): 963–75.

media reveal discrepancies between candidates' claims and their records and between the images that candidates seek to project and the underlying realities.

At the same time, politicians have become ever more reliant on news coverage, especially favorable coverage. National political leaders and journalists have had symbiotic relationships, at least since Franklin Delano Roosevelt's presidency. Initially, politicians were the senior partners. Thus, for example, reporters did not publicize potentially embarrassing information, widely known in Washington, D.C., about the personal lives of such figures as Roosevelt and John F. Kennedy. Today, the balance has shifted. Often it seems the journalists have the upper hand. Now that individual politicians have become heavily dependent on media to reach their constituents, journalists no longer need fear that their access to information can be restricted in retaliation for negative coverage. It is not uncommon today to hear the White House press corps challenge the president's press liaison or even the president himself.

Freedom gives the media enormous power. The media can make or break reputations, help launch or destroy political careers, and build support for or rally opposition against programs and institutions.[51] Wherever there is so much power, at least the potential for its abuse or overly zealous use exists. All things considered, free media are so critically important to the maintenance of a democratic society that we may be willing to take the risk that the media will occasionally abuse their power. The forms of government control that would prevent the media from misusing their power would also certainly pose a serious risk to our freedom.

For Further Reading

Ansolabehere, Stephen, Roy Behr, and Shanto Iyengar. *The Media Game: American Politics in the Television Age*. New York: Macmillan, 1993.

Arnold, R. Douglas. *Congress, the Press, and Political Accountability*. Princeton, NJ: Princeton University Press, 2004.

Bagdikian, Ben. *The New Media Monopoly*. Boston: Beacon Press, 2004.

reader selection

Baum, Matthew, A. *Soft News Goes to War: Public Opinion and American Foreign Policy in the New Media Age*. Princeton, NJ: Princeton University Press, 2003.

Cook, Timothy. *Governing with the News: The News Media as a Political Institution*. Chicago, IL: University of Chicago Press, 1997.

Fenton, Tom. *Bad News: The Decline of Reporting, the Business of News, and the Danger to Us All*. New York: HarperCollins, 2005.

51 See Martin Linsky, *Impact: How the Press Affects Federal Policy Making* (New York: Norton, 1991).

Fritz, Ben, Bryan Keefer, and Brendan Nyhan. *All the President's Spin.* New York: Touchstone Books, 2004.

Goldberg, Bernard. *Bias: A CBS Insider Exposes How the Media Distort the News.* New York: Regnery, 2002.

Groseclose, Tim. *Left Turn.* New York: St. Martin's Press, 2011.

Groseclose, Timothy, and Jeffrey Milyo. "A Measure of Media Bias." *Quarterly Journal of Economics* 120, no. 4 (November 2005): 1191–1237.

Hamilton, James T. *All the News That's Fit to Sell: How the Market Transforms Information into News.* Princeton, NJ: Princeton University Press, 2003.

Iyengar, Shanto. *Media Politics: A Citizen's Guide.* Second Edition. New York: Norton, 2011. **reader selection**

Kellner, Douglas. *Media Spectacle and the Crisis of Democracy: Terrorism, War, and Election Battles.* Boulder, CO: Paradigm, 2005.

Merritt, Davis. *Knightfall: Knight Ridder and How the Erosion of Newspaper Journalism Is Putting Democracy at Risk.* New York: Amacom Books, 2005.

Norris, Pippa, Montague Kern, and Marion R. Just, eds. *Framing Terrorism: The News Media, the Government, and the Public.* New York: Routledge, 2003.

Schudson, Michael. "The News Media as Political Institutions." *Annual Review of Political Science* 5 (June 2002): 249–69.

Starr, Paul. *The Creation of the Media.* New York: Basic Books, 2004.

Visit **wwnorton.com/studyspace/** to access free review materials such as:

- Vocabulary Flashcards of All Key Terms
- Chapter Review Quizzes
- Complete Study Outlines

reader selection

Highlighted selections are included in *Readings in American Politics: Analysis and Perspectives*, Second Edition.

Appendix

The Declaration of Independence

In Congress, July 4, 1776

When in the course of human events, it becomes necessary for one people to dissolve the political bands which have connected them with another, and to assume among the Powers of the earth, the separate and equal station to which the Laws of Nature and of Nature's God entitle them, a decent respect to the opinions of mankind requires that they should declare the causes which impel them to the separation.

We hold these truths to be self-evident, that all men are created equal, that they are endowed by their Creator with certain unalienable rights, that among these are Life, Liberty, and the pursuit of Happiness. That to secure these rights, Governments are instituted among Men, deriving their just powers from the consent of the governed. That whenever any Form of Government becomes destructive of these ends, it is the Right of the People to alter or to abolish it, and to institute new Government, laying its foundation on such principles and organizing its powers in such form, as to them shall seem most likely to effect their Safety and Happiness. Prudence, indeed, will dictate that Governments long established should not be changed for light and transient causes; and accordingly all experience hath shown, that mankind are more disposed to suffer, while evils are sufferable, than to right themselves by abolishing the forms to which they are accustomed. But when a long train of abuses and usurpations, pursuing invariably the same Object evinces a design to reduce them under absolute Despotism, it is their right, it is their duty, to throw off such Government, and to provide new Guards for their future security.—Such has been the patient sufferance of these Colonies; and such is now the necessity which constrains them to alter their former Systems of Government. The history of the present King of Great Britain is a history of repeated injuries and usurpations, all having in direct object the establishment of an absolute Tyranny over these States. To prove this, let Facts be submitted to a candid world.

He has refused his Assent to Laws, the most wholesome and necessary for the public good.

He has forbidden his Governors to pass Laws of immediate and pressing importance, unless suspended in their operation till his Assent should be obtained; and when so suspended, he has utterly neglected to attend to them.

He has refused to pass other Laws for the accommodation of large districts of people, unless those people would relinquish the right of Representation in the Legislature, a right inestimable to them and formidable to tyrants only.

He has called together legislative bodies at places unusual, uncomfortable, and distant from the depository of their public Records, for the sole purpose of fatiguing them into compliance with his measures.

He has dissolved Representative Houses repeatedly, for opposing with manly firmness his invasions on the rights of the people.

He has refused for a long time, after such dissolutions, to cause others to be elected; whereby the Legislative powers, incapable of Annihilation, have returned to the People at large for their exercise; the State remaining in the mean time exposed to all dangers of invasion from without, and convulsions within.

He has endeavored to prevent the population of these States; for that purpose obstructing the Laws of Naturalization of Foreigners; refusing to pass others to encourage their migrations hither, and raising the conditions of new Appropriations of Lands.

He has obstructed the Administration of Justice, by refusing his Assent to Laws for establishing Judiciary powers.

He has made Judges dependent on his Will alone, for the tenure of their offices, and the amount and payment of their salaries.

He has erected a multitude of New Offices, and sent hither swarms of Officers to harass our People, and eat out their substance.

He has kept among us, in times of peace, Standing Armies without the Consent of our legislature.

He has affected to render the Military independent of and superior to the Civil Power.

He has combined with others to subject us to a jurisdiction foreign to our constitution, and unacknowledged by our laws; giving his Assent to their Acts of pretended Legislation:

For quartering large bodies of armed troops among us:

For protecting them, by a mock Trial, from Punishment for any Murders which they should commit on the Inhabitants of these States:

For cutting off our Trade with all parts of the world:

For imposing taxes on us without our Consent:

For depriving us in many cases, of the benefits of Trial by jury:

For transporting us beyond Seas to be tried for pretended offences:

For abolishing the free System of English Laws in a neighboring Province, establishing therein an Arbitrary government, and enlarging its Boundaries so as to render it at once an example and fit instrument for introducing the same absolute rule into these Colonies:

For taking away our Charters, abolishing our most valuable Laws, and altering fundamentally the Forms of our Governments:

For suspending our own Legislatures, and declaring themselves invested with Power to legislate for us in all cases whatsoever.

He has abdicated Government here, by declaring us out of his Protection and waging War against us.

He has plundered our seas, ravaged our Coasts, burnt our towns, and destroyed the lives of our people.

He is at this time transporting large armies of foreign mercenaries to compleat the works of death, desolation, and tyranny, already begun with circumstances of Cruelty & perfidy scarcely paralleled in the most barbarous ages, and totally unworthy the Head of a civilized nation.

He has constrained our fellow Citizens taken Captive on the high Seas to bear Arms against their Country, to become the executioners of their friends and Brethren, or to fall themselves by their Hands.

He has excited domestic insurrections amongst us, and has endeavored to bring on the inhabitants of our frontiers, the merciless Indian Savages, whose known rule of warfare, is an undistinguished destruction of all ages, sexes, and conditions.

In every stage of these Oppressions We have Petitioned for Redress in the most humble terms: Our repeated Petitions have been answered only by repeated injury. A Prince, whose character is thus marked by every act which may define a Tyrant, is unfit to be the ruler of a free people.

Nor have We been wanting in attention to our British brethren. We have warned them from time to time of attempts by their legislature to extend an unwarrantable jurisdiction over us. We have reminded them of the circumstances of our emigration and settlement here. We have appealed to their native justice and magnanimity, and we have conjured them by the ties of our common kindred to disavow these usurpations, which, would inevitably interrupt our connections and correspondence. They too must have been deaf to the voice of justice and of consanguinity. We must, therefore, acquiesce in the necessity, which denounces our Separation, and hold them, as we hold the rest of mankind, Enemies in War, in Peace Friends.

WE, THEREFORE, the Representatives of the UNITED STATES OF AMERICA, in General Congress, Assembled, appealing to the Supreme Judge of the world for the rectitude of our intentions, do, in the Name, and by Authority of the good People of these Colonies, solemnly publish and declare, That these United Colonies are, and of Right ought to be FREE AND INDEPENDENT STATES; that they are Absolved from all Allegiance to the British Crown, and that all political connection between them and the State of Great Britain, is and ought to be totally dissolved; and that as Free and Independent States, they have full Power to levy War, conclude Peace, contract Alliances, establish Commerce, and to do all other Acts and Things which Independent States may of right do. And for the support of this Declaration, with a firm reliance on the Protection of Divine Providence, we mutually pledge to each other our Lives, our Fortunes, and our sacred Honor.

The foregoing Declaration was, by order of Congress, engrossed, and signed by the following members:

John Hancock

NEW HAMPSHIRE
Josiah Bartlett
William Whipple
Matthew Thornton

MASSACHUSETTS BAY
Samuel Adams
John Adams
Robert Treat Paine
Elbridge Gerry

RHODE ISLAND
Stephen Hopkins
William Ellery

CONNECTICUT
Roger Sherman
Samuel Huntington
William Williams
Oliver Wolcott

NEW YORK
William Floyd
Philip Livingston
Francis Lewis
Lewis Morris

NEW JERSEY
Richard Stockton
John Witherspoon
Francis Hopkinson
John Hart
Abraham Clark

PENNSYLVANIA
Robert Morris
Benjamin Rush
Benjamin Franklin
John Morton
George Clymer
James Smith
George Taylor
James Wilson
George Ross

DELAWARE
Caesar Rodney
George Read
Thomas M'Kean

MARYLAND
Samuel Chase
William Paca
Thomas Stone
Charles Carroll,
of Carrollton

VIRGINIA
George Wythe
Richard Henry Lee
Thomas Jefferson
Benjamin Harrison
Thomas Nelson, Jr.
Francis Lightfoot Lee
Carter Braxton

NORTH CAROLINA
William Hooper
Joseph Hewes
John Penn

SOUTH CAROLINA
Edward Rutledge
Thomas Heyward, Jr.
Thomas Lynch, Jr.
Arthur Middleton

GEORGIA
Button Gwinnett
Lyman Hall
George Walton

Resolved, That copies of the Declaration be sent to the several assemblies, conventions, and committees, or councils of safety, and to the several commanding officers of the continental troops; that it be proclaimed in each of the United States, at the head of the army.

The Articles of Confederation

Agreed to by Congress November 15, 1777; ratified and in force March 1, 1781

To all whom these Presents shall come, we the undersigned Delegates of the States affixed to our Names send greeting. Whereas the Delegates of the United States of America in Congress assembled did on the fifteenth day of November in the Year of our Lord One Thousand Seven Hundred and Seventy seven, and in the Second Year of the Independence of America agree to certain articles of Confederation and perpetual Union between the States of Newhampshire, Massachusetts-bay, Rhodeisland and Providence Plantations, Connecticut, New-York, New-Jersey, Pennsylvania, Delaware, Maryland, Virginia, North-Carolina, South-Carolina and Georgia in the Words following, viz. "Articles of Confederation and perpetual Union between the states of Newhampshire, Massachusetts-bay, Rhodeisland and Providence Plantations, Connecticut, New-York, New-Jersey, Pennsylvania, Delaware, Maryland, Virginia, North-Carolina, South-Carolina and Georgia.

Art. I. The Stile of this confederacy shall be "The United States of America."

Art. II. Each state retains its sovereignty, freedom and independence, and every Power, Jurisdiction and right, which is not by this confederation expressly delegated to the United States, in Congress assembled.

Art. III. The said states hereby severally enter into a firm league of friendship with each other, for their common defence, the security of their Liberties, and their mutual and general welfare, binding themselves to assist each other, against all force offered to, or attacks made upon them, or any of them, on account of religion, sovereignty, trade, or any other pretence whatever.

Art. IV. The better to secure and perpetuate mutual friendship and intercourse among the people of the different states in this union, the free inhabitants of each of these states, paupers, vagabonds and fugitives from Justice excepted, shall be entitled to all privileges and immunities of free citizens in the several states; and the people of each state shall have free ingress and regress to and from any other state, and shall enjoy therein all the privileges of trade and commerce, subject to the same duties, impositions and restrictions as the inhabitants thereof respectively, provided that such restriction shall not extend so far as to prevent the removal of property imported into any state, to any other state of which the Owner is an inhabitant; provided also that no imposition, duties or restriction shall be laid by any state, on the property of the united states, or either of them.

If any Person guilty of, or charged with treason, felony, or other high misdemeanor in any state, shall flee from Justice, and be found in any of the united states, he shall upon demand of the Governor or executive power, of the state from which he fled, be delivered up and removed to the state having jurisdiction of his offence.

Full faith and credit shall be given in each of these states to the records, acts and judicial proceedings of the courts and magistrates of every other state.

Art. V. For the more convenient management of the general interests of the united states, delegates shall be annually appointed in such manner as the legislature of each state shall direct, to meet in Congress on the first Monday in November, in every year, with a power reserved to each state, to recall its delegates, or any of them, at any time within the year, and to send others in their stead, for the remainder of the Year.

No state shall be represented in Congress by less than two, nor by more than seven Members; and no person shall be capable of being a delegate for more than three years in any term of six years; nor shall any person, being a delegate, be capable of holding any office under the united states, for which he, or another for his benefit receives any salary, fees or emolument of any kind.

Each state shall maintain its own delegates in a meeting of the states, and while they act as members of the committee of the states.

In determining questions in the united states, in Congress assembled, each state shall have one vote.

Freedom of speech and debate in Congress shall not be impeached or questioned in any Court, or place out of Congress, and the members of congress shall be protected in their persons from arrests and imprisonments, during the time of their going to and from, and attendance on congress, except for treason, felony, or breach of the peace.

Art. VI. No state without the Consent of the united states in congress assembled, shall send any embassy to, or receive any embassy from, or enter into any conference, agreement, or alliance or treaty with any King, prince or state; nor shall any person holding any office or profit or trust under the united states, or any of them, accept of any present, emolument, office or title of any kind whatever from any king, prince or foreign state; nor shall the united states in congress assembled, or any of them, grant any title of nobility.

No two or more states shall enter into any treaty, confederation or alliance whatever between them, without the consent of the united states in congress assembled, specifying accurately the purposes for which the same is to be entered into, and how long it shall continue.

No state shall lay any imposts or duties, which may interfere with any stipulations in treaties, entered into by the united states in congress assembled, with any king, prince or state, in pursuance of any treaties already proposed by congress, to the courts of France and Spain.

No vessels of war shall be kept up in time of peace by any state, except such number only, as shall be deemed necessary by the united states in congress assembled, for the defence of such state, or its trade; nor shall any body of forces be kept up by any state, in time of peace, except such number only, as in the judgment of the united states, in congress assembled, shall be deemed requisite to garrison the forts necessary for the defence of such state; but every state shall always keep up a well regulated and disciplined militia, sufficiently armed and accoutred, and shall provide and constantly have ready for use, in public stores, a due number of field pieces and tents, and a proper quantity of arms, ammunition and camp equipage.

No state shall engage in any war without the consent of the united states in congress assembled, unless such state be actually invaded by enemies, or shall have received certain advice of a resolution being formed by some nation of Indians to invade such state, and the danger is so imminent as not to admit of a delay, till the united states in congress asssembled can be consulted; nor shall any state grant commissions to any ships or vessels of war, nor letters of marque or reprisal, except it be after a declaration of war by the united states in congress assembled, and then only against the kingdom or state and the subjects thereof, against which war has been so declared, and under such regulations as shall be established by the united states in congress assembled, unless such state be infested by pirates; in which case vessels of war may be fitted out for that occasion, and kept so long as the danger shall continue, or until the united states in congress assembled shall determine otherwise.

Art. VII. When land-forces are raised by any state for the common defence, all officers of or under the rank of colonel, shall be appointed by the legislature of each state respectively by whom such forces shall be raised, or in such manner as such state shall direct, and all vacancies shall be filled up by the state which first made the appointment.

Art. VIII. All charges of war, and all other expences that shall be incurred for the common defence or general welfare, and allowed by the united states in congress assembled, shall be defrayed out of a common treasury, which shall be supplied by the several states, in proportion to the value of all land within each state, granted to or surveyed for any Person, as such land and the buildings and improvements thereon shall be estimated according to such mode as the united states in congress assembled, shall from time to time direct and appoint. The taxes for paying that proportion shall be laid and levied by the authority and direction of the legislatures of the several states within the time agreed upon by the united states in congress assembled.

Art. IX. The united states in congress assembled, shall have the sole and exclusive right and power of determining on peace and war, except in the cases mentioned in the sixth article—of sending and receiving ambassadors—entering into treaties and alliances, provided that no treaty of commerce shall be made whereby the legislative power of the respective states shall be restrained from imposing such imposts and duties on foreigners, as their own people are subjected to, or from prohibiting the exportation of any species of goods or commodities whatsoever—of establishing rules for deciding in all cases, what captures on land or water shall be legal, and in what manner prizes taken by land or naval forces in the service of the united states shall be divided or appropriated—of granting letters of marque and reprisal in times of peace—appointing courts for the trial of piracies and felonies committed on the high seas and establishing courts for receiving and determining finally appeals in all cases of captures, provided that no member of congress shall be appointed a judge of any of the said courts.

The united states in congress assembled shall also be the last resort on appeal in all disputes and differences now subsisting or that hereafter may arise between two or more states concerning boundary, jurisdiction or any other cause whatever; which authority shall always be exercised in the manner following. Whenever the legislative or executive authority or lawful agent of any state in controversy with another shall present a petition to congress stating the matter in question and praying for a hearing, notice thereof shall be given by order of congress to the legislative or executive authority of the other state in controversy, and a day assigned for the appearance of the parties by their lawful agents, who shall then be directed to appoint by joint consent, commissioners or judges to constitute a court for hearing and determining the matter in question: but if they cannot agree, congress shall name three persons out of each of the united states, and from the list of such persons each party shall alternately strike out one, the petitioners beginning, until the number shall be reduced to thirteen; and from that number not less than seven, nor more than nine names as congress shall direct, shall in the presence of congress be drawn out by lot, and the persons whose names shall be so drawn or any five of them, shall be commissioners or judges, to hear and finally determine the controversy, so always as a major part of the judges who shall hear the cause shall agree in the determination: and if either party shall neglect to attend at the day appointed, without shewing reasons, which congress shall judge sufficient, or being present shall refuse to strike, the congress shall proceed to nominate three persons out of each state, and the secretary of congress shall strike in behalf of such party absent or refusing; and the judgment and sentence of the court to be appointed, in the manner before prescribed, shall be final and conclusive; and if any of the parties shall refuse to submit to the authority of such court, or to appear to defend their claim or cause, the court shall nevertheless proceed to pronounce sentence, or judgment, which shall in like manner be final and decisive, the judgment or sentence and other proceedings being in either case transmitted to congress, and lodged among the acts of congress for the security of the parties concerned: provided that every commissioner, before he sits in judgment, shall take an oath to be administered by one of the judges of the supreme or superior court of the state, where the cause shall be tried, "well and truly to hear and determine the matter in question, according to the best of his judgment, without favour, affection or hope of reward:" provided also that no state shall be deprived of territory for the benefit of the united states.

All controversies concerning the private right of soil claimed under different grants of two or more states, whose jurisdictions as they may respect such lands, and the states which passed such grants are adjusted, the said grants or either of them being at the same time claimed to have originated antecedent to such settlement of jurisdiction, shall on the petition of either party to the congress of the united states, be finally determined as near as may be in the same manner as is before prescribed for deciding disputes respecting territorial jurisdiction between different states.

The united states in congress assembled shall also have the sole and exclusive right and power of regulating the alloy and value of coin struck by their own authority, or by that of the respective states—fixing the standard of weights and measures throughout the united states—regulating the trade and managing all affairs with the Indians, not members of any of the states, provided that the legislative right of any state within its own limits be not infringed or violated—establishing and regulating post-offices from one state to another, throughout all the united states, and exacting such postage on the papers passing thro' the same as may be requisite to defray the expences of the said office—appointing all officers of the land forces, in the service of the united states, except regimental officers—appointing all the officers of the united states—making rules for the government and regulation of the said land and naval forces, and directing their operations.

The united states in congress assembled shall have the authority to appoint a committee, to sit in the recess of congress, to be denominated "A Committee of the States," and to consist of one delegate from each state; and to appoint such other committees and civil officers as may be necessary for managing the general affairs of the united states under their direction—to appoint one of their number to preside, provided that no person be allowed to serve in the office of president more than one year in any term of three years; to ascertain the necessary sums of Money to be raised for the service of the united states, and to appropriate and apply the same for defraying the public expences—to borrow money, or emit bills on the credit of the united states, transmitting every half year to the respective states an account of the sums of money so borrowed or emitted,—to build and equip a navy—to agree upon the number of land forces, and to make requisitions from each state for its quota, in proportion to the number of white inhabitants in such state; which requisition shall be binding, and thereupon the legislature of each state shall appoint the regimental officers, raise the men and cloath, arm and equip them in a soldier like manner, at the expence of the united states, and the officers and men so cloathed, armed and equipped shall march to the place appointed, and within the time agreed on by the united states in congress assembled: But if the united states in congress assembled shall, on consideration of circumstances judge proper that any state should not raise men, or should raise a smaller number than its quota, and that any other state should raise a greater number of men than the quota thereof, such extra number shall be raised, officered, cloathed, armed and equipped in the same manner as the quota of such state, unless the legislature of such state shall judge that such extra number cannot be safely spared out of the same, in which case they shall raise, officer, cloath, arm and equip as many of such extra number as they judge can be safely spared. And the officers and men so cloathed, armed and equipped, shall march to the place appointed, and within the time agreed on by the united states in congress assembled.

The united states in congress assembled shall never engage in a war, nor grant letters of marque and reprisal in time of peace, nor enter into any treaties or alliances, nor coin money, nor regulate the value thereof, nor ascertain the sums and expences necessary for the defence and welfare of the united states, or any of them, nor emit bills, nor borrow money on the credit of the united states, nor appropriate money, nor agree upon the number of vessels of war, to be built or purchased, or the number of land or sea forces to be raised, nor appoint a commander in chief of the army or navy, unless nine states assent to the same: nor shall a question on any other point, except for adjourning from day to day be determined, unless by the votes of a majority of the united states in congress assembled.

The congress of the united states shall have power to adjourn to any time within the year, and to any place within the united states, so that no period of adjournment be for a longer duration than the space of six Months, and shall publish the Journal of their proceedings monthly, except such parts thereof relating to treaties, alliances or military operations as in their judgment require secresy; and the yeas and nays of the delegates of each state on any question shall be entered on the Journal, when it is desired by any delegate; and the delegates of a state, or any of them, at his or their request shall be furnished with a transcript of the said Journal, except such parts as are above excepted to lay before the legislatures of the several states.

Art. X. The committee of the states, or any nine of them, shall be authorised to execute, in the recess of congress, such of the powers of congress as the united states in congress assembled, by the consent of nine states, shall from time to time think expedient to vest them with; provided that no power be delegated to the said committee, for the exercise of which, by the articles of confederation, the voice of nine states in the congress of the united states assembled is requisite.

Art. XI. Canada acceding to this confederation, and joining in the measures of the united states, shall be admitted into, and entitled to all the advantages of this union: but no other colony shall be admitted into the same, unless such admission be agreed to by nine states.

Art. XII. All bills of credit emitted, monies borrowed and debts contracted by, or under the authority of congress, before the assembling of the united states, in pursuance of the present confederation, shall be deemed and considered as a charge against the united states, for payment and satisfaction whereof the said united states and the public faith are hereby solemnly pledged.

Art. XIII. Every state shall abide by the determinations of the united states in congress assembled, on all questions which by this confederation are submitted to them. And the Articles of this confederation shall be inviolably observed by every state, and the union shall be perpetual; nor shall any alteration at any time hereafter be made in any of them; unless such alteration be agreed to in a congress of the united states, and be afterwards confirmed by the legislatures of every state.

AND WHEREAS it hath pleased the Great Governor of the World to incline the hearts of the legislatures we respectively represent in congress, to approve of, and to authorize us to ratify the said articles of confederation and perpetual union. KNOW YE that we the undersigned delegates, by virtue of the power and authority to us given for that purpose, do by these presents, in the name and in behalf of our respective constituents, fully and entirely ratify and confirm each and every of the said articles of confederation and perpetual union, and all and singular the matters and things therein contained: And we do further solemnly plight and engage the faith of our respective constituents, that they shall abide by the determination of the united states in congress assembled, on all questions, which by the said confederation are submitted to them. And that the articles thereof shall be inviolably observed by the states we respectively represent, and that the union shall be perpetual. In Witness whereof we have hereunto set our hands in Congress. Done at Philadelphia in the state of Pennsylvania the ninth Day of July in the Year of our Lord one Thousand seven Hundred and Seventy-eight and in the third year of the independence of America.

The Constitution of the United States of America

Annotated with references to *The Federalist Papers*

Federalist Paper Number (Author)

[PREAMBLE]

We the People of the United States, in Order to form a more perfect Union, establish Justice, insure domestic Tranquility, provide for the common defence, promote the general Welfare, and secure the Blessings of Liberty to ourselves and our Posterity, do ordain and establish this Constitution for the United States of America. 84 (Hamilton)

ARTICLE I

Section 1

[LEGISLATIVE POWERS]

All legislative Powers herein granted shall be vested in a Congress of the United States, which shall consist of a Senate and House of Representatives. 10, 45 (Madison)

Section 2

[HOUSE OF REPRESENTATIVES, HOW CONSTITUTED, POWER OF IMPEACHMENT]

The House of Representatives shall be composed of Members chosen every second Year by the People of the several States, and the Electors in each State shall have the Qualifications requisite for Electors of the most numerous Branch of the State Legislature. 39, 45, 52–53, 57 (Madison)

No Person shall be a Representative who shall not have attained to the Age of twenty-five Years, and been seven Years a Citizen of the United States, and who shall not, when elected, be an inhabitant of that State in which he shall be chosen. 52 (Madison) 60 (Hamilton)

Representatives and *direct Taxes*[1] shall be apportioned among the several States which may be included within this Union, according to their respective Numbers, *which shall be determined by adding to the whole Number of free Persons, including those bound to Service for a Term of Years,* and excluding Indians not taxed, *three-fifths of all other Persons.*[2] The actual Enumeration shall be made within three Years after the first Meeting of the Congress of the United States, and within every subsequent Term of ten Years, in such Manner as they shall by Law direct. The Number of Representatives shall not exceed one for every thirty Thousand, but each State shall have at Least one Representative; *and until such enumeration shall be made, the State of New* 54, 58 (Madison) 55–56 (Madison)

1 Modified by Sixteenth Amendment.

2 Modified by Fourteenth Amendment.

Hampshire shall be entitled to chuse three, Massachusetts eight, Rhode-Island and Providence Plantations one, Connecticut five, New-York six, New Jersey four, Pennsylvania eight, Delaware one, Maryland six, Virginia ten, North Carolina five, South Carolina five, and Georgia three.[3]

When vacancies happen in the Representation from any State, the Executive Authority thereof shall issue Writs of Election to fill such Vacancies.

79 (Hamilton)

The House of Representatives shall chuse their Speaker and other Officers; and shall have the sole Power of Impeachment.

Section 3

[THE SENATE, HOW CONSTITUTED, IMPEACHMENT TRIALS]

39, 45 (Madison)
60 (Hamilton)

The Senate of the United States shall be composed of two Senators from each State, *chosen by the Legislature thereof,*[4] for six Years; and each Senator shall have one Vote.

62–63 (Madison)
59, 68 (Hamilton)

Immediately after they shall be assembled in Consequence of the first Election, they shall be divided as equally as may be into three Classes. The Seats of the Senators of the first Class shall be vacated at the Expiration of the second Year, of the second Class at the Expiration of the fourth Year, and of the third Class at the Expiration of the sixth Year, so that one third may be chosen every second Year: *and if vacancies happen by Resignation, or otherwise, during the Recess of the Legislature of any State, the Executive thereof may make temporary Appointments until the next Meeting of the Legislature, which shall then fill such Vacancies.*[5]

62 (Madison)
64 (Jay)

No person shall be a Senator who shall not have attained to the Age of thirty Years, and been nine Years a Citizen of the United States, and who shall not, when elected, be an Inhabitant of that State for which he shall be chosen.

The Vice-President of the United States shall be President of the Senate, but shall have no Vote, unless they be equally divided.

The Senate shall chuse their other Officers, and also a President pro tempore, in the Absence of the Vice-President, or when he shall exercise the Office of President of the United States.

39 (Madison)
65–67, 79 (Hamilton)

The Senate shall have the sole Power to try all Impeachments. When sitting for that Purpose, they shall be on Oath or Affirmation. When the President of the United States is tried, the Chief Justice shall preside: And no Person shall be convicted without the Concurrence of two-thirds of the Members present.

84 (Hamilton)

Judgment in Cases of Impeachment shall not extend further than to removal from Office, and disqualification to hold and enjoy any Office of honor, Trust or Profit under the United States: but the Party convicted shall nevertheless be liable and subject to Indictment, Trial, Judgment and Punishment, according to Law.

Section 4

[ELECTION OF SENATORS AND REPRESENTATIVES]

59–61 (Hamilton)

The Times, Places and Manner of holding Elections for Senators and Representatives, shall be prescribed in each State by the Legislature thereof; but the

3 Temporary provision.

4 Modified by Seventeenth Amendment.

5 Modified by Seventeenth Amendment.

Congress may at any time by Law make or alter such Regulations, except as to the Places of chusing Senators.

The Congress shall assemble at least once in every Year, and such Meeting shall be on the first Monday in December, unless they shall by Law appoint a different Day.[6]

Section 5

[QUORUM, JOURNALS, MEETINGS, ADJOURNMENTS]

Each House shall be the Judge of the Elections, Returns and Qualifications of its own Members, and a Majority of each shall constitute a Quorum to do Business; but a smaller Number may adjourn from day to day, and may be authorized to compel the Attendance of absent Members, in such Manner, and under the Penalties as each House may provide.

Each House may determine the Rules of its Proceedings, punish its Members for disorderly Behavior, and, with the Concurrence of two-thirds, expel a Member.

Each House shall keep a Journal of its Proceedings, and from time to time publish the same, excepting such Parts as may in their Judgment require Secrecy; and the Yeas and Nays of the Members of either House on any questions shall, at the Desire of one-fifth of the present, be entered on the Journal.

Neither House, during the Session of Congress, shall, without the Consent of the other, adjourn for more than three days, nor to any other Place than that in which the two Houses shall be sitting.

Section 6

[COMPENSATION, PRIVILEGES, DISABILITIES]

The Senators and Representatives shall receive a Compensation for their Services, to be ascertained by Law, and paid out of the Treasury of the United States. They shall in all Cases, except Treason, Felony and Breach of the Peace, be privileged from Arrest during their Attendance at the Session of their respective Houses, and in going to and returning from the same; and for any Speech or Debate in either House, they shall not be questioned in any other Place.

No Senator or Representative shall, during the time for which he was elected, be appointed to any civil Office under the authority of the United States, which shall have been created, or the Emoluments whereof shall have been encreased during such time; and no Person holding any Office under the United States, shall be a Member of either House during his Continuance in Office.

55 (Madison)
76 (Hamilton)

Section 7

[PROCEDURE IN PASSING BILLS AND RESOLUTIONS]

All Bills for raising Revenue shall originate in the House of Representatives; but the Senate may propose or concur with Amendments as on other Bills.

66 (Hamilton)

Every Bill which shall have passed the House of Representatives and the Senate, shall, before it become a Law, be presented to the President of the United States; if he approve he shall sign it, but if not he shall return it, with his Objections to that House in which it shall have originated, who shall enter the Objections at large on their Journal, and proceed to reconsider it. If after such Reconsideration

69, 73 (Hamilton)

6 Modified by Twentieth Amendment.

two-thirds of that House shall agree to pass the Bill, it shall be sent, together with the Objections, to the other House, by which it shall likewise be reconsidered, and if approved by two-thirds of that House it shall become a Law. But in all such Cases the Votes of both Houses shall be determined by Yeas and Nays, and the Names of the Persons voting for and against the Bill shall be entered on the Journal of each House respectively. If any Bill shall not be returned by the President within ten Days (Sundays excepted) after it shall have been presented to him, the Same shall be a Law, in like Manner as if he had signed it, unless the Congress by their Adjournment prevent its Return, in which Case it shall not be a Law.

69, 73 (Hamilton) Every Order, Resolution, or Vote to which the Concurrence of the Senate and House of Representatives may be necessary (except on a question of Adjournment) shall be presented to the President of the United States; and before the Same shall take Effect, shall be approved by him, or being disapproved by him, shall be repassed by two-thirds of the Senate and House of Representatives, according to the Rules and Limitations prescribed in the Case of a Bill.

Section 8

[POWERS OF CONGRESS]

The Congress shall have Power

To lay and collect Taxes, Duties, Imposts and Excises, to pay the Debts and
30–36 (Hamilton) provide for the common Defence and general Welfare of the United States; but
41 (Madison) all Duties, Imposts and excises shall be uniform throughout the United States;

To borrow Money on the Credit of the United States;

56 (Madison) To regulate Commerce with foreign Nations, and among the several States,
42, 45, 56 and with the Indian Tribes;

(Madison) To establish an uniform Rule of Naturalization, and uniform Laws on the
32 (Hamilton) subject of Bankruptcies throughout the United States;

To coin Money, regulate the Value thereof, and of foreign Coin, and fix the
42 (Madison) Standard of Weights and Measures;

To provide for the Punishment of counterfeiting the Securities and current
42 (Madison) Coin of the United States;

To establish Post Offices and post Roads;

42 (Madison) To promote the Progress of Science and useful Arts, by securing for limited
42, 43 (Madison) Times to Authors and Inventors the exclusive Right to their respective Writings and Discoveries;

81 (Hamilton) To constitute Tribunals inferior to the supreme Court;

42 (Madison) To define and Punish Piracies and Felonies committed on the high Seas, and Offences against the Law of Nations;

41 (Madison) To declare War, grant Letters of Marque and Reprisal, and make Rules concerning Captures on Land and Water;

23, 24, 26 (Hamilton) To raise and support Armies, but no Appropriation of Money to that Use shall be for a longer Term than two Years;

41 (Madison) To provide and maintain a Navy;

To make Rules for the Government and Regulation of the land and naval forces;

29 (Hamilton) To provide for calling for the Militia to execute the Laws of the Union, suppress Insurrections and repel Invasions;

To provide for organizing, arming, and disciplining, the Militia, and for governing such Part of them as may be employed in the Service of the United States, reserving to the States respectively, the Appointment of the Officers, and the Authority of training the Militia according to the discipline prescribed by Congress; 29 (Hamilton) 56 (Madison)

To exercise exclusive Legislation in all Cases whatsoever, over such District (not exceeding ten Miles square) as may, by Cession of particular States, and the Acceptance of Congress, become the Seat of the Government of the United States, and to exercise like Authority over all Places purchased by the Consent of the Legislature of the State in which the Same shall be, for the Erection of Forts, Magazines, Arsenals, dock-Yards, and other needful Buildings;—And 32 (Hamilton) 43 (Madison)

To make all Laws which shall be necessary and proper for carrying into Execution the foregoing Powers, and all other Powers vested by this Constitution in the Government of the United States, or in any Department or Officer thereof. 29, 33 (Hamilton) 44 (Madison)

Section 9

[SOME RESTRICTIONS ON FEDERAL POWER]

The Migration or Importation of such Persons as any of the States now existing shall think proper to admit, shall not be prohibited by the Congress prior to the Year one thousand eight hundred and eight, but a Tax or Duty may be imposed on such Importation, not exceeding ten dollars for each Person.[7] 42 (Madison)

The privilege of the Writ of *Habeas Corpus* shall not be suspended, unless when in Cases of Rebellion or Invasion the public Safety may require it. 83, 84 (Hamilton)

No Bill of Attainder or ex post facto Law shall be passed. 84 (Hamilton)

No Capitation, or other direct, Tax shall be laid, unless in Proportion to the Census or Enumeration herein before directed to be taken.[8]

No Tax or Duty shall be laid on Articles exported from any State.

No Preference shall be given by any Regulation of Commerce or Revenue to the Ports of one State over those of another; nor shall vessels bound to, or from, one State, be obliged to enter, clear, or pay Duties in another. 32 (Hamilton)

No Money shall be drawn from the Treasury, but in Consequence of Appropriations made by Law; and a regular Statement and Account of the Receipts and Expenditures of all public Money shall be published from time to time.

No Title of Nobility shall be granted by the United States: And no Person holding any Office of Profit or Trust under them, shall, without the Consent of the Congress, accept of any present, Emolument, Office or Title, of any kind whatever, from any King, Prince, or foreign State. 39 (Madison) 84 (Hamilton)

Section 10

[RESTRICTIONS UPON POWERS OF STATES]

No State shall enter into any Treaty, Alliance, or Confederation; grant Letters of Marque and Reprisal; coin Money; emit Bills of Credit; make any Thing but gold and silver Coin a Tender in Payment of Debts; pass any Bill of Attainder, ex post facto Law, or Law impairing the Obligation of Contracts, or grant any Title of Nobility. 33 (Hamilton) 44 (Madison)

7 Temporary provision.

8 Modified by Sixteenth Amendment.

No State shall, without the Consent of the Congress, lay any Imposts or Duties
32 (Hamilton) on Imports or Exports, except what may be absolutely necessary for executing its
44 (Madison) inspection Laws: and the net Produce of all Duties and Imposts, laid by any State
on Imports or Exports, shall be for the Use of the Treasury of the United States;
and all such Laws shall be subject to the Revision and Control of the Congress.

No State shall, without the Consent of Congress, lay any Duty of Tonnage, keep Troops, or Ships of War in time of Peace, enter into any Agreement or Compact with another State, or with a foreign Power, or engage in War, unless actually invaded, or in such imminent Danger as will not admit of Delay.

ARTICLE II

Section 1

[EXECUTIVE POWER, ELECTION, QUALIFICATIONS OF THE PRESIDENT]

39 (Madison) The executive Power shall be vested in a President of the United States of
70, 71, 84 America. *He shall hold his Office during the Term of four years and, together with the Vice-*
(Hamilton) *President, chosen for the same Term, be elected, as follows:*[9]

68, 69, 71, 77 Each State shall appoint, in such Manner as the Legislature thereof may
(Hamilton) direct, a Number of Electors, equal to the whole Number of Senators and Rep-
39, 45 (Madison) resentatives to which the State may be entitled in the Congress: but no Senator
or Representative, or Person holding an Office of Trust or Profit under the
United States, shall be appointed an Elector.

66 (Hamilton) *The electors shall meet in their respective States, and vote by ballot for two Persons, of
whom one at least shall not be an Inhabitant of the same State with themselves. And they shall make a List of all the Persons voted for, and of the Number of Votes for each; which List they shall sign and certify, and transmit sealed to the Seat of the Government of the United States, directed to the President of the Senate. The President of the Senate shall, in the Presence of the Senate and House of Representatives, open all the Certificates, and the Votes shall then be counted. The Person having the greatest Number of Votes shall be the President, if such Number be a Majority of the whole Number of Electors appointed; and if there be more than one who have such Majority and have an equal Number of Votes, then the House of Representatives shall immediately chuse by Ballot one of them for President; and if no person have a Majority, then from the five highest on the List the said House shall in like Manner chuse the President. But in chusing the President, the Votes shall be taken by States, the Representation from each State having one Vote; A quorum for this Purpose shall consist of a Member or Members from two-thirds of the States, and a Majority of all the States shall be necessary to a Choice. In every Case, after the Choice of the President, the person having the greatest Number of Votes of the Electors shall be the Vice-President. But if there should remain two or more who have equal vote, the Senate shall chuse from them by Ballot the Vice-President.*[10]

The Congress may determine the Time of chusing the Electors, and the Day on which they shall give their Votes; which Day shall be the same throughout the United States.

---

9 Number of terms limited to two by Twenty-second Amendment.

10 Modified by Twelfth and Twentieth Amendments.

No Person except a natural born Citizen, or a Citizen of the United States, at the time of the Adoption of this Constitution, shall be eligible to the Office of President; neither shall any Person be eligible to that Office who shall not have attained to the Age of thirty-five Years, and been fourteen Years a Resident within the United States. 64 (Jay)

In Case of the Removal of the President from Office, or his Death, Resignation, or Inability to discharge the Powers and Duties of the said Office, the same shall devolve on the Vice-President, and the Congress may by Law provide for the Case of Removal, Death, Resignation, or Inability, both of the President and Vice-President, declaring what Officer shall then act as President, and such Officer shall act accordingly, until the Disability be removed, or a President shall be elected.

The President shall, at stated Times, receive for his Services, a Compensation, which shall neither be encreased nor diminished during the Period for which he shall have been elected, and he shall not receive within that Period any other Emolument from the United States, or any of them. 73, 79 (Hamilton)

Before he enter on the Execution of his Office, he shall take the following Oath or Affirmation:—"I do solemnly swear (or affirm) that I will faithfully execute the Office of President of the United States, and will to the best of my Ability, preserve, protect and defend the Constitution of the United States."

Section 2
[POWERS OF THE PRESIDENT]

The President shall be Commander in Chief of the Army and Navy of the United States, and of the Militia of the several States, when called into the actual Service of the United States; he may require the Opinion, in writing, of the principal Officer in each of the executive Departments, upon any Subject relating to the Duties of their respective Offices, and he shall have Power to grant Reprieves and Pardons for Offences against the United States, except in Cases of Impeachment. 69, 74 (Hamilton)

He shall have Power, by and with the Advice and Consent of the Senate, to make Treaties, provided two-thirds of the Senators present concur; and he shall nominate, and by and with the Advice and Consent of the Senate, shall appoint Ambassadors, other public Ministers and Consuls, Judges of the Supreme Court, and all other Officers of the United States, whose Appointments are not herein otherwise provided for, and which shall be established by Law: but the Congress may by Law vest the Appointment of such inferior Officers, as they think proper, in the President alone, in the Courts of Law, or in the Heads of Departments. 42 (Madison) 64 (Jay) 66, 69, 76, 77 (Hamilton)

The President shall have Power to fill up all Vacancies that may happen during the Recess of the Senate, by granting Commissions which shall expire at the End of their next Session. 67, 76 (Hamilton)

Section 3
[POWERS AND DUTIES OF THE PRESIDENT]

He shall from time to time give to the Congress Information of the State of the Union, and recommend to their Consideration such Measures as he shall judge necessary and expedient; he may, on extraordinary Occasions, convene both Houses, or either of them, and in Case of Disagreement between them, with Respect to the Time of Adjournment, he may adjourn them to such Time 69, 77, 78 (Hamilton) 42 (Madison) as he shall think proper; he shall receive Ambassadors and other public Ministers; he shall take Care that the Laws be faithfully executed, and shall Commission all the Officers of the United States.

Section 4

[IMPEACHMENT]

39 (Madison) The President, Vice-President and all civil Officers of the United States
69 (Hamilton) shall be removed from Office on Impeachment for, and Conviction of, Treason, Bribery, or other high Crimes and Misdemeanors.

ARTICLE III

Section 1

[JUDICIAL POWER, TENURE OF OFFICE]

65, 78, 79, 81, 82 (Hamilton) The judicial Power of the United States, shall be vested in one supreme Court, and in such inferior Courts as the Congress may from time to time ordain and establish. The Judges, both of the supreme and inferior Courts, shall hold their Offices during good Behavior, and shall, at stated Times, receive for their Services, a Compensation, which shall not be diminished during their Continuance in Office.

Section 2

[JURISDICTION]

80 (Hamilton) The judicial Power shall extend to all Cases, in Law and Equity, arising under this Constitution, the Laws of the United States, and Treaties made, or which shall be made, under their Authority;—to all Cases affecting Ambassadors, other public Ministers and Consuls;—to all Cases of admiralty and maritime Jurisdiction;—to Controversies to which the United States shall be a party;—to Controversies between two or more States;—*between a State and Citizens of another State;*—between Citizens of different States,—between Citizens of the same State claiming Lands under Grants of different States, *and between a State,* or the Citizens thereof, *and foreign States, Citizens or Subjects.*[11]

81 (Hamilton) In all Cases affecting Ambassadors, other public Ministers and Consuls, and those in which a State shall be Party, the supreme Court shall have original Jurisdiction. In all the other Cases before mentioned, the supreme Court shall have appellate Jurisdiction, both as to Law and Fact, with such Exceptions, and under such Regulations as Congress shall make.

83, 84 (Hamilton) The Trial of all Crimes, except in Cases of Impeachment, shall be by Jury; and such Trial shall be held in the State where the said Crimes shall have been committed; but when not committed within any State, the Trial shall be at such Place or Places as the Congress may by Law have directed.

11 Modified by Eleventh Amendment.

Section 3
[TREASON, PROOF, AND PUNISHMENT]

Treason against the United States, shall consist only in levying War against them, or in adhering to their Enemies, giving them Aid and Comfort. No Person shall be convicted of Treason unless on the Testimony of two Witnesses to the same overt Act, or on Confession in open Court. 43 (Madison) 84 (Hamilton)

The Congress shall have Power to declare the Punishment of Treason, but no Attainder of Treason shall work Corruption of Blood, or Forfeiture except during the Life of the Person attained. 43 (Madison) 84 (Hamilton)

ARTICLE IV

Section 1
[FAITH AND CREDIT AMONG STATES]

Full Faith and Credit shall be given in each State to the public Acts, Records, and judicial Proceedings of every other State. And the Congress may by general Laws prescribe the Manner in which such Acts, Records and Proceedings shall be proved, and the Effect thereof. 42 (Madison)

Section 2
[PRIVILEGES AND IMMUNITIES, FUGITIVES]

The Citizens of each State shall be entitled to all Privileges and Immunities of Citizens in the several States. 80 (Hamilton)

A person charged in any State with Treason, Felony or other Crime, who shall flee from Justice, and be found in another State, shall on Demand of the executive Authority of the State from which he fled, be delivered up to be removed to the State having Jurisdiction of the Crime.

No person held to Service or Labour in one State, under the Laws thereof, escaping into another, shall, in Consequence of any Law or Regulation therein, be discharged from such Service or Labour, but shall be delivered up on Claim of the Party to whom such Service or Labour may be due.[12]

Section 3
[ADMISSION OF NEW STATES]

New States may be admitted by the Congress into this Union; but no new State shall be formed or erected within the Jurisdiction of any other State; nor any State be formed by the Junction of two or more States, or Parts of States, without the Consent of the Legislatures of the States concerned as well as of the Congress. 43 (Madison)

The Congress shall have Power to dispose of and make all needful Rules and Regulations respecting the Territory or other Property belonging to the United States; and nothing in this Constitution shall be so construed as to Prejudice any Claims of the United States, or of any particular State. 43 (Madison)

12 Repealed by Thirteenth Amendment.

Section 4

[GUARANTEE OF REPUBLICAN GOVERNMENT]

39, 43 (Madison) The United States shall guarantee to every State in this Union a Republican Form of Government, and shall protect each of them against Invasion; and on Application of the Legislature, or of the Executive (when the Legislature cannot be convened) against domestic Violence.

ARTICLE V

[AMENDMENT OF THE CONSTITUTION]

39, 43 (Madison) 85 (Hamilton) The Congress, whenever two-thirds of both Houses shall deem it necessary, shall propose Amendments to this Constitution, or, on the Application of the Legislatures of two-thirds of the several States, shall call a Convention for proposing Amendments, which, in either Case, shall be valid to all Intents and Purposes, as Part of this Constitution, when ratified by the Legislatures of three-fourths of the several States, or by Conventions in three-fourths thereof, as the one or the other Mode of Ratification may be proposed by the Congress; *Provided that no Amendment which may be made prior to the Year One thousand eight hundred and eight shall in any Manner affect the first and fourth Clauses in the Ninth Section of the first Article;*[13] and that no State, without its Consent, shall be deprived of its equal Suffrage in the Senate.

ARTICLE VI

[DEBTS, SUPREMACY, OATH]

43 (Madison) All Debts contracted and Engagements entered into, before the Adoption of this Constitution, shall be as valid against the United States under this Constitution, as under the Confederation.

27, 33 (Hamilton) 39, 44 (Madison) This Constitution, and the Laws of the United States which shall be made in Pursuance thereof; and all Treaties made, or which shall be made, under the Authority of the United States, shall be the supreme Law of the Land; and the Judges in every State shall be bound thereby, any Thing in the Constitution or Laws of any State to the Contrary notwithstanding.

27 (Hamilton) 44 (Madison) The Senators and Representatives before mentioned, and the Members of the several State Legislatures, and all executive and judicial Officers, both of the United States and of the several States, shall be bound by Oath or Affirmation, to support this Constitution; but no religious Test shall be required as a Qualification to any Office or public Trust under the United States.

ARTICLE VII

[RATIFICATION AND ESTABLISHMENT]

39, 40, 43 (Madison) The Ratification of the Conventions of nine States, shall be sufficient for the Establishment of this Constitution between the States so ratifying the Same.[14]

13 Temporary provision.

14 The Constitution was submitted on September 17, 1787, by the Constitutional Convention, was ratified by the conventions of several states at various dates up to May 29, 1790, and became effective on March 4, 1789.

Done in Convention by the Unanimous Consent of the States present the Seventeenth Day of September in the Year of our Lord one thousand seven hundred and Eighty seven and of the Independence of the United States of America the Twelfth. *In Witness* whereof We have hereunto subscribed our Names,

G:[0] WASHINGTON—
Presidt, and Deputy
from Virginia

NEW HAMPSHIRE
John Langdon
Nicholas Gilman

MASSACHUSETTS
Nathaniel Gorham
Rufus King

CONNECTICUT
Wm Saml Johnson
Roger Sherman

NEW YORK
Alexander Hamilton

NEW JERSEY
Wil: Livingston
David Brearley
Wm Paterson
Jona: Dayton

PENNSYLVANIA
B Franklin
Thomas Mifflin
Robt Morris
Geo. Clymer
Thos. FitzSimons
Jared Ingersoll
James Wilson
Gouv Morris

DELAWARE
Geo Read
Gunning Bedfor Jun
John Dickinson
Richard Bassett
Jaco: Broom

MARYLAND
James McHenry
Dan of St Thos Jenifer
Danl Carroll

VIRGINIA
John Blair—
James Madison Jr.

NORTH CAROLINA
Wm Blount
Richd Dobbs Spaight
Hu Williamson

SOUTH CAROLINA
J. Rutledge
Charles Cotesworth Pinckney
Charles Pinckney
Pierce Butler

GEORGIA
William Few
Abr Baldwin

Amendments to the Constitution

Proposed by Congress and Ratified by the Legislatures of the Several States, Pursuant to Article V of the Original Constitution.

Amendments I–X, known as the Bill of Rights, were proposed by Congress on September 25, 1789, and ratified on December 15, 1791. *The Federalist Papers* comments, mainly in opposition to a Bill of Rights, can be found in number 84 (Hamilton).

AMENDMENT I

[FREEDOM OF RELIGION, OF SPEECH, AND OF THE PRESS]

Congress shall make no law respecting an establishment of religion, or prohibiting the free exercise thereof; or abridging the freedom of speech, or of the press; or the right of the people peaceably to assemble, and to petition the Government for a redress of grievances.

AMENDMENT II

[RIGHT TO KEEP AND BEAR ARMS]

A well regulated Militia, being necessary to the security of a free State, the right of the people to keep and bear Arms, shall not be infringed.

AMENDMENT III

[QUARTERING OF SOLDIERS]

No Soldier shall, in time of peace be quartered in any house, without the consent of the Owner, nor in time of war, but in a manner to be prescribed by law.

AMENDMENT IV

[SECURITY FROM UNWARRANTABLE SEARCH AND SEIZURE]

The right of the people to be secure in their persons, houses, papers, and effects, against unreasonable searches and seizures, shall not be violated, and no Warrants shall issue, but upon probable cause, supported by Oath or affirmation, and particularly describing the place to be searched, and the persons or things to be seized.

AMENDMENT V

[RIGHTS OF ACCUSED PERSONS IN CRIMINAL PROCEEDINGS]

No person shall be held to answer for a capital, or otherwise infamous crime, unless on a presentment or indictment of a Grand Jury, except in cases arising in the land or naval forces, or in the Militia, when in actual service in time of

War or in public danger; nor shall any person be subject for the same offence to be twice put in jeopardy of life or limb; nor shall be compelled in any Criminal Case to be a witness against himself, nor be deprived of life, liberty, or property, without due process of law; nor shall private property be taken for public use, without just compensation.

AMENDMENT VI

[RIGHT TO SPEEDY TRIAL, WITNESSES, ETC.]

In all criminal prosecutions, the accused shall enjoy the right to a speedy and public trial, by an impartial jury of the State and district wherein the crime shall have been committed, which district shall have been previously ascertained by law, and to be informed of the nature and cause of the accusation; to be confronted with the witnesses against him; to have compulsory process for obtaining Witnesses in his favor, and to have the Assistance of Counsel for his defence.

AMENDMENT VII

[TRIAL BY JURY IN CIVIL CASES]

In suits at common law, where the value in controversy shall exceed twenty dollars, the right of trial by jury shall be preserved, and no fact tried by a jury shall be otherwise re-examined in any Court of the United States, than according to the rules of the common law.

AMENDMENT VIII

[BAILS, FINES, PUNISHMENTS]

Excessive bail shall not be required, nor excessive fines imposed, nor cruel and unusual punishments inflicted.

AMENDMENT IX

[RESERVATION OF RIGHTS OF PEOPLE]

The enumeration in the Constitution, of certain rights, shall not be construed to deny or disparage others retained by the people.

AMENDMENT X

[POWERS RESERVED TO STATES OR PEOPLE]

The powers not delegated to the United States by the Constitution, nor prohibited by it to the States, are reserved to the States respectively, or to the people.

AMENDMENT XI

[Proposed by Congress on March 4, 1794; declared ratified on January 8, 1798.]

[RESTRICTION OF JUDICIAL POWER]

The Judicial power of the United States shall not be construed to extend to any suit in law or equity, commenced or prosecuted against one of the United States by Citizens of another State, or by Citizens or Subjects of any Foreign State.

AMENDMENT XII

[Proposed by Congress on December 9, 1803; declared ratified on September 25, 1804.]

[ELECTION OF PRESIDENT AND VICE-PRESIDENT]

The Electors shall meet in their respective states, and vote by ballot for President and Vice-President, one of whom, at least, shall not be an inhabitant of the same state with themselves; they shall name in their ballots the person voted for as President, and in distinct ballots the person voted for as Vice-President, and they shall make distinct lists of all persons voted for as President, and of all persons voted for as Vice-President, and of the number of votes for each, which lists they shall sign and certify, and transmit sealed to the seat of the government of the United States, directed to the President of the Senate;—The President of the Senate shall, in presence of the Senate and House of Representatives, open all the certificates and the votes shall then be counted;—The person having the greatest number of votes for President, shall be the President, if such number be a majority of the whole number of Electors appointed; and if no person have such majority, then from the persons having the highest numbers not exceeding three on the list of those voted for as President, the House of Representatives shall choose immediately, by ballot, the President. But in choosing the President, the votes shall be taken by states, the representation from each state having one vote; a quorum for this purpose shall consist of a member or members from two-thirds of the states, and a majority of all states shall be necessary to a choice. And if the House of Representatives shall not choose a President whenever the right of choice shall devolve upon them, before the fourth day of March next following, then the Vice-President, shall act as President, as in the case of the death or other constitutional disability of the President. The person having the greatest number of votes as Vice-President, shall be the Vice-President, if such a number be a majority of the whole number of Electors appointed, and if no person have a majority, then from the two highest numbers on the list, the Senate shall choose the Vice-President; a quorum for the purpose shall consist of two-thirds of the whole number of Senators, and a majority of the whole number shall be necessary to a choice. But no person constitutionally ineligible to the office of President shall be eligible to that of Vice-President of the United States.

AMENDMENT XIII

[Proposed by Congress on January 31, 1865; declared ratified on December 18, 1865.]

Section 1

[ABOLITION OF SLAVERY]

Neither slavery nor involuntary servitude, except as a punishment for crime whereof the party shall have been duly convicted, shall exist within the United States, or any place subject to their jurisdiction.

Section 2

[POWER TO ENFORCE THIS ARTICLE]

Congress shall have power to enforce this article by appropriate legislation.

AMENDMENT XIV

[Proposed by Congress on June 13, 1866; declared ratified on July 28, 1868.]

Section 1

[CITIZENSHIP RIGHTS NOT TO BE ABRIDGED BY STATES]

All persons born or naturalized in the United States, and subject to the jurisdiction thereof, are citizens of the United States and of the State wherein they reside. No state shall make or enforce any law which shall abridge the privileges or immunities of citizens of the United States; nor shall any State deprive any person of life, liberty, or property, without due process of law; nor deny to any person within its jurisdiction the equal protection of the laws.

Section 2

[APPORTIONMENT OF REPRESENTATIVES IN CONGRESS]

Representatives shall be apportioned among the several States according to their respective numbers, counting the whole number of persons in each State, excluding Indians not taxed. But when the right to vote at any election for the choice of electors for President and Vice-President of the United States, Representatives in Congress, the Executive and Judicial officers of a State, or the members of the Legislature thereof, is denied to any of the male inhabitants of such State, being twenty-one years of age, and citizens of the United States, or in any way abridged, except for participation in rebellion, or other crime, the basis of representation therein shall be reduced in the proportion which the number of such male citizens shall bear to the whole number of male citizens twenty-one years of age in such State.

Section 3

[PERSONS DISQUALIFIED FROM HOLDING OFFICE]

No person shall be a Senator or Representative in Congress, or elector of President and Vice-President, or hold any office, civil or military, under the United States, or under any State, who, having previously taken an oath, as a member of Congress, or as an officer of the United States, or as a member of any State legislature, or as an executive or judicial officer of any State, to support the Constitution of the United States, shall have engaged in insurrection or rebellion against the same, or given aid or comfort to the enemies thereof. But Congress may by a vote of two-thirds of each House, remove such disability.

Section 4

[WHAT PUBLIC DEBTS ARE VALID]

The validity of the public debt of the United States, authorized by law, including debts incurred for payment of pensions and bounties for services in suppressing insurrection or rebellion, shall not be questioned. But neither the United States nor any State shall assume or pay any debt or obligation incurred in aid of insurrection or rebellion against the United States, or any claim for the loss or emancipation of any slave; but all such debts, obligations and claims shall be held illegal and void.

Section 5

[POWER TO ENFORCE THIS ARTICLE]

The Congress shall have power to enforce, by appropriate legislation, the provisions of this article.

AMENDMENT XV

[Proposed by Congress on February 26, 1869; declared ratified on March 30, 1870.]

Section 1

[NEGRO SUFFRAGE]

The right of citizens of the United States to vote shall not be denied or abridged by the United States or by any State on account of race, color, or previous condition of servitude.

Section 2

[POWER TO ENFORCE THIS ARTICLE]

The Congress shall have power to enforce this article by appropriate legislation.

AMENDMENT XVI

[Proposed by Congress on July 12, 1909; declared ratified on February 25, 1913.]

[AUTHORIZING INCOME TAXES]

The Congress shall have power to lay and collect taxes on incomes, from whatever source derived, without apportionment among the several States, and without regard to any census or enumeration.

AMENDMENT XVII

[Proposed by Congress on May 13, 1912; declared ratified on May 31, 1913.]

[POPULAR ELECTION OF SENATORS]

The Senate of the United States shall be composed of two Senators from each State, elected by the people thereof, for six years; and each Senator shall have one vote. The electors in each State shall have the qualifications requisite for electors of the most numerous branch of the State Legislature.

When vacancies happen in the representation of any State in the Senate, the executive authority of such State shall issue writs of election to fill such vacancies: Provided, That the Legislature of any State may empower the executive thereof to make temporary appointment until the people fill the vacancies by election as the Legislature may direct.

This amendment shall not be so construed as to affect the election or term of any Senator chosen before it becomes valid as part of the Constitution.

AMENDMENT XVIII

[Proposed by Congress December 18, 1917; declared ratified on January 29, 1919.]

Section 1

[NATIONAL LIQUOR PROHIBITION]

After one year from the ratification of this article the manufacture, sale, or transportation of intoxicating liquors within, the importation thereof into, or the exportation thereof from the United States and all territory subject to the jurisdiction thereof for beverage purposes is hereby prohibited.

Section 2

[POWER TO ENFORCE THIS ARTICLE]

The Congress and the several states shall have concurrent power to enforce this article by appropriate legislation.

Section 3

[RATIFICATION WITHIN SEVEN YEARS]

This article shall be inoperative unless it shall have been ratified as an amendment to the Constitution by the legislatures of the several states, as provided in the Constitution, within seven years from the date of the submission hereof to the states by the Congress.[15]

AMENDMENT XIX

[Proposed by Congress on June 4, 1919; declared ratified on August 26, 1920.]

[WOMAN SUFFRAGE]

The right of the citizens of the United States to vote shall not be denied or abridged by the United States or by any state on account of sex.

Congress shall have power to enforce this article by appropriate legislation.

AMENDMENT XX

[Proposed by Congress on March 2, 1932; declared ratified on February 6, 1933.]

Section 1

[TERMS OF OFFICE]

The terms of the President and Vice-President shall end at noon on the 20th day of January, and the terms of the Senators and Representatives at noon on the 3rd day of January, of the years in which such terms would have ended if this article had not been ratified; and the terms of their successors shall then begin.

Section 2

[TIME OF CONVENING CONGRESS]

The Congress shall assemble at least once in every year, and such meeting shall begin at noon on the 3rd day of January, unless they shall by law appoint a different day.

15 Repealed by Twenty-first Amendment.

Section 3

[DEATH OF PRESIDENT-ELECT]

If, at the time fixed for the beginning of the term of the President, the President-elect shall have died, the Vice-President-elect shall become President. If a President shall not have been chosen before the time fixed for the beginning of his term, or if the President-elect shall have failed to qualify, then the Vice-President-elect shall act as President until a President shall have qualified; and the Congress may by law provide for the case wherein neither a President-elect nor a Vice-President-elect shall have qualified, declaring who shall then act as President, or the manner in which one who is to act shall be selected, and such person shall act accordingly until a President or Vice President shall have qualified.

Section 4

[ELECTION OF THE PRESIDENT]

The Congress may by law provide for the case of the death of any of the persons from whom the House of Representatives may choose a President whenever the right of choice shall have devolved upon them, and for the case of the death of any of the persons from whom the Senate may choose a Vice-President whenever the right of choice shall have devolved upon them.

Section 5

[AMENDMENT TAKES EFFECT]

Sections 1 and 2 shall take effect on the 15th day of October following ratification of this article.

Section 6

[RATIFICATION WITHIN SEVEN YEARS]

This article shall be inoperative unless it shall have been ratified as an amendment to the Constitution by the legislatures of three-fourths of the several States within seven years from the date of its submission.

AMENDMENT XXI

[Proposed by Congress on February 20, 1933; declared ratified on December 5, 1933.]

Section 1

[NATIONAL LIQUOR PROHIBITION REPEALED]

The eighteenth article of amendment to the Constitution of the United States is hereby repealed.

Section 2

[TRANSPORTATION OF LIQUOR INTO "DRY" STATES]

The transportation or importation into any State, Territory, or Possession of the United States for delivery or use therein of intoxicating liquors, in violation of the laws thereof, is hereby prohibited.

Section 3

[RATIFICATION WITHIN SEVEN YEARS]

This article shall be inoperative unless it shall have been ratified as an amendment to the Constitution by conventions in the several States, as provided in the Constitution, within seven years from the date of the submission hereof to the States by the Congress.

AMENDMENT XXII

[Proposed by Congress on March 21, 1947; declared ratified on February 26, 1951.]

Section 1

[TENURE OF PRESIDENT LIMITED]

No person shall be elected to the office of President more than twice, and no person who has held the office of President or acted as President for more than two years of a term to which some other person was elected President shall be elected to the Office of the President more than once. But this Article shall not apply to any person holding the office of President when this Article was proposed by the Congress, and shall not prevent any person who may be holding the office of President, or acting as President, during the term within which this Article becomes operative from holding the office of President or acting as President during the remainder of such term.

Section 2

[RATIFICATION WITHIN SEVEN YEARS]

This Article shall be inoperative unless it shall have been ratified as an amendment to the Constitution by the legislatures of three-fourths of the several states within seven years from the date of its submission to the States by the Congress.

AMENDMENT XXIII

[Proposed by Congress on June 21, 1960; declared ratified on March 29, 1961.]

Section 1

[ELECTORAL COLLEGE VOTES FOR THE DISTRICT OF COLUMBIA]

The District constituting the seat of Government of the United States shall appoint in such manner as the Congress may direct:

A number of electors of President and Vice-President equal to the whole number of Senators and Representatives in Congress to which the District would be entitled if it were a State, but in no event more than the least populous State; they shall be in addition to those appointed by the States, but they shall be considered, for the purposes of the election of President and Vice-President, to be electors appointed by a State; and they shall meet in the District and perform such duties as provided by the twelfth article of amendment.

Section 2

[POWER TO ENFORCE THIS ARTICLE]

The Congress shall have power to enforce this article by appropriate legislation.

AMENDMENT XXIV

[Proposed by Congress on August 27, 1963; declared ratified on January 23, 1964.]

Section 1

[ANTI-POLL TAX]

The right of citizens of the United States to vote in any primary or other election for President or Vice-President, for electors for President or Vice-President, or for Senator or Representative of Congress, shall not be denied or abridged by the United States or any State by reasons of failure to pay any poll tax or other tax.

Section 2

[POWER TO ENFORCE THIS ARTICLE]

The Congress shall have power to enforce this article by appropriate legislation.

AMENDMENT XXV

[Proposed by Congress on July 7, 1965; declared ratified on February 10, 1967.]

Section 1

[VICE-PRESIDENT TO BECOME PRESIDENT]

In case of the removal of the President from office or his death or resignation, the Vice-President shall become President.

Section 2

[CHOICE OF A NEW VICE-PRESIDENT]

Whenever there is a vacancy in the office of the Vice-President, the President shall nominate a Vice-President who shall take the office upon confirmation by a majority vote of both houses of Congress.

Section 3

[PRESIDENT MAY DECLARE OWN DISABILITY]

Whenever the President transmits to the President pro tempore of the Senate and the Speaker of the House of Representatives his written declaration that he is unable to discharge the powers and duties of his office, and until he transmits to them a written declaration to the contrary, such powers and duties shall be discharged by the Vice-President as Acting President.

Section 4

[ALTERNATE PROCEDURES TO DECLARE AND TO END PRESIDENTIAL DISABILITY]

Whenever the Vice-President and a majority of either the principal officers of the executive departments, or of such other body as Congress may by law provide, transmit to the President pro tempore of the Senate and the Speaker of the House of Representatives their written declaration that the President is unable to discharge the powers and duties of his office, the Vice-President shall immediately assume the powers and duties of the office as Acting President.

Thereafter, when the President transmits to the President pro tempore of the Senate and the Speaker of the House of Representatives his written declaration that no inability exists, he shall resume the powers and duties of his office unless the Vice-President and a majority of either the principal officers of the executive departments, or of such other body as Congress may by law provide, transmit within four days to the President pro tempore of the Senate and the Speaker of the House of Representatives their written declaration that the President is unable to discharge the powers and duties of his office. Thereupon Congress shall decide the issue, assembling within 48 hours for that purpose if not in session. If the Congress, within 21 days after receipt of the latter written declaration, or, if Congress is not in session, within 21 days after Congress is required to assemble, determines by two-thirds vote of both houses that the President is unable to discharge the powers and duties of his office, the Vice-President shall continue to discharge the same as Acting President; otherwise, the President shall resume the powers and duties of his office.

AMENDMENT XXVI

[Proposed by Congress on March 23, 1971; declared ratified on June 30, 1971.]

Section 1

[EIGHTEEN-YEAR-OLD VOTE]

The right of citizens of the United States, who are eighteen years of age or older, to vote shall not be denied or abridged by the United States or by any State on account of age.

Section 2

[POWER TO ENFORCE THIS ARTICLE]

The Congress shall have power to enforce this article by appropriate legislation.

AMENDMENT XXVII

[Proposed by Congress on September 25, 1789; ratified on May 7, 1992.]

No law varying the compensation for the services of the Senators and Representatives shall take effect until an election of Representatives shall have intervened.

Federalist Papers

NO. 10: MADISON

Among the numerous advantages promised by a well-constructed Union, none deserves to be more accurately developed than its tendency to break and control the violence of faction. The friend of popular governments never finds himself so much alarmed for their character and fate as when he contemplates their propensity to this dangerous vice. He will not fail, therefore, to set a due value on any plan which, without violating the principles to which he is attached, provides a proper cure for it. The instability, injustice, and confusion introduced into the public councils have, in truth, been the mortal diseases under which popular governments have everywhere perished, as they continue to be the favorite and fruitful topics from which the adversaries to liberty derive their most specious declamations. The valuable improvements made by the American constitutions on the popular models, both ancient and modern, cannot certainly be too much admired; but it would be an unwarrantable partiality to contend that they have as effectually obviated the danger on this side, as was wished and expected. Complaints are everywhere heard from our most considerate and virtuous citizens, equally the friends of public and private faith and of public and personal liberty, that our governments are too unstable, that the public good is disregarded in the conflicts of rival parties, and that measures are too often decided, not according to the rules of justice and the rights of the minor party, but by the superior force of an interested and overbearing majority. However anxiously we may wish that these complaints had no foundation, the evidence of known facts will not permit us to deny that they are in some degree true. It will be found, indeed, on a candid review of our situation, that some of the distresses under which we labor have been erroneously charged on the operation of our governments; but it will be found, at the same time, that other causes will not alone account for many of our heaviest misfortunes; and, particularly, for that prevailing and increasing distrust of public engagements and alarm for private rights which are echoed from one end of the continent to the other. These must be chiefly, if not wholly, effects of the unsteadiness and injustice with which a factious spirit has tainted our public administration.

By a faction I understand a number of citizens, whether amounting to a majority or minority of the whole, who are united and actuated by some common impulse of passion, or of interest, adverse to the rights of other citizens, or to the permanent and aggregate interests of the community.

There are two methods of curing the mischiefs of faction: the one, by removing its causes; the other, by controlling its effects.

There are again two methods of removing the causes of faction: the one, by destroying the liberty which is essential to its existence; the other, by giving to every citizen the same opinions, the same passions, and the same interests.

It could never be more truly said than of the first remedy that it was worse than the disease. Liberty is to faction what air is to fire, an aliment without which it instantly expires. But it could not be a less folly to abolish liberty, which is essential to political life, because it nourishes faction than it would be to wish the annihilation of air, which is essential to animal life, because it imparts to fire its destructive agency.

The second expedient is as impracticable as the first would be unwise. As long as the reason of man continues fallible, and he is at liberty to exercise it, different opinions will be formed. As long as the connection subsists between his reason and his self-love, his opinions and his passions will have a reciprocal influence on each other; and the former will be objects to which the latter will attach themselves. The diversity in the faculties of men, from which the rights of property originate, is not less an insuperable obstacle to a uniformity of interests. The protection of these faculties is the first object of government. From the protection of different and unequal faculties of acquiring property, the possession of different degrees and kinds of property immediately results; and from the influence of these on the sentiments and views of the respective proprietors ensues a division of the society into different interests and parties.

The latent causes of faction are thus sown in the nature of man; and we see them everywhere brought into different degrees of activity, according to the different circumstances of civil society. A zeal for different opinions concerning religion, concerning government, and many other points, as well of speculation as of practice; an attachment to different leaders ambitiously contending for pre-eminence and power; or to persons of other descriptions whose fortunes have been interesting to the human passions, have, in turn, divided mankind into parties, inflamed them with mutual animosity, and rendered them much more disposed to vex and oppress each other than to co-operate for their common good. So strong is this propensity of mankind to fall into mutual animosities that where no substantial occasion presents itself the most frivolous and fanciful distinctions have been sufficient to kindle their unfriendly passions and excite their most violent conflicts. But the most common and durable source of factions has been the various and unequal distribution of property. Those who hold and those who are without property have ever formed distinct interests in society. Those who are creditors, and those who are debtors, fall under a like discrimination. A landed interest, a manufacturing interest, a mercantile interest, a moneyed interest, with many lesser interests, grow up of necessity in civilized nations, and divide them into different classes, actuated by different sentiments and views. The regulation of these various and interfering interests forms the principal task of modern legislation and involves the spirit of party and faction in the necessary and ordinary operations of government.

No man is allowed to be judge in his own cause, because his interest would certainly bias his judgment and, not improbably, corrupt his integrity. With equal, nay with greater reason, a body of men are unfit to be both judges and parties at the same time; yet what are many of the most important acts of legislation but so many judicial determinations, not indeed concerning the rights of single persons, but concerning the rights of large bodies of citizens? And what are the different classes of legislators but advocates and parties to the causes which they determine? Is a law proposed concerning private debts? It is a question to which the creditors are parties on one side and the debtors on the other. Justice ought to hold the balance between them. Yet the parties are, and must be, themselves the judges; and the most numerous party, or in other words, the most powerful faction must be expected to prevail. Shall domestic manufacturers be encouraged, and in what degree, by restrictions on foreign manufacturers? are questions which would be differently decided by the landed and the manufacturing classes, and probably by neither with a sole regard to justice and the public good. The apportionment of taxes on the various descriptions of property is an act which seems to require the most exact impartiality; yet there is, perhaps, no legislative act in which greater opportunity and temptation are given to a predominant party to trample on the rules of justice. Every shilling with which they overburden the inferior number is a shilling saved to their own pockets.

It is in vain to say that enlightened statesmen will be able to adjust these clashing interests and render them all subservient to the public good. Enlightened statesmen will not always be at the helm. Nor, in many cases, can such an adjustment be made at all without taking into view indirect and remote considerations, which will rarely prevail over the immediate interest which one party may find in disregarding the rights of another or the good of the whole.

The inference to which we are brought is that the *causes* of faction cannot be removed and that relief is only to be sought in the means of controlling its *effects*.

If a faction consists of less than a majority, relief is supplied by the republican principle, which enables the majority to defeat its sinister views by regular vote. It may clog the administration, it may convulse the society; but it will be unable to execute and mask its violence under the forms of the Constitution. When a majority is included in a faction, the form of popular government, on the other hand, enables it to sacrifice to its ruling passion or interest both the public good and the rights of other citizens. To secure the public good and private rights against the danger of such a faction, and at the same time to preserve the spirit and the form of popular government, is then the great object to which our inquiries are directed. Let me add that it is the great desideratum by which alone this form of government can be rescued from the opprobrium under which it has so long labored and be recommended to the esteem and adoption of mankind.

By what means is this object attainable? Evidently by one of two only. Either the existence of the same passion or interest in a majority at the same time must be prevented, or the majority, having such coexistent passion or interest, must be rendered, by their number and local situation, unable to concert and carry into effect schemes of oppression. If the impulse and the opportunity be suffered to coincide, we well know that neither moral nor religious motives can be relied on as an adequate control. They are not found to be such on the injustice and violence of individuals, and lose their efficacy in proportion to the number combined together, that is, in proportion as their efficacy becomes needful.

From this view of the subject it may be concluded that a pure democracy, by which I mean a society consisting of a small number of citizens, who assemble and administer the government in person, can admit of no cure for the mischiefs of faction. A common passion or interest will, in almost every case, be felt by a majority of the whole; a communication and concert results from the form of government itself; and there is nothing to check the inducements to sacrifice the weaker party or an obnoxious individual. Hence it is that such democracies have ever been spectacles of turbulence and contention; have ever been found incompatible with personal security or the rights of property; and have in general been as short in their lives as they have been violent in their deaths. Theoretic politicians, who have patronized this species of government, have erroneously supposed that by reducing mankind to a perfect equality in their political rights, they would at the same time be perfectly equalized and assimilated in their possessions, their opinions, and their passions.

A republic, by which I mean a government in which the scheme of representation takes place, opens a different prospect and promises the cure for which we are seeking. Let us examine the points in which it varies from pure democracy, and we shall comprehend both the nature of the cure and the efficacy which it must derive from the Union.

The two great points of difference between a democracy and a republic are: first, the delegation of the government, in the latter, to a small number of citizens elected by the rest; secondly, the greater number of citizens and greater sphere of country over which the latter may be extended.

The effect of the first difference is, on the one hand, to refine and enlarge the public views by passing them through the medium of a chosen body of citizens, whose wisdom may best discern the true interest of their country and whose patriotism and love of justice will be least likely to sacrifice it to temporary or partial considerations. Under such a regulation it may well happen that the public voice, pronounced by the representatives of the people, will be more consonant to the public good than if pronounced by the people themselves, convened for the purpose. On the other hand, the effect may be inverted. Men of factious tempers, of local prejudices, or of sinister designs, may, by intrigue, by corruption, or by other means, first obtain the suffrages, and then betray the interests of the people. The question resulting is, whether small or extensive republics are most favorable to the election of proper guardians of the public weal; and it is clearly decided in favor of the latter by two obvious considerations.

In the first place it is to be remarked that however small the republic may be the representatives must be raised to a certain number in order to guard against the cabals of a few; and that however large it may be they must be limited to a certain number in order to guard against the confusion of a multitude. Hence, the number of representatives in the two cases not being in proportion to that of the constituents, and being proportionally greatest in the small republic, it follows that if the proportion of fit characters be not less in the large than in the small republic, the former will present a greater option, and consequently a greater probability of a fit choice.

In the next place, as each representative will be chosen by a greater number of citizens in the large than in the small republic, it will be more difficult for unworthy candidates to practise with success the vicious arts by which elections are too often carried; and the suffrages of the people being more free, will be more likely to center on men who possess the most attractive merit and the most diffusive and established characters.

It must be confessed that in this, as in most other cases, there is a mean, on both sides of which inconveniencies will be found to lie. By enlarging too much the number of electors, you render the representative too little acquainted with all their local circumstances and lesser interests; as by reducing it too much, you render him unduly attached to these, and too little fit to comprehend and pursue great and national objects. The federal Constitution forms a happy combination in this respect; the great and aggregate interests being referred to the national, the local and particular to the State legislatures.

The other point of difference is the greater number of citizens and extent of territory which may be brought within the compass of republican than of democratic government; and it is this circumstance principally which renders factious combinations less to be dreaded in the former than in the latter. The smaller the society, the fewer probably will be the distinct parties and interests composing it; the fewer the distinct parties and interests, the more frequently will a majority be found of the same party; and the smaller the number of individuals composing a majority, and the smaller the compass within which they are placed, the more easily will they concert and execute their plans of oppression. Extend the sphere and you take in a greater variety of parties and interests; you make it less probable that a majority of the whole will have a common motive to invade the rights of other citizens; or if such a common motive exists, it will be more difficult for all who feel it to discover their own strength and to act in unison with each other. Besides other impediments, it may be remarked that, where there is a consciousness of unjust or dishonorable purposes, communication is always checked by distrust in proportion to the number whose concurrence is necessary.

Hence, it clearly appears that the same advantage which a republic has over a democracy in controlling the effects of faction is enjoyed by a large over a small republic—is enjoyed by the Union over the States composing it. Does this advantage consist in the substitution of representatives whose enlightened views and virtuous sentiments render them superior to local prejudices and to schemes of injustice? It will not be denied that the representation of the Union will be most likely to possess these requisite endowments. Does it consist in the greater security afforded by a greater variety of parties, against the event of any one party being able to outnumber and oppress the rest? In an equal degree does the increased variety of parties comprised within the Union increase this security? Does it, in fine, consist in the greater obstacles opposed to the concert and accomplishment of the secret wishes of an unjust and interested majority? Here again the extent of the Union gives it the most palpable advantage.

The influence of factious leaders may kindle a flame within their particular States but will be unable to spread a general conflagration through the other

States. A religious sect may degenerate into a political faction in a part of the Confederacy; but the variety of sects dispersed over the entire face of it must secure the national councils against any danger from that source. A rage for paper money, for an abolition of debts, for an equal division of property, or for any other improper or wicked project, will be less apt to pervade the whole body of the Union than a particular member of it, in the same proportion as such a malady is more likely to taint a particular county or district than an entire State.

In the extent and proper structure of the Union, therefore, we behold a republican remedy for the diseases most incident to republican government. And according to the degree of pleasure and pride we feel in being republicans ought to be our zeal in cherishing the spirit and supporting the character of federalist.

PUBLIUS

NO. 51: MADISON

To what expedient, then, shall we finally resort, for maintaining in practice the necessary partition of power among the several departments as laid down in the Constitution? The only answer that can be given is that as all these exterior provisions are found to be inadequate the defect must be supplied, by so contriving the interior structure of the government as that its several constituent parts may, by their mutual relations, be the means of keeping each other in their proper places. Without presuming to undertake a full development of this important idea I will hazard a few general observations which may perhaps place it in a clearer light, and enable us to form a more correct judgment of the principles and structure of the government planned by the convention.

In order to lay a due foundation for that separate and distinct exercise of the different powers of government, which to a certain extent is admitted on all hands to be essential to the preservation of liberty, it is evident that each department should have a will of its own; and consequently should be so constituted that the members of each should have as little agency as possible in the appointment of the members of the others. Were this principle rigorously adhered to, it would require that all the appointments for the supreme executive, legislative, and judiciary magistracies should be drawn from the same fountain of authority, the people, through channels having no communication whatever with one another. Perhaps such a plan of constructing the several departments would be less difficult in practice than it may in contemplation appear. Some difficulties, however, and some additional expense would attend the execution of it. Some deviations, therefore, from the principle must be admitted. In the constitution of the judiciary department in particular, it might be inexpedient to insist rigorously on the principle: first, because peculiar qualifications being essential in the members, the primary consideration ought to be to select that mode of choice which best secures these qualifications; second, because the permanent tenure by which the appointments are held in that department must soon destroy all sense of dependence on the authority conferring them.

It is equally evident that the members of each department should be as little dependent as possible on those of the others for the emoluments annexed to their offices. Were the executive magistrate, or the judges, not independent of the legislature in this particular, their independence in every other would be merely nominal.

But the great security against a gradual concentration of the several powers in the same department consists in giving to those who administer each department the necessary constitutional means and personal motives to resist encroachments of the others. The provision for defense must in this, as in all other cases, be made commensurate to the danger of attack. Ambition must be made to counteract ambition. The interest of the man must be connected with the constitutional rights of the place. It may be a reflection on human nature that such devices should be necessary to control the abuses of government. But what is government itself but the greatest of all reflections on human nature? If men were angels, no government would be necessary. If angels were to govern men, neither external nor internal controls on government would be necessary. In framing a government which is to be administered by men over men, the great difficulty lies in this: you must first enable the government to control the governed; and in the next place oblige it to control itself. A dependence on the people is, no doubt, the primary control on the government; but experience has taught mankind the necessity of auxiliary precautions.

This policy of supplying, by opposite and rival interests, the defect of better motives, might be traced through the whole system of human affairs, private as well as public. We see it particularly displayed in all the subordinate distributions of power, where the constant aim is to divide and arrange the several offices in such a manner as that each may be a check on the other—that the private interest of every individual may be a sentinel over the public rights. These inventions of prudence cannot be less requisite in the distribution of the supreme powers of the State.

But it is not possible to give to each department an equal power of self-defense. In republican government, the legislative authority necessarily predominates. The remedy for this inconveniency is to divide the legislature into different branches; and to render them, by different modes of election and different principles of action, as little connected with each other as the nature of their common functions and their common dependence on the society will admit. It may even be necessary to guard against dangerous encroachments by still further precautions. As the weight of the legislative authority requires that it should be thus divided, the weakness of the executive may require, on the other hand, that it should be fortified. An absolute negative on the legislature appears, at first view, to be the natural defense with which the executive magistrate should be armed. But perhaps it would be neither altogether safe nor alone sufficient. On ordinary occasions it might not be exerted with the requisite firmness, and on extraordinary occasions it might be perfidiously abused. May not this defect of an absolute negative be supplied by some qualified connection between this weaker branch of the stronger department, by which the latter may be led to support the constitutional rights of the former, without being too much detached from the rights of its own department?

If the principles on which these observations are founded be just, as I persuade myself they are, and they be applied as a criterion to the several State constitutions, and to the federal Constitution, it will be found that if the latter does not perfectly correspond with them, the former are infinitely less able to bear such a test.

There are, moreover, two considerations particularly applicable to the federal system of America, which place that system in a very interesting point of view.

First. In a single republic, all the power surrendered by the people is submitted to the administration of a single government; and the usurpations are guarded against by a division of the government into distinct and separate departments. In the compound republic of America, the power surrendered by the people is first divided between two distinct governments, and then the portion allotted to each subdivided among distinct and separate departments. Hence a double security arises to the rights of the people. The different governments will control each other, at the same time that each will be controlled by itself.

Second. It is of great importance in a republic not only to guard the society against the oppression of its rulers, but to guard one part of the society against the injustice of the other part. Different interests necessarily exist in different classes of citizens. If a majority be united by a common interest, the rights of the minority will be insecure. There are but two methods of providing against this evil: the one by creating a will in the community independent of the majority—that is, of the society itself; the other, by comprehending in the society so many separate descriptions of citizens as will render an unjust combination of a majority of the whole very improbable, if not impracticable. The first method prevails in all governments possessing an hereditary or self-appointed authority. This, at best, is but a precarious security; because a power independent of the society may as well espouse the unjust views of the major as the rightful interests of the minor party, and may possibly be turned against both parties. The second method will be exemplified in the federal republic of the United States. Whilst all authority in it will be derived from and dependent on the society, the society itself will be broken into so many parts, interests and classes of citizens, that the rights of individuals, or of the minority, will be in little danger from interested combinations of the majority. In a free government the security for civil rights must be the same as that for religious rights. It consists in the one case in the multiplicity of interests, and in the other in the multiplicity of sects. The degree of security in both cases will depend on the number of interests and sects; and this may be presumed to depend on the extent of country and number of people comprehended under the same government. This view of the subject must particularly recommend a proper federal system to all the sincere and considerate friends of republican government, since it shows that in exact proportion as the territory of the Union may be formed into more circumscribed Confederacies, or States, oppressive combinations of a majority will be facilitated; the best security, under the republican forms, for the rights of every class of citizen, will be diminished; and consequently the stability and independence of some member of the government, the only other security, must be proportionally increased. Justice is the end of government. It is the end of civil society. It ever has been and ever will be pursued until it be obtained, or until liberty be lost in the pursuit. In a society under the forms of which the stronger faction can readily unite and oppress the weaker, anarchy may as truly be said to reign as in a state of nature, where the weaker individual is not secured against the violence of the stronger; and as, in the latter state, even the stronger individuals are prompted, by the uncertainty of their condition, to submit to a government which may protect the weak as well as themselves; so, in the former state, will the more powerful factions or parties be gradually induced, by a like motive, to wish for a government which will protect all parties, the weaker as well as the more powerful. It can be little doubted that if the State of Rhode Island was separated from the Confederacy and left to itself, the insecurity of rights under the popular form of government within such narrow limits would be displayed by such reiterated oppressions of factious majorities that some power altogether independent of the people would soon be called for by the voice of the very factions whose misrule had proved the necessity of it. In the extended republic of the United States, and among the great variety of interests, parties, and sects which it embraces, a coalition of a majority of the whole society could seldom take place on any other principles than those of justice and the general good; whilst there being thus less danger to a minor from the will of a major party, there must be less pretext, also, to provide for the security of the former, by introducing into the government a will not dependent on the latter, or, in other words, a will independent of the society itself. It is no less certain than it is important, notwithstanding the contrary opinions which have been entertained, that the larger the society, provided it lie within a practicable sphere, the more duly capable it will be of self-government. And happily for the *republican cause,* the practicable sphere may be carried to a very great extent by a judicious modification and mixture of the *federal principle.*

PUBLIUS

Glossary

administrative adjudication The application of rules and precedents to specific cases to settle disputes with regulated parties.

administrative legislation Rules made by **regulatory agencies** and commissions.

adverse selection The problem of incomplete information—of choosing alternatives without fully knowing the details of available options.

affirmative action A policy or program designed to redress historic injustices committed against specific groups by making special efforts to provide members of these groups with access to educational and employment opportunities.

after-the-fact authority The authority to follow up on the fate of a proposal once it has been approved by the full chamber.

agenda power The control over what a group will consider for discussion.

agenda-setting effect The power to bring attention to particular issues and problems.

agency loss The difference between what a principal would like an agent to do and the agent's performance.

agency representation The type of representation according to which representatives are held accountable to their constituents if they fail to represent them properly. That is, constituents have the power to hire and fire their representatives.

agents of socialization The social institutions, including families and schools, that help shape individuals' basic political beliefs and values.

amicus curiae "Friend of the court," an individual or group who is not party to a lawsuit but seeks to assist the court in reaching a decision by presenting an additional brief.

Articles of Confederation and Perpetual Union America's first written constitution. Adopted by the Continental Congress in 1777, the Articles of Confederation and Perpetual Union were the formal basis for America's national **government** until 1789, when they were superseded by the Constitution.

Australian ballot An electoral format that presents the names of all the candidates for any given office on the same ballot. Introduced at the end of the eighteenth century, the Australian ballot replaced the partisan ballot and facilitated split-ticket voting.

authoritarian government A system of rule in which the **government** recognizes no formal limits but may nevertheless be restrained by the power of other social institutions.

autocracy A form of **government** in which a single individual rules.

bandwagon effect A shift in electoral support to the candidate whom public opinion polls report as the front-runner.

bicameralism The division of a legislative assembly into two chambers, or houses.

bicameral legislature A legislative assembly composed of two chambers, or houses.

Bill of Rights The first 10 amendments to the U.S. Constitution, adopted in 1791. The Bill of Rights ensures certain rights and liberties to the people.

block grants Federal funds given to state **governments** to pay for goods, services, or programs, with relatively few restrictions on how the funds may be spent.

brief A written document in which an attorney explains—using case precedents—why the Court should rule in favor of his or her client.

bureaucracy The complex structure of offices, tasks, rules, and principles of organization that are employed by all large-scale institutions to coordinate the work of their personnel.

bureaucratic drift The oft-observed phenomenon of bureaucratic implementation that produces policy more to the liking of the **bureaucracy** than faithful to the original intention of the legislation that created it, but without triggering a political reaction from elected officials.

by-product theory The idea that groups provide members with private benefits to attract membership. The possibility of group **collective action** emerges as a consequence.

Cabinet The secretaries, or chief administrators, of the major departments of the federal **government**. Cabinet secretaries are appointed by the president with the consent of the Senate.

casework An effort by members of Congress to gain the trust and support of constituents by providing personal service. One important type of casework consists of helping constituents obtain favorable treatment from the federal **bureaucracy**.

categorical grants-in-aid Funds given by Congress to states and localities that are earmarked by law for specific categories, such as education or crime prevention.

caucus system A normally closed meeting of a political or legislative group to select candidates, plan strategy, or make decisions regarding legislative matters.

causation A relationship or association between two variables such that one causes the other.

census A comprehensive enumeration of all individuals in a population.

checks and balances The mechanisms through which each branch of **government** is able to participate in and influence the activities of the other branches.

chief justice The justice on the **Supreme Court** who presides over the Court's public sessions.

civil law A system of jurisprudence, including private law and governmental actions, for settling disputes that do not involve criminal penalties.

civil liberties The protection of citizens from improper governmental action.

civil rights The legal or moral claims that citizens are entitled to make on the **government**.

class-action suit A lawsuit in which a large number of persons with common interests join together under a representative party to bring or defend a lawsuit, as when hundreds of workers join together to sue a company.

clear and present danger The criterion used to determine whether speech is protected or unprotected, based on its capacity to present a "clear and present danger" to society.

clientele agency A department or bureau of **government** whose mission is to promote, serve, or represent a particular interest.

closed primary A primary election in which voters can participate in the nomination of only those candidates of the party in which they have been enrolled for a period of time before primary day. Contrast with **open primary**.

closed rule The provision by the House Rules Committee that prohibits the introduction of amendments during debate.

cloture A rule allowing a supermajority of the members of a legislative body to set a time limit on debate over a given bill.

coalitional drift The prospect that enacted policy will change because the composition of the enacting coalition is temporary and provisional.

collective action The pooling of resources and the coordination of effort and activity by a group of people (often a large one) to achieve common goals.

commander in chief The power of the president as commander of the national military and the state national guard units (when called into service).

commerce clause Article I, Section 8, of the Constitution, which delegates to Congress the power "to regulate Commerce with foreign Nations, and among the several States, and with the Indian Tribes." This clause was interpreted by the **Supreme Court** to favor national power over the economy.

concurrent powers The authority possessed by *both* state and national **governments**, such as the power to levy taxes.

conference committee A joint committee created to work out a compromise for House and Senate versions of a piece of legislation.

congressional caucus An association of members of Congress based on party, interest, or social characteristics such as gender or race.

conservative Today this term refers to those who generally support the social and economic status quo and are suspicious of efforts to introduce new political formulas and economic arrangements. Many conservatives also believe that a large and powerful **government** poses a threat to citizens' freedoms.

constituency The district making up the area from which an official is elected.

constitutional government A system of rule in which formal and effective limits are placed on the power of the **government**.

cooperative federalism A type of **federalism** existing since the New Deal era, in which **grants-in-aid** have been used strategically to encourage states and localities (without commanding them) to pursue nationally defined goals. Also known as intergovernmental cooperation.

correlation A relationship or association between two variables.

court of appeals (appellate court) A court that hears the appeals of trial-court decisions.

criminal law The branch of law that deals with disputes or actions involving criminal penalties (as opposed to **civil law**).

de facto segregation Racial segregation that is not a direct result of law or **government** policy but is, instead, a reflection of residential patterns, income distributions, or other social factors.

de jure segregation Racial segregation that is a direct result of law or official policy.

delegate A representative who votes according to the preferences of his or her **constituency.**

delegated powers Constitutional powers assigned to one governmental agency but exercised by another agency with the express permission of the first.

delegation The transmission of authority to some other official or body for the latter's use (though often with the right of review and revision).

democracy A system of rule that permits citizens to play a significant part in the governmental process, usually through the selection of key public officials.

deregulation The policy of reducing or eliminating regulatory restraints on the conduct of individuals or private institutions.

devolution The policy of removing a program from one level of **government** by deregulating it or passing it down to a lower level, such as from the national government to the state and local governments.

dissenting opinion A decision written by a justice who voted with the minority opinion in a particular case, in which the justice fully explains the reasoning behind his or her opinion.

distributive tendency The tendency of Congress to spread the benefits of a policy over a wide range of members' districts.

divided government The condition in American **government** in which the presidency is controlled by one party while the opposing party controls one or both houses of Congress.

double jeopardy The Fifth Amendment right providing that a person cannot be tried twice for the same crime.

dual federalism The system of **government** that prevailed in the United States from 1789 to 1937, in which most fundamental governmental powers were shared between the federal and state governments, with the states exercising the most important powers. Compare with **cooperative federalism**.

due process Proceeding according to law and with adequate protection for individual rights.

Duverger's Law Law of politics, formalized by Maurice Duverger, stating that plurality-rule electoral systems will tend to have two political parties.

electoral college The presidential electors from each state who meet in their respective state capitals after the popular election to cast ballots for president and vice president.

eminent domain The right of the **government** to take private property for public use, with reasonable compensation awarded for the property.

equal protection clause The provision of the Fourteenth Amendment guaranteeing citizens "the equal protection of the laws." This clause has served as the basis for the **civil rights** of African Americans, women, and other groups.

equal time rule The requirement that broadcasters provide candidates for the same political office an equal opportunity to communicate their messages to the public.

establishment clause The First Admendment clause that says, "Congress shall make no law respecting an establishment of religion." This law means that a wall of separation exists between church and state.

exclusionary rule The ability of courts to exclude evidence obtained in violation of the Fourth Amendment.

executive agreement An agreement between the president and another country that has the force of a treaty but does not require the Senate's "advice and consent."

Executive Office of the President (EOP) The permanent agencies that perform defined management tasks for the president. Created in 1939, the EOP includes the Office of Management and Budget, the Council of Economic Advisers, the National Security Council, and other agencies.

executive order The rule or regulation issued by the president that have the effect and formal status of legislation.

executive privilege The claim that confidential communications between the president and the president's close advisers should not be revealed without the consent of the president.

expressed power The notion that the Constitution grants to the federal government only those powers specifically named in its text.

fairness doctrine An FCC requirement that broadcasters who air programs on controversial issues provide time for opposing views.

federalism The system of **government** in which a constitution divides power between a central government and regional governments.

Federal Reserve System (the Fed) Consisting of 12 Federal Reserve districts, the Fed facilitates exchanges of cash, checks, and credit; it regulates member banks; and it deploys monetary policies to fight inflation and deflation.

fighting words Speech that directly incites damaging conduct.

filibuster A tactic used by members of the Senate to prevent action on legislation they oppose by continuously holding the floor and speaking until the majority backs down. Once given the floor, senators have unlimited time to speak, and it requires a **cloture** vote of three-fifths of the Senate to end a filibuster.

fiscal policy The government's use of taxing, monetary, and spending powers to manipulate the economy.

formula grants **Grants-in-aid** in which a formula is used to determine the amount of federal funds a state or local **government** will receive.

framing The power of the media to influence how events and issues are interpreted.

free exercise clause The First Amendment clause that protects a citizen's right to believe and practice whatever religion he or she chooses.

free riding Enjoying the benefits of some good or action while letting others bear the costs. See also **public good**.

full faith and credit clause The provision in Article IV, Section 1, of the Constitution requiring that each state normally honors the public acts and judicial decisions that take place in another state.

gatekeeping authority The right and power to decide if a change in policy will be considered.

gender gap A distinctive pattern of voting behavior reflecting the differences in views between women and men.

gerrymandering The apportionment of voters in districts in such a way as to give unfair advantage to one political party.

going public The act of launching a media campaign to build popular support.

government The institutions and procedures through which a land and its people are ruled.

grand jury A jury that determines whether sufficient evidence is available to justify a trial. Grand juries do not rule on the accused's guilt or innocence.

grants-in-aid A general term for funds given by Congress to state and local **governments**. See also **categorical grants-in-aid**.

Great Compromise An agreement reached at the Constitutional Convention of 1787 that gave each state an equal number of senators regardless of its population but linked representation in the House of Representatives to population.

home rule The power delegated by the state to a local unit of **government** to manage its own affairs.

illusion of salience The impression conveyed by polls that something is important to the public when it actually is not.

impeachment The charging of a governmental official (president or otherwise) with "Treason, Bribery, or other high Crimes and Misdemeanors" and bringing him or her before Congress to determine guilt.

implementation The efforts of departments and agencies to translate laws into specific bureaucratic routines.

implied powers Powers derived from the **necessary and proper clause** (Article I, Section 8) of the Constitution. Such powers are not specifically **expressed** but are **implied** through the expansive interpretation of **delegated powers**.

incumbency Holding a political office for which one is running.

informational benefits Special newsletters, periodicals, training programs, conferences, and other information provided to members of groups to entice others to join.

inherent powers Powers claimed by a president that are not expressed in the Constitution but are inferred from it.

initiative A process by which citizens may petition to place a policy proposal on the ballot for public vote.

institutions The rules and procedures that provide incentives for political behavior, thereby shaping politics.

instrumental Done with purpose, sometimes with forethought, and even with calculation.

interest group An organized group of individuals or organizations that makes policy-related appeals to **government**.

intermediate scrutiny The test used by the Supreme Court in gender discrimination cases. Intermediate scrutiny places the burden of proof partially on the government and partially on the challengers to show that the law in question is constitutional.

issue voting An individual's propensity to select candidates or parties based on the extent to which the individual agrees with one candidate more than others on specific issues.

judicial activism The judicial philosophy that posits that the Court should see beyond the text of the Constitution or a statute to consider broader societal implications for its decisions.

judicial restraint The judicial philosophy whose adherents refuse to go beyond the text of the Constitution in interpreting its meaning.

judicial review The power of the courts to declare actions of the legislative and executive branches invalid or unconstitutional. The **Supreme Court** asserted this power in *Marbury v. Madison* (1803).

jurisdiction The domain over which an institution or member of an institution has authority.

kitchen cabinet An informal group of advisers to whom the president turns for counsel and guidance. Members of the official **cabinet** may or may not also be members of the kitchen cabinet.

legislative initiative The president's inherent power to bring a legislative agenda before Congress.

legislative supremacy The preeminent position assigned to Congress by the Constitution.

Lemon test Rule articulated in *Lemon v. Kurtzman* according to which governmental action in respect to religion is permissible if it is secular in purpose, does not lead to "excessive entanglement" with religion, and neither promotes nor inhibits the practice of religion.

libel A written statement made in "reckless disregard of the truth" and considered damaging to a victim because it is "malicious, scandalous, and defamatory."

liberal A liberal today generally supports political and social reform; extensive government intervention in the economy; the expansion of federal social services; more vigorous efforts on behalf of the poor, minorities, and women; and greater concern for consumers and the environment.

line-item veto The power of the executive to veto specific provisions (lines) of a bill passed by the legislature.

lobbying An attempt by a group to influence the policy process through persuasion of **government** officials.

logrolling A legislative practice wherein reciprocal agreements are made between legislators, usually in voting for or against a bill. In contrast to bargaining, logrolling unites parties that have nothing in common but their desire to exchange support.

majority leader The elected leader of the party holding a majority of the seats in the House of Representatives or the Senate. In the House, the majority leader is subordinate in the party hierarchy to the Speaker.

majority party The party that holds the majority of legislative seats in either the House or the Senate.

majority rule A type of electoral system in which, to win a seat in a representative body, a candidate must receive a majority (50 percent plus 1) of all the votes cast in the relevant district.

material benefits Special goods, services, or money provided to members of groups to entice others to join.

mean The average value of a variable.

measurement error The failure to identify the true distribution of opinion within a population because of errors such as ambiguous or poorly worded questions.

median The numerical value separating the higher half of a sample or population from the lower half; also called the fiftieth percentile.

median-voter theorem A proposition predicting that when policy options can be arrayed along a single dimension, majority rule will pick the policy most preferred by the voter whose ideal policy is to the left of half of the voters and to the right of exactly half of the voters.

minority leader The elected leader of the party holding less than a majority of the seats in the House or Senate.

Miranda rule The convention derived from the **Supreme Court**'s 1966 ruling in the case of *Miranda v. Arizona* whereby persons under arrest must be informed of their legal rights, including their right to counsel, before undergoing police interrogation.

monetary policy Policies that control the supply of money, the price of money (interest rate), and the availability of credit.

mootness A criterion used by courts to avoid hearing cases that no longer require resolution.

moral hazard Not knowing all aspects of the actions taken by an agent (nominally on behalf of the principal but potentially at the principal's expense).

multiple-member district An electorate that selects several candidates at large from an entire district, with each voter given the number of votes equivalent to the number of seats to be filled.

National Security Council (NSC) A presidential foreign policy advisory council composed of the president, the vice president, the secretaries of state, defense, and the treasury, the attorney general, and other officials invited by the president.

necessary and proper clause Article I, Section 8, of the Constitution, which enumerates the powers of Congress and provides Congress with the authority to make all laws "necessary and proper" to carry them out; also referred to as the elastic clause.

nomination The process by which political parties select their candidates for election to public office.

oligarchy A form of **government** in which a small group of landowners, military officers, or wealthy merchants controls most of the governing decisions.

open primary A primary election in which voters can choose on the day of the primary which party to enroll in to select candidates for the general election. Contrast with **closed primary**.

open rule The provision by the House Rules Committee that permits floor debate and the addition of amendments to a bill.

opinion The written explanation of the **Supreme Court**'s decision in a particular case.

oral argument The stage in **Supreme Court** proceedings in which attorneys for both sides appear before the Court to present their positions and answer questions posed by the justices.

oversight The effort by Congress, through hearings, investigations, and other techniques, to exercise control over the activities of executive agencies.

party activist A partisan who contributes time, energy, and effort to support a party and its candidates.

party caucus (party conference) A normally closed meeting of a political or legislative group to select candidates or leaders, plan strategy, or make decisions regarding legislative matters.

party identification An individual voter's psychological ties to one party or another.

party machine In the late nineteenth and early twentieth centuries, the local party organization that controlled local politics through patronage and the nominations process.

party vote A **roll-call vote** in the House or Senate in which at least 50 percent of the members of one party take a particular position and are opposed by at least 50 percent of the members of the other party. Party votes are less common today than they were in the nineteenth century.

path dependency The idea that certain possibilities are made more or less likely because of the historical path taken.

patronage The resources available to higher officials, usually opportunities to make partisan appointments to offices and confer grants, licenses, or special favors to supporters.

pluralism The theory that all interests are and should be free to compete for influence in the **government**. The outcome of this competition is compromise and moderation.

plurality rule A type of electoral system in which victory goes to the individual who gets the most votes in an election, but not necessarily a majority of the votes cast.

pocket veto A veto that is effected when Congress adjourns during the time a president has to approve a bill and the president takes no action on it. See also **veto.**

police power The power reserved to the **government** to regulate the health, safety, and morals of its citizens.

political action committee (PAC) A private group that raises and distributes funds for use in election campaigns.

political caucus A normally closed meeting of a political or legislative group to select candidates, plan strategy, or make decisions regarding legislative matters.

political party An organized group that attempts to influence government by electing its members to office.

political socialization The induction of individuals into the political culture; the process of learning the underlying beliefs and values on which the political system is based.

politics The conflicts and struggles over the leadership, structure, and policies of government.

pork-barrel legislation The appropriations made by legislative bodies for local projects that often are not needed but are created so that local representatives can carry their home district in the next election.

precedents Prior cases whose principles are used by judges as the bases for their decisions in present cases.

priming A process of preparing the public to take a particular view of an event or a political actor.

principal-agent relationship The relationship between a principal and his or her agent. This relationship may be affected by the fact that each is motivated by self-interest, yet their interests may not be well aligned.

prior restraint An effort by a government agency to block the publication of material it deems libelous or harmful in some other way; censorship. In the United States, the courts forbid prior restraint except under the most extraordinary circumstances.

privatization The act of moving all or part of a program from the public sector to the private sector.

privileges and immunities The provision from Article IV, Section 2, of the Constitution stating that a state cannot discriminate against someone from another state or give its own residents special privileges.

probability sampling A method used by pollsters to select a representative sample in which every individual in the population has an equal probability of being selected as a respondent.

project grants Grant programs in which state and local **governments** submit proposals to federal agencies and for which funding is provided on a competitive basis.

proportional representation (PR) A multiple-member district system that allows each political party representation in proportion to its percentage of the vote.

proposal power The capacity to bring a proposal before the full legislature.

prospective voting Voting based on the imagined future performance of a candidate.

public good A good that (1) may be enjoyed by anyone if it is provided and (2) may not be denied to anyone once it has been provided. See also **free riding**.

public law Cases involving the action of public agencies or officials.

public opinion Citizens' attitudes about political issues, leaders, institutions, and events.

public-opinion poll The scientific instrument for measuring public opinion.

purposive benefits **Selective benefits** of group membership that emphasize the purpose and accomplishments of the group.

push polling A polling technique in which the questions are designed to shape the respondent's opinion.

random digit dialing A poll in which respondents are selected at random from a list of 10-digit telephone numbers, with every effort made to avoid bias in the construction of the sample.

recall The removal of a public official by popular vote.

referendum A measure proposed or passed by a legislature to the vote of the electorate for approval or rejection.

regulatory agency A department, bureau, or independent agency whose primary mission is to eliminate or restrict certain behaviors defined as negative in themselves or negative in their consequences.

reserved powers Powers, derived from the Tenth Amendment to the Constitution, that are not specifically **delegated** to the national government or denied to the states; these powers are reserved to the states.

retrospective voting Voting based on the past performance of a candidate.

right of rebuttal An FCC regulation giving individuals the right to have the opportunity to respond to personal attacks made on a radio or TV broadcast.

right to privacy The right to be let alone, which has been interpreted by the Supreme Court to entail free access to birth control and abortions.

roll-call votes Votes in which each legislator's yes or no vote is recorded.

rule making A quasi-legislative administrative process that produces regulations by **government** agencies.

rule of four The rule that *certiorari* will be granted only if four justices vote in favor of the petition.

salient interest An attitude or view that is especially important to the individual holding it.

sample A small group selected by researchers to represent the most important characteristics of an entire population.

sampling error A polling error that arises on account of the small size of the sample.

selection bias A polling error in which the sample is not representative of the population being studied, so that some opinions are over- or underrepresented.

selective benefits Benefits that do not go to everyone but, rather, are distributed selectively—only to those who contribute to the group enterprise.

senatorial courtesy The practice whereby the president, before formally nominating a person for a federal judgeship, finds out whether the senators from the candidate's state support the nomination.

seniority The priority or status ranking given to an individual on the basis of length of continuous service on a congressional committee.

"separate but equal" rule The doctrine that public accommodations could be segregated by race but still be equal.

separation of powers The division of governmental power among several institutions that must cooperate in decision making.

signing statement Announcement made by the president when a bill is signed into law.

single-member district An electorate that is allowed to elect only one representative from each district—the typical method of representation in the United States.

slander An oral statement made in "reckless disregard of the truth" and considered damaging to a victim because it is "malicious, scandalous, and defamatory."

solidary benefits Selective benefits of group membership that emphasize friendship, networking, and consciousness-raising.

sovereignty Supreme and independent political authority.

spatial issue An issue for which a range of possible options or policies can be ordered, say, from liberal to conservative or from most expensive to least expensive.

Speaker of the House The chief presiding officer of the House of Representatives. The Speaker is elected at the beginning of every Congress on a straight **party vote**. He or she is the most important party and House leader.

speech plus Speech accompanied by activities such as sit-ins, picketing, and demonstrations. Protection of this form of speech under the First Amendment is conditional, and restrictions imposed by state or local authorities are acceptable if properly balanced by considerations of public order.

staff agencies The agencies responsible for providing Congress with independent expertise, administration, and **oversight** capability.

standing The right of an individual or an organization to initiate a court case.

standing committee A permanent legislative committee that considers legislation within its designated subject area; the basic unit of deliberation in the House and Senate.

stare decisis Literally "let the decision stand." The doctrine whereby a previous decision by a court applies as a precedent in similar cases until that decision is overruled.

state sovereign immunity A legal doctrine holding that states cannot be sued for violating an act of Congress.

states' rights The principle that states should oppose increases in the authority of the national **government**. This view was most popular before the Civil War.

supremacy clause A clause of Article VI of the Constitution that states that all laws passed by the national **government** and all treaties are the supreme laws of the land and superior to all laws adopted by any state or any subdivision.

supreme court The highest court in a particular state or in the United States. This court primarily serves an appellate function.

survey A study of a relatively small subset of individuals that is used to make inferences about an entire population.

third party A party that organizes to compete against the two major American political parties.

Three-fifths Compromise An agreement reached at the Constitutional Convention of 1787 stipulating that for purposes of the apportionment of congressional seats, every slave would be counted as three fifths of a person.

totalitarian government A system of rule in which the **government** recognizes no formal limits on its power and seeks to absorb or eliminate other social institutions that might challenge it.

transaction costs The cost of clarifying each aspect of a principal-agent relationship and monitoring it to make sure arrangements are complied with.

trial court The first court to hear a criminal or civil case.

trustee A representative who votes based on what he or she thinks is best for his or her **constituency**.

tyranny Oppressive **government** that employs the cruel and unjust use of power and authority.

unfunded mandates National standards or programs imposed on state and local **governments** by the federal government without accompanying funding or reimbursement.

valence issue An issue or aspect of a choice for which all voters prefer a higher value, in contrast to a **spatial issue**. For example, voters prefer their politicans to be honest, and honesty is a valence issue.

variable A categorization or numerical representation of all values of a given characteristic.

veto The president's constitutional power to turn down acts of Congress within 10 days of their passage while Congress is in session. A presidential veto may be overridden by a two-thirds vote of each house of Congress.

veto power The ability to defeat something even if it has made it on to the agenda of an institution.

War Powers Resolution A resolution of Congress declaring that the president can send troops into action abroad only by authorization of Congress or if U.S. troops are already under attack or seriously threatened.

whip system A communications network in each house of Congress. Whips poll the membership to learn their intentions on specific legislative issues and assist the **majority** and **minority leaders** in various tasks.

White House staff The analysts and advisers to the president, often given the title "special assistant."

writ of *certiorari* A formal request by an appellant to have the Supreme Court review a decision of a lower court. *Certiorari* is from a Latin word meaning "to make more certain."

writ of *habeas corpus* A court order demanding that an individual in custody be brought into court and shown the cause for detention. *Habeas corpus* is guaranteed by the Constitution and can be suspended only in cases of rebellion or invasion.

Index

Page numbers in *italics* refer to figures and tables.